797,885 Books

are available to read at

Forgotten Books

www.ForgottenBooks.com

Forgotten Books' App
Available for mobile, tablet & eReader

ISBN 978-1-331-17107-2
PIBN 10153636

This book is a reproduction of an important historical work. Forgotten Books uses state-of-the-art technology to digitally reconstruct the work, preserving the original format whilst repairing imperfections present in the aged copy. In rare cases, an imperfection in the original, such as a blemish or missing page, may be replicated in our edition. We do, however, repair the vast majority of imperfections successfully; any imperfections that remain are intentionally left to preserve the state of such historical works.

Forgotten Books is a registered trademark of FB &c Ltd.
Copyright © 2015 FB &c Ltd.
FB &c Ltd, Dalton House, 60 Windsor Avenue, London, SW19 2RR.
Company number 08720141. Registered in England and Wales.

For support please visit www.forgottenbooks.com

1 MONTH OF FREE READING

at

www.ForgottenBooks.com

By purchasing this book you are eligible for one month membership to ForgottenBooks.com, giving you unlimited access to our entire collection of over 700,000 titles via our web site and mobile apps.

To claim your free month visit:
www.forgottenbooks.com/free153636

* Offer is valid for 45 days from date of purchase. Terms and conditions apply.

English
Français
Deutsche
Italiano
Español
Português

www.forgottenbooks.com

Mythology Photography **Fiction**
Fishing Christianity **Art** Cooking
Essays Buddhism Freemasonry
Medicine **Biology** Music **Ancient Egypt** Evolution Carpentry Physics
Dance Geology **Mathematics** Fitness
Shakespeare **Folklore** Yoga Marketing
Confidence Immortality Biographies
Poetry **Psychology** Witchcraft
Electronics Chemistry History **Law**
Accounting **Philosophy** Anthropology
Alchemy Drama Quantum Mechanics
Atheism Sexual Health **Ancient History**
Entrepreneurship Languages Sport
Paleontology Needlework Islam
Metaphysics Investment Archaeology
Parenting Statistics Criminology
Motivational

THE

CABINET OF CURIOSITIES,

OR

Wonders of the World Displayed;

FORMING

A REPOSITORY OF WHATEVER IS REMARKABLE

IN THE

REGIONS OF NATURE AND ART,

EXTRAORDINARY EVENTS,

Eccentric Biography,

&c. &c.

" Nothing pleaseth but rare accidents."
SHAKSPEARE.

LONDON:

PRINTED FOR J. LIMBIRD, 143, STRAND.

1824.

LONDON: PRINTED BY A. APPLEGATH, STAMFORD-STREET.

INDEX.

ABYSSINIAN disease, 181.
Adams the astrologist, 97.
Albay, volcanic mountains of, 386.
Alphabet for the blind, 165.
America, natural wonders in, 319.
Anaconda, the, 408.
Animal flower, 126.
Anthony the lunatic, 122.
Apparition of Souter Fell, 326.
Art, minute wonders of, 367.
Assassin of Cologne, 341.
Auto-da-fé, 401.
Baker, the conjurer, 41.
Barber overjoyed, the, 42.
Battalia the stone-eater, 12.
Bartholomew, Mr. C. memoir of, 597.
Barrett, Mrs. Starr, 267.
Biography Eccentric, 12, 26, 44, 58, 77, 94, 109, 121, 141, 157, 171, 187, 204, 220, 238, 252, 280, 300, 317, 328, 347, 365, 378, 396, 414, 426.
Blashe de Manfre, 177.
Bogs of butter, 25.
Bolton, Frances, 78.
Bonaparte and his familiar, 279.
Bottle conjurer, the, 23.
Boots, Old, 190, 273.
Booty's ghost, 104.
Boyd, Zachary, account of, 144.
Branagh, Roger, 221.
Brown, Phebe, memoir of, 13.
Browne, Simon, account of, 34.
Buckhorse, account of, 300.
Calculations, curious, 287.
Caleb Quotem, a Lincolnshire, 27.
Calvados, the abbé of, 418.
Cannibals, account of, 17.
Canning, Elizabeth, account of, 57.
Capper, J., memoir of, 414.
Cat-eaters, 11.
—— adventures of a, 130.
Cathcart, lady, 121.
Cataract of Paràna, 133.
Cavern crystallized, 301.
Caraboo, Princess, 169.
Champagne, the savage girl of, 370, 388, 411.
Charlatan, French, 119.
Charles XI., vision of, 53.
Chilton, the somnambulist, 419.
Conscience, a guilty, 64.
Corbeau Renee, account of, 67.
Crystal summer-house, 98.
Cuckoo-spittle, 318.
Darney, Jenny, 61.
Dawber, Mrs. Sarah, 317.
Davis, the somnambulist, 348.
Deaf and dumb amateur, 207.
Deafness cured, 79.
Death simulated, 359.
Delusion, extraordinary, 394.
D'Eon, Chevalier, 94, 293.
Demetriuses, the, 281.
Dimsdale, Sir Harry, 209.
Dog of Montargis, 233.

Dorislaus, assassination of, 417.
Dryden's superstition, 269.
DWARFS, THE BOOK OF, 134, 185, 250, 344.
East, Mary, the female husband, 44.
Echo, singular, 125.
Edwards the Welsh conjurer, 137.
Elephant, wild, 350.
Elm, family, 10.
Escapes, singular, 208, 254.
Evidence, whimsical, 46.
Execution of an innocent man, 428.
Family afflictions, singular, 70.
——, gifted, 354.
Fear, fatal effects of, 335.
Fecundity of fish, 334.
—————— of flies, 404.
Female executed, recovered, 152.
Fielding, Sir John, 298.
Forests, subterraneous, 324.
————, Indian, 367.
Fortunate youth, the, 200, 214.
Fossil animal of Maestricht, 311.
Francœur the lunatic, 204.
Game of Turks and Christians, 382.
Ganesa, the Hindoo deity, 385.
Gascoigne, Mr., memoir of, 238.
Ghost, mode of bringing to light, 333.
—— story, 376.
GIANTS, THE BOOK OF, 115, 155, 199.
Glebe, Rev. E. 381.
Groaning tree, the, 48.
Grottoes and caverns, 422.
Gunpowder Plot Conspirators, 129.
Hals, Frank, 254.
Hartop, Jonathan, 237.
Hastings, Sir George, 427.
Hatching chickens in Egypt, 71.
Hebrew, learned, 75.
Henrietta, Queen, anecdote of, 31.
Hermitess of Salem, 365.
Heroic mother, the, 99.
Highwaymen, the, 26.
Himalaya mountains, 375.
Hindoo and Mussulman devotees, 337.
Hoax aquatic, 364.
Hoaxes and Impostures, in every number.
Hobbies—Hermits, 296.
Hohenlohe, Prince, 89, 105.
Honeywood, Mrs. M., 220.
Hope, Old, life of, 14.
Horns, human, 211.
Howe, the absent husband, 77.
Hudson, Jeffery, in the pie, 321.
Hudson, Thomas, 173.
Hurricane at Lucknow, 40.
Hydrophobia, case of, 36.
Ice Islands, 405.
Icebergs, 406.
Identity extraordinary, 346.
Imbecility extraordinary, 302.
Impostor, royal, 234.
Inundation in Worcestershire, 361.
Jacob, John, life of, 28.
Java, boiling mud lake of, 132.

INDEX

Jetzer, Friar, 313.
Jurullo, volcano of, 6.
Kettlewell, Lumley, memoir of, 252.
Lambert, the infant, 334.
———, Mr. Daniel, 378.
Langley, Mr., 285.
Levi, Marcus, 239.
Lightning, effects of, 360.
Lisbon conspirators, 33.
Lizards in chalk rock, 287.
Littleness, wonders of, 83.
Lolkes, Wybrand, 225.
Longevity, anecdotes of, 14, 28, 61, 75, 92, 107, 119, 140, 156, 187, 237, 267, 284, 346, 426.
Lyttleton, Lord, presentiment of, 86.
Maestricht, vaults of, 357.
Mackay the fatalist, 101.
Maniac, ferocious, 194.
Manufacture, celerity of, 10.
Marble ponds of Persia, 159.
Marriot the glutton, 145.
Mapp, Mrs., the bone-setter, 187.
Martyrdom, recent, 430.
Medusæ, the, 8.
Mermaid, the, 383.
Microscope, wonders of the, 101.
Minds, the cats' Raphael, 59.
Mine of frogs, 131.
Moll Cut Purse, 194.
Monkeys, mischievous, 191.
Monster, American, 437.
Monument of Vulong, 50.
Moore, Ann, of Tutbury, 257
Moran, the ventriloquist, 74.
Mourner, amateur, 26.
Moving earth, 256.
Mulled Sack, life of, 49.
Murder in India, 47.
——— Russia, 79.
——— America, 139.
———, the Cornish, 327.
———, discovery of a, 333.
Negro boy, the spotted, 65.
Negroes, white, 183.
Negress, white, 303.
Nurse, Indian, 11.
Oak, extraordinary, 30.
O'Brien, Mary, 30.
Occupations, trifling, 224.
Odd family, the, 126.
Oliver, Helen, the rustic D'Eon, 171.
Parr, Old, life of, 107.
Parricide punished, the, 54.
Pasaic, falls of the, 175.
Patient, a good, 14.
Patriarchs, 61, 62, 92, 140, 156, 119.
Peeke's combat, 81.
Penitents, procession of, 153.
Pentheney, Mr. A., 268.
Pett, the miser, 157.
Pitch lake of Trinidad, 126.
Pompey's pillar, 1.
Powder magazine, explosion of, 63.
Pranforce, the fanatic, 102.
Presentiment of death, 32.
Pressing to death, law of, 42
Ptolemy's mirror, 241.
Pyramids, the, 206, 239, 309.
Quill, Maurice, memoir of, 396

Reade, lady, 28.
Resemblances, singular, 350.
Revenge, fatal, 83.
Rio de la Plata, phenomenon in, 175.
Rocking stones, 87.
Russian longevity, 30
Rutland cavern, 271.
Sabbatei-Sevi, 116.
Salt mines in Cheshire, 230.
Scrap Book, in every number.
Scylla and Charybdis, 226.
Sea, island risen from the, 179.
Senses, confusion of the, 72.
Seven, mystical number, 244.
Ship on fire at sea, 4.
Shrimp-man, musical, 348.
iva, the Hindoo god, 369.
Slave ship, wreck of a, 114.
Snakes, American, 296, 299.
Spectre of the Broken, 197.
Spider, the gossamer, 383.
Starvation, voluntary, 21.
Stone-eater, 138.
Strength, anecdotes of, 392.
Stukely, the perpetual-motion man, 109
Sulphur mountains of Iceland, 168.
Swift's ballad on a murder, 7.
Strong, the blind mechanic, 141.
Storm, violent, 286.
Stretch, Samuel, memoir of, 347.
Stylites, Simeon, 328.
Superstition, singular, 255.
———, the best doctor, 399.
Swan, a whistling, 399.
Sympathies and antipathies, 273, 322.
Tailor, blind, 111.
Terrors, midnight, 398.
Theatre of puppets, 174.
Three, the mystical number, 190.
Thunder storms, remarkable, 246.
Tiger and crocodile, fight of, 353.
Tiquet, execution of Madame, 161.
Toothless company, 176.
Trenck, Baron, 431.
Trial, whimsical, 248.
——— for murder, 261.
Tude, Henry Masers de la, 6.
Turpin, the highwayman, 424.
Typhon, violent, 146.
Urselin, Barbara, 113.
"Vade in Pace," terrible, 51.
Vampire of the ocean, 363.
Vampires and vampirism, 147, 166, 355.
Varieties, in every number.
Vegetables, fecundity of, 265.
Victims, human, 361.
Vine-fretter, 373.
Vishnu, incarnation of, 305.
Volcanoes in the sun, 150.
Vortex, singular, 341.
War and weather, 222.
Warning, supernatural, 123.
Water-drinkers, 111, spouts 335, quack, 425.
Welch, Mr. S. 75.
Well, remarkable, 31.
Whirlwinds, 73, 178.
Williamson, Peter, 241.
Winifred's well, St. 85.
Wonders, transatlantic, 266.

THE CABINET OF CURIOSITIES;
OR,
𝔚onders of the 𝔚orld 𝔇isplayed.

A world of wonders, where creation seems
No more the works of Nature but her dreams.—MONTGOMERY.

No. 1.]   PRICE TWO-PENCE.

POMPEY'S PILLAR.

BRITISH SAILORS ON POMPEY'S PILLAR.

The spirit of daring is so prominent a feature in the character of British sailors, that scarcely any thing they undertake can excite much surprise among those to whom their adventurous disposition is known; and yet the circumstance of a few hardy sons of Neptune drinking a bowl of punch on the top of Pompey's Pillar might have staggered our belief, had not the fact been too well authenticated to admit of doubt.

Pompey's Pillar is situated about a quarter of a league from the southern gate of Alexandria, a city of Lower Egypt, and once its capital. It is composed of red granite; the capital which is nine feet high is Corinthian, with palm leaves, and not indented. The shaft and the upper member of the base are of one piece of granite, ninety feet long and nine feet in diameter. The base, which is one solid block of marble, fifteen feet square, rests on two layers of stone, bound together with lead. The whole column is one hundred and fourteen feet high. It is perfectly well polished, and only a little shivered on the eastern side. Nothing can equal the majesty of this monument, which seen from a distance overtops the town and seems as a signal for vessels. Approaching it nearer, Pompey's Pillar produces astonishment mixed with awe: and the beauty of the capital, the length of the shaft, and the extraordinary simplicity of the pedestal excite the admiration of all travellers.

It was not however to mere admiration that a party of English sailors confined themselves. These jolly sons of Neptune had been pushing the can about on board their ship in the harbour of Alexandria, when they determined to go on shore and drink a bowl of punch on the top of Pompey's Pillar. The eccentricity of the idea was sufficient to make it be immediately adopted, and its apparent impossibility a certain spur for putting it into execution. On arriving at the spot many contrivances were tried but without effect, and the British tars began to despair of success, when the officer who had planned the frolic suggested the means of accomplishing it by a paper kite, for which one of the men was despatched to the city.

The inhabitants were by this time apprized of what was going forward, and flocked in crowds to witness the exploit. The governor of Alexandria was told that the English seamen were about to pull down Pompey's Pillar, but he would not interfere, saying, the English were too great patriots to injure the remains of Pompey. He knew little however of the disposition of the people engaged in the undertaking; for had the Turkish empire risen in opposition it would not perhaps at this moment have deterred them.

The kite was brought and flown directly over the pillar, by which means a cord was carried over the capital. This accomplished, a rope was then drawn over, and one of the seamen ascended by it to the top, where being arrived, other ropes were handed to him by the same conveyance, and in little more than an hour a regular set of shrouds was erected, by which the whole company went up, and drank their bowl of punch amidst the shouts of several thousand people collected to see what they termed a miracle, as no one had before been known to have seen the top of that stupendous edifice, which overtops the highest buildings of the city. To the eye below, the capital does not appear capable of holding more than one man, but our seamen found it would contain no less than eight persons very conveniently; they also discovered what before was unknown, that there was originally a statue on this pillar, of gigantic size, of which the foot and ancle are the only parts now remaining. The only injury the pillar sustained was the loss of one of its volutes, which fell down and was brought to England by one of the captains. The sailors, after painting the initials of their names in large letters, just beneath the capital, descended, to the great astonishment of the Turks, who to this day speak of it as the madcap experiment.

Our engraving presents a beautiful and correct view of Pompey's Pillar, with the shrouds, &c. by which our tars ascended to its top—a combination of one of the wonders of the ancients with as extraordinary an exploit as was perhaps ever attempted even by British sailors.

TO THE PUBLIC.

If an editor who commences a new work renders it worthy of the public patronage he will have no occasion to apologize for having added one more to the numerous periodicals of the day; and if, on the contrary, he fails of success, he will need no aggravation of his punishment. The Editor of THE CABINET OF CURIOSITIES, or WONDERS OF THE WORLD DISPLAYED, is conscious of the ordeal he has to pass, but he has the courage to brave it.

The Editor is also aware that his second title of "Wonders of the World," may be deemed somewhat astounding for a periodical; and may excite some doubt as to whether the work is to be a collection of facts or romances. To such the Editor has no hesitation in saying, that it his intention to adhere to facts, curious and well authenticated: and if travellers are absurd in relating wonders, the world would be equally absurd in disbelieving them altogether.

"I knew," says a modern writer, "a very worthy g n man who never was believed, and yet never told a falsehood; but he had given himself a habit of relating every thing extraordinary which his observant mind had collected in a long life, and never mentioned any ordinary occurrence." Such is often the fate of travellers. Bruce was considered a sort of Baron Munchausen, though subsequent travellers have confirmed so much of his narrative as to entitle him to the highest credit; and when the same traveller spoke of a camera obscura which would hold a large company, it appeared apocryphal, till a common showman exhibited the same in our streets.

The most marvellous accounts have generally some foundation in truth. The wonderful story of the Upas, to be found in the notes to Dr. Darwin's poem of the Botanic Garden, seems only an exaggeration of the qualities of the poison-tree, well known in some parts of America, or of the marsh miasma, which Townsend searched for in Spain; and the fish whose similitude to the human figure gave rise to the fable of the mermaid, is common on the coast of Africa. The unicorn is evidently the rhinoceros, and the griffin a mere picture drawn by terror, in describing some tremendous snake.

The most marvellous anecdote related by any traveller can scarcely seem to us so incredible as it must be to an Abyssinian, that we can walk under water for hours together by the diving bell; that by mere vapour we can traverse the ocean; or that by means of balloons we can soar in the air; and yet these are facts so common that they no longer excite surprise among us. Then, as to narratives of occurrences, it is universally acknowledged that the most fertile imagination never invented fictions half so remarkable or extravagant as many of the realities of life.

So much in regard to Curiosities and Wonders generally, we may observe that, "The Cabinet of Curosities" is intended to form a record of every thing remarkable in the regions of Nature and Art—in times past or present—a sort of museum in which every collector may deposit his *rara avis*, secure of its being kept in good preservation, and handed down to posterity.

The ancients boasted of their Seven Wonders: it shall be our endeavour to provide our readers with seven times seven every week; though we cannot promise that each Wonder in our Cabinet will stretch so far as the Colossus at Rhodes, or cover so large a space as one of the Pyramids of Egypt. We shall—but Shakspeare, in himself, one of the greatest Wonders the world ever produced, has anticipated all we intended to say of our work, and therefore shall furnish the description of its miscellaneous contents. In the course then of our editorial labours in "The Cabinet of Curiosities," we shall speak

—"Of most disastrous chances;
Of moving accidents by flood and field;
Of hair breadth 'scapes i' th' imminent
    deadly breach;
Of antres vast, and deserts idle;
Rough quarries, rocks, and hills whose
    heads touch heaven;
And of the Cannibals that each other eat:
The Anthropophagi, and men whose heads
Do grow beneath their shoulders."

*** The Cabinet of Curiosities will be published every Wednesday morning, at Six o'Clock. Each Number will contain thirty-two columns, neatly printed on good paper, and embellished with a spirited wood Engraving, from original designs by the first artists. Price Twopence.

SHIP ON FIRE AT SEA.

PERHAPS the most aggravating circumstances under which shipwreck can occur, are when it is occasioned by fire. It is then that death stares the mariner in the face in the most hideous form, while his means of counteracting the danger, or escaping from it, are more limited and ineffectual. Few disasters of this nature have been so calamitous as the burning of a French East Indiaman, *The Prince*. She sailed from Port l'Orient on the 19th of February, 1752, on a voyage outbound. She suffered much in the passage from being driven on a sand bank. In June she was discovered to be on fire. While the captain hastened on deck, lieutenant de la Fond ordered some sails to be dipped in the sea and the hatches to be covered with them, in order to prevent access of air. Every one was employed in procuring water; all the buckets were used, the pumps plied, and pipes introduced from them into the hold; but the rapid progres of the flames baffled every exertion to subdue them, and augmented the general consternation. The boatswain and three others took possession of the yawl and pushed off; but those on board still continued as active as ever. The master boldly went down into the hold, but the intense heat compelled him to return, and had not a quantity of water been dashed over him he would have been severely scorched. In attempting to get the long-boat out, it fell on the guns and could not be righted.

Consternation now seized on the crew, nothing but sighs and groans resounded through the vessel, and the animals on board, as if sensible of the impending danger, uttered the most dreadful cries. The chaplain who was now on the quarter deck, gave the people general absolution, still cheering them to renewed exertions, but,

"With fruitless toil the crew oppose the flame;
No art can now the spreading mischief tame,
Some chok'd and smother'd did expiring lie,
Burn with the ship and on the waters fry;
Some, when the flames could be no more withstood,
By wild despair directed, midst the flood,
Themselves in haste from the tall vessel threw,
And from a dry to liquid ruin flew.
Sad choice of death! when those who shun the fire,
Must to as fierce an element retire,
Uncommon sufferings did these wretches wait,
Both burnt and drown'd they met a double fate."

Self-preservation now was the only object; each was occupied in throwing overboard whatever promised the slender chance of escape, yards, spars, hencoops, and every thing to be met with was seized in despair, and thus employed. Some leaped into the sea, as the mildest death that awaited them; others, more successful, swam to fragments of the wreck, while some crowded on the ropes and yards, hesitating which alternative of destruction to choose. A father was seen to snatch his son from the flames, clasp him to his breast and then plunging into the waves perished in each other's embrace.

"What ghastly ruin then deformed the deep?
Here glowing planks, and flowing ribs of oak,
Here smoking beams, and masts in sunder broke."

The floating masts and yards were covered with men struggling with the watery element, many of whom now perished by balls discharged from the guns as heated by the fire, forming thus a third means of destruction. M. de la Fond, who had hitherto borne the misfortune with the greatest fortitude, was now pierced with anguish to see that no further hope remained of preserving the ship, or the lives of his fellow-sufferers. Stripping off his clothes, he designed slipping down a yard, one end of which dipped in the water, but it was so covered with miserable beings shrinking from death, that he tumbled over them and fell into the sea. There a drowning soldier caught hold of him. Lieutenant de la Fond made every exertion to disengage himself, but in vain; twice they plunged below the surface, but still the man held him until the agonies of death were passed, and he became loosed from his grasp. After clearing his way through the dead bodies, which covered the surface of the ocean, he seized on a yard, and afterwards gained a spritsail covered with people, but on which he was nevertheless permitted to take a place. Hence he got on the mainmast, which having been consumed below, fell overboard, and after killing some in its fall, afforded a temporary succour to others.

Eighty persons were now on the mainmast, including the chaplain, who by his discourse and example, taught the duty of resignation. Lieutenant de la Fond, seeing the worthy man quit his hold and drop into the sea, lifted him up. "Let me go," said he, "I am already half drowned, and it is only protracting my sufferings."—"No, my friend," the lieutenant replied, "when my strength is exhausted, but not till then, we will perish together."

The flames still continued raging in the vessel; and the fire reached the magazine, when the most thundering explosion ensued. A thick cloud intercepted the light of the sun, and amidst the terrific darkness, nothing but pieces of flaming timber, projected aloft in the air, could be seen, threatening to crush to atoms in their fall numbers of miserable beings, already struggling in the agonies of death. As night approached, they providentially discovered a cask of brandy, about fifteen pounds of pork, a piece of scarlet cloth, about twenty yards of linen, a dozen of pipestaves, and a small piece of cordage. The scarlet cloth was substituted for a sail, an oar was erected for a mast, and a plank for a rudder. This equipment was made in the darkness of the night; yet a great difficulty remained, for wanting charts and instruments, and being nearly two hundred leagues from land, the party felt at a loss how to steer.

Eight days and nights passed in miserable succession without seeing land, the party all the while exposed to the scorching heat of the sun by day, and to the intense cold by night; suffering too from the extremities of hunger and of thirst.

When every thing seemed to predict a speedy termination to the sufferings of this unfortunate crew, they discovered the distant land on the 3d of August. It would be difficult to describe the change which the prospect of deliverance created. Their strength was renovated, and they were roused to precautions against being drifted away by the current. They reached the coast of Brazil and entered Treason Bay. As soon as they reached the shore, they prostrated themselves on the ground, and in transports of joy rolled on the sand. They exhibited the most frightful appearance; some were quite naked, others had only shirts in rags, and scarcely any thing human characterised any of them. When deliberating on the course they should follow, about fifty Portuguese of the settlement advanced, and seeing their wretched condition, pitied their misfortunes, and conducted them to their dwellings, where they were hospitably entertained.

Nearly three hundred persons perished in this dreadful catastrophe. The survivors reached Lisbon on the 17th of December, and thence sailed to Port L'Orient.

DEAN SWIFT'S BALLAD ON A MURDER.

In the year 1726, Catherine Hayes murdered her husband, under circumstances of the most horrible description. After she and two men, who were her accomplices, had killed him with a hatchet, they cut off his head and threw it into the Thames, in order to conceal their crime; but God, who seeth in secret, made the murder manifest, and all the parties were taken. One of the men, Wood, died in prison; the other, Billings, was executed, and then hung in chains. Catherine Hayes was condemned to be burnt, and on the day of execution being brought to the stake, was chained thereto with an iron chain, running round her waist, and under her arms, and a rope round her neck, which was drawn through a hole in the post; then the faggots, intermixed with light brushwood and straw, being piled all round her, the executioner put fire thereto in several places, which immediately blazing out, as soon as the same reached her, she with her arms pushed down those which were before her, when she appeared in the middle of the flames as low as the waist; upon which the executioner got hold of the end of the cord which was round her neck, and pulled it tight, in order to strangle her, but the fire soon reached his hand, and burned it, so that he was obliged to let it go again; more faggots were immediately thrown upon her, and in about three or four hours she was reduced to ashes. Horrible as this murder was, and the annals of crime scarcely present its parallel, Dean Swift made it the subject of a punning ballad, of which the following is a copy.

A SONG
ON THE MURDER OF MR. HAYES.

To the Tune of *Chevy Chase.*

In Tyburn road a man there liv'd,
  A just and honest life;
And there he might have lived still,
  If so had pleas'd his wife.

But she to vicious ways inclin'd
  A life most wicked led;
With tailors, and with tinkers too,
  She oft defil'd his bed.

Full twice a day to church he went,
  And so devout would be;
Sure never was a saint on earth,
  If that no saint was he!

This vex'd his wife unto the heart,
  She was of wrath so full,
That finding no hole in his coat,
  She pick'd one in his scull.

But then her heart 'gan to relent,
  And griev'd she was so sore;
That quarter to him for to give,
  She cut him into four.

All in the dark and dead of night,
  These quarters she convey'd;
And in a ditch at Marybone
  His marrow-bones she laid.

His head at Westminster she threw,
  All in the Thames so wide;
Says she, my dear, the wind sets fair,
  And you may have the tide.

But heav'n, whose pow'r no limit knows
  On earth, or on the main,
Soon caus'd his head for to be thrown
  Upon the land again.

The head being found, the justices
  Their heads together laid;
And all agreed there must have been
  Some body to this head.

But since no body could be found,
  High mounted on a shelf,
They e'en set up the head to be
  A witness for itself.

Next, that it no self-murder was,
  The case itself explains,
For no man could cut off his head,
  And throw it in the Thames.

Ere many days had gone and past,
  The deed at length was known,
And Cath'rine she confess'd, at last,
  The fact to be her own.

God prosper long our noble king,
  Our lives and safeties all,
And grant that we may warning take
  By Cath'rine Hayes's fall."

Varieties.

THE MEDUSÆ.

The Polar sea has a peculiar colour, which is caused by the great quantity of medusæ and other minute animals. They are most abundant in the sea water, which is of an olive-green colour. Capt. Scoresby, during one of his voyages to the Arctic regions, examined a quantity of the olive-green sea water, and found the medusæ immense. They were about one-fourth of an inch asunder. In this proportion a cubic inch of water would contain 64; a cubic foot 110,592; a cubic fathom 23,887,872, and a cubic mile about 23,888,000,000,000. From soundings made in the situation where these animals were found, it is probable the sea is upwards of a mile in depth, but whether these substances occupy the whole depth is uncertain. Provided however the depth to which they extend be but 250 fathoms, the above immense number of one species may occur in a space of two miles square. It may give a better conception of the amount of medusæ in this extent, if we calculate the length of time that would be requisite for a certain number of persons to count this number. Allowing that one person could count a million in seven days, which is barely possible, it would have required that 80,000 persons should have started at the creation of the world to complete the enumeration at the present time.

What a stupendous idea does this fact give of the immensity of creation! But if the number of animals in a space of two miles square be so great, what must be the amount requisite for discolouring the sea through an extent of twenty or thirty thousand miles.

WILD PIGEONS.

The accounts of the enormous flocks in which the passenger, or wild pigeons, fly about in North America, seem to an European like the tales of Baron Munchausen; but the travellers are "all in a story." In Upper Canada, says Mr. Howison, in his entertaining "*Sketches*," you may kill 20 or 30 at one shot out of the masses which darken the air. And in the United States, according to Wilson the ornithologist, they sometimes desolate and lay waste a tract of country 40 or 50 miles long, and 5 or 6 broad, by making it their breeding-place. While in the state of Ohio, Mr. Wilson saw a flock of these birds which extended, he judged, more than a mile in breadth, and continued to pass over his head at the rate of one mile in a minute, during four hours—thus making its whole length about 240 miles.—According to his moderate estimate, this flock contained two thousand two hundred and thirty millions two hundred and seventy-two pigeons.

THE VOLCANO OF JURULLO, IN MEXICO.

The most elevated summit of the intendancy of Valladolid in Mexico, is the Pic de Tancitaro, to the east of Tuspan. To the east of this peak is the extraordinary volcano of Jurullo, which was formed in the night of the 29th September, 1759. The great catastrophe by which this mountain rose from the earth, and by which a considerable extent of ground totally changed its appearance, is perhaps one of the most extraordinary physical revolutions on record. A vast plain extends from the hills of Eguasarco to near the villages of Teipa and Petatlan, both equally celebrated for their fine plantations of cotton. This plain is only from two thousand one hundred and sixty to two thousand six hundred and twenty-four feet above the level of the sea. In the middle of this space basaltic cones appear, the summits of which are crowned with ever-green oaks of a laurel and olive foliage, intermingled with palm trees. This beautiful vegetation forms a singular contrast with the aridity of the plain which was laid waste by volcanic fire. Till the middle of the 18th century, fields cultivated with sugar-cane and indigo occupied the extent of ground between the two brooks Cuitamba and San Pedro. These fields, watered by artificial means, belonged to one of the greatest and richest plantations in the country. In the month of June, 1759, a subterraneous noise was heard. Hollow noises of a most alarming nature were accompanied by frequent earthquakes, which succeeded one another for from fifty to sixty days, to the great consternation of the neighbouring inhabitants. From the beginning of September, every thing seemed to announce the complete reestablishment of tranquillity, when, in the night between the 28th and 29th, the horrible subterraneous noise recommenced. The affrighted Indians fled to the mountains for safety. A track of ground, from three to four square miles in extent, which goes by the name of Malpays, rose up in the shape of a bladder. The bounds of this convulsion are still distinguishable in the fractured strata. The ground thrown up is, near its edges, thirty-nine feet in height above the old level of the plain; but it rises progressively towards the centre, to an elevation of five hundred feet. Those who witnessed this great catastrophe from the top of the mountain of Aguasarco, assert, that flames were seen to issue forth for an extent of more than half a square league; that fragments of burning rocks were thrown up to prodigious heights; and that, through a thick cloud of ashes, illumined by volcanic fire, the softened surface of the earth was seen to swell up like an agitated sea. The rivers of Cuitamba and San Pedro rushed into the burning chasms, and contributed to exasperate the flames, which were distinguishable at the city of Pascuaro, though situated on a very extensive table land, four thousand five hundred feet above the plains of Jurullo. Eruptions of mud, and especially of strata of clay, enveloping balls of decomposed basaltes, in concentrical layers, appear to indicate that subterraneous water had no small share in producing this extraordinary revolution. Thousands of small cones, from six to nine feet in height, called by the natives ovens, issued from the ground while it was under the influence of this confusion; and, although the heat of these volcanic ovens has suffered a great diminution, Humboldt mentions that he has seen the thermometer rise to two hundred and two degrees of Fahrenheit, on being plunged into fissures, which exhale an aqueous vapour. From each small cone the vapour arises to the height of forty or fifty feet. In many of them a subterraneous noise is heard, resembling that occasioned by the boiling of a fluid. In the midst of the ovens, six large masses, elevated from one thousand three hundred to one thousand six hundred feet above the old level of the plains, sprung up from the chasm. The most elevated of these masses is the great volcano of Jurullo. It is continually burning, and has thrown up an immense quantity of lavas. These great eruptions of the central volcano continued till the month of February, 1760. In the following years they became less frequent; and the Indians having been gradually accustomed to the terrific noises of the new volcano, had advanced towards the mountains to admire the streams of fire discharged from an infinity of great and small volcanic apertures. At the first explosion of this volcano, the roofs of the houses of Queretaro were covered with ashes, though distant more than forty-eight leagues. The subterraneous fire appears now far from violent; and the desolated ground, as well as the great volcano, begin to be covered with vegetables. The air, however, is still heated to such a degree by the ovens, as to raise the thermometer to one hundred and nine degrees of Fahrenheit.

THE FAMILY ELM.

In the village of Crawley there is an Elm of great size, in the hollow trunk of which a poor woman gave birth to an infant, and where she afterwards resided for a long time. The tree which is a great curiosity is still standing, but as the parish is not willing to be burthened with all the young elms that might be brought forth from the trunk of this singular tree, the lord of the manor has very wisely put up a door to the entrance of this new lying-in-hospital, which is kept locked, except upon particular occasions, when the neighbours meet to enjoy their pipe, and tell old tales in the cavity of the elm, which is capable of containing a party of more than a dozen. The interior of this tree is paved with bricks, and in other respects made comfortable for its temporary occupants.

CELERITY OF MANUFACTURE.

Gen. M'Clure made a bet of 50 dollars, that he would take wool, in the fleece and manufacture a suit of satinet cloth in ten hours. The bet was decided entirely in his favour, having completed the suit and put it on, in eight hours and forty-six minutes. The colour was a blue mixture; the wool was coloured in thirty-five minutes; carded, spun, and wove in two hours and twenty-five minutes; fulled, napped, dyed, sheared, and dressed in one hour and fifty-nine minutes; carried in four minutes three quarters of a mile, to Mr. Gilmore's tailor's shop, who, with the assistance of seven hands, completed the coat, jacket, and overalls in three hours and forty-nine minutes. There was half a yard of the cloth left, being in the whole eight yards and a half, and of such quality as was estimated to be worth one dollar per yard. The General offers to double the bet that he will make a better suit in less than eight hours, and dares the advocates of John Bull's manufactures to take him up.

There was a great collection of people assembled on this occasion. Col. Barnard, with the officers, commissioned and non-commissioned, of his regiment, a full band of music, and many citizens, escorted the General from the village to the factory; when, after partaking of this worthy citizen's usual liberality, the procession returned to the village, the air resounding with many hearty cheers.—*American Paper*.

THE INDIAN NURSE.

Captain Franklin (R. N.) in his narrative of his journey to the Polar Seas, says,—" The Chipewyan Indians profess strong affection for their children, and some regard for their relations, who are often numerous, as they trace very far the ties of consanguinity. A curious instance of the former was mentioned to us, so well authenticated, that I shall venture to give it in the words of Dr. Richardson's Journal.—' A young Chipewyan had separated from the rest of his band for the purpose of trenching beaver, when his wife, who was his sole companion, and in her first pregnancy, was seized with the pains of labour. She died on the third day, after having given birth to a fine boy. The husband was inconsolable, and vowed in his anguish never to take another woman to wife, but his grief was in some degree absorbed in anxiety for his infant son. To preserve its life he descended to the office of nurse, so degrading in the eyes of a Chipewyan, as partaking of the duties of a woman. He swaddled it in soft moss, fed it with broth made from the flesh of the deer, and to still its cries applied it to his breast, praying most earnestly to the great Maker of Life, to assist his endeavours. The force of the powerful passion by which he was actuated, produced the same effect in his case, as it has done in some others which are recorded; a flow of milk actually took place from his breast. He succeeded in rearing his child, taught him to be a hunter, and when he attained the age of manhood, chose him a wife from the tribe. The old man kept his vow in never taking a second wife himself, but he delighted in tending his son's children, and when his daughter-in-law used to interfere, saying that it was not the occupation of a man, he was wont to reply, that he had promised to the great Master of Life, if his child was spared, never to be proud, like the other Indians. He used to mention, too, as a certain proof of the approbation of Providence, that although he was always obliged to carry his child on his back while hunting, yet that it never roused a mouse by its cries, being always particularly still at those times. Our informant (Mr. Wentzel, the guide to the expedition) added, that he had often seen this Indian in his old age, and that his left breast, even then, retained the unusual size it had acquired in his occupation of nurse.'"

CAT EATERS.

Some years ago, for a wager of 50*l*. a fellow, who lived near the race-course of Kildare, in Ireland, devoured five fox cubs, and literally began eating each while alive. It is, however, to be observed, that the devourer was a natural fool, having been born deaf, dumb, and without a palate. Another story is told, that " a fellow, a shepherd at Beverley, in Yorkshire, about eleven years ago, for a bet of five pounds, was produced, who was to devour a living cat. The one produced was a large black tom cat, which had not been fed for the purpose; but was chosen, as being the largest in that neighbourhood. The day appointed was the fair-day at Beverley. The parties met. The man produced was a raw-boned fellow, about forty. The cat was then given to him; on which he took hold of his four legs with one hand, and closing his mouth with the other, he killed him by biting his head to pieces immediately, and in less than a quarter of an hour, devoured every part of the cat, tail, legs, claws, bones, and every thing. The man who laid the wager gave the fellow *two guineas* for doing it, and the shepherd appeared perfectly satisfied with the reward."—After he had done it, he walked about the fair the whole afternoon, and appeared neither sick nor sorry. He took no emetic, nor had this repast any effect upon him whatever.

Eccentric Biography.

"Mankind are various, and the world is wide."

FRANCIS BATTALIA, THE STONE-EATER.

Man generally comes into the world and goes out of it empty handed; we say generally, for this rule, like most others, is not without an exception, as will be seen in the memoir we are about to give of an Italian who lived in London about the middle of the seventeenth century. For this account we are indebted to a tract by Dr. John Bulwer, published in 1753, and entitled "Man Transformed, or the Artificial Changeling."

I saw in London, the other day (says the Doctor), an Italian, one Francis Battalia by name, about thirty years of age, who was born with two stones in one hand and one in the other; who as soon as he was born, having the breast offered unto him refused to suck; and when they would have fed him with pap he utterly rejected that also; whereupon the midwife and nurse, entering into consideration of the strangeness of his birth and refusal of all kind of nourishment, consulted with some physicians what they should do in this case.

When the physicians saw that the child rejected all usual nourishment, they stated their opinion that the child brought its meat with it in the world, and that it was to be nourished with stones. The experiment was tried, the three stones which he held in his hands when born (some accounts say five) were successively swallowed; and the nurse now fed him with nothing but small pebbles, which constituted his only solid food, not only from his birth to manhood, but during the remainder of his life.

Dr. Bulwer, who saw him when he was thirty years of age, says: "His manner is to put three or four stones into a spoon, and so putting them into the mouth together, to swallow them all down one after another; then he drinks a glass of beer after them. He devours about half a peck of these stones every day; and when he chinks upon his stomach, or shakes his body, you may hear the stones rattle as if they were in a sack; all which in twenty-four hours are resolved: after which digestion of them he hath a fresh appetite to these stones, as we have to our victuals; and by these, with a cup of beer and a pipe of tobacco, he has his whole subsistence. He hath attempted to eat meat and bread, broth, milk, and such kind of food, upon which other mortals commonly live; but he could never brook any, neither would they stay with him to do him any good.

He is a black, swarthy, little fellow, active and strong enough; and hath been a soldier in Ireland, where he hath made good use of this property; for having the advantage of this strange way of alimony, he sold his allowance of provision at great rates; and he told me that at Limerick, in Ireland, he sold a sixpenny loaf and two pennyworth of cheese for twelve shillings and sixpence.

It seems that when Battalia first came over to this country, he was suspected to be an impostor, and was by the order of the government shut up for a month with the allowance of two pots of beer and half an ounce of tobacco every day. At the end of this time he was discharged and acquitted of all deceit.

Mr. Boyle, in his Experimental Philosophy, notices Battalia, of whom he says, " Not long ago, there was here in England, a private soldier very famous for digesting of stones; and a very inquisitive man assures me that he knew him familiarly, and had the curiosity to keep in his company for twenty-four hours together to watch him; and observed that he ate nothing but stones in that time."

PHEBE BROWN.

The greatest wonder I ever saw (says Mr. Hutton, of Birmingham) was Phebe Brown. She is five feet six inches in height, is about thirty, well proportioned, round face, and ruddy; has a dark penetrating eye, which, the moment it fixes upon your face, sees your character, and that with precision. Her step (pardon the Irishism) is more manly than a man's, and can cover forty miles a day. Her common dress is a man's hat, coat, with a spencer over it, and men's shoes. She is unmarried.

She can lift one hundred weight in each hand, and carry fourteen score; can sew, knit, cook, and spin, but hates them all, and every accompaniment to the female character, that of modesty excepted. A gentleman at the New Bath had recently treated her rudely: " She had a good mind to have knocked him down." She assured me she never knew what fear was. She gives no affront, but offers to fight any man who gives her one. If she never has fought, perhaps it is owing to the insulter having been a coward, for the man of courage would disdain to offer an insult to a female.

Phebe has strong sense, an excellent judgment, says smart things, and supports an easy freedom in all companies. Her voice is more than masculine, it is deep toned. With the wind in her favour, she can send it a mile; she has neither beard nor prominence of breast; she undertakes any kind of manual labour, as holding the plough, driving a team, thatching the barn, using the flail, &c.; but her chief avocation is breaking horses, for which she charges a guinea a week each. She always rides without a saddle, is thought to be the best judge of a horse or cow in the country, and is frequently employed to purchase for others at the neighbouring fairs.

She is fond of Milton, Pope, and Shakspeare, also of music; is self-taught, and performs on several instruments, as the flute, violin, and harpsichord, and supports the bass viol in Mallock church. She is a markswoman, and carries the gun on her shoulder. She eats no beef or pork, and but little mutton. Her chief food is milk, which is also her drink, discarding wine ale, and spirits.

A GOOD PATIENT.

At the Lincoln Assizes in March 1817, an action was brought by Mr. Wright, an apothecary of Bottesford, against a Mr. Jessop, a bachelor of opulence, residing near Lincoln, to recover the sum of 787*l.* 18*s.* for medicine and attendance, during 25 years. By the statement of plaintiff's counsel, it appeared that the defendant was of a hypochondriacal turn, and had taken pills for a great number of years; he used to have from 600 to 2000 pills sent to him at a time; and in one year he took 51,000! being at the rate of 150 a-day. There were also thousands of bottles of mixture. From the ravenous propensity of the patient for physic, it was deemed necessary to call in two physicians, who inquiring of the defendant what was the course of medicine and nourishment he pursued through the day, answered as follows:—At half past two o'clock in the morning I take two spoonsful and a half of jalap, and then a quantity of electuary; then I sleep till seven, and repeat the dose of both jalap and electuary; at nine o'clock I take 14 pills of No. 9, and 11 pills of No. 10, to whet my appetite for breakfast; at breakfast I eat a basin of milk, at eleven I have an acid and alkali mixture, afterwards I have a bolus, and at nine at night I have an anodyne mixture and go to sleep." After some progress had been made in the evidence, a compromise took place, the plaintiff accepting a verdict for 450*l.*!

Anecdotes of Longevity.

The great age attained by man in the early history of the world, might in the present day be questioned, did it not rest on the best of all authorities—the Sacred Scriptures. Immediately after the creation, when the world was to be peopled by one man and one woman, the ordinary age was 900 years and upwards. Immediately after the flood when there were three persons to stock the world, their age was cut shorter, and none of those Patriarchs, but Shem, arrived at 500. In the second century we find that none reached 240; and in the third Terah alone reached 200 years. The world by this time had become so well peopled, that they had built cities and were cantoned out into distant regions. By degrees, as the number of people increased, their longevity diminished, until it came down to 70 or 80 years, and there it stood, and has continued to stand ever since the time of Moses; though that many thousands have passed far beyond this general limit to the age of man, our anecdotes of longevity will shew. In commencing perhaps our readers will expect that we should begin with Henry Jenkins, or old Parr, the two most remarkable instances of longevity this country has produced; we prefer, however, taking a more recent instance, that of a Negro who lived to the great age of 140 years. For this account we are indebted to a Jamaica Paper for the year 1819.

OLD HOPE.

Roger Hope Elletson died at Hope estate on Monday the 31st of May, 1819, aged upwards of 140 years.

His age cannot be positively proved by any written document or record, and must therefore be inferred from his own account of himself, combined with what collateral testimony may be collected, and the circumstances connected with it. His own account is, that he was born at Merryman's Hill, an old sugar-estate, in St. Andrew's, and was a father at the time of the great earthquake in 1692, which destroyed Port-Royal; that he was at home, when that event took place, and perfectly remembered the violence of the shocks, far exceeding any he had felt since. The particulars of the immediate consequences resulting from that dreadful convulsion of nature, had faded from his memory, but the general scene of desolation and distress he very well remembered. Being asked, about two years since, if he recollected any thing remarkable to have happened a short time either before or after the great earthquake, he replied, "Yes; a great storm, and an attempt of the French to land on the island;" but he could not tell which event preceded the other. The first was in 1689, the second in 1694; and it is by no means strange that he could not recollect these circumstances so correctly as the earthquake; because the predominating magnitude of that awful event, its dreadful violence, and shocking consequences, must naturally have made a deeper impression on his mind. He could not tell how long it was since he had done any work, but that it was a great many years: that he had never been sick, and had never drank rum, nor any ardent spirit, in the whole course of his life.

Mr. Long, in his History of Jamaica, speaking of the healthiness of the climate, and the consequent longevity of its inhabitants, says, " I conversed with a negro man, who remembered perfectly well the great earthquake which destroyed Port-Royal in 1692; and, by his account, he could not have been much under 18 or 20 when that event happened. This person was not, as in northern countries, decrepid, or bedridden, but lively, and able to stir about, his appetite good, and his faculties moderately sound." It is very probable that OLD HOPE was the man he conversed with; especially when we consider that Mr. Long's book was published in 1774, and that his conversation with the old man was five years at least before that, which brings it to 1769, 77 years after the earthquake, to which, if we add 18 years, his supposed age at the time, it makes him to have been then 95 years old: add 50 years that have elapsed since, and it amounts to 145—about the age that he professed himself to be.

OLD HOPE was a strong man, of full six feet in height. Many years ago he lost the sight of his right eye, by being too near the blasting of a rock with gunpowder, but he could see perfectly well with the other; his other senses were very good, as well as his mental faculties. He had some teeth remaining; he had some grey hairs, but so few, that at a little distance it could scarcely be perceived he had any. His head was well covered, without baldness in any part. He did not stoop more than, nor so much as, many men not half his age; and in October, 1817, when his portrait was painted, he used to walk to town with ease, whenever he was required to sit:—He would then drink some wine sangaree to recruit himself, but never more than was requisite to quench his thirst; and would generally leave some in the glass for his grandson. He sat very patiently, and was much pleased to observe the progress of the portrait; and was highly gratified with the idea of the Admiral's taking it home, and shewing it to the *King* and *Nobility of England.* Neither his father nor mother were uncommonly old. The only survivor derived from him is his grandson *Richard,* a boy about twelve years old, who constantly attended him. Young Richard is the son of *Quashie,* now living on the estate, who married OLD HOPE's youngest daughter, and only remaining child. She died in 1813, of a consumption, aged about 45 years; so that he must have been near a hundred years old when he became her father; and it reflects the highest credit to the old man's feelings, to know that he attended and nursed her with the tenderest care, and most unremitting attention, during a lingering illness.

At last his own time drew nigh. Perceiving himself to get weaker and weaker, and being conscious he could not exist much longer, he grew very desirous to be baptized, or, as he called it, to be made a Christian of; and, in compliance with his earnest wishes, was sent to the church at St. Andrew's, and was baptized by the Rev. Mr. Campbell, on the 11th of April, being Easter Sunday, by the name of ROGER HOPE ELLETSON. After his baptism, he continued to decline by imperceptible gradations, without any bodily pain or mental uneasiness, until Whit Monday, the 31st of May, when he quietly expired at about three o'clock in the afternoon.

The Scrap Book.

AN EGG OF EGGS.

ON Easter Monday, March 31, 1823, at breakfast, boiled eggs being a part, my wife breaking one, discovered a second therein; the first appeared, in every respect, a perfect egg, before and after being opened, containing yolk and white in a perfect state; the second, the size of a partridge's egg, perfectly round, enclosed in a strong membrane or skin, containing slime or white only. On opening this second egg we therein discovered a third, enveloped as the former; of a firm texture, of the natural or common shape, and of the size of a snow-bird or chippy's egg. This is retained and preserved for the inspection of the curious; and may be seen at the sign of the *Traveller's Rest,* M'GREWSBURGH. —*Philadelphia Paper.*

PROGRESS OF THE MARVELLOUS.

THE Nuremberg Correspondent gives an account of a gigantic Vat, made for Stretton and Co. the London Brewers, which, it says, is 34 feet high and 96 in diameter; and quite outdoes the famous ton of Heidelberg. This stupendous vat is stated by the same authority to have been installed in the brewery by dining 796 persons within its bounds at once, with abundance of elbow room!

Published by J. LIMBIRD, 355, *Strand,* (*East End of Exeter 'Change*); *and sold by all Newsmen and Booksellers. Printed by* A. APPLEGATH, *Stamford-street.*

THE CABINET OF CURIOSITIES;
OR,
Wonders of the World Displayed.

A world of wonders, where creation seems
No more the works of Nature but her dreams.—MONTGOMERY.

No. 11.]　　　PRICE TWO-PENCE.

CANNIBALS.

In almost every age of the world there have been barbarous nations who followed the horrible practice of cannibalism, and

>———" devour'd each other like the beasts
Gorging on human flesh."

Homer speaks of anthropophagy, or cannibalism being frequent in the age immediately preceding his own; and Herodotus relates that the Essedonian Scythians mixed up the flesh of men who died with that of beasts and made a feast. The Messagetæ were still more ferocious: they did not wait until death did its office, but when any person grew old, they killed him and eat his flesh. If he died of sickness they buried him. The same historian relates, that several Indian nations killed all their old people and their sick to feed on the flesh; and persons in health were sometimes accused of being ill in order to afford a pretence for devouring them. The Greek writers all represent cannibalism as universal before the time of Orpheus; and according to Sextus Empiricus, the first laws that were made were for the prevention of this barbarous practice.

We have equally good evidence of the custom of eating human flesh in later times. All

c

the Romish missionaries who visited the internal parts of Africa, and some parts of Asia, speak of it as quite common. Herrera states, that there are great markets in China furnished wholly with human flesh for the higher orders of the people; and other writers mention it as common to the inhabitants of Concha, Java, Siam, the islands in the gulf of Bengal, &c.

The philosophers Diogenes, Chrysippus, and Zeno, followed by the whole sect of Stoics, maintain that there is nothing unnatural in the eating of human flesh; and that it is very reasonable to use dead bodies for food rather than give them a prey to worms and putrefaction.

In Egypt, in the thirteenth century, the habit of eating human flesh pervaded all classes of society; and extraordinary snares were spread for physicians in particular. They were called to attend persons, who pretended to be sick, but who were only hungry; and it was not in order to consult, but to devour them. An historian of great veracity, Abd-Allatif, has related, how a practice which at first inspired dread and horror, soon occasioned not the slightest surprise. He says:

"When the poor began to eat human flesh, the horror and astonishment caused by repasts so dreadful were such, that these crimes furnished the never ceasing subject of every conversation. But at length the people became so accustomed to it, and conceived such a taste for this detestable food, that people of wealth and respectability were found to use it as their ordinary food, to eat it by way of regale, and even to lay in a stock of it. Thus flesh was prepared in different ways, and the practice being once introduced, spread into the provinces, so that examples of it were found in every part of Egypt. It then no longer caused any surprise; the horror it had at first inspired vanished, and it was mentioned as an indifferent and ordinary thing. This fury of devouring one another became so common among the poor, that the greater part perished in this manner. These wretches employed all sorts of artifices to seize men by surprise, or decoy them into their houses under false pretences. This happened to three physicians among those who visited me; and a bookseller, who sold me books, an old and very corpulent man, fell into their snares, and escaped with great difficulty.

"All the facts we relate as ocular witnesses fell under our observation accidentally, for we generally avoided seeing spectacles which inspired us with so much horror."

When America was discovered, cannibalism was found to be almost universal; so much so, that several authors have supposed it to be occasioned through a want of food, or through the indolence of the people to seek for it, though others ascribe its origin to a spirit of revenge. But although it is known that anthropophagy and the practice of human sacrifices, with which it is often connected, are found in all parts of the globe, and among people of very different races; yet what strikes us more in the study of history is, to see human sacrifices retained in a state of civilisation somewhat advanced, and that the nations, who hold it a point of honour to devour their prisoners, are not always the rudest and most ferocious. This observation, which has something in it distressing and painful, has not escaped such of the missionaries as are sufficiently enlightened to reflect on the manners of the surrounding tribes. The Cabres, the Guipunavis, and the Caribbees, have always been more powerful and more civilized than the other hordes of the Oronooko; and yet the former two are as much addicted to anthropophagy, as the last are repugnant to it. We must carefully distinguish the different branches into which the great family of the Caribbee nation is divided. These branches are as numerous as those of the Monguls, and the western Tartars or Turcomans. The Carribbees of the continent, those who inhabit the plains between the Lower Oronooko, the Rio Branco, the Essequibo, and the sources of the Oyapoc, hold in horror the practice of devouring their enemies. This barbarous custom at the first discovery of America existed only among the Caribbees of the West Indies.

The cannibalism of the nations of Guyana is never caused by the want of subsistence, or by the superstitions of their religion, as in the islands of the South Sea; but it is generally the effect of the vengeance of a conqueror, and (as the missionaries say) "of a vitiated appetite." Victory over a hostile horde is celebrated by a repast, in which some parts of the body of a prisoner are devoured. Sometimes a defenceless family is surprised in the night; or an enemy who is met with by chance in the woods, is killed by a poisoned arrow. The body is cut to pieces, and carried as a trophy to the hut. It is civilisation only, that has made man feel the unity of the human race; which has revealed to him, as we may say, the ties of consanguinity, by which he is linked to beings to whose language and manners he is a stranger. Savages know only their own family; and a tribe appears to them but a more numerous assemblage of relations. When those who inhabit the missions see Indians of the forest, who are unknown to them, arrive, they make use of an expression which has struck us by its simple candour: "They are no doubt my relations; I understand them when they speak to me." But these very savages detest all, who are not of their family, or their tribe; and hunt the Indians of a neighbouring tribe, who live at war with their own, as we hunt game. They know the duties of family and of relationship, but not those of humanity, which require the feeling of a common tie with beings framed like ourselves. No emotion of pity prompts them to spare the wives or children of a hostile race; and the latter are devoured in preference, at the repasts given at the conclusion of a battle, or of a warlike incursion.

The hatred which savages for the most part feel for men, who speak another idiom, and appear to them to be *barbarians* of an inferior race, is sometimes rekindled in the missions, after having long slumbered. A short time before our arrival at Esmeralda, says Humboldt, an Indian, born in the forest, behind the Duida, travelled alone with another Indian, who, after having been made prisoner by the Spaniards on the banks of the Ventuario, lived peaceably in the village, or, as it is expressed here, "within the sound of the bell," debaxo de la campana. The latter could only walk slowly, because he laboured under one of those fevers, to which the natives are subject when they arrive in the missions, and abruptly change their diet. Wearied of his delay, his fellow traveller killed him, and hid the body behind a copse of thick trees, near Esmeralda. This crime, like many others among the Indians would have remained unknown, if the murderer had not made preparations for a feast on the following day. He tried to induce his children, born in the mission, and become Christians, to go with him for some parts of the dead body. They had much difficulty in persuading him to desist from his purpose; and the soldier who was posted at Esmeralda, learned from the domestic squabble caused by this event, what the Indians would have hidden from his knowledge.

In the island of Sumatra, human flesh is still eaten by the Batta people, but by them only. "They do not eat human flesh," says Mr. Marsden, "as a means of satisfying the cravings of nature, owing to a deficiency of other food; nor is it sought after as a gluttonous delicacy, as it would seem among the *New Zealanders*. The *Battas* eat it as a species of ceremony; as a mode of shewing their detestation of crimes, by an ignominious punishment, and as a horrid indication of revenge and insult to their unfortunate enemies. The objects of this barbarous repast are the prisoners taken in war, and offenders convicted and condemned for capital crimes. Persons of the former description may be ransomed or exchanged, for which they often wait a considerable time; and the latter suffer only when their friends cannot redeem them by the customary fine of twenty *beenchangs*, or eighty dollars. These are tried by the people of the tribe where the fact was committed; but cannot be executed till their own particular *raja*, or chief, has been acquainted with the sentence; who, when he acknowledges the justice of the intended punishment, sends a cloth to put over the delinquent's head, together with a large dish of salt and lemons. The unhappy object, whether prisoner of war, or malefactor, is then tied to a stake; the people assembled throw their lances at him from a certain distance, and when mortally wounded, they run up to him, as if in a transport of passion, cut pieces from the body with their knives, dip them in the dish of salt and lemon-juice, slightly broil them over a fire prepared for the purpose, and swallow the morsels, with a degree of savage enthusiasm. Sometimes (I presume according to the degree of their animosity and resentment) the whole is devoured; and instances have been known, where with barbarity still aggravated, they tear the flesh from the carcass with their mouths. To such a depth of depravity may man be plunged, when neither religion nor philosophy enlighten his steps! All that can be said in extenuation of the horror of this diabolical ceremony, is, that no view appears to be entertained of torturing the sufferers; of increasing or lengthening out the pangs of death: the whole fury is directed against the corse; warm indeed with the remains of life, but past the sensation of pain. I have found a difference of opinion in regard to their eating the bodies of their enemies *slain* in battle. Some persons long resident there, and acquainted with their proceedings, assert that it is not customary; but as one or two particular instances have been given by other people, it is just to conclude, that it sometimes takes place, though not generally. It was supposed to be with this intent that *Raja Neabin* maintained a long conflict for the body of Mr. Nairne, a most respectable gentleman and valuable servant of the India Company, who fell in an attack upon the campong of that chief, in the year 1775."

UNPARALLELED INSTANCE OF VOLUNTARY STARVATION.

(From a Paris Paper.)

In the year 1822, Louis Antoine Viterbi, was tried before the Court of Cassation in Paris as an accomplice in the assassination of a person named Frediani—a crime which he denied to the last moment. He was condemned to death, and towards the end of November was confined in the prison of Basria, where he was guarded in the usual manner. Viterbi determined not to die on the scaffold, but to be his own executioner, though not by any desperate act of suicide.

To effect this purpose, he abstained from food during three days, and then ate voraciously, and to a forced excess, in the hope that after fasting so long, he should thereby put an end to his existence. Nature deceived him; and on the 2d of December, he determined to starve himself to death. From that day nothing could subdue this terrible resolve: although Viterbi, who had already sustained two dangerous attacks of illness, did not expire until the night of the 21st of that month.

During the three first days, Viterbi, as was the case when he made the first attempt, felt himself progressively tormented by hunger, and did not endure these early sufferings with less courage than he had shewn on the former occasion. Under these circumstances, a report was made to the public minister, who ordered bread, water, wine, and soup, to be taken daily to his cell, and placed conspicuously in view. This order was punctually executed until the day of his death: but Viterbi always caused the provisions of the preceding day to be distributed amongst his fellow-prisoners, without ever tasting the fresh supply. No debility was manifest during these three days—no irregular muscular movement was remarked—his intellect continued sound, and he wrote with his usual facility.

From the 5th to the 6th, to famishment insensibly succeeded the much more grievous suffering of thirst, which became so acute, that on the 6th, without ever deviating from his resolution, he began to moisten his lips and mouth occasionally, and to gargle with a few drops of water, to relieve the burning pain in his throat; but he let nothing pass the organs of deglutition, being desirous not to assuage the most insupportable cravings, but to mitigate a pain which might have shaken his resolution. On the 6th, his physical powers were a little weakened; his voice was nevertheless still sonorous, pulsation regular, and a natural heat extended over his whole frame. From the 3d to the 6th, he had continued to write; at night, several hours of tranquil sleep seemed to suspend the progress of his sufferings; no change was observable in his mental faculties, and he complained of no local pain.

Until the 10th, the burning anguish of thirst became more and more insupportable; Viterbi merely continued to gargle, without once swallowing a single drop of water; but in the course of the day of the 10th, overcome by excess of pain, he seized the jug of water, which was near him, and drank immoderately. During the last three days, debility had made considerable progress, his voice became feeble, pulsation had declined, and the extremities were cold. Viterbi, however, continued to write: and sleep, each night, still afforded him several hours' ease.

From the 10th to the 12th, the symptoms made a slight progress. The constancy of Viterbi never yielded an instant; he dictated his journal, and afterwards approved and signed what had thus been written agreeably to his dictation. During the night of the 12th, the symptoms assumed a more decided character; debility was extreme, pulsation scarcely sensible, his voice extraordinarily feeble; the cold had extended itself all over his body, and the pangs of thirst were more acute than ever. On the 13th, the unhappy man, thinking himself at the point of death, again seized the jug of water, and drank twice, after which the cold became more severe; and congratulating himself that death was near, Viterbi stretched himself on the bed, and said to the gendarmes who were guarding him, "Look how well I have laid myself out." At the expiration of a quarter of an hour he asked for some brandy; the keeper not having any, he called for some wine, of which he took four spoons-full. When he had swallowed these, the cold suddenly ceased, heat returned, and Viterbi enjoyed a sleep of four hours.

On awaking (on the morning of the 13th) and finding his powers restored, he fell into a rage with the keeper, protesting that they had deceived him, and then began beating his head violently against the wall of the prison, and would inevitably have killed himself, had he not been prevented by the gendarmes.

During the two following days he resisted his inclination to drink, but continued to gargle occasionally with water. During the two nights he suffered a little from exhaustion, but in the morning found himself rather relieved.

On the 16th, at five o'clock in the morning, his powers were almost annihilated, pulsation could hardly be felt, and his voice was almost wholly inaudible; his body was benumbed with cold; and it was thought he was on the point of expiring. At ten o'clock he began to feel better, pulsation was more sensible, his voice strengthened, and, finally, heat again extended over his frame, and in this state he continued during the whole of the 17th. From the latter day, until the 20th, Viterbi only became more inexorable in his resolution to die; he inflexibly refused all offers of aliment, and even resisted the torturing pangs of thirst; not a drop of water did he swallow, although he still, from time to time, moistened his parched lips, and sometimes his burning eyelids, from which he found some relief to his agony.

During the 19th the pangs of hunger and thirst appeared more grievous than ever; so insufferable, indeed, were they, that, for the first time, Viterbi let a few tears escape him. But his invincible mind instantly spurned this human tribute. For a moment he seemed to have resumed his wonted energy, and said, in presence of his guards and the gaoler, "I will persist, whatever may be the consequence; my mind shall be stronger than my body; my strength of mind does not vary, that of my body daily becomes weaker."

A short time after this energetic expression, which shewed the powerful influence of his moral faculties over his physical necessities, an icy coldness again assailed his body, the shiverings were frequent and dreadful, and his loins, in particular, were seized with a stone-like coldness, which extended itself down his thighs.

During the 19th, a slight pain, at intervals, affected his heart, and, for the first time, he felt a ringing sensation in his ears. At noon, on this day, his head became heavy; his sight however, was perfect, and he conversed almost as usual, making some signs with his hands.

On the 20th, Viterbi declared to the gaoler and physician, that he would not again moisten his mouth, and feeling the approach of death, he stretched himself on the bed, and asked the gendarmes, as he had done on a former day, whether he was well laid out, and added, "I am prepared to leave this world." Death did not this time betray the hopes of a man who, perhaps, of all others invoked it with the greatest fervour, and to whom it seemed to deny its cheerless tranquillity. Until the day of his death, this inconceivable man had regularly kept his journal. On the 21st, Viterbi was no more.

Hoaxes and Impostures.
No. I.
THE BOTTLE-CONJURER.

'When conjurers the quality can bubble,
And get their gold with very little trouble,
By putting giddy lies in public papers,—
As jumping in quart bottles,—such like vapours;
And further yet, if we the matter strain,
Wou'd pipe a tune upon a walking cane;
Nay, more surprising tricks! he swore he'd shew,
Grannams who died a hundred years ago:—
'Tis whimsical enough, what think ye, Sirs?
The quality can ne'er be conjurers,——
The de'el a bit;—no, let me speak in brief,
The audience fools, the conjurer a thief.
London Magazine for 1749.

We cannot perhaps select a more appropriate commencement for our hoaxes and impostures, than that remarkable hoax which was played upon the good people of the metropolis in the year 1749, by the facetious Duke of Montague, and which has ever since been referred to as a proof of human credulity. This nobleman being in company with some friends, the conversation turned on public curiosity, when the duke said it went so far, that if a person advertised that he would creep into a quart bottle, he would get an audience. Some of the company could not believe this possible, a wager was the result, and the duke, in order to decide it, caused the following advertisement to be put in all the papers.

"AT the *New Theatre* in the *Hay Market*, on *Monday* next, the 16th inst. to be seen a person who performs the several most surprising things following, viz. first, he takes a common walking-cane from any of the spectators, and thereon plays the music of every instrument now in use, and likewise sings to surprising perfection. Secondly, he presents you with a common wine-bottle, which any of the spectators may first examine; this bottle is placed on a table in the middle of the stage and he (without any equivocation) goes into it in sight of all the spectators, and sings in it; during his stay in the bottle, any person may handle it, and see plainly that it does not exceed a common tavern bottle.

Those on the stage or in the boxes may come in masked habits, (if agreeable to them) and the performer (if desired) will inform them who they are.

Stage 7s. 6d. Boxes 5s. Pit. 3s. Gallery 2s. To begin at half an hour after six o'olock.

Tickets to be had at the theatre.

⁎ The performance continues about two hours and a half.

N.B. If any gentleman or lady, after the above performauces (either singly or in company, in or out of mask) are desirous of seeing a representation of any deceased person, such as husband or wife, sister or brother, or any intimate friend of either sex, (upon making a gratuity to the performer) shall be gratified by seeing and conversing with them for some minutes as if alive: likewise (if desired) he will tell you the most secret thoughts in your past life; and give you a full view of persons who have injured you, whether dead or alive.

For those gentlemen and ladies who are desirous of seeing this last part, there is a private room provided.

These performances have been seen by most of the crowned heads of *Asia, Africa,* and *Europe,* and never appeared public any where but once; but will wait of any at their houses, and perform as above, for five pounds each time.

⁎ There will be a proper guard to keep the house in due decorum."

The following advertisement was also published at the same time, which one would have thought sufficient to prevent the former having any effect.

" *Lately arrived from Italy,*

Signor Capitello Jumpedo, a surprising dwarf, no taller than a common tavern tobacco pipe; who can perform many wonderful equilibres, on the slack or tight rope: likewise he'll transform his body in above ten thousand different shapes and postures; and after he has diverted the spectators two hours and a half, he will open his mouth wide, and jump down his own throat. He being the most wonderfullest wonder of wonders as ever the world wondered at, would be willing to join in performance with that surprising musician on *Monday* next, in the *Hay Market.*

He is to be spoke with at the *Black Raven* in *Golden-lane* every day from seven till twelve, and from twelve all day long."

The bait however took even better than could have been expected. The playhouse was crowded with dukes, duchesses, lords, ladies, and all ranks and degrees to witness the bottle-conjurer. Of the result, we quote the following account from the journals of the time.

" Last night (viz. *Monday* the 16th) the much expected drama of the bottle-conjurer of the *New Theatre* in the *Hay Market,* ended in the tragi-comical manner following. Curiosity had drawn together prodigious numbers. About seven the theatre being lighted up, but without so much as a single fiddle to keep the audience in good-humour, many grew impatient. Immediately followed a chorus of catcalls, heightened by loud vociferations, and beating with sticks; when a fellow came from behind the curtain, and bowing, said, that if the performer did not appear, the money should be returned. At the same time a wag crying out from the pit, that if the ladies and gentlemen would give double prices, the conjurer would get into a pint bottle, presently a young gentleman in one of the boxes seized a lighted candle, and threw it on the stage. This served as the charge for sounding to battle. Upon this the greater part of the audience made the best of their way out of the theatre; some losing a cloak, others a hat, others a wig, and others hat, wig, and swords also. One party however staid in the house, in order to demolish the inside, when the mob breaking in, they tore up the benches, broke to pieces the scenes, pulled down the boxes, in short dismantled the theatre entirely, carrying away the particulars abovementioned into the street, where they made a mighty bonfire; the curtain being hoisted on a pole, by way of a flag. A large party of guards were sent for, but came time enough only to warm themselves round the fire. We hear of no other disaster than a young nobleman's chin being hurt, occasioned by his fall into the pit, with part of one of the boxes, which he had forced out with his foot. 'Tis thought the conjurer vanished away with the bank. Many enemies to a late celebrated book, concerning the ceasing of miracles, are greatly disappointed by the conjurer's non-appearance in the bottle; they imagining, that his jumping into it would have been the most convincing proof possible, that miracles are not yet ceased."

Several advertisements were printed afterwards, some serious, others comical, relating to this whimsical affair; among the rest was the following, which, we hope, may be a means of curing this humour for the future.

" *This is to inform the Public,* That notwithstanding the great abuse that has been put upon the gentry, there is now in town a man, who, instead of creeping into a quart or pint bottle, will change himself into a rattle; which he hopes will please both young and old. If this person meets with encouragement to this advertisement, he will then acquaint the gentry where and when he performs."

The reason assigned, in another humorous advertisement, for the conjurer's not going into the *quart bottle*, was, that after searching all the taverns, not one could be found due measure.

BOGS OF BUTTER.

" At Stramore, in the county of Monaghan, near the town of Glaslough," say the newspapers of 1813, " a short time ago a quantity of butter was found in a bog on the lands of Thomas Johnson, of Armagh, Esq. at the depth of twenty feet beneath the surface of the ground. In consequence of the antiseptic qualities of the bog, the butter was found in a state of the most perfect preservation; its colour a statuary white. The person who found this butter, mixed it with other unctuous matter, and formed it into candles for family use. It was more condensed in substance than butter usually is, but perfectly sweet in taste, and free from any disagreable odour. About seven years ago, a quantity of peat, ten feet in depth, had been cut of the same bog. At that period, therefore, the butter must have lain under a pressure of thirty feet of moss."

THE HIGHWAYMEN.

A BILL in the Exchequer was brought by a highwayman named Evetre, against his companion Williams, to compel him to account for a moiety of the partnership effects. The bill stated, that the plaintiff was skilled in *dealing* in several commodities, such as plate, rings, watches, &c.; that the defendant applied to him to become a partner; that they entered into partnership, and it was agreed that they should equally provide all sorts of necessaries, such as horses, saddles, bridles, and equally bear all expenses on the roads, and at inns, taverns, or ale-houses, or at markets or fairs. " And your Orator and the said Joseph Williams proceeded jointly with good success in the said business, on Hounslow-heath, where they dealt with a gentleman for a gold watch; and afterwards the said Joseph Williams told your Orator, that Finchley, in the County of Middlesex, was a good and convenient place to deal in, and that commodities were very plentiful at Finchley aforesaid, and it would be almost all clear gain to them; that they went accordingly, and dealt with several gentlemen for divers watches, rings, swords, canes, hats, cloaks, horses, bridles, saddles, and other things; that about a month afterwards the said Joseph Williams informed your Orator that there was a gentleman at Blackheath who had a good horse, saddle, bridle, watch, sword, cane, and other things, *to dispose of*, which he believed might be had for little or *no money*; that they accordingly went, and met with the said gentleman, and after *some small discourse*, they dealt for the said horse, &c. That your Orator and the said Joseph Williams continued their joint dealings together in several places, viz. at Bagshot, in Surrey; Salisbury, in Wiltshire; Hampstead, in Middlesex; and elsewhere, to the amount of two thousand pounds and upwards." The rest of this bill was in the ordinary form for a partnership account. The parties concerned, however, were foiled in their modest application. The bill was referred for scandal and impertinence! The worthy solicitors were attached and fined, and the equally worthy counsel who signed the bill was directed to pay the costs. The plaintiff was afterwards executed; and one of the solicitors convicted of a robbery and transported! This case was referred to by Lord Kenyon, in *Ridley and Morse: Append. Cliff. Rep. of Southwark Elec.*

Eccentric Biography.

AN AMATEUR MOURNER.

MR. L. was a gentleman of an independent fortune, which he exhausted in the course of a few years, in gratifying one of those whims which we learn from the investigation into Lord Portsmouth's case, was not peculiar to himself. Like his Lordship, the principal enjoyment of Mr. L. was attending funerals. When he heard of the death of any great man, through the channel of the papers, he immediately made the circuit of the whole town, to know who had the job, and then prepared to accompany it. He has often been to York and the confines of Scotland, to be present at the interment of a nobleman or gentleman; and in this respect he was no way biassed by party, or religion; it was the same to him if he was Whig or Tory, out or in; whether a Roman Catholic, or a Protestant, a Jew, or a Presbyterian, they equally commanded his respect and attention, provided the funeral was magnificent. His highest ambition was to obtain one of the little escutcheons, which he considered as so many trophies of his glory; and being known to most of the undertakers, and a constant companion in their peregrinations, they seldom or ever refused him this request. Being entirely inattentive to his own affairs, he found himself in a state of distress, when he did not expect it; yet, though reduced to almost the want of the common necessaries of life, his passion for death-hunting still prevailed; and when he could not ride, he walked on foot. But whenever the journey was of any length, ' he bribed the hearse-driver to let him be an inside passenger with the corpse. In this doleful state he traversed England more than once: but unfortunately fell a martyr, at length, to his strange whim. Being an inside passenger, on one of these solemn occasions, in very hot weather, and there being no air hole, as there usually is, in the hearse, when they took out the corpse, they found poor Mr. L. dead from suffocation.

A LINCOLNSHIRE CALEB QUOTEM.

On Monday the 25th of January, 1813, Mr. John Thompson, of Kirton, near Boston, Lincolnshire, departed this life, a character most singular and well known. The occupations " multiform and vast," of the erudite *Caleb Quotem*, were nothing in comparison to those that served to fill up the busy life of the departed ornament of Kirton. When to the following *poetical* enumeration of the most prominent of his occupations, (which was published while he lived,) we add that he was *three times married*, a tolerable idea of the numerous *duties* Mr. Thompson had to perform, may be entertained. That monster *ennui* certainly never laid him under contribution:—

At Kirton, near Boston, (my story is true,)
Lives a curious character, equall'd by few;
His vocations, (tho' num'rous) in each he does shine,
If not quite the first in the very first line:
As an *artist*, his temples well merit a wreath,
His colours on canvass seem almost to breathe;
In *portrait* or *landscape* there's few to excel him,
Of rivals in *shaving* presume not to tell him;
As *grocer* and *hosier* his fame is well known,
As *carver* and *gilder* and *graver* of stone;
As *vender* of *music* and noted *musician*;
A *butcher*, a *cobbler*, a learned *optician*;
A *hanger of rooms*, and what is more curious,
A *vender* of *medicines*, *patent* — not spurious.
As a *sportsman* not equall'd, a *dealer* in guns,
A *pieman*, a *toyman*, a *maker of buns*.
As *chymist* his name is deservedly known,
His *ointment* excels all the patents in town;
As *stationer*, *varnisher*, *miller*, and *baker*,
Barometer-seller and *violin-maker*;
With other professions distinguished he stands,
And business extensive in each he commands.

Ye book-learn'd, ye curious, *virtuosi* and all
Who pass by his door pray give him a call:
His paintings are beautiful, Westall's no better,
Tho' to a master he ne'er was a debtor,
But as *footman* and *butler* was known when a boy,
Then *thrashing* and reaping became his employ.
But for genius inventive his compeers are few,
Tho' to see him, perhaps, you might think him a Jew,
As a compound of trades he's a challenge to any,
Then call at his shop where he *shaves for a penny*.

BIRD FANCIER.

Lady Reade, of Shipton in Oxfordshire, when advanced in years, devoted all her time, and a considerable portion of her property, to her aviary, which was the most extensive and the most diversified of any in this country. When she travelled between London and Shipton, she attracted almost as much attention as monarchy itself. At the inns where she stopped, the gates were usually shut, to afford her an opportunity of disembarking and landing her cargo of parrots, monkies, and other living attendants, who were stowed in and about her carriages.

Anecdotes of Longevity.

JOHN JACOB.

In one of the foreign journals, published in the month of Oct. 1790, we find the following account of an old man, who had attained to the great age of 118:

"The phenomenon of a life extended beyond the ordinary bounds, interests us for two reasons; because it prolongs our hopes, and excites our reflections. We imagine that we see nature suspending its general laws, and performing a miracle, which we all flatter ourselves may be operated in our favour. Beside this, we affix to the fond idea of a long existence, the striking ideas of strength and antiquity, and we behold a veteran, who has withstood the power of years, with the same respect and veneration, as a column defaced by time, but still raising its head amid surrounding ruins. In a journey, which I lately made, I twice enjoyed this spectacle, but in a different manner. Being at the castle of St. Julian, situated in the bosom of the mountains of the *Franche-Comté*, and not far distant from those of Jura and the Alps, I imagined that I was walking in the path of ages, and I thought I perceived marks of their passage in that multitude of rocks, half undermined, which seemed to nod on their summits, and to threaten destruction by their fall. There, formerly, the Roman, the Gallic, and the Teutonic armies passed. While I was admiring the antiquity of this place, and, on this occasion observing the contrast which is always formed between the short duration of man, and the long duration of things, I was told of an old man, aged 118, who lived at the distance of a league from St. Julian, on the estate of Montaigu. Thinking that this wonder was exaggerated, as generally happens, I wished to examine the truth of it, and the clergyman of St. Julian, and that of Montaigu, conducted me to the house in which the old man lodged. When we arrived, we found him seated on a stone-bench at the door, where he every day goes to repose, or rather to revive himself in the rays of the sun. When we first saw him he was asleep. His sleep seemed to be very profound; his respiration was easy; his pulse beat very regularly; the veins of his forehead were of a lively and transparent blue colour, and his whole appearance was remarkably calm and venerable. Hair, white as snow, fell carelessly over his neck, and was scattered over his cheeks, upon which were displayed the vivid tints of youth and healthfulness. I for some time surveyed, with the utmost attention, this old man, while enjoying his sleep; but when those around awakened him, in order that he might speak to me, he appeared to be less blooming and less beautiful; that is to say, not so fresh when awake as when asleep. He could with difficulty lift his eyelids, and in the open day, he scarcely receives light enough to direct his steps. I found also that he was deaf, and that he did not hear, unless when one spoke in his ears with a loud voice. He had been in this state only for about three years. At the age of 115, he seemed to be no more than eighty, and at 110 he could perform almost any labour. In the meadows he cut grass as the head of the mowers, whom he astonished by his vigour, and animated by his activity; and at table he distinguished himself, no less by his appetite, than by his songs, which he sung with a full and strong voice. At the same age, having conceived a desire of revisiting the place of his nativity, he repaired thither at a time when the inhabitants carried on a lawsuit against their lord, respecting a cross which he had erected at a great distance from boundaries till then acknowledged by custom and tradition, and which consequently would have deprived them of a considerable portion of common. When the old man arrived, he heard mention made of this process, and as he had been a witness of the past, he became also a judge of the present. Having conducted a great number of the inhabitants, who accompanied him, to a high pile of stones, situated at the distance of a league, he began to remove them, and discovered the ancient and real cross, which had occasioned the lawsuit, and which also brought it to a conclusion.

"This old man, we are told, whose name is John Jacob, was born at Charme, a bailiwick of Orgelet, on the 10th of November, 1669. Mr. de Caumartin de Sainte-Ange, Intendant of Franche-Comté, having in the year 1785 heard of him, and having satisfied himself respecting his age, and learned that he had need of assistance, proposed to the minister of the finances to grant him a pension of 200 livres, to enable him to terminate his long career in peace, and to add to it a present of 1200 more. This proposal was agreed to in the month of September 1785, and since that period he has enjoyed this mark of beneficence conferred upon old age. On the 20th of October, last year, he was conducted to Paris, and presented to the king, who viewed him with equal attention and surprise, and who treated with much kindness this extraordinary man, who had been a subject to Louis XIV. and Louis XV. as well as to himself. Though reduced almost to a state of vegetation, he still vegetates with pleasure; and he has retained three passions, vanity, anger, and avarice, which are those, undoubtedly, that continue longest; but with these he unites gratitude, a virtue which generally dies young.

"By the manner in which he blessed the king, it appeared that he had a heart still young and tender. This old man was to be seen at Paris in November 1789, in the new street called *des Bons Enfans*, in the passage to the *Palais-royal*."

MARY O'BRIEN.

There was living in 1813, at the house of Mr. J. Mathews, gardener, Armagh, a woman, named Mary O'Brien, aged 103.—Four generations of her lineal descendants reside with her. There is a probability, from her health and strength, that she may live to see her granddaughter's grandchild, when she may be enabled to say, "Rise up daughter, go to your daughter, for your daughter's daughter has got a daughter."— Old Jenkins, the Englishman, lived to the vast age of 169. It is a curious speculation, that if thirty-three men were each to attain the same age of Jenkins, one coming into the world at the precise moment his immediate predecessor left it, the first of these venerable personages might have shaken hands with Adam, and the remotest of thirty-five such persons would have been coeval with the world.

RUSSIA.

The tables of longevity published for the year 1817, in the Russian empire, give the following results:

Amongst 826,561 persons who have died, all belonging to the Greek church, there appear to have been as follows:

1 above 140 years of age
1 do. 135 do.
7 do. 130 do.
21 do. 125 do.
51 do. 120 do.
83 do. 115 do.
784 do. 100 do.

The banks of Lake Champlain, in the United States of America, afford an instance of longevity which has seldom been equalled since the period of holy writ; the individual alluded to is a German by birth, aged 135 years. This venerable character belonged to Queen Anne's guards, at her coronation in the year 1702, at which time he was eighteen years old; and having served to the end of the war, he then went to America. He is still robust, and very strong—he sees and hears perfectly, and still preserves his hair; he has a soldierlike air, and is proud of his temperance, in having always abstained from spirituous liquors. His youngest son is twenty-seven years of age.

Varieties.

THE OAK.

This useful tree grows to such a surprising magnitude, that were there not many well authenticated instances of this in our own country, they would certainly appear difficult of belief. In the 18th volume of the *Gentleman's Magazine*, we have the dimensions of a leaf twelve inches in length, and seven in breadth; and all the leaves of the same tree were equally large. On the estate of Woodhall, purchased in 1775 by Sir Thomas Rumbold, Bart. an oak was felled which measured twenty-four feet round, and sold for 43*l*.: and we are also told of one in Millwood forest, near Chaddesley, which was in full verdure in winter, getting its leaves again after the autumn ones had fallen off.

Gough, in his edition of Camden, thus describes the Greendale oak which had been noticed in Evelyn's Sylva. "The Greendale oak with a road cut through it still bears one great branch. Such branches as have been cut or broken off are guarded from wet by lead. The diameter of this tree at the top whence the branches issue is fourteen feet two inches; at the surface of the ground eleven and a half feet; circumference there thirty-five feet; height of the trunk fifty-three feet; height of the arch 107, width six feet."

HENRIETTA OF ENGLAND.

HENRIETTA, the daughter of Charles the First, and the first wife of Monsieur, brother to the King of France, was poisoned. On the morning of her death d'Effeat, a creature of the Chevalier Lorraine, who had been driven from the Duke's service by Madame, was seen rubbing the inside of a cup with paper, out of which Madame was accustomed to drink. About twelve o'clock she called for some endive water; after drinking it out of the cup, she cried out that she was poisoned. She was put to bed and expired in the greatest torments an hour or two after midnight. The poison must have been of the most violent and subtile nature, for the cup was obliged to be passed through the fire before it could be again used with safety. The ghost of Madame was said to wander for a considerable time after about a fountain in the park of St. Cloud; and a laquais of Mareschal Clerambault, who saw a white figure near the spot one night, which rose up at his approach, fled in the utmost affright towards the house, protested most solemnly that he had seen the shade of Madame, took to his bed and died.

REMARKABLE WELL.

ON the 19th of February, 1815, a paper by Dr. Storer was read to the Royal Society, giving an account of a well dug in Bridlington harbour, Yorkshire, within high water-mark. The bottom of the harbour is a bed of clay, through which they bored to the bed below; a tinned copper pipe was then put into the circular cavity, and the whole properly secured. The cavity was soon filled with pure water. When the tide rises to within about fifty inches of the mouth of this well, the fresh water begins to flow over, and the quantity flowing increases as the tide rises; and the flow continues till the tide sinks more than fifty inches below the mouth of the well. During storms, the water flows in waves similar to the waves of the sea. Mr. Milne accounts for the flowing of this singular well in this way: the whole bay, he conceives, has a clay bottom. The water between the clay and the rock can flow out nowhere except at the termination of the clay, which is under the sea. As the tide rises, the obstruction to this mode of escape of the water will increase. Hence less will make its way below the clay, and of course it will rise and flow out of the mouth of the well.

PRESENTIMENT OF DEATH.

IN 1813, Mrs. Eagen, wife of a dealer in marine stores, of Little Drury-lane, went to an opposite neighbour's and expressed an earnest desire to see his eldest daughter. On being informed she was from home, she appeared highly disappointed, and said, although she was then in perfect health, she had a strong presentiment that she should not long survive; this was, of course, treated with levity. She then took the hand of another daughter, and a niece of her neighbour, saying, "God bless you girls, I shall never see you again." She next called on a Mrs. Chaplain, who works for Morgan and Saunders, in Catherine-street, and informed her she was shortly to die, and requested her to perform the accustomed offices on such occasions. She likewise took leave of a woman who keeps a chandler's shop near Clare-market. The same evening she spent cheerfully, in company with her husband and a female friend, and retired to rest at her usual hour. She slept well in the night, nor did she complain of indisposition when her husband rose at seven in the morning; but, about eight, on attempting to rise, she was seized with a violent vomiting; this was succeeded by an acute pain in the head, which speedily became so alarming, that two medical practitioners were called to her aid, but without effect, as she continued in a state of insensibility, and lingered until seven in the evening, when she expired.

The Scrap Book.

HUGH WILLIAMS.

In the year 1664, on the 5th of December, a boat on the Menai, crossing that strait, with eighty-one passengers, was upset, and only one passenger, named Hugh Williams, was saved. On the same day, in the year 1785, was upset another boat, containing about sixty persons, and every soul perished, with the exception of *one*, whose name also was Hugh Williams. And on the 5th of August, 1820, a third boat met the same disaster; but the passengers of this were no more than twenty-five, and singular to relate, the whole perished with the exception of *one*, whose name was Hugh Williams.—*Bristol Mercury.*

SINGULAR EWE.

Mr. W. Hewitt of Harrington Mill, has a ewe, which, this spring, yeaned a lamb, of which the following is a description: the eyes were placed in the middle of the forehead without any division betwixt them, one eyelid covering both: the nostrils opened into the mouth, and the under jaw was turned up in an oval shape. It was unable to suck, and died in the course of the day.

A DOMESTICATED ROBIN.

A ROBIN is now sitting her eggs in a bedroom at Tatton-park, the seat of Wilbraham Egerton, Esq. M.P., which is constantly occupied. The male bird pays every attention to his mate by bringing her daily food, which he begins to perform at an early hour in the morning; and for this purpose the window is regularly thrown open at the time of rising, by the person who occupies the room.

Published by J. LIMBIRD, 355, Strand, (East End of Exeter 'Change); and sold by all Newsmen and Booksellers. Printed by A. APPLEGATH, Stamford-street.

THE CABINET OF CURIOSITIES;
OR,
Wonders of the World Displayed.

A world of wonders, where creation seems
No more the works of Nature but her dreams.—MONTGOMERY.

No. III.]   PRICE TWO-PENCE.

EXECUTION OF THE LISBON CONSPIRATORS.

It is well known that the Jesuits were the actual sovereigns of Paraguay, while they acknowledged the King of Spain for its master. The Spanish court had, by a treaty of exchange, ceded certain districts of these lands to King Joseph of Portugal, of the house of Braganza. The Jesuits were accused of having opposed this cession, and of causing the people to revolt who were to have submitted to the government of the Portuguese. This, joined to a number of other injuries, occasioned the Jesuits to be driven from the court of Lisbon.

Some time after, the Tavora family, and particularly the Duke d'Aveiro, uncle to the young Countess Ataïde d'Atouguia, the old Marquis and Marchioness of Tavora, the parents of the young Countess, and, in short, Count Ataïde, her husband, and one of this unfortunate lady's brothers, imagining that they had received from the king an irreparable injury, resolved to revenge themselves. Vengeance and superstition are mutually linked. The meditators of a wicked attempt will always seek casuists and confessors to encourage them in their villainy; and this family,

D

thinking themselves thus abused, concerted with three Jesuits, viz. Malagrida, Alexander, and Mathos. These casuists declared, that to take away the life of the king was only committing a sin that they termed venial.

On the 3d of September, 1758, the conspirators, furnished with their pardon for the other world, waited the king's return to Lisbon from a little country-house, alone, without domestics, and in the night: they fired into his coach, and dangerously wounded him in the arm, but he recovered. All the accomplices, except one domestic, were seized. The young Countess d'Ataïde, whose husband was executed, went, by order of the king, to bewail in a convent those horrible misfortunes which she was thought to be the cause of. The rest were tried, convicted, and condemned to death in various ways as represented in our engraving.

On Saturday, January 13, 1759, being the day appointed for the execution, a scaffold had been built in the square, opposite to the house where the prisoners were confined, and eight wheels fixed upon it. On one corner of the scaffolding was placed Antonio Alvares Ferreira, and on the other corner the effigy of Joseph Policarpio de Azevedo, who was missing; these being the two persons that fired at the back of the king's equipage. About half an hour after eight in the morning, the execution began. The criminals were brought out one by one, each under a strong guard. The Marchioness of Tavora was the first that was brought upon the scaffold, where she was beheaded at one stroke. Her body was afterwards placed upon the floor of the scaffolding, and covered with a linen cloth. Young Joseph Maria of Tavora, the young Marquis of Tavora, the Count of Atouguia, and three servants of the Duke of Aveiro, were first strangled at a stake, and afterwards their limbs broken with an iron instrument; the Marquis of Tavora, general of horse, and the Duke of Aveiro, had their limbs broken alive. The duke, for greater ignominy, was brought bareheaded to the place of execution. The body and limbs of each of the criminals, after they were executed, were thrown upon a wheel, and covered with a linen cloth. But when Antonio Alvarez Ferreira was brought to the stake, whose sentence was to be burnt alive, the other bodies were exposed to his view, the combustible matter, which had been laid under the scaffolding, was set on fire, and the whole machine, with the bodies, were consumed to ashes, and thrown into the sea.

SIMON BROWNE, THE MAN WITHOUT A SOUL

The "Adventurer" has made very generally known the extraordinary case of Mr. Simon Browne, the dissenting clergyman, who was afflicted with a species of melancholy, unparalleled in the history of human nature. He conceived that he had fallen under the displeasure of God, who had caused his natural soul gradually to perish, and left him only an animal life in common with brutes. The following is a copy of an original letter sent by him to the Rev. Mr. Read of Bradford in Wilts, shortly after he was seized with this phantasy, of which it gives a very full developement.

"Reverend Sir,

'I doubt not you have been in earnest with God in my behalf, since you left the city, who expressed so much tender concern for me while you were in it. I wish I could write any thing to you that might turn your compassion into thanksgiving, and your prayers into praises; but alas! nothing of that kind is to be expected from one who has lived a life of defiance to God under a Christian profession and a sacred character; and is now through his just displeasure in the most forlorn state a man can be in on earth—perfectly empty of all thought, reflection, conscience, or consideration; destitute, entirely destitute, of the knowledge of God and Christ and his own soul, and the things both of time and eternity; being unable to look backward or forward, inward or outward, upward or downward; having no conviction of sin or duty, no capacity of reviewing his conduct or looking forward with expectation of either good or evil; and in a word, without any principles of religion or even of reason, and without the common sentiments or affections of human nature; insensible even to the good things of life, incapable of tasting any present enjoyments, or expecting future ones; dead to his children, friends, and country; having no interest, either bodily or spiritual, temporal or eternal, to value or mind, but converted into a mere beast that can relish nothing but present bodily enjoyments, without tasting them by anticipation or recollection.

"*This is my true condition;* thus am I thrown down from my excellency. Because I had not, God has taken away the things that I had.—Indeed I have not those horrors on my mind to which you were a witness; I am grown more calm, because more insensible, and every day since you saw me has this insensibility been growing upon me; nor can it be removed without a miracle of grace; and for this grace I cannot pray, having lost all sight of God and tenderness of soul towards him. Such an instance of divine displeasure the world hardly ever saw, much less one recovered by divine grace out of such a condition. I doubt whether you have room to pray; but if you think you have, I doubt not but you will be fervent at the throne of grace in your resquests. But I am so changed that I must first be made *a man* before I can be made a *Christian;* having now none of that knowledge or common sentiments on which a saving change must be founded. I am utterly incapable of any business in life, and must quit my present station; and think, as soon as I can, to be retiring into my own country, there to spend out the wretched remains of a miserable life, which yet I am continually prompted to destroy. I thought you would be willing to hear from me; and though you cannot be pleased with the account, I am obliged to give you a true one; and beg an interest in your prayers, which will turn to your own account, if it avails nothing towards the salvation of the most wretched and wicked sinner, who would yet, if he was able, be

"Your friend and servant,
"Simon Browne."

A singular letter this was, to come from a man of no thinking powers? so clear, so acute, so elegant, so correct, in all but the theory on which it proceeds. But it was one of the peculiarities attending this extraordinary case, that though no arguments were of force sufficient to induce Mr. Browne to relinquish the absurd notion that his soul had been taken from him, it was observed by his friends that at no time did his judgment, except in this single point, appear strange, or his conceptions clearer.

Having resigned his pastoral office in London, from an idea that a man who was himself without a soul, could not very well take charge of the souls of others, Browne retired to spend the rest of his days at his native place, Shepton Mallet. Although he was here lost in solitude, deprived of all conversation with the learned, and almost without any assistance from books, his mind lost nothing of its vigour, and to the close of his life he devoted himself with ardour and success to the cultivation of literature. Among his productions during this period, was an able "Defence of the Religion of Nature and the Christian Religion," (although himself as he averred no "*Christian*") against the attack made upon them in Tindal's "Christianity as old as the Creation." He intended to dedicate this work to Queen Caroline, and did actually write a dedication of it to her Majesty, but of so strange a sort, that his friends were glad to prevail upon him to suppress it; wisely considering that a book with such an introduction would be condemned without examination, as written by a man really out of his wits. A copy of it is however preserved in the work to which we have alluded.

MELANCHOLY CASE OF HYDROPHOBIA.

It appears by the newspapers that several mad dogs have been observed in the neighbourhood of London; and in order to shew what dreadful consequences arise from them, we publish the following account —:

On the 8th of December, 1818, Mr. John Hubbard, nephew of Mr. Thompson, of Frognall Priory, near Hampstead, a healthy young man, twenty-five years of age, was bitten in the fleshy part of the inner surface of the right hand by a large Newfoundland dog, which, for several days previously, had shewn symptoms of some slight disease. His mother immediately applied some common Friar's balsam to the wound, and he proceeded in a few hours afterwards to consult Mr. Rodd, surgeon, of Hampstead; but that gentleman being absent, the lacerated part was treated by his assistant as a common wound, there being no suspicion that the dog's complaint was madness.

On the following day, Mr. Rodd examined his hand, and being informed by Mr. Hubbard that the animal had broken from confinement and had bitten another dog, he deemed it prudent to dress the sore with caustic. He applied the *argenti nitras* in so effectual a manner, that it was confidently hoped all danger, to be apprehended from the bite, was removed. In a short time the wound healed comfortably, and Mr. Hubbard pursued his usual occupations, not suspecting any unhappy sequel.

On the 21st January, 1819, forty-four days after being bitten, he perceived a degree of tenderness in the part of the hand which had been wounded; and soon afterwards he felt a pain and sense of stiffness in the arm, which he attributed to his having worked several hours with a saw. During the interval, to the 24th, the pain increased daily, and extended to his right breast, from which he suffered severely, and was otherwise indisposed. His mother, conceiving it to be a rheumatic attack, rubbed his arm with an embrocation, and caused him to put on a flannel waistcoat. On the above day he rose at ten o'clock, and drank two cups of tea at breakfast; but feeling a general sense of languor and weakness, he returned to his bed. He had no desire for food; and when tea was brought to him in the afternoon, he was unable to drink it. During the latter part of the day the pain in the right side of the thorax increased, and a spasmodic breathing, with a sense of suffocation, supervened. He took some gruel, but found much difficulty in swallowing it. He was no longer able to obtain his usual rest, but passed a most disturbed and sleepless night.

On the 25th he rose at ten o'clock; his suffering and sense of strangulation were so violent as to prevent him from walking steadily without support. A basin of water being brought near him, it was observed he turned his head from it; on his mother putting a wet cloth to his face he started, and his breathing became spasmodic and suffocating.

On the 25th January, (writes Dr. Pinckard,) I was called to visit him at his father's house, Battle Bridge. On my arrival, I found him sitting in the parlour with scarcely any appearance of illness, except an occasional deep and hurried respiration. This was repeated every eight or ten minutes, the eyes being rather widely opened, and the countenance betraying some expression of anxiety; but during the intervals he was tranquil and composed. He related to me the circumstance of the dog's attack, answering whatever questions were put to him in the most distinct and collected manner.

Being desirous of ascertaining whether copious and speedy depletion might have any effect in arresting the progress of this most direful disease, I directed bleeding until syncope should be induced. Whilst the blood was flowing, he remarked that the pain of the arm and breast was diminished. He held the basin himself, very steadily, while the blood was allowed to trickle down the arm; but when it was suffered to pass into the basin in a stream, he became agitated, the convulsive catching of the breath was increased, and he cried out, "it almost strangles me." When about thirty ounces of blood were drawn, he grew faint, turned exceedingly pale, and perspired profusely. Before the ligature could be fastened, he was seized with a spasmodic attack, and fell from the chair in a violent struggle, during which the pupil of the eyes dilated and contracted in extreme degrees with uncommon rapidity. The convulsion recurred, with less severity, in the course of a few minutes, after which he sunk into a state of languid composure.

Having witnessed, in former cases, the great distress occasioned by presenting fluids to patients in a similar situation, I could not but regard it as an act of cruelty to bring them before him; I suggested, therefore, to his own discretion, whether he would attempt to swallow liquids;

or to use the warm bath. The conversation upon these subjects increased the spasms, and disturbed him exceedingly; but he expressed a desire to effect the bathing, and said, that notwithstanding the impossibility of drinking, he might, perhaps, swallow as much as a tea spoon full of drops, when he was more composed.

At two o'clock, I saw him again, when he appeared more tranquil; but the interruptions of his breathing were more frequent, and according to his own expression, "suffocating." His pulse had increased, being 112, the tongue whitish, and the skin cold and damp. He remarked, that his mental faculties were "as strong as ever," and that he was "quite composed and collected." Yielding to my intimation, he attempted to take a few drops; but before the tea spoon reached his lips, he was seized with convulsive startings, which raised him from his pillow and nearly threw him out of bed. The attempt to use the bath was equally unsuccessful; on entering it, the convulsive breathing became so distressing, as to compel him to spring out hastily, to save himself, as he expressed it, "from being strangled."

At six o'clock the pulse had increased to 120. The bleeding was repeated. When about twenty ounces were drawn, he became faint and was thrown upon the floor in strong convulsions, and after he was lifted up, the general convulsion was twice or thrice repeated. The scene now became singularly awful and impressive. His person was distorted by spasmodic contractions, he struggled with preternatural strength, stamped violently upon the floor, and struck his hands forcibly against his forehead; his breathing was convulsive, almost to suffocation—his whole frame was shaken with dreadful agitation—a wild anxiety overspread his countenance, and, in a trembling, hurried accent, he exclaimed:—"What is the matter? What is it? What ails me?"

Being put into bed again, he moaned deeply, but at length became more composed; he felt rather sleepy, which was attributed to the effect of the opium I had caused to be administered. It was too manifest that the disease was uninterrupted and rapidly advancing in its usual train. The spasms returned in quick succession; his eyes were widely extended, and his countenance assumed a strong expression of watchfulness and anxiety; he inquired, in a hurried manner, for his mother and aunt, and, though sleepy, could obtain no repose; he closed his eyes for a minute or two; but the convulsions, and a sense of strangulation, recurred still oftener and with increased violence. The night was more wretched than can be described; his distress was truly piteous. He complained constantly of the parched dryness of his mouth, yet was unable to endure any thing of a moistening quality. He endeavoured to apply the corner of a wet cloth to cool his parched lips; but even this was not effected without vehement struggles, and the horrors of being strangled.

On the morning of the 26th the thirst and dryness became insupportably distressing, and he gave vent to loud and piteous wailing, calling for something to relieve him; but no relief could be administered; for not only was the sight of fluids intolerable to him to a degree which threatened instant suffocation from spasmodic inspirations; but from a morbid increase of sensibility, the impression of objects upon any of the senses produced excessive irritability. Odours reaching his nose, any one touching his person, and even the light sound of his sister sighing in an adjoining room, brought on convulsive startings, which threw him across the bed. Under all these afflicting feelings, his intellectual faculties remained unimpaired. He conversed calmly, and was perfectly collected; he desired to have his hands held during these convulsive struggles, remarking that it seemed to lessen the violence of the spasms. He requested to see his relations, and talked with them composedly, addressing them in the most considerate and affectionate manner. He complained that some of them were absent, and said, he could die tranquilly, if he had his friends about him.

Presently afterwards, he was thrown into violent agitation, breathed convulsively, and, starting up, cried out in a furious accent, "Throw the window open some perfume is choking me." It arose from some pills with musk and opium, which had been brought to him to take. A similar effect was produced by my taking my handkerchief out of my pocket at his bedside, when he called out impatiently,"There's lavender in it—I can't bear that perfume—it strangles me." He referred the feeling of suffocation more to the region of the stomach, than on the preceding day; during the night he stamped and tore in the most violent manner.

On the morning of the 27th, the condition and appearance were such as to excite the most heartfelt commiseration. All the afflicting symptoms of his disorder were so increased in strength and frequency, as to allow scarcely any intermission. Every movement was hurried and convulsive; his eyes expanded in wild and staring watchfulness, and the pupils contracted and dilated in rapid alternation, while he raved in frantic exclamation, "I shall go mad!" Every violent symptom continued to increase; at one o'clock he rolled on the bed in convulsive writhings and contortions, his countenance exhibiting a fearful portrait of agitation and suffering. Still the powers of his mind seemed perfectly rational and collected. At this period he desired to see his friends, and tenderly took leave of those who came around his bed, requesting them to convey his dying remembrance to others who were absent; then apportioning little gifts to the respective branches of his family, and calmly contemplating his speedy dissolution, he named the persons whom he wished to follow him to the grave.

At half-past one, whilst conversing with his friends, he was seized with a severe convulsive paroxysm. The whole frame became rigid. The frothy mucus issued from his mouth, and he was no longer able to speak. Presently the throat swelled, the face became bloated, respiration was more and more impeded, the right hand assumed a livid hue, while the left took on the sallow hue of a corpse. He remained insensible; the pulsation of the arteries ceased, and at a quarter after two, this closing spasm relaxed in death.

DESCRIPTION OF A HURRICANE AT LUCKNOW.

"This evening, the heat being very oppressive, I was sitting in my apartment on the terrace-roof of the house, when a sudden gloom and distant thunder induced me to go out on the terrace. The wind, which had been easterly, was now perfectly lulled. A very dark blue cloud arose from the west, and at length covered half the sky. The thunder was not loud, and the air was perfectly still. The birds were flying very high, and making a terrible screaming. At length a dark brown cloud appeared on the western horizon, and came on with considerable rapidity. The whole town of Lucknow, with its numerous minars, was between me and the cloud, and the elevation of my terrace gave me an excellent opportunity of observing it. When at about the distance of a mile, it had all the appearance of a smoke from a vast fire, volume rolling over volume in wild confusion, at the same time raising itself high in the air. As it approached, it had a dingy red appearance: and, by concealing the most distant minars from my view, convinced me that it was sand borne along by a whirlwind. The air with us continued perfectly still; the clouds of sand had a defined exterior: nor did the wind a moment precede it. It came on with a rushing sound, and at length reached us with such violence, as to oblige me to take shelter in my eastern veranda. Even there the dust was driven with a force that prevented me from keeping my eyes open. The darkness became every moment greater, and at length it was black as night. It might well be called palpable darkness; for the wind now changing a little to the southward, brought on the storm with tenfold violence, and nearly smothered us with dust. It blew so violently, that the noise of the thunder was frequently drowned by the whistling of the wind in the trees and buildings. The total darkness lasted about ten minutes; when at length it gradually gave way to a terrifically red but dingy light, which I, at first, attributed to a fire in the town. The rain now poured down in torrents, and the wind changed to due south. In about an hour from its commencement the sky began to clear, the tufaun went off to the eastward, and the wind immediately returned to that quarter. The air was perfectly cool, and free from dust. Although all my windows and doors had been kept closed, and there were tattys on the outside, yet the sand was so penetrating, that it had covered my bed and furniture with a complete coat of dust. Mr. Paul tells me, he once was caught in a north-wester on the banks of the Ganges, when the darkness lasted for several hours. This, however, was one of the most tremendous that had ever been beheld at Lucknow. One person was literally frightened to death. There is, indeed, no danger from the storm itself, but the fires in the houses are in such situations that a blast might easily drive a spark against their thatched roofs, heated already by the sun; in which case, the darkness would probably preclude the possibility of saving any part of the town. It is equally probable that a roof may be blown in, which would have the same melancholy consequences. The long drought had pulverized so much of the country, and so completely annihilated vegetation on the sandy plains, that the tufaun brought with it more sand than usual; and to that alone must be attributed the perfect darkness. It was the most magnificent and awful sight I ever beheld; not even excepting a storm at sea. The wind in both cases was of equal violence, but neither the billows nor the sense of danger affected my mind so much as this unnatural darkness.

Hoaxes and Impostures.
No. II.
CONJURER BAKER.

RICHARD Baker, of Westleigh, in the parish of Burliscombe, Somersetshire, a small farmer (but better known by the name of " *Conjurer* Baker") died in 1819, full of years and iniquities, being seventy years old, and having, during the far greater part of his life, practised the gainful tactics of the "Black Art." In noticing the death of a character who, for nearly half a century, has been daily and hourly employed in alternately counting the wages of his villainies, and in laughing at the follies of a cheated multitude, it would be no unfit opportunity for taxing the risibility of our readers, by portraying the deceased knave with all the mirthful embellishments of which his life and occupations are so abundantly susceptible. In common justice, we might for once laugh at him, who has, in so many thousand instances, amused and profited himself by making a jest of others; but his life is too much clogged with the heaviness of a guilty account, to allow one redeeming ray to qualify the lurid aspect of his mortal reckoning. It may surprise the distant reader, whose ears have never been afflicted with the doleful superstitions of the western counties, to be informed, that such was the fame of the deceased wizard, that the educated as well as the uninstructed of all classes, were in the habit of resorting to him from all parts of this and the neighbouring counties for the exercise of his cabalistic skill,' and on a Sunday, which was the day for his high orgies, vehicles of superior as well as of lowly descriptions were found to bring him an eager throng of votaries. His reputation was universal, and his gains proportionate. The wonders of his art would fill the Alexandrian library. Bad crops, lost cattle, lost treasure, and lost hearts, brought their respective sufferers in ceaseless crowds to his door. They were all *overlooked*, he said; and they overlooked his knavery in their confidence of his skill. He foretold to the Southcottians that the Shiloh would *not* come, and who but a conjurer would have known this? The tenant of sterile land was, after a careful inspection of his presiding star, advised to provide a certain quantity of manure, which being spread over his ground in the form of rams' horns at twelve o'clock precisely on the full moon night, would infallibly secure a good crop. This astonishing prediction has been repeatedly verified! Strayed stock and mislaid property have been strangely recovered, by only being well looked after, provided the wise man had once taken the matter in hand; and many a relenting Phillis, who had parted with her Strephon in a *huff*, has been heard to exclaim, on finding him return at the very hour calculated by the conjurer, that "sure Baker and the devil were in partnership." If to juggling artifices and petty fooleries of this description, the man had limited his imposture, he might have left the world with the simple reputation of a knave; but his avarice led him to delude the victim of disease into a fatal reliance on his affected skill, and very numerous are the instances of this description. Charmed powders and mystic lotions were confided in, to the exclusion of rational advice and proper remedies, and the death of the old and young has been the consequent penalty, of such deplorable imbecility. A child died at Wellington, a martyr to its mother's folly of this nature. She consulted the heartless villain, and was assured that the infant was "overlooked." Some powders were given to her, accompanied with the slang verbosity of his craft, which the little sufferer was compelled to swallow, notwithstanding the mother, declared that "it made her heart bleed to see the agonies of her child while taking the dose." The consequence was as we have stated; and thus the guilt of a cold-blooded murder, is superadded to the atrocities which have marked the career of this miscreant through life. His habits were those of an unsocial drunkard; but his necromancy, notwithstanding the expense of his selfish indulgence, enabled him to leave some property.

THE OVERJOYED BARBER.

The following instance of mischievous imposition may be depended on as a fact, having occurred a few years ago. On the drawing of one of the large prizes, some person who was in the hall, and knew the disposition of a poor barber, who belonged to a lottery club at Limehouse, the numbers of their tickets, &c. immediately set off to make a false report of their good fortune, which was performed with so much plausibility, that the breaking of all the things in the barber's shop (before determined on, in case of good luck) was directly put in practice; and, as the populace were invited to assist in this rude demonstration of joy, a fire was made before the door, where wig-blocks, band-boxes, &c. &c were actually burning, before the fraud was discovered. A public-house would have been opened, if the landlord had not been rather incredulous. The author of this sport took care to withdraw before its conclusion.

PRESSING TO DEATH.

A most barbarous law formerly prevailed in this country which imposed the punishment of pressing an individual to death if he refused to plead on his trial. Several instances of its being put into execution have occurred in the history of the English criminal code.

The Yorkshire Tragedy, a play, which some critics attribute to Shakspeare, is founded on the tragical tale of Mr. Calverly, a gentleman of good family in the north of England, who in a fit of jealousy killed his wife, and refused to plead that he might preserve his estate to his child: he was pressed to death.

At the Nottingham Assizes in 1735, a person commonly reputed deaf and dumb from his infancy, committed a murder. When brought to trial, two persons swore positively that he had been heard to speak. He was desired to plead but pleaded not. He was taken into an adjoining room and actually pressed to death, without uttering a word, which there is reason to believe he never could do.

At the Kilkenny Assizes, in 1740, one Matthew Ryan was tried for highway robbery. When he was apprehended he pretended to be a lunatic, stripped himself in the gaol, threw away his clothes, and could not be prevailed on to put them on again, but went as he was to the court to take his trial. He then affected to be dumb, and would not plead; on which the judges ordered a jury to be impanneled, to inquire and give their opinion whether he was mute and lunatic by the hand of God, or wilfully so. The jury returned in a short time, and brought in a verdict of "Wilful and affected dumbness and lunacy." The judges on this desired the prisoner to plead; but he still pretended to be insensible to all that was said to him. The law now called for the *peine forte et dure*; but the judges compassionately deferred awarding it until a future day, in the hope that he might in the mean time acquire a juster sense of his situation. When again brought up however, the criminal persisted in his refusal to plead; and the court at last pronounced the dreadful sentence, that he should *be pressed to death*. This sentence was accordingly executed upon him two days after, in the public market place of Kilkenny. As the weights were heaping on the wretched man, he earnestly supplicated to be hanged; but it being beyond the power of the sheriff to deviate from the mode of punishment prescribed in the sentence, even this was an indulgence which could no longer be granted to him.

Another instance is related in the annals of Newgate of one William Spiggot, who suffered in the same manner.

Before he was put into the press, the ordinary of Newgate endeavoured to dissuade him from hastening his own death in such a manner; and thereby depriving himself of that time which the law allowed him to repent in: to which he only answered, if you come to take care of my soul, I shall regard you; but if you come about my body, I must desire to be excused; for I cannot hear one word. At the next visit the chaplain found him lying in the vault, upon the bare ground, with three hundred and fifty pound weight upon his breast, and then prayed by him, and several times asked him why he would hazard his soul by such obstinate kind of self-murder. But all the answer that he made was, pray for me, pray for me. He sometimes lay silent under the pressure, as if insensible of pain, and then again would fetch his breath very quick and short. Several times he complained that they had laid a cruel weight upon his face, though it was covered with nothing but a thin cloth; which was afterwards removed, and laid more light and hollow; yet he still complained of the prodigious weight upon his face, which might be caused by the blood's being forced up thither, and pressing the veins as violently as if the force had been externally on his face.

When he had remained half an hour under this load, and fifty pounds weight more laid on him, being in all four hundred, he told those that attended him he would plead.

Immediately the weights were at once taken off, the cords cut asunder, he was raised up by two men, some brandy was put into his mouth to revive him, and he was carried to take his trial.

The reasons he gave for enduring the press were, that his effects might be preserved for the good of his family, that none might reproach his children by telling them their father was hanged, and that Joseph Lindsey might not triumph in saying, he had sent him to Tyburn. He seemed to be much incensed against this Lindsey; for, says he, I was once wounded, and in danger of my life, by rescuing him when he was near being taken, and yet he afterwards made himself an evidence against me.

The Press-yard in Newgate was so named because it was the place for inflicting this punishment.

Eccentric Biography.

MARY EAST THE FEMALE HUSBAND.

ABOUT the year 1736, a young fellow courted one Mary East, and for him she conceived the greatest liking; but he, going upon the highway, was tried for a robbery and cast, but was afterwards transported: this so affected our heroine, that she resolved ever to remain single. In the same neighbourhood lived another young woman, who had likewise met with many crosses in love, and had determined on the like resolution; being intimate, they communicated their minds to each other, and determined to live together ever after. After consulting on the best method of proceeding, they agreed that one should put on man's apparel, and that they would live as man and wife in some part where they were not known: the difficulty now was who was to be the man, which was soon decided, by the toss up of a halfpenny, and the lot fell on Mary East, who was then about sixteen years of age, and her partner seventeen. The sum they were then possessed of together, was about 30*l*.; with this they set out, and Mary, after purchasing a man's habit, assumed the name of James How, by which we will for awhile distinguish her. In the progress of their journey, they happened to light on a little public-house at Epping, which was to let, they took it, and lived in it for some time: about this period a quarrel happened between James How and a young gentleman. James entered an action against him, and obtained damages of 500*l*. which was paid him. Possessed of this sum, they sought out for a place in a better situation, and took a public-house in Limehouse-hole, where they lived many years, saving money, still cohabiting as man and wife, in good credit and esteem: they afterwards left this and removed to the White Horse at Poplar, which they bought, and after that several more houses.

About the year 1750, one Mrs. Bentley, who lived on Garlick-hill, and was acquainted with James in her younger days, knowing in what good circumstances she lived in, and of her being a woman, thought this a good scheme to build a project on, and accordingly sent to her for 10*l*. at the same time intimating that if she would not send it, she would discover her sex. James, fearful of this, complied with her demand,

and sent the money. It rested here for a considerable time, in which time James lived with his supposed wife in good credit, and had served all the parish offices in Poplar, excepting constable and churchwarden, from the former of which she was excused by a lameness in her hand, occasioned by the quarrel already mentioned; the other she was to have been next year, if this discovery had not happened: she had been several time foreman of juries; though her effeminacy indeed was remarked by most. At Christmas 1765, Mrs. Bentley sent again with the same demand for 10*l.* and with the like threatening obtained it: flushed with success, and not yet contented, she within a fortnight after sent again for the like sum, which James at that time happened not to have in the house: however, still fearful and cautious of a discovery, she sent her 5*l.* The supposed wife of James How now died, and the same conscionable Mrs. Bentley now thought of some scheme to enlarge her demand: for this purpose she got two fellows to execute her plan, the one a mulatto, who was to pass for one of justice Fielding's gang, the other to be equipped with a short pocket staff, and to act as constable. In these characters they came to the White Horse, and inquired for Mr. How, who answered to the name; they told her that they came from justice Fielding to take her into custody for a robbery committed by her thirty-four years ago, and moreover that she was a woman. Terrified to the greatest degree on account of her sex, though conscious of her innocence in regard to the robbery, an intimate acquaintance, one Mr. Williams, a pawnbroker, happening to be passing by, she called to him, and told him the business those two men came about, and withal added this declaration to Mr. Williams, I am really a woman, but innocent of their charge. On this sincere confession he told her she should not be carried to Fielding, but go before her own bench of justices; that he would just step home, put on a clean shirt, and be back in five minutes. At his departure, the two fellows threatened James How, but at the same time told her, that if she would give them 100*l.* they would trouble her no more; if not, she would be hanged in sixteen days, and they should have 40*l.* a piece each for hanging her. Notwithstanding these threatenings she would not give them the money, waiting with impatience till the return of Mr. Williams: on her denial, they immediately forced her out, and took her near the fields, still using the same threats; adding with imprecations, had you not better give us the 100*l.* than be hanged: after awhile they got her through the fields, and brought her to Garlick-hill to the house of the identical Mrs. Bentley, where with threats they got her to give a draft on Mr. Williams to Bentley, payable in a short time; which, when they had obtained, they sent her about her business. Williams came back punctual to his promise, and was surprised to find her gone: he immediately went to the bench of justices to see if she was there, and not finding her, went to Sir John Fielding's, and not succeeding, came back, when James soon after returned; when she related to him all that had passed. The discovery was now public. On Monday, July 14, 1766, Mrs. Bentley came to Mr. Williams with the draft, to know if he would pay it, being due the Wednesday after: he told her if she came with it when due, he should know better what to say; in the mean time, he applied to the bench of justices for advice, and Wednesday being come, they sent a constable with others to be in the house. Mrs. Bentley punctually came for the payment of the draft, bringing with her the mulatto man, both of whom were taken into custody, and carried to the bench of justices sitting at the Angel in Whitechapel, where Mr. Williams, attended with James How, dressed in the proper habit of her sex, now again under her real name of Mary East. The alteration of her dress from that of a man to that of a woman appeared so great, that together with her awkward behaviour in her new assumed habit, it caused great diverson.

In the course of their examination Mrs. Bentley denied sending for the 100l.; the mulatto declared likewise, if she had not sent him for it he should never have gone. In short, they so contradicted each other, that they discovered the whole villainy of their designs. In regard to the ten pounds which Bentley had before obtained, she in her defence urged that Mary East had sent it to her. After the strongest proof of their extortion and assault, they were denied any bail, and both committed to Clerkenwell Bridewell to be tried for the offence: the other man made off, and was not afterwards heard of. At the following session the mulatto, whose name was William Barwick, was tried for defrauding the female husband of money, and was convicted; when he was sentenced to four years imprisonment, and to stand four times in the pillory.

During the whole of their cohabiting together as man and wife, which was thirty-four years, they lived in good credit and esteem, having during this time traded for many thousand pounds, and been to a day punctual to their payments: they had also by honest means saved up between 4000l. and 5000l. between them. It is remarkable that it has never their been observed that they ever dressed a joint of meat in their whole lives, nor ever had any meetings or the like at their house. They never kept either maid or boy; but Mary East, the late James How, always used to draw beer, serve, fetch in and carry out pots always herself, so peculiar were they in each particular.

Varieties.

WHIMSICAL EVIDENCE.

The following whimsical evidence appears in the course of the trial of J. Carrick and Molony for a street robbery.

Court. Mr. Young, by what light did you see the prisoners when they robbed you?

Mr. Young. I saw them plainly by the chairman's lanthorn. When Carrick was going to rifle me, he bid one of them go over the way: but Molony asked Carrick what he sent him away for; and calling to the chairman, d—n ye, villains, says he, come back, or I will run ye through. And the chairman coming back, Molony stood over him with his sword. He bid the chairmen hold their hats before their face, but they held them a little on one side, so that they could see what was done.

Carrick. Pray, sir, which side of the chair was I on when you say I robbed you?

Mr. Young. On the left side.

Carrick. Now that is a lie, for I was on the right side. I shall catch you again presently. What coloured coat had I?

Mr. Young. Black.

Carrick. I can prove the reverse.—What sort of a wig?

Mr. Young. A light tie-wig

Carrick. That is another lie of your's—for you know, Mr. Molony, that you and I changed wigs that night, and your's is a dark brown. Had I two pistols in one hand, or one in each hand?

Mr. Young. I saw but one pistol.

Carrick. Then your eyesight failed ye.

MURDER IN INDIA.

One Khrisnoo Doss, a carpenter, residing at Benyapookur of Etally, in the eastern suburbs of Calcutta, suspected his wife, a very beautiful young woman, to have fallen in love with one of her neighbours. On the evening of the 26th of April, while the woman and her paramour were passing their happiest moments in her own chamber, the carpenter returned; and so much pressed was he with hunger, that without paying the least attention to any thing that was going on before his eyes, he, as usual, cried out from the very door, " Bow, kolah geli bhat de;" that is, " Come, wife, set my dinner before me." The voice of her husband filled her mind with terror, and she came out to give him a pot of water to wash his feet, and then went to light up the lamp. The carpenter took his seat upon the lower beam of the door, and the gallant seeing no other means left of making his escape but breaking through the outside wall, he in that manner effected his retreat. The noise made upon this occasion escaped not the attention of the carpenter, who, thus knowing the treachery of his wife, discovered not the least symptom of anger, but with the same tone as before told her, " Mah ami aur bhai khabo noh; amar boro matha dhoriacce; cholo gye sooya thaki;" or " I won't dine now; I have got a severe headach; let us go to rest." They then went to bed and entered into a long conversation; and about midnight, seeing his wife wrapped in profound sleep, the carpenter rose up, and to satisfy the violent passion which he had hitherto suppressed, he cruelly thrust a knife into her throat, and thus at once put an end to her days. The perpetration of this criminal act gave rise to a variety of reflections in his mind, and he at last came to the conclusion that his own life must pay for the murder which he had committed. Very early next morning he locked the door of his house, and went to Callee Ghaut, where having offered a grand Pajoo to the goddess Calloe, he came back to the Kutcherry, at Allipoor, with a garland of Jova (a red flower) on his neck, and a spot of vermillion on the forehead, after they had been offered to the goddess. Upon his return, and finding the house to be a scene of great noise and tumult, he cried out, " What's all this clamour about?"—" How came your wife," rejoined the Thannadar, " to be murdered?" At this Khrisnoo-Doss candidly confessed his crime, saying, " It is I who have killed her; no one else; therefore bind me." Moreover he boldly related every particular attending the murder of his wife, which induced the Thannadar to secure him and take him before Mr. Barwell, the Judge of Allipoor.—*Sungbaud Cowmuddy.*

GROANING TREE IN LINCOLNSHIRE.

I HAVE a letter by me, says Clarke in his "Looking Glass," dated July 7, 1606, written by one Mr. Ralph Bovy, to a godly minister in London, wherein he thus writes :—

"Touching news, you shall understand, that Mr. Sherwood hath received a letter from Mr. Arthur Hildersam, which containeth this subsequent narrative; viz. that at Brampton, in the parish of Toksey, near Gainsborough, in Lincolnshire, an ash-tree shaketh in body and boughs thereof, sighing and groaning like a man troubled in his sleep, as if it felt some sensible torment. Many have climbed to the top of it, who heard the groans more easily than they could below. But one among the rest, being on the top thereof, spake to the tree, but presently came down much aghast, and lay grovelling on the earth three hours speechless: in the end, reviving he said, Brampton, Brampton, thou art much bound to pray. The Earl of Lincoln caused one of the arms of the ash to be lopped off, and a hole to be bored through the body, and then was the sound or hollow voice heard more audibly than before, but in a kind of speech which they could not comprehend."

The Scrap Book.

AN IRISH WILL.

THE following is a copy of a will made by a miser in Ireland : " I give and bequeath to my sister-in-law Mary Dennis, four old worsted stockings, which she will find underneath my bed; to my nephew Charles Macartney, two other pair of stockings, lying in the box where I keep my linen; to Lieutenant Johnson, of his Majesty's fifth regiment of foot, my only pair of white cotton stockings, and my old scarlet great-coat; and to Hannah Bourke, my housekeeper, in return for her long and faithful services, my cracked earthen pitcher." Hannah, in anger, told the other legatees, that she resigned to them her *valuable* share of the property, and then retired. In equal rage, Charles kicked down the pitcher; and, as it broke, a multitude of guineas burst out, and rolled along the floor. This fortunate discovery induced those present to examine the stockings, which, to their great joy, were crammed with money.

CANINE NURSE.

IN 1805, a small mongrel bitch, the property of a gentleman in Truro, having a litter of puppies, and being detained from them for the space of three or four days, upon her return found that another bitch (her offspring in a former litter, and then about seven months old) had adopted the litter as her own; and, though she never had borne puppies herself, actually suckled her adopted children : and so copiously did the milk flow from this virgin nurse, that she alone nourished and reared the whole litter, while their own mother abandoned them.

Published by J. LIMBIRD, 355, Strand, (East End of Exeter 'Change); and sold by all Newsmen and Booksellers. Printed by A. APPLEGATH, Stamford-street.

OR
Wonders of the World Displayed.

A world of wonders where creation seems
No more the works of Nature but her dreams.—MONTGOMERY.

No. IV.]   PRICE TWOPENCE.

MULLED SACK.

JOHN COTTINGTON, better known by the name of Mulled Sack, was one of the most notorious highwaymen this country has produced. He was the son of a haberdasher in Cheapside, who having exhausted his property died poor, and was buried by the parish, leaving fifteen daughters and four sons, of whom our hero was the youngest. At eight years of age he was put apprentice to a chimney-sweeper of St. Mary-le-bow, with whom he remained about five years: as soon as he entered his teens he ran away; and soon afterwards received the name, by which he was best known, of Mulled Sack, from his drinking sack mulled, morning, noon and night. To support a life of dissipation he turned pickpocket; and one of his first robberies of this sort was committed on Lady Fairfax, from whom he got a rich gold watch: and his depredations were afterwards so numerous, that his biographers state "the many various neat tricks Mulled Sack played upon Ludgate-hill, by making stops of coaches and carts, and the money that he and his consorts got there by picking pockets, would have been almost enough to have built St. Paul's Cathedral."

Mulled Sack was detected in picking the pocket of Oliver Cromwell as he came out of the Parliament House; but escaped hanging by the political changes of the times. He next turned highwayman, and was so audacious as to rob Colonel Hewson when marching over Hounslow at the head of his regiment, in company with one Tom Cheney. They were pursued by a body of troopers; Mulled Sack escaped, but his companion, after defending himself against eighteen horsemen, was overpowered and taken: he was tried at the Old Bailey, convicted, and executed at Tyburn. Mulled Sack, afterwards, along with several other of his companions, waylaid a waggon which was conveying £4,000 to Oxford and Gloucester, and seized the money, which they soon spent: he also robbed the house of the Receiver-General of Reading of £6,000, which he was preparing to send up to town. For this offence Mulled Sack, who was taken, was tried at Reading, but acquitted; it is said, by bribing the jury. He had not been long at liberty before he killed one John Bridges, for which he was obliged to quit the kingdom, and went to Cologne, where he robbed King Charles II. then in exile, of as much plate as was valued at £1,500. On returning to England he promised to give Oliver Cromwell some of his Majesty's papers, but, says his biographer, "not making good his promise, he was sent to Newgate, and receiving sentence of death was hanged in Smithfield rounds, in April 1659, aged fifty-five years."

Our engraving is copied from an old print, beneath which is the following inscription:—

"I walke the Strand and Westminster
  and scorne
To march t' the cittie; though I beare
  the horne,
My feather and my yellow band accord
To prove me courtier, my boots, spur, and
  sword,
My smoking pipe, scarf, garter, rose on
  shoe
Showe my brave mind, t' affect what
  gallants do,
I singe, dance, drinke, and merrily pass
  the day,
And like a chimney sweep all care away."

CURIOUS MONUMENT OF VICTORY.

About two miles to the north of Lambourne, in Berkshire, is White Horse Hill, on the summit of which is a large Roman entrenchment, called Uffington Castle, from its overlooking the village of Uffington in the adjacent valley. And a little below this fortification, on the steep of the same hill, facing the north west, is the figure of a white horse, the dimensions of which are extended over about an acre of ground. Its head, neck, body and tail, consist of one white line, as does also each of its four legs. The lines are formed by cutting trenches in the chalk, two or three feet in depth, and about ten feet in breadth. The chalk of the trench being of a brighter colour than the surrounding turf of the hill, the whole figure, when the midday sun darts his rays upon it, is visible at more than twelve miles distance. A white horse is known to have been the Saxon standard, and some have thence supposed, that this figure was made by Hengist, one of the Saxon kings.

But Mr. Wise, the author of a letter on this subject, addressed to Dr. Mead, and published in 1738, brings several arguments to prove, that this figure was formed by order of Alfred, during the reign of Ethelred his brother, as a monument of his victory gained over the Danes in the year 871, at Ashdown, now called Ashen, or Ashbury park, near Ashbury, not far from this hill. Others, however, suppose it to have been partly the effect of accident, and partly the work of the shepherds, who observing a rude figure somewhat resembling a horse, as there are in the veins of wood and stone many figures that resemble trees, caverns, and other objects, reduced it by degrees to a more regular figure. But however this be, it has been a custom immemorial for the neighbouring peasants to assemble on a certain day about midsummer, to clear away the weeds from this white horse, and trim the edges, to preserve its colour and shape, which they call "Scouring the horse," after which the evening is spent in mirth and festivity.

At the foot of White Horse Hill, and almost directly under the horse, is a large barrow, which the inhabitants there call Dragon-hill; and their tradition is, that "Here St. George killed the dragon." They shew besides a bare place on the top of it, which is a plain about fifty or sixty yards over, where the turf does not protrude, which they say proceeds "from the venomous blood that issued from the dragon's wound." That this was a funeral monument can hardly be doubted, and it is most probable it was erected by the Britons, to the memory of one of their kings who was killed in battle. H.

THE TERRIBLE "VADE IN PACE."

In the monastery of the Predicant Friars, at Toulouse, lived a young and lively monk, named Agostino, whose skill in music enabled him to play some most delightful airs on the organ, with which, on religious festivals, he accompanied the pious psalmody. The Superior accordingly relaxed in some degree the severity of the usual discipline, and permitted this youth occasionally to go out of the monastery for the purpose of perfecting himself in this elegant accomplishment; and Agostino, by his frequent visits to the house of his music-master, became intimate with one of his daughters, to whom, at the request of the father himself, he gave a few lessons on the harp. A young man who had an attachment to this damsel became jealous of the Monk, because such opportunities of familiar intercourse were allowed to him, while he himself could only gratify his curiosity by watching the steps of his beloved as she walked to church, or to the theatres. At length he plotted a dark scheme against his imagined rival; and after some time, when the young lady happened to be indisposed, he suborned the principal physician in the town, with whom he was on intimate terms, to declare, when called in to give his advice, that it was a case of pregnancy. The father was fired with indignation; and without inquiring into the reality of the imputation, immediately visited the Superior, and charged the Monk with the deed. The latter, in utter astonishment, appeared in the presence of the incensed Prior, and maintained his innocence without shrinking; honestly confessing that he admired the beauty of this fair damsel, but asserting that he was entirely guiltless not only of any action but of any expression bordering on vice; and asseverating that the very thought of such a prostitution of religion, of such an act of treason to the rights of friendship and hospitality, filled his mind with horror. The Prior made no reply, but, darting on the Monk a penetrating and freezing glance, he ordered him to retire to his cell, and there await the punishment which he deserved. A cold chill ran through the blood of the poor youth, who, pale and trembling, with a confused vision before his eyes, sank down senseless on his pallet.

In the mean time, the Superior assembled all the members of the convent, related to them the particulars of the charge, and maintained that one who had thus dared to violate his vows merited condign punishment. Those whose rank and age qualified them to pronounce their judgment answered, that the delinquent ought to be closed in the *Vade in pace*, that subterraneous prison in which fated culprits are doomed to expire. No consideration of Agostino's youth, of his amiable manners, and of his elegant accomplishments, could touch their unfeeling hearts with pity. The Monks rushed to the cell, where he had scarcely recovered the full use of his senses, and dragged him again into the presence of the Superior, who in a loud voice pronounced the sentence, *Vade in pace*. Agostino was scarcely yet in possession of his faculties, but when he heard those awful words, he exclaimed in phrensy:——' What—without inquiry, without trial, am I, who am innocent, condemned to a den of darkness, there to be buried alive, and to suffer an existence worse than a thousand deaths? and are ye the ministers of a merciful God? the chosen of a meek Redeemer? Do you call yourselves my brethren, you who are my executioners? Blasphemous wretches'—More he would have said, but the Monks thundered forth a psalm, covered his face with a black veil, tied his hands, and commenced the horrible procession which was to conduct him to a living sepulchre. One monk went before the others, carrying a cross wrapped in mourning; the rest followed, chaunting in a deep and dismal tone the *De profundis*; in the middle was the miserable Agostino, and the Prior walked last in the funeral procession. In this order the monks descended the dark subterraneous passages of the monastery, and arrived at the mouth of a deep vault, just wide enough to admit a single body, from which not only the light of the day but every breath of healthful atmosphere was excluded. An iron portal barred the access, above which was a small aperture, where they placed the pittance of bread and water with which the poor wretch, when deposited beneath, was for a time to be supported. The procession advanced towards this abyss of death, when the Prior seized the hand of Agostino, who stood like a victim at the altar, and, with the assistance of the other monks, hurled him downwards, closing over him the dismal portal. Agostino heard the grating of the rusty hinges, and the shutting of that door which to him would be shut for ever. After some few days had elapsed, in a fit of phrensy he dashed his head against the wall; his eyeballs burst from their sockets, and his brains from his skull; and his body lay weltering in his blood, a pitiable spectacꞏe to the monks who ran in to witness the calamity.—*Lavater's Travels of Petrarch.*

VISION OF CHARLES XI. OF SWEDEN.

The following singular narration occurs in the Rev. J. T. James's Travels in Sweden, Prussia, Poland, &c. during the years 1813 and 1814.—The most marvellous part of the affair is, that, as the reader will see, no less than six persons (the monarch inclusive) concur in attesting the reality of the pretended vision.

Charles XI, it seems, sitting in his chamber between the hours of eleven and twelve at night, was surprised at the appearance of a light in the window of the hall of the diet: he demanded of the grand chancellor, Bjelke, who was present, what it was that he saw, and was answered that it was only the reflection of the moon: with this, however, he was dissatisfied; and the senator, Bjelke, soon after entering the room, he addressed the same question to him, but received the same answer. Looking afterwards again through the window, he thought he observed a crowd of persons in the hall: upon this, said he, Sirs, all is not as it should be—in the confidence that he who fears God need dread nothing, I will go and see what this may be. Ordering the two noblemen before-mentioned, as also Oxenstiern and Brahe, to accompany him, he sent for Grunsten, the door-keeper, and descended the staircase leading to the hall

Here the party seem to have been sensible of a certain degree of trepidation, and no one else daring to open the door, the king took the key, unlocked it, and entered first into the ante-chamber: to their infinite surprise, it was fitted up with black cloth: alarmed by this extraordinary circumstance, a second pause occurred; at length the king set his foot within the hall, but fell back in astonishment at what he saw; again, however, taking courage, he made his companions promise to follow him, and advanced. The hall was lighted up and arrayed with the same mournful hangings as the antechamber: in the centre was a round table, where sat sixteen venerable men, each with large volumes lying open before them: above was the king, a young man of sixteen or eighteen years of age, with the crown on his head and sceptre in his hand. On his right hand sat a personage about forty years old, whose face bore the strongest marks of integrity; on his left an old man of seventy, who seemed very urgent with the young king that he should make a certain sign with his head, which as often as he did, the venerable men struck their hands on their books with violence.

Turning my eyes, says the king, a little further, I beheld a scaffold and executioners, and men with their clothes tucked up, cutting off heads one after the other so fast, that the blood formed a deluge on the floor: those who suffered were all young men. Again I looked up and perceived the throne behind the great table almost overturned; near to it stood a man of forty, that seemed the protector of the kingdom. I trembled at the sight of these things, and cried aloud—"It is the voice of God!—What ought I to understand?—When shall all this come to pass?" A dead silence prevailed; but on my crying out a second time, the young king answered me, saying, "This shall not happen in your time, but in the days of the sixth sovereign after you. He shall be of the same age as I appear now to have, and this personage sitting beside me gives you the air of him that shall be the regent and protector of the realm. During the last year of the regency, the country shall be sold by certain young men, but he shall then take up the cause, and, acting in conjunction with the young king, shall establish the throne on a sure footing; and this in such a way, that never was before, or ever afterwards shall be seen in Sweden so great a king. All the Swedes shall be happy under him; the public debts shall be paid; he shall leave many millions in the treasury, and shall not die but at a very advanced age: yet before he is firmly seated on his throne shall an effusion of blood take place unparalleled in history. "You," added he, "who are king of this nation, see that he is advertised of these matters: you have seen all; act according to your wisdom."

Having thus said, the whole vanished, and (adds he) we saw nothing but ourselves and our flambeaus, while the ante-chamber through which we passed on returning was no longer clothed in black.—"Nous entrâmes dans mes appartemens, et je me mis aussitôt à écrire ce que j'avois vu: ainsi que les avertissements, aussi bien que je le puis. Que le tout est vrai, je le jure sur ma vie et mon honneur, autant que le Dieu m'aide le corps et l'ame.

"Charles XI. aujourd'hui Roi de Suède. L'an 1791, 17 Dec."

"Comme témoins et présents sur les lieux nous avons vu tout ce que S. M. a rapporté, et nous l'affermons par notre serment, autant que Dieu nous aide pour le corps et l'ame. H. L. Bjelke, Gr. Chancelier du Royaume,—Bjelke, Sénateur,—Brahe, Sénateur,—Ax. Oxenstiern, Sénateur, —Petre Grunsten, Huissier."

"The whole story" says Mr. James, "is curious, and well worth attention; but unless the young king's ghostly representative made an error in his chronological calculation, it will be difficult to reconcile the time specified with that which is yet to come. I can offer no explanation, and bequeath the whole, like the hieroglyphic in Moore's Almanack, 'to the better ingenuity of my readers.'"

THE PARRICIDE PUNISHED.

THE following very singular adventure is related as a fact in a French work, entitled *La Nouvelle Bibliothèque de Société*; and is said to have happened in one of the provinces of France. It is related in a letter to a friend.

The adventure which I am going to relate to you, my dear friend, is of so strange and dreadful a nature, that you are the only person to whom I must ever disclose the secret.

The nuptials of Mademoiselle de Vildac were celebrated yesterday; at which, as a neighbour, custom and good manners required my attendance. You are acquainted with M. de Vildac: he has a countenance which never pleased me; his eyes have often a wild and suspicious glare, a something which has always given me disagreeable sensations for which I could in no way account. I could not help observing yesterday, that, in the midst of joy and revelry, he partook not of pleasure: far from being penetrated with the happiness of his new son and daughter, the delight of others seemed to him a secret torment.

The feast was held at his ancient castle; and, when the hour of rest arrived, I was conducted to a chamber immediately under the Old Tower at the north end. I had just fallen into my first sleep, when I was awakened and alarmed by a heavy kind of noise over head. I listened, and heard very distinctly the footsteps of some one slowly descending, and dragging chains that clanked upon the stairs, the noise approached, and presently the chamber-door was opened, the clanking of the chains redoubled, and he who bore them went towards the chimney. There were a few embers half extinguished; these he scraped together, and said in a sepulchral voice—'Alas! how long it is since I have seen a fire!' I own my friend, I was terrified: I seized my sword, looked between my curtains, and saw by the glimmer of the embers a withered old man half naked, with a bald head and a white beard. He put his trembling hands to the wood, which began to blaze, and soon afterwards turned towards the door by which he entered, fixed his eyes with horror upon the floor, as if he beheld something most dreadful, and exclaimed with agony, "My God! my God!"

My emotion caused my curtains to make a noise, and he turned affrighted. "Who is there?" said he. "Is there any one in that bed?"—"Yes," I replied: "and who are you?" Contending passions would not for a while suffer him to speak; at last he answered, "I am the most miserable of men. This, perhaps, is more than I ought to say; but it is so long, so many years, since I have seen or spoken to a human being, that I cannot resist. Fear nothing; come towards the fire; listen to my sorrows, and for a moment soften my sufferings!"

My fear gave place to pity; I sat down by him. My condescension and my feelings moved him; he took my hand, bathed it with his tears, and said—"Generous man! let me desire you first to satisfy my curiosity. Tell me why you lodge in this chamber, where no man has lodged before for so many years; and what mean the rejoicings I have heard? what extraordinary thing has happened to-day in the castle?'

When I had informed him of the marriage of Vildac's daughter, he lifted up his hands to heaven—"Has Vildac a daughter? and is she married? Almighty God grant she may be happy! grant she may never know guilt!" He paused for a moment—"Learn who I am," said he. "You see, you speak to the father of Vildac—the cruel Vildac! Yet what right have I to complain? Should I—should I call man or tiger cruel?"—"What!" exclaimed I with astonishment, "is Vildac your son? Vildac! the monster! shut you from the sight of man! load you with chains! And lives there such a wretch?"

"Behold," said he, "the power, the detestable power of riches. The hard and pitiless heart of my unhappy son is impenetrable to every tender sentiment: insensible to love and friendship, he is also deaf to the cries of nature; and, to enjoy my lands, has hung these eating irons on me.

"He went one day to visit a neighbouring young nobleman,

who had lately lost his father; he saw him encircled by vassals, and occupied in receiving their homage and their rents: the sight made a shocking impression upon the imagination of Vildac, which had long been haunted with a strong desire to enjoy his future patrimony. I observed at his return a degree of thoughtfulness and gloom about him that was unusual. Five days afterwards I was seized during the night, carried off naked by three men masked, and lodged in this tower. I know not by what means Vildac spread the report of my death; but I guessed, by the tolling of the bells and funeral dirges, more solemn than for inferior persons, they were performed for my interment. The idea was horrid; and I entreated most earnestly to be permitted to speak for a moment to my son, but in vain: those who brought me my food, no doubt, supposed me a criminal condemned to perish in prison. It is now twenty years since I was first confined here. I perceived this morning that my door was not secured, and I waited till night to profit by the accident: yet I do not wish to escape; but the little liberty of a few yards more is much to a prisoner."

"No," cried I, "you shall quit that dishonourable habitation. Heaven has destined me to be your deliverer, defender, support, and guide. Every body sleeps; now is the time; let us be gone!"

"It must not be!" said he, after a moment's silence. "Solitude has changed my ideas, and my principles. Happiness is but in opinion. Now that I am inured to suffer, why should I fly from my fate? What is there for me to wish in this world? The die is thrown, and this tower must be my tomb!"

"Surely you dream," answered I. "Let us not lose time; the night is advanced: we shall presently have but a moment. Come!"

"I am affected," replied he: "but cannot profit by your kindness. Liberty has no charms for my small remains of life. Shall I dishonour my son; or which way has his daughter given me offence, to whom I was never known, by whom I was never seen? This sweet innocent sleeps happily in the arms of her husband, and shall I overwhelm her with infamy? Yet might I but behold her! might I but lock her in these feeble arms, and bedew her bosom with my tears! 'Tis in vain! It cannot be! I never must look upon her!

"Adieu! day begins to break, and we shall be surprised. I will return to my prison."

"No," said I, stopping him; "I will not suffer it. Slavery has enfeebled your soul; I must inspire you with courage. Let us be gone; we will afterwards examine whether it be proper to make the matter public. My house, my friends, my fortune, are at your service. No one shall know who you are; and, since it is necessary, Vildac's crime shall be concealed. What do you fear?"

"Nothing! I am all gratitude! Oh, no! it cannot be! Here I will remain!"

"Well, act as you please; but if you refuse to fly with me, I will go immediately to the governor of the province, tell him who you are, and return armed with his authority and his power, to wrest you from the barbarity of an inhuman child."

"Beware what you do! abuse not my confidence. Leave me to perish. You know me not. I am a monster! Day and the blessed sun would sicken at my sight. Infamous I am, and covered with guilt—guilt most horrible! Turn your eyes upon that wall; behold these boards; sprinkled with blood, a father's blood!—murdered by his son; by me!—Ha! look! behold! do you not see him! He stretches forth his bleeding arms! he begs for pity! the vital stream flows out! he falls! he groans! Oh, horror! madness! despair!"

The miserable wretch fell convulsed with terror on the floor; and when fear and passion in part subsided, he durst not turn his guilty eyes towards me, where I stood transfixed with horror. As soon as he had the power, he approached the door:—"Farewell," said he; "be innocent, if you would be happy! The wretch who so lately moved your pity, is now become detestable to you as well as to himself: he goes unlamented to the dungeon, whence alive he never shall return!"

I had neither the power to speak or move. The castle was become a place most abominable; and I departed in the morning. I must leave the neighbourhood; I cannot bear the sight of Vildac, nor the remembrance of this night. How, my friend, is it possible that humanity can produce wickedness so intolerable and unnatural!

Hoaxes and Impostures.
No. III.
ELIZABETH CANNING.

I was in London, says Voltaire, in the year 1753, when the adventures of Elizabeth Canning made so much noise. Elizabeth had quitted the house of her parents, and disappeared for a month; when she returned thin, emaciated, and her clothes in rags—"Good God! in what condition are you returned! where have you been? whence are you come? what has befallen you?"— "Alas, my dear aunt, as I passed through Moorfields, in order to return home, two strong ruffians threw me down, robbed me, and carried me off to a house ten miles from London." Her aunt and her neighbours wept at this tale. "Oh, my dear child! was it not to the house of that infamous Mrs. Webb, that the ruffians conveyed you? for she lives about ten miles from town." "Yes, aunt, it was to Mrs. Webb's."—"To a great house on the right?"—"Yes, aunt." The neighbours then described Mrs. Webb; and the young Canning agreed, that she was exactly such a woman as they described her. One of them told Miss Canning, that people played all night in that woman's house; that it was a cut-throat place, where young men resorted to lose their money and ruin themselves. "Indeed it is a cut-throat place," replied Elizabeth Canning. "They do worse," said another neighbour, "those two ruffians, who are cousins to Mrs. Webb, go on the highway, take up all the pretty girls they meet, and oblige them to live on bread and water until they consent to abandon themselves to the gamblers in the house."—"Good God! I suppose they obliged you, my dear niece, to live upon bread and water?"—"Yes, aunt." She was asked, whether the ruffians had not offered violence to her chastity, and whether she had not been ruined? She answered; "That she had resisted them; that they beat her to the ground, and put her life in danger." Then the aunt and the neighbours began to cry out and weep.

They conducted the little girl to the house of one Adamson, who had been long a friend of the family; he was a man of fortune, and of great consequence in the parish. He mounted his horse, and took with him some friends, as zealous as himself, to reconnoitre the house of Mrs. Webb. On viewing the house, they thought there could be no doubt of the girl's having been confined there; and on perceiving an outhouse where there was some hay, they concluded that to have been the place of her confinement. The pity of the good man Adamson was excited; he described the place on his return, which Elizabeth acknowledged she had been confined in. He interested the whole neighbourhood in her behalf, where a subscription was set on foot, in favour of a young woman so cruelly treated.

In proportion as Canning recovered her appearance and beauty, the people grew warm in her interest. Mr. Adamson presented a formal complaint to the sheriff in behalf of injured innocence. Mrs. Webb, and all those who lived in her house, while tranquil and unapprehensive in the country, were arrested and thrown into a dungeon. The sheriff, in order to be the better informed of the truth of this transaction, commenced his proceedings by enticing amicably to him a young woman who was a servant to Mrs. Webb; and engaging her by gentle words to say all that she knew. The servant, who had never seen or heard of Miss Canning, answered ingenuously at first, that she knew nothing of the person he spoke of. But when the sheriff told her, she must answer in a court, and that she would certainly be hanged if she did not confess, she said every thing he wished her to say. In short, a jury was assembled, and nine persons were condemned to be hanged!

The time drew near in which these nine persons were to be exexcuted; when the paper, called the *Session-Paper*, fell into the hands of a philosopher, named Ramsay. He read the account of the trial, and found the whole of it absurd. He was moved with indignation; and sat down to write a pamphlet, in which he stated it as a principle, that it is the first obligation of a juryman to be possessed of common sense, He shewed, that Mrs. Webb, her two cousins, and the rest of the family, must have been different from the rest of mankind, if they obliged young girls to fast on bread and water with a view to prostitute them; for, on the contrary, they should have dieted and dressed them well, in order to render them agreeable; because, in all cases, merchants who have goods to dispose of, take care not to injure or tear them. He shewed, that Miss Canning had never been at the house of Mrs. Webb, and that she had only repeated the foolish things which her aunt had suggested to her, and that the good Mr. Adamson had, by the excess of his zeal, occasioned this extravagant prosecution: in short, that in all probability, the lives of nine of his majesty's subjects would be sacrificed, because Miss Canning was handsome and would tell falsehoods. The servant, who had been induced in an amicable manner, to say before the sheriff what was not true, could not safely contradict herself before the court. A person, who has given false testimony through passion or fear, commonly adheres to what he has said, and lies, from fear of passing for a liar.

It is in vain, said Mr. Ramsay, the law has ordained that two witnesses should be sufficient to prove a capital crime, and to take away the life of a citizen. If the Lord Chancellor and the Archbishop of Canterbury should swear that they have seen me assassinate my father and mother, and in half an hour eat them all for my breakfast, the Chancellor and the Archbishop should be put in Bedlam, rather than I should be burnt upon their evidence. If on the one hand a thing be impossible and absurd, and on the other there be ten thousand witnesses and a thousand reasoners, the impossibility of the thing should determine it against the evidences and reasonings. This little pamphlet opened the eyes of the sheriff and the jury. They were obliged to revise the proceedings. It was alleged, that Miss Canning was a little impostor, who had retired to lie in, while she pretended to have been in prison at Mrs. Webb's; and all the city of London, which had espoused her cause, was as much ashamed as it had been when a wag proposed to jump into a quart bottle, brought two thousand people to see the spectacle, carried off their money, and left them the bottle.

For an interesting account of the hoax here alluded to by Voltire, see "The Cabinet of Curiosities," No. II.

Eccentric Biography.

GOTTFRIED MINDS, THE CATS RAPHAEL.

In the year 1815, there died at Berne, in Switzerland, of an apoplexy, Gottfried Minds, a painter, celebrated for his extraordinary delineations of bears and cats. Minds died in the forty-sixth year of his age.

His father, still living in Berne, is a native of Lipsch, in Upper Hungary, and learned the trade of a cabinet-maker at Kremnitz. The son was a pupil of Frudenberger, and his extraordinary talents in the representation of various species of animals, but especially those abovementioned, in paintings in water-colours, are attested not only by the numerous productions of his pencil in the portfolios of various amateurs at Berne, Zurich, Basle, and other places, but also by the high encomiums passed upon his performances by many artists of the highest eminence. Madame Lebrun, of Paris, perhaps the first living female painter, never failed, in her different journies through Switzerland, to purchase several of Minds's performances, declaring at the same time that they were real master-pieces of their kind, and would be acknowledged as such even in the French metropolis. It was she who first gave to our artist the appellation of *Le Raphael des Chats*—(the Raphael of Cats)—which he has ever since retained, and by which many strangers inquired for him at Berne. Minds was certainly well worthy of this name, not only on account of the correctness of his drawings of those animals, and the true though dignified delineation of their forms, but also more especially on account of the life and spirit which he transfused into them in his pictures. The particular and individual physiognomy which distinguished each of his cats; the half-fawning, half tiger-like, look which is common to them all; the graceful movements of his kittens, three or four of which are sometimes represented sporting about the mother; the silky hair, which, looks as though you could blow it up—in a word, whatever is characteristic of the animal, we find in his works with such truth and such complete illusion, that the spectators would scarcely be surprised if the eyes of his figures began to roll, if the paws were raised for a spring, and the well-known cry were to issue from the paper. The affection of Minds for the feline race might be termed fraternal. When he was at work, a favourite puss generally sat by his side, and a kind of conversation was kept up between them, partly in words and partly by gestures. He was often seen employed at his table with an old cat on his lap, and two or three kittens upon both shoulders, or even in the hollow formed at the back of his neck by the inclination of his head, while the whole family purred forth their delight at having found such comfortable quarters, in sounds resembling those of a spinning-wheel. Thus encumbered, he would sit for hours together at his work, and abstain from every motion that could in the least incommode his beloved favourites. In 1809, the general massacre of cats at Berne, rendered their friend almost inconsolable. Eight hundred of those animals were slaughtered in the space of twenty-four hours, because one had gone mad and bitten several others. Minds had indeed carefully concealed and preserved his darling Minette, but the melancholy sight, which every moment met his view, of dead or living cats carried by men, maids, or boys, to the skinner, wounded him to the heart. In winter evenings, Minds used to amuse himself with carving bears, cats, and other animals, in miniature, out of wild chestnut tree, with such accuracy and skill that they had a rapid sale, and were bought up by many as ornaments for their chimney-pieces. It is to be regretted that insects soon attacked the wood and thus destroyed the pretty little figures. He passed many of his happiest hours at the Bears' Den, in Berne, where from remote antiquity two live bears have been continually kept. Between him and these animals, a peculiar sympathy seemed to subsist. No sooner did Friedli, by which name he was best known at Berne, make his appearance, than the bears hastened to him with a friendly grunt, and saluted him with a bow, upon which they were invariably rewarded with a piece of bread, or an apple, from the pocket of their benefactor and friend.—Next to cats and bears, Minds received the greatest delight from looking over works of art, particularly prints in which animals were introduced. Among these, however, the lions of Rubens, some pieces by Rembrandt and Potter, and Riedinger's stags, were the only copies that he allowed to be excellent. With the other animals by Riedinger he found fault, almost without exception, as incorrect. The bears, by the same artist, he characterised as absolute monsters: neither did he entertain a much more favourable opinion of the celebrated cats of Cornel, Vicher, and Hollar. On other works, such chiefly as hunting and historical composition, he often pronounced most severe opinions, without the least regard to the celebrity of the master; and on other matters, notwithstanding his secluded life, he displayed profound penetration and correct judgment.—The following parody of the verses of Catullus, on Lesbia's sparrow, has been proposed as an appropriate inscription for this artist:

> Lugete, o feles, ursique lugete!
> Mortuus est vobis amicus:—

which might be thus rendered:—

> Ye weeping cats, your sorrows mew;
> Your griefs ye soften'd Bruins bellow;
> Mourn him whom death has snatch'd from you,
> Forsooth ye'll never find his fellow!

JENNY DARNEY.

An inoffensive individual of the name of Jenny Darney is well known in the southern parts of the county of Cumberland. It has been impossible to ascertain any thing of her family, friends, or where she was born. The country people know her by the appellation of Jenny Darney, from the manner, I presume, in which she used to mend her clothes. Her present garb is entirely of her own manufacture. She collects the small parcels of wool which lie about the fields in sheep-farms, spins it on a rock and spindle of her own making; and, as she cannot find any other method of making the yarn into cloth, she knits it on wooden needles, and by that means procures a warm, comfortable dress. In the lifetime of the late Charles Lutwidge, Esq. of Holm Rook, she took possession of an old cottage, or rather cow-house, on his estate, in which she has ever since been suffered to continue. Her intellects seem at certain times greatly deranged, but her actions are harmless, and her language inoffensive. On that score she is caressed by all the villagers, who supply her with eatables, &c. for money she utterly refuses. She seems a person, in her lucid intervals, of much shrewdness, and her understanding is much above the common level. This has also been improved by a tolerable education. Her appearance has been much the same for these twenty years, so that she must now be nearly ninety years of age; but of this, as well as her family and name, she is always silent. She seems to have chosen out the spot where she now lives, to pass the remainder of her days unknown to her friends, and in a great measure from a distaste of a wicked world, to "prepare herself," as she often in her quiet hours says, "for a better."

Anecdotes of Longevity.

GREEK PATRIARCH.

Hufeland, in his Art of prolonging Life, says: "The most extraordinary instances of longevity are to be found among those classes of mankind who, amidst bodily labour, and in the open air, lead a simple life, agreeable to nature; such as farmers, gardeners, hunters, soldiers, and sailors. In these situations, man still attains to the age of 140 and even 150." He then enumerates several persons who attained a great age, among whom are Henry Jenkins and Thomas Parr; the former of whom, at the time of his death, was 169 years old, and the latter upwards of 152. Draakenburg, the Dane, who died in 1772, in the 146th year of his age; J. Effingham, who died in Cornwall, in the 144th; and the old Prussian soldier, Mittelstedt, who died in 1792, in the 112th year of his age. These are some of the most remarkable instances given by Dr. Hufeland; but in turning over a Dutch dictionary, "Het Algemeen historisch, geographisch en genealogisch Woordenboek," by Luiscius, we have found the following still more extraordinary instance of a man who attained to the age of 180. As it is little known, we have translated the whole article from the above work. "Czartan (Petrarch), by religion a Greek, was born in the year 1539, and died on the 5th of January, 1724, at Kofrosch, a village four miles from Temeswar, on the road leading to Karansebes. He had lived, therefore, a hundred and eighty years. At the time when the Turks took Temeswar from the Christians he was employed in keeping his father's cattle. A few days before his death he had walked, with the help of a stick, to the post-house at Kofrosch, to ask charity from the travellers. His eyes were much inflamed, but he still enjoyed a little sight. His hair and beard were of a greenish white colour, like mouldy bread; and he had a few of his teeth remaining. His son, who was ninety-seven years of age, declared his father had once been a head taller; that at a great age he married for the third time; and that he was born in this last marriage. He was accustomed, agreeably to the rules of his religion, to observe fast days with great strictness, and never to use any other food than milk, and certain cakes, called by the Hungarians *kollatschen*, together with a good glass of brandy, such as is made in the country. He had descendants in the fifth generation, with whom he sometimes sported, carrying them in his arms. His son, though ninety-seven, was still fresh and vigorous. When field marshal Count Wallis, the commandant of Temeswar, heard that this old man was taken sick, he caused a portrait of him to be painted, and when it was almost finished, he expired." This account is extracted from a letter dated January the 29th, 1724; and written by Hamelbranix, the Dutch envoy at Vienna, to their High Mightinesses the States General.

ENGLISH PATRIARCH.

At Oxhey, in Saddleworth, on the 8th of December, 1817, died, aged 91, Mr. William Heginbottom, son of the late Rev. John Heginbottom, many years an eminent, zealous, and pious minister of the parish church there. He will be long remembered by an extensive circle of vocal performers, as one of the most eminent of the musical profession. He was a man of the strictest honour and integrity, and a most zealous supporter of the Established Church. He was father to ten, father-in-law to ten, grandfather to 131, great grandfather to 153, and great great grandfather to one, in all 305. The last of whom, he walked thirty-two miles to see, in his 90th year. He saw his grandfather, his own father, his own sons, his grandsons, the sons of his grandsons, and the daughter of his grandson's son, even seven generations. He was followed to the tomb by nine of his own children, (whose united ages amount to 533 years) fifty-nine of his grandchildren, and a numerous sorrowing assemblage of other relatives, friends, and domestics, to St. Thomas's Chapel, Frier Mear, where he was interred by torch light, after the solemn funeral anthems had been sung.

Varieties.

EXPLOSION OF A POWDER MAGAZINE AT DANTZIC.

DANTZIC.—On Wednesday the 6th of December, 1815, about nine o'clock in the morning, the remaining gunpowder, consisting of about 60 cwt. besides the filled bombs and shells, were to be removed from the powder magazine, close to the rampart, within the city, near St. James's Gate. For this purpose, twelve cannoneers, a subaltern officer, and an artificer, went into it, when just as the last man was going in, (as it is reported,) the magazine blew up. The effect of the explosion was dreadful; those who lived at a distance, took it for an earthquake, for the doors and windows flew open, the household furniture was thrown down, and the bells, set in motion by the pressure of the air, rang of themselves; the hissing of the balls in the air confirmed the idea that it was an earthquake, but the true cause was soon discovered by the balls that fell in the remote parts of the city, and by the lamentations of the wounded. A third part of the city, and precisely that inhabited by the poorer class, between six and seven hundred houses; the churches of St. James and St. Bartholomew, the Schusseldam, the market-place, the Pfeifferstadt and the adjacent streets have particularly suffered. Corpses, which, from mutilation and dust, were hardly recognised as human; lay in heaps around, and were envied by the half living, who, with their limbs crushed, and howling with pain, endeavoured to crawl from underneath the ruins. Those who had escaped with moderate wounds were asking, or digging, with their faces and hands covered with blood, which the cold made to freeze upon them, after their friends and their property. There lay, still convulsed, the torn members of a human body. A mother lamented over three children whom she missed; the children were found, but none of them were alive. Almost more shocking was the sight in a long street leading to the powder magazine, which served as a market-place for the country people, who came here with little sledges loaded with wood, from Cassuben. It happened to be market time. Twenty of these poor people lay crushed under the horses and oxen, which were likewise crushed, and under their overturned sledges. Round the stump of a lamp-post was a horse, whose bones was broken, twisted round like a cord. The instances of miraculous escapes are many. Some persons were saved merely by the falling beams, &c. forming a kind of an arch over them. The extent of the damage may be conceived, from the circumstance, that for the distance of above half a league round the magazine, in every direction, it rained, as one may say, balls, bombs, shells, cannister shot, pieces of brickwork, &c. The number of the killed and wounded is between 300 and 400, that of the houses damaged, 600 or 700, and the loss sustained not to be made good for half a million of dollars.

Glass is wanting to mend the windows, which were almost universally broken by the pressure of the air.

EFFECTS OF A GUILTY CONSCIENCE.

The Gazette de France of November 10, 1815, gives the following remarkable instance of the deep impression made by a theatrical representation:—A young woman, the mother of three children, went with her husband to see the performance of "The Guilty Mother," a play by Beaumarchais; the situation and the remorse of the heroine affected her the more deeply, as she had a similar fault to reproach herself with; this recollection, which, for a long time, she endeavoured to stifle without success, took such lively possession of her soul, that she could not support the heart-rending scenes in the fourth act. She was conveyed home in great agitation of mind, and the next day, after a long struggle and anguish, she confessed to her husband, a fault which he had never suspected, and which he pardoned. But the blow was struck, and she survived this confession three days only, in spite of the care and assurance of tenderness which her husband lavished upon her.

The Scrap Book.

AWFUL CALCULATION.

If we reckon with the ancients, that a generation lasts 30 years, then in that space 800,000,000 of human beings are born, and die; consequently 74,039 must be dropping off into eternity every day, 3,044 every hour, and about 51 every minute.—How awful the reflection!

A SOMNAMBULIST.

The son of Abel Moore, aged eight years, of the Royal Oak, in West-street, Chichester, on Sunday night, the 8th instant, at half past ten o'clock, rose from his bed on the second floor, and passed through a large room; he then opened the window and got over a frame containing flower-pots, and descended into the street without injury; being all the while asleep. Two persons, who witnessed the circumstance, awoke the youth, and reconducted him into the house.

SPRING AT HARDINGFORDBURY.

In the parish of Hardingfordbury, about two miles from Essenden, in Hertfordshire, is a spring of water, known by the name of *Aquatile-hole*, vulgo, *Akerley-hole*, now in the tenure or occupation of Samuel Whitbread, Esq. of the most copious or singular nature in the island, supposed to deliver a quantity of water at the mouth, or opening, sufficient for the discharge of a pipe of the bore of three feet and a half in diameter. This spring rises within one hundred yards of the river Lea, into which it disembogues; and in that short space, actually furnishes a greater quantity of water than what is contained in the river itself, which is well known to take the aggregate springs from Leagrove-marsh, near Dunstable, in Bedfordshire, to that place.

Published by J. LIMBIRD, 355, Strand, (East End of Exeter 'Change); and sold by all Newsmen and Booksellers. Printed by A. APPLEGATH, Stamford-street.

THE CABINET OF CURIOSITIES,
OR
Wonders of the World Displayed.

A world of wonders where creation seems
No more the works of Nature but her dreams.—MONTGOMERY.

No. V.]   PRICE TWOPENCE.

THE SPOTTED NEGRO BOY.

GEORGE ALEXANDER GRATTON, the Spotted Negro Boy, whose portrait embellishes our present number, was well known to the inhabitants of the metropolis and its vicinity, about twelve years ago, at which time he was exhibited at the fairs, by Richardson, a famous purveyor of objects of entertainment at those places of popular festivity.

Both the parents of George Alexander were black, and natives of Africa. He was born in the island of St. Vincent, on the plantation of Mr. Alexander, of which one Gratton was overseer, about the month of June, 1808; and the curiosity of his appearance was such, that he was shewn, in the capital of his native island, at the price of a dollar each person. It is added, that the superstitious prejudices of the

F

negroes placed his life in some danger, and that he was, on that account, shipped for England. Probably the prospect of a profitable disposal of him, in this country, was an equally powerful motive for his removal.

The child was only fifteen months old, when, in September, 1809, being brought to Bristol, in the ship called the Friends of Emma, Mr. Richardson, the proprietor, as before intimated, of a travelling theatre, was applied to, and an engagement entered upon, by which he was consigned to Mr. Richardson's care for three years.

His skin and hair were every where party-coloured, transparent brown and white. On the crown of his head, several triangles, one within the other, were formed by alternations of the colours of his hair. In figure and countenance he might truly be called a beautiful child. His limbs were well-proportioned, his features regular and pleasing, his eyes bright and intelligent, and the whole expression of his face both mild and lively. His voice was soft and melodious; and, as his mind began to develope itself, much quickness and penetration were betrayed.

When nearly five years of age, he was unfortunately attacked with a swelling in the jaw, and died on the 3d of February, 1813. Mr. Richardson, who had always treated him with a parental kindness while alive, was sincerely afflicted at his death. Soon after he had been placed with him, he had caused him to be baptized at the parish church of Newington, in the county of Surrey, and, on his death, he was buried at Great Marlow, in Buckinghamshire, in a brick vault, which Mr. Richardson caused to be purposely constructed. Mr. Richardson, fearful that the body might be stolen, had previously kept it unburied for the space of three months.

In the vestry of the church of Great Marlow hangs a fine painting of this extraordinary natural phenomenon, executed from the life, by Coventry; and presented to the corporation of Buckingham by Mr. Richardson; who finally closed his displays of affectionate regard for a child, which was not originally more recommended to his attention by his curiosity, than he was afterward endeared to him by disposition and manners, by erecting a monument to his memory at Great Marlow, and placing upon it the following inscription and epitaph:—

TO THE MEMORY

OF

GEORGE ALEXANDER GRATTON,

THE SPOTTED NEGRO BOY,

From the Carribee Islands, in the West Indies, died February 3d, 1813, aged four years and three quarters.

This Tomb, erected by his only Friend and Guardian, Mr. John Richardson, of London.

Should this plain simple tomb attract thine eye,
Stranger, as thoughtfully thou passest by,
Know that there lies beneath this humble stone,
A child of colour, haply not thine own.

His parents born of Afric's sun-burnt race,
Tho' black and white were blended in his face,
To Britain brought, which made his parents free,
And shew'd the world great Nature's prodigy.

Depriv'd of kindred that to him were dear,
He found a friendly Guardian's fost'ring care,
But, scarce had bloom'd, the fragrant flower fades,
And the lov'd infant finds an early grave,

To bury him his lov'd companions came,
And drop't choice flowers, and lisp'd his
  early fame;
And some that lov'd him most, as if un-
  blest,
Bedew'd with tears the white wreath on
  his breast.

But he is gone, and dwells in that abode,
Where some of every clime must joy in
  God!

RENEE CORBEAU.

In the year 1594, a young gentleman, whose family dwelt in the town of Sues, in Normandy, came to the university of Angiers, in order to study the law. There he saw Reneé Corbeau, the daughter of a citizen of that place. This amiable girl was young, prudent, handsome, and witty. Though her parents were not rich, yet she inspired in the heart of the young student a passion so vehement, and love inspired him with such eloquence, that, in a very short time their attachment, become mutual, was so fervent, that in his transports he offered to espouse her, and gave her a solemn promise in writing. The young woman, agreeably deluded by his putting this paper into her hands, forfeited her honour. The consequence was, a child. Her parents reproached her in severe terms, and began to consult about the means by which her error might be repaired. The result of their deliberations was, that she should make her lover an appointment at their country-house, and thus give her parents an opportunity of surprising them together.

This scheme was effectually carried into execution, and while love possessed the heart of the young inamorato, he gave the daughter a contract of marriage.

The moment he had put his hand to this instrument, it filled him with disgust. Those charms, which had pierced his heart a few hours before, now lost their force, and the fair one, from being the most lovely of her sex, now appeared the least agreeable. After a few days, he left her abruptly and returned home to his father, whom, without the least reserve, he related the unlucky event. The father was extremely chagrined at this story of his son's, and disapproving of the match, he told him there was but one way left, and that, if he would regain his favour, he must follow it immediately. The young gentleman, in obedience to his father's directions, entered into holy orders, and was actually ordained a priest; so that it was impossible for him to perform his contract.

Renee Corbeau heard this news with the utmost grief, nor was it possible for her to dissemble the anger she conceived against her lover, for committing so black an act of perfidy. It is very likely, however, that her wrath would have vented itself in complaints, and all her threatenings evaporated in words; but her father immediately accused the young man before the magistrate for seduction, and on hearing the cause he was found guilty. However, he appealed to the parliament of Paris, and the cause was moved to the Tournelle, where Monsieur de Villeroy at that time presided. On the hearing all parties, the behaviour of this young gentleman appeared so gross, and capable of so little alleviation, that the court decided, that he should either marry the woman or suffer death. The first was impossible, because he had taken orders; the court, therefore, directed that he should be led to execution. Accordingly, he was put into the hands

F 2

of the executioner, and the confessor drew near, who was to assist him in his last moments. Then it was that Renee Corbeau found her bosom agitated with the most exquisite affliction, which was still heightened when she saw the pomp of justice about to take place, and her lover on the point of being led to the scaffold.

Furious, through despair, and guided only by her passion, she rushed with such impetuosity through the crowd that she got into the inner chamber before the judges were separated, and then, her face bathed in tears, and all in disorder, she addressed them in the following terms: "Behold! my Lords! the most unfortunate lover that ever appeared before the face of justice. In condemning him I love, you seem to suppose that either I am not guilty of any thing, or that, at least, my crime is capable of excuse, and yet you adjudge me to death, which must befall me with the same stroke that takes away my lover. You subject me to the most grievous destiny, for the infamy of my lover's death will fall upon me, and I shall go to my grave more dishonoured than him. You desire to repair the injury done to my honour, and the remedy you bring will load me with eternal shame; so that at the moment you give your opinion, that I am rather unhappy than criminal, you are pleased to punish me with the most severe and most intolerable pains. How agrees your treatment of me with your equity, and with the rules of that humane justice which should direct your court? You cannot be ignorant of the hardship I sustain; for you were men before you were judges. You must have been sensible of the power of love, and you cannot but have some idea of the torment which must be felt in a breast, where the remembrance dwells of having caused the death, the infamous death, of the dear object of her love. Can there be a punishment equal to this, or, after it, could death be considered in any other light than as the highest blessing of heaven?

"Stay! Oh, stay, my Lords! I am going to open your eyes. I am going to acknowledge my fault, to reveal my secret crime, which hitherto I have concealed, that, if possible, the marriage of my lover might have restored my blasted honour. But, urged now by remorse of conscience, I am constrained to confess that I seduced him. Yes, my lords, I loved first! It was I, that to gratify my passion, informed him of my attachment, and thus I made myself the instrument of my own dishonour. Change then, my lords, the sentiments you have hitherto entertained of this affair. Look upon me as the seducer; on my lover as the person injured; punish me; save him. If justice is inexorable, and there is a necessity for some victim, let it be me.

"You look upon it as a crime that he took holy orders, and thereby rendered it impossible for him to comply with his contract; but this was not his own act; it was the act of a barbarous father, whose tyrannous commands he could not resist. A will in subjection, my Lords, is no will at all to deserve punishment. The offender must be free; his father could only be guilty; and were he not the father of my love, I would demand justice of you on him. Is it not clear then, my Lords, that your last sentence contradicts your first? You decreed that he should have his choice to marry me, or to die, and yet you never put the first in his power. How odious must I appear in your eyes, when you choose rather to put a man to death, than to allow him to marry me. He has declared, that his present condition will not allow him to marry, and, in consequence of this declaration, you have condemned him to death; but what signifies that declaration; his meaning was, that he would have married me if he could, and if so, your sentence is unjust; for, by your former decree, he was to have his option. But you will say, a priest can't marry. Ah! my Lords, love has taught me better. Love brings things instantly to our minds that may be of service to the object of our loves. The Pope, my Lords, can dispense with his vow: you cannot be ignorant of this, and therefore his choice may be yet in his power. We expect every moment the legate of his holiness; he has all the plenitude of power delegated to him, which is in the sovereign pontiff. I will solicit him for this dispensation, and my passion tells me, that I shall not plead in vain; for what obstacle will it not be able to surmount, when it has overcome that of your decree. Have pity then, my Lords! Have pity on two unfortunate lovers; mitigate your sentence, or, at least, suspend it till I have time to solicit the legate for a dispensation. You look on my lover, it is true, as a man guilty of a great crime; but what crime too great to be expiated by the horrors he has already sustained? Has he not felt a thousand times the pains of death since the pronouncing his sentence? Besides, could you enter into my breast, and conceive what torments I have endured, you would think our fault, foul as it is, fully atoned. I see among your Lordships some who are young, and some who are advanced in years; the first cannot sure have their breasts already steeled against the emotions of a passion natural to their sex; and I may hope the latter have not forgot the tender sentiments of their junior years. From both I have a right to pity; and if the voices for me are few, let the humanity of their sentiments prevail against the number of their opponents. But if all I have said is vain, at least afford me the melancholy pleasure of sharing his punishment, as I shared his crime. In this, my Lords, be strictly just; and, as we have lived, let us die, together."

This amiable woman was heard with equal silence and compassion; there was not a word lost of her discourse, which she pronounced with a voice so clear, and with a tone so expressive of her affliction, that it struck to the hearts of the judges. Her beauty, her tears, her eloquence, had charms too powerful not to incline the most frozen hearts to think with her. The judges receded unanimously from their opinions. Monsieur de Villeroy having collected their sentiments, and declared that he agreed with them, proceeded to suspend the last edict, and to allow the criminal six months to apply for a dispensation.

The legate immediately after entered France. It was the great Cardinal de Medicis, afterwards Pope, by the name of Clement the Eleventh, though he enjoyed the chair not quite a month. He heard the whole of this affair, and inquired narrowly into all its circumstances, but finding that he took holy orders with a premeditated design to avoid the performance of his contract, he declared, that he was unworthy of a dispensation, and that he would not respite such a wretch from the death he deserved.

Renee Corbeau had a passion too strong to be overcome; she threw herself at the feet of the king, Henry the Fourth. He heard her with attention, answered with tenderness, and going to the legate in person, requested the dispensation in such terms, that it could not be refused. He had the goodness to deliver it the lady with his own hands; the criminal gladly accepted Renee for his wife; they were publicly married, and lived long together in the happiest union.

SINGULAR FAMILY AFFLICTION.

[We are indebted to a very amiable young lady, on whose veracity we can rely, for the following unpublished circumstantial narrative, of a most extraordinary case, which occurred in the parish of Wattisham, in the county of Suffolk, in the year 1762. The statement, which was written at the time, was then communicated to an ancestor of our fair correspondent; who has permitted us to copy it from the original attested document.—Ed.]

"On Sunday, January 10, 1762, Mary, daughter of John Weatherset, alias Downing, aged sixteen years, was taken with a pain in her left leg, which in an hour or two sunk into her foot and toes. The next day her toes were much swelled, and black spots appeared upon them. By degrees the whole foot became swelled and black; the pain, which was now chiefly in her toes, was, she said, as if dogs were gnawing them, and the blackness and swelling increasing upwards by slow degrees, until it came near the knee, when the flesh of her leg putrified and came off at the ancle with the foot, leaving the leg bones bare. Her other foot and leg were affected in a few days, and decayed nearly in the same degree and manner. Her thighs both swelled, and under her ham an abscess was formed. The surgeon seeing no perfect separation, did on the 17th of April following, attempt to take off one of the limbs near the knee, just above the corrupted flesh; but such an effusion of blood ensued as to stop his attempt: he afterwards took off both her legs near the knee, but, after living a few weeks, she died.

"Very soon after the death of the daughter, Mary, the mother, was taken with the same sort of pain under her left foot; her toes, foot and leg, were affected in the same manner as her daughter's, and in a few days her other foot and leg became affected; both her feet fell off at the ancles, and the flesh dropped from the bones of the legs. Her hands and arms became benumbed and her fingers were contracted, but not black, but she afterwards recovered the free use of her arms and fingers, and gave promise of living many years.

"Elizabeth, the second daughter, aged fourteen years, was seized on Monday, January 11, 1762, in one leg and foot only, which she could not set on the floor for three weeks, but stood all that time upon the other,' leaning against the chimney. Afterwards she was taken in the same manner in the other foot, when in a short time her foot came off at the ancle, and the other leg at the knee : but she is still alive, and is married.

"Sarah, the next child, aged ten years, was taken on the same day like her sister Elizabeth, ill in one foot, which mortified and came off about the ancle. The toes of the other foot were affected, but recovered.

"Robert, aged seven years, was taken on the Tuesday or Wednesday following in both legs, which came off at the knees.

"Edward, aged four years, was at the same time taken ill in both feet, which came off a little below the ancle.

"An infant, aged two months, was taken from the mother's breast as soon as she was seized with the disorder. It was put out to nurse and died within two months; when dead its feet and hands turned black.

"John, the father of this unhappy family, was seized with the same disorder, about three weeks after the first was taken ill, in both his hands. His fingers were benumbed, contracted, and black; the nails of some of them came off, and two of them broke, but healed again. He complained much of darting pains in his hands, arms, legs, and back.
Signed,
"James Bones, Curate."

"N.B. The mother and her two daughters, Elizabeth and Sarah, and the two sons, Robert and Edward, are still living, and in good health. Three of them are married; namely, Robert, who has two children; Elizabeth, who has borne one daughter; and Sarah, who is but lately married."

CURIOUS METHOD OF HATCHING CHICKENS IN EGYPT.

"Before daylight in the morning, Sept. 5," says Dr. Clarke, in his Travels, "we went to the village of Rerinbal, to see the manner of hatching poultry, by placing their eggs in ovens, so frequently mentioned by authors, and so well described by one of our ablest travellers, George Sandys. Notwithstanding this, the whole contrivance, and the trade connected with it are accompanied by such extraordinary circumstances, that it required all the evidence of one's senses to give them credibility. We were conducted to one of the principal buildings constructed for the purpose; and entered by a narrow passage, on each side of which were two rows of chambers, in two tiers, one above the other, with cylindrical holes, as passages, from the lower to the upper tier. The floor of the upper tier is grated and covered with mats, on which is laid camel's dung; somewhat resembling the manner of placing hops, for drying, in English oast-houses. We counted twenty chambers, and in each chamber had been placed 3000 eggs; so that the aggregate of the eggs then hatching amounted to the astonishing number of sixty thousand. Of these, above half are destroyed in the process. The time of hatching continues from autumn until spring. At first all the eggs are put in the lower tier. The most important part of the business consists, of course, in a precise attention to the requisite temperature; this we would willingly have ascertained by the thermometer, but could not adjust it to the nice test adopted by the Arab superintendent of the ovens. His manner of ascertaining it is very curious. —Having closed one of his eyes, he applies an egg to the outside of his eyelid; and if the heat be not great enough to cause any uneasy sensation, all is safe; but if he cannot bear the heat of the egg thus applied to his eye, the temperature of the ovens must be quickly diminished, or the whole hatch will be destroyed. During the first eight days of hatching, the eggs are kept carefully turned. At the end of that time the culling begins. Every egg is then examined, being held between a lamp and the eye; and thus the good are distinguished from the bad, which are cast away. Two days after this culling, the fire is extinguished—then half the eggs upon the lower are conveyed to the upper tier, through the cylindrical passages in the floor; and the ovens are closed. In about ten days more the chickens are hatched. At this time, a very singular ceremony ensues. An Arab enters the ovens, stooping and treading upon stones placed so that he may walk among the eggs without injuring them, and begins clucking like a hen, continuing this curious mimicry until the whole are disclosed. We heard this noise, and were equally surprised and amused by the singular adroitness of the imitation. The chickens thus hatched are then sold to persons employed in rearing them. Many are strangely deformed; and great numbers die, not only in rearing, but even during the sale; for to add to the extraordinary nature of the whole undertaking, the proprietors of those ovens do not give themselves the trouble of counting the live chickens in order to sell them by number, but dispose of them, as we should say, by the gallon, heaping them into a measure containing a certain quantity, for which they ask the low price of a *parah*, rather more than a farthing of our money.

CONFUSION OF THE SENSES.

Some years ago there was a woman residing in the neighbourhood of Lyons, who seemed to have the quality of one sense transferred to another. A very learned physician, a writer in the *Journal de Santé*, gives an account of having visited this woman at Lyons. He says, " To believe in apparent impossibilities, is often the necessity of men of science; but it is their good fortune likewise to discover, that the world contains many more miracles than is at first imagined; that nothing is impossible, as referred to the omnipotence of the Deity; and that impossibilities are much rarer in the combination of human life than the vanity of science will acknowledge.

" The woman whom I visited, and to whom I presented several sorts of medicines, powders, simples, compounds, and many other substances, which I am convinced she never saw before, told me their several tastes, as nearly, and with as much precision as taste could pronounce. She described them, indeed, with astonishing exactness, and frequently when my own palate was confounded.

" Her eyes were next bound with a thick bandage, and I drew from my pockets several sorts of silk ribbands. All those that differed in the original colours she immediately told me. It was in vain to attempt puzzling her;

she made no mistake; she passed the ribband merely through her hand, and immediately decided on its peculiar colour. She could, in fact, discover the quality of any thing by the touch or taste, as accurately as I could do with my eyes.

"The organs of hearing were then closed, as well as the contrivance of stuffing the ears would answer the purpose. I then commenced a conversation with a friend in the apartment, and spoke in almost inaudible whispers. She repeated, with great power of memory, every word of the conversation. In short, I came away a convert, in other words, believed what I had seen. A philosopher knows the fallibility of the senses; but he should know, likewise, that science ought not to reject because it cannot have demonstration."

THE WHIRLWINDS, MIRAGE, AND LOCUSTS OF EGYPT.

A STRONG wind that arose this day leads me to mention some particulars of the phenomena that often happen in Egypt. The first I shall notice is the *whirlwinds*, which occur all the year round, but especially at the time of the camseen wind, which begins in April, and lasts fifty days. Hence the name of camseen, which in Arabic signifies fifty. It generally blows from the southwest, and lasts four, five, or six days without varying, so very strong, that it raises the sands to a great height, forming a general cloud, so thick that it is impossible to keep the eyes open, if not under cover. It is troublesome even to the Arabs; it forces the sand into the houses through every cranny, and fills every thing with it. The caravans cannot proceed in the deserts; the boats cannot continue their voyages; and travellers are obliged to eat sand in spite of their teeth. The whole is like a chaos. Often a quantity of sand and small stones gradually ascends to a great height and forms a column sixty or seventy feet in diameter, and so thick, that were it steady on one spot, it would appear a solid mass. This not only revolves within its own circumference, but runs in a circular direction over a great space of ground, sometimes maintaining itself in motion for half an hour, and where it falls it accumulates a small hill of sand. God help the poor traveller who is caught under it!

The next phenomenon is the *mirage*, often described by travellers, who assert having been deceived by it, as at a distance it appears to them like water. This is certainly the fact; and I must confess that I have been deceived myself, even after I was aware of it. The perfect resemblance to water, and the strong desire for this element, made me conclude, in spite of all my caution not to be deceived, that it was really water I saw. It generally appears like a still lake, so unmoved by the wind, that every thing above is to be seen most distinctly reflected by it, which is the principal cause of the deception. If the wind agitate any of the plants that arise above the horizon of the mirage, the motion is seen perfectly, at a great distance. If the traveller stand elevated much above the mirage, the apparent water seems less united and less deep; for, as the eyes look down upon it, there is not thickness enough in the vapour on the surface of the ground to conceal the earth from the sight. But, if the traveller be on a level with the horizon of the mirage, he cannot see through it, so that it appears to him clear water. By putting my head first to the ground, and then mounting a camel, the height of which from the ground might have been about ten feet at the most, I found a great difference in the appearance of the mirage. On approaching it, it becomes thinner, and appears as if agitated by the wind, like a field of ripe corn. It gradually vanishes as the traveller approaches, and at last entirely disappears when he is on the spot.

The third phenomenon is the *locusts*. These animals I have seen in such clouds, that twice the number in the same space would form an opaque mass, which would wholly intercept the rays of the sun, and cause complete darkness. They alight on fields of corn, or other vegetables, and in a few minutes devour their whole produce. The natives make a great noise to frighten them away, but in vain; and, by way of retaliation, they catch and eat them when fried, considering them a dainty repast. They are something like the grasshopper in form, about two inches in length. They are generally of a yellow or gold colour, but there are some red and some green."—*Belzoni's Travels*.

Hoaxes and Impostures.
No. IV
MORAN THE VENTRILOQUIST.

Some years ago one Moran, a slater, possessed the faculty of ventriloquism in a very extraordinary degree: from the tops of the houses he could accost travellers in the streets, in a voice that seemed to proceed from the next passenger. This man was employed to work at the new episcopal palace, built by Primate Robinson, at Armagh. One morning, a labourer, who wrought about the premises, was terrified by a hollow and dismal voice, that proceeded from a dark cellar in a house that had belonged to the late Thomas Ogle, which his Grace the Primate had given orders to pull down. He was summoned, in a manner that he found it impossible to resist, to descend into the dark terrific vault. Trembling, agitated and perspiring at every pore, he obeyed the awful mandate. When he was in the cellar, profound silence prevailed for a few minutes. The same voice then solemnly uttered these tremendous words : " I am the spirit of a murderer; to-night I will visit you in the little room of your kitchen, and communicate to you the horrid crimes I have committed. If you regard your life here, or your salvation hereafter, meet me in that room at twelve o'clock.".The poor labourer was unable to utter a syllable, and with trembling knees he betook himself to his house, sent for the vicar of his parish, and encouraged by his presence, awaited the approach of the awful hour. Twelve o'clock, however, came, but the spirit came not.—Next morning he was obliged to resume his work; when he came opposite the same spot, the same voice again accosted him, but in a more elevated and angry tone, " Beware how you bring with you the vicar to our interview. This night let me meet you alone, at twelve o'clock, or your destruction will ensue." The wretched labourer, thus beset, as he thought, by preternatural powers, obeyed. At a quarter before twelve o'clock, he was seated at a little table in his room. His apparatus, for defence against the spiritual visitant, was a bible, a sword, and a bottle of whiskey. His pallid lips were alternately applied in ejaculating pious prayers to Heaven, or swallowing exhilarating drams; and his trembling hands now and then grasped, and then dropped the useless steel, as his courage rose and fell. Meanwhile, his wife and daughters stood almost breathless at the outside of the door, counting the tickings of a cuckoo clock. At length, at the first sound of the expected hour, a deep groan was heard in the room, and a noise, which, to their affrighted ears, seem to resemble the fall of a thunderbolt. The poor labourer had dropped down, powerless on the floor. His imagination had overpowered him, and at the first stroke of the clock, he had tumbled on the ground, a senseless lump. All his vital powers were suspended for a long time; and, after their revival, the poor fellow was deprived for a considerable period of the exercise of his understanding; and, if it had not been for the humanity of William Johnson, father to the celebrated architect, of Dublin, he would have perished, a wretched victim to the tricks of Moran, the ventriloquist.

A LEARNED HEBREW.

When M. Cailland, the French mineralogist, was travelling in Egypt, he one day indulged his genius in sporting with the penetration and antiquarian knowledge of a contemporary traveller, then at Thebes; a gentleman well informed in matters of general observation, but not generally skilled in the finer shades and more precise discrimination of profound research. M. Cailland instructed an Arab to present him with a pipe, on which had been engraven, with some art, several hieroglyphical characters. This amateur of rarities was a stranger to the bychante pipes commonly used in Abyssinia; he examined the pipe with great care and conceiving it to be an object extremely interesting, became an eager purchaser, and gave the mysterious Bedouin thirty dollars for what was not worth accepting.

Anecdotes of Longevity.

MR. SAMUEL WELCH.

Mr. Samuel Welch, now living at Bow (United States) has advanced more than eight months in the *one hundred and twelfth year of his age*. He was born in Kingston, September 1, 1710. Mr. Welch has resided in Bow nearly fifty years. His life has been marked by no extraordinary vicissitude; he was never sick but once during his long life, and then of a slight fever. He was always temperate. Through life he has been a man of hard labour; and appears to have been of a retiring disposition, preferring the most obscure retreats to the noise and the vexations and dangers of society. We lately visited this old man, and found him sitting in his chair—his present wife, now eighty-four years of age, smoothing his white locks with her comb, and exhibiting the utmost interest in his welfare. He is now unable to walk, except by holding upon chairs or the arms of his attendants, though his health does not appear rapidly to decline. When at the age of 105, he used to work about his little farm, cut his firewood, &c. and until the last two years he walked out of doors without assistance. He is in person rather above the middle size, of Grecian features, with dark penetrating eyes. His locks are of a clayed white, looking as if they had already mouldered in the grave. His frame is now feeble—the least movement causes his bones to grate at the joints; and we feel a momentary chill at the presence of a man whose appearance speaks such a lesson of decay and gradual dissolution! His hands are withered, dry, and cold—the expanded veins starting out in ruddy fulness. His countenance is fair, though wrinkled with the cares of a century and an eighth. His mental faculties appear to be little impaired; his memory, however, as his wife informed us, begins to fail, and he cannot connect his ideas with much precision. He is still amiable and social, and were it not that his hearing is somewhat affected, he would be a most interesting person in conversation. We asked him many questions, to all which he made very sensible replies. His life, he said, was but a span, though he had lived more than half the time since the landing of our fathers at Plymouth rock. It had now become a burthen to him, and he was willing to depart when it should please the Almighty.—In the annals of longevity in this state, there are but three to be found who have reached the age of Mr. Welch. Those three are Mr. Lovewell, of Dunstable, who lived to be 120; William Perkins, of Newmarket, 116; and Robert Macklin, of Wakefield, 115. The two first are supposed to have been born in England; the last was a native of Scotland. We cannot recal to recollection a single instance of any one born in the State of New Hampshire who has arrived at the age of Mr. Welch.—*American Paper.*

James Sands, of Horborn in Staffordshire, lived to the age of 140 years, and his wife 120. He outlived five leases of twenty-one years each after his marriage, and died about the year 1625.

On Sunday, the 23d of March, was interred, at Pilling, Ann Grime, widow. She was married the first time at the age of seventeen, was a wife eighteen years, then continued a widow fourteen years; married again and was a wife twenty-seven years; again a widow four years; at the age of eighty she married for the last time, and continued a wife thirteen years. She died at the age of ninety-three, being only a widow a few months. She had no children save to her first husband, from whose loins sprung upwards of three hundred children and grandchildren, forty of whom were great great grandchildren.

Died lately at Six-mile Bridge, county Clare, at the advanced age of 100 years, Mr. Edward Byrne, formerly an eminent clothier; he retained his faculties to the last; his wife still survives him, and she is in her 105th year, to whom he was married nearly eighty years; she possesses her faculties, with the exception of sight.

As a proof of the salubrity of the air in Newcastle, we need only observe, that in 1743, two old men, the father and son, were subpœnaed to an assize held in that town, as witnesses, from a neighbouring village; the father was one hundred and thirty-five years of age, and his son ninety-five, both of them hearty, and retaining their sight and hearing; and the next year, one Adam Turnbull died in Newcastle, aged one hundred and twelve, who had married four wives, and the last when he was near a hundred years of age.

Eccentric Biography.

MR. HOWE, THE ABSENT HUSBAND.

About the year 1706, I knew (says Dr. King) one Mr. Howe, a sensible well-natured man, possessed of an estate of 700*l.* or 800*l.* per annum; he married a young lady of good family, in the West of England; her maiden name was Mallet, she was agreeable in her person and manners, and proved a very good wife. Seven or eight years after they had been married, he rose one morning very early, and told his wife he was obliged to go to the Tower to transact some particular business: the same day at noon, his wife received a note from him, in which he informed her, that he was under the necessity of going to Holland, and should probably be absent three weeks or a month. He was absent from her *seventeen years*, during which time she never heard from him or of him. The evening before he returned, whilst she was at supper, and with some of her friends and relations, particularly one Dr. Rose, a physician, who had married her sister, a billet, without any name subscribed, was delivered to her, in which the writer requested the favour of her to give him a meeting the next evening in the Birdcage Walk, in St. James's Park. When she had read the billet, she tossed it to Dr. Rose, and laughing, said, "You see, brother, old as I am, I have a gallant." Rose, who perused the note with more attention, declared it to be Mr. Howe's handwriting: this surprised all the company, and so much affected Mrs. Howe, that she fainted away; however, she soon recovered, when it was agreed that Dr. Rose and his wife, with the other gentlemen and ladies who were then at supper, should attend Mrs. Howe the next evening to the Birdcage Walk: they had not been there more than five or six minutes, when Mr. Howe came to them, and after saluting his friends and embracing his wife, walked home with her, and they lived together in great harmony from that time to the day of his death. But the most curious part of my tale remains to be related. When Howe left his wife, they lived in a house in Jermyn-street, near St. James's church: he went no farther than to a little street in Westminster, where he took a room, for which he paid five or six shillings a week, and changing his name, and disguising himself by wearing a black wig (for he was a fair man) he remained in this habitation during the whole time of his absence! He had two children by his wife when he departed from her, who were both living at that time; but they both died young in a few years after. However, during their lives, the second or third year after their father disappeared, Mrs. Howe was obliged to apply for an Act of Parliament to procure a proper settlement of her husband's estate, and a provision for herself out of it during his absence, as it was uncertain whether he was alive or dead; this act he suffered to be solicited and passed, and enjoyed the pleasure of reading the progress of it in the votes, in a little coffee-house, near his lodging, which he frequented. Upon his quitting his house and family in the manner I have mentioned, Mrs. Howe at first imagined, as she could not conceive any other cause for such an abrupt elopement, that he had contracted a large debt unknown to her, and by that means involved himself in difficulties which he could not easily surmount; and for some days she lived in continual apprehensions of demands from creditors, of seizures, executions, &c. But nothing of this kind happened; on the contrary, he did not only leave his estate quite free and unencumbered, but he paid the bills of every tradesman with whom he had any dealings; and upon examining his papers, in due time after he was gone, proper receipts and discharges were found from all persons, whether tradesmen or others, with whom he had any manner of transactions or money concerns. Mrs. Howe, after the death of her children, thought proper to lessen her family of servants and the expenses of her housekeeping; and therefore removed from her house in Jermyn-street to a small house in Brewer-street, near Golden-square. Just over against her lived one Salt, a corn-chandler. About ten years after Howe's abdication, he contrived to make an acquaintance with Salt, and was at length in such a degree of intimacy with him, that he usually dined with him once or twice a week. From the room in which they ate, it was not difficult to look into Mrs. Howe's dining-room, where she generally sat, and received her company; and Salt, who believed Howe to be a bachelor, frequently recommended his own wife to him as a suitable match. During the last seven years of this gentleman's absence, he went every Sunday to St. James's church, and used to sit in Mr. Salt's seat, where he had a view of his wife, but could not easily be seen by her. After he returned home, he would never confess, even to his most intimate friends, what was the real cause of such a singular conduct; apparently there was none; but whatever it was, he was certainly ashamed to own it. Dr. Rose has often said to me that he believed his brother Howe would never * have returned to his wife, if the money which he took with him, which was supposed to have been 1000*l.* or 2000*l.* had not been all spent: and he must have been a good economist, and frugal in his manner of living, otherwise his money would scarcely have held out; for I imagine he had his whole fortune by him, I mean what he carried away with him in money or bank-bills, and daily took out of his bag, like the Spaniard in Gil Blas, what was sufficient for his expenses.—*King's Anecdotes.'*

FRANCIS BOLTON.

On the 23d of June 1811, died, at Boroughbridge, Yorkshire, aged eighty-three, Francis Bolton, pauper, of that place, one of the

* "And yet I have seen him, after his return, addressing his wife in the language of a young bridegroom. And I have been assured, by some of his most intimate friends, that he treated her, during the rest of their lives, with the greatest kindness and affection."

most eccentric characters perhaps ever known. He was born at Spofforth, in Yorkshire, and was said, in his youthful days, to be a remarkably handsome man, and the first person, as a farmer's servant, in that part of the country, who wore white stockings. His constant custom, from his infancy, was to throw large quantities of cold water upon his head. The manner he performed this was very singular: in the most inclement winter, he would go to some neighbouring pump, and fill his hat with water, and having drank as much as he thought proper, he would put his hat on, and the contents would run down his body. His shirt, when washed, he would put on wet, and for the last twenty years of his life he refused to lie on a bed; as a substitute he used wet straw, on which he used to lie without any covering but the clothes he put off; and during the winter season he has many times been found frozen to the ground. When able, he travelled the country as a beggar.

Varieties.

MURDER IN RUSSIA.

An extraordinary murder was lately committed at Petersburgh. The servant of a family, on going into the kitchen, found a basket containing an infant, together with a letter and purse of 200 roubles. The letter escaped her notice, and, tempted by the money, the inhuman wretch resolved to destroy the child. She threw it into the large stove used in that country, where the poor innocent was speedily consumed, the money secreted, and every thing likely to lead to suspicion put away, by the time that the family, which had been abroad, returned home. The master, however, a humane and respectable man, by accident found the letter, which informed him of the deposit, and stated that he should receive 200 roubles every quarter while the infant, whom circumstances forced its parents to conceal, lived under his charge. He called up the servant, who at first denied all knowledge of the fact; but being closely questioned at last confessed her crime, to the enormity of which the ashes from the stove bore horrible testimony. —She was committed to prison, and paid her forfeit life to the laws.

DEAFNESS CURED.

It is mentioned in a German Journal, that in 1750, a merchant of Cleves, named Jorrissen, who had become almost totally deaf, sitting one day near a harpsichord, where some persons were playing, and having a tobacco-pipe in his mouth, the bowl of which rested against the body of the instrument, was agreeably surprised to hear all the notes in the most distinct manner. By a little reflection and practice he again obtained the use of this valuable sense, which as Bonnee says, connects us with the moral world; for he soon learned by means of a piece of hard wood, one end of which he placed against his teeth, to keep up a conversation, and to be able to understand the least whisper. He soon afterwards made his beneficial discovery the subject of an inaugural dissertation, published at Halle, in 1754. Perolie has given some excellent observations on the capability of hard bodies to conduct sound, in the *Memoirs of the Academy of Turin*, for 1790 and 1791. The effect is the same if the person who speaks rests the stick against his throat or his breast; or when one rests the stick which he holds in his teeth against some vessel into which the other speaks.

FASHIONABLE RAT.

In December 1815, a full grown rat was caught in a shop here, the neck of which was found to be embellished with the very unusual decoration of two finger rings; these were of the description manufactured as baubles for children, and were fancifully disposed round the neck of the animal, the stone of one gracing the breast, while that of the other adorned the centre of the neck behind. Conjecture is at a loss to account for the circumstance of the rat becoming so oddly equipped: the rings were so small as to be even less than half the circumference of the head and the skin around the neck, exposed to the tight friction of the rings, had become completely excoriated; beneath them the hair was entirely worn off, and the flesh protruded in some parts over the rings. This sufficiently indicates that the poor animal must have become possessed of this piece of troublesome finery when very young, and leads to the conclusion of the rings having been stolen by the parent rat and carried to her nest, where, by a singular fatality, this one of her progeny might have put its head severally through both, and been afterwards unable to extricate itself from either. It is well known that these animals are extremely fond of trinkets, and in the present case, several rings of the same description had been, at some distance of time, missed from the shop where the rat was caught. It having been killed in the taking, a gentleman in town had it stuffed, which has been admirably performed by an ingenious mechanic, in Large, of the name of Wilson, and it is now in the possession of the former.—*Glasgow Paper.*

The Scrap Book.

SILKWORM.

In a communication to the Society of Arts and Manufactures, it is stated, by Miss Henrietta Rhodes, that one line of the silkworm, when unwound, measured 404 yards, and, when dry, weighed three grains. Hence it follows, that one pound avoirdupois of the thread, as spun by the worm, may be extended into a line 535 miles long, and that a thread which would encompass the earth, would weigh no more than forty-seven pounds.

PETRIFYING SPRING AT LUTTERWORTH.

Near the town of Lutterworth in Leicestershire, is the celebrated petrifying spring, the water of which is exceedingly cold, and so strongly impregnated with petrifying particles, that in a very little time, it converts wood and several other substances into stone.

SINGULAR DENTITION.

A female, of the name of Mary Thompson, residing at Little Smeaton, near Pontefract, at the advanced age of *ninety-six* years, has, within a few months back, cut four new teeth. The last tooth perforated the gum about six weeks ago.

Published by J. LIMBIRD, 355, Strand (East End of Exeter 'Change); and sold by all Newsmen and Booksellers. Printed by A. APPLEGATH, Stamford-street.

THE CURIOSITIES,
OR
Wonders of the World Displayed.

A world of wonders where creation seems
No more the works of Nature but her dreams.—MONTGOMERY.

No. VI.]   PRICE TWOPENCE.

PEEKE'S COMBAT WITH THREE SPANIARDS.

IT would be a very difficult matter to persuade the public that one Englishman will not at any time beat three Frenchmen; indeed to doubt it for a moment would be deemed heresy. In the field we have often done much more, as the ensanguined plains of Cressy, Poictiers, Agincourt, and Minden, bear witness. It has however been generally considered that our national superiority lay more in our physical strength than in generalship, though in this we have, to say the least of it, always been a match for the French.

A singular instance of English skill and valour furnishes the subject of our present engraving, which is copied from a very scarce tract, entitled "Three to One. Being an English Spanish combat. Performed by a westerne Gentleman of Tavystoke in Devonshire, with an English Quarterstaffe, against three Spanish Rapiers and Poniards. at Sherries in Spain, the 15th day of November, 1625. In the presence of Dukes, Condes, Marquisses and other great Dons of Spain, being the Counsel of Warre. The author of this book and actor in this encounter, R. Peeke."

Richard Peeke was a native of Tavistock, who had been a voyage

G

to Algiers, entered as a volunteer in the expedition against Cales in Spain, and who, to use his own phrase, "performed some desperate service" at the castle of Puntall, on that coast. On the surrender of the castle, the English troops landed, when some of them, wandering up the country for plunder, were set upon by the Spaniards and killed. Peeke, who landed after them, hearing there was no danger in venturing up the country, set out alone. He had scarcely proceeded a mile on his way when he discovered the bodies of three Englishmen dead, and one just dying; he resolved if possible to carry the wounded man on board the English ship, and set out with him on his back. He was pursued by a Spanish horseman, whom he threw to the ground, and then began to rifle his pockets; but a party of fourteen musketeers came up at the time and took him prisoner. He was led a prisoner into the town of Cales, where he reports to have seen "Englishmen's heads kicked about the streets like footballs, and their ears cut off and worn in Spanish hats in scorn."

After Peeke had been confined eighteen days in prison at Cales, he was ordered to Xeres, about three leagues distant, to take his trial, where he underwent a long examination before several of the nobles, who passed bitter taunts and jokes on his countrymen. One Spaniard compared the English to *hens*, which so roused Peeke's indignation, that he said if the English were hens, the Spaniards were chickens and pullets. The duke of Medina, who was present, frowned, and asked Peeke if he dared fight with one of those pullets. This was readily accepted; a combatant was brought forward, but Peeke soon disarmed him, and presented his weapons, rapier and poniard to the nobles. He was then asked if he would engage another Spaniard. "Another," says Peeke, "ay, for the honour of my country I will do good service against any six, and that without any other weapon than a halberd, deprived of its head."

The noblemen present thinking six persons too many for one man to encounter, restricted the number to three, who were armed with two weapons, a rapier and poniard each. Peeke modestly excuses his presumption in undertaking so unequal a contest by saying, "To die I thought most certain, but to die basely I would not; for three to kill one, had been to me no dishonour, to them (weapons considered) no glory. Upon these thoughts I fell to it."

The Spaniards made many desperate thrusts with their rapiers, which Peeke parried, and at length by a well directed blow laid one of his adversaries dead at his feet. The other two were soon so handled, that they both took to their heels, one running to the band of soldiers for protection, and the other sheltering himself behind the judges. The Spaniards who were assembled, seeing their countrymen thus defeated, became clamorous against the Englishman; but the duke of Medina Sidonia immediately declared it death to any man that dared to injure him. A collection of nearly five pounds was made for him by the judges; he was presented to the king at Madrid, who offered him a place, but he refused, and returning to England, published the narrative from which this account is taken.

THE FATAL REVENGE.

On the eighth of September, 1727, some strollers took a puppet shew to the village of Barnwell, in Cambridgeshire, for the purpose of exhibiting it in a large thatched barn; but just as the shew was about to begin, an idle fellow attempted to enter the barn without paying, which the owners of the shew prevented, and a quarrel ensued. After some altercation, the fellow departed, and the door being fastened, all was quiet; but this execrable villain, to revenge the supposed injury he had received from the showman, went to a heap of hay and straw which stood close to the barn, and secretly set it on fire. The spectators of the shew, who were in the midst of their entertainment, were soon alarmed by the flames, which had now communicated rapidly to the barn. In the sudden terror, which instantly seized the whole assembly, every one rushed towards the door, which unfortunately happened to open inwards; and the crowd that was behind still urging those that were before, they pressed so violently against it, that it could not be opened; and being too well secured to give way, the whole company, consisting of more than one hundred and twenty persons, were kept confined in the building till the roof fell in, which covered them with fire and smoke: some were suffocated in the smouldering thatch, and others were consumed alive in the flames: six only escaped with life; the rest, among whom were several young ladies of fortune, and many innocent children, were reduced to one undistinguishable heap of mangled bones and flesh, the bodies being half consumed, and totally disfigured. The surviving unhappy friends of the dead, not knowing which were the relics they sought, a large hole was dug in the churchyard, and all were promiscuously interred together in one grave: and what contributed still more to heighten this horrible event was the escape of the villain without any punishment being inflicted on him.

WONDERS OF LITTLENESS.

Pliny and Ælian relate that Myrmecides, wrought out of ivory a chariot with four wheels and four horses, and a ship with all her tackling, both in so small a compass, that a bee could hide either with its wings. Nor should we doubt this, when we find it recorded in our own domestic history, on less questionable authority, that in the twentieth year of Queen Elizabeth's reign, a blacksmith of London, of the name of Mark Scaliot, made a lock of iron, steel, and brass, of eleven pieces, and a pipe key, all of which only weighed one grain. Scaliot also made a chain of gold, of forty-three links, which he fastened to the lock and key, and put it round the neck of a flea, which drew the whole with perfect ease. The chain, key, lock, and flea, altogether weighed but one grain and a half!

Hadrianus Junius saw at Mechlin in Brabant, a cherrystone cut into the form of a basket; in it were fourteen pair of dice distinct, the spots and numbers of which were easily to be discerned with a good eye.

But still more extraordinary than this basket of dice, or any thing we have yet mentioned, must have been a set of turnery shewn at Rome, in the time of Pope Paul the Fifth, by one Shad of Mitelbrach, who had purchased it from the artist Oswaldus Norhingerus. It consisted of *sixteen hundred* dishes, which were all perfect and complete in every part, yet so small and slender, that the whole could be easily enclosed in a case fabricated out of a peppercorn of the ordinary size! The Pope is said to have himself counted them, but with the help of a pair of spectacles, for they were so very small as to be almost invisible to the naked eye. Although his holiness thus satisfied his own eyes of the fact, he did not, we are assured, require of those about him to subscribe to it on the credit of his infallibility; for he gave every one an opportunity of examining and judging for himself, and among the persons thus highly favoured, particular reference is made to Gaspar Schioppins, and Johannes Faber, a physician of Rome.

Turrianus, of whose skill so many wonderful things are related, is said to have fabricated iron mills, which moved of themselves, so minute in size, that a monk could carry one in his sleeve; and yet it was powerful enough to grind, in a single day, grain enough for the consumption of eight men.

In penmanship, the productions of this class have been very numerous, and some of them not a little extraordinary. In the reign of Queen Elizabeth, as Dr. Heylin, in his life of King Charles, relates. "There was one who wrote the Ten Commandments, the Creed, the Pater Noster, the queen's name, and the year of our Lord, within the compass of a penny; and gave her majesty a pair of spectacles, of such an artificial making, that by the help thereof, she did plainly and distinctly discern every letter."

A gentleman now living in Liverpool, has written the whole of Mr. Roscoe's poem of " Mount Pleasant," in a square of $3\frac{1}{4}$ inches, by $2\frac{7}{10}$th inches; Goldsmith's Poem of " The Traveller" (488 lines) in a square of $3\frac{1}{2}$ inches by $3\frac{1}{2}$ inches; the book of the Prophet Malachi, in a kind of pyramid, not exceeding an ordinary little finger in bulk; and the Lord's Prayer, in the circle of $\frac{3}{16}$ths of an inch, which may be distinctly read with a magnifying glass, and by some without that help.

This astonishing instance of industry and perseverance was produced by the exertions of Mr. Beedle, of Ottery St. Mary, whose skill in minute penmanship has placed him far beyond the reach of competition. He has just executed another specimen, comprehending *ninety-three thousand four hundred and eighty* letters in a space $3\frac{1}{2}$ inches by $3\frac{1}{2}$ inches, exceeding his former attempt within the same limits by many thousand letters. The following are the pieces he has chosen, and which are written without the slightest abbreviation:—Goldsmith's Traveller, Deserted Village, Essay on Education, Distresses of a disabled Soldier, the tale of Azim, Essay on Justice and Generosity, on the Irresolution of Youth, on the Frailty of Man, on Friendship, on the Genius of Love, and the National Anthem of God save the King. In the central circle he had delineated Ottery church, all the shades and lines of which form part of the writing. Though written without the aid of glasses, it requires microscopic powers to distinguish the characters. We understand that Mr. Beedle will make no further attempt, in consequence of the injury it has occasioned his sight, and the confidence that what he has now done cannot be surpassed.

ST. WINIFRID'S WELL, FLINTSHIRE.

THE town of Holywell takes its name from this spring, which lies at the bottom of three hills at its east end, and is covered by a small gothic building of some antiquity, and remarkable for its neatness. The work forms a canopy on the inside over the well, which has a shield charged with a coat of arms, long since effaced by time, in its centre. The portrait of St. Winifrid still remains on the walls, which were formerly painted.

The water here passes through an arch into a small court. The well forms an oblong, being about twelve feet long and seven feet wide. The walls are hung round with votive memorials of the efficacy of this spring, that, however, seem to be exaggerated; but this is by no means wonderful, when it is considered that the general prejudices of the vulgar here, of whom no small number are of the Roman Catholic persuasion, have magnified some naturally curious circumstances into the bulk of miracles. The well is indeed extremely clear, and has incontestably been proved serviceable in some complaints; it boils up like a caldron with vast force, and sends forth an amazing quantity of water in a short space of time, which turns a mill at a small distance; and, in a printed description, it has been pretended to emit no less than a hundred tons per minute. At the bottom are several stones spotted with red, whose affinity to blood appears to some weak minds to countenance the following legend, which we insert for the entertainment, we could not be so absurd as to introduce it to engage the belief, of our readers.

Once on a time, it is generally related to be in the seventh century, a young maiden whose name was Winifrid, then living under the care of her pious uncle Bueno, a professor and warm admirer of a monastic life, a neighbouring tyrannical and lascivious prince, called Cradoc, attempted first to bend her to his desires, and afterwards to commit a rape on her person. Being struck with horror, the trembling virgin fled, to escape the violence intended to her chastity; but this savage chief pursuing and overtaking her, his lust was changed into such a fit of rage, that he drew his sword and instantly struck off her head, which took its way down the valley, where a spring of sovereign virtues directly burst from the earth; but in commemoration of the event the stones at the bottom of this stream were marked with indelible stains of blood. The virgin's loss was soon after repaired by Bueno, who coming that way, took up the head, which he well knew, and, finding the body, united them again; but Cradoc was struck dead, and the ground opening, his blackened corpse was conveyed to the infernal regions, as a deserved punishment for his monstrous wickedness. The good Winifrid, who lived fifteen years after this restoration, so timely effected by Bueno's piety, used to send him an annual token or present when he went over to Ireland; to expedite the despatch of which, she had only to place the gift on the stream of the well, and from

LORD LYTTLETON'S PRESENTIMENT OF HIS OWN DEATH.

The singular circumstances attending the death of the celebrated Lord Lyttleton, are thus related by his friend Miles Peter Andrews, Esq.

About a week before Lord Lyttleton died, he said he went to bed, pretty well, but restless; soon after his servant had left him, he heard a footstep at the bottom of his bed; he raised himself in order to see what it could be, when one of the most angelic female figures that imagination could possibly paint, presented itself before him, and, with a commanding voice and action, bade him attend, and prepare himself, for on such a night, and at the *hour of twelve*, he would surely die! He attempted to address the vision, but was unable, and the ghost vanished, and left him in a state more easily conceived than could be described. His valet found him in the morning more dead than alive, and it was some hours before his Lordship could be recovered sufficiently to send for his friends, to whom he thought it necessary to communicate this extraordinary circumstance. Mr. Miles Peter Andrews was one of the number sent for, being at that time one of his most intimate associates. Every person to whom Lord L. told the tale, naturally turned it into ridicule—all knowing him to be very nervous and superstitious, and tried to make him believe it was a dream; as they certainly considered so themselves. Lord L. filled his house with company, and appeared to think as his friends would wish him. Mr. M. P. Andrews had business which called him to Dartford, and therefore soon took his leave, thinking Lord Lyttleton quite composed on this subject, so that his friend's dream dwelt so little on his imagination, that he did not even recollect the time when it was predicted that the event would take place. One night after he left Pitt-place, the residence of Lord Lyttleton, he supposed he might have been in bed half an hour, when endeavouring to compose himself, suddenly his curtains were pulled open, and Lord L. appeared before him at his bedside, standing in his robe de chambre and night-cap. Mr. A. looked at him some time, and thought it so odd a freak of his friend's that he began to reproach him for his folly, in coming down to Dartford Mills without notice, as he could find no accommodation; however, said he, I'll get up and see what can be done. He turned to the other side of the bed, and rung the bell, when Lord L. disappeared. Mr. Andrews's servant soon after entered, when his master inquired, where is Lord Lyttleton? The servant, all astonishment, declared he had not see any thing of his Lordship since they left Pitt-place. Pshaw, you fool, replied Mr. A. he was here this moment at my bedside. The servant persisted that it was not possible. Mr. A. dressed himself, and, with the servants, searched every part of the house and garden, but no Lord L. was to be found; still Mr. A. could not help believing that Lord L. had played him this trick for his disbelief of his vision, till, about four o'clock he next day, an express arrived to inform him of Lord L.'s death, and the manner of it, by a friend who was present, and gave the following particular account of it. That on the morning before Lord L. died, he entered the breakfast room between ten and eleven o'clock; appeared rather thoughtful, and did not answer any inquiries made by his friends respecting his health, &c. At dinner he seemed much better, and, when the cloth was taken away, he exclaimed "Richard's himself again!" but, as night came on, the gloom of the morning returned. However, as this was the predicted night of dissolution, his friends agreed that it would be right to alter the clocks and watches in the house. This was managed by the steward, without Lord L. suspecting any thing of it, his own watch, which lay on his dressing-table, being altered by his valet. During the evening they got him into some pleasant discussion, in which he distinguished himself with peculiar wit and pleasantry. At *half past eleven*, as he conceived it, from the alteration of the clocks, (but it was only eleven,) he said he was tired, and would retire to bed; bade them a good night, and left them all delighted with his calm appearance. During the day, not the least hint was given by any one to him of the dream. But of course, as soon as he had withdrawn, the conversation instantly turned upon it. The discourse continued till nearly twelve o'clock, when the door being hastily opened, Lord L.'s valet entered, pale as death, crying out, "My Lord is dying!" His friends flew to his bedside; but he expired before they could all assemble round him! Lord L.'s valet gave to them the following statement, viz. That Lord L. made his usual preparations for bed; that he kept every now and then looking at his watch; that when he got into bed, he ordered his curtains to be closed at the foot. It was now within a minute or two of *twelve*, by his watch, he asked to look at mine, and seemed pleased to find it nearly keep time with his own. His Lordship then put them both to his ear, to satisfy himself if they went. When it was more than a quarter after twelve by our watches, he said, "*This mysterious lady is not a true prophetess, I find.*"—When it was near the *real* hour of twelve, he said, "Come, I'll wait no longer; get me my medicine; I'll take it, and try to sleep!" I just stepped into the dressing-room to prepare the physic, and had mixed it, when I thought I heard my Lord breathing very hard—I ran to him, and found him in the agonies of death!

ROCKING STONES.

PLINY tells us, that at Harpasa, a town of Asia, there was a rock of such a wonderful nature, that if touched with the finger it would shake, but could not be moved from its place with the whole force of the body. Ptolemy Hephestion mentions a stone near the ocean, which was agitated when struck by the stalk of an asphodel, but could not be removed by a great exertion of force.

In Britain there are many stones of this description. In the parish of St. Leven, Cornwall, there is a promontory called Castle Treryn. On the western side of the middle group, near the top, lies a very large stone, so evenly poised, that any hand may move it from one side to another; yet it is so fixed on its base, that no lever, nor any mechanical force, can remove it from its present situation. It is called the Logan Stone, and is at such a height from the ground, that no person can believe that it was raised to its present position by art.

Other rocking stones are so shaped, and so situated, that there can be no doubt they were erected by human strength. Of this kind, Borlase thinks the great *Quoit*, or *Karn-lehau*, in the parish of Tywidnek, to be. It is thirty-nine feet in circumference, and four feet thick at a medium, and stands on a single pedestal. There is also a remarkable stone of the same kind in the Island of St. Agnes, in Scilly. It is poised on a mass of rock, which is ten feet six inches high, forty-seven feet round the middle, and touches the ground with no more than half its base. From this the rocking stone rises on one point only, and is so nicely balanced, that two or three men with a pole can move it. It is eight feet six inches high, and forty-seven feet in circumference. On the top there is a bason, hollowed out, three feet eleven inches in diameter, at a medium, but wider at the brim, and three feet deep. From the globular shape of this upper stone, it is highly probable that it was rounded by human art, and perhaps, even placed on its pedestal by human strength.

In Sithney parish, near Helston, in Cornwall, stood the famous *Logan*, or rocking stone, commonly called *Men Amber*, *Men-au-bar*, or the top stone. It was eleven feet by six, and four high, and so nicely poised on another stone, that a little child could move it, and all travellers who passed this way desired to see it. But Shrubsall, Cromwell's governor of Pendennis, with much ado, caused it to be undermined, to the great grief of the country. There are some marks of the tool upon it, and, by its quadrangular shape, it was probably dedicated to Mercury.

In the parish of Kirkmichael, in Scotland, there is a very remarkable stone of this description. It stands on a flat topped eminence, surrounded at some distance by steep rocky hills. It rests on the plain surface of a rock, level with the ground. Its shape is quadrangular, approaching to the figure of a rhombus, of which the greater diagonal is seven feet, and the lesser five. Its medium thickness is about two feet and a half; its solid contents will, therefore, be about fifty-one cubical feet. As it is of very hard and solid whinstone, its weight, reckoning the cubical foot at eight stone three pounds, may be reckoned to be 418 stone five pounds, or within thirty pounds of three tons. It touches the rock on which it rests only in one line, which is in the same plane with the lesser diagonal, and its lower surface is convex towards the extremities of the greater diagonal. By pressing down either of the extreme corners, and withdrawing the pressure alternately, a rocking motion is produced, which may be increased so much, that the distance between the lowest depression and highest elevation is a full foot. When the pressure is wholly withdrawn, the stone will continue to rock till it has made twenty-six or more vibrations, from one side to the other, before it settles in its naturally horizontal position. Both the lower side of the stone, and the surface of the rock on which it rests, appear to be worn and roughened by mutual friction.

Hoaxes and Impostures.
No. V.
PRINCE HOHENLOHE.

THE Roman Catholic Church has ever boasted of its miracles, and human credulity is still heavily taxed by the artful representation, or mistaken zeal of monks and bigots. We say mistaken zeal, for we are far from accusing the Roman Catholic Clergy of knowingly fabricating all the relations of pretended miracles; though this is not unfrequently the case.

The barefaced impostures of priests in former times, had become so notorious, as to throw a general discredit on all Catholic miracles, and hence they were not very frequent. They have lately however, been revived in several instances, but in none so strikingly as in Prince Alexander of Hohenlohe, whose extraordinary feats in curing diseases, in all parts of the world, the newspapers are now recording.

This Prince, whose elder brother is now serving in the French army in Spain, is of one of the oldest families in Germany. His ancestors were among the first to embrace the reformed religion, but returned to the Catholic Church in 1667. In 1744, the houses of Hohenlohe were elevated to the rank of Princes of the holy Roman empire by Charles VII. They are divided into two reigning families, or houses, viz. of Neuenstein and of Waldenburg, to the latter of which the Rev. Prince Hohenlohe belongs. He is one of the canons of the noble Chapter of Olmutz, and a knight of Malta.

In June, 1821, Prince Hohenlohe visited Wurzburgh, where he preached frequently, and celebrated high mass, after which he commenced his miracles, which Father Baur, his biographer, thus briefly sums up:—

"With perfect confidence he has restored persons declared incurable; he has made the blind see—the deaf hear—the lame walk; and paralytics he has perfectly cured. The number of these already amounts to *thirty-six* persons, amongst whom is the Princess Matilda of Schwartzenberg. Amongst others who have been restored to sight, the mother of Mr. Polzano, the man-milliner, deserves to be mentioned. She is the general subject of conversation throughout the city. By firm confidence in God, with God and in God, he performs these cures. *This is his secret, his magnetic power, and his sympathy.*"

Such miraculous doings naturally attracted a great concourse of people from town and country, and the house of the Prince was surrounded by thousands: the cures, which on the 27th of June amounted to thirty-six, had, on the following day, increased to sixty; but the cure on which the Prince's historian most dwells, is that of the Princess of Schwartzenberg, who had been lame from her eighth to her seventeenth year; 80,000 florins had been spent in medical advice for her, and fourteen days before the Prince saw her, her life was despaired of,—

"It was only," says Father Baur, "with the most violent pain that she could lie in a horizontal position, and only by means of a machine, constructed by Mr. Heine, could she be something freer from pain in bed; because it supported her and brought her nearer to a perpendicular direction; and in this state the Prince of Hohenlohe found her, where, praying with him and his disciple Martin Michel, and with full confidence in God, at his command to arise, she was instantly cured. She stepped out of bed alone, threw the machine from her, was dressed, and walked afterwards in the court-yard and in the garden, performed her devotions the next morning in the church, with praises and thanksgivings, visited the garden of the court and Julius' Hospital, and went on the 24th instant, in company with her Serene Highness the Princess of Lichtenstein, horn Princess of Esterhazy; his Serene Highness the Duke of Aremberg, also her uncle his Serene Highness the Prince of Baar, and others, to the sermon of the Prince of Hohenlohe, in the Collegiate Church of Haug, and continues to this hour perfectly well."

" The public will do well to reflect on this," says Father Baur, " and the more so, as on the preceding day, as well as on the 20th of June in the morning, the Princess could neither turn herself in bed nor stand on either of her feet !!! The Crown Prince of Bavaria, who was deaf, was also restored to his hearing, on which he exclaimed, full of joy, ' How happy I am that I can now hear the birds sing, and the clock strike !' " Great gratifications certainly, but we should have thought there might have been higher pleasures derived from it.

When the Prince left Wurzburgh for a short time for Bamberg, he met a great number of invalids on the roads; " he stopped, got out of his carriage, and healed them." At Bamberg " he restored two sisters to the use of their limbs, who had not left their beds for ten years." The Rev. Mr. Sollner of Hallstadt, " in the presence of a number of persons, was cured of the gout as he sat in his carriage, and immediately alighted and went through the town on foot."

On the return of the Prince to Wurzburg, he continued his healing powers :—

" In the morning of Saturday, the 30th of June, a chaise drove up to Staufenberg's hotel. It was immediately conjectured that it brought some poor creature in need of help; and actually, an old man, by trade a butcher, was carried out of it in sheets into the hotel; for all his members were so crippled, that he could not be touched with hands. The crowd assembled in the place before the hotel, were astonished to see a person so extremely afflicted, and many said aloud,— ' If this man is cured, the finger of God will be manifest.' The whole multitude were full of expectation for the event. After some time a lady was heard in the hotel, calling out of the window to those in the windows of the adjoining house—' Good God! the man is cured ! he can walk already !' The crowd below were now more eager with expectation: when another lady called out to them—' Clear the way before the door, the man is coming out—let him have a free passage !' The man came out, and walked to his chaise; but, after driving a little way, he stopped the coachman, and desired him to take him back to the gracious Prince, as, through excessive joy, he had forgotten to return him thanks."

The miracles of the Prince do not stop here, for other remarkable cures follow:—

"The sister of Mrs. Brioli, the grocer, who lay under the physician's care almost dead, was healed on the spot, and now enjoys full health and vigour. Likewise on a bookkeeper of hers, a native of Volkach, whose speech was greatly affected by a disorder in his tongue, but who now speaks perfectly well.

"The child of Mr. Gulemann, who was attended by medical men, being entirely blind; but restored on the spot, and to this hour remains blessed with perfect sight.

"A most remarkable case was the cure of the wife of the forester Kiesling, and that of the clerk of the courts, Mr. Kandler, who had almost given up all hopes of relief from physicians, and was perfectly healed of a lingering disease.

"Moreover, the daughter of Mel, the King's cellarer, who was deaf; she ran about the house, crying out for joy,—' I can hear perfectly well!'

"Previous to his departure on the 11th of July, his Serene Highness worked the following cures, among many others, which are certainly miraculous in their kind:

"A boy of four years old was brought from Grossenlangheim, who, for three years and a half had one of his eyes entirely covered by the eyelid, so that no one could tell whether the eye existed at all; and his other eye was covered with a film. This boy was so perfectly restored by the prayers of the Prince, that both his eyes are now sound and well, and the same afternoon he went up and down all the steps of the Quanteischer House in this place.

"A wine-merchant came from Konigshofen, whose hands and feet had been for four years so much contracted, that his hands were fast clenched like a fist, and he could scarcely use them at all. This man was instantaneously restored, so that he can stand upright on his feet and walk, and also open and shut his hands, and enjoys the perfect use of them.

"A man from Schwemelsbach, who had not been able for eight years to raise himself once in his bed, was brought in a carriage before the residence of the Rev. Prince, who was just about to begin a journey. The Prince was in the greatest haste, but still wished to relieve this afflicted man, and accordingly opened his window, and began to pray from it, desiring the sick to pray at the same time. After giving him his blessing, he called out to the man to arise. This he could not do, and the prayer was repeated, whereupon the sick man raised himself a little, and declared that he was quite free from pain. The prayer was again repeated, and then the man arose entirely by himself, got out of the vehicle, went from thence to the Collegiate Church of Haug, and there returned thanks to God for his deliverance."

Such are a proof of the miracles related by Father Baur, in his life of Prince Hohenlohe; in our next we shall give some still more surprising feats attributed to this miracle monger.

To those who are well read in the history of the Roman Catholic religion, these absurdities or known impostures will not excite much surprise. We do not mean to deny that imagination may have considerable influence on many diseases, but imagination will not give eyes to the blind, ears to the deaf, or feet to the lame. Besides, with regard to the cures said to have been performed by the Prince, although we are told they are all well attested, yet there is not a single affidavit or attestation given. On the contrary, the *chef-d'œuvre* of the Prince, the cure of the Princess of Schwartzenberg, is partially contradicted, at least, as to her debilitated state, by her medical attendant. The fact appears to be, that the Princess was so far recovered as to be able to walk before the Prince of Hohenlohe saw her. Mr. Heine, her surgeon, says, that " she was enabled to perform the full functions of the lower extremities, namely the backward and forward steps in walking, without any difficulty ;" and that this was her state the day before the Prince saw her, though, for fear of overstraining, it was not thought advisable to encourage any desire to go alone. What, therefore, was there remarkable that, when encouraged, she should make the experiment of walking, and succeed.

[*To be continued.*]

Anecdotes of Longevity.

THE CUMBERLAND PATRIARCH.

THE northern counties of England have produced numerous instances of longevity, and we have now to add to the list the name of R. Bowman, who died at Irthington, near Carlisle, on the 13th of June, 1823, in the 118th year of his age.

This Cumberland patriarch was born at Bridgewood-Foot, a hamlet, about two miles from Irthington, in the month of Oct. 1705, in the house where his grandfather had resided, and where his father was also born, both of whom were brought up to husbandry. His ancestors were Roman Catholics, and in the early part of his life he professed that religion ; but many years ago he became a member of the Church of England, and was a constant and orderly attendant upon divine worship, until prevented by age and infirmity. From early youth he had been a laborious worker, and was at all times healthy and strong, having never taken medicine, nor been visited with any kind of illness, except the measles when a child, and the hooping-cough when he was above one hundred years of age. During the course of his long life he was only once intoxicated, which was at a wedding ; and he never used tea or coffee ; his principal food having been bread, potatoes, hasty-pudding, broth, and occasionally a little meat. He scarcely ever tasted ale or spirits, his chief beverage being water, or milk and water mixed ;—this abstemiousness arose partly from a dislike to strong liquors, but more from a saving disposition, being remarkably careful of his money, and strongly attached to the things of this world ; for the same reason, as he himself acknowledged, he never used snuff or tobacco. With these views his habits of industry and disregard of personal fatigue were extraordinary ; having often been up for two or three nights in a week, particularly when bringing home coals or lime. In his younger days he was rather robust, excellent in bodily strength, and was considered a master in the art of wrestling—an exercise to which he was particularly attached. He was of low stature, being not above five feet five inches in height, with a large chest, well-proportioned limbs, and weighing about twelve stone. His vigour never forsook him till far advanced in life; for in his 108th year he walked to and from Carlisle (sixteen miles) without the help of a staff, to see the workmen lay the foundation of Eden-bridge. In the same year he actually reaped corn, made hay, worked at hedging, with apparently as much energy as the stoutest of his sons. His education was very limited; but he possessed a considerable share of natural sense, with much regularity and prudence. His memory was very tenacious. He remembered the rebellion in 1715, when he was ten years of age, and witnessed a number of men running away from the danger. In the second rebellion in the year 1745, he was employed in cutting trenches round Carlisle; but fled from his disagreeable situation as soon as the opportunity afforded for escaping. He did not marry till he was fifty years of age, and his wife lived with him fifty-two years: dying in 1807, aged eighty-one. In 1810 one of his brothers died at the age of ninety-nine, and in 1819, a cousin died, aged ninety-six; another cousin is now living, eighty-seven years old. He has left six sons, the youngest of whom is fifty-years of age, and the eldest sixty-two; his grandchildren are twenty in number, and his great grandchildren only eleven. He never had any daughters. About the year 1779, he lost all his teeth, but no mark of debility appeared about his person before 1813, when he took to his bed, and never was able to use his limbs afterwards. During the first nine years of his confinement his health and spirits continued good, and he was free from corporal pain; but for the last twelve months his intellect became rather impaired. At length, on Thursday, the 12th ult. he was seized with illness, which in fourteen hours put a period to his protracted existence. He grew weaker and weaker as the day declined, but experienced no sickness: and about eight in the evening slept silently away in the arms of death, at the extraordinary age of one hundred and seventeen years and eight months.

J. WOODS.

DIED, at Gortnagally, near Dungannon, Ireland, in May 1818, J. Woods, an industrious farmer, at the advanced age of one hundred and twenty-two years. He lived a regular and sober life. His wife died about two years ago, aged eighty-two. He was forty-two years old the day of her birth. He was born Anno Domini 1696, in the reign of William III. of course he has lived in the reigns of five monarchs; and the reign of the late King has been longer than that of any other who ever ascended the throne.

SOLOMON NIBLETT.

DIED, on November 15, 1815, in Laurens District, South Carolina, Mr. Solomon Niblett, aged 143. He was born in England, where he lived until he was nineteen years old; he then emigrated to America, and resided in the state of Maryland, until about fifty-five years ago, when he went to

South Carolina, where he resided until his death. He never lost his teeth nor his eyesight. A few days before his death, he joined a hunting party, and actually killed a hare.

Eccentric Biography.

CHEVALIER D'EON.

The Chevalier d'Eon, who was well known in London, was employed on diplomatic missions, and figured in some affairs of honour, passed many years of his life as a female. The Chevalier was born at Tounerre in Burgundy, in 1728, and when of a proper age was, through the interest of the Prince of Conti, presented with a cornetcy of dragoons. He was afterwards employed as Secretary of Legation, in important embassies to Russia and England; and served as aide-de-camp to Marshal Broglio on the Rhine: he acquitted himself so well on these several occasions, as to be invested with the order of St. Louis, by the French King.

It was about the year 1771, that doubts first publicly arose in England as to the sex of the Chevalier d'Eon, although it had previously been the subject of conversation at St. Petersburgh. The English, who wish to decide every disputed point by a wager, made the Chevalier's sex a sporting subject. Considerable bets were laid, and gambling policies of insurance to a large amount were effected on his sex. In 1777, an action was brought on one of these before Lord Mansfield, for the recovery of £700. The plaintiff was a surgeon, of the name of Hayes, and the defendant, Jaques, a broker, who received premiums of fifteen guineas, for every one of which he engaged to return £100, whenever it should be proved that the Chevalier was a woman. The plaintiff brought two French witnesses, who swore that the Chevalier was a female. Lord Mansfield reprobated the transaction, but held the wager fair; in consequence of which, a verdict was given for the plaintiff. The matter was afterwards solemnly pleaded before his Lordship, when the defendant pleading the act of parliament, which rendered legally null all gambling debts above ten pounds, the insurers in this shameful transaction were deprived of their expected gains.

The Chevalier was now regarded as a woman, and accused of being an accomplice in these gambling transactions, and a sharer of the plunder, he was compelled to leave England.

He however previously published the following letter in the newspapers:—

"By an article of advice (or caution) inserted in the Morning Post of the 13th and 14th Nov. 1775, Nos. 951 and 952, I had most earnestly desired the public of England, who have always testified their benevolence towards me, not to renew any policy on my sex. I declared that I would not manifest it juridically, while any policies were made, and till the old ones were annulled: but, if that was impossible, I should be obliged to retire from this country, that I esteemed as next to my native one.

"The avidity that my enemies have proved for money, the *auri sacri fames* that possess them, has unhappily prevailed. They have not only renewed the old policies, but they have also obtained, on Tuesday, the first of July last, a judgment at the tribunal of the King's Bench to decide my sex.

"In consequence, I keep, with regret, my word with the public: I leave, with pain, my dear England, and where I believed I had found tranquillity and liberty, to retire to my native country, to be near to an august master, whose protection and goodness will prove a greater assurance of tranquillity than all the Magna Chartas of this island.

"If the parties, interested and losing in those policies, would take my advice, I would counsel them not to pay any thing yet; because the judgment of the King's Bench, where they have decided the question of my sex, was given without my being privy to it, and against my consent; because I will oppose myself to that judgment when the tribunal of the King's Bench shall have resumed their sittings, and that the King my master will permit me to return to England. It will then be the proper time and place to offer all my reasons against the three witnesses who gave evidence on my sex.

"I had rather perish than be triumphant from the weakness of the sex imputed to me. I have never made use of aught but my quality of Captain of dragoons to combat my enemies, when they have had the heart. How sad for me to have had to do, since my misfortunes in England, with only a set of avaricious wretches and poltroons? My sex was never inquired into when I was sent to fight and negociate with the enemies of my country. I am always unus et idem.

"Being unwilling to abuse the public patience, though on the eve of my departure, and that it will very likely be for the last time, I here declare authentically, that, if any one, whether in France or in England, can convict me, in any court of justice, of being interested for a single shilling in any one or more policies, I will distribute all I am worth in the world to such hospital or charity that the said tribunal shall indicate

"Le Chev. D'EON."

London, 10th Aug. 1777,
Brewer-street, Golden-square.

On his return to France, we find him confirming the rumours against him by assuming the female dress. In excuse for this, it was said that this was not a matter of choice, but insisted on by the French court. The female garb once assumed was never relinquished.

In 1785 the Chevalier returned to England, living on his pension, until deprived of it by the French Revolution. In 1795, he issued an advertisement, in which the Chevalier d'Eon, states "That at the age of sixty-eight, she embraces the resource of her skill, and long experience in the science of arms, to cut *her* bread with her sword, and instead of idly looking up for support from professed friends, she relies on the liberality of Britons at large, to protect an unfortunate woman of quality from the 'stings and arrows of outrageous fortune' in a foreign land, and in the vale of years."

The appeal was not made in vain, the Chevalier, who was well skilled in fencing, opened an Academy, and "cut *her* bread with *her* sword," until the year 1810, when the Chevalier died; and *her* friends were for the first time enabled with full confidence to say to all the world,

"THIS WAS A MAN."

The Scrap Book.

NUMBER OF LETTERS IN VOLTAIRE'S WORKS.

In a number of the *Journal de la Libraire*, published at Paris in 1817, a new and complete edition of Voltaire's works is announced, in twelve vols. octavo. The bookseller apprizes the public, that each volume will contain a thousand pages, each page fifty lines, and each line fifty-five letters. By a little simple calculation, it will be found that the literature, poetry, philosophy and history of Voltaire, are comprised in thirty-three millions of letters!

PETRIFIED CORPSE

On the 31st May, 1781, a grave was opened to make way for another coffin at Hathersedge, in Derbyshire, a village on the road between Castleton and Sheffield. In this grave Benjamin Ashton had been buried on the 29th of December 1725, aged forty-two, his coffin was opened either from accident or curiosity, when his body was discovered, the whole mass quite petrified, not incrusted, but the whole substance changed to stone. The appearance induced the people to take it out of the coffin, in doing which, the head was broken off, and shewed that the whole substance was become a solid mass.

The likeness remained so strong that some who knew him when alive, remembered his features perfectly.—His face and belly were swarthy, the underparts of a somewhat different colour. It was replaced in the coffin and buried again. The coffin which was made of oak plank, one inch and a half thick, was as sound as when put into the ground, and was without any appearance of petrifaction about it!

There was a strong spring of water in the grave, which had made its way into the coffin, yet had made no change in that, nor has it been otherwise known to possess a petrifying quality.

A TRINITARIAN.

There is now living in a country village, a man who has been *three times married;* each of his wives names were the *same;* he had *three children* by *each*, and *each* lived with him *three years.* He was a *widower* between *each* marriage *three years*, has *three children living,* the *third* by *each wife,* and whose birth days are within *three days of each other;*—his last wife has been dead *three years,* and he expects to be married again in *three months.*

DELICATE SPINNING.

Some years ago a pair of worsted stockings were made of such delicate texture, that they could be drawn through a lady's ring of ordinary size; and a machine has since been invented, which spins woollen yarn much superior in fineness. By this machine a pound of yarn may be rendered worth ten guineas, producing ninety-five hands of five hundred and sixty yards each in length, 55,200 yards, or thirty miles and four hundred yards.

Published by J. LIMBIRD, 355, Strand, (East End of Exeter 'Change); and sold by all Newsmen and Booksellers. Printed by A. APPLEGATH, Stamford-street.

THE CABINET OF CURIOSITIES,
OR
Wonders of the World Displayed.

A world of wonders where creation seems
No more the works of Nature but her dreams.—MONTGOMERY.

No. VII.] PRICE TWOPENCE.

JACK ADAMS THE ASTROLOGER.

JACK ADAMS, "Professor of the Celestial Sciences, Clerkenwell-green," lived in the reign of Charles the Second, and was in his day an important personage. His biographer calls him "a blind buzzard, that pretended to have the eye of an eagle." He was chiefly employed in horary questions relative to love and marriage, and knew, upon proper occasions, how to soothe the passions and flatter the expectations of those who consulted him; as a man might have had much better fortune from him for five guineas, than for the same number of shillings. He affected a singular dress, and cast his horoscopes with great solemnity. When he failed in his predictions, he declared that the stars did not absolutely force, but powerfully incline; and threw the blame

H

upon wayward and perverse fate! he maintained that their tendency was intrinsically right, when they intimated such things as were never verified; and that they were only wrong, as the hand of a clock, made by a skilful workman, when it is moved forward or backward by any external and superior force. He assumed the character of a learned and *cunning* man, but was no otherwise cunning than as he knew how to overreach those credulous mortals who were as willing to be cheated as he was to cheat them; and who relied implicitly upon his art. In the original print from which our engraving is taken, Jack Adams is thus designated:—

"Magnifico Smokentissimo Custardissimo Astrologissimo, Cunningmanissimo, Rabbinissimo Vero JACKO ADAMS, de Clarkenwell Greeno, hanc lovelissiman sui Picturam. Hobbedeboody, pinxit et scratchabat.

The following curious description accompanies the portrait:—

View here the wonder of Astrologers,
How solemnly he with himself confers,
Sure by his leaning posture we may guess
Some serious things his noddle doth' possess.
The drum, tops, whips and rattles, by his head,
He seems to slight; whilst fortune he doth read.
Unto which purpose with what earnestness
See how the gallant doth his counsel press;
So earnestly as not to be denied,
Longing to have a Princess for his bride.
Joan, Queen of Sluts, as earnest doth importune,
His worship would be pleased to tell her fortune,
Whilst he looks down with an intentive look,
On the twelve houses and poor Robin's book.
The medal which before him hangs on pin,
Is that which the Great Turk did send to him.
Nought else remaineth, that we should describe,
But horn-book and napkin by his side;
His pipe's at girdle, which he calls his gun;
His inkhorn a porridge pot; and so we have done.

A CRYSTAL SUMMER HOUSE.

FURETIERE has given a description of a very curious summer house, invented for the King of Siam, and which is in one of his country palaces. The tables, the chairs, closets, &c., are all composed of crystals. The walls, the ceiling, and the floors, are formed of pieces of ice, of about an inch thick, and six feet square, so nicely united by a cement, which is as transparent as glass itself, that the most subtile water cannot penetrate. There is but one door, which shuts so closely, that it is as impenetrable to the water as the rest of this singular building. A Chinese engineer has constructed it thus, as a certain remedy against the insupportable heat of the climate. This pavilion is twenty-eight feet in length, and seventeen in breadth; it is placed in the midst of a great basin, paved and ornamented with marble of various colours. They fill this basin with water in about a quarter of an hour, and it is emptied as quickly. When you enter the pavilion, the door is immediately closed, and cemented with mastich, to hinder the water from entering; it is then they open the sluices; and this great basin is filled, so that the pavilion is entirely under water, except the top of the dome, which is left untouched, for the benefit of respiration. Nothing is more charming than the agreeable coolness of this delicious place, while the extreme fervour of the sun boils on the surface of the freshest fountains.

THE HEROIC MOTHER.

In the month of June, 1818, a pedlar and his wife presented themselves at nightfall at the door of a little farm house, near the village of the Brie, in France, and requested of the farmer permission to sleep there; his wife was still confined to her bed, having lately lain-in. A small room was assigned to them, where they passed the night quietly. The next day being Sunday, the farmer and his servants went to mass to a neighbouring village. The pedlar also expressed a wish to go, and there remained in the house only the wife of the farmer, the pedlar's wife, who complained that she was not well, and a child of six years of age.

Scarcely had the people gone out, when the pedlar's wife, armed with a knife, presented herself at the bed of the lying-in woman, and demanded her money, threatening to kill her in case of refusal.—The latter, sick and weak, did not oppose the slightest resistance, and delivered up the keys of her drawers, at the same time desiring the little boy to conduct the woman who had to look for something in them. She rose softly from her bed, followed the pedlar's wife without being heard, and having beckoned the child out of the room, locked the robber up in the chamber. She then desired the child to run to the village, to apprize his father, and desire him to bring assistance.

The child did not lose an instant; but by an inconceivable fatality met on the road the pedlar, who had left the church, no doubt, to join his wife. Having asked the child where he was going, the latter answered ingenuously he was going to seek his father, as an attempt was made to rob them. The pedlar took the child by the hand, and said it would be unnecessary, and that he would himself go and protect his mother.

They returned to the farm where the farmer's wife was shut up; they knocked at the door, but this woman not recognising the voice of her husband, obstinately refused to open it; the pedlar made vain efforts to induce her to it, and being unable to attain his end, threatened to cut her child's throat, if she did not instantly decide upon it. Furious at not being able to prevail upon her, he executed his horrible threat, and killed the child, almost under the eyes of its mother, who heard without being able to give succour, the cries and last sighs of her son.

After having committed this useless crime, he endeavoured to penetrate into the house to save his wife; time pressed, they might each moment return from mass, and he could not succeed in getting admission but by mounting on the roof and descending down the chimney. During all this time he exhausted his rage in menaces and imprecations against the farmer's wife, who, almost fainting, saw nothing to deliver her from her certain death. This wretch had already got into the chimney, and was about to enter into the chamber, when the farmer's wife, collecting all her force, drew by sudden inspiration, the paillasse of her bed to the edge of the hearth, and there set it on fire. The smoke in a few minutes enveloped the assassin, who not being able to reascend, very soon fell into the fire, half suffocated. The farmer's courageous wife lost not her presence of mind, but struck him several blows with the poker, which put him beyond the chance of recovering his senses. Finally, exhausted with fatigue and mental agony, she fell senseless on the carpet of her chamber, and remained in this situation till the moment when the farmer and his servants returned from church to be witnesses of this horrible occurrence. The dead body of the child, at the gate of the farm house, was the first spectacle that struck the eyes of this unhappy father. They forced open the gate, and after having recalled to life the farmer's wife, they seized the two culprits, who were delivered up to justice. The pedlar survived his wounds, and both received the punishment due to their crimes

JOHN MACKAY THE FATALIST.

THE subject of the following melancholy tale has long ceased to exist, and there is not in the place of his nativity a being who bears his name. The recital will, therefore, wound the feelings of no one; nor will it disturb the ashes of the dead, to give to the world the story of his madness, rather than his crime.

The name of John Mackay appears on the criminal records of the town of Belfast, in the north of Ireland. He was the murderer of his own child. It is unnecessary to dwell on the character of this unhappy man; suffice it that, from early education, and deeply-rooted habits, he was a fatalist. An enthusiastic turn of mind had been warped into a superstitious dread; and the fabric that might have been great and beautiful, became a ruin that betokened only death and gloom. Yet in his breast the Creator had infused much of the milk of human kindness, and his disposition peculiarly fitted him to be at peace with all men. The poison had lain dormant in his bosom, but it rankled there. Domestic sorrows contributed to strengthen his gloomy creed; and its effects were darker as it took a deeper root. Life soon lost all its pleasures for him; his usual employments were neglected; his dress and appearance altered; his once animated countenance bore the traces of shame or guilt; and a sort of suspicious eagerness was in every look and action.

He had an only child; one of the loveliest infants that ever blessed a father's heart. It was the melancholy legacy of the woman he had loved; and never did a parent doat with more affection on an earthly hope. This little infant, all purity and innocence, was destined to be the victim of his madness. One morning his friend entered his apartment, and what was his horror at beholding the child stretched on the floor, and the father standing over it, his hands reeking with the blood of his babe. "God of heaven!" exclaimed his friend, "what is here?" Mackay approached, and calmly welcomed him, bidding him behold what he had done. His friend beat his bosom, and sunk on a chair, covering his face with his hands. "Why do you grieve?" asked the maniac; "why are you unhappy? I was the father of that breathless corpse, and I do not weep; I am even joyful when I gaze on it. Listen, my friend, listen; I knew I was predestined to murder, and who was so fit to be my victim as that little innocent, to whom I gave life, and from whom I have taken it? He had no crime to answer for; besides, how could I leave him in a cold world, which would mock him with my name?" Even before the commission of the crime, he had sent to a magistrate, whose officers shortly entered, and apprehended him. He coolly surrendered himself, and betrayed no emotion; but he took from his bosom a miniature of his wife, dipped in the blood of his babe, and, without a sigh or a tear, departed. It was this circumstance that made many loath him, and created against him a sentiment of general abhorrence; but when he afterwards, in prison, declared to his friend the storm of passions to which that horrid calm succeeded—that he had torn his hair until the blood trickled down his forehead, while his brain seemed bursting his scull; his friend was satisfied and still loved him. In the prison he was with him: though all others deserted him, he pitied and wept. Still, even to the last he believed he had but fulfilled his duty in the death of his child; and often when he described the scene, and told how the infant smiled on its father at the moment he was prepared to kill it, lisping his name as the weapon was at its throat, he would start with horror at his own tale, and curse the destiny which had decreed it, but always spoke of it as a necessary deed. The time appointed for his trial approached; he contemplated it without dread, and talked of the fate that awaited him without a shudder. But his friend had exerted himself to procure such testimony of the state of his mind, previous to his committing the dreadful act, as to leave little dread of the result; yet he feared to awaken hopes in the unhappy prisoner which might be destroyed, and never mentioned it to him.

The morning of his trial arrived; he was brought to the bar; his hollow eyes glared unconsciously on his judge, and he gave his plea, as if the words "not guilty" came from a being without life. But his recollection seemed for a moment to return; he opened his lips and gasped faintly, as if he wished to recall them. The trial commenced, and he listened with the same apathy; but once betraying feeling, when he smiled on his friend beside him. The evidence had been heard; the jury had returned to their box, and were about to record a verdict of insanity, when a groan from the prisoner created a momentary pause, and he dropped lifeless in the dock. He had for some minutes shadowed his countenance with his hand, and no one but his friend perceived its dreadful alteration. He attributed it to the awful suspense of the moment, the agony between hope and despair. Its cause was a more awful one;—he had procured poison, had taken it, and with an almost superhuman strength, had struggled with its effects until he fell dead before the court. He was buried in the churchyard of his native village, where a mound of earth marked his grave, but there was neither stone nor inscription to preserve the name of one so wretched.

WONDERS OF THE MICROSCOPE.

Upon examining the edge of a very keen razor by the microscope, it appears as broad as the back part of a very thick knife: rough, uneven, full of notches and furrows, and so far from any thing like sharpness, that an instrument so blunt as this seemed to be, would not serve even to cleave wood.

An exceedingly small needle being also examined, the point thereof appeared above a quarter of an inch in breadth; not round nor flat, but irregular and unequal; and the surface, though extremely smooth and bright to the naked eye, seemed full of ruggedness, holes and scratches. In short, it resembled an iron bar out of a smith's forge.

But the sting of a bee, viewed through the same instrument, showed every where a polish amazingly beautiful, without the least flaw, blemish or inequality; and ended in a point too fine to be discerned.

A small piece of exceedingly fine lawn appeared, from the large distances of holes between its threads, somewhat like a hurdle or lattice; and the threads themselves seemed somewhat coarser than yarn wherewith ropes are made for anchors.

Some Brussels lace, worth five pounds a yard, looked as if it were made of a thick, rough, uneven, hair line, entwisted, fastened or clotted together in a very inartful manner.

But a silkworm's web being examined, appeared perfectly smooth and shining, every where equal, and as much finer than any thread the finest spinster in the world made, as the smallest twine is finer than the thickest cable. A pod of this silk being wound off, was found to contain nine hundred and thirty yards; but it is proper to take notice, that as two threads are glued together by the worm through its whole length, it makes really double the above number, or one thousand eight hundred and sixty yards: which, being weighed with the utmost exactness, were found no heavier than two grains and a half. What an exquisite fineness was here! and yet this is nothing when compared to the web of a small spider, or even with the silk, that issues from the mouth of this very worm when newly hatched from the egg.

Let us examine things with a good microscope, and we shall be immediately convinced that the utmost power of art is only a concealment of deformity, an imposition upon our want of sight; and that our admiration of it arises from our ignorance from what it really is.

This valuable discoverer of truth will prove the most boasted performances of art to be ill-shaped, rugged and uneven as if they were hewn with an axe, or struck out with a mallet and chisel; it will shew bungling inequality and imperfection in every part, and that the whole is disproportionate and monstrous. Our finest miniature paintings appeared before this instrument as mere daubings, plastered on with a trowel, and entirely void of beauty, either in the drawing or the colouring. Our most shining varnishes, our smoothest polishings, will be found to be mere roughness, full of gaps and flaws.

PRANPOREE, THE INDIAN FANATIC.

PRANPOREE, adopted by an Hindoo devotee, and educated by him in the rigid tenets of his religion, when yet young commenced a course of extraordinary mortifications. The first vow which the plan of life he had chosen to himself induced him to make, was to continue perpetually upon his legs, and neither to sit down upon the ground nor lay down to rest, for the space of twelve years. All this time, he told me, says Turner, in his Embassy to Teshoo Lama, he had employed in wandering through different countries. When I inquired how he took the indispensable refreshment of sleep when wearied with fatigue, he said, that at first, to prevent his falling, he used to be tied with ropes to some tree or post, but that this precaution, after some time, became unnecessary, and he was able to sleep standing without such support.

The complete term of this first penance being expired, the next he undertook was to hold his hands, locked in each other, over his head, the fingers of one hand dividing those of the other, for the same space of twelve years. He was still determined not to dwell in any fixed abode; so that, before the term of this last vow could be accomplished, he had travelled over the greater part of the continent of Asia. He first set out by crossing the peninsula of India, through Guzerat; he then passed by Surat to Bussora, and thence to Constantinople; from Turkey he went to Ispanhan, and sojourned so long among different Persian tribes as to obtain a considerable knowledge of their language, in which he conversed with tolerable ease. In his passage from thence towards Russia, he fell in with the Kussaucs (hordes of Cossacks) upon the borders of the Caspian sea, where he narrowly escaped being condemned to perpetual slavery: at length he was suffered to pass on, and reached Moscow; he then travelled along the northern boundary of the Russian empire, and through Siberia, arrived at Pekin, in China, from whence he came through Tibet, by the way of Teshoo Lomboo and Nepaul down to Calcutta. When I first saw him at this place, in the year 1783, he rode upon a piebald Tangun horse from Bootau, and wore a satin embroidered dress given to him by Teshoo Lama, of which he was not a little vain. He was robust and hale, and his complexion, contrasted with a long bushy black beard, appeared really florid. I do not suppose that he was then forty years of age.

Two Goseins attended him, and assisted him in mounting and alighting from his horse. Indeed, he was indebted to them for the assistance of their hands on every occasion; his own, being immoveably fixed in the position in which he had placed them, were of course perfectly useless. The circulation of blood seemed to have forsaken his arms: they were withered, and void of sensation, and inflexible; yet he spoke to me with confidence of recovering the use of them, and mentioned his intention to take them down the following year, when the term of his penance would expire.

To complete the full measure of his religious penance, I understood that there still remained two other experiments for Pranporee to perform. In the first of these the devotee is suspended by the feet to the branch of a tree over a fire, which is kept in a continued blaze, and swung backwards and forwards, his hair passing through the flame, for one pahr and a quarter, that is three hours and three quarters. Having passed through this fiery trial, he may then prepare himself for the last act of probation, which is to be buried alive, standing upright in a pit dug for that purpose, the fresh earth being thrown in upon him, so that he is completely covered; in this situation he must remain for one pahr and a quarter, or three hours and three quarters; and, if at the expiration of that time, on the removal of the earth, he should be found alive, he will ascend into the highest rank, among the most pure of the Yogee."

OLD BOOTY'S GHOST.

THE following is a remarkable observation which was entered in Mr. Spink's Journal; with an account of Mrs. Booty's trial at the Court of King's Bench, concerning her husband, a brewer in London.

"Tuesday, May the 12th, this day the wind was S. S. W. and a little before four in the afternoon, we anchored in Manser Road, where lay Captains Bristo, Brian, and Barnaby, all of them bound to Lucera to load. Wednesday, May the 13th, we weighed anchor, and in the afternoon I went on board of Captain Barnaby, and about two o'clock, we sailed all of us for the island of Lucera, wind W. S. W. and bitter weather. Thursday the 14th, about two o'clock, we saw the island, and all came to an anchor in twelve fathoms' water, the wind was W. S. W. and on the 15th day of May, we had an observation of Mr. Booty in the following manner: Captains Bristo, Brian and Barnaby went on shore shooting of colues on Strombolo: when we had done we called our men together, and about fourteen minutes after three in the afternoon, to our great surprise, we saw two men run by us with amazing swiftness; Captain Barnaby says, Lord bless me, the foremost man looks like my next door neighbour, Old Booty; but said, he did not know the other behind; Booty was dressed in grey clothes, and the one behind him in black; we saw them run into the burning mountain in the midst of the flames, on which we heard a terrible noise, too horrible to be described; Captain Barnaby, then desired us to look at our watches, pen the time down in our pocket books, and enter it in our journals, which we accordingly did. When we were laden, we all sailed for England, and arrived at Gravesend on the 6th of October, 168. ; Mrs. Barnaby and Mrs. Brian came to congratulate our safe arrival, and after some discourse, Captain Barnaby's wife, says my dear, I have got some news to tell you, Old Booty is dead. He swore an oath, and said, we all saw him run into 'hell.'"

Sometime afterwards, Mrs. Barnaby met with a lady of her acquaintance in London, and told her what her husband had seen, concerning Mr. Booty; it came to Mrs. Booty's ears; she arrested Captain Barnaby in 1000l. action, he gave bail, and it came to trial at the court of King's Bench, where Mr. Booty's clothes were brought into court. The sexton of the parish, and the people that were with him during his illness swore to the time when he died, and we swore to our journals, and they came within two minutes; twelve of our men swore that the buttons of his coat were covered with the same grey cloth, and it appeared to be so; the jury asked Mr. Spink if he knew Mr. Booty in his lifetime, he said he never saw him till he saw him go by him into the burning mountain. The judge then said,

"Lord, grant I may never see the sight that you have seen; one, two or three, may be mistaken, but twenty or thirty cannot;" so the widow lost the cause.

N.B. It is now in the Records at Westminster. James the Second, 1687.

HERBERT, Chief Justice.
WYTHENS,
HOLLOWAY, } Justices.
AND WRIGHT.

Hoaxes and Impostures.
No. VI.
PRINCE HOHENLOHE.
[Concluded from our last.]

It would far exceed the limits of our work to attempt to chronicle all the miracles said to be performed by the wonder-working Prince Hohenlohe; in fact, no journal could keep pace with him, since to him time and distance are no obstacles; for he can work miracles by the post, as well as when present—at least, so the Catholics assure us—nay, even a Protestant physician bears testimony to one of his cures—not however as a miracle, but as the effect of imagination. This was the case of a Miss Barbara O'Connor, a nun, in the convent of New-hall, near Chelmsford; who had been attacked with a swelling in the thumb, which extended along the arm to the elbow, defying the most skilful treatment of the surgeons. At length Prince Hohenlohe was applied to. He writes a letter, telling the nun that at eight o'clock on the 3rd of May, 1822, he will offer up prayers for her recovery, and bidding her pray at the same time. "On the 2d of May," says Dr. Badeley, "I was requested to look at Miss O'Connor's hand and arm, which I found as much swollen and as bad as I had ever seen them. The fingers looked ready to burst, and the wrist was fifteen inches in circumference."

The next day, Miss O'Connor went through the religious process prescribed by Prince Hohenlohe. "Mass being nearly ended," says Dr. Badeley, "Miss O'Connor not finding the immediate relief she expected, exclaimed, 'Thy will be done, oh! Lord! thou hast not thought me worthy of this cure.' Almost immediately after, she felt an extraordinary sensation through the whole arm to the end of her fingers. The pain instantly left her, and the swelling gradually subsided; but it was some weeks before the hand resumed its natural size and shape."

Our next, and the last miracle we shall mention, rests entirely on the authority of a Catholic priest, and the world knows that things of this sort lose nothing in such hands. It is a letter from the Rev. Mr. O'Connor to Dr. Doyle, and we subjoin it without comment.

Maryborough, June, 1823.

MY LORD,

In compliance with your request, I send you a statement of the facts relative to Miss Lalor, which I have heard from others and witnessed myself.

I am now in the house where she was first deprived of her speech. She is at present in the eighteenth year of her age; and as she is connected with most of the respectable Catholic families in this country, and has had frequent intercourse with them, her privation of speech during six years and five months, is established beyond contradiction. Her hearing and understanding remained unimpaired, and she carried a tablet and pencil to write what she could not communicate by signs.

Medical aid was tried by Dr. Ferris of Athy, and Surgeon Smith of Mountrath, but without effect. The latter gentleman (as a similar case never occurred in the course of his practice) resolved to have it submitted to the most eminent physicians in Dublin, eight of whom were consulted by him, and the result was, that no hopes could be entertained of her recovery. This decision was imparted by Dr. Smith to her father, apart from Mrs. and Miss Lalor; all which circumstances the doctor recollected on the 14th instant, when he saw Miss Lalor, heard her speak, and declared the cure to be miraculous.

You, my Lord, are already aware, that according to your directions, written to me on the 1st of June, I waited on Mr. Lalor, and communicated to him and to his family, all that you desired. They observed it with every exactness; and on the morning of the 10th inst. having heard Miss Lalor's confession by signs, and disposed her for receiving the holy communion, I read to her again from your lordship's letter, the directions of the Prince, namely, that she would excite within her a sincere repentance, a firm resolution of obeying God's commands, a lively faith, and unbounded confidence in his mercy, an entire conformity to his holy will, and a disinterested love of him.

I had previously requested the clergy of this district to offer up for Miss Lalor the holy sacrifice of the mass, at twelve minutes before eight o'clock in the morning of the 10th, keeping the matter a secret from most others, as you had recommended; however, as it transpired somewhat, a considerable number collected in the chapel, when my two coadjutors, with myself, began mass at the hour appointed. I offered the holy sacrifice in the name of the church. I besought the Lord to overlook my own unworthiness, and regard only Jesus Christ, the Great High Priest and Victim, who offers himself in the mass to his Eternal Father, for the living and the dead. I implored the Mother of God, of all the Angels and Saints, and particularly of St. John Nepomuscene; I administered the sacrament to the young lady, at the usual time, when she heard, as it were, a voice distinctly saying to her, "*Mary you are well*"—when she exclaimed, "O Lord am I!" and, overwhelmed with devotion, fell prostrate on her face. She continued in this posture for a considerable time, whilst I hastened to conclude the mass; but was interrupted in my thanksgiving immediately after by the mother of the child, pressing her to speak.

When at length she was satisfied in pouring out her soul to the Lord, she took her mother by the hand, and said to her, 'dear mother,' upon which Mrs. Lalor called the clerk, and sent for me, as I had retired to avoid the interruption, and on coming to where the young lady was, I found her speaking in an agreeable, clear, and distinct voice, such as neither she nor her mother could recognise as her own.

As she returned home in the afternoon, the doors and windows in the street through which she passed were crowded with persons, gazing with wonder at this monument of the power and goodness of Almighty God.

Thus, my lord, in obedience to your commands, I have given you a simple statement of facts, without adding to, or distorting what I have seen and heard, the truth of which, their very notoriety places beyond all doubt; and which numberless witnesses, as well as myself, could attest by the most solemn appeal to heaven. I cannot forbear remarking to your lordship, how, our Lord confirms now the doctrine of his church, and his own presence upon our altars, by the same miracles to which he referred the disciples of John, saying, "Go tell John the dumb speak," &c. as a proof that he was the Son of God who came to save the world.

I remain your lordship's dutiful and affectionate servant in Christ, N. O'CONNOR.
To the Right Rev. Dr. Doyle Old Derrig, Carlow.

Anecdotes of Longevity.

OLD PARR.

THOMAS PARR, was the son of John Parr, a husbandman of Winnington, in the parish of Alderbury, in the county of Salop, where he was born in the year 1483. Though he lived to the vast age of upwards of 152 years, yet the tenour of his life admitted but of little variety. He appears to have been the son of a husbandman; he laboured hard, and lived on coarse fare. Taylor the Water Poet, says of him,

Good wholesome labour was his exercise,
Down with the lamb, and with the lark would rise;
In mire and toiling sweat he spent the day,
And to his team he whistled time away:
The cock his night clock, and till day was done,
His watch and chief sun-dial was the sun.
He was of old Pythagoras' opinion,
That green cheese was most wholesome with an onion;
Coarse maslin bread, and for his daily swig,
Milk, butter-milk, and water, whey and whig:
Sometimes metheglin, and by fortune happy;
He sometimes sipp'd a cup of ale most nappy,
Cyder or perry, when he did repair
T' a Whitsun ale wake, wedding, or a fair;
Or when in Chrismas-time he was a guest
At his good landlord's house amongst the rest:
Else he had little leisure-time to waste;
Or at the ale-house huff-cap ale to taste,
- - - - - - - - - - -
- - - - - - - - - - -
His physic was good butter, which the soil
Of Salop yields, more sweet than Candy oil;
And garlick he esteem'd above the rate
Of Venice treacle, or best mithridate.
He entertain'd no gout, no ache he felt,
The air was good and temperate where he dwelt;
While mavisses and sweet-tongued nightingales
Did chant him roundelays and madrigals.
Thus living within bounds of Nature's laws,
Of his long lasting life may be some cause.

And the same writer describes him in the following two lines:

From head to heel, his body had all over
A quick set, thick set, natural hairy cover.

The manner of his being conducted to London is also noticed in the following terms: "The Right Hon. Thomas, Earl of Arundel and Surrey, Earl Marshal of England, on being lately in Shropshire, to visit some lands and manors which his Lordship held in that county, or for some other occasions of importance which caused his Lordship to be there, the report of this aged man was signified to his Honour, who hearing of so remarkable a piece of antiquity, his Lordship was pleased to see him; and in his innate, noble, and christian piety, he took him into his charitable tuition and protection, commanding that a litter and two horses (for the more easy carriage of a man so feeble and worn with age) to be provided for him; also that a daughter of his, named Lucy, should likewise attend him, and have a horse for her own riding with him: and to cheer up the old man and make him merry, there was an antiqued-faced fellow with a high and mighty beard, that had also a horse for his carriage. These were all to be brought out of the country to London by easy journeys, the charge being allowed by his Lordship; likewise one of his Lordship's own servants, named Bryan Kelly, to ride on horseback with them, and to attend and defray all manner of reckonings and expenses.

" In London, he was well entertained and accommodated with all things, having all the aforesaid attendance at the sole charge and cost of his Lordship."

When brought before the King, his majesty, with more acuteness than good-manners, said to him, "You have lived longer than other men, what have you done more than other men?" He answered, "I did penance when I was a hundred years old." "For shame, old man," said the King, "to recollect nothing but your vices."

This journey, however, proved fatal to him; owing to the alteration in his diet, the change of the air, and his general mode of life, he lived but a very short time, dying the 5th of November, 1635, and was buried in Westminster Abbey.

After his death his body was opened, and an account was drawn up by the celebrated Dr. Harvey, some part of which we shall extract.

" Thomas Parr was a poor countryman of Shropshire, whence he was brought up to London by the Right Hon. Thomas Earl of Arundel and Surrey, and died after he had outlived nine Princes, in the tenth year of the tenth of them, at the age of 152 years and nine months.

" He had a large breast, lungs not fungous, but sticking to his ribs, and distended with blood; a lividness in his face, as he had a difficulty of breathing a little before his death, and a long lasting warmth in his armpits and breast after it; which sign, together with others, were so evident in his body, as they use to be on those that die by suffocation. His heart was great, thick, fibrous, and fat. The blood in the heart blackish and diluted. The cartilages of the sternum not more bony than in others, but flexile and soft. His viscera were sound and strong, especially the stomach; and it was observed of him, that he used to eat often by night and day, though contented with old cheese, milk, coarse bread, small-beer, and whey; and which is more remarkable, that he eat at midnight a little before he died.

" The cause of his death was imputed chiefly to the change of food and air; forasmuch as coming out of a clear, thin, and free air, he came into the thick air of London; and after a constant plain and homely country diet, he was taken into a splendid family, where he fed high and drank plentifully of the best wines, whereupon the natural functions of the parts of his body were overcharged, his lungs obstructed, and the habit of the whole body quite disordered; upon which there could not but ensue a dissolution.

"The brain was sound, entire, and firm; and though he had not the use of his eyes, nor much of his memory, several years before he died, yet he had his hearing and apprehension very well, and was able even to the hundred and thirtieth year of his age to do any husbandman's work, even threshing of corn."

Taylor the Water Poet, says, that Parr took his last lease of his landlord for his life, but being desirous for his wife's sake to renew it for years, which his landlord would not consent to, he, to give himself the appearance of rejuvenescence, adopted the following trick: "Having been long blind, sitting in his chair by the fire, his wife looked out of the window, and perceiving Edward Porter, the son of his landlord, to come towards their house, she told her husband, saying, 'Our landlord is coming hither:' 'Is it so,' said old Parr, 'I prithee, wife, lay a pin on the ground near my foot, or at my right toe;' which she did; and when young master Porter, yet forty years old, was come into the house, after salutations between them, the old man said, 'Wife, is not that a pin on the ground near my foot?' 'Truly, husband,' quoth she, 'it is a pin indeed;' so she took up the pin, and Master Porter was half in a maze, that the old man had recovered his sight again. But it was quickly found out to be a witty conceit, thereby to have them suppose him to be more lively than he was, because he hoped to have his lease renewed for his wife's sake."

Rubens saw Parr at Shrewsbury, when he was above 140 years of age, and painted him. The picture represents Parr with a complexion as delicately incarnated as that of a young woman.

Eccentric Biography.

MR. STUKELEY THE PERPETUAL MOTION SEEKER.

MR. STUKELEY was a gentleman of fortune bred to the law, but relinquished the profession, and retired into the country filled with the project of discovering the perpetual motion. During a period of thirty years, he never went abroad but once, which was when he was obliged to take the oath of allegiance to King George the First; this was also the only time he changed his shirt and clothes, or shaved himself, during the whole time of his retirement.

Mr. Stukeley was at once the dirtiest and the cleanliest man; washing his hands twenty times a day, but his hands only. His family consisted of two female servants, one lived in the house, and the other out of it. He never had his bed made. After he had relinquished the project of the perpetual motion, he devoted himself to observing the works and economy of ants; and stocked the town so plenteously with that insect, that the fruits in the gardens were devoured by them.

During the reign of Queen Anne, whenever the Duke of Marlborough opened the trenches against a city in Flanders, he broke ground at the extremity of a floor in his house, made with lime and sand, according to the custom of that country, and advanced in his approaches regularly with his pickaxe, gaining work after work, chalked out on the ground according to the intelligence in the gazette; by which he took the town in the middle of the floor at Bideford, the same day the duke was master of it in Flanders; thus every city cost him a new floor.

Sterne no doubt had Mr. Stukeley in his eye, when he drew the character of My Uncle Toby.

Mr. Stukeley never sat on a chair, and when he chose to warm himself, he made a pit before the fire, into which he leapt, and thus sat on the floor. He suffered no one to see him, but the heir to his estate, his brother and sister; the first never but when he sent for him, and that very rarely; the others sometimes once a year, and sometimes seldomer, when he was cheerful, talkative, and a lover of the tittle-tattle of the town. Notwithstanding his apparent avarice, he was by no means a lover of money; for, during his seclusion, he never received nor asked for any rent from many of his tenants; those who brought him money, he would often keep at an inn more than a week, and then pay all their expenses, and dismiss them without receiving a shilling. He lived well in his house, frequently gave to the poor, always ate from large joints of meat, never saw any thing twice at table; and at Christmas divided a certain sum of money amongst the necessitous of the town. He seemed to be afraid of two things only; one, being killed for his riches; the other being infected with disease; for which reasons he would send his maid sometimes to borrow a half-crown from his neighbours, to hint he was poor; and always received the money which was paid him in a basin of water, to prevent taking infection from those who paid him. He did not keep his money locked up, but piled it on the shelves before the plates in his kitchen. In his chamber, which no servant had entered during the time of his remaining at home, he had two thousand guineas on the top of a low chest of drawers, covered with dust, and five hundred on the floor, where it lay five and twenty years; this last sum a child had thrown down, which he was fond of playing with, by oversetting a table that stood upon one foot; the table continued in the same situation also; through this money he had made two paths, by kicking the pieces on one side, one of which led from the door to the window, the other from the window to the bed. When he quitted the Temple in London, he left an old portmanteau over the portal of the ante-chamber, where it had continued many years, during which time, the chambers had passed through several hands; at length a gentleman who possessed them, ordered his servant to pull it down; it broke, being rotten, and out fell four or five hundred pieces of gold, which were found to belong to him, from the papers enclosed. It was generally supposed at his death, that he had put large sums in the hands of a banker, or lent it to some tradesman in London, without taking any memorandum; all which was lost to his heirs, as he would never say to whom he lent it, through fear, perhaps, lest he should hear it was lost; which some minds can bear to suspect, though not to know positively. After more than thirty years living a recluse, he was at last found dead in his bed, covered with vermin. Thus ended the life of this whimsical being, at the age of seventy.

The gentleman who accompanied him to the Town Hall, when he went to take the oath of allegiance, talked with him on every subject he could recollect, without discovering in him the least tincture of madness. He rallied himself on the perpetual motion, laughed at the folly of confining himself in-doors, and said he believed he should come abroad again, like other men. He was always esteemed a person of good understanding before his shutting himself up. At the time of his death, he was building a house, the walls of which were seven feet thick.—*Percy Anecdotes.*

Varieties.

BLIND TAILOR.

The late family tailor of Mr. Macdonald, of Clanronald, in South Uist, Inverness-shire, lost his sight fifteen years before his death; yet he still continued to work for the family as before; not indeed with the same expedition, but with equal correctness. It is well known how difficult it is to make a Tartan dress, because every stripe and colour (of which there are many) must fit each other with mathematical exactness: hence it is that very few tailors, who enjoy their sight, are capable of executing this task. Blind Macquarrie having received orders to make for Mr. Macdonald a complete suit of Tartan, within a given time, proceeded to work without delay. It so happened, that Mr. Macdonald passed at a late 'hour at night through the room where the blind tailor was working, and hearing some low singing, he asked, who was there? to which the poor blind tailor answered, "I am here, working at your honour's hose." "How," says the gentleman, forgetting that he was blind, "can you work without a candle?" "Oh! please your honour," rejoined the tailor, "midnight darkness is as clear to me as noonday." In fact, by the sense of touch only, he was enabled to distinguish all the different colours in the Tartan.

WATER DRINKERS.

Catherine Beausergaut had been distinguished from the most tender age by a thirst which nothing could quench. In her infancy she drank two pailfulls of water every day. When her parents endeavoured to prevent her drinking water so abundantly she procured it clandestinely, in summer from the river, from fountains, and from the houses of the neighbours even in the streets; and in winter from pieces of ice, or from snow, which she melted privately night and day. The harsh manner in which her family treated her on account of this propensity, induced her at length to quit her paternal mansion.—She went to Paris, and entered into the service of some persons more indulgent than her parents, and who left her at liberty to drink as much water as she chose. Her conduct in this service was irreproachable. At twenty-two years of age she was married to a man named Ferry, a cordwainer, from whom she concealed her ardent thirst, through fear that he would not espouse her. She had had nine children in 1719. During the months she was in the family way, her thirst increased: she refused constantly to quench it with any other drink than fresh water, of which she drank three or four pints at one time. In the winter of 1788, being then near her time of delivery, she drank nearly two pailfulls of water in twenty-four hours: water at that time cost six sous per pail. Her husband went and collected snow and ice, and thawed it. It was extraordinary, she never could drink a glass of wine without pain and shivering.

The Foreign Journals of 1753, mention a young woman, aged twenty years, who had felt for fourteen years a great desire for drink. She drank usually, in twenty-four hours, eighteen or twenty pints of water; making the quantity drank in the course of fourteen years 95,000 pints.

The Scrap Book.

A RARE CIRCLE OF FRIENDS.

SIR HENRY BLACKMAN, of Lewes, on being knighted in 1782, gave a dinner to sixteen friends, with an invitation to them to dine with him annually for forty years; four of them died during the first four years, but twenty-eight years rolled round before another seat became vacant at the festive board. In 1814 two died, aged between eighty and ninety; so that ten remained of the original number at the thirty-third anniversary, held in July, 1815!

THE CANINE PATIENT.

A DOG having been run over by a carriage, had his leg broken, and a humane surgeon passing, had the animal brought home, set his leg, and, having cured his patient, discharged him,—aware that he would return to his old master: the dog, whenever he met the surgeon afterwards, never failed to recognise him by wagging his tail, and other demonstrations of joy.—One day a violent barking was heard at the surgeon's door, which was found to be occasioned by this dog, who it appeared was striving to procure admittance for another dog, who had just had his leg broken!

JUVENILE INDISCRETION.

IN the year 1817, was married at the Collegiate Church, Manchester, after being a widower the immense space of *nine weeks*, Mr. Davies, of Long Millgate, aged seventy, to Mrs. Bowden, of the same place, aged seventy-two, being the fourth appearance of this *young* lady in the character of a bride!

A MIRACLE MONGER.

A PRIEST in extreme poverty resolved to get credit for a miracle. He put the yolks of several eggs in a hollow cane, and stopped the end with butter; then walking into an ale house he begged to fry a single egg for his dinner; the smallness of his repast excited curiosity, and they gave him a morsel of lard; he stirred the lard with his cane, and to the wonder of the surrounding peasants produced a handsome omelet. This miracle established his fame. He sold amulets, and grew rich by his ingenuity.

Published by J. LIMBIRD, 355, Strand, (East End of Exeter 'Change); and sold by all Newsmen and Booksellers. Printed by A. APPLEGATH, Stamford-street

THE CABINET OF CURIOSITIES,
OR
Wonders of the World Displayed.

A world of wonders where creation seems
No more the works of Nature but her dreams.—MONTGOMERY.

No. VIII.] PRICE TWOPENCE.

BARBARA URSELIN.

IN the year 1655, the female whose portrait this week forms our *embellishment*, was exhibited for money. Her name was Augusta Barbara; she was the daughter of Balthazar Urselin, and was then in her twenty-second year. Her whole body, and even her face, was covered with curled hair of a yellow colour, and very soft, like wool; she had besides a thick beard that reached to her girdle, and from her ears hung long tufts of yellowish hair. She had been married above a year, but then had no issue. Her husband's name was Vaubeck, and he married her merely to make a show of her, for which purpose he visited various countries of Europe, and England among others. Barbara Urselin is believed to be the hairy girl mentioned by Bartoline, and appears not to differ from her whom Borelli describes by the name of Barba, who he believed improved, if not procured, that hairiness by art.

WRECK OF A SLAVE SHIP.

The following extract of a letter from Philadelphia, dated November 11, 1762, gives an account of the melancholy disaster that befel the Phœnix, Capt. M'Gacher, in lat. 37° N. and longitude 72° W. from London, bound to Potomack, in Maryland, from the coast of Africa, with 332 slaves on board.

" On Wednesday the 20th of October 1762, at six o'clock in the evening, came on a most violent gale of wind at south, with thunder and lightning, the sea running very high, when the ship sprung a leak, and we were obliged to lie-to under bare poles, the water gained on us with both pumps constantly working. At 10 p. m. endeavoured to put the ship before the wind to no purpose. At twelve the sand ballast having choked our pumps, and there being seven feet water in the hold, all the casks afloat, and the ballast shifted to leeward, cut away the rigging of the main and mizen masts, both which went instantly close by the deck, and immediately after the foremast was carried away about twenty feet above. Hove overboard all our guns, upon which the ship righted a little. We were then under a necessity of letting all our slaves out of irons, to assist in pumping and baling.

"Thursday morning being moderate, having gained about three feet on the ship, we found every cask in the hold stove to pieces, so that we only saved a barrel of flour, 10 lbs. of bread, twenty-five gallons of wine, beer, and shrub, and twenty-five gallons of spirits. The seamen and slaves were employed all this day in pumping and baling; the pumps were frequently choked, and brought up great quantities of sand. We were obliged to hoist one of the pumps up, and put it down the quarter deck hatchway. A ship this day bore down upon us, and, though very near, and we making every signal of distress, she would not speak to us.

"On Friday, the men slaves being very sullen and unruly, having had no sustenance of any kind for forty-eight hours, except a dram, we put one half of the strongest of them in irons.

" On Saturday and Sunday, all hands night and day could scarce keep the ship clear, and were constantly under arms.

" On Monday morning, many of the slaves had got out of irons, and were attempting to break up the gratings; and the seamen not daring to go down in the hold to clear the pumps, we were obliged, for the preservation of our own lives, to kill fifty of the ringleaders and stoutest of them.

It is impossible to describe the misery the poor slaves underwent, having had no fresh water for five days. Their dismal cries and shrieks, and most frightful looks, added a great deal to our misfortunes; four of them were found dead, and one drowned herself in the hold. This evening the water gained on us, and three seamen dropped down with fatigue and thirst, which could not be quenched, though wine, rum, and shrub were given them alternately. On Thursday morning the ship had gained, during the night, above a foot of water, and the seamen quite worn out, and many of them in despair. About ten in the forenoon we saw a sail; about two she discovered us, and bore down; at five spoke to us, being the King George, of Londonderry, James Mackay, master; he immediately promised to take us on board, and hoisted out his yawl, it then blowing very fresh. The gale increasing, prevented him from saving any thing but the white people's lives, not even any of our clothes, or one slave, the boat being scarcely able to live in the sea the last trip she made. Captain Mackay and some gentlemen passengers he had on board, treated us with great kindness and humanity."   T. C. W.

The Book of Giants.

"And there were giants in those days."

Chapter I.

THE extravagant accounts which the romances of all ages give of giants of incredible size and strength, has had the effect of making many disbelieve entirely their existence. They contend that the stature of man hath been the same in all ages; and some have even gone so far as to pretend to demonstrate mathematically the impossibility of the existence of giants. Among these theorists, Mr. Laurin was, perhaps, the most explicit and ingenious, but the whole of his arguments are inconclusive; and leave the existence of giants to rest on the credibility of the accounts we have from those who pretend to have seen them, and not on any arguments drawn *à priori.*

In Scripture, giants are frequently mentioned; and although in some cases it is contended that the word translated giants, does not imply extraordinary stature, yet in the case of Og, King of Bashan, and Goliah of Gath, such is its evident meaning. Profane historians have given seven feet as the height of Hercules their first hero; but we have in our own days seen men above eight feet high.

If we could credit the accounts of the gigantic bones said to have been discovered, eight feet would be nothing; but while we give these accounts which are recorded in history, we certainly must acknowledge our conviction that they are generally fabulous.

The Athenians are said to have found near their city, two famous skeletons, one of thirty-four, and the other of thirty-six feet. At Totu, in Bohemia, we are told, a skeleton was found in the year 758, the head of which could scarcely be fathomed by the arms of two men together, and whose legs, which they still keep in the castle of that city, were twenty-six feet long. The skull of the giant found in Macedonia, September, 1691, held two hundred and ten pounds of corn. Near Mazarino, in Sicily, was found a giant 30 feet high; his head was the size of a hogshead, and each of his teeth weighed five ounces. Near Palermo, in the valley of Mazara, in Sicily, a skeleton of a giant thirty feet long was found in the year 1548; and another, thirty-three feet high, in 1550. Many curious persons, historians assure us, have preserved several of those gigantic bones.

The Chevalier Scory, in his voyage to the Peake of Teneriffe, says, they found in one of the sepulchral caverns of that mountain, the head of a Guanche which had eighty teeth, and the body was not less than fifteen feet long. In Rouen, in 1509, in digging the ditches near the Dominicans, they found a stone tomb containing a skeleton, whose skull held a bushel of corn, and whose shin bone reached up to the girdle of the tallest man there, being about four feet high, consequently the body must have been seventeen or eighteen feet high. On the tomb was a plate of copper with this inscription:—

"In this tomb lies the noble and puissant Lord, the Chevalier Ricon de Vallemont and his bones."

Platerus, a famous physician, declares that he saw at Lucerne, the true human bones of a subject, which must have been nineteen feet high. Valence, in Dauphiny, boasts of possessing the bones of the giant Bucart, tyrant of the Vivarais, who was slain by an arrow, by the Count de Cabillon his vassal. The Dominicans had a part of the shin bones with the articulation of the knee, and his figure painted in fresco, with an inscription, shewing that this giant was twenty-two feet and a half high, and that his bones were found in 1705, near the banks of the Morderi, a little river at the foot of the mountains of Crussol, upon which, tradition says, the giant dwelt.

On the 11th of January, 1613, some masons digging near the ruins of a castle in Dauphiny, in a field which had long been traditionally called the giant's field, found, at the depth of eighteen feet, a brick tomb, thirty feet long, twelve feet wide, and eight feet high, on which was a grey stone, with the words *Theutobochus Rex*, engraved on it. When the tomb was opened they found a human skeleton entire, twenty-five feet and a half long, ten feet wide across the shoulders, and five feet deep from the breast bone to the back. His teeth were each about the size of an ox's foot, and his shin bone measured four feet.

The celebrated Sir Hans Sloane, who wrote a learned treatise on the subject, does not doubt these facts, but thinks the bones were those of elephants, whales, or other enormous animals: but neither the bones, much less the head, of an elephant or whale, could be imposed on any anatomist, or even a connoisseur, for those of a man, however gigantic. The evidence, however, rests on too slender an authority to be deemed conclusive.

Hoaxes and Impostures.
No. VII.
SABBATEI-SEVI.

DURING the siege of Candia, in the year 1669, an affair happened among the Turks, that drew the attention of all Europe and Asia. A general rumour was spread at that time, founded on an idle curiosity, that the year 1666 was to be remarkable for some great revolution. The source of this opinion was the mystic number of 666, found in the book of Revelation. Never was the expectation of the antichrist so general. On the other hand, the Jews pretended that their Messiah was to come this year.

A Smyrna Jew, named Sabbatei-Sevi, who was a man of some learning, and son of a rich broker belonging to the English factory, took advantage of this general opinion, and set up for the Messiah. He was eloquent, and of a graceful figure; he affected modesty, recommended justice, spoke like an oracle, and proclaimed, wherever he came, that the times were fulfilled. He travelled at first in Greece and Italy. At Leghorn he ran away with a girl, and carried her to Jerusalem, where he began to preach to his brethren. It is a standing tradition among the Jews, that their Shiloh, or Messiah, their avenger and king, is not to appear till the coming of Elijah; and they are persuaded that they have had one Elijah, who is to appear again at the renewing of the world. Elijah, according to them, is to introduce the great sabbath, the great Messiah, and the general revolution of all things. This notion has been even received among Christians. Elijah is to come to declare the dissolution of this world, and a new order of things. Almost all the different sects of fanatics expect an Elijah. The prophets of the Cevennes, who came to London in 1707 to raise the dead, pretended to have seen Elijah, and to have spoken to him, and that he was to shew himself to the people. In 1724, the lieutenant of the police at Paris, sent two Elijahs to prison, who fought with each other, who should be accounted the true one. It was therefore necessary that Sabbatei-Sevi should be announced to his brethen by an Elijah, otherwise his pretended mission would have been treated as an imposture.

He met with one Nathan, a Jewish rabbin, who thought there was something to be gained by playing a part in this farce. Accordingly Sabbatei declared to the Jews of Asia Minor and Syria, that Nathan was Elijah; and Nathan on his part insisted that Sabbatei was the Messiah, the Shiloh, expected by the chosen people. They both performed great works at Jerusalem, and reformed the synagogue. Nathan explained the prophecies, and demonstrated that at the expiration of that year, the sultan would be dethroned, and Jerusalem become mistress of the world. All the Jews of Syria were convinced. The synagogues resounded with ancient prophecies. They grounded themselves on these words of Isaiah: "Awake, awake, put on thy strength, O Zion, put on thy beautiful garments O Jerusalem, the holy city, for henceforth, there shall no more come into thee the uncircumcised and the unclean." All the rabbins had the following passage in their mouths: "And they shall bring all your brethren for an offering unto the Lord, out of all nations, upon horses, and in chariots, and in litters, and upon mules, and upon swift beasts, to my holy mountain Jerusalem." In short, their hopes were fed by these and a thousand other passages, which both women and children were for ever repeating. There was not a Jew but prepared lodgings for some of the ten dispersed tribes. So great was their enthusiasm, that they left off trade every where, and held themselves ready for the voyage to Jerusalem.

Nathan chose twelve men at Damascus, to preside over the twelve tribes. Sabbatei-Sevi went to shew himself to his brethren at Smyrna, and Nathan wrote to him thus: "King of kings, Lord of lords, when shall we be worthy to put ourselves under the shadow of your ass? I prostrate myself to be trod under the soles of your feet." At Smyrna, Sabbatei deposed some doctors of the law, who did not acknowledge his authority, and established others more tractable. One of his most violent enemies, named Samuel Pennia, was publicly converted, and proclaimed him to be the Son of God. Sabbatei having presented himself one day before the cadi of Smyrna, with a multitude of his followers, they all declared they saw a column of fire betwixt him and the cadi. Some other miracles of this sort set his divine mission beyond all doubt. Numbers of Jews were impatient to lay their gold and their precious stones at his feet.

The bashaw of Smyrna would have arrested him; but he set out for Constantinople with his most zealous disciples. The grand vizir, Achmet Cuprogli, who was getting ready for the siege of Candia, gave orders for him to be seized on board the vessel that brought him to Constantinople, and to be confined. The Jews easily obtained admittance into the prison for money, as is usual in Turkey; they went and prostrated themselves at his feet, and kissed his chains. He preached to them, exhorted them, and gave them his blessing, but never complained. The Jews of Constantinople, believing that the coming of the Messiah would cancel all debts, refused to pay their creditors. The English merchants at Galata waited upon Sabbatei in jail, and told him, that, as king of the Jews, he ought to command all his subjects to pay their debts. Sabbatei wrote the following words to the persons complained against: "To you, who expect the salvation of Israel, &c. discharge your lawful debts; if you refuse it, you shall not enter with us in our joy, and into our empire."

Sabbatei, during his imprisonment, was continually visited by his followers, who began to raise some disturbances in Constantinople. At that time the people were greatly dissatisfied with Mahomet IV. and it was apprehended that the Jewish prophecy might occasion some disturbance. Under these circumstances, one would imagine, that such a severe government as that of the Turks, would have put the person, calling himself King of Israel, to death. Yet they only removed him to the castle of the Dardanelles. The Jews then cried out, that it was not in the power of man to take away his life.

His fame had reached even the most distant parts of Europe; at the Dardanelles he received deputations from the Jews of Poland, Germany, Leghorn, Venice, and Amsterdam: they paid very dear for kissing his feet; and probably this was what preserved his life. The distributions of the Holy Land were made very quietly in the tower of the Dardanelles. At length the fame of his miracles was so great, that Sultan Mahomet had the curiosity to see the man, and to examine him himself. The king of the Jews was brought to the seraglio. The sultan asked him in the Turkish language, whether he was the Messiah. Sabbatei modestly answered, he was; but as he expressed himself incorrectly in this tongue, "You speak very ill," said Mahomet to him, "for a Messiah, who ought to have the gift of languages. Do you perform any miracles?"—"Sometimes," answered the other. "Well then," said the sultan, "let him be stripped stark naked; he will be a very good mark for the arrows of my pages, and if he is invulnerable, we will acknowledge him to be the Messiah." Sabbatei flung himself upon his knees, and confessed it to be a miracle above his strength. It was proposed to him immediately, either to be impaled, or to turn Mussulman, and go publicly to the Turkish mosque. He did not hesitate in the least, but embraced the Turkish religion directly. Then he preached that he had been sent to substitute the Turkish for the Jewish religion, pursuant to the ancient prophecies. Yet the Jews of distant countries believed in him a long time. The affair, however, was not attended with bloodshed, but increased the shame and confusion of the Jewish nation.

FRENCH CHARLATAN.

ABOUT four years ago, a man of imposing figure, wearing a large sabre and immense mustachios, arrived at one of the principal inns of a provincial city in France, accompanied with a female of agreeable shape and enchanting mien. He alighted at the moment that dinner was serving up at the *table d'hôte*. At his martial appearance all the guests rose with respect; they felt assured that it must be a lieutenant-general, or a major-general at least. A new governor was expected in the province about this time, and every body believed that it was he who had arrived *incognito*. The officer of gendarmerie gave him the place of honour, the comptroller of the customs and the receiver of taxes sat by the side of Madame, and exerted their wit and gallantry to the utmost. All the tit-bits, all the most exquisite wines, were placed before the fortunate couple. At length the party broke up, and every one ran to report through the city that Monsieur the governor had arrived. But oh! what was their surprise, when the next day his excellency, clad in a scarlet coat, and his august companion dressed out in a gown glittering with tinsel, mounted a small open calash, and preceded by some musicians, went about the squares and public ways, selling Swiss tea and balm of Mecca. How shall we describe the fury of the guests? They go and complain to the mayor, and demand that the audacious quack should be compelled to lay aside the characteristic mark of the brave. The prudent magistrate assembled the common council; and those respectable persons, after a long deliberation, considering that nothing in the charter forbids the citizens to let their beard grow on their upper lip, dismissed the complaint altogether. The same evening the supposed governor gave a serenade to the complainants, and the next day took his leave, and continued his journey amidst the acclamations of the people; who, in small as well as in great cities, are very apt to become passionately fond of charlatans.

Anecdotes of Longevity.

PATRIARCHAL FAMILIES.

A DUBLIN paper of 1819 has the following paragraph:—" A few days ago, two old men went on board a Whitehaven vessel, at George's-quay, to purchase coals. One of them had a little boy by the hand, apparently about three or four years old. 'This (observed the Captain) is your grandson, I suppose.'—'Nay, (replied the other) he is my son.'—'Your son!'—'Yes; and that old fellow there is another of my sons; but there is a distance of *seventy* years in their ages.' This turned out to be the fact—the father is *a hundred*, and about four years ago, he married a girl of *twenty-two*, by whom he had this youngest child."

CRANMER'S DESCENDANT.

In the parish of Acton, Middlesex, still exist the lineal posterity of the famous Bishop Cranmer, who was burnt at the stake by order of Queen Mary, nearly 300 years ago. One of them, an old lady named Whytell, has completed her 112th year, and retains her intellectual and bodily faculties to a surprising extent. She usually devotes her morning hours to attend on the neighbouring poor, and in the evening secludes herself in her room.

JEAN MOUSTIE.

On the 1st of Jan. died at Monheurt, in the department of Lot and Garonne, Jean Moustie, aged one hundred and fifteen years. He was born in January, 1698, and married in 1720. By this marriage he had seven children, one daughter and six sons; the eldest of whom would now be 85 years old, had not a fatal accident terminated his life; the youngest aged 57, carries on his father's business as a tile-maker. Jean Moustie was for some time in the army, during the minority of Louis XV.: but having returned to his trade, he worked at it without interruption to the age of 109 years, and was never confined to his bed by illness, except for about 24 hours before his death. Every Sunday, in all weathers, this venerable man went to Monheurt, where, seated beneath the aged elm, which overshadows the public place, amidst generations, whose birth he remembered, he beheld with delight the amusements of youth, and emptied at leisure the little flask with which he had taken care to provide himself. At sunset he returned to his family, in which he knew how to keep up invariable happiness and mirth. A sober, active, and laborious life, an upright mind and sound judgment, rendered Jean Moustie a pattern of honour and integrity; his gaiety made the young fond of his society; his mild and even temper, and kind disposition, gained him the love of all who knew him. His memory is venerated in the country where he lived.

MR. ELDRED.

On the 6th of January, 1818, died, at the very advanced age of one hundred years, Mr. Eldred, page to the king. His first master was George the Second, and though, from that time to the present, he had been incessant in his attentions at the palace, he had not been thought a fit person to be promoted. As his length of years makes him somewhat remarkable, his court biographer has taken pains to furnish us with some characteristics in his life and manners. He tells us, for instance, that he was a joker; but the only *bon mot* on record is, that he never got a hearty dinner but in the sprat-season, by which somewhat ambiguous declaration, the old gentleman meant to express a sarcastic contempt at the smallness of his board wages, which prevented the purchase of a plentiful meal, except of cheap articles. In his taste he was, we are happy to hear, decidedly English, for his favourite disb was a rump-steak; his penchant for which had, it appears, at least one useful effect, for it made him take long walks in order to procure the best in the markets. Again, he was much fonder of porter than spirits, and as a proof of his patriotism it is recorded, that when he did take the latter, his beverage was always *British* gin. He had also one more taste, which, though now somewhat declining in England, is of good old English origin, he was a continual smoker of tobacco. This is all that has reached us of this eminent person, except that he retained his health to the last, and carried a heavy mace before the Regent on the last occasion of his Royal Highness going to St. James's chapel.

Eccentric Biography.

LADY CATHCART.

LADY CATHCART (who died the 11th of August) was one of the four daughters of —— Malyn, Esq. of Southwark and Battersea, in Surrey. She was four times married, but never had any issue: First, to James Fleet, Esq. of the city of London, lord of the manor of Tewing (believed to be the son and heir to Sir John Fleet, lord mayor of London in 1693, and to have died April 30, 1733.) Secondly, to Captain Sabine, younger brother to General Joseph Sabine, of Quinohall, in Tewing aforesaid. Thirdly, in 1739, to the Right Hon. Charles, eighth Lord Cathcart, of the kingdom of Scotland, Commander in Chief of the Forces in the West Indies, who died at Dominica, Dec. 20, 1740: And fourthly, May 18, 1745, to Hugh Macguire, an officer in the service of the Queen of Hungary, for whom she bought a lieutenant-colonel's commission in the British service, and whom she also survived, but was not encouraged, by his treatment of her, to verify her resolution, which she inscribed as a poesy on her wedding ring:

" If I survive,
" I will have five."

Her avowed motives for these multifarious engagements were, the first to please her parents, the second for money, the third for title, and the fourth because " the devil owed her a grudge, and would punish her for her sins." In the last she met with her match. The Hibernian fortune-hunter wanted only her money. Soon after she married him, she found that she had made a grievous mistake, for that he was desperately in love, not with the widow, but with the "widow's jointured land;" and apprehending that he designed to carry her off, and to get the absolute power of all her property, she endeavoured to prepare for the worst, by having some of her jewels plaited in her hair, and others quilted in her petticoat, and constantly wearing them. The Colonel's mistress insinuated herself into his wife's confidence so well, that she learnt where her will was; and Macguire getting sight of it, insisted on her altering it in his favour, threatening to shoot her. Her apprehensions proved to be not without foundation; for one morning, when she and her *caro sposo* went out to take an airing from Tewing in the coach, she proposed to return, but he desired to go a little further. The coachman drove on; she remonstrated, " they should not be back by dinner-time." At length the Colonel told her, that " she might make herself easy, for they should not dine that day at Tewing; they were on the high road to Chester, and to Chester they should go." Her efforts and expostulations were vain. Upon her disappearing, her friends found out what had happened, and whither she was gone. They sent an attorney in pursuit of her, with a writ of *habeas corpus* or *ne exeat regno*, who overtook her at an inn at Chester. The Colonel was not deficient in expedients. The attorney found him, and demanded a sight of my lady, but he did not know her person. The Colonel told him, that he should see her immediately, and he would find that she was going with him to Ireland with her own free consent. The Colonel persuaded a woman, whom he had properly tutored, to personate her. The attorney asked the supposed captive, if she was going with Col. Macguire to Ireland of her own free will? "Perfectly so," said the woman. Astonished at such an answer, he begged her pardon, made her a low bow, and set out again for London. The Colonel thought that possibly Mr. Attorney might recover his senses, find how he had been deceived, and yet stop his progress; and in order to make all safe, sent two or three fellows after him, with directions to plunder him of all he had, and particularly his papers. They faithfully executed their commission; and when the Colonel had the writ in his possession, he knew that he was safe. He then took my lady over to Ireland, and kept her there, in a solitary place in the country, till his death, which, to her great satisfaction, happened in or about 1764. While she was in this state of confinement, she sent, by a crazy woman whom she could depend on, her jewels to a Mrs. Johnson, to be taken care of. After some time, Mrs. Johnson's husband failed, and she returned all the jewels safe to the owner, and in reward for her fidelity, my lady bought her son a commission. When the Colonel died, his widow returned in triumph to her house at Tewing, which he had let to Mr. Joseph Steele; but her ladyship at her return turned him out, and on his resisting her ejectment, she brought a suit against him at the assizes, which she attended in person, and cast him. She danced at Welwyn assembly, with the spirit of a young woman, when she was past 80.

ANTHONY.

The history of Anthony is one of the most extraordinary of any which have been preserved in the annals of madness. I have read the following account of him in a very curious manuscript. Something like it may be found in the works of Jacob Spon.

Anthony was born at Brieu in Lorrain; his parents were Catholics, and he was educated by the Jesuits at Pont à Mousson. The preacher Feri, at Metz, induced him to embrace the Protestant religion. On his return to Nanci, he was persecuted as a heretic; and if a friend had not exerted himself to save him, he would have been hanged. He sought an asylum at Sedan, where he was suspected to be a Roman Catholic, and with difficulty escaped assassination.

Seeing, that by some strange fatality, his life was in danger among Papists and Protestants, he went to Venice and turned Jew. He was thoroughly convinced, even to the last moments of his life, that the Jewish religion was alone authentic; for, he observed, if it was once the true religion, it must be always so. The Jews did not circumcise him, lest they should have some difference with the magistrates; but he was inwardly a Jew. He went to Geneva, were he concealed his faith, became a preacher, a president in a college, and at last what is called a minister.

The perpetual contention in his mind between the religion of Calvin, which he was under a necessity of preaching, and that of Moses, the religion he believed in, occasioned a long illness. He grew melancholy, and becoming quite mad, he often cried out in his paroxysms, that he was a Jew. The ministers came to visit him, and tried to restore him to his senses; but he continually said, that he adored none but the God of Israel; that it was not possible God should change; that he could never have given a law, and written it with his own hand, intending that it should be abolished. He spoke to the disadvantage of Christianity, and afterwards retracted what he had said, and even delivered up a confession of faith to escape punishment; but after having written it, the unfortunate persuasion of his heart would not suffer him to sign it. The council of the city assembled the preachers to consider what was to be done with the unfortunate Anthony. The smaller number of those preachers were of opinion, that he should be pitied, and that some attempts should be made to cure his disease, rather than punish him. The greater number determined he should be burnt, and he was burnt accordingly. This transaction is of the year 1632. A hundred years of reason and virtue are hardly sufficient to atone for such a determination

SUPERNATURAL WARNING.

The age of superstition is past, and there are few, except in the lower rank of society, who will now give credit to improbable tales, however well they may be persuaded of the respectability of their source, unless they have the means of being acquainted with their truth and authenticity. Superstition, however, has still her votaries; and in spite of the enlightened and civilized state of society, at the present time, there are few who will not feel some interest at the recital of a story, in which any thing connected with supernatural agency is introduced, and more particularly so when that story is in the most remote manner founded on fact. The tale I am about to narrate deviates but very slightly from one which has been well authenticated, and at the time when it was fresh upon our memory, was almost universally believed.

A young gentleman, by the name of C——, was, some years ago, residing with a clergyman in the north of England, for the purpose of completing his education. He was heir to a large fortune, particularly amiable, of a lively disposition, gay in his manners, and entirely free from any taint of superstitious belief. He was strong and healthy, and very unlikely, in any manner, to give credit to the workings of his imagination, or to believe in dreams. I mention this because there are some people whose weak state of health, or whose melancholy disposition, might make them more liable to be exposed to the impression produced by any sudden alarm, or any unusual agitation. One morning, however, at breakfast, his haggard and pale looks, and his thoughtful manner, attracted the attention of his friends, who were accustomed to see him animated and healthy, and upon their pressing him to account for this sudden alteration, he confessed that he had, during the night, had a dream, which had made so strong an impression upon him, that he could not drive it from his thoughts. He said, that he had seen a young woman enter his room softly, with a light in one hand, and a knife in the other; that she made several attempts to stab him, but upon his resistance, she had disappeared. He then described her person and dress, both of which, he said, were so deeply impressed upon his memory, that they never could be effaced.

His friends treated the matter lightly, and endeavoured to ridicule him for giving so much credit to a dream; and Mr. C—— himself, as if ashamed of his weakness, tried to banish it from his thoughts. Several months passed away, and he resumed his usual gaiety of manner; every thing appeared forgotten; and when his dream intruded itself upon his recollection, he laughed at himself for having ever thought of such a trifle.

Years had elapsed, and Mr. C—— having come into the possession of a large property, proposed to an intimate friend to visit the Continent. They left England together; and after having travelled through most of the countries in Europe, were returning home, in the autumn of ——. A long and tedious day's journey brought them very late one evening to a retired village on the borders of Hun_ary; there was but one inn in the place, and that, from its appearance, did not promise them very comfortable accommodation. However, they had no choice; it was too late to proceed, and they alighted. There was nothing remarkable in their reception, they were proceeding to the apartment which was allotted to them, when Mr. C—— suddenly stopped short, and uttered a scream of horror; his friend ran to his assistance, surprised at an emotion for which he could not account, but Mr. C—— having closed the door, immediately related the circumstances of the dream which had made so much impression upon him some years before, adding, at the same time, that the female servant who had lighted them up stairs, was the same person, both in face, appearance, and dress, who had appeared to him in his vision. The sudden and unexpected recollection of a circumstance which had been so long forgotten, could not fail to agitate Mr. C—— exceedingly; but as there was nothing suspicious in the manners of the inhabitants of the inn, the friends retired to rest, having first taken care to fasten the door, and place their pistols near them.

Overcome by the fatigue of travelling, they were soon both asleep; but Mr. C—— awaking suddenly, beheld, to his extreme horror, the same woman, standing over him, with a light in one hand, and a knife in the other, having the blade directed towards his breast, apparently about to strike. In his agony of horror, he uttered a scream, which awoke his friend, who springing from his bed, was just in time to catch her arm. * * * *

N. G

THE UNCONSCIOUS POET.

In the year 1758, John Wilson, a young man of slender education, was condemned to suffer death for a riot. The contrition he evinced for the crime he had committed, with his youth and good character, induced his Majesty, on the representation of several respectable persons, to extend the most amiable prerogative of the crown, the royal mercy. In a few hours after the reprieve reached the repentant convict, he poured forth the effusions of his grateful heart in the following verses, which he wrote with his own hand, though it was never known that he had ever attempted any thing of the kind before:

And live I yet, by Power divine?
. And have I still my course to run?
Again brought back in its decline,
   The shadow of my parting sun?

Wond'ring I ask, Is this the breast,
   Struggling so late with grief and pain?
The eyes which upward look'd for rest,
   And dropt their wearied lids again?

The recent horrors still appear:
   Oh, may they never cease to awe!
Still be the King of Terrors near,
   Whom late in all his pomp I saw

Torture and grief prepar'd his way,
   And pointed to a yawning tomb;
Darkness behind eclips'd the day,
   And check'd my forward hopes to come

But now the dreadful storm is o'er,
   Ended at last the doubtful strife!
And, living, I the hand adore,
   That gave me back again my life.

God of my life, what just return
   Can sinful dust and ashes give?
I only live my sins to mourn,
   To love my God, I only live.

To thee, benign and sacred Power,
   I consecrate my lengthen'd days;
While, mark'd with blessings, ev'ry hour
   Shall speak thy co-extended praise.

Varieties.

SOUND.

Every observer knows that when a gun is fired at a considerable distance from him, he perceives the flash a certain time before he hears the report; and the same thing is true with respect to the stroke of a hammer, or of a hatchet, the fall of a stone, or, in short, any visible action which produces a sound or sounds. In general, sound travels through the air at the rate of 1142 feet in a second, or about thirteen miles in a minute. This is the case with all kinds of sounds, the softest whisper flying as fast as the loudest thunder. Sound, like light, after it has been reflected from several places, may be collected into one point as a focus, where it will be more audible than in any other part.

SINGULAR ECHO.

The most remarkable echo recorded, is at the palace of a nobleman, within two miles of Milan, in Italy. The building is of some length in front, and has two wings jetting forward; so that it wants only one side of an oblong figure. About one hundred paces before the mansion, a small brook glides gently; and over this brook is a bridge forming a communication between the mansion and the garden. A pistol having been fired at this spot, fifty-six reiterations of the report were heard. The first twenty were distinct; but in proportion as the sound died away, and was answered at a greater distance, the repetitions were so doubled that they could scarcely be counted, the principal sound appearing to be saluted in its passage by reports on either side at the same time. A pistol of a larger caliber having been afterwards discharged, and consequently with a louder report, sixty distinct reiterations were counted.

THE ODD FAMILY.

In the reign of William the Third, there lived in Ipswich, in Suffolk, a family, which, from the number of peculiarities belonging to it, was distinguished by the name of the *Odd Family*. Every event remarkably good or bad happened to this family on an odd day of the month, and every one of them had something odd in his or her person, manner, and behaviour; the very letters in their christian names always happened to be an odd number. The husband's name was Peter, and the wife's Rabah; they had seven children, all boys, viz: Solomon, Roger, James, Matthew, Jonas, David, and Ezekiel. The husband had but one leg, his wife but one arm. Solomon was born blind of the left eye, and Roger lost his right eye by accident; James had his left ear pulled off by a boy in a quarrel, and Matthew was born with only three fingers on his right hand; Jonas had a stump foot, and David was humpbacked; all these, except David, were remarkably short, while Ezekiel was six feet two inches high at the age of nineteen; the stump-footed Jonas and the humpbacked David got wives of fortune; but no girl would listen to the addresses of the rest. The husband's hair was as black as jet, and the wife's remarkably white, yet every one of the children's was red. The husband had the peculiar misfortune of falling into a deep saw-pit, where he was starved to death, in the year 1701; and his wife, refusing all kind of sustenance, died in five days after him. In the year 1703, Ezekiel enlisted as a grenadier, and although he was afterwards wounded in twenty-three places, he recovered. Roger, James, Matthew, Jonas, and David, died at different places on the same day in 1713, and Solomon and Ezekiel were drowned together in crossing the Thames, in the year 1723.

PITCH LAKE OF TRINIDAD.

Near Point la Braye, Tar Point, the name assigned to it on account of its characteristic feature, in the island of Trinidad, is a lake which at the first view appears to be an expanse of still water, but which, on a nearer approach, is found to be an extensive plain of mineral pitch, with frequent crevices and chasms filled with water. On its being visited in the autumnal season, the singularity of the scene was so great, that it required some time for the spectators to recover themselves from their surprise, so as to examine it minutely. The surface of the lake was of an ash colour, and not polished or smooth, so as to be slippery, but of such a consistence as to bear any weight. It was not adhesive, although it received in part the impression of the foot, and could be trodden without any tremulous motion, several head of cattle browsing on it in perfect security. In the summer season, however, the surface is much more yielding, and in a state approaching to fluidity; as is evidenced by pieces of wood and other substances, recently thrown in, having been found enveloped in it. Even large branches of trees, which were a foot above the level, had, in some way, become enveloped in the bituminous matter. The interstices, or chasms, are very numerous, ramifying and joining in every direction; and being filled with water in the wet season, present the only obstacle to walking over the surface. These cavities are in general deep in proportion to their width, and many of them unfathomable: the water they contain is uncontaminated by the pitch, and is the abode of a variety of fishes. The arrangement of the chasms is very singular, the sides invariably shelving from the surface, so as nearly to meet at the bottom, and then bulging out towards each other with a considerable degree of convexity. Several of them have been known to close up entirely, without leaving any mark or seam.

The pitch lake of Trinidad contains many islets covered with grass and shrubs, which are the haunts of birds of the most exquisite plumage. Its precise extent cannot, any more than its depth, be readily ascertained, the line between it and the neighbouring soil not being well defined; but its main body may be estimated at three miles in circumference. It is bounded on the north and west sides by the sea, on the south by a rocky eminence, and on the east by the usual argillaceous soil of the country.

ANIMAL FLOWER.

The inhabitants of St. Lucie have lately discovered a most singular plant. In a cavern of that isle, near the sea, is a large basin, from twelve to fifteen feet deep, the water of which is very brackish, and the bottom composed of rocks. From these, at all times proceed certain substances, which present, at first sight, beautiful flowers, of a bright shining colour, and pretty nearly resembling our marigolds, only that their tint is more lively. These seeming flowers, on the approach of a hand or instrument retire, like a snail, out of sight. On examining their substance closely, there appear, in the middle of the disk, four brown filaments, resembling spiders' legs, which move round a kind of petals with a pretty brisk and spontaneous motion. These legs have pincers to seize their prey; and, upon seizing it, the yellow petals immediately close, so that it cannot escape. Under this exterior of a flower is a brown stalk, of the bigness of a raven's quill, and which appears to be the body of some animal. It is probable that this strange creature lives on the spawn of fish, and the marine insects thrown by the sea into the basin.

A GOOD SHOT.

"It is now," said Von Wyk, "more than two years since, in the very place where I stand, I ventured to take one of the most daring shots that ever was hazarded. My wife was sitting within the house near the door, the children were playing about her, and I was without, busied in doing something to a waggon, when suddenly, though it was mid-day, an enormous lion appeared, came up, and laid himself quietly down in the shade, upon the very threshold of the door! My wife, either frozen with fear or aware of the danger attending any attempt to fly, remained motionless in her place, while the children took refuge in her lap. The cry they uttered attracted my attention, and I hastened towards the door; but my astonishment may well be conceived, when I found the entrance to it barred in such a way.—Although the animal had not seen me, unarmed as I was, escape seemed impossible; yet I glided gently, scarcely knowing what I meant to do, to the side of the house, up to the window of my chamber, where I knew my loaded gun was standing. By a most happy chance, I had set it in the corner close by the window, so that I could reach it with my hand; for, the opening was too small to admit of my having got in; and still more fortunately, the door of the room was open, so that I could see the whole danger of the scene. The lion was beginning to move, perhaps with the intention of making a spring. There was no longer any time to think: I called softly to the mother not to be alarmed, and, invoking the name of the Lord, fired my piece.—The ball passed directly over the hair of my boy's head, and lodged in the forehead of the lion immediately above his eyes, which shot forth, as it were, sparks of fire, and stretched him on the ground, so that he never stirred more."—*Lichtenstein's Travels in South Africa.*

The Scrap Book.

SINGULAR FUNERAL.

Mr. G. Scoray died at Minsteed in 1811, aged eighty-three years. At his wedding, about fifty-two years before, he preserved three candles, one of which he burnt at the funeral of his wife, and another at that of a relation; and he ordered that the third should be burnt when his own funeral took place; and that some mead, preserved also at the marriage feast, with all the cider and liquors in the house, should then be drank. His friends followed his remains to Minsteed church, witnessed the funeral rites, and heard an excellent sermon; after which they returned to his house, burnt the candle, and drank out all the liquor.

SINGULAR RECOGNITION.

A few weeks ago, (says the daily papers,) two gentlemen, who were travelling in different directions, stopped at the Bell Inn, Hounslow, when the host, Mr. Strange, while attending them and other guests, remarked a great similarity of countenance between these strangers, which produced a conversation, in which they recognised each other as brothers. A gentleman present, many years resident in that town, named Stables, who is unfortunately blind, appeared deeply interested in the explanation, and claimed the same affinity. The recognition was a scene difficult to describe. The youngest brother is in his fiftieth year, and their last meeting was in his infancy.

PERPETUAL FIRE.

In the peninsula of Abeheron, in the province of Schirwan, formerly belonging to Persia, but now to Russia, there is found a perpetual, or as it is there called, an eternal fire. It rises or has risen from time immemorial from an irregular orifice of about twelve feet in depth, and one hundred and twenty feet in width, with a constant flame. The flame rises to the height of from six to eight feet, is unattended with smoke, and yields no smell. The finest turf grows about the borders, and at the distance of two toises are two springs of water.

Published by J. LIMBIRD, 355, Strand, (East End of Exeter 'Change); and sold by all Newsmen and Booksellers. Printed by A. APPLEGATH, Stamford-street.

THE CABINET OF CURIOSITIES,
OR
Wonders of the World Displayed.

A world of wonders where creation seems
No more the works of Nature but her dreams.—MONTGOMERY.

No. IX.] PRICE TWOPENCE.

GUNPOWDER PLOT CONSPIRATORS.

THERE is not, we are well assured, one of our readers that is unacquainted with Guy Fawkes and the Gunpowder Plot. Indeed no historical event is perhaps better known, nor can the remembrance of it cease as long as schoolboys get a holiday by making bonfires, firing pop-guns, or burning "Old Guy" on the 5th of November.

Well however as the fact is known, the gunpowder treason is involved in much obscurity; and it is really difficult to believe either, that because the Jesuits were not sufficiently indulged by James the First, that they should form the plan of destroying him, his parliament, and family at once, or that men could be found willing to undertake the hellish project: and yet, if we are to believe the concurring testimony of historians, the evidence of facts, and the memoirs of the individuals, such was really the case.

The plot appears to have been first concerted between Catesby and Piercy, or rather perhaps Catesby first communicated it to Piercy, and told him that the plan was to get barrels of gunpowder placed under the Parliament House, which were to be fired on the first day of sitting, when the king and the royal family were to be present. Several other persons were enlisted in the plot, and Fawkes, an officer in the Spanish service, was sent for to Flanders. A house was hired next to the Parliament House, towards the end of the year 1604; a hole was cut through the wall, though three feet thick; and at last even the vault itself under the House of Parliament was hired. Several barrels of gunpowder and faggots of wood were introduced, and all was ready; when, fortunately for humanity, an event, which would have stamped the British annals with a crime unparalleled, was averted.

Ten days before the meeting of Parliament, Lord Monteagle, a Catholic, received a letter, warning him not to go to Parliament that day, in order to avoid a terrible calamity. Lord Monteagle took the letter to Lord Salisbury, the Secretary of State. The day before the meeting of Parliament the vaults were searched, the gunpowder found, and Fawkes ready to carry the dreadful project into effect. He was seized and committed to the Tower.

The eight principal conspirators, whose portraits we have prefixed to this article, were Thomas Bates, Robert Winter, Christopher Wright, John Wright, Thomas Piercy, Guido Fawkes, Robert Catesby, and Thomas Winter. Of these, Catesby and Piercy, who fled into Staffordshire, were killed with one shot, in resisting an attempt to arrest them. Guy Fawkes was executed in 1606, in company with Thomas Winter. John Wright was killed in the same struggle as Catesby and Piercy; and Thomas Bates was executed. They were all men of terrible daring, and would not have shrunk from their purpose, appalling as it was.

THE ADVENTURES OF A CAT.

Two elderly ladies, who for many years resided in Leeds, had a favourite cat, which was brought up by them from a kitten. One of the ladies dying in September last, the other shortly afterwards shut up her house at Leeds, and came to reside at Cowley, in Ecclesfield, about six miles from this town. She brought her cat with her in a small hamper, which was placed under the seat of the carriage. The cat remained at her new residence very quietly for nearly two months, when a servant one day beat her for some fault. On this affront she ran away, and in a few days afterwards was seen at Leeds by a neighbour, sitting and watching at the kitchen-door of the house lately occupied by her mistress. There she remained three days without intermission. On the evening of the third day she came into the neighbour's house, who left her in the kitchen all night. There the servant found her the following morning, but on opening the kitchen door she ran out, and in a few days afterwards returned to her mistress's habitation in a most deplorable state, being almost reduced to a skeleton, and so feeble for several days that she could scarcely take any food. One eye appeared much inflamed, as if from cold, and since then she has utterly lost the sight of it. She is now living, and evinces her attachment to her mistress by sitting daily at her side. The cat was absent about ten days. The distance from Cowley to Leeds, through Barnsley and Wakefield, is 28 miles.—*Sheffield Iris.*

A MINE OF FROGS.

The following account of a Mine of Frogs is related by Dr. Williams, of the state of Vermont, in America :—

"There are several accounts in natural history of toads being found in the hearts of trees, and in solid rocks, wholly enclosed and shut up from the air and all appearance of food, and being taken alive out of such situations. In the Memoirs of the Academy of Sciences there is an account, that, in the year 1731, a toad was found in the heart of an old oak, near Nantz, without any visible entrance to its habitation. From the size of the tree, it was concluded, that the toad must have been confined in that situation, at least eighty or a hundred years. We have several instances in Vermont, equally extraordinary. At Windsor, a town joining to Connecticut river, in September 1790, a living frog was dug up at the depth of nine feet from the surface of the earth. Stephen Jacobs, Esq. from whom I have this account, informs me, that the place where this frog was found, was about half a mile from the river, on the interval lands, which are annually overflowed by its waters. At Castleton, in the year 1779, the inhabitants were engaged in building a fort near the centre of the town. Digging into the earth five or six feet below the surface, they found many frogs, apparently inactive, and supposed to be dead. Being exposed to the air, animation soon appeared, and they were found to be alive and healthy. I have this account from General Clarke and a Mr. Moulton, who were present when these frogs were dug up. Upon viewing the spot, it did not appear to me that it had ever been overflowed with water, but it abounded with springs. A more remarkable instance was at Burlington, upon Onion river. In the year 1788, Samuel Lane, Esq. was digging a well near his house. At the depth of twenty-five or thirty feet from the surface of the earth, the labourers threw out with their shovels something which they suspected to be ground-nuts, or stones covered with earth. Upon examining these appearances, they were found to be frogs, to which the earth every where adhered. The examination was then made of the earth, in the well where they were digging; a large number of frogs were found covered with the earth, and so numerous that several of them were cut in pieces by the spades of the workmen. Being exposed to the air, they soon became active; but, unable to endure the direct rays of the sun the most of them perished. This account is from Mr. Lane, and Mr. Lawrence, one of the workmen, who were both present when the frogs were dug up. From the depth of earth with which these frogs were covered, it cannot be doubted but that they must have been covered over in the earth for many years, or rather centuries. The appearances denote that the place from whence these frogs were taken, was once the bottom of a channel or lake, formed by the waters of Onion river. In digging the same well, at the depth of forty-one feet and a half from the surface, the workmen found the body of a tree eighteen or twenty inches in diameter, partly rotten, but the biggest part sound. The probability is, that both the tree and the frogs were once at the bottom of the channel of a river, or lake ; that the waters of Onion river, constantly bringing down large quantities of earth, gradually raised the bottom; that by the constant increase of earth and water, the water was forced over its bounds, forming for itself a new channel or passage in its descent into Lake Champlain. How vigorous and permanent must the principle of life be in this animal! Frogs placed in a situation in which they were perpetually supplied with moisture, and all waste and perspiration from the body prevented, preserve the powers of life from age to age! Centuries must have passed since they began to live in such a situation; and had that situation continued, nothing appears but that they would have lived for many centuries yet to come.

BOILING MUD LAKE OF JAVA.

A PARTY of gentlemen having received an extraordinary account of a natural phenomenon in the plains of Grobogna, fifty paals north-east of Solo, they set off from Solo the 25th of September, 1814, to examine it. On approaching the dass or village of Kuhoo, they saw between the tops of two trees in a plain, an appearance like the surf breaking over rocks, with a strong spray falling to leeward. Alighting, they went to the " Bluddugs," as the Javanese call them. They are situated in the village of Kuhoo, and by Europeans are called by that name. "We found them," says the narrator, "to be an elevated plain of mud about two miles in circumference, in the centre of which immense bodies of soft mud were thrown up to the height of ten or fifteen feet, in the form of large bubbles, which bursting, emitted great volumes of dense white smoke. These large bubbles, of which there were two, continued throwing up and bursting seven or eight times in a minute; at times they threw up two or three tons of mud. The party got to leeward of the smoke, and found it to stink like the washings of a gun barrel. As the bubbles burst, they threw the mud out from the centre, with a pretty loud noise, occasioned by the falling of the mud on that which surrounded it, and of which the plain is composed. It was difficult and dangerous to approach the large bubbles, as the ground was all a quagmire, except where the surface of the mud had become hardened by the sun; upon this, we approached cautiously to within fifty yards of one of the largest bubbles, or mud-pudding, as it might properly be called, for it was of the consistency of custard-pudding, and was about a hundred yards in diameter: here and there, where the foot accidentally rested on a spot not sufficiently hardened to bear, it sunk, to the no small distress of the walker.

" We also got close to a small bubble, (the plain was full of them, of different sizes,) and observed it attentively for some time. It appeared to heave and swell, and, when the internal air had raised it to some height, it burst, and the mud fell down in concentric circles; in which state it remained quiet until a sufficient quantity of air again formed internally to raise and burst another bubble, and this continued at intervals of from about half-a minute to two minutes.

" From various other parts of the pudding round the large bubbles, there were occasionally small quantities of sand shot up like rockets to the height of twenty or thirty feet, unaccompanied by smoke: this was in parts where the mud was of too stiff a consistency to rise in bubbles. The mud, at all the places we came near, was cold.

"The water which drains from the mud is collected by the Javanese, and, being exposed in the hollows of split bamboos to the rays of the sun, deposits crystals of salt. The salt thus made is reserved exclusively for the use of the Emperor of Solo; in dry weather it yields thirty dudgins of one hundred catties each, every month, but, in wet or cloudy weather, less.

"Next morning we rode two and a half paals to a place in a forest called Ram am, to view a salt lake, a mud hillock, and various boiling pools.

"The lake was about half a mile in circumference, of a dirty looking water, boiling up all over in gurgling eddies, but more particularly in the centre, which appeared like a strong spring. The water was quite cold, and tasted bitter, salt, and sour, and had an offensive smell.

"About thirty yards from the lake stood the mud-hillock, which was about fifteen feet high from the level of the earth. The diameter of its base was about twenty-five yards, and its top about eight feet, and in form an exact cone. The top is open, and the interior keeps constantly boiling and heaving up like the bluddugs. The hillock is entirely formed of mud which has flowed out of the top. Every rise of the mud was accompanied by a rumbling noise from the bottom of the hillock, which was distinctly heard for some seconds before the bubble burst; the outside of the hillock was quite firm. We stood on the edge of the opening and sounded it, and found it to be eleven fathoms deep. The mud was more liquid at the bluddugs, and no smoke was emitted either from the lake, hillock, or pools.

"Close to the foot of the hillock was a small pool of the same water as the lake, which appeared exactly like a pot of water boiling violently; it was shallow, except in the centre, into which we thrust a stick twelve feet long, but found no bottom. The hole not being perpendicular, we could not sound it without a line.

"About two hundred yards from the lake were two very large pools or springs, eight or twelve feet in diameter; they were like the small pool, but boiled more violently and stunk excessively. We could not sound them for the same reason which prevented our sounding the small pool.

"We heard the boiling thirty yards before we came to the pools, resembling the noise of a waterfall. These pools did not overflow—of course the bubbling was occasioned by the rising of air alone. The water of the bluddugs and of the lake is used medicinally by the Javanese."

THE CATARACT OF PARANA.

THE rivers Yguazu, Paragua, and Uruguay, are larger than the largest rivers in Europe; D'Azara, thinks that the Parana, after its junction with the Paragua, is equal to a hundred of the greatest rivers in Europe; and that when, after receiving the waters of the Uruguay, it assumes the name of La Plata, it may be considered as one of the greatest rivers in the world, and perhaps equal to those of Europe united. The Parana includes an innumerable multitude of isles, of which some are very large. Notwithstanding the enormous volume of its waters, the Parana is not navigable through its whole extent, as it is intersected by shoals and cataracts. At one of these cataracts, which the author called de Guayra, the Parana, which is 4,200 yards wide, is suddenly contracted into a channel of sixty yards, in which the whole mass of waters is precipitated with indescribable fury. It does not fall perpendicularly, but in an inclined plane of fifty degrees. The vapours which rise when the water dashes against the interior sides of the rock, is seen at the distance of several leagues in the form of columns in the air; and nearer, they form, when the sun shines, different rainbows of the most vivid colours. The noise is heard at the distance of six leagues; and the rocks in the vicinity seem to experience the concussion of an earthquake.

In order to obtain a view of the cataract it is necessary to make a journey of thirty leagues through a desert from the town of Curuguaty, to the river Gatemy. On reaching this spot, we look out for one or two large trees, each of which is sufficient for the conveyance of travellers with their provisions and baggage. It is necessary to leave on shore a party of men well armed, in order to guard the horses, as this tract abounds with wild Indians, who give no quarter. Those who intend to visit the cataract, pass thirty leagues up the Gatemy, taking every precaution against the Indians, who are concealed in the woods on the banks of the river. Travellers are sometimes obliged to drag their canoes over numerous shoals which impede the navigation; and sometimes even to carry them on their shoulders. At last they reach the Parana, when they are only three leagues distant from the cataract, which they may travel either by water or on foot, along the banks, by skirting a wood, where we do not meet with a single bird, either great or small, but only occasionally with some *yagareté*, a wild beast of more tremendous ferocity than tigers or lions. From the bank above we may measure the cataract with ease, and even survey the inferior part by penetrating the wood. But the rain is so constant in the environs, that it is necessary to strip to the skin in order to approach it.

The Book of Dwarfs.

We are men my liege.
Ay, in the catalogue ye go for men;
As hounds and greyhounds, mungrels,
    spaniels, curs,
Showghes, water-rugs, and demi-wolves
    are cleped,
All by the name of dogs.—SHAKSPEARE.

CHAPTER I.

THE most ancient dwarfs of which mention is made are the pigmies; but these people so famous for their battles with the storks, may have never existed; at least, in searching after all the parts where they have been placed, no vestige is found of them; whence it is very probable that this pretended nation is indebted for its origin only to some foreign name, ill interpreted by the Greeks, as we have several examples of such mistakes. It is, however, certain that Homer is the first who spoke of them, comparing in his Iliad, the Trojans attacking the Greeks in the absence of Achilles, to storks falling impetuously on the pigmies. But Homer wanted a comparison that might make an agreeable picture, and not to discuss a point of history. It would be laying too great a restraint on the imagination of a poet, to subject him to historical exactness, when we only require from him fire and vivacity. Let us therefore give up to him the nation of the pigmies, and examine what more serious authors have said of Dwarfs. Still we shall here find enough of the fabulous: witness the dwarf cited by Nicephorus, which was seen at the court of Constantine, and was not bigger than a partridge; the historian on this occasion might have had a somewhat poetical imagination. The Romans, especially under the first emperors, placed dwarfs among the objects of their luxury and ostentation. Augustus had one whose statue it is pretended he had ordered to be made, and he so little spared the expense, that the apples of the eyes were represented by precious stones; this dwarf, as Suetonius relates, was less than two feet in height, weighed seventeen pounds, and had a very strong voice. This statue, formerly in the cabinet of the king of France, showed that Augustus was not so nice in this affair, as the statue represented a ricketty subject, ill-proportioned, and with nothing of that air, of a little adolescent, which dwarfs usually have. He might be supposed to be about thirty years old.

Tiberius admitted a dwarf to his table, and indulged him in the boldest questions, which the dwarf taking advantage of, hastened the punishment of a state criminal. Mark Antony had one below two feet, whom by way of irony he had called Sisyphus. Domitian had assembled a number of dwarfs that he formed into a little troop of gladiators.

Nor only the emperors entertained dwarfs, but the princesses and even considerable ladies kept some. History has preserved to us the name of Conopas, the dwarf of the Princess Julia, daughter of Augustus, who was two feet nine inches high: and this taste remained till the reign of Alexander Severus; but that prince having expelled the male and female dwarfs from his court, the mode of them soon ceased throughout the empire.

The passion which the Romans then had for these little men, had made them an object of commerce; and interest, an occasion of cruelty. The dealer, in order to have a greater number of dwarfs to sell, hit upon the project of squeezing up children in boxes and bandages contrived with art. It is evident that such of these children as could survive this cruel torture, were in no respect dwarfs, but deformed and maimed men.

The desire of having dwarfs did not seem afterwards to be so considerable. Johnson, however, relates, that the first wife of Joachim Frederic, Elector of Brandenberg, seemed to improve on the Roman ladies; having assembled a number of dwarfs of both sexes, in order to marry them with a view of multiplying their species, but her attempt was fruitless, and none of them left issue. Hoffman and Peter Messic cite Catherine of Medicis as having had the same taste, but with as little success, which need excite no surprise.

Dwarfs are also appendages to the dignity of the Grand Seignor, and when deaf and dumb are deemed invaluable. Domenichino has placed dwarfs in the suite of the Emperor Otho, Raphael has done the same in a series of paintings of the history of Constantine, and Velasquez has painted some of the Spanish court. Dwarfs formed a part of the revenue of William Duke of Normandy, and at that time were the usual pages of every lord. They were employed to hold the bridle of the King's horses in grand processions.

Russia and Poland have been long celebrated for the great number and diminutive size of their dwarfs. We have read of some of them who were cradled in a lady's slipper, and held up to be christened in a soup-plate. Such miniatures of our kind are sometimes called *lusus naturæ*, or sports of nature; but nothing can argue more strongly a want of refinement, or positive barbarism, than to make them compose the sports of man. Peter the Great, who travelled into different parts of Europe to learn the trade of a carpenter, whatever were his other great qualities, did not show himself much above a carpenter in the vulgar pleasure which he received from assembling and tormenting these diminutive creatures; and thus displaying the defects and weakness of our nature. It is no less barbarous and unfeeling to expose to ridicule an assemblage of dwarfs, than an assemblage of hunchbacks or of cripples. Having expressed our disapprobation of a species of amusement which could not now find a place in the refined court of St. Petersburgh, we lay before our readers a curious passage, extracted from the memoirs of a Scotch gentleman, called Bruce, giving an account of a dwarf wedding which he witnessed at Moscow, and which delighted and enchanted the courtiers of Czar Peter, a little more than a century ago:—

" The Princess Natalia, only sister to the Czar by the same mother, ordered preparations to be made for a grand wedding for two of her dwarfs who were to be married; on which occasion several small coaches were made, and little Shetland horses provided to draw them; and all the dwarfs in the kingdom were summoned to celebrate the nuptials, to the number of ninety-three. They went in grand procession through all the streets of Moscow. Before them went a large open waggon drawn by six horses, with kettle-drums, trumpets, French horns, and hautboys. Then followed the Marshal and his attendants, two and two, on horseback. Then the bridegroom and bride in a coach and six, attended by their brideman and maid, who sat before them in the coach. They were followed by fifteen small coaches, each drawn by six Shetland horses, and each containing four dwarfs. It was somewhat surprising to see such a number of little creatures in one company together; especially as they were furnished with an equipage conformable to their stature. Two troops of dragoons attended the procession to keep off the mob, and many persons of fashion were invited to the wedding, who attended in their coaches to the church where the small couple were married. From thence the procession returned in order to the Princess's palace, where a grand entertainment was prepared for the company. Two long tables were covered on each side of a long hall where the company of dwarfs dined together. The Princess, with her two nieces, Princesses Ann and Elizabeth, the Czar's daughters, were at the trouble themselves to see them all seated and well attended, before they sat down to their own table. At night, the Princesses, attended by the nobility, conducted the married couple to bed in grand state. After that ceremony the dwarf company had a large room allotted them to make merry among themselves; the entertainment concluded with a ball, which lasted till day-light. The company which attended the Princesses on this occasion was so numerous that they filled several rooms."

What improvement has taken place in the age since 1713.—The present Emperor's accomplished sister, the late Queen of Wirtemberg, would no more have thought of arranging and superintending a dwarf wedding, than of exhibiting punch's puppetshow in her drawing-room.

Hoaxes and Impostures.
No. VIII.

EDWARDS, THE WELCH CONJURER.

At the Flintshire Great Sessions in April, 1818, a trial came on which exhibited a singular instance of superstition and imposture. The prosecution was Edward Pierce against John Edwards, for obtaining money under false pretences.

The nature of the case will be best understood from the evidence.

Edward Pierce examined by Mr. Temple.—I live at Llandyrnog, in the county of Denbigh. I saw John Edwards at his own house, called Berth-ddu, in the parish of Northop, in the month of April, 1815. I understood I had been put in Fynnon Elian; I mean my name had been put in. I thought something was the matter with me. I saw every thing going cross. I was informed that John Edwards pulled people out of the well; I went to him in order to be pulled out. I told him something was the matter with me. He immediately observed my name was put in Fynnon Elian. I trembled! He said it was not then a fit time to take my name out, but desired me to wait till the next full moon, when he would take me out. He requested me in the interim to read the following Psalms 6, 7, 20, 68, 109, and 118; afterwards he would let me know when to go to Fynnon Elian, as there were other people to go with us—it was absolutely necessary to go there. I went to his house in May following, to inquire about the proper time to go to the well. He said he would go on the following Sunday, and desired me to meet him at St. Asaph. We met there at seven o'clock on the Sunday evening; it was then full moon. Edwards fixed the day. When I saw him at St. Asaph, he desired me to go on one side with him to pay the money, which he said was to be given to the woman of the well, for taking my name out; he said, if I paid him, my name would be taken out; I was to pay 15s.; but I told him I had only 14s. 6d. by me, which he accepted. He then engaged to take my name out, and pay the money to the woman of the well. He told me, that in consequence of having my name taken out, I should have my health and authority as I wished to have; I am sure he told me so; I paid the money in order that my name might be taken out. John Edwards, myself, and two other men on the same business, then started for the well; we arrived there from 12 to half-past 12 on Sunday night; I never saw the well before; Edwards called me to the well, and showed it me; we went to a stile near the well; he bid us three go over and remain there till he fetched the key from the house where the woman of the well lived. He told me he would then pay the woman; he did not say where the house was; the well was inside a fence; I did not see a key; there was no door on it to my knowledge. Edwards was absent about 10 minutes; when he returned, he desired one of the men to follow him; one of the strangers went with him; they were absent about a quarter of an hour or 20 minutes; when the man returned, I went in his stead. I found Edwards at the well; he bid me stand on one side of the well, and say the Lord's Prayer; I did so; he then emptied the well with a small wooden cup; when emptying it, he prayed to Father, Son, and Holy Ghost; the well then filled again. He then put some water into the cup, and desired me to drink some of it, and throw the remainder over my head; he said I must do so three times; I complied: after this, Edwards said, now we will look for your name. He put his hand a little above near where the water goes into the well; he found something immediately, and said, "Here is something," which he gave to me. He desired me to put my hand in; I did so, but could find nothing. What he gave me was a piece of slate, a cork, a piece of sheet-lead, rolled up and tied together with a wire. I did not open it till I got home; it was in my possession till then.

When I opened the sheet-lead, I found a piece of parchment inside, with the letters E. P. upon it; there were also some crosses. It was too dark to read at the well. When Edwards gave it me, he said he thought it was my name, and said every thing would be right and go on well with me, and that I should come on better than usual. I gave the slate, &c. to Mr. Edward Thelwell; I had them in my possession till then.

After some other witnesses were examined, Mr. Manley addressed the Jury on behalf of the defendant, but called no witnesses.

The Chief Justice then proceeded to sum up the evidence, and animadverted much on the enormity of the offence.

The Jury, after a few minutes' deliberation, found the defendant Guilty.—He was then remanded, and ordered to be brought up for judgment the following day; when the court intimated, that the offence of which he had been convicted subjected him to transportation; but in consideration of its being the first offence, and of his imprisonment since last Great Session, sentenced him to be confined in the county gaol for twelve calendar months.

STONE-EATER.

At Avignon, in 1760, a Stone-Eater was exhibited, he not only swallowed flints of an inch and a half long, a full inch broad and half an inch thick; but stones, such as marbles and pebbles, which he could reduce to powder he made up in paste, and this was to him a most agreeable and wholesome food. On examination, his gullet was found to be very large, his teeth exceeding strong, his saliva very corrosive, and his stomach lower than ordinary, which was imputed to the number of flints he swallowed, averaging one day with another, four and twenty a day. His keeper stated that three years before this he was found on a northern island by the crew of a Dutch ship. He would eat raw flesh with stones, but he could not be prevailed upon to swallow bread. He would drink water, wine, and brandy, which last liquor gave him great pleasure. He slept sitting on the ground with one knee, over the other, and his chin resting on his right knee, for at least twelve hours a day, and he smoked almost all the time that he was not either asleep or eating. The flints he swallowed were, when voided, somewhat corroded and diminished in weight, and the rest of his excrements resembled mortar. Some physicians contrived to get him bled, and found that his blood had little or no serum, and in two hours became as fragile as coral. He could pronounce only a few words; had been taught to make the sign of the cross, showed great respect to ecclesiastics, and was baptized in the church of St. Come, at Paris.

MURDER IN AMERICA.

A MAN who resided near the Drylands, in New York, having to pay a sum of 800*l.* called on a neighbour, who kept a public-house, and mentioned the circumstance, observing, that he had the whole amount at home, except 15*l.* which he wished to borrow. The landlord agreed to lend him the above sum, but stated that he must wait till the next day, as he should go out to collect some debts, when, if he would call, he should have what he wanted. He accordingly went at the appointed time, and having waited the whole evening, was prevailed on by the landlord's wife to stay all night, her husband not having come home, on whose return she promised to call him; he accordingly retired to bed, but was soon disturbed by terrifying dreams, on which he awoke a pedlar, who had taken up his residence in the same room for the night, and informed him that he had dreamed his house was on fire, and his wife and children enveloped in the flames. The pedlar endeavoured to pacify him, but without effect, as he determined on going home immediately; finding he could not prevail on him to return to his bed, and feeling interest in the dream, he agreed to accompany him, taking with him a pair of pistols well loaded. On approaching the house, they were alarmed (the night being dark) by observing a bright light in the lower apartment, and on approaching the window, they beheld three men with blackened faces, counting out money on the table. Each of the spectators singled out his man, and shot two of the plunderers dead; the third was met at the door, endeavouring to escape, but, being overcome with conscious guilt, he made very little resistance, and soon shared the fate of his companions. The agitated husband then went into his bed-room, where he found his wife and three young children weltering in their blood, having apparently been murdered in their sleep. On washing the faces of the robbers, they proved to be near neighbours, who were

Anecdotes of Longevity.

THE HIGHLAND PATRIARCH.

IN the course of the summer of 1822, a gentleman travelling in the north of Scotland, was told at the manse of Lethnot of a Highlander, living in that parish, who had reached the unusual age of 108, and still preserved the faculties of his mind unimpaired.—Curiosity induced him to visit the old man's cottage. He found him, as had been represented, still vigorous of mind, though greatly enfeebled in body. He had been out, he said, *in the Forty-five*; a phrase by which the survivors of that unhappy period express their having taken arms in behalf of the Pretender. Where had he fought? " I stuck to the Prince," said Patrick Grant, for that is the old man's name, " frae first to last; I was wi' him in England, and I was wi' him on the bluidy field o' Culloden. Oh! waefu', waefu' day!" He proceeded, at his visitor's request, to relate the particulars of the battle very nearly as they are represented in the histories of that period, and brought out the " braid sword" which he had used on the occasion, and, waving it over his head, shewed how " *other* fields were won." On inquiring into his circumstances his visitor was sorry to learn that he depended entirely for support on the charity of his neighbours, and was destitute of all the comforts which declining age require. " But for myself," said Patrick, " I ha'e nae meikle now to care for; it 'ill no be lang now till I'm below the eird. But there's my puir lassie there," pointing to a silent old woman, sitting by the inglecheek, " I am unco fear'd they'll forget her whan auld Patrick's dead and gane."—" Never fear, Patrick," said the worthy clergyman of the parish, who accompanied the stranger, " while I am minister of Lethnot she shall never want."

On leaving the cottage, the stranger suggested to Mr. S——, the clergyman, that were a representation of the old man's patriarchial age and destitute situation, laid before the king, there was every thing to hope from his majesty's generosity, never more strongly shewn than it has been to many followers of the exiled house. Mr. S—— approved of the idea, and, since the stranger's return to the metropolis, the Rev. gentleman forwarded to him the petition to his majesty, of which the subjoined is a copy. It was immediately submitted to the king, through the medium of Sir Benjamin Bloomfield, Bart. and an answer as promptly returned, stating that his majesty had been most graciously pleased to order out of his private purse, a pension to Patrick Grant and his daughter, and the survivor of them, of one guinea per week. His majesty had the generous condescension to add, that he was only sorry he had not made an earlier application.

PETITION OF PATRICK GRANT TO HIS MAJESTY.

" The humble petition of Patrick Grant, residing at Westside, parish of Lethnot, county of Forfar.

" May it please your majesty,

" The fame of your majesty's distinguished generosity and benevolence having reached your petitioner in this remote corner of your empire, he is therefore emboldened to approach his sovereign with a representation no less urgent than true.

"May it please your majesty,

"The years of your petitioner are many, being no less than one hundred and eight; and he is, perhaps, the oldest enemy your majesty has now alive, having fought at Culloden. Educated a Roman Catholic, and in all the prejudices of the times, he drew his sword in behalf of another family, and fought with all the energy of a Highlander; but time and experience have corrected his views. Under the mild administration of your royal predecessors, he has seen the nation flourish, and its glory upheld by their wise, able, and vigorous measures. With equal zeal, then, would he gladly draw the sword in defence of that monarch, who now fills the throne, and who he trusts in God, for the good and happiness of his people, will continue to do so for many years to come!

"But, alas! my royal sire, though the soul of the aged Highlander is still ardent, the frost of age has chilled his vigour. He who in former times had experienced all the luxury of a comfortable independence, is now, in the evening of his age, reduced to poverty and want; for he has not even strength left to travel in search of his daily bread: and to aggravate his distress, to one affectionate daughter, Ann, the only solace of her aged and surviving parent, your petitioner can only bequeath poverty and rags.

"May it, therefore, please your majesty to take your petitioner's case into your royal consideration, and to grant such relief as his circumstances may seem to merit; and your petitioner shall ever pray.

"PATRICK GRANT.
"Al. Symers, Minister, Witness.
"James Young, Elder, Witness.
"Thomas Mollison, Elder, Witness.
"James Gordon, Elder, Witness.
"James Speed, Elder, Witness."

Eccentric Biography.

JOSEPH STRONG, THE BLIND MECHANIC.

Mr. Joseph Strong, of Carlisle, who was living in 1780, and had been blind from his infancy, followed the business of a diaper-weaver, and was allowed, even by people of the same occupation, to be not only a good but an expeditious workman. He lived to be somewhat advanced in years, but his mechanical abilities were not impaired in any considerable degree. In the exercise of these, besides making almost every article of household furniture, he constructed various pieces of machinery; one of which was the model of a loom, and the figure of a man working it. As an appendage, he added a brace of puppets, representing two women buffeting each other, or, as he interpreted them to his visitors, "boxing for the web."

At different times he dressed himself with articles entirely the work of his own hands. The instances of his admirable execution are too various to be enumerated here.

To show his strong propensity to produce, by his own ingenuity and labour, whatever he thought worthy of possessing, we shall add the following circumstances:

When he was about fifteen years of age, he concealed himself one afternoon in the cathedral during the time of service; after which, the congregation being gone, and the doors shut, he got into the organ loft, and examined every part of the instrument. This had engaged his attention till about midnight, when, having satisfied himself respecting the general construction, he proceeded to try the tones of the different stops, and the proportion they bore to each other. This experiment was not to be conducted in so silent a manner as his former inquiries. In short, the noise alarmed the neighbourhood of the church, and the circumstance of the organist having died a short time before, and no successor having been appointed, caused great consternation in the ears of all who heard it.

After some deliberation, a party, less intimidated than the rest, summoned resolution enough to enter the church at that tremendous hour; and Joseph, not less confounded than his unexpected visitors, was obliged to abandon his studies for that time. The next day he was taken before the Dean, who, after reprimanding him for the steps he had taken to gratify his curiosity, permitted him to visit the organ at all seasonable times. In consequence of this he set about making a chamber organ, which he completed without the assistance of any person.

He sold this instrument to a merchant in the Isle of Man, who afterwards removed to Dublin, where it was considered as a great curiosity.

Soon after his disposing of that, he made another, upon which he played for his amusement and devotion; having a set of chaunts (his own composition) which he frequently used as a religious exercise, and to which he joined long and irregular lines, expressive of various devotional subjects.

He walked from Carlisle to London to visit Mr. Stanley, the celebrated organist and composer; on which occasion he made, for the first time, a pair of shoes.

Varieties.

PTOLEMY'S MIRROR.

WE read in several ancient authors, that Ptolemy Evergetes caused to be placed in the tower of Pharos, at Alexandria, a mirror which represented accurately every thing which was transacted throughout all Egypt, both on water and on land! Some writers affirm, that with this mirror an enemy's fleet could be seen at the distance of 600,000 paces; others say 500 parasangs, or more than 100 leagues!

Abulfeda, in his description of Egypt, says that the mirror was of Chinese iron, and that soon after Mahometanism prevailed, the Christians destroyed it by stratagem.

Buffon thinks that by Chinese iron, Abulfeda meant polished steel; but there seems more plausibility in the conjecture of an acute anonymous writer, (*Phil. Mag.* 1805,) who supposes the metal to have been what is known to us by the name of *tutanag*, a Chinese metallic compound, which might be valued then as it is now, for the high polish it receives.

The existence of this wonderful mirror has been very generally treated as a fiction. Some celebrated opticians, who have been so far staggered by the positive terms in which the fact stands recorded, as to hesitate about discrediting it entirely, think that, at all events, it could be nothing else than the effect of magic. Such is the opinion of Father Kircher among others, who includes it among " those delusions of the devil, which we should shun with all our might; and, after the example of our Holy Mother church, condemn and execrate." Experience, however, has taught us, that many facts, once reckoned chimerical by a number of learned men, having been better examined by other learned men, have been found not only possible, but in actual existence. Father Abbat, in his *Amusements Philosophiques*, a work first published at Marseilles, in 1763, but now extremely scarce, has a very acute and ingenious dissertation, in which he endeavours to show, that to a certain extent, the fact is in itself " neither impossible nor difficult, but, on the contrary, very probable."

" If this mirror," says Abbat, " existed, it is probable that it was the only one of its kind, and that no other means had been then found of viewing distant objects distinctly. It must, therefore, have been considered as a great wonder in those times, and must have filled with astonishment all who saw its effects. Even though its effects had not been greater than those of a small telescope, it could not fail to be regarded as a prodigy. Hence it is natural to think, that those effects were exaggerated beyond all probability, and even possibility, as commonly happens to rare and admirable machines and inventions. If we abstract then from the accounts of the Mirror of Ptolemy, the evident exaggerations of ignorance, nothing will remain but that at some distance, provided nothing was interposed between the objects and the mirror, those objects were seen more distinctly than with the naked eye; and that with the mirror many objects were seen, which, because of their distance, were imperceptible without it."

Here is nothing but what is both possible and probable; and nobody, we think, after perusing Father Abbat's proofs and illustrations, need blush for their philosophy in acknowledging a belief in the actual existence of the long reputed fable of Ptolemy's Mirror.

A SENSIBLE HORSE.

We do not think the records of *Instinct* ever contained a more extraordinary instance than we are now about to relate, and for the truth whereof we pledge ourselves. A few days since, Mr. J. Lane, of Fascombe, in the parish of Ashelworth, in Gloucestershire, on his return home, turned his horse into a field in which it had been accustomed to graze. A few days before this the horse had been shod, all-fours, but unluckily had been pinched in the shoeing of one foot.—In the morning Mr. Lane missed the horse, and caused an active search to be made in the vicinity, when the following singular circumstances transpired:—The animal, as it may be supposed, feeling lame, made his way out of the field by unhanging the gate with his mouth, and went straight to the same farrier's shop, a distance of a mile and a half; the farrier had no sooner opened his shed than the horse, which had evidently been standing there some time, advanced to the forge and held up the ailing foot. The farrier instantly began to examine the hoof, discovered the injury, took off the shoe, and replaced it more carefully—on which the horse immediately turned about and set off at a merry pace for his well-known pasture. Whilst Mr. Lane's servants were on the search, they chanced to pass by the forge, and on mentioning their supposed loss, the farrier replied, " Oh, he has been here, and shod and gone home again!!" which on their returning they found to be actually the case.

The Scrap Book.

VEGETABLE PHENOMENON.

In June 1823, was growing in the garden of Messrs. Hutton, Nurserymen, of Carlisle, a white moss-rose in full bloom, which has produced a *red* rose from the same stem, without having been either budded or grafted. This extraordinary plant, which justly excites the admiration of the curious, was brought from London, among many other deciduous trees and shrubs, without any knowledge of its wonderful property of producing different coloured flowers, so contrary to the nature of its species.

CYPRESS TREE OF PATRA.

About two miles to the south of Patra, is the famous cypress tree, the trunk of which was eighteen feet in circumference when Spon visited Greece. A recent traveller, Mr. Dodwell, says, " I found its circuit twenty-three feet; it has therefore grown five feet in one hundred and thirty years. Its body appears perfectly sound, and its wide spreading branches form a dense shade, impenetrable to the sun: near it are four others of considerable size, but of a different form from the large one, and tapering towards the top. The people have a kind of religious veneration for this tree, which they shew to strangers with pride.

ZACHARY BOYD.

In the reign of Charles the Second, a Professor of Glasgow, named Zachary Boyd, translated the Bible into rhyme, and left the MS. to that University, with a legacy of 3000*l.* to defray the expenses of printing it. The University refused to accept the money, but retained the MS. That they consulted both their own credit and that of the testator, in not publishing it, will appear from the following specimen:—

" Jonah was three days in the whale's belly, without fire or candle,
" And had nothing all the while but cold fish guts to handle!"

A hive of bees, belonging to Mr. John Stordy, of Great Orton, swarmed on the 29th of May 1823. On the 2d and 4th of June, the same hive again swarmed; and on the 15th of that month, they swarmed a fourth time! An adjoining hive also swarmed three times in the same period. The whole seven casts took place within twenty days.

Published by J. LIMBIRD, 355, Strand, (East End of Exeter 'Change); and sold by all Newsmen and Booksellers. Printed by A. APPLEGATH, Stamford-street.

THE CABINET OF CURIOSITIES,
OR
𝔚onders of the 𝔚orld Displayed.

A world of wonders where creation seems
No more the works of Nature but her dreams.—MONTGOMERY.

No. X.]   PRICE TWOPENCE.

MARRIOTT THE GLUTTON.

MARRIOTT, was a lawyer of Gray's Inn, who piqued himself on the brutal qualification of a voracious appetite, and a powerful digestive faculty, attainments which at most could only rank him in the same scale of beings as the cormorant or the ostrich.

Marriott increased his natural capacity for food by art and application, and had as much vanity in eating to excess as any monk ever had in abstinence.

Under the print of Marriott, from which our engraving is copied, are the following lines:

" Here to your view's presented the great eater,
Marriott the lawyer, Gray's Inn's cormorant;
Who for his gut is become a mere cheater;
Those that will feed him counsel shall not want."

Great eaters have been found in all ages, from the time of

L

Herodotus, the wrestler of Megara, who would eat as much as ought to serve his whole company; down to the fellow backed by Sir John Lade, some years ago, against a glutton provided by the Duke of Queensbury. We do not recollect how much these fellows devoured, but the umpires declared that one man beat the other by a pig and an apple-pie.

VIOLENT TYPHON.

"The autumnal equinoctial gale," says Colnett, in his voyage to the South Atlantic, "came on us the 23d of March, and held upwards of four days, with frequent claps of thunder, accompanied by lightning, hail, and rain. It blew as hard as I ever remember, and, for several hours, we could not venture to show any sail. At the same time a whirlwind, or typhon, arose to windward, from whence, in one of the squalls, two balls of fire, about the size of cricket-balls, fell on board. One of them struck the anchor, which was housed on the forecastle, and, bursting into particles, struck the chief mate and one of the seamen, who fell down in excruciating tortures. On examining them, several holes appeared to have been burned in their clothes, which were of flannel; and in various parts of their bodies there were small wounds, as if made with a hot iron, of the size of a sixpenny piece. I immediately ordered some of the crew to perform the operation of the Otaheiteans, called roro mee, which consists in grasping the fleshy parts of the body, legs, and arms, and working it with the fingers. This caused a considerable abatement of their pains, but several days elapsed before they were perfectly recovered. The other ball struck the funnel of the caboose, made an explosion equal to that of a swivel gun, and burned several holes in the mizen stay-sail and mainsail, which were handed. At the height of it the barometer was 28°. The alarm which we may be supposed to have experienced during the whirlwind was not allayed by the noise of the birds, who, not considering the ship to be a place of safety, as is the case in common gales, appeared, by the violence of their shrieks and the irregularity of their flight, to be sensible of the danger; for, as the squall approached them, numbers plunged into the sea, to avoid it; while those who could not escape its influence were whirled, in a spiral manner, out of sight, in an instant. It very fortunately reached us only within two cables' length of each beam, and so passed ahead of the ship to the north. From our first seeing, to our losing sight of it, was about half an hour. In this gale I lost the greatest part of my live stock, together with all the vegetables that hung at the stern of the ship."

It may not be generally known to the lovers of Natural History, that the trout species will prey on the lizard. An instance of this was discovered in a trout, caught by a gentleman on Friday last, in the lake of Buttermere. The fish weighed a pound and a half; and when opened, was found to contain a full grown lizard. They who are fond of the rural diversion of angling, may profit from the hint, by trying the experiment of baiting for trout with animals of the lizard species — *Whitehaven Gazette, May,* 1823.

ON VAMPIRES AND VAMPIRISM.

Although superstition is perhaps more prevalent in the North than in any other part; yet there is strong reason to suppose that the belief in Vampires originated in the East ;—in Arabia, it had long been quite common, but it did not reach the Greeks until after the establishment of Christianity. On the division of the Latin and Greek churches, the superstition assumed its present form, the idea becoming prevalent, that a Latin body could not corrupt if buried in the territory of the Greeks ; it gradually increased and formed the subject of many wonderful stories still extant, of the dead rising from their graves, and feeding upon the blood of the young and beautiful. The superstition, with very little variation, extended itself all over Austria, Hungary, Lorraine, and Poland, and even in Iceland it became quite prevalent; and there is little doubt of the superstition having once prevailed in this island. It is in the highest degree probable, that our custom of driving a stake through the body of a *felo-de-se*, had its origin in the popular horror of the self-murderer ; in the apprehension of his being a vampire, and in the design of preventing his body from leaving its unhallowed grave.

Sir Walter Scott, in his translation of Eyrbyggia Saga, relates a traditionary story of several vampires, who committed dreadful ravages in Iceland, in the year 1000, so that, in a household of thirty servants, eighteen died. These vampires were not bloodsuckers, the sucking of blood being only a particular feature of the general superstition concerning vampires ; all vampires were not suckers of blood, but despatched their victims by inflicting on them a contagious disease. At length, a singular means of getting rid of them was adopted, no less than that of instituting judicial proceedings against the spectres. The inhabitants were regularly summoned to attend upon the inquest, as in a cause between man and man ; a tribunal was constituted with the usual legal solemnities,—charges were preferred against the individual spectres, accusing them of molesting the mansion, and introducing death among the inhabitants. All the solemn rites of judicial procedure were observed on this singular occasion ; evidence was adduced, charges given, and the cause formally decided. It does not appear that the vampires put themselves on their defence, so that the sentence of ejectment was pronounced against them individually, in due and legal form. Each of the spectres, as they heard their individual sentence, left the place, saying something that indicated their unwillingness to depart. The priest afterwards entered with holy water, and the celebration of a solemn mass followed ; this completed the conquest over the goblins, which had been commenced by the power and authority of the Icelandic law.

In Dr. More's Antidote against Atheism, there are some curious accounts of vampires in more modern times. Among the Hungarians and the Moravians it is a very general notion, that certain dead persons possess the power of returning, by night, to molest the living, especially those with whom they have been intimate ; to suck their blood, and by such refreshment to continue their own terrestrial existence at the expense of their victims, who furnish them with the means of subsistence. This absurd prejudice is also, more or less, accredited among the Polanders, the Silesians, the Servians, and the Greeks; to whom others might be added. The Hungarians have almost reduced the persuasion and its consequences to a system: they discover, by infallible signs, attendant on dead bodies, whether they have the power of returning to prey on the living; they employ means to counteract this power, and to preserve themselves from such disastrous assaults. Moreover, from these people is derived the name *Vampires*, given to the dead who possess the power of self-resuscitation, and of maintaining this second life by sucking blood: the name imports *bloodsuckers*. The Greeks, who are alive to every impulse of superstition, are infected with nearly the same notions; and have invented an appellation, barbarous enough, to denote these supernatural bloodsuckers: they call them *Broucocolakoi*; and by this name they are known as well on the continent, as among the islands of the Archipelago. Tournefort, in his Travels into Greece, relates a history that places this superstition and its consequences in a striking point of view.

"The man whose story we are going to relate, was a peasant of Mycone, naturally *ill-natured* and *quarrelsome*; circumstances to be noticed, as truly important, in such cases: he was murdered in the fields, nobody knew how, or by whom. Two days after his burial in a chapel in the town, it was rumoured that this quarrelsome fellow, ever restless, was seen to walk in the night with great rapidity through the town; that he tumbled people's goods about, put out their lamps, griped them *à posteriori*, tore their clothes, forced open doors, broke windows, found his way to the wine-cellars, and emptied the bottles most heroically; with a thousand other mad pranks and diabolical performances. At first, the thing was treated as ridiculous; and the losers who complained were laughed at: but on a sudden, the affair took another turn; the better sort of people began to be involved in apprehension; the *papas* (priests) gave credit to the fact, and the traveller hints at reasons more sagacious than gracious for this sanction on their part. Masses must be said; and masses were repeatedly said; but, *non obstante*, the ill-natured peasant continued to play his former antics; and paid no deference to exorcisms and holy water. I have never seen (says Tournefort) so pitiable a state as this island was in, at that time; the whole population was struck with alienation of mind. All ranks were equally affected: it was truly a scene of universal brain fever; no less dangerous than absolute insanity and canine madness. Entire families were seen, in all parts, forsaking their houses, and flocking from the extremities of the town into the public square, bringing their beds with them, for the sake of passing the night in company, and in hope of at least partial safety, and of obtaining *some* repose. Every individual had a new insult to complain of. At the approach of night nothing was heard but groans and lamentations from all quarters. The most considerate withdrew into the country. How was it possible to withstand the madness of a whole people? Those who inferred from our silence that we doubted the truth of the fact, came and reproached our incredulity: they brought evidence in proof that such things as *Broucocolakoi* really do exist; and quoted the *Buckler of Faith*, the work of a Jesuit missionary, and therefore true; ay, and doubly true.

"The chief people of the city held meetings, at which the priests and the monks assisted; these meetings 'Resolved,' that it was necessary, in consequence of certain rites performed, or to be performed, to wait nine days after the interment; and in the mean while to stay proceedings. On the tenth day, a mass was said in the chapel, in order to expel the devil who might peradventure be there, whether from custom, or from curiosity; then they took up the body, and got every thing ready for pulling out the seat of this supernatural vitality, the heart. At this moment the whole assembly began crying out *Broucocolas*; and *Broucocolas* re-echoed from the chapel vault to the roof, and from the roof to the vault: throughout the whole of every street nothing was to be heard but shouts of *Broucocolas!!* —except an intermixture of heavy and indignant curses on the malevolent deceased, for not being thoroughly dead; but suffering himself to be reanimated by a devil, and then returning to plague and terrify his neighbours. They determined, as the wisest course, to burn the heart on the seashore; and the heart was burnt accordingly.—In vain; the numbers of nocturnal assaults and batteries increased beyond what even Westminster-hall can conceive of after a general election. Where the doors were strongly bolted and fastened, the *Broucocolas* opened the roof and descended—who but he? As to clattering of windows, creaking of doors, howlings in the chimnies, subterranean noises, and, as aforesaid, cracking of bottles, and emptying of casks, the culprit had acquired as much additional impudence, and perhaps dexterity too, as if he had been instructed by a dozen accusations and acquittals at the Old Bailey. The rascal had the knack of being every where, at once, in his burglaries.

"Some of the citizens," says Tournefort, "who were most eminently zealous for the public good, saw clearly enough where the error lay:—the priests, they argued, had said mass *before* they pulled out the heart: had they said mass *afterwards*, the devil would as lieve be——as return to his old haunt: whereas, the cunning dog of a devil—(and it was a *very* cunning dog of a devil they had to do with,) had only fled for a while, and after the danger was over, back he came again, as rampant as ever. Not withstanding these dead certainties, they found their perplexities increase: they met in the council-chamber night and morning: they debated and discussed—and determined nothing: they made processions three days and three nights: they obliged the *papas* to fast: and these religious were called to all parts, were never off their legs, running from house to house, incessantly plying the holy water sprinkler; scattering the element in all directions; washing the doors with it; nay, they even poured it abundantly into the mouth of the insensible *Broucocolas*.

"Alas! for the wit and wisdom of mortal man! An acute Albanese, who happened to be at Mycone, observed, that it was no wonder the devil continued *in*— for, how could he *get out?* if they deluged the body with holy water, could the devil come through *that?* if they stuck naked swords by dozens over his grave—which they did—the sword-handles, being crosses, terrified the devil from passing *them*. He, therefore, recommended Turkish scimitars; and Turkish scimitars were tried—without efficacy: the wine-tubs of those who were so foolish as to leave them exposed, were continually emptied; and though Turks abhor pork, yet whether that abhorrence extended to the devil in question, our author does not say; but he hints very shrewdly at the loss as well of bacon as of eggs.

" The advice of the learned Albanese was eventually found to be fruitless; the inhabitants had prayed to every saint of their acquaintance in heaven, without obtaining a hearing—or, if the saints *did* hear, they were as much at a loss as their votaries; unless, indeed, by way of answer, they sent down a general inspiration among their petitioners aforesaid, who now began to bawl with universal vociferation, that the *Broucocolas* should be burnt entire; and then, let the devil lurk in it, if he could. With this the magistrates complied, seeing the island was in danger of being deserted; for all the best families were packing up in preparation for departure to Syra or Tinos:— accordingly, the carcass was reduced to ashes, January 1, 1701. The Myconians now boasted that the devil had met with his match: they had made the *Broucocolas* too hot to hold him; and their poets sported a number of humorous ballads, and treated their late disturber with some excellent jokes, and abundance of wit and ridicule. All would have ended well, if the Turks, at their next visit to receive the capitation-tax, had not laid a fine on the island, and turned the whole adventure to the profit of the Grand Signior's treasury: not forgetting that of his officers, through whose hands the money was *supposed to pass.*"

[*To be continued.*]

VOLCANOES IN THE SUN.

A German journal contains the following curious facts, by Count Moscati and his assistant M. Quirio Mauri, which were drawn up at Milan, having been deduced from observations of the former in that city:—

" On the 3d of October, 1814," says that astronomer, " the craters of the three volcanoes lately discovered in the surface of the sun, appeared quite distinct, but elliptical: they were situated about the edge of the sun, in the form of a transverse belt. On the 4th, the two nearest to the edge were invisible, owing to the sun's revolution, and the contour of the other was less distinctly marked than before. On the opposite edge, however, appeared very plainly on the sun's disk, two detached planetary masses, in conjunction; on the 5th was observed, a single but thicker mass of the same kind, likewise in conjunction. On the 7th, half of the middle crater of the 3d was seen nearly circular, because it had approached to the centre of the solar disk. On the 9th, the circumference of this crater appeared lengthened, and the crater observed on the 4th, seemed almost round, and nearest to the centre of the disk, as did, in its turn, the last and only one visible on the 4th. On the 17th were remarked three different planetary masses in conjunction, like those abovementioned, but not so large: on the 18th appeared three small but probably similar masses; on the 19th, three smaller; on the 23d, three still smaller; on the 29th, five, little different from the preceding; and, finally, on the 30th, near the edge of the sun, a small portion of one of the craters described above. All these masses, without exception, were in the abovementioned zone. The powers of the telescope would not allow of any farther discoveries during the time specified."

From these phenomena M. Maura deduces the following inferences:—

"The sun must be considered as a body, containing a matter capable of producing distinct volcanoes, because it has recently exhibited traces of such craters, and the projected masses really, or at least to appearance, covered the luminous surface in several places. There is every reason to believe that the sun is a solid, not a fluid, body; because the volcanic craters were distinctly to be seen open for a considerable time together. The sun is, on the other hand, a cold body, not so hot as to melt or produce a red glow; because the parts observed in these abysses, were not fiery, but black. The sun has, for the promotion of fertility, a luminous, slightly fluid, envelope, like the green carpet that covers our fields; because some folds of luminous matter inclined downward, in order to cover the bare places on some of the interior edges of the craters. The sun, underneath the abovementioned envelope, is not luminous, because the interior of the newly opened craters was quite dark as well as the masses thrown up by them. The sun has, probably a warmth nearly approaching to the temperature of our earth; because volcanoes which are hotter than the rest of the mass of the earth, make their appearance there. The sun reproduces the luminous envelope, wherever the latter is broken through; because the volcanoes are gradually covered again with it, after the manner of an organic, and, to us, unknown matter. The sun accomplishes its daily revolution in about one hundred and eight hours of our time. This period is ascertained by the reappearance of the individual craters discernible by us on the surface of the sun; and on this occasion it may be affirmed, that the spots, as they are called, upon the sun, which have hitherto been considered as attached to its body, are either atmospheric phenomena, or aërolites, passing about it, because they change their situation with respect to each other. Perhaps they may be wrecks from that remote catastrophe described by Moses: perhaps fragments though of smaller dimensions, yet of a similar nature with those which we have in a former place denominated planetary masses: fragments of that kind, which I remarked in diverging columns, more or less fan-shaped, which accompanied the last beautiful comet, like an atmosphere illuminated in opposition with the sun, and through which, on account of the inferior power of reflecting light, I discovered the real, opaque nucleus of that meteor. I could appeal, for the truth of this to the testimony of various eye witnesses, and among the rest of a professor, who observed it with me, and who entertained no doubt of the reality of the phenomenon. The sun has, on its surface, prodigious concavities, and proportionate protuberances; because the situation of the elliptic axis of the crater differed from that of those which would have been produced on a perfectly level sphere. Besides its annual and diurnal motion, the sun has a conical revolution round its pole, which is performed by its axis in about twenty-seven days of our time; because the last portion of crater, in the zone originally discovered, reappeared in that period, after the positive passage of the craters into other zones. I might mention some other discoveries worthy of notice; but this letter is already long enough. Allow me, however, to express my ardent wish, that astronomers, possessed of the requisite instruments and skill, would examine and confirm the discovery of the latest planets that have issued from the sun. The three largest seemed to me to belong to the class of Venus and Mercury. If the sun's light should preclude observations of them at present, in their elliptical situation, they might be found hereafter in a more favourable position. The discoverers might then give them what appellation they please, with the exception of the three largest, which I reserve to myself the right of naming."

SINGULAR RECOVERY OF A FEMALE UNJUSTLY EXECUTED.

The following account of the case of a poor girl who was unjustly executed in 1766, is given by a celebrated French author, as an instance of the injustice which was often committed by the equivocal mode of trial used in France:—

"About seventeen years since, a young peasant girl, possessed of a very agreeable figure, was placed at Paris in the service of a man depraved by all the vices consequent on the corruption of great cities. Smitten with her charms, he tried every method to seduce her; but she was virtuous, and resisted. The prudence of this girl only irritated the passion of her master, who, not being able to make her submit to his desires, determined on the most black and horrible revenge. He secretly conveyed into her box many things belonging to him, marked with his name. He then exclaimed that he was robbed, called in a commissaire (a ministerial officer of justice,) and made his deposition. The girl's box was searched, and the things were discovered. The unhappy servant was imprisoned. She defended herself only by her tears; she had no evidence to prove that she did not put the property in her box; and her only answer to the interrogatories was, that she was innocent. The judges had no suspicion of the depravity of the accuser, whose station was respectable, and they administered the law in all its rigour; a rigour undoubtedly excessive, which ought to disappear from our code to give place to a simple but certain penalty which would leave fewer crimes unpunished. The innocent girl was condemned to be hanged. The dreadful office was ineffectually performed, as it was the first attempt of the son of the great executioner. A surgeon had purchased the body for dissection, and it was conveyed to his house. On that evening, being about to open the head, he perceived a gentle warmth about the body. The dissecting knife fell from his hand, and he placed in his bed her whom he was about to dissect. His efforts to restore her to life were effectual; and at the same time he sent for a priest, on whose discretion and experience he could depend, in order to consult with him on this strange event, as well as to have him for a witness to his conduct. The moment the unfortunate girl opened her eyes, she believed herself in the other world, and perceiving the figure of the priest, who had a marked and a majestic countenance, (for I know him, and it is from him that I have this fact,) she joined her hands tremblingly, and exclaimed, 'Eternal Father, you know my innocence, have pity on me!' In this manner she continued to invoke the ecclesiastic, believing, in her simplicity, that she beheld her God. They were long in persuading her that she was not dead—so much had the idea of the punishment and of death possessed her imagination. Nothing could be more touching and more expressive than the cry of an innocent being, who thus approached towards him whom she regarded as her Supreme Judge; and, independently of her affecting beauty, this single spectacle was sufficient to create the most lively interest in the breast of an observing and sensible man. What a scene for a painter! What a moral for a philosopher! What a lesson for a legislator!

"The process was not submitted to a new revision, as was stated in the *Journal de Paris*. The servant having returned to life, recognised a man in him whom she had adored, and who directing her prayers towards the only adorable Being, quitted the house of the surgeon, who was doubly unquiet on her account and his own. She retired to hide herself in a distant village, fearing to meet the judges or the officers, who, with the dreadful tree, incessantly haunted her imagination. The villainous accuser remained unpunished, because his crime, though manifested to the eyes of two individual witnesses, was not so clear to the eyes of the magistrates and of the laws. The people subsequently became acquainted with the resurrection of this girl, and loaded with reproaches the execrable author of her misery; but, in this immense city, his offence was soon forgotten, and the monster perhaps still breathes; at least, he has not publicly suffered the punishment which he deserves.

"A book should be published, containing a collection of cases in which innocent persons have been punished, in order, by showing the causes of error, to avoid them for the future.—Perhaps some man of the law may undertake this important work."

PROCESSION OF PENITENTS IN SPAIN AND PORTUGAL.

UNTIL the French revolution, an extraordinary procession took place in all the principal towns of Spain and Portugal. It is called the Procession of Penitents, and is composed of all the religious orders both regular and secular, of the several parishes in the city and their fraternities; of all the tribunals and corporations, and of the several companies of tradesmen. The players also bore a part with the rest;

and, in Madrid and Lisbon, the whole of the royal family frequently attended.

The penitents in this procession walked each with a sword by his side, and a wax taper in his hand; and every nobleman was followed by a great many footmen with torches. An air of gloom appeared in every part of the ceremony; the several parties of soldiers had their arms in mourning, and the horses were led by grooms in sable attire. There were also men clothed in black and masked, holding various musical instruments in their hands, such as trumpets, drums, flutes, &c. The drums were covered with black, and beat a dead march. The crosses and banners of the several parishes were also covered with black crape. Heavy and cumbersome machines, raised on scaffolds, were drawn along, being painted with figures representing the mysteries of our Saviour's passion. At this ceremony, all the ladies appeared at their windows or balconies, dressed as on their wedding-day, and leaning on rich and sumptuous carpets. All the penitents, or *self-scourgers*, of the city, never failed of making a part in this procession. They wore on their heads a long lawn cap, three feet long, and sloped like a cone, on which a piece of linen cloth was fixed that fell down and covered their faces. They whipped themselves in cadence, with a scourge made of whipcord, at the ends of which were small round lumps of wax, stuck full of pointed pieces of glass. He who scourged himself with the greatest courage and dexterity, was looked upon as the bravest man; and such as did otherwise, were hooted by the women, who are so used to this cruel and bloody spectacle, that they cannot forbear breaking out into injurious expressions against those who do not whip themselves as severely as they would have them. Sometimes, however, these penitents had so little devotion in this part as to return the reproaches that were cast upon them, and even to insult the spectators as they passed along. Whenever they observed a fine woman, they were so dexterous at scourging as to make the blood spirt just upon them; and the ladies who were thus distinguished never failed to return thanks for the honour. But they proceeded much further when in sight of their mistress's house; for then they lay on with so much violence and fury, that they almost tore the flesh from their backs and shoulders; and the lady who saw this from the balcony, and who was conscious that it was all done for her sake, was highly pleased with it, and very grateful for the favour. These penitents were persons of all degrees and conditions, from those of the highest quality to the meanest plebeian; and some of them practised austerities of a much more severe nature than the abovementioned. These went barefooted, and had a mat tied on tight about them, which covered their arms and part of their bodies to the waist. Some drew after them a cross of a prodigious weight, others carried drawn swords, fixed in the back and arms, which made very deep wounds every time they happened to stumble. Others, being stripped to their shirts, had themselves tied to a cross at the church door, when they broke out into long and doleful lamentations. The persons who practised these austerities were always masked, as were the servants who attended upon them; and whether these penitents, or self-scourgers, whipped themselves from devotion or gallantry, it is certain that these mortifications were the death of a great many of them every year.

The Book of Giants.

"And there were giants in those days."

CHAPTER II.

WANLEY, though he calls his work the "Wonders of the Little World," contrives to squeeze some tolerably large marvels into it. He however gives his authority, and consequently incurs no more responsibility than we wish to do in quoting from him our second chapter of the Book of Giants.

"As the tallest ears of corn," says Wanley, "are the lightest in the head, and houses built many stories high have their uppermost rooms the worst furnished, so those human fabrics which nature hath raised to a giant-like height, are observed not to have so happy a composition of the brain as other men: like the pyramids of Egypt, they are rather for ostentation than use, and are remembered in history not for any accomplishment of mind, but only for the magnitude of their bodies.

"Artacæas, of the family of the Achæmenidæ, a person in great favour with Xerxes, was the tallest man of the rest of the Persians; for he lacked but the breadth of four fingers of full five cubits by the royal standard, which in our measure must be near seven feet.

"Walter Parsons, born in Staffordshire, was first apprentice to a smith; when he grew so tall, that a hole was made for him in the ground, to stand therein up to the knees, so as to make him adequate with his fellow-workmen: he was afterwards porter to king James; because gates being generally higher than the rest of the building, it was proper that the porter should be taller than other persons. He was proportionable in all parts, and had strength equal to his height, valour equal to his strength, and good temper equal to his valour; so that he disdained to do an injury to any single person: he would take two of the tallest yeomen of the guard in his arms at once, and order them as he pleased. He was seven feet four inches in height.

"William Evans was born in Monmouthshire, and may justly be counted the giant of our age for his stature, being full two yards and a half in height; he was porter to king Charles the First, succeeding Walter Parsons in his place, and exceeding him two inches in stature; but far beneath him in equal proportion of body; for he was not only knockkneed and splayfooted, but also halted a little; yet he made a shift to dance in an antimask at court, where he drew little Jeffery the king's dwarf out of his pocket, to the no small wonder and laughter of the beholders.

"The tallest man, (says Pliny,) that hath been seen in our age was one named Gabara, who, in the days of Claudius the late emperor, was brought out of Arabia: he was nine feet nine inches high.

"I saw a young girl in France,

(says Barthollett,) of eighteen years of age, who was of a giant like stature and bigness; and though she descended of parents of mean and small stature, yet her hand was equal to the hands of three men, if they were joined together.

"Jovianus the emperor was of a pleasant countenance, grey-eyed, and of a vast stature; so that for a long time there was no royal robe that was found to answer the height of his body.

"Maximinus the emperor was eight feet and a half in height: he was a Thracian, barbarous, cruel, and hated of all men: he used the bracelet or armlet of his wife as a ring for his thumb, and his shoe was longer by a foot than that of another man.

"There was a young man at Lunenburg, called Jacobus Damman, who for his extraordinary stature was carried throughout Germany to be seen. Anno 1613, he was brought to us at Basil: he was then twenty-three years of age and a half; beardless as yet, strong of body and limbs, save that at that time he was somewhat sick and lean; he was eight feet high complete; the length of his hand was one foot and four inches: he surpassed the common stature of man two feet.

"I saw, (says Wierus,) a maid, who, for the gigantic proportion of her body, was carried from one city and country to another, on purpose to be seen, as a monstrous representation of the human figure. I diligently inquired into all things concerning her, and was informed, both by the mother and her mighty daughter, that both her parents were but of low stature; nor were there any of her ancestors who were remembered to exceed the common stature of men. This maid herself, to the twelfth year of her age, was of a short and mean stature; but being about that time seized with a quartan ague, after she had been troubled with it for some months, it perfectly left her; and then she began to grow to that wonderful greatness; all her limbs being proportionably answerable to the rest. She was, when I beheld her, about twenty-five years of age, to which time it had never been with her as is usual to women; her complexion somewhat swarthy; stupid and dull; and slow as to her whole body."

Anecdotes of Longevity.

WELSH PATRIARCH.

THE following copy of a very remarkable instance of longevity, and a numerous offspring, is extracted from an old register belonging to the parish of Tregauan, which is part of the rectory of Llangesney, in the county of Anglesea, and transcribed into the new register thereof, for the satisfaction of posterity.

There died the 11th of March, 1581, in the said parish of Tregauan, in the said county of Anglesea, one William Aphowelaph Yerweth, aged one hundred and five. He had been thrice married; his first wife was Ellen serch William; by her he had twenty-two children. The second wife was Katherine serch Richard; by her he had ten children. The third wife was Ellen uch William, now living; by her he had four children. His eldest son was Griffith ap William, now living, aged eighty-four: he has children's children to the fourth generation in abundance. His youngest son is also called Griff ap William, aged two years and a half, now living in the said parish, and the difference between the two brothers' age is eighty-one years and a half, for the eldest was of that age when the youngest was born : his eldest daughter is called Alice serch William, aged seventy-two ; she has been twice married, and has a numerous progeny : there being living now of the old man's offspring in the said parish eighty persons, and at his funeral there were computed to be about three hundred persons that were descended from him. The said old man was of a middle stature, of good complexion, never troubled with cholic, gout, or stone, seldom sick, of moderate diet, lived by tillage, exercised himself in fishing and fowling, and had his senses to the last.

HENRY BROWN

A NEW York paper contains the following :—Henry Brown, a native of New Jersey, residing near Beavertown, was born Jan. 1686 : consequently is now in his 129th year. He is a black man, with long straight hair, and wears it tied. He was in General Braddock's defeat, in 1755, and then was fifty-nine years old. He had been a slave seventy years.—Has been a free man fifty-eight years—is now in good health, can walk pretty well, has a good appetite at times, but is getting weak. He was never married ; and says he wishes to die, but fears he never shall.—1814.

FEMALE IN CALABRIA.

THERE was living in Drosi, a little village of Calabria, a woman whose age was 125 years, and who has lived in three different centuries. She enjoys all her faculties, as well moral as physical, and what renders her age the more extraordinary is, the fact that the air of the village has been long considered unhealthy. She was married four times : her first marriage took place 105 years ago.

Eccentric Biography.

THOMAS PETT THE MISER.

THOMAS PETT, who died in Clifford's Passage, on the 2d of June, 1803, was a native of Warwickshire. At the age of ten years he came to London with a solitary shilling in his pocket. As he had neither friends nor relations in the capital, he was indebted to the humanity of an old woman, that sold pies, for a morsel of bread, till he could procure himself a crust. In the course of a few days he was engaged as an errand-boy by a tallow-chandler. Mrs. Dip, a lady of London mould, however, could not reconcile herself to his rustic manners and awkward gait ; so that she dismissed him one cold winter's evening, with this observation, " Your master hired you in my absence, and I'll pack you off in his." The good husband did not desert Tom ; he found him out, and bound him apprentice to a butcher, in the Borough of Southwark. He behaved so well during his apprenticeship, that his master recommended him, when he was out of his time, to a brother of the cleaver in Claremarket, as a journeyman. Tom's maxim was, that honesty was not the shortest road to wealth, but that it was by far the surest. For the first five years he was engaged at twenty-five pounds a year, meat and drink. The accumulation of money, and the abridgement of expense, were the two sole objects of his thoughts. His expenses were reduced to these three heads, lodging, clothing, and washing: as to the first, he fixed on a back room on the second floor, with one window, that occasionally admitted a straggling sunbeam. As to dress, every article was second-hand, nor was he choice in the colour or quality; jocosely observing, when he was twitted on his garb, that, according to Solomon, there was nothing new under the sun; and that, as to colour, it was a mere matter of fancy; and that that was the best which stuck longest to its integrity: then, as to washing, he used to say, a man did not deserve a shirt that would not wash it himself; and that the only fault he had to find with Lord North was the duty he imposed on soap. There was one expense, however, that lay heavy on his mind, and which robbed him of many a night's sleep, and that was shaving; he often lamented that he had not learnt to shave himself; he used to console himself by hoping, that beards would one day be in fashion, and that even the Bond-street loungers would be driven to wear artificial ones. He made a promise one night when he was very thirsty, that as soon as he had accumulated a thousand pounds, he would treat himself to a pint of porter every Saturday. Fortune soon put it in his power to perform this promise, and he continued to observe it till the additional duty was laid on porter; he then sunk to half a pint, as he thought that sufficient for any man that did not wish to get drunk, and, of course, die in a workhouse. If he heard of an auction in the neighbourhood, he was sure to run for a catalogue, and when he had collected a number together, he used to sell them for waste paper. When he was first told that the Bank was restricted from paying in specie, he shook loudly, as Klopstock the poet says; took to his bed, and could not be prevailed on to taste a morsel, or wet his lips, till he was assured that all was right. On Sundays, after dinner, he used to lock himself up in his room, and amuse himself with reading an old newspaper, or writing rhymes, many of which he left behind him on slips of paper. The following will serve as a specimen of his talents in this way:

On hearing that Small-beer was raised.
They've rais'd the price of table drink;
What is the reason, do you think?
The tax on malt, the cause I hear:
But what has malt to do with table-beer?

He was never known, even in the depth of the coldest winter, to light a fire in his room, or to go to bed by candlelight.

He was a great friend to good cheer at the expense of another. "Every man," said he, "ought to eat when he can get it—an empty sack cannot stand."

If his thirst at any time got the better of his avarice, and water was not at hand, he would sometimes venture to step into a public-house, and call for a pennyworth of beer. On trying occasions, he was always sure to sit in the darkest corner of the taproom, in order that he might drink in every thing that was said with thirsty ear. He was seldom or ever known to utter a word, unless Bonaparte or a parish dinner were mentioned, and then he would draw a short contrast between French kickshaws and the roast beef and plumb-pudding of Old England, which he called the staple commodity of life. Once on a time he was prompted, by what demon I cannot tell, to purchase a *pint* of small beer; but the moment he locked it up in his closet, he repented, tore the hair out of his wig, and threw the key out of the window, lest he should be tempted, in some unlucky moment, to make too free with it.

Thus far of the life of Thomas Pett, whose pulse, for the last twenty years of his life, rose and fell with the funds; who never lay down or rose that he did not bless the first inventor of compound interest; whose constant saying was, "that gold was the clouded cane of youth, and the crutch of old age;" who, for forty-two years lived in Claremarket as a journeyman butcher; who lodged thirty years in one gloomy apartment, which was never brightened with coal, candlelight, or the countenance of a visitant; who never treated man, woman, or child, to a glass of any kind of liquor; who never lent or borrowed a penny; who never spoke ill or well of any one; who never ate a morsel at his own expense; who never said a civil thing, as far as is known, to that part of the creation which renders life tolerable; who would not trust a washerwoman with a pocket-handkerchief; who looked on all mankind to be fools, or mad, who did not pile up yellow dirt; and who wanted to bargain for a coffin half an hour before he died.

About three days before his dissolution, he was pressed by his mistress to make his will, which he at last reluctantly assented to, observing, as he signed his name, that it was a hard thing that a man should sign away all his property with a stroke of a pen.

He left 2,475*l.* in the three per cents, to distant relations, not one of whom he had ever seen or corresponded with.

The following list of his wearing apparel, &c. was taken after his death by a wag in the neighbourhood.

An old bald wig.
A hat as limber as a pancake.
Two shirts that might pass for fishing-nets.
A pair of stockings embroidered with threads of different colours.
A pair of shoes, or rather sandals.
A bedstead instead of a bed.
A toothless comb.
An almanack out of all date.
A gouty chair and a leafless table.
A looking-glass that had outlived reflection.
A leathern bag, with a captive guinea, &c. &c.

Varieties.

MARBLE PONDS OF PERSIA.

THESE wonders of nature consist of certain pools, or plashes, whose indolent waters, by a slow and regular process, stagnate, concrete, and petrify; producing that beautiful transparent stone, commonly called Tabriz marble, much used in the burial places of Persia, and in their best edifices. These ponds are contained within the circumference of half a mile, and their position is distinguished by heaps of stone, which have accumulated as the excavations have increased. The petrifactive process may be traced from its commencement to its termination: in one part, the water is clear; in a second, it appears thicker and stagnant; in a third quite black; and in its last stage it is white like a hoar frost. When the operation is complete, a stone thrown on its surface makes no impression, and a man may walk over it without wetting his shoes. Such is the constant tendency of this water to become stone, that when it exudes from the ground in bubbles, the petrifaction assumes a globular shape, as if the bubbles of a spring, by a stroke of magic, had been arrested in their play, and metamorphosed into stone. The substance thus produced is brittle, transparent, and sometimes richly streaked with green, red, and copper-coloured veins. It admits of being cut into very large slabs, and takes a good polish. So much is this stone looked on as an article of luxury, that none but the king, his sons, and persons privileged by special firman, are permitted to take it.

CASCADE IN BUCKINGHAMSHIRE.

At the village of Blidlow, in Buckinghamshire, there is a natural curiosity close by the church-yard. It is a cavity of about thirty feet deep, twenty-one wide, and fifty long, formed of solid rock, from whose sides innumerable streams of water issue, and falling into one (the noise of which much resembles that of a waterfall) rolls gently on, and uniting with another stream about half a mile distant, flows through Wycombe, &c. till joining the canal at Uxbridge in Middlesex, it falls into the Thames afterwards. Nothing is wanting to give this a picturesque appearance, for its sides are encircled with woodbine and ivy, and its top crowned with spreading oaks and weeping willows, whose roots are discernible at some distance from the surface of the earth; and the bottom is so dry that I have passed many a half-hour at it, surveying with wonder and admiration this "dream of nature." S.

The Scrap Book.

RICHARDSON THE FIRE-EATER.

The following is an extract from Evelyn's Diary:

"Oct. 8. 1672.—I took leave of my Lady Sunderland, who was going to Paris to my Lord, now ambassador there. She made me stay dinner at Leicester-house, and afterwards sent for Richardson, the famous fire-eater. He before us devoured brimstone on glowing coals, chewing and swallowing them. He melted a beere glasse, and eate it quite up; then taking a live coal on his tongue, he put on it a raw oyster; the coal was blown on with bellows till it flam'd and sparkl'd in his mouth, and so remain'd till the oyster gap'd and was quite boil'd; then he melted pitch and wax with sulphur, which he drank down as it flam'd. I saw it flaming in his mouth a good while."

Great numbers of persons are daily viewing the large oak tree, which has lately been felled in Tooley Park, Leicestershire. This surprising oak is ten yards round the butt, of solid timber, and is valued at about two hundred guineas. The bark is estimated at three tons; and the tree and branches now fallen cover half an acre of land. It is supposed to have been been growing several hundred years. Many of the branches are from three to four yards long.

Published by J. LIMBIRD, *355, Strand, (East End of Exeter 'Change); and sold by all Newsmen and Booksellers. Printed by A.* APPLEGATH, *Stamford-street.*

THE CABINET OF CURIOSITIES,
OR
Wonders of the World Displayed.

A world of wonders where creation seems
No more the works of Nature but her dreams.—MONTGOMERY.

No. XI.]   PRICE TWOPENCE.

EXECUTION OF MADAM TIQUET.

MADAM TIQUET was the daughter of Monsieur Carlier, a bookseller at Metz, who left behind him a million of French livres, or 50,000*l*. She was born in the year 1657, and lost her father when she was but fifteen years old. Her natural qualifications were shining, and they had received all the embellishments which could be derived from education.

Among her numerous admirers was M. Tiquet, counsellor of parliament. He might in all probability have sighed with a train of hopeless lovers, if he had not made use of an old aunt, who had a great ascendency over his fair mistress; and, by a present of 4000 livres, so effectually persuaded her of his passion, that she was continually speaking to her niece in his praise. Having observed in the

M

young lady herself an extravagant fondness for magnificence and expense, he one day took an opportunity of presenting her with a fine nosegay of flowers, intermixed with diamonds, to the value of 15,000 livres. These dazzled her eyes and wounded her heart; that is to say, they induced her to prefer M. Tiquet to the rest of her lovers, because she looked on him to be the richest and most generous of them all.

The aunt improved the kind sentiments she entertained for this gentleman; while he, on the other hand, never examined the temper or qualities of his mistress, but believing all things about her were as fair as her person, resolved at all events to marry her, if he could gain her consent. Assiduities like his are seldom continued long, without producing their effect: the lady was not more inexorable than the rest of her sex; her aunt's lectures, and M. Tiquet's presents, at length subdued her heart, or to speak more properly, procured her hand, which, with great seeming tenderness, she gave to M. Tiquet.

The first months of their marriage were happy, and in due time Madam Tiquet brought her husband, at one birth, a son and a daughter, to be the pledges of their love.

But this marriage, concluded without consideration, little answered the expectations of either of the parties. Madam Tiquet thought of nothing but her husband's riches, and how she might waste them in subserviency to her pleasures. The counsellor was so taken up with the beauty and fortune of his wife, that he made no question of her virtue, which, to his cost, he found afterwards was a point he ought to have considered.

The happy day over, the excessive expenses of Madam Tiquet obliged her husband to endeavour to set some bounds to them, though against his will. The Sieur Mongeorge, captain in the guards, a person who had all the qualities of a fine gentleman, so dazzled the eyes of Madam, that she and this officer quickly indulged themselves in the criminal passion they had for each other. The jealousy of the husband, excited by these proceedings, increased in Madam Tiquet the aversion she had conceived for her spouse.

M. Tiquet in debt, which was increased by the expenses he had incurred by his marriage, was now exposed to the pursuit of his creditors. This circumstance, added to his constantly watching his wife's steps, in order to interrupt her pleasures, raised her hatred to such a pitch, that it turned at last to fury, and she resolved to have him assassinated. She had some knowledge of a vile character, one Augustus Cattelain, whom, with her porter, she employed to assassinate him. They waylaid him in the night, but failed in their object. She next mixed poison in some broth, but the valet-de-chambre by whom she sent it, suspecting it, made a false step and threw it down: he then left the service.

This irritated the lady so much, that she determined within herself to find out a short remedy, by recurring to her first project. She opened her scheme on this head to her porter, and directed him to find persons who could execute it.

It happened that M. Tiquet went to pay a visit to a neighbour of his, one Madam de Villemur, and staid there pretty late. His servants sitting up for him, heard several pistol-shots in the street before the door; upon which, running out in a hurry, they found their master assassinated, and weltering in his blood. When they came to his assistance, he desired that they would carry him back to Madam de Villemur's, which was done; his domestics then went to acquaint their lady. She, pretending great surprise, went immediately to the house where he was, to inquire how he did, but that was all she could do; for he having earnestly desired that she might not enter the room where he was, she was constrained to go back without seeing him, at which she affected some concern. He had received three wounds, but none of them were mortal. The commissary of that quarter of the town came to see and to examine M. Tiquet, as soon as his wounds were dressed. The first question he asked him was, "What enemies have you?" The poor gentleman answered, "I know of none except my wife." This answer confirmed the suspicions of the world, which, as soon as the affair was known, fell immediately upon her. She did not, however, betray the least signs of guilt; but manifested a constancy scarcely to be accounted for.

She was advised to flee, and on the eighth day, a Theatine came hastily into her chamber, and addressed her thus:—"Madam, there is no time to be lost; in a few moments you will be apprehended: I have brought you one of the habits of my order; slip it on; get down stairs; there is a sedan waits, which will carry you to a place where there is a post-chaise in which you may go immediately to Calais, and from thence to England, till we see what turn things will take."—"Such measures," replied Madam Tiquet, "are proper for the guilty; innocence is every where secure; these reports are spread by my husband, to prejudice me in the eyes of the world, and to intimidate me so far as to leave my country, that he may get my fortune into his hands; but his skill shall fail him; I am not frightened; I will fall into the hands of the law, for I doubt not but the law will do me justice."

The next day the Sieur Deffita, lieutenant-criminel, entered the room. Madam Tiquet arose, and paid him her compliments with great gravity, "You needed not, Sir," said she, "have brought this mighty escort. I never had any intention to fly, and if you had come alone, I should have gone with you wherever you were pleased to carry me."

On coming, however, to the Chatelet, she changed colour; but she presently recovered it, and appeared as serene as ever. Augustus Cattelain put himself into the hands of justice, making an open confession, that, three years before, Madam Tiquet had engaged him in a conspiracy to murder her husband, in which also her porter was concerned: it was upon this that she was apprehended; for as to the last assassination, there was no proof against her. Her crime, therefore, was not the actual causing her husband to be assassinated, but for having been concerned in a conspiracy for that purpose, which had not, however, taken effect. For this offence she incurred a capital punishment, and the judges of the Chatelet, on the 3d of June, 1699, passed sentence upon her and upon the porter, by which she was adjudged to have her head cut off, and he to be hanged. This was afterwards confirmed by an arret of Parliament. Augustus Cattelain, notwithstanding his being an evidence, was condemned to the gallies for life.

M. Tiquet, being cured of his wounds, went to Versailles, accompanied by his two children, and threw himself at the feet of the king. "Sire," said he, "I implore your mercy for Madam Tiquet; be not more severe than God himself, who doubtless has pardoned her on her repentance. Has your justice been more offended than I? Yet I freely forgive her; and my children lift for their mother their pure and innocent hands to your majesty. The crime she intended has been expiated by the terrors and afflictions she has felt in the deplorable condition she is now in, ready to fall a sacrifice to justice; as her crime, then, is done away, do not, Sire, inflict death for repentance." The king, however, was inexorable; nevertheless he granted to M. Tiquet all the effects of his wife, which would otherwise have fallen to the crown, that his own and his children's circumstances might be made more easy. The brother of this unhappy woman, who was a captain in the guards, as well as the Sieur Mongeorge, used all their interest to save her. At last his majesty yielded: but the archbishop of Paris, the famous cardinal de Noailles, interposed, and told him, that if such a crime escaped with impunity, it would become frequent; that the security of married men's lives depended on the death of Madam Tiquet; since the grand penitentiary's ears were already stunned with the confessions of women, who charged themselves with having attempted their husband's lives. This remonstrance determined the king, who declared that Madam Tiquet should be made an example.

When she was brought before the lieutenant-criminel, he ordered her sentence to be read, looking all the while steadfastly upon her, that he might perceive what effects it produced. Madam Tiquet heard it without the least emotion or change of colour. The lieutenant-criminel exhorted her to confess her crime, and she acknowledged all. They asked her if the Sieur de Mongeorge had any knowledge of this affair? upon which she cried out, "Alas! if I had communicated the least tittle of it to him, I should have lost his esteem beyond retrieving." The parson of St. Sulpice was then admitted to her. She heard with great docility all his instructions. She frequently entreated him to beg pardon of her husband, and assure him, that in death she had for him all that tenderness which had made the first year of their marriage so delightful. There was perhaps never seen in Paris so great a crowd, as in the streets through which Madam Tiquet passed to Le Grève. She went in a coach, and the curate of St. Sulpice with her; the porter was there before her, and had with him a confessor. At the sight of the amazing multitude, her spirits began to sink; the clergyman who was with her endeavoured to console her. Revived and encouraged by his words, she lifted up her hood, and looked upon the spectators with an air at once modest and resolved.

When Madam Tiquet was brought to the place where she

was to suffer, there fell so great a rain that they were obliged to defer the execution till it was over. She had, during this space, all the apparatus of her punishment in view, and at the same time a mourning coach with six horses, covered with black cloth, which was to carry away her body. When she saw the porter executed, she lamented his destiny so much that she seemed to forget her own. When she was directed to mount the scaffold, she gave her hand to the executioner, that he might help her. When she was on the scaffold, she kissed all the instruments of death, and did every thing with an air as if she had studied her part. She accommodated her hair and head-dress in a moment, and was instantly on her knees in a posture ready to suffer; but the executioner was so agitated, that he could hardly perform his office: he missed his blow thrice, and when her head fell from her body all the spectators set up a loud cry. Though Madam Tiquet was forty-two years old when she suffered, her beauty was not in the least decayed; and, as she died in full health and vigour, her face retained an agreeable air even after her head was struck off.

ALPHABET FOR THE BLIND.

The string alphabet is formed by so knotting a cord, a ribbon, or the like, that the protuberances made upon it may be qualified by their shape, size, and situation, for signifying the elements of language. The letters of this alphabet are distributed into seven classes, which are distinguished by certain knots, or other marks; each class comprehends four letters, except the last, which comprehends but two. The first, or A class, is distinguished by a large round knot; the second, or E class, by a knot projecting from the line; the third, or I class, by the series of links, vulgarly called the drummer's plait; the fourth, or M class, by a simple noose; the fifth, or Q class, by a noose with a line drawn through it; the sixth or U class, by a noose with a net knot cast upon it; and the seventh, or Y class, by a twisted noose. The first letter of each class is denoted by the simple characteristic of its respective class; the second by the characteristic, and a common knot close to it; the third by the characteristic, and a common knot, half an inch from it; and the fourth by the characteristic, and a common knot, an inch from it. Thus A is simply a large round knot; B is a large round knot, with a common knot close to it; C is a large round knot, with a common knot half an inch from it, and D is a large round knot, with a common knot an inch from it, and so on. The alphabet above described is found by experience to answer completely the purpose for which it was invented. The inventors, Robert Milne and David Macbeath, who are both blind, being in the habit of corresponding by its means, not only with each other, but with several individuals whom they have taught its use. It must readily occur to every one, that the employment of an alphabet, composed in the manner which has been explained, will ever be necessarily tedious; but it should be borne in mind, that there is no supposable system of tangible figures, significant of thought, that is not more or less liable to the same objection. The inventors are aware, that among the different methods by which people at a distance might be enabled to hold mutual intercourse through the medium of a language addressed to the touch, there are some that would doubtless be more expeditious than theirs; but they flatter themselves, that when all the advantages and disadvantages of each particular method are duly considered, the plan which they have been led to adopt will appear, upon the whole, decidedly the best. There can scarcely be any system of tangible signs, which it would be less difficult either to learn or to remember; since a person of ordinary intellect may easily acquire a thorough knowledge of the string alphabet in an hour, and retain it for ever. Yet the inventors can assure their readers, that it is impossible for the pen or the press to convey ideas with greater precision. Besides the highly important properties of simplicity and accuracy which their scheme unites, and in which it has not been surpassed, it possesses various minor, nor yet inconsiderable, advantages, in which, it is presumed, it cannot be equalled by any thing of its kind. For example, its tactile representations of articulate sounds are easily portable—the materials of which they are constructed may always be procured at a trifling expense, and the apparatus necessary for their construction is extremely simple. In addition to the letters of the alphabet, there have been contrived arithmetical figures, which, it is hoped, will be of great utility, as the remembrance of numbers is often found peculiarly difficult. Palpable commas, semicolons, &c. have likewise been provided to be used, when judged requisite. The inventors have only to add, that, sensible of the happy results of the invention to themselves, and commiserating the fate of their fellow-prisoners of darkness, they most earnestly recommend to all intrusted with the education of persons deprived of sight, carefully to instruct them in the principles of orthography, as the blind being in general unable to spell, is the chief obstacle to their deriving from the new mode of signifying thought, the much-wanted benefit which it is designed to extend to their circumstances.

ON VAMPIRES AND VAMPIRISM.
(Continued from p. 147.)

The worst part of the theory of Vampirism remains to be told: this faculty proved contagious; and those who had been sucked by a vampire, felt themselves condemned to become vampires, in their turn. They faded away; every body saw it; they became mere walking skeletons: they had no enjoyment of life. In vain they rubbed themselves with turfs and earth taken from the grave of their tormentor: in vain their tormentor was disinterred, and treated with the customary indignities due to his malevolence. About the year 1732, the affair of vampirism made a great noise in the Austrian states; and the report resounded through Europe. A heyduke, named Arnold Paul, was crushed to death under a load of hay. Report affirmed, that this Hungarian had been, when living, sucked by a vampire: consequently, he being now dead, began to suck, in his turn, the inhabitants of the town. In a short time it was believed, that four persons had died from the effects of his nocturnal visitations. The baillie of the place proceeded to take cognizance of the facts : the tombs of this vampire and his victims were opened with all the solemnities of justice. The symptoms of vampirism were obvious, were demonstrated : in the presence of the magistrate the bodies had a stake driven through each of them, and suffered a posthumous decollation. The minds of the people were apparently calmed, for a moment; but the calm was in appearance, and momentary only : every body believed that the country continued subject to the selfsame suffering; for, it was proved, that Arnold Paul had not only killed four inhabitants by his suctions, but that he had sucked the cattle also, and there could be no doubt, not the least in the world, but that those who had eaten of the flesh of such cattle, and those who should hereafter eat of such as were not yet brought to market, would become vampires also, after their death. Where could this end? What was infection by the smallpox, or by a sweeping pestilence, to this? Not less than seventeen tombs were opened by way of precaution; and the usual proceedings against vampires were resorted to. The bodies were eventually burned, and the ashes were thrown into the river. The whole was conducted under the inspection of a military commission appointed by the government; and the *process-verbal* was duly forwarded to Vienna. The learned Germans *got up* dissertations on vampires and vampirism : the French press did the same: the most moderate (among whom was Dom. Calmet himself,) did not dare wholly to deny the possibility of the reappearance of deceased persons; though they inclined to discharge the devil from the imputation of creating vampires. The Doctors of the Sorbonne commended the work of Dom. Calmet for avoiding two rocks, equally fatal, said they, on the subject of reappearances—that of *vain credulity*, on the one hand, that of *dangerous phyrrhonism*, on the other. It should seem, therefore, that he concluded, somewhat like Dr. Johnson, "Why, Sir, all testimony is for it; and all argument is against it."

In Dr. Moore's Antidote against Atheism, previously referred to, there is a singular account of a shoemaker, at Breslau, in Silesia, who committed suicide in the year 1591, but whose violent death was concealed by his family, and he had Christian burial. In about two months after his interment, it is stated that he appeared to several persons in his exact shape and habit, not only at night but at mid-day; "those that were asleep it tempted with horrible visions: those that were waking it would strike, pull, or press, lying heavy upon them like an *ephialtes*, so that there were perpetual complaints every morning of their last night's rest through the whole town."

For nearly eight months these proceedings continued, when the magistrates were determined to do something to put a period to them, though they did not, like the Icelanders, adopt a judicial process; they dug up his body, which was found entire, "his joints limber and flexible as in those that are alive." They kept his body out of earth six days, but the "unquiet stirs" did not cease for all this; they then buried it under the gallows; but this did not do. At length they took up his body again, "cut off the head, arms, and legs of the corpse, and opening his back, took out his heart, which was as fresh and entire as in a calf new killed; these, together with his body, they put on a pile of wood, and burnt them to ashes, which they, carefully sweeping together, and putting into a sack, (that none might get them for wicked uses,) poured into the river, after which the *spectrum* was never seen more."

THE SULPHUR MOUNTAIN OF ICELAND.

This mountain is distant about three miles from the village of Krisuvik, in Iceland. At the foot of the mountain is a small bank, composed chiefly of white clay and sulphur, from every part of which steam issues. Having ascended this bank, a ridge presents itself, immediately beneath which is a deep hollow, whence a profusion of vapour arises, with a confused noise of boiling and splashing, accompanied by steam escaping from narrow crevices in the rock. This hollow being, as well as the whole side of the mountain opposite, covered with sulphur and clay, it was very hazardous to walk over a soft and steaming surface of such a description. The vapour concealing the party from each other occasioned much uneasiness; and there was some hazard of the crust of sulphur breaking, or of the clay sinking beneath their feet. They were thus several times in danger of being scalded, as, indeed, happened to one of the party, Mr. Bright, who accidentally plunged one of his legs into the hot clay. When the thermometer was immersed in it, to the depth of a few inches, it generally rose to within a few degrees of the boiling point. By stepping cautiously, and avoiding every little hole from which steam issued, they soon ascertained how far they might venture. Their good fortune, however, observes Sir George Mackenzie, (from whose Travels in Iceland we take the account,) ought not to tempt any person to examine this wonderful place, without being provided with two boards, with which every part of the banks may be traversed in perfect safety. At the bottom of the hollow, above described, they found the cauldron of mud, which boiled with the utmost vehemence. They approached within a few yards of it, the wind favouring them in viewing every part of this singular scene. The mud was in constant agitation, and often thrown up to the height of six or eight feet. Near this spot was an irregular space filled with water, boiling briskly. At the foot of the hill, in a hollow formed by a bank of clay and sulphur, steam rushed with great force and noise from among the loose fragments of rock.

In ascending the mountain, our travellers met with a spring of cold water, which was little to be expected in such a place. At a greater elevation, they came to a ridge, composed entirely of sulphur and clay, joining two summits of the mountain. The smooth crust of sulphur was beautifully crystallized; and beneath it was a quantity of loose granular sulphur, which appeared to be collecting and crystallizing, as it was sublimed along with the steam. On removing the sulphureous crust, steam issued, and annoyed the party so much, that they could not examine this place to any depth.

Beneath the ridge, on the farther side of this great bed of sulphur, an abundance of vapour escaped with a loud noise. Having crossed to the side of the mountain opposite, they walked to what is called the principal spring. This was a task of much apparent danger, as the side of the mountain, to the extent of about half a mile, was covered with loose clay, into which the feet of our travellers sunk at every step. In many places there was a thin crust, beneath which the clay was wet, and extremely hot. Good fortune attended them; and, without any serious inconvenience, they reached the object they had in view. A dense column of steam, mixed with a small portion of water, forced its way impetuously through a crevice in the rock, at the head of a narrow valley, or break in the mountain. The violence with which it rushed out was so great, that the noise, thus occasioned, might often be heard at the distance of several miles. During night, while the party lay in their tent at Krisuvik, they more than once listened to it with mingled awe and astonishment. Behind the column of vapour was a dark coloured rock, which added to the sublimity of the effect.

"It is quite beyond my power," observes Sir George Mackenzie, "to offer such a description of this extraordinary place, as would convey adequate ideas of its wonders, or of its terrors. The sensations of a person, even of firm nerves, standing on a support which feebly sustains him, over an abyss where, literally, fire and brimstone are in dreadful and incessant action; having before his eyes tremendous proofs of what is going on beneath him, enveloped in thick vapours; his ears stunned with thundering noises; must be experienced before they can be understood."

Hoaxes and Impostures.
No. IX
PRINCESS CARABOO.

SOME few years ago, a singular female impostor appeared, and attracted great attention at Bath and Bristol. She was supposed to be some Eastern Princess, who had either been wrecked on our coast or put on shore, but as she did not speak any language that was known here, her history was not easy to come at. Dr. Wilkinson of Bath, very humanely interested himself in her behalf. As she could write, pen, ink, and paper were furnished her, and she wrote a letter which was sent to one or both of the Universities to decipher, but without effect. At length it was discovered that Miss Caraboo was a Devonshire girl, who had in her life "played many parts."

The following account of her early life, and the ballad, will we are assured be acceptable to our readers:—

This girl was born at Witheridge, in Devonshire, in the year 1792. From a very early age, she was accustomed to roaming about. Her mother taught her to spin wool, and obliged her to work as much as she could, and in the season she was employed in weeding in the corn fields; but Mary evinced strong inclination to follow the occupations and amusements of a boy. When fatigued, she would go into the water. Her mother being uneasy at her way of life, procured her a place of service at Exeter;

but she soon left it, and commenced in earnest the life of a wandering mendicant. Sometimes she met with encouragement, and sometimes with rebuffs; but she soon acquired a habit of tearing her clothes to tatters, and to appear as miserable as possible. In a word, she became a proficient in all the artifices, and was exposed to all the vicissitudes of the trade she had chosen.

From Exeter she wandered to Taunton, sleeping under hayricks and in barns, always exciting compassion rather than importuning for alms. In this way Mary's stars guided her to Bristol a few years ago. When she had expended all the money she had collected on the road, she applied to the *Strangers' Friend Society*; but an inquiry having been set on foot as to her character and history, she deemed it prudent to decamp, and set off for London.

On the road she was taken ill, and the future Princess of Javasu, was conveyed in a humble waggon to St. Giles's hospital, where she was confined a considerable time with a frenzy fever. Her youth and engaging manners induced the chaplain of the institution to commiserate her forlorn situation, and he humanely procured her a situation, as servant in a family, with whom she remained three years; but her mistress being very strict, and refusing to allow her as much liberty as she wished, Mary packed up her little wardrobe, and bade her mistress farewell.

She now assumed the male attire, and procured a place as *footman*; and in this disguise she actually lived in her native place, close to her father's house, without exciting the least suspicion, having acquired the art of altering her features so completely that no one knew her.

After residing at Witheridge some time, she removed to a neighbouring village; but being sent with a message during the deep snow about three years before she was overwhelmed, and lay buried all night. In the morning she was benumbed and insensible. The removal of her wet clothes discovered her sex, and she was obliged to leave the place, and set out in pursuit of new adventures.

This young woman is the same person who, a few years previous, passed with some respectable families in Ayrshire, in the west of Scotland, under the name of *Mrs. Mackrinkan*.

CARABOO—A NEW BALLAD.
Respectfully inscribed to Dr. W——n, of Bath.

O Bristol, 'mongst numerous evils,
  Thou hast always been prone to a *hoax*,
Witness *Lukin*, from whom went seven devils,
  The *Haystack*, and *Chatterton's* jokes;
But, guided by fashion and science,
  What could tradesmen and simple folks do?
Can we wonder they plac'd such reliance
  On the tale of the sweet Caraboo!

To have *seen* her—in *that* there was danger—
  The Doctor's *account* must content us;
'Tis well while we burn'd for the stranger,
  That her shy and coy mien would prevent us;
But her sufferings we prize at a high rate,
  When England first meeting her view,
She swam *many leagues* from a pirate,
  Who threatened the chaste Caraboo.

Did she leave her fine garments behind her,
  When she plung'd in the sea in a huff?
Or did those who first happen'd to find her,
  Meet the beautiful creature *in buff!*
She breasted thy waves, Bristol channel,
  Sans petticoat, stocking, or shoe,
'Till landed, *a Fay* brought her flannel,
  'Stead of fig leaves, for poor Caraboo.

By the same more than mortal director,
  A "*couch*, in a *cottage*" was shewn her;
In she popp'd, and there met a protector—
  She *couldn't* ask leave of the owner!

Such eyes, nose and chin, and complexion,
  Apelles of old never drew;
Venus' self had not won his affection,
  Had he seen thy "*sweet smile*," Caraboo.

But oh! every passionate lover
  Thanks his stars 'tis *not often* he can die.
When he finds the fair pilgrim discover
  Such aversion to *men* and to *brandy*.
By *signs* were her wishes unravell'd,
  Or by *words* not unlike the *Hindoo;*
No interpreters ever had travell'd
  To the land which produced Caraboo.

Then she wrote such a delicate hand
  In style not unlike *European*—
But the characters none understand,
  Nor the wisest of linguists agree on;
Blunt Oxford knew nothing about it—
  Learned Raffles was posed with it too—
The Doctor alone didn't doubt it,
  That thou wrot'st *heathen Greek,*
    Caraboo.

Once a week she climb'd up to the attic,
  (*Allah Tallah* said this must be done)
There worshipp'd with fervour ecstatic,
  The rise and the fall of the sun:
Of a gold chain she seem'd to declare,
  Round the neck of one *Jessee Mandue,*
Of the Isle *Javasu* the Lord Mayor,
  And the father of dear Caraboo.

She fences with " dagger and sword"—
  As to trinkets she has but a few on;
Though she carries a magical " chord,
  " Not unlike the Chinese *suon-puon*."
None can harbour the slightest suspicion
  But apathy's niggardly crew;
By the India House soon a provision
  Will be made for the lorn Caraboo.

As the food of her country was fish,
  With them she was fed without grudg-
    ing;
Every day brought her favourite dish,
  And she fed *a good while upon gudgeon;*
A scar on her back, after stripping,
  (Haply done by an Indian *tattoo*)
Was seen—who shall say 'twas a whipping
  Thus flayed thy nice skin Caraboo?

One morning when gorged to the full,
  She stole from her cage like a squirrel;
Glumdalchtch ne'er griev'd for *her* gull—
  Like the gull of all gulls, Mrs. W——rr——ll.
" Hue and cry—search the whole of the
    nation;
" She's stol'n by some *Macratoo!*
" I've lost my outlandish *Circassian*—
  " O! where, and O! where's Caraboo?

To Bath, unassisted and single,
  Having *guess'd* the right way, she had
    hied her;
The scar on her back 'gan to tingle,
  As the *tail of a cart* pass'd beside her;

In *this*, with the *English* tongue gifted,
  Her journey she *begged* to pursue;
In the cart she was instantly lifted—
  But the man never *touched* Caraboo.

The Doctor has giv'n us the sequel—
  At Bath how she ask'd for her tea;
Her story can scarce find an equal
  If she *really did figure a tree;*
Here the Lady of Knowle overtook her—
  What a scene it presented to view!
How she griev'd that she ever forsook her!
  How repentant was poor Caraboo!

" Truth will out," says the saw, " in the
    end"—
So she told them the whole imposition;
  How she dup'd " her benevolent friend,"
Bamboozling the learn'd Physician.
The Doctor now says " D—l take her!
  " The *journal* is none of it true—
" Caraboo is become Mary Baker!
  " And I shall be dubb'd Caraboo."

Eccentric Biography.

HELEN OLIVER THE RUSTIC D'EON.

IN the spring of 1822, a female was discovered to have been working for some time as a plasterer, in a man's dress. The following detailed account of this eccentric character, is given in the Glasgow Chronicle:—

She belonged originally to Saltcoats, is about twenty-seven years of age, and for better than four years she has, of her own free choice, worn the attire, and discharged the laborious duties, of one of the male sex. Her real name is Helen Oliver; but she has assumed the name of her brother John. About six years ago, while she was a maid servant in a farm house in West Kilbride, a particular intimacy took place between her and a person in a neighbouring house, who officiated as ploughman. Being frequently seen walking together in quiet and sequestered places, they were regarded as lovers; ultimately however, this " ploughman" turned out to be also a female; and it is believed by Helen's relatives and acquaintances, that it was the arguments of this personage which induced her to abandon the female dress and duties. Upon Sunday the 4th of January, 1818, while in her parent's house at Saltcoats, she requested her mother to give her her "wee cutty pipe," and she would give her two new ones in exchange. To this unusual demand the mother, after some questions, assented; and Helen immediately afterwards began to write a letter, which, in answer to an inquiry from her parent, she said was to inform the people in Greenock, to whom she was hired as a servant, that she would not be with them for some time for several reasons she then alleged. Early on the following morning, Helen helped herself to a complete suit of her brother's clothes and disappeared, without giving the least intimation of her future prospects, or where she intended to fix her residence. Dressed in her new attire, she reached the house of a cousin in Glasgow on the same day. Her relative was not sufficiently intimate with the person of the fair impostor to detect the fraud. Never doubting in the least that she was "the real John Oliver," among other inquiries for absent relatives "sister Helen" was not forgotten. A plasterer stopt at the time in her cousin's house, and she resolved to learn that business. Accordingly she went for trial to a person in the Calton; but having fallen out with her master, she left the town. She then went to Paisley, where she wrought for about three months, and she was next employed for about half a year in Johnstone. There, either for amusement, or to prevent suspicion, and ensure concealment, she courted a young woman, and absolutely carried the joke so far as to induce the girl to leave her service to be married. Travelling one night between Johnstone and Paisley, she was accosted by a lad from Saltcoats, who was intimate with her person, parents, and history; and in consequence she removed to Kilmarnock, where she remained six months. Besides the places already mentioned, she has been in Lanark and Edinburgh, working always at plastering, except a short time she was employed by a Glasgow flesher, about the Bell-street Market.—A variety of circumstances have frequently impelled this rustic D'Eon to change not only her master and house of residence, but also the town in which she was comfortably employed, particularly as she was often, or rather almost always, obliged to board and share her lodgings with some neighbour workman; and though for obvious reasons she seldom detailed more of her previous history than mentioned the towns she had visited and the masters she had served, yet some sagacious females have been known to declare that "Johnnie must have been a sodger or a sailor," because "when he likes himself he can brawly clout his breeks, darn his stockings, mak' his ain meat, and wash his ain claise." At the beginning of February last, Helen applied for employment to a master plasterer in Hutchesontown. She said she was seventeen years of age, and stated that she and a sister were left orphans at an early age; urged her forlorn condition, and that having already had some practice, she was very anxious to be bound an apprentice, that she might obtain an ample knowledge of the business. Eventually she was employed, and though she had the appearance of a little man, she was in reality a tall woman, being about five feet four inches high. By no means shy of a lift, times without number she has carried the heavy hod full of lime for the Irish labourer in attendance. Steady, diligent, and quiet, she gave her master every satisfaction, and he, considering her rather a delicate boy, feelingly kept her at light ornamental work, and paid her seven shillings a week. Some time since a workman was employed by the same master, to whom Helen was intimately known. The master having learned the facts of the case, placed her apart at work from the men, and took a favourable opportunity to speak with her. She indignantly denied her metamorphosis, offered to produce letters from her sister, declared that she was a freemason, and besides had been a flesher, a drummer in the Greenock volunteers, and made a number of statements with a view to escape detection. One day, an Irishman, with characteristic confidence, sprang upon the heroine, hugged her like a brother bruin, and cried in his genuine Doric, "Johnny, they tell me you're a woman, and dang it, I mane to know, for I love a pruty girl." The agile female extricated herself in an instant, and with a powerful kick drove him from her; at the same time exclaiming, with an oath, she would soon convince him she was not a woman. Ultimately, however, the truth was wrung from her, and she has consequently left the town. She writes a good hand, and previous to her departure, she addressed a card to her master, in which she bade him farewell, and requested him not to make much talk about H. Oliver.

THOMAS HUDSON.

HUDSON was a native of Leeds in Yorkshire, and in the earlier part of his life, filled a respectable situation as clerk in a government office in London: while in this employment, he came in possession of a considerable fortune by the death of an aunt; upon which, he retired into Staffordshire, where he remained for some years, in the enjoyment of every earthly happiness; till unfortunately he became a party to the celebrated South-Sea scheme; and so sanguine was he of its success, that he ventured the whole of his fortune in that disastrous project.

Misfortune now became his intimate companion, the news of the failure of his darling scheme, arrived at the time when he had to witness the decease of an affectionate wife. These severe reverses were too much for him: he left his favourite residence, in a state of bankruptcy, and made the best of his way for London. From this period he became in a manner insane; and Tom of Ten Thousand (as he used to call himself,) was like Poor Joe —all alone!

The peculiarity of his dress, and deformity of figure, attracted particular notice; wrapped in a rug, and supported by a crutch, without either shoes or stockings, did this poor creature perambulate, even in the coldest weather, the fields about Chelsea, craving assistance. Sterne says, with truth and feeling, that

The Lord tempers the wind for the shorn lamb.

Let us hope, therefore, that the

chilling blasts of winter, were rendered as congenial to poor Hudson as the balmy breezes of a summer's day.

After many years of misery, death took this "son of misfortune" from his earthly troubles, in the year 1767, at a very advanced age.

Varieties.

THEATRE OF PUPPETS

"Among other sights in Milan," says a traveller, "I went to Girolamo's theatre of puppets (le Marionette,) and laughed more than at any exhibition I ever beheld. You may perhaps think this entertainment was childish enough; so it was. But you don't know it, nor have you ever seen any thing like it, nor any thing so superlatively ludicrous. The puppets were about five feet, or perhaps less in height; and Girolamo, the master and owner of the theatre, was the animating soul and voice of these grotesque images. He had to speak and modulate his voice in the characters of nine or ten different *dramatis personæ*, male and female. He was, of course, invisible. After an overture from a most miserable orchestra, in which there was neither time nor tune, nor any thing like tolerable music, the curtain, on which was a very clever painting, drew up, and a little deformed black, in a suit of brown, with scarlet stockings, and an immense cocked hat, moved forward upon the stage, and began a soliloquy, which was interrupted by the entrance of another strange figure, a female, who entered into a smart dialogue with the little black, whose gestures, grimaces, and contortions of limb, were amazingly absurd, although perfectly in unison, in point of time and Italian manner, with the recitation which seemed to proceed from his inflexible lips. Had it not been for a certain awkward rigidity in their sidelong motions, when moving from one part of the stage to another, and for the visibility of the wire attached to their heads, and descending from the roof above the stage, one might have been deceived for a little, into a belief of the animal existence of these strange personages. They walked about very clumsily, to be sure; but then they bowed, and curtsied, and flourished with their arms, and twisted themselves about, with as much energy and propriety of effect, as most of those worthy living puppets who infest the stages of the little theatres in London. There were two skeletons, who played their parts admirably. They glided about, and accompanied their hollow-voiced speeches with excellent gesticulations, while their fleshless jaws moved quite *naturally*. Then, to crown all, there was a *ballet* of about a dozen of these puppets; and they danced with all the agility of Vestris, and cut much higher than he ever did in his life. They actually did cut extremely well in the air. You know the technical meaning of that word in the dancing-master's vocabulary. All the airs and graces of the French opera-dancers, their *pirouettes*, spinning round with a horizontal leg, &c., were admirable quizzed. One of these dancers, dressed like a Dutchman, stopped short, after a few capers, and, drawing a snuff-box from his pocket, took a pinch; then replaced the box, and set off again with a most exalted example of the *entrechat*.

His partner helped herself, from a *pocket-pistol*, to a dram, and then recommenced her furious exertion!"

THE FALLS OF THE PASSAIC.

At Patterson, in the state of New Jersey, and about twenty miles distant from New York, are the beautiful and romantic Falls of the Passaic. They are at a short distance from the village, are from seventy to ninety feet high, and are seen in many places with great effect; but the best is from the top of the rock on the opposite side, as it discloses to the view of the spectator, the river which supplies the fall, winding in a serpentine direction, the banks covered with trees of the most luxuriant foliage, in which nature seems to have blended all her varieties; the blue distance rising in mountains of majestic forms, whilst the rich foreground, with the immense body of water, rushing over the fall into the abyss below, till it gently rolls along the silent vale, tends to form a scene inexpressibly grand and beautiful.

The face of the country, from New York to the village of Patterson, is generally very picturesque and well cultivated. The road lies principally along the banks of the river, which is very romantic and well shaded with trees; and, in the summer months, is a great relief to the traveller from the scorching heat of the sun.

AGE OF TREES.

There are various opinions respecting the full age or natural life of trees. Mr. Evelyn, and others, imagine, that from three to four hundred years form the natural life of the oak tree. An oak tree was felled in April, 1791, in the park of Sir John Rushout, Bart. at Northwick, near Blackley, in Worcestershire, judged to be about three hundred years old. It was perfectly sound; contained 634 cubical feet of timber in the trunk, and the arms were estimated at two hundred feet more. In Mr. Gilpin's work on Forest Scenery, there is an account of oak trees in the New Forest which had marks of existing before the conquest. The tree in the same forest, against which the arrow of Sir Walter Tyrrel glanced and killed King William Rufus, remains still a tree, though much mutilated. In Mr. Robert Lowe's View of the Agriculture of Nottinghamshire, several trees are said to have been lately felled in Sherwood Forest, which were found to have cut into them I. R. or 'In R. (*Rex*) and some had a crown over the letters. Mr. M'William, in his Essay on the Dry Rot, goes still farther; he says, that many trees might be mentioned in this and other countries, which bear sufficient testimony of their being far above a thousand years old; and he gives reasons for believing, that several trees now exist, more than three thousand years old!

SINGULAR PHENOMENON IN THE RIO DE LA PLATA.

In the year 1793 the waters of this river were forced, in the month of April, by a most violent current of wind, to the distance of ten leagues, so that the neighbouring plains were entirely inundated, and the bed of the river was left dry. A number of ships which had been sunk in the river for upwards of thirty years were uncovered; and, among others, an English vessel which was cast away in the year 1762. Several persons repaired to the bed of the river, on which they could walk without wetting their feet, and returned laden with silver and other riches, which had been long buried under the water. This phenomenon continued three days, at the end of which the wind ceased, and the water returned with great violence to its native bed.

The Scrap Book.

THE TOOTHLESS COMPANY.

A VERY old gentleman told me that he was once invited to dine with a lady of some distinction at Bath, about his own age, and where he met a party of inmates to the number of *eight*, the lady herself making one. On sitting down to the table, the seven guests looked at the dinner with some surprise, there being nothing solid to be seen in any one of the dishes; no joint of any sort, but soups, minced meats, stewed vegetables, jellies, syllabubs, creams, &c. This old lady amused herself a short time with witnessing the strange looks of her company, before she explained to them the mystery. She then told them that, having an exact knowledge of their circumstances, and a sympathetic feeling towards them, she had resolved to make a *feast* for the whole party, suitable to their condition; that she had reason to know, that though eight in number, they had not *one tooth* amongst them all, and she had therefore ordered a dinner, upon which they need not bestow a thought upon the lost power of mastication. Such an odd piece of kindness, as the old gentleman told me, kept them so laughing all dinner time, that they found the toothless meat almost as difficult to swallow as if it had consisted of bones.—*Heraldic Anomalies.*

AUSTRALASIAN MONSTER.

At LIVERPOOL, New South Wales, two men voluntarily made affidavits, that they had seen in a bush, two miles and a half out of town, a tremendous snake, which to the best of their belief, was *forty-five feet in length, and three times in circumference* of the human body!!! He who first saw it, thinking it dead, threw a stick at it, when it reared its monstrous body five feet from the ground. A third person offered to corroborate on oath the depositions. A party of respectable gentlemen went in quest of this extraordinary object, but succeeded only in finding its track, which bore the impression of immense scales, and confirmed the reports. Some conjecture it must be a species of crocodile, from a mark in the earth fourteen inches long, apparently indented by its jaw.

TRADITION has handed down from father to son a story of a man having hanged himself with a hay-rope over a hay-rick at Berrybush, in the county of Selkirk, one hundred and five years ago. Two men, lately employed in casting peats remembering the tale, curiosity prompted them to dig about the spot; and, to their astonishment, they discovered the body of a man, with a hay-rope about his neck, by which they pulled him out of the moss: neither body nor clothes were the least decayed.—*Border Courier.*

Published by J. LIMBIRD, 355, Strand, (East End of Exeter 'Change): and sold by all Newsmen and Booksellers. Printed by A. APPLEGATH, Stamford-street.

THE CABINET OF CURIOSITIES,
OR
Wonders of the World Displayed.

A world of wonders where creation seems
No more the works of Nature but her dreams.—MONTGOMERY.

No. XII.]   PRICE TWOPENCE.

BLASH DE MANFRE, THE WATER SPOUTER.

BLASH DE MANFRE, commonly called the Water Spouter, rendered himself famous for drinking water in large quantities and discharging it from his stomach converted into various sorts of wine, simple waters, beer, oil and milk. This he performed before the emperor and several continental kings. He is said to have been one of the most wonderful jugglers that ever appeared, and was considered as a magician by many. He travelled through most of the countries of Europe, but declined going to Spain on account of the Inquisition, where a horse that had been taught to tell the spots on the cards, the hour of the day, was with its owner put on a charge of having dealt with the devil. The supposed human criminal soon convinced the Inquisitors that he was an honest juggler, and that his horse was as innocent as any ass of the Inquisition. Blash de Manfre died in 1651, at the age of seventy-two.

WHIRLWINDS.

On the 30th of October, 1669, about six in the evening, the wind being then westwardly, a formidable whirlwind, scarcely of the breadth of sixty yards, and which spent itself in about seven minutes, arose at Ashley, in Northamptonshire. Its first assault was on a milkmaid, whose pail and hat were taken from off her head, and the former carried many scores of yards from her, where it lay undiscovered for some days. It next stormed a farm-yard, where it blew a waggon body off the axle-trees, breaking in pieces the latter and the wheels, three of which, thus shattered, were blown over a wall. Another waggon, which did not, like the former, lie across the passage of the wind, was driven with great speed against the side of the farm house. A branch of an ash-tree, so large that two stout men could scarcely lift it, was blown over a house without damaging it, although torn from a tree a hundred yards distant. A slate was carried nearly two hundred yards, and forced against a window, the iron bar of which it bent. Several houses were stripped; and in one instance, this powerful gust, or stream of air, forced open a door, breaking the latch; whence it passed through the entry, and, forcing open the dairy door, overturned the milk pans, and blew out three panes of glass. It next ascended to the chambers, and blew out nine other panes. Lastly, it blew a gate-post, fixed two feet and a half in the ground, out of the earth, and carried it many yards into the fields.

On the 30th of October, 1731, at one in the morning, a very sudden and terrific whirlwind, having a breadth of two hundred yards, was experienced at Cerne-Abbas, in Dorsetshire. From the south-west side of the town it passed to the north-east, crossing the centre, and unroofing the houses in its progress. It rooted up trees, broke others in the middle, of at least a foot square, and carried the tops a considerable distance. A sign-post, five feet by four, was broken off six feet in the pole, and carried across a street forty feet in breadth, over a house opposite. The pinnacles and battlements of one side of the church-tower were thrown down, and the leads and timber of the north aisle broken in by their fall.

About the middle of August, 1741, at ten in the morning, several peasants being on a heath near Holkham in Norfolk, perceived a wind like a whirlwind approach, pass through the field where they were ploughing, and tear up the stubble and grass in the ploughed ground, for two miles in length, to the breadth of thirty yards. In reaching an enclosure at the top of a rising ground, it appeared like a great flash or ball of fire, emitting smoke, and accompanied by a noise similar to that of carts passing over a stony ground. Both before and after the wind passed, there was a strong smell of sulphur; and the noise was heard long after the smoke had been perceived. This fiery whirlwind moved so slowly forward, that it was nearly ten minutes in proceeding from the enclosure to a farm house in the vicinity, where it did much mischief.

AN ISLAND THAT ROSE OUT OF THE SEA.

The following surprising account of a new island, that rose out of the sea in the year 1707, among the Islands of the Archipelago, and near the Island of Santorini, is translated from the French of a Jesuit Missionary, who presented the account to M. de Seriol, at that time Ambassador from the French Court, at Constantinople:

The ancient name of Santorini, was that of Thera, or Theramena, and famous for its gulf, in which a new island appeared about two hundred years before the birth of Christ. It is now called the great Cameni, or great burning island, to distinguish it from another of less magnitude, which, like the former, rose out of the same gulf in the year 1573. Between these two burning islands, and in the same gulf, the island, which is the subject of this little history, rose out of the sea in the year 1707. On the 23d of May, as soon as the light of the morning had rendered objects visible, the island in question was seen to rise out of the sea, about a league from Santorini. A slight earthquake preceded its appearance, doubtless occasioned by the motion of that enormous mass of matter, which was then breaking from the bottom and gradually ascending towards the surface of the water. A company of seamen perceiving something at a distance, that seemed to float on the water, imagined it must be part of a wreck, and went towards it in their boats; but on finding their mistake, and that what they at first imagined to be the remains of a ship, was, in reality, a prodigious mass of rocks and earth, which continued to rise higher and higher above the surface of the sea, they were greatly terrified, and returned with the utmost expedition to Santorini, where their report spread a general consternation over the whole island.

For some time the inhabitants, who ran in crowds to the sea shore, were lost in astonishment; but at last curiosity and courage got the better of their fears, and some of them resolved to examine this strange object themselves. Accordingly they went in boats to the new island, and, seeing no danger, landed upon it. In passing from one rock to another, they observed the ground was everywhere covered with white stones, resembling bread, and as easily broken. They found also a large number of oysters sticking to the rocks, and were preparing to fill their boats with them; but perceiving the rocks to move and rise under their feet, they were alarmed, and immediately made off in their boats. This trembling was occasioned by the rising of the island, which in a few days gained above twenty feet in height, and forty in breadth; so that by the beginning of June it was elevated more than thirty feet above the surface of the water, and near five hundred paces in circumference. But the five or six following days, its increase being almost imperceptible, it was imagined it would rise no higher. The part now visible was of a circular figure, and covered with a white earth; whence the inhabitants called it the White Island.

The various motions of the island, and the rocks that were detached from it, which sometimes rose above the surface of the sea, and sometimes sunk below it, often changed the colour of the water. Sometimes it was tinctured green, sometimes yellow, and sometimes reddish, according to the nature of the minerals thrown up from the abyss. Sulphur was found in the greatest quantity, so that the waters were tinged with it twenty miles round. The boiling of the sea round this new island was very extraordinary; and on approaching the island, the heat became excessive. All the shores were covered with dead fish, and the air tainted with a loathsome stench, which extended as far as Santorini.

During the whole of June, and the half of July, things continued nearly in the same state; but on the 16th of July, the inhabitants of Santorini were struck with a new phenomenon, more terrible than any of the former. Towards sunset there appeared, about sixty paces from the island, a large column, consisting of eighteen black rocks, arising out of a part of the gulf, which was so deep that all attempts to fathom it had proved fruitless. These eighteen rocks, which at first appeared at a little distance from one another, being united, formed a second island, called the Black Island, and which was soon after joined to the other.

Hitherto neither fire nor smoke had been seen. But upon the appearance of these eighteen rocks, clouds of smoke, mixed with flames, began to appear during the night; and at the same time the most dreadful noises, which seemed to come from the center of the island, were heard. The White Island emitted neither fire nor smoke; but the black island threw out both with such velocity, and in such amazing quantities, that both the pillar of fire, and column of smoke, were seen at Candia, which is thirty-two leagues from Santorini.

In proportion as the black island rose higher, and the breaches in it became larger, the fire increased. The sea became more agitated; the boiling of the waters more violent; and the air, which every day became more noisome, joined with the smoke which the island threw out in amazing quantities, almost took away the breath at Santorini, and totally destroyed all the vines on the island.

During the night between the first and second of August, a noise was heard like the discharge of cannon; and at the same time two sheets of flame burst out from one of the mouths of the black island. The following days the noise increased, and resembled the most dreadful claps of thunder, so that most of the doors and windows in Santorini were broke and burst open. Red hot stones of an enormous size were now seen flying in the air. From the largest mouth of the volcano issued astonishing columns of smoke mixed with ashes; which, being driven by the wind, covered all the neighbouring parts. Some of the ashes were carried as far as the isle of Ansi, eight leagues from Santorini; and a shower of red hot stones, falling upon the Lesser Cameni, formed a scene, which, on a less dreadful occasion, would have been very pleasing. Every day presented something new to the beholders. Sometimes after the usual noises, the appearance of innumerable rockets, were projected from the large opening; and at others, sheaves of fire: which, after mounting to a prodigious height, fell down again on the white island, which became entirely illuminated.

In this manner the volcano continued its eruption several times in a day, till January 1708. But on the 10th of February, the fire, the smoke, the subterraneous noises, the boiling of the sea, and the projection of red hot stones, became more dreadful than ever, and increased by the 15th of April to such a degree, that it was imagined the new island must have been destroyed. But after that time the claps of thunder became less dreadful, the waters more calm, and the stench scarcely perceivable. The smoke however grew still thicker, the shower of ashes still continued to fall, and the southern part of the island still continued to increase.

On the 5th of July, some ecclesiastics ventured near a part of the island where there was neither fire nor smoke, with an intention to land. But, when they came within two hundred paces, they observed the water grow hotter as they advanced. They sounded, but found no bottom with ninety-five fathoms of line. While they were deliberating how they should proceed, they perceived that the pitch on the bottom of their bark melted, upon which they immediately returned to Santorini. They were hardly landed before the large mouth of the volcano began its usual eruptions, and threw out an amazing quantity of red hot stones, which fell on the place they had just left. On measuring this new island from proper stations on the Greater Cameni, it was found to be two hundred feet high, one hundred broad, and five thousand round.

All now continued quiet till the year 1710, when its volcano again vomited out torrents of fire and smoke, and the sea boiled to a considerable distance from the island. No appearance of its increase was, however, observed for some time; but in the year 1712, it was twelve leagues round. The fury of the larger mouth was greatly abated; no subterraneous noises were heard; but considerable quantities of smoke continued to issue, and the sea was often tinged of different colours for more than a league from the island.

We shall conclude this short narrative with observing, that, according to Pliny, the island of Santorini itself rose out of the sea; and that many other islands in the Archipelago are said to have been produced in the same manner.

AN ABYSSINIAN DISEASE.

In Abyssinia there are various kinds of complaints which the natives say are caused by the agency of the devil. One of these called the Tegretier, is thus described by Nathaniel Pearce, the English sailor, who passed some years in that country.

"A complaint, called the *tegretier*, both in Tegri and Ammerrer, which is not so frequent among men as women, is for a certainty very surprising; and I think the devil must have some hand in it. It is very common among them, and when I have been told in what manner they acted I would never believe it until it came to my own wife's chance, who had lived with me five years. At the first appearance of this complaint, she was five or six days very ill, and her speech so much altered that I could scarcely understand her. Her friends and relations who came to visit her, told me that her complaint was the tegretier, which, from what I had heard, frightened me, and I would at the instant have turned her away, only for fear they might think me a brute for turning away my wife when afflicted with sickness. Her parents, however, persuaded me to bear it with patience, and say nothing, for if I were to be angry it would cause her death, and that they would cure her as all others were cured in this country. After the first five or six days' sickness, she began to be continually hungry, and would eat five or six times in the night, never slept, and in the day time she would go about, followed by *some of her parents*, to all her neighbours, borrowing rings and other ornaments for her neck, arms, and legs. I did not like the thing at all; but for the sake of seeing the curiosity, I endeavoured to hold my tongue and be patient. Her speech I could scarcely understand at all; and she, like all others troubled with this complaint, called a man she and a woman he. One day, she called unto me in the presence of her friends after the manner of calling a woman, which vexed me so much that I swore she should not stop in the house. But the moment she saw me in a passion she fell as if in a fit, and I can assure you that I saw the blood run from her eyes as if they had been pricked with a lance."

This made Pearce fearful she would die, and he determined to say nothing more until the day appointed for her cure, " or the devil to be drove out of her," which was done in the following manner:—

" Her friends had hired as many trumpeters and drummers, who go about the country for the purpose, as they thought sufficient; and early in the morning of the day appointed, they loaded her neck, arms, and legs, with silver ornaments, and dressed her with a dress which the great men wear at reviews after battle, which the owners readily lend on such an occasion. After she was sufficiently dressed, she was taken to a plain appointed by herself, about a mile from the town, where hundreds of boys, girls, and men and women of low class follow. Her friends and relations take a great many large jars of maize and swoir for them to drink; I had often seen people go out of the town for the same purpose, but would not for shame follow to see them. However, for the sake of curiosity, I was determined to see the last of this, and I therefore went to the place appointed before daylight, and waited until they came; a cradle was placed in the middle of the spot covered with a carpet, and a great many large jars of maize were placed round it. As soon as she came near, she began to dance, and the trumpeters all began to play in two parties; when one party were tired, the other relieved them, so that the noise constantly might be heard; the drink being continually served out by her friends to all, kept them singing and shouting; she still dancing and jumping sometimes four or five feet from the ground, and every now and then she would take off an ornament and throw it down. Some one being appointed to take care they might not be lost, picked them up, and put them into a basket. She kept on jumping and dancing in this manner without the least appearance of being tired, until nearly sunset, when she dropped the last ornament, and as soon as the sun disappeared, she started; and I am perfectly sure, that for as good as four hundred yards, when she dropped as if dead, the fastest running man in the world could not have come up with her. The fastest running young man that can be found is employed by her friends to run after her with a matchlock well loaded, so as to make a good report; at the moment she starts, he starts with her, but before she has run the distance where she drops as if dead, he is left half way behind; as soon as he comes up to her, he fires right over her body, and asks her name, which she then pronounces, although during the time of her complaint, she denies her Christian name, and detests all priests or churches. Her friends afterwards take her to church, where she is washed with holy water, and is thus cured."

ACCOUNT OF WHITE NEGROES.

THE following account of the White Negro shewn before the Royal Society, is in a letter to the Right honourable the Earl of Morton, President of the Royal Society, from James Parsons, M.D. F.R.S. and printed in the fifty-fifth volume of the Philosophical Transactions.

It appears that the father and mother of this boy were brought down above three hundred miles from an inland country to the Gold Coast in Africa, and were bought, among a great number of others, and put on board a ship bound to Virginia; where they arrived in the year 1755.

They became the property of Colonel Benjamin Chambers, of the Falling-springs, in Cumberland county, in Pennsilvania; and are now employed upon an estate in Virginia.

The father and mother of this child are perfectly black, and were both very young when landed; the woman not being above sixteen years old, and her husband not more than six years older; and when they landed, being asked, how far she was gone with child? answered, so as to be understood to mean, that she was with child something more than six moons, and that this was her first pregnancy. They also declared, that they had never seen a white person before they came to the shore where the Europeans were employed in buying black slaves.

This child was born about six or seven weeks after his parents landed in Virginia, in the year 1755; and was purchased by Mr. Hill Clark, of Colonel Chambers, in 1764, so that he appears not to be quite ten years old; and his mother has had two children since, who are both as black as the parents.

Now, though this deviation of colour in the child, from the contrary hue of both parents, is very singular, and something preternatural, yet instances of the same kind have happened before. We had one about four years ago here in London, which was a white girl, something younger than this boy, but exactly similar in colour, wool, &c.

To this remarkable case I shall subjoin two others, one of which I saw myself, and the other was given me by a gentleman of undoubted veracity; which, though they differ in some circumstances from the above, yet have so much relation to each other as will prevent their being censured as digressions from the subject.

The first is a black man who married a white woman in York several years ago; of which I had an account from an eye witness. She soon proved with child, 'and in due time brought forth one entirely black, and in every particular of colour and features resembling the father, without the least participation from the mother. This was looked upon as a very singular case, because people naturally expect the issue of such a marriage would be tawny; which indeed is the usual effect produced by the congress of black and white persons.

The second case was of a black man, servant to a gentleman who lived somewhere in the neighbourhood of Gray's-inn. This black man married a white woman, who lived in the same family; and when she proved with child, took a lodging for her in Gray's-inn Lane: when she was at her full time, the master had business out of town, and took his man with him, and did not return till ten or twelve days after this woman was delivered of a girl, which was as fair a child to look at as any born of white parents, and her features exactly like the mother's. The black at his return was very much disturbed at the appearance of the child, and swore it was not his; but the nurse who attended the lying-in woman soon satisfied him; for she undressed the infant, and shewed him the right buttock and thigh, which were as black as the father, and reconciled him immediately to both mother and child. I was informed of the fact, and went to the place, where I examined the child, and found it true; this was in the spring of the year 1747.

About nineteen years ago, in a small plantation which belonged to a widow, two of her slaves, both black, were married; and the woman brought forth a white girl; and as the circumstances of this case were very particular, I shall make mention of them here, both for the entertainment of the society, and to shew that this is exactly similar to the case of the boy before us. When the poor woman was told that the child was like the children of white people, she was in great dread of her husband, declaring, at the same time, that she never had any thing to do with a white man in her life; and therefore begged they would keep the place dark that he might not see it. When he came to ask her how she did, he wanted to see the child, and wondered why the room was shut up, as it was not usual; the woman's fears increased when he had it brought into the light; but while he looked at it he seemed highly pleased, returned the child, and behaved with extraordinary tenderness. She imagined he dissembled his resentment, till she should be able to go about, and that then he would leave her; but in a few days he said to her: "You are afraid of me, and therefore keep the room dark, because my child is white; but I love it the better for that, for my own father was a white man, though my grandfather and grandmother were as black as you and myself; and although we came from a place where no white people ever were seen, yet there was always a white child in every family that was related to us." The woman did well, and the child was shewn about as a curiosity; and was, about the age of fifteen, sold to Admiral Ward, and brought to London in order to be shewn to the Royal Society; but, finding that one of the sailors had illtreated the girl he immediately resolved to put her under the care of a captain returning to America, and sent her back to her own country.

Admiral Franklin had taken a Spanish ship, in war time, and brought her into Carolina; and, upon searching, found a picture of a boy who was as beautifully mottled all over with black and white spots as any dog that ever was seen; it is uncertain which was the ground, or what colour the spots were of; several copies of the picture were taken in Carolina; and they said it was the portrait of a child born of negro parents upon the Spanish main; the ship was bound to old Spain. Several other well authenticated instances have occurred, not only of white, but also of piebald and mottled negroes, some of which we shall hereafter mention.

The Book of Dwarfs.

We are men my liege.
Ay, in the catalogue ye go for men;
As hounds and greyhounds, mungrels, spaniels, curs,
Showghes, water-rugs, and demi-wolves are cleped,
All by the name of dogs.—SHAKSPEARE.

CHAPTER II.

IN our last chapter we spoke of dwarfs generally, and the favour in which they were held at different periods and in different countries. We shall now give an account of some of the most distinguished dwarfs of antiquity as recorded by the best historians.

Julia, the niece of Augustus, had a little dwarfish fellow, called Conopas, whom she set great store by; he was not above two feet and a handbreadth in height; and Andromeda, a freed maid of Julia, was of the same height.

Marcus Varus reported that Marius Maximus and Marcus Tullius were but two cubits, or two feet eleven inches high, and yet they were both gentlemen and knights of Rome; and, in truth, we ourselves have seen their bodies, as they lie embalmed, which testify the same thing.

In the time of Theodosius there was seen in Egypt a pigmy, so small of body that he resembled a partridge; yet did he exercise all the functions of a man, and could sing tunably; he lived to the twentieth year of his age.

I have seen (says an ancient historian) some men of a very small stature, not by reason of any crookedness in the spine of the back, or legs, but such as were so from their birth, though straight in all their bones; of this number was John de Estrix of Mechlin, whom I saw when he was brought through Basil to the Duke of Parma, then in Flanders, anno 1592. He was aged thirty-five; he had a long beard, and was no more than three feet high; he could not go up stairs, much less could he get upon a form, but was always lifted up by a servant: he was skilled in three tongues, ingenious and industrious; with whom I played at tables.

There was once a dwarf, at the court of Wirtemberg, at the nuptials of the Duke of Bavaria: the little gentleman armed cap-a-pié, girt with a sword, and with a spear in his hand, was put into a pie, that he might not be seen, and the pie set upon the table; when raising the lid, he stepped out, drew his sword, and, after the manner of a fencer, traversed his ground upon the table, to the equal laughter and diversion of them that were present.

M. Antonius is said to have

had Sisyphus, a dwarf, who was not of the full height of two feet, and yet of a lively wit.

Anno 1610, I saw John Ducker, an Englishman, whom some of his own countrymen carried up and down to get money by the sight of him. I have his picture by me, drawn at full length: he was about forty-five years of age, as far as might be discerned by his face, which now began to be wrinkled; he had a long beard, and was only two feet and a half high; otherwise of straight and thick limbs, and well proportioned, less than he I have never seen.

Augustus Cæsar exhibited in his plays one Lucius, a young man born of honest parents: he was not full two feet high, saith Ravisius: he weighed but seventeen pounds, yet he had a strong voice.

In the time of Iamblicus, lived Alypius of Alexandria, a most excellent logician, and a famous philosopher, but of so small and little a body that he hardly exceeded a cubit, or one foot five inches and a half in height. Such as beheld him would think he was scarcely any thing but spirit and soul: so little grew that part of him which was liable to corruption, that it seemed to be consumed into a kind of divine nature.

Characus was a man of exceedingly small stature, yet was he the wisest counsellor that was about Saladine, that great conqueror of the east.

Anno 1306, Uladislaus Cubitalis, that pigmy King of Poland reigned, and fought more battles, and obtained more glorious victories therein, than any of his longshanked predecessors. "*Nullam virtus respuit staturam:*" Virtue refuseth no stature: but commonly vast bodies and extraordinary statures have sottish, dull and leaden spirits.

Cardan saith, that he saw a man at full age in Italy, not above a cubit high, carried about in a parrot's cage. This would have passed my belief, had I not been told by a gentleman of a clear reputation, that he saw a man at Sienna, about two years since, not exceeding the same stature. He was a Frenchman of the country of Limosin, with a formal beard, who was also shewn in a cage for money, at the end whereof was a little hutch, into which he retired; and when the assembly was full, came forth, and played on an instrument.

C. Licinius Calvus, was an orator of that reputation, that he a long time contended with Cicero himself, which of them two should bear away the prize, and chiefest praise of eloquence; yet was this man of a very small and low stature. One time he had pleaded in an action against Cato; and when he saw that Asinius Pollio, who was the accuser, was compassed about with the clients of Cato in Cæsar's market-place, he required them about him to set him upon some turfs thereby; being got upon these, he openly swore that in case Cato should do any injury unto Asinius Pollio, who was his accuser, that then he himself would swear positively to that whereof he had been accused. And after this time Asinius Pollio was never hurt either in word or deed, either by Cato, or any of his advocates.

There were two of the Molones, who were remarkable for the noted brevity and shortness of their stature; the one of them was an actor in plays and interludes, the other was a famous robber on the highway, both of them were so little that the name of them passed into a proverb, men using to say of a little man, "that he was as very a dwarf as Molone."

Anecdotes of Longevity.

LONGEVITY IN ONE FAMILY.

FIVE brothers and one sister dined together at the Eight Bells, in Canterbury, some years ago, whose united ages amounted to 452 years, viz.

Mrs. Burgess 80	And. Smith 72
John Smith 78	Benj. Smith 69
Edw. Smith 76	Henry Smith 77

The youngest brother has 32 grandchildren; and, what is remarkable, there had not been a death of either a brother or sister of the abovenamed persons for the preceding seventy years.

LONGEVITY OF ARTISTS.

An incessant devotion to the arts and sciences is often supposed to be unfavourable both to health and longevity. The following lists of the ages of several famous musicians and sculptors, will shew how very unfounded this supposition is:

AGES OF EMINENT MUSICIANS.

Tallis, 85; Bird, 80; Child, 90; Wilson, 79; Turner, 88; Holder, 82; Creighton and Burridge 90; Pepusch, 85; Handel, 75; Arne, 74; Stanley, 70; Boyce, 89; Harrington, 89; Burney, 86; Randall, 80; Paesiello, 84; Castrucci, 80; Tartoni, 78; Guglielmi, 76; Geminianæ, 82; Hays, 80; Cervetto, 104.

AGES OF CELEBRATED SCULPTORS.

Michael Angelo, 90; Bernini, 82; Donatello, 83; Puget, 73; Tubi, 70; G. de Pologna, 84; Ghiberti, 83; Bardinelli, 72; Sarazin, 70; St. Guilliard, 77; Giradon, 85; Coyswox, 80; Le Fautre, 84; Vaucleve, 87; M. Anguin, 85; F. Angwir, 76; Coston, 75; Le Moyne, 74; Adam, 77; Rhysbrack, 75; Reynauldin, 79.

Among these names will be found some of the most laborious and remarkable of those who have devoted their live to either of these arts.

Eccentric Biography.

MRS. MAPP, THE BONE-SETTER, OR SHAPE-MISTRESS.

THIS masculine woman, whose maiden name was *Wallis,* learned the principles of her art from her father, who practised as a bone-setter at *Hindon,* in the county of Wiltshire; but quarrelling with him, she wandered about the country sometime, calling herself *Crazy Sally.*

When she first set up as a bone-setter in London does not appear, but meeting with uncommon success in her profession she married, August 11, 1736,* one *Hill Mapp,* a servant to Mr. *Ibbetson,* mercer, on Ludgate-hill. In most cases her success was rather owing to the strength of her arms, and the boldness of her undertakings, than to any knowledge of anatomy, or skill in chirurgical operations. The following particulars relative to her, are collected from the *Grub-street* journal, and other publications of the day, and serve at least to shew, that she was a

* Some verses on this event were printed in the Gentleman's Magazine, 1736, p. 484.

August 19, 1736.—" We hear that the husband of Mrs. Mapp, the famous bone-setter at Epsom, ran away from her last week, taking with him upwards of one hundred guineas, and such other portable things as lay next hand."

" Several letters from Epsom mention that the footman, whom the female bone-setter married the week before, had taken a sudden journey from thence with what money his wife had earned; and that her concern at first was very great; but soon as the surprise was over she grew gay, and seemed to think the money well disposed of, as it was like to rid her of a husband. He took just one hundred and two guineas."

The following verses were addressed to her in August, 1736.

Of late, without the least pretence to skill,
Ward's grown a fam'd physician by a pill,*
Yet he can but a doubtful honour claim,
While envious death oft blasts his rising fame.
Next travell'd Taylor, fill'd us with surprise,
Who pours new light upon the blindest eyes;
Each journal tells his circuit thro' the land;
Each journal tells the blessing of his hand:
And lest some hireling scribbler of the town
Injure his history, he writes his own.
We read the long accounts with wonder o'er;
Had he wrote less, we had believ'd him more.

* General Churchill was " the primary puffer of Ward's pill at court;" and Lord Chief Baron Reynolds soon after published " its miraculous effects on a maid servant," as I learn by some doggerel verses of Sir William Browne, addressed to "Dr. Ward, a quack of merry memory," under the title of the Pill-Plot, or the Daily Courant's miraculous Discovery, upon the ever-memorable 28th of November, 1734, from the Doctor himself being a Papist, and distributing his pills to the poor gratis, by the hands of the Lady Gage, also a Papist, that the pill must be beyond all doubt a deep-laid plot to introduce Popery.

Let these, O Mapp! thou wonder of the age!
With dubious arts endeavour to engage
While you, irregularly strict to rules,
Teach dull collegiate pedants they are fools:
By merit, the sure path to fame pursue;
For all who see thy art, must own its true."

September 2, 1736. — " On Friday, several persons who had the misfortune of lameness, crowded to the White Hart Inn, in Whitechapel, on hearing Mrs. Mapp the famous bone-setter was there. Some of them were admitted to her, and were relieved as they apprehended. But a gentleman, who happened to come by, declared Mrs. Mapp was at Epsom, on which the woman thought proper to move off."

September 9, 1736.—" Advertisement.—Whereas it has been industriously (I wish I could say truly) reported, that I had found great benefit from a certain female bone-setter's performance, and that it was to a want of resolution to undergo the operation, that I did not meet with a perfect cure: this is therefore to give notice, that any person afflicted with lameness (who are willing to know what good or harm others may receive, before they venture on desperate measures themselves) will be welcome any morning to see the dressing of my leg, which was sound before the operation, and they will then be able to judge of the performance, and to whom I owe my present unhappy confinement to my bed and chair.

" Thomas Barber, Tallow-Chandler, Saffron-hill."

September 16, 1736.—" On Thursday, Mrs. Mapp's plate of ten guineas was run for at Epsom. A mare, called Mrs. Mapp, won the first heat; when Mrs. Mapp gave the rider a guinea, and swore if he won the plate she would give him one hundred; but the second and third heats were won by a chesnut mare."

"We hear that the husband of Mrs. Mapp is returned, and has been kindly received."

September 23, 1736.—" Mrs. Mapp continues making extraordinary cures: she has now set up an equipage, and on Sunday waited on her Majesty."

Saturday, October 16, 1636.— "Mrs. Mapp the bone-setter, with Dr. Taylor the oculist, was at the playhouse in Lincoln's-inn Fields, to see a comedy called 'The Husband's Relief, with the Female Bone-setter and Worm Doctor;' which occasioned a full house, and the following epigram:

"While Mapp to th' actors shew'd a kind regard,
On one side Taylor sat, on the other Ward:
When their mock persons of the drama came,
Both Ward and Taylor thought it hurt their fame;
Wonder'd how Mapp cou'd in good humour be—
Zoons! cries the manly dame, it hurts not me;
Quacks without art may either blind or kill;
But *demonstration** shews that mine is skill."

And the following was sung upon the stage.

"You surgeons of London, who puzzle your pates,
To ride in your coaches, and purchase estates,

---

* This alludes to some surprising cures she performed before Sir Hans Sloane at the Grecian Coffee-house, (where she came once a week from Epsom in her chariot with four horses;) viz. a man of Wardour-street, whose back had been broke nine years, and stuck out two inches; a niece of Sir Hans Sloane in the like condition; and a gentleman who went with one shoe-heel six inches high, having been lame twenty years of his hip and knee, whom she set straight, and brought his leg down even with the other."—*Gent. Mag.* 1736, p. 617.

Give over, for shame, for your pride has a fall,
And the doctress of Epsom has outdone you all.
Derry down, &c.

What signifies learning, or going to school,
When a woman can do, without reason or rule,
What puts you to non-plus, and baffles your art?
For petticoat-practice has now got the start.
Derry down, &c.

In physics, as well as in fashions, we find
The newest has always the run with mankind;
Forgot is the bustle 'bout Taylor and Ward;
Now Mapp's all the cry, and her fame's on record.
Derry down, &c.

Dame nature has given her a doctor's degree,
She gets all the patients, and pockets the fee,
So if you don't instantly prove it a cheat,
She'll loll in her chariot, whilst you walk the street.
Derry down, &c.

October 19, 1736, London Daily Post.—"Mrs. Mapp being present at the acting of the Wife's Relief, concurred in the universal applause of a crowded audience. This play was advertised by the desire of Mrs. Mapp, the famous bone-setter from Epsom."

October 21, 1736,—"On Saturday evening there was such a concourse of people at the theatre royal in Lincoln's-inn Fields, to see the famous Mrs. Mapp, that several gentlemen and ladies were obliged to return for want of room. The confusion at going out was so great that several gentlemen and ladies had their pockets picked, and many of the latter lost their fans, &c. Yesterday she was elegantly entertained by Dr. Ward, at his house in Pall-Mall."

"On Saturday and yesterday Mrs. Mapp performed several operations at the Grecian Coffee-house, particularly one upon a niece of Sir Hans Sloane, to his great satisfaction and her credit. The patient had her shoulder-bone out for about nine years."

"On Monday, Mrs. Mapp performed two extraordinary cures; one on a young lady of the Temple, who had several bones out from the knees to her toes, which she put in their proper places: and the other on a butcher, whose knee-pans were so misplaced that he walked with his knees knocking one against another. Yesterday she performed several other surprising cures; and about one set out for Epsom, and carried with her several crutches, which she calls trophies of honour."

November 25, 1736.—" Mrs. Mapp, the famous bone-setter, has taken lodgings in Pall-Mall, near Mr. Joshua Ward's, &c.

" In this bright age three wonder-workers
  rise,
Whose operations puzzle all the wise—
To lame, and blind, by dint of manual
  slight,
Mapp gives the use of limbs, and Taylor
  sight.
But greater Ward, &c."

December 16, 1736.—" On Thursday Polly Peachum (Miss Warren, that was sister to the famous Mrs. Mapp) was tried at the Old Bailey for marrying Mr. Nicholas; her former husband, Mr. Somers, being living, &c."

December 22, 1737.—" Died last week, at her lodgings near the Seven Dials, the much-talked-of Mrs. Mapp, the bone-setter, so miserably poor that the parish was obliged to bury her."

Many of her advertisements may be found in Mist's Journal, and still more accounts of her cures in the periodical publications of her time.

OLD BOOTS.

THE name of this singular character is not known. Among the vast variety of human countenances, none perhaps ever excited more public curiosity than that of Old Boots; he was formed by nature, with a nose and chin so tenderly endearing, that they used to embrace each other; so much so, that he could hold a piece of money between them.

The appellation of Old Boots was given him on account of his being employed at an inn, at Rippon, to clean boots. He always went into the rooms, with a boot jack and a pair of slippers. The urbanity of his manners always pleased the company, who frequently gave him money, on condition that he would hold it between his nose and chin, which request he always complied with, and bore off the treasure with great satisfaction. He remained at the above inn till his death.

Varieties.

THE MYSTICAL NUMBER THREE.

ODD numbers seem to have been much regarded, particularly the number 3, as having a beginning, a middle, and an end. The adoption of this number probably arose from the Trinity, and is generally made use of as follows: If the eyes were sore, they were washed 3 times; in sacrifices the priests sprinkle 3 times; in the Salian dance they beat the ground 3 times; in execrations they spat 3 times upon the earth; Jupiter's thunderbolt had 3 forks; the trident of Neptune had 3 prongs; Cerberus, the dog of Pluto, had 3 heads; the Pythian priestess sat on a tripod, the 3 legs of which signified the knowledge of the gods, as distinguished by the past, the present, and the future;

there were likewise 3 parcæ, 3 furies, and 3 several capacities to the sun, as Sol, Apollo, and Liber; there were 3 capacities also to the moon, as Hecate, Diana, and Luna; the Sabines prayed 3 times a day; and many nations in performing acts of adoration bow 3 times; in this country, people are dipped in holy water 3 times; and diseases were cured by 3 circumlocutions; in approaching royalty it is customary to bow 3 times, once on entering the presence chamber, then half-way to the sovereign, and lastly at the foot of the throne; Shakspeare, in Macbeth, has 3 witches, and their dances have been generally performed 3 times, or 3 times 3; Gay in his fourth pastoral also alludes to this number.

MISCHIEVOUS MONKEYS.

Mr. Forbes, in his Oriental Memoirs, states the following curious facts:—On his arrival at Dhuboy, while the durbar was repairing, he resided in a house, the back part of which was separated by a narrow court from that of a principal Hindoo; this being a shady side, he usually retired to a veranda there during the heat of the afternoon; and reposed on a sofa with his book. Here small pieces of mortar and tiles frequently fell about him, to which he paid no attention, till one day the annoyance became considerable, and a blow from a larger piece of the tile than usual, made him turn to discover the cause: the opposite roof was covered with monkeys; they had taken a dislike to his complexion, and had commenced a system of hostilities which left the governor no alternative but that of changing his lodgings; for, he says, he could neither make reprisals nor expect quarter. One very singular use is made of this active tribe at Dhuboy. Duelling and boxing are equally unknown among the Hindoos; the tongue, however, in their quarrels makes amends for the inactivity of the hands, and vituperation, as in our own vulgar tongue, seeks to stigmatize the object of abuse, by disparaging his nearest relation; but it does not, as with us, confine its reproaches to the mother of the offending party; wife, sister, and daughter, all come in for their share of the slander. Here it is that the Hindoo's sense of honour is vulnerable, such an affront can only be wiped out by the retort discourteous; and he who fails in this, or disdains to employ it, has recourse to the monkeys instead of the lawyers. The tiles in Hindostan are not fastened on the roof with mortar, but laid regularly one over the other; just before the wet season commences they are all turned and adjusted; being placed in order then they keep the house dry while the rains last; during the other eight months it matters not if they are misplaced. It is when they have just been turned, and the first heavy rain is hourly expected, that the monkeys are called in. The injured person goes by night to the house of his adversary, and contrives to strew a quantity of rice or other grain over the roof. The monkeys speedily discover it, and crowd to pick it up; they find that much has fallen between the tiles, and make no scruple of nearly unroofing the house—when no workmen can be procured to repair the mischief. Down comes the rain, soaks through the floor, and ruins the furniture and the depositories of grain, which are generally made of unbaked clay, dried and rubbed over with cow-dung.

The Scrap Book.

ELEPHANT DESTROYER.

ELEPHANTS, though from their size and strength formidable to all the other inhabitants of the forest, themselves live in continual apprehension of a small reptile, against which neither their sagacity nor their prowess can at all defend them. This diminutive creature gets into the trunk of the elephant, and pursues its course till it finally fixes in his head, and, by keeping him in continual agony, at length torments the stupendous animal to death. So dreadfully afraid are the elephants of this dangerous enemy, that they use a variety of precautions to prevent his attacks; and never lay their trunks to the ground, except to gather or separate their food.

LIZARD IN AN EGG.

"In July 1822, the wife of the man who superintends the decoy ponds in the parish of Great Oakley, near Harwich, took an egg from a hen's nest, in which was a remarkable discolouration. She kept it about a week, and, upon breaking it, observed something within alive, which so alarmed her, that she let it fall, and ran for her husband who was close by, and immediately came, and found lying on the ground, surrounded with the contents of the egg, an animal of the lizard species alive, but incapable, from weakness, of getting away. The contents of the egg were fœtid, contained a very small portion of yolk, and with the albumen, not more than sufficient to half fill the shell. The animal proved to be a land swift, speckled belly, about four inches in length, nothing remarkable in its form, except its hind legs being longer than usual. It died shortly after being out of the egg. The man has it dried for the inspection of the curious."—*Colchester Gazette.*

CANINE SAGACITY.

A GENTLEMAN residing at Gosport was, when visiting Portsmouth, usually accompanied by his dog in the ferry-boat. One day it so happened that the dog lost his master somewhere in Portsmouth, and surmising that he had recrossed the water for Gosport, sped his way to the house of a bookseller in High-street, and intimating by every possible means his misfortune—" What!" exclaimed the shopman, "you have lost your master, have you? Well, here is a penny for your fare across the water." The dog snatched up the coin, ran directly to Point Beach, dropped the penny into the hand of the waterman, and was ferried across with the other passengers.

A GLUTTON.

TITUS ANGLES of Darlington, has again shewn symptoms of a voracious appetite, by devouring five pounds and a half of old bacon, nauseous to the extreme. After finishing his repast he was taken in triumph round the town in a cart, and afterwards ducked in the Skerne.—*Durham Paper.*

Published by J. LIMBIRD, 355, *Strand,* (*East End of Exeter 'Change*): *and sold by all Newsmen and Booksellers. Printed by* A. APPLEGATH, *Stamford-street.*

THE CABINET OF CURIOSITIES,
OR
Wonders of the World Displayed.

A world of wonders where creation seems
No more the works of Nature but her dreams.—MONTGOMERY.

No. XIII.]   PRICE TWOPENCE.

MOLL CUT PURSE.

MARY FRITH, or as she was more generally called, Moll Cut Purse, was a woman of masculine figure and spirit, who lived in the reign of Charles the First. She was a participator in most of the crimes and wild frolics of her time; and was notorious as a fortune-teller, a pickpocket, and a receiver of stolen goods. In this she acted much on the same plan that was afterwards adopted by Jonathan Wild, keeping a correspondence with most of the thieves of that time. She was particularly intimate with Mulled Sack, (whose life and portrait we gave in No. IV of "THE CABINET OF CURIOSITIES,") until he once left her in pawn for a tavern score, when she dropped his acquaintance.

Moll Cut Purse once robbed General Fairfax on Hounslow Heath, for which offence she was sent to Newgate, but by the proper application of a large sum of money she soon obtained her liberty. She lived a life of iniquity which was extended to the age of seventy-five years. Moll was very fond of smoking tobacco, which her early biographer thinks hastened her death; but the smokers of the present day would deny such an inference. Moll's character and exploits are alluded to by Butler and Swift. Her portrait we have copied from an old print of the time.

A FEROCIOUS MANIAC.

PATRICK WALSH, a native of Castlebar, in Ireland, aged about forty-seven years, was admitted into the New Bedlam on the 6th of August, 1818, but was formerly in Old Bethlem Hospital, for some time at a mad-house at Hoxton, and has been confined altogether about twelve years.

This ferocious maniac, from the first period of his confinement, has uniformly evinced a character of desperation, vengeance, and sanguinary cruelty, scarcely conceivable; even under the deplorable frenzy by which he is afflicted; and more characteristic of a tiger than a human being, even deprived of the rational faculties.

Indeed his history, previously to his confirmed insanity, has been marked by a disposition naturally fierce and cruel; and it is not improbable that the intolerable stings of a tortured conscience, reflecting on the sanguinary deeds in which he had been an active accomplice, formed the source of that frenzy, which neither length of years, the natural abatement of passion, coercion, or mild treatment, have been able to mitigate in the slightest degree.

This wretched man was a ringleader of the mutinous and murderous crew of his Majesty's frigate the Hermione, commanded by Captain Pigott, who with his officers were massacred by that crew, in the year 1797. This lamentable catastrophe took place in the West Indies, on the 22d of September, when Captain Pigott and all his officers (excepting the surgeon and master's mate,) with most part of the marines on board, were murdered. One of the principal mutineers was Captain Pigott's own cockswain, who had sailed with him for four years; and this fellow found his way into the captain's cabin when he was asleep, and cut off his head, while his accomplices were at their bloody work in other parts of the ship. The miscreants afterwards carried the frigate into Laguira, and sold her to the Spanish Governor. In the course of the war much the greater number of the mutineers were taken on board of other ships, and suffered the punishment justly due to their crimes.

Walsh, the maniac, however, escaped that fate; and from the stories elicited from him, at intervals more lucid and less furious, it appears that he had been afterwards both in the British navy and army, and deserted several times from each. By his own account, he has murdered with his own hand nine or ten persons. He acknowledges to have been a ringleader in the mutiny on board the Hermione: and being asked his motives, he says the treatment by his officers was so tyrannical, that he and his shipmates could stand it no longer. The project was first started by a butcher on board, who belonged to the forecastle: this man came and consulted with Walsh and a few others, who agreed on the horrible project; and one day the parties rushed from between decks, seized the ship, effected the massacre, carried the frigate into Laguira, sold her, and divided the purchase-money amongst them. After he had spent his share of the money he rambled about the colony; and when all was gone, he contrived to find his way to England, where he enlisted in a regiment of dragoons. He deserted from that, and enlisted in the 42d Highland regiment, and was with that corps under Sir Ralph Abercrombie in Egypt. He deserted again from that regiment, and entered as a seaman on board one of his Majesty's ships, from which he was afterwards drafted on board the Victory, and was close to the immortal Nelson when he fell in the fight off Trafalgar.

From the first time of his confinement in Bethlem Hospital, it has been found necessary to keep him always strongly ironed; notwithstanding which, he found means to kill two persons in Bethlem and Hoxton, before he was removed to this establishment. For a long time after his admission here he conducted himself pretty calmly, and was under no very great restraint, until the month of April, 1820. About that time the Commissioners of the Roads had given to the governors of the hospital a large quantity of road-drift, for the purpose of raising the lower part of the airing-ground, which was low and damp. Amongst this rubbish were unfortunately brought in the blade of an old knife and one half of an old pair of scissars. These were discovered by Walsh; and he carefully concealed them until he found private opportunities of grinding the knife to a sharp edge and point, like the killing-knife of a hog-butcher; and watching a treacherous opportunity, when no one could have the slightest suspicion of his purpose, on Sunday, the 30th of April, 1820, he sprung with fury upon a sickly patient named Dennis Leonard, while sitting down, and before he was observed or could be prevented, he inflicted upon the poor man twelve or fourteen wounds, many of which were mortal. The poor victim was carried into the house, but expired almost immediately.

A coroner's inquest was held on the body, who returned a verdict of wilful murder against Walsh; but agreed to add that he was in a state of frantic derangement when he committed the act. He was, however, taken to Guildford, in Surrey, on the 4th of August following, to be tried at the assizes for the murder; but the grand jury of the county, on inquiring into the circumstances, ignored the bill, and the maniac was sent back to this hospital. This fatal occurrence was the first burst of his ferocity since he was admitted here, and he has been under constant restraint ever since. He is naturally a man of powerful strength, which is greatly increased by the paroxysms of his frenzy. He had put on him at first a pair of handcuffs of extraordinary strength, made purposely for himself, which he broke in a very short time. The keeper then put on him, by order, two pairs of the common handcuffs; but these, within two hours afterwards, he smashed into a hundred pieces. It was then found necessary to contrive other means for his restriction, consisting of an iron cincture that surrounds his waist, with strong handcuffs attached to it, sufficient to check his powers of manual mischief, but with liberty enough for all his requisite occasions of food, drink, taking snuff, &c. &c. Such are the means for his restraint by day: not painful to him, but merely for the safety of others. At night it is found necessary to fasten him by one hand and leg to his bedstead, with strong locks and chains. He is never permitted to associate with any other of the patients. He goes out alone into the airing-ground every morning until breakfast time; in summer from six o'clock to eight, and in winter from seven to half past eight; afterwards he is kept alone in the dining-room from morning until bedtime; excepting only when the other patients are there at meal-times, when he is locked up in his own room, the door of which, as well as that of the dining-room, are made of remarkable strength, with double bolts, and perfectly secure, for he would break through the common bed-room doors instantly.

But bloodshed and massacre are the constant topics of his frenzied discourse, and seem to afford him high gratification and delight.

After the murder of poor Leonard, he used to declare repeatedly. " that he was better pleased at what he had done, than if he had all the riches of India, for that it made his mind happy and contented." His vengeance against the poor victim was excited by some dispute about religion. Leonard, he said, had spoken profanely of the Almighty and the Virgin Mary (in a language not to be repeated.) This was the cause of his anger, and he had waited for an opportunity of punishment until the fatal day in which it was accomplished. He rejoiced at what he had done. He told the coroner's jury, that if he could obtain the King's crown, and all the riches of the universe, he would not forego the pleasure of killing him, for all would be nothing to the ease of mind he felt in putting him out of the way.

Yet he has sometimes said, but evidently in dissimulation, " that he was sorry for killing the poor lad;" hoping by his pretended contrition to obtain some snuff, of which he is passionately fond.

But his propensity to mischief, malice, and personal abuse, are as incessant as his taste for bloodshed and slaughter. He has contrived, notwithstanding his restriction of hands and feet, to break above seventy panes of glass, within the last two years, in the dining-room windows, although guarded on the inside by a strong iron wire lattice-work. This amusement he contrived to effect by standing on a form placed at some distance from the windows, and taking the bowl of his wooden spoon in his mouth, he poked the handle through the meshes of the wire-work, and thus broke the pane. This has caused, for some time past, the seats to be still further removed from the windows.

He is continually venting blasphemous imprecations, and the grossest abuse against his fellow-patients, whose names he knows, or adapts others to them. "Stinking Lloyd," " rascally Jack Hallwood," " thieving old Coates," " lousy Jenkins," " sneaking Pocock," " damned Welch," " black Dams," and a poor Greek, whom he calls " a lousy Spaniard."

Even his very dreams, when he sleeps, are occupied with scenes of fury and vengeance : and he takes delight in detailing them the next morning. When he dreams of having murdered any, and sometimes all, of the patients abovenamed, he awakes quite pleased, and details the scene with much satisfaction ; and the manner in which he has gratified his vengeance, and what fine fun he had in seeing them die. He thought he had a sword, with which he first cut all their throats, and then walked round them to see which should live longest; that when they were all dead, or nearly so, he split their skulls, and then transposed the brains from Hallwood's head into that of Lloyd's ; Lloyd's into Coates's ; his to Jenkins's ; his again into the Spaniard's ; and his again to Hugh Dams's. He then ripped up their bellies, and changed their entrails in like manner : and then he hanged and burned them all. But the only thing that grieved him was to hear them all talking in the gallery next morning. He stamps and raves most of the day, and nearly all night, with a piece of blanket crammed into his mouth, gnawing and tearing their souls out, as he imagines and terms it. He picks up pieces of glass, old nails, bones, and spoons, which he grinds to a point, stones of a convenient size for flinging, and indeed every thing that is likely to enable him to do mischief, to which he is always inclined if he has an opportunity.

He stamps on the ground like a cart-horse, which has rendered his feet almost as hard as hoofs, and gladdens himself with the idea that he is trampling some of the persons beforementioned under his feet. He will at times turn with the wildest ferocity to some particular spot, where he pictures to his disordered fancy some of those objects of his vengeance prostrate, and then jumps and stamps with the wildest rage, exclaiming, " Die you rascals, die and be damned !" "hang him up !" "jump his soul out !" "ha, you vagabond, die !" with numberless other expressions of rage and revenge: and this fit over, he comes away, seemingly quite pleased, and sings and whistles, elated beyond description, until he conjures up another imaginary group, on whom he repeats in fancy the same operations. Every voice he hears he supposes to be that of some one abusing him, and even the ducks in the pond he has charged with calling him abusive names, and abuses them in his turn, in furious terms, and tells the steward, with an oath, that if he could get at them he would tear out their windpipes. He swears and blasphemes most shockingly, talks most impiously, and uses the most indecent language : but any topic of murder or bloodshed is his chief delight. He is a strong, hardy fellow ; his aspect wild, brutal, and terrific beyond description. He presents a hideous and appalling specimen of the human savage deprived of reason, and exposed to all the hurricanes of unbridled passions and the delusions of a bewildered fancy.

SPECTRE OF THE BROKEN

That celebrated optical delusion, called the Spectre of the Broken, is thus described from personal observation, by two distinguished philosophers, M. Haue and M. Gmelin. M. Haue, in his diary of an excursion to the Hartz mountains in Hanover, of which the Broken is one, writes as follows: "After having been here for the thirtieth time, I was at length so fortunate as to have the pleasure of seeing this atmospheric phenomenon, and perhaps my description may afford satisfaction to others who visit the Broken through curiosity. The sun rose about four o'clock, and the atmosphere being quite serene towards the east, his rays could pass without any obstruction over the Heinrichshöhe. In the south-west, however, towards Achtermannshöhe, a brisk west wind carried before it thin transparent vapours, which were not yet condensed into thick heavy clouds.

About a quarter past four I went towards the inn, and looked round to see whether the atmosphere would permit me to have a free prospect to the south-west, when I observed at a very great distance, towards Achtermannshöhe, a human figure of a monstrous size. A violent gust of wind having almost carried away my hat, I clapped my hand to it, by moving my arm towards my head, and the colossal figure did the same. The pleasure which I felt on this discovery can hardly be described; for I had already walked many a weary step, in the hope of seeing this shadowy image, without being able to gratify my curiosity. I immediately made another movement, by bending my body, and the colossal figure before me repeated it. I was desirous of doing the same thing once more, but my Colossus had vanished. I remained in the same position, waiting to see whether it would return, and in a few minutes it again made its appearance on the Achtermannshöhe. I paid my respects to it a second time, and it did the same to me. I then called the landlord of the Broken; and having both taken the same position which I had taken alone, we looked towards the Achtermannshöhe, but saw nothing. We had not however stood long, when two such colossal figures were formed over the above eminence, which repeated our compliments by bending their bodies as we did; after which they vanished. We retained our position, kept our eyes fixed on the same spot, and in a little time the two figures again stood before us, and were joined by a third. Every movement that we made by bending our bodies, these figures imitated, but with this difference, that the phenomenon was sometimes weak and faint, sometimes strong and well defined.

"Having thus had an opportunity of discovering the whole secret of this phenomenon, I can give the following information to such of my readers as may be desirous of seeing it themselves. When the rising sun (and, according to analogy, the case will be the same at the setting sun) throws his rays over the Broken, upon the body of a man standing opposite to fine light clouds, floating around or hovering past him, he need only fix his eyes steadfastly upon them, and in all probability he will see the singular spectacle of his own shadow extending to the length of five or six hundred feet at the distance of about two miles before him. This is one of the most agreeable phenomena I ever had an opportunity of remarking on the great observatory of Germany."

M. Gmelin in his account says: "The first time I was deceived by this extraordinary phenomenon, I had clambered up to the summit of the Broken very early in the morning, in order to wait there for the inexpressibly beautiful view of the sun rising in the east. The heavens were already streaked with red, the sun was just appearing above the horizon in full majesty, and the most perfect serenity prevailed throughout the surrounding country, when the other Hartz mountains in the south-west, towards the Worm mountains, &c. lying under the Broken, began to be covered by thick clouds. Ascending at that moment the granite rocks called Teufelskanzel, there appeared before me, but at a great distance, the gigantic figure of a man as if standing on a large pedestal. Scarcely had I discovered it, when it began to disappear; the clouds sunk down speedily, and I saw the phenomenon no more. The second time, however, I saw this spectre somewhat more distinctly, a little below the summit of the Broken, as I was looking at the sun rising, about four o'clock in the morning. The weather was rather tempestuous; the sky towards the level country was pretty clear, but the Hartz mountains had attracted several thick clouds which had been hovering around them, and which beginning to settle on the Broken, confined the prospect. In these clouds, soon after the rising of the sun, I saw my own shadow, of a monstrous size, move itself for a couple of seconds exactly as I moved; but I was soon involved in clouds, and the phenomenon disappeared.

"It is impossible," adds M. Gmelin, "to see this phenomenon, except when the sun is at such an altitude as to throw his rays upon the body in a horizontal direction; for if he is higher, the shadow is thrown rather under the body than before it."

The Book of Giants.

"And there were giants in those days."

Chapter III.

In the time of Augustus Cæsar there were two persons, called Idusio and Secundilla, each of them was ten feet high, and somewhat more: their bodies after their death were kept and preserved for a wonder, in a sepulchre within the Salustian gardens.

In the 58th Olympiad, by the admonition of the Oracle, the body of Orestes was found at Tegæ by the Spartans; and the just length of it was seven cubits, which is upwards of ten feet.

The son of Euthymenes of Salamina, at the age of three years, was three cubits, or four feet four inches in height; but he was slow of pace, dull of sense, had a strong voice: soon after he was seized with manifold diseases, and, by immoderate afflictions of sickness, made an overamends for the precipitate celerity of his growth.

We find it left in the monuments and writings of the ancients as a most received truth, that in the Cretan war the rivers and waters rose to unusual height, and made sundry breaches in the earth. When the floods were gone, in a great cleft, and the fall of the earth, there was found the carcass of a man, of the length of thirty and three cubits, or near forty-two feet. Lucius Flaccus the then Legate, and Metellus himself, allured with the novelty of the report, went on purpose to the place to take a view of it; and there they saw that which upon hearsay they had imagined was a fable.

Antonius was born in Syria in

the reign of Theodosius; he exceeded the measure of human stature; for he was five cubits and an hand breadth, or seven feet seven inches high: but his feet did not answer in proportion to the magnitude of his body. He lived no longer than twenty-five years, saith Nicophorus.

Vitellius sent Darius, the son of Artabanes, an hostage to Rome, with divers presents, amongst which there was a man seven cubits, or ten feet two inches high, a Jew born; he was named Eleazar, and was called a giant by reason of his greatness.

That is a memorable example of a giant, reported by Thuanus, anno 1575, where, discoursing of an inroad made by the Tartars upon the Polonian territories, he speaks of a Tartar, of a prodigious bigness, slain by a Polander; his words are, "There was one found of a prodigious bulk, slain (saith Leonardus Gorecius) by James Niazabilovius; his forehead was twenty-four fingers broad, and the rest of his body of that magnitude, that the carcass, as it lay upon the ground, would reach to the navel of any ordinary person that stood by it!

As I travelled by Dirnen, says an old writer, anno 1565, I was showed a girl of five years of age, who was playing with the children; she was bigger than any woman. After I had looked more nearly upon her, and measured her, I found that her thighs were thicker than the neck of my horse: the calves of her legs bore the proportion of the thigh of a lusty and strong man. Her father and mother being set together might be compassed within the girdle which she commonly wore about her middle. Her parents told me, that before she was a year old, she weighed as much as a sack of wheat that held eight modii, or bushels. Anno 1566, I saw her again; for Count Henry of Faustenburg lodging at my house, she was brought to him; and there both of us were amazed at her wonderful bigness; but in a few years after she died.

In December 1671, there came to the city of Coventry, one Mr. Thomas Birtles, a Cheshire man, living near unto Maxfield: he had been at London, where, and in his journey homeward, he made a public show of himself for his extraordinary stature: his just height, as he said himself, was somewhat about seven feet, although upon trial it appeared to want something. His father he said, was a man of moderate stature; his mother was near two yards high; and he himself had a daughter, who being about sixteen years of age, had already arrived to the height of sixteen feet complete.

Hoaxes and Impostures.
No. X.
THE FORTUNATE YOUTH.

As the newspapers have recently stated that the "Fortunate Youth" had been ordained, but that the bishop, on learning who he was, suspended the exercise of his clerical functions; we give a Memoir of this famous impostor.——CAWSTON, jun. the hero of the tale, at the time of his imposture in 1817, was about eighteen years of age, and is the youngest son of a respectable family residing on the Chippenham estate, near Newmarket. The early talents and solidity of character displayed by him, attracted general notice; and he appeared a boy of such promise, that no expense was spared to cultivate his mind and qualify him for the church. A neighbouring clergyman was his first tutor, and thence he was sent to Dr. Butler's seminary, at Shrewsbury. There was some doubt as to the regularity of his conduct whilst at that seminary, for he did not himself make favourable report of it when questioned on the subject at a late period; but it is now understood that Dr. B. gives him the highest character for general conduct whilst under his care. Young Cawston had stated, that amongst other causes for reproof, he obtained more money than Dr. B. approved, and a letter was sent to his friends, remonstrating against the indulgence of his extravagance; it is now believed that he procured his money, if he had any excess, which may be doubted, from a family in the neighbourhood, although he sought to convert the incident of his riches at that time into one of the proofs of his subsequent fable. Still he pursued his education so as to acquire the reputation of an excellent scholar; and during his vacations he conducted himself with so much propriety, that he was always a welcome guest with a family who patronised him; and his manners were so prepossessing, that notwithstanding a countenance which was not, if strictly examined, a letter of credit, he became a general favourite with every visitor.

In October, 1817, a report prevailed that young C. had come into possession of an immense fortune, under most extraordinary circumstances. The father first mentioned the general fact, and the son soon afterwards authenticated the statement, and gave the following detail of the adventure which rendered him so fortuitously one of the richest subjects in the world:—

About eighteen months previously he had been on his return to school. A schoolfellow who was to have accompanied him had, by some mistake, preceded him the day before, and he was left to go alone in the stage. On his arrival at Birmingham, he was shewn into the parlour of an inn, where an old gentleman was sitting, and who became his companion for the rest of the journey to Shrewsbury. In the course of it the old gentleman and himself entered into a warm altercation on the subject of the South American contest. The dispute continued to the journey's end, and they parted as adversaries.

The next morning, to his great surprise, the old man sent for him, and on his coming into the room, said: "Young man, you were right in your argument yesterday. I admire your spirit, candour, and bold maintenance of your opinions. You shall find in me from henceforth a friend." From that time he lavished many favours on him; money to the amount which attracted Dr. B.'s notice and displeasure, and the envy of all his comrades, who, nevertheless, paid homage to the superiority which he acquired by the power of conferring favours; and thus, in his boyhood, he proved the irresistible influence of gold.

Some months afterwards, the old man, who had hitherto promised only a considerable establishment in the church, sent for him, and declaring that he felt his life was ebbing fast away, announced his intention to make over to him immediately, by a deed of gift, the whole of his immense property. "If," added he, "I should live, contrary to my expectations, I shall be a dependent on your gratitude and bounty." From that moment the old man initiated him in all his secrets, directed him how to conduct his extensive pecuniary transactions, gave him a list of the various names he was obliged to assume to conceal his property in foreign countries, and related all the adventures of his extraordinary and, in some respects, criminal life.—Many of these secrets he had sworn never to divulge, and others he should only unfold as the developement became necessary for the execution of his trust and management of his fortune.

Six weeks afterwards the old man died at a nameless village near Shrewsbury; and, in conformity with his last commands, a lawyer of great eminence and respectability at Liverpool (Mr. S.) was sent for, and who took back with him all the parchments, papers, &c. belonging to the old man, except the deed of gift, which young C. would never part with out of his own possession. At the expiration of six months, the lawyer (Mr. S.) returned and gave him up all the title-deeds, papers, &c.; and at the same time communicated to him that he had almost boundless wealth, but the preservation of the greater part depended on his prudence, secrecy, and conformity to the injunctions and proceedings of the old man, his deceased benefactor. The title-deeds were immediately buried in a garden of one of the estates, and the only person (except one of his schoolfellows of eleven years old, who saw the interment of the strong box) to whom he confided any part of the momentous story of his fortune, was his mother, and who avowed she had been in possession of the secret of his affluence without ever having betrayed the confidence.

The moment was now arrived when he might extend that confidence, but not yet give full publicity to the amount of wealth he possessed. Indeed, some of his property was derived from sources which affected the most serious interests of the highest personages in every country. The great object of the old man, his benefactor, had been to acquire secret influence, by getting as many people as possible into his trammels; nay, the desire of this mysterious dominion had been in him a stronger passion even than avarice. Most of the foreign sovereigns, therefore, owed him money. The Empress of Russia was a debtor to the amount of a hundred thousand pounds, but she regularly paid 6,000*l.* per ann. interest. Prince Eugene was also in his list for a large sum; and on the King of Spain he had immense claims. His principal estates lay, indeed, in that country, but he had also large estates in Germany, Italy, Sicily, and in England—many great mortgages and reversions unknown to the presumed successors, and amongst the latter he cited the painful case of his being one day obliged to dispossess his dearest friend of an inheritance on which he relied, or make him a dependent on his generosity for the restitution.— Exclusive of three millions in the funds, he had palaces in Madrid and Naples; many sets of diamonds; and he intimated that the old man had been largely concerned in the diamond trade, and that he owed the foundation of his fortune to that traffic. At another time he stated that his benefactor had been the soul of the South American insurrection, and that he had solemnly sworn to him on his death-bed to continue the same aids; he was now, therefore, sending out great supplies of ships, arms, &c.; he named two ships, the Asia and Fortitude, as belonging to him, and represented that he met with a deputy on the high road whenever he wished confidential communication, as he dared not trust the utterance of his secrets where there was any possibility of his being overheard or suspected. When speaking on the South American subject, tears came into his eyes at the mention of two of his Spanish friends who had perished in that country under the most cruel tortures. The South American affairs were, indeed, his favourite theme and inexhaustible topic. At every communication he, however, concluded with the most solemn injunctions of secrecy, since he must leave the country if any of the above particulars transpired, being resolved never to submit to any legal jurisdiction which would infallibly be attempted. To frustrate inquiry, he had forbidden all his agents, bankers, &c. to acknowledge any transaction with him, but still he was in continual anxiety on that subject, and had reason to apprehend that attempts had already been made to intercept and peruse his papers and correspondence. He, however, had warned those of his family, whom he suspected, against the indulgence of a curiosity ruinous to himself and inevitably fatal to them. Some few days afterwards most of the above details having appeared in a country paper, and being copied into the London papers, young C. pretended to be almost frantic, and accused his family of having betrayed his interest to gratify a pernicious vanity, but when he was appeased, he pledged himself to continue the liberal arrangements he had resolved on making for the provision of his relatives. Half a million of money was to be appropriated to this noble object, and the details of appropriation were such as augmented the general estimation of his principles and knowledge.

His brother immediately took suitable measures to enter into Emanuel College, with an income of 6,000l. per annum; and young C. on being asked what his father had said on the information being given that he was to have an estate purchased for him with the 100,000l. destined to be his portion, replied, with emotion, "He burst into tears."

For some reasons, which young C. would not assign, the realization of his promises was to be deferred until the 1st of January, 1818; but to sustain his statements in the interval, and lull the suspicions of an anxious suspense, he desired his father to take him to Mr. Weatherby, of Newmarket, who, after the first introduction was over, and the father had retired, received directions from young C. to make his will. To the observation that he was a minor, he replied, that the property being personal he had the legal right. In the next interview, he desired Mr. W. to be one of his executors, to which he agreed, if the father or brother were joined with him; and at a third interview he insisted that Mr. W. should accept of a legacy to a considerable amount, but this Mr. W. refused, although young C. always affirmed he had acceded to the proposition. The will was made, and a copy of it given to young C. From that time the interviews with Mr. W. became more frequent; and Mr. W. receiving instructions to purchase various estates, opened a correspondence with the agent of Lord Cholmondeley, &c. The knowledge of this fact made proselytes of the most sceptical; and applications from all quarters, and on all subjects, were addressed to young C. in the view of deriving benefit from the distribution of his treasures. Every one who had any thing to sell, whether of real or personal property, made their offers, and no one received direct refusals. Negotiations were opened at the same time for change of name, armorial honours, and such distinctions as his pride suggested, or his wealth seemed to justify; but although he sometimes affirmed that a British earldom would be added to his Spanish titles of nobility, it is not believed that he was warranted in such an assertion by any direct arrangement with his Majesty's ministry. The want of ready money was, no doubt, for some time, a subject of much solicitude to the Crœsus of 1818, but his tale had acquired so much confidence, that a relative, to whom he said 100,000*l.* had been promised on the great pay day, entreated him to make use of 1,200*l.* laying idle in Oaks's bank at Bury. The offer was accepted, and young C. was so eager to grasp the prize, that his servant arrived with the check at the bank before the doors were opened. This circumstance, and the employment of a common groom as the receiver of such a large sum, excited some suspicion, and the clerk was sent over to young C. with the money. Young C. gave him one pound for his trouble, put 99*l.* into his purse, which was soon carelessly left about, to be seen full of bank notes, and 1,100*l.* were placed in the bank of Messrs. Hammond and Eden, at Newmarket, who afterwards opened a credit of 1,000*l.* in favour of young C. with their correspondents, Messrs. Cox and Biddulph, Charing Cross.

The 1,100*l.* placed in Hammond's hands were augmented, by report of others, to 5,000*l.*; and the source from whence the original sum was obtained, although known to several, was never mentioned, for in the conviction of young C.'s story being true to its fullest extent, it should seem it was thought right to give him all possible consequence, that might tend to impress the neighbourhood with similar belief.

[*To be continued.*]

Eccentric Biography.

FRANCŒUR THE LUNATIC.

SOME years ago, there was stationed on the island of Ratoneau, the centre of three islands on the coast of Marseilles, and the most deserted of the three, an invalid of the name of Francœur, who, with his wife and daughter and another invalid, composed the whole population of the island. Francœur had been once deranged in his mind, and confined in the Hotel de St. Lazare, near Marseilles, a hospital for the reception of lunatics; but, after a time, was discharged as perfectly cured. His comrade and his wife, however, perceiving that he began to shew symptoms of derangement, sent information of it to the governor-general of the three islands, who resided on one of them, named the Chateau d'If. The governor, not choosing to attempt seizing Francœur singly, for fear of incensing him, sent an order for the whole party to appear before him, hoping, in this way, to get the lunatic quietly and without difficulty into his power. Francœur prepared with the rest to obey the summons; but, at the moment of their embarking, when the other invalid was already in the boat, being seized with a sudden phrensy, he attempted to stab, first his wife, and then his daughter. They both escaped by jumping hastily into the boat; when, pushing off before he had time to follow them, and hastening to the Chateau d'If, they left him alone on the island.

His first movement, on finding himself without control, was to take possession of a small fort, where were two or three guns mounted, with a little powder and ball; and, shutting himself up in it, he began a cannonade upon the governor's house, which did some damage. The governor on this sent a boat with five invalids of his own garrison, bearing an order to Francœur to appear before him; but the latter, shut up in his fort, told those who brought the summons, to carry back this answer: "That his father was governor of the island of Ratoneau, and being his sole heir, the right of domain there had devolved entirely on him, nor would he yield it up while a drop of blood remained in his veins." He immediately fired on the men, who, not being amused with the joke, hastily withdrew. Francœur then began a second cannonade on the governor's chateau; but, after firing a few shots, he was diverted from this object by perceiving a vessel in the bay within gun shot, to which his battery was now directed. The captain, greatly surprised at finding himself treated in this inhospitable manner, sent to inquire the reason of it, when my lord governor replied, that he wanted a supply of biscuit and wine, and if they were not sent immediately, he would sink the vessel. The captain, glad to compromise matters so easily, sent the supplies required, the weather being such that he could not stand out to sea at the moment; but as soon as it was in his power, he hastened to remove from so disagreeable a neighbour. Three or four other vessels which had the presumption to approach within reach of my lord governor's guns, were, in like manner, laid under contribution; nor were the fishermen spared, but were obliged to furnish their quota towards the supply of his lordship's table.

The governor of the Chateau d'If, still unwilling to sacrifice the life of the unfortunate lunatic, sent a second party from his garrison, with orders to seize him, under pretence of demanding a conference; but either from having taken their measures ill, or from cowardice, they were obliged to return without accomplishing their purpose. Extremely emharrassed how to proceed with a man, who, though not accountable for his actions, was in a situation where he might do mischief, the governor of the Chateau d'If sent to the Duke de Villars, who, as governor of Provence, was then at Marseilles, to consult him what was to be done. The Duke immediately despatched a party of five and twenty grenadiers, with a serjeant at their head, who had orders to land in the night, and get possession of the fort by means of scaling ladders while the governor was asleep. This was done accordingly, and his lordship was extremely surprised when he awoke in the morning to find himself surrounded by an armed force. Perceiving that resistance was impossible, he said that he was ready to surrender to the Duc de Villars on honourable terms, but that on no account would he enter into any negotiation with the governor of the Chateau d'If. The terms he proposed were that for the accommodation of his sovereign, he would consent to exchange his government of the island of Ratoneau, for that of the house of St. Lazare, whither he had sense enough to perceive, he should be reconducted; but he insisted on being permitted to march out of the fort with the honours of war, and an instrument drawn up in the proper form; which should confirm to himself and his heirs for ever the government of St. Lazare; while it contained his renunciation of all his rights to the island of Ratoneau.

A promise was made that these stipulations should be faithfully fulfilled; when, shouldering a musket, he marched out of the fort with great solemnity, and there grounding it, walked on quietly to the boat. Thus ended his sovereignty of three days over an island without subjects.

Varieties.

A SCENE OF EXTREME HORROR IN THE PYRAMIDS OF EGYPT.

Some French travellers attempting to explore the vaults of the Egyptian Pyramids, had already traversed an extensive labyrinth of chambers and passages; they were on their return, and had arrived at the most difficult part of it,—a very long and winding passage, forming a communication between two chambers; its opening narrow and low. The ruggedness of the floor, sides, and roof, rendered their progress slow and laborious, and these difficulties increased rapidly as they advanced. The torch with which they had entered became useless, from the impossibility of holding it upright, as the passage diminished its height. Both its height and width, at length, however, became so much contracted, that the party were compelled to crawl on their bellies. Their wanderings in these interminable passages (for such, in their fatigue of body and mind they deemed them) seemed to be endless. Their alarm was very great, and their patience already exhausted, when the headmost of the party cried out, that he could discern the light at the exit of the passage, at a considerable distance ahead, but that he could not advance any further, and that in his efforts to press on, in hopes to surmount the obstacle without complaining, he had squeezed himself so far into the reduced opening, that he had now no longer sufficient strength even to recede! The situation of the whole party may be imagined: their terror was beyond the power of direction or advice; while the wretched leader, whether from terror, or the natural effect of his situation, swelled so that, if it was before difficult, it was now impossible for him to stir from the spot he thus miserably occupied. One of the party, at this dreadful and critical moment, proposed, in the intense selfishness to which the feeling of vital danger reduces all, as the only means of escape from this horrible confinement,—this living grave, to cut in pieces the wretched being who formed the obstruction, and clear it by dragging the dismembered carcass piecemeal past them! He heard this dreadful proposal, and contracting himself in the agony at the idea of this death, was reduced by a strong muscular spasm to his usual dimensions, and was dragged out, affording room for the party to squeeze themselves past over his prostrate body. This unhappy creature was suffocated in the effort, and was left behind a corpse.

DEAF AND DUMB AMATEUR.

It is a singular fact that the deaf and dumb are not excluded from the pleasures arising from music; a remarkable proof of this is related of an artist of the name of Arrowsmith, a member of the Royal Academy, who resided some months at Winnington, about the year 1816, exercising his profession of a miniature and portrait painter.—" He was," says Mr. Chippendale of Winnick, who relates the anecdote, " quite deaf.' It will scarcely be credited, that a person thus circumstanced should be fond of music; but this was the case with Mr. Arrowsmith. He was at a gentleman's glee club, of which I was President at that time, and as the glees were sung, he would place himself near some article of wooden furniture, or a partition, door, or window-shutter, and would fix the extreme end of his finger nails, which he kept rather long, upon the edge of some projecting part of the wood, and there remain until the piece under performance was finished; all the time expressing, by the most significant gestures, the pleasure he felt in the perception of musical sounds. He was not so much pleased with a solo as with a pretty full clash of harmony; and if the music was not very good, or rather if it was not correctly performed, he would show the slightest sensation of pleasure. But the most extraordinary circumstance in this case is, that he was evidently most delighted with those passages in which the composer displayed his science in modulating the different keys. When such passages happened to be executed with precision, he could scarcely repress the emotions of pleasure which he received within any bounds; for the delight he evinced seemed to border on ecstasy. This was expressed most remarkably at our club, when the glee was sung with which we often conclude; it is by Stevens, and begins with the words " Ye spotted snakes," from Shakspeare's *Midsummer Night's Dream*. In the second stanza, on the words, " Weaving spiders come not here," there is some modulation of the kind above alluded to, and here Mr. Arrowsmith would be in raptures, such as would not be exceeded by any one who was in immediate possession of the sense of hearing."

SINGULAR ESCAPE.

In 1817, as some sailors were endeavouring to split some old bomb-shells on the beach at Margate, by driving iron tapering bolts in the fusee holes, one thirteen-inch shell, which had been lying on the beach some years, resisted all their power to rend it, and not being able to withdraw the bolt, they took it to Mr. Chapman's forge, and heated it red hot. Observing it make a hissing noise, they apprehended danger, and withdrew some little distance from it, when it made an explosion as loud as a six pounder, drove out the iron bolt through an adjoining partition, and the shell itself took a direction through the front window of the shop, and carrying away the jamb of the window, struck the front of Mr. Bamford's house on the opposite side of the street, at an elevation of seven feet from the fire whereat it was heated. It went with such velocity as to drive in the flints five inches, breaking some to pieces, and others into powder. The shell weighed two cwt. and was not the least damaged, and providentially no person was hurt.

The Scrap Book.

NUMBER OF EYES IN THE BEETLE AND HORSE FLY.

The eyes of insects are immoveable, and many of them seem cut into a multitude of little planes or *facets*, like the facets of a diamond, and have the appearance of net-work. Each of these facets is supposed to possess the power and properties of an eye, and Leuenhoeck counted *three thousand one hundred and eighty one* of them in the cornea of a beetle, and *eight thousand* in those of a horse-fly!

SINGULAR WILL.

An inhabitant of Montgaillard, lately deceased, left the following testament:—"It is my will that any one of my relations who shall presume to shed tears at my funeral shall be disinherited; he, on the other hand, who laughs most heartily, shall be sole heir. I order, that neither the church nor my house shall be hung with black cloth; but that on the day of my burial, the house and church shall be decorated with flowers and green boughs. Instead of the tolling of bells, I will have drums, fiddles, and fifes. All the musicians of Montgaillard and its environs shall attend the funeral. Fifty of them shall open the procession with hunting tunes, waltzes, and minuets." This will create the more surprise, as the deceased had always been denominated by his family, the Misanthrope, on account of his gloomy and reserved character.

KING OF OTTER HUNTERS.

Mr. W. Williamson, papermaker, Milnthorp, claims this title, having caught in his life time thirty-six otters, three of which he tamed, being as familiar with him as lap-dogs; they would frequently follow him even miles from home, would at all times obey him, and at his command would perform a variety of entertaining actions. One of these animals slept with him every night during a whole winter; and it would not suffer any person to molest him.

REMARKABLE FAMILY.

In January 1823, there lived at Wonersh, near Guildford, a woman of the name of Punteen, at the age of ninety-six years, whose daughter is the mother of sixteen children, one of whom (a daughter) has had sixteen children, one of whom has also become the mother of sixteen children: consequently the old lady has sixteen grandchildren, sixteen great-grandchildren, and sixteen great-great-grandchildren, all living.

Published by J. LIMBIRD, 355, Strand, (East End of Exeter 'Change); and sold by all Newsmen and Booksellers. Printed by A. APPLEGATH, Stamford-street.

THE CABINET OF CURIOSITIES,
OR
Wonders of the World Displayed.

A world of wonders where creation seems
No more the works of Nature but her dreams.—MONTGOMERY.

No. XIV.]   PRICE TWOPENCE.

SIR HARRY DIMSDALE, MAYOR OF GARRATT.

SOME doubt exists as to the origin of the Mayors of Garratt; though they are generally believed to have taken their rise from a frolic towards the close of the seventeenth century, when some watermen, during an election, determined on passing a merry day at Garratt, a district in the parish of Wandsworth, in Surry, took into their heads to choose one of their company representative of that place. Ever since, at a general election, the custom has been generally kept up, and the Mayor, who is usually a cripple or an idiot, is elected. The crowd collected on such occasions, occasioned a sort of fair, and the election, on this account, perhaps, was principally encouraged. The last Mayor of Garratt was *Sir* Harry Dimsdale, as he was called; for the power

P

which made him representative of Garratt, conferred on him the honour of knighthood.

This poor idiot was born in Shug-lane, Haymarket, in the year 1758. Of his early pursuits little is known; but we find him in 1788, receiving parochial relief from St. Martin's parish: his trade at that time was vending " bobbins, thread, and stay-laces for the ladies:" he next commenced muffin dealer; by which he rendered himself very conspicuous about the streets of London. His harmless behaviour gained him many customers, and life rolled on gaily and smoothly, till ' ambition fired his soul;' and he aspired to the honour of representing the borough of Garratt, on the death of that celebrated character Sir Jeffrey Dunstan; and in which he was successful. Sir Harry was elected to fill the *important* station of Mayor of Garratt, during four parliaments; though not without experiencing violent opposition in the persons of Squire Jobson the bill-sticker, Lord Goring the ministerial barber, and others. The following is a copy of his address to his constituents, at the general election 1807.

> To the worthy, free, and independent electors of the ancient borough of Garratt.
>
> Gentlemen,
>
> Once more you are called on to exercise your invaluable right, the elective franchise, for your ancient and honourable borough, and once more your faithful representative, for the three last parliaments, offers himself a candidate.
>
> Gentlemen, as all the Talents were lately dismissed, disgracefully, it is requisite I should declare to you, I held no place under them. I am, gentlemen, no milk and water patriot—I am no summer insect—I have always been a champion for the rights and privileges of my constituents—and as we have now an entire change of men, I hope, as they are called by many all the Blocks, they will see the necessity of calling to their aid and assistance, men who have long been hid in obscurity—men, whose virtue and integrity may shine at this awful crisis—and, gentlemen, should they at length see their interest so clear, as to call into action my abilities, I declare I am ready to accept any place under them, but I am determined to act on independent principles, as my worthy colleague, Lord Cochrane, so loudly and so often swore on the hustings, at Covent Garden.
>
> Gentlemen, I congratulate you on the defeat of Sixpenny Jack,* he was obliged to hop off and leave the laurel of victory to Sir Francis Burdett and my worthy colleague Lord Cochrane, and should any Quixotic candidate be hardy enough to contest with me the high honour of representing your ancient borough, I have no doubt, by your manly exertions, you will completely triumph over my opponent. In times past, you have had confidence in my wisdom and integrity—you have looked up to me as your guardian angel—and I hope you have not been deceived; for, believe me, when I repeat what I so often have done, I am ready to sacrifice life, health, and fortune, in defence of the invaluable rights, privileges, and immunities of your ancient and honourable borough.
>
> I am, &c.
> SIR HARRY DIMSDALE.
> From my attic chamber,
> The dirty end of Monmouth-street,
> June 10, 1807.

* John E——t, Esq.

In this contest, Sir Harry was again successful, and his procession to Garratt-lane, exceeded *any thing of the kind* ever seen in London. He was placed (or rather, tied) on an eminence in a carriage somewhat resembling a triumphal car, drawn by four horses, which were profusely decorated with dyed wood shavings—a substitute for ribands. The dress of Sir Harry was perfectly *en suite;* and the *tout ensemble* a rare display of eccentric magnificence. Solomon, in all his glory, was not arrayed like the Mayor of Garratt, on this memorable day.

And now, for a short time, all was sunshine with Sir Harry; yet, he found something was wanting to complete his happiness, and he resolved on taking to his bosom a wife; a suitable object presenting herself in the person of an inmate of St. Ann's workhouse. In a few weeks after the consummation of their nuptials, his *rib*, with the utmost *good-nature*, presented him with a son and heir, of which he was very proud.

In addition to his office of Mayor, he was nominated as a proper person to be opposed to the then all-powerful Buonaparte, whereupon he was elected Emperor. His garb now assumed all the show of royalty; but unlike most monarchs, he carried his crown in his hand; it not being correct, he said, for him to wear it till he had ousted his more powerful rival. In this character, Sir Harry levied pretty handsome contributions on the good people of London; but the novelty of his person at length lost most of its attractions; he became neglected; illness seized him; and he died in the year 1811, in the 53d year of his age.

By his death, the boys were deprived of an object of ridicule, and the compassionate man spared the painful task of witnessing so harmless a being tormented and ill-used by the unfeeling and the heedless: for, as Shakspeare says,

God made him,
Therefore let him pass for a man.

ON HUMAN HORNS
BY SIR EVERARD HOME, BART. F.R.S.

HORNY excrescences arising from the human head have not only occurred in this country, but have been met with in several other parts of Europe; and the horns themselves have been deposited as valuable curiosities in the first collections in Europe.

In giving the history of a disease so rare in its occurrence, and in its effects so remarkable as almost to exceed belief, it might be thought right to take some pains in bringing proofs to ascertain that such a disease does really exist: I consider the doing so as less necessary at present, there being two women now (1791) alive, and residing in England, who are affected by the complaint. I shall, however, in the course of this paper, bring other evidence from the testimony of the most respectable authors who have considered this subject.

The two following cases contain a very accurate and distinct history of the progress of the disease through its different stages, and make any further detail of the symptoms entirely unnecessary.

Mrs. Lonsdale, a woman fifty-six years old, a native of Horncastle in Lincolnshire, fourteen years ago, observed a moveable tumor on the left side of her head, about two inches above the upper arch of the left ear, which gradually increased in the course of four or five years to the size of a pullet's egg, when it burst, and for a week continued to discharge a thick, gritty fluid. In the center of the tumor, after the fluid was discharged, she perceived a small soft substance, of the size of a pea, and of a reddish colour on the top, which at that time she took for proud flesh. It gradually increased in length and thickness, and continued pliable for about three months, when it first began to put on a horny appearance. In two years and three months from its first formation, made desperate by the increased violence of the pain, she attempted to tear it from her head; and with much difficulty, and many efforts, at length broke it in the middle, and afterwards tore the root from her head, leaving a considerable depression which still remains in the part where it grew. Its length altogether is about five inches, and its circumference at the two ends about one inch; but in the middle rather less. It is curled like a ram's horn contorted, and in colour much resembling isinglass.

From the lower edge of the depression another horn is now growing, of the same colour with the former, in length about three inches, and nearly the thickness of a small goosequill; it is less contorted, and lies close upon the head.

A third horn, situated about the upper part of the lambdoidal suture, is much curved, above an inch in length, and more in circumference at its root: its dirction is backwards, with some elevation from the head. At this place two or three successive horns have been produced, which she has constantly torn away; but, as fresh ones have speedily followed, she leaves the present one unmolested in hopes of its dropping off.

Besides these horny excrescences, there are two tumors, each of the size of a large cockle; one upon the upper part, the other about the middle of the left side of the head: both of them admit of considerable motion, and seem to contain fluids of unequal consistence; the upper one affording an obscure fluctuation, the other a very evident one.

The four horns were all preceded by the same kind of incisted tumors, and the fluid in all of them was gritty; the openings from which the matter issued were very small, the cists collapsed and dried up, leaving the substance from which the horn proceeded distinguishable at the bottom. The cists gave little pain till the horns began to shoot, and then became very distressing, and continued with short intervals till they were removed. This case is drawn up by the surgeon who attended the woman for many years, which gave him frequent opportunities of seeing the disease in its different stages, and acquiring an accurate history of its symptoms.

Mrs. Allen, a middle-aged woman, resident in Leicestershire, had an incisted tumor upon her head, immediately under the scalp, very moveable, and evidently containing a fluid. It gave no pain unless pressed upon, and grew to the size of a small hen's egg. A few years ago it burst, and discharged a fluid; this diminished in quantity, and in a short time a horny excrescence, similar to those above-mentioned, grew out from the orifice, which has continued to increase in size; and in the month of November 1790, the time I saw it, it was about five inches long, and a little more than an inch in circumference at its base. It was a good deal contorted, and the surface very irregular, having a laminated appearance. It moved readily with the scalp, and seemed to give no pain upon motion; but, when much handled, the surrounding skin became inflamed. This woman came to London, and exhibited herself as a show for money; and it is highly probable, that so rare an occurrence would have sufficiently excited the public attention to have made it answer her expectations in point of emolument, had not the circumstance been made known to her neighbours in the country, who were much dissatisfied with the measure, and by their importunity obliged her husband to take her into the country.

That the cases which I have related may not be considered as peculiar instances from which no conclusions can be drawn, it may not be amiss to take notice of some of the most remarkable histories of this kind, mentioned by authors, and see how far they agree with those I have stated, in the general characters that are sufficiently obvious to strike a common observer; for the vague and indefinite terms in which authors express themselves on this subject, shew plainly that they did not understand the nature of the disease, and their accounts of it are not very satisfactory to their readers.

In the Ephemerides Academiæ Naturæ Curiosorum there are two cases of horns growing from the human body. One of these instances was a German woman, who had several swellings, or ganglions, upon different parts of her head, from one of which a horn grew. The other was a nobleman, who had a small tumor, about the size of a nut, growing upon the parts covering the two last or lowermost vertebræ of the back. It continued for ten years, without undergoing any apparent change; but afterwards enlarged in size, and a horny excrescence grew out from it.

In the history of the Royal Society of Medicine, there is an account of a woman, ninety-seven years old, who had several tumors on her head, which had been fourteen years in growing to the state they were in at that time: she had also a horn which had originated from a similar tumor. The horn was very moveable, being attached to the scalp, without any adhesion to the skull. It was sawn off, but grew again, and although the operation was repeated several times, the horn always returned.

Bartholine, in his Epistles, takes notice of a woman who had a tumor under the scalp, covering the temporal muscle. This gradually enlarged, and a horn grew from it, which had become twelve inches long in the year 1646, the time he saw it. He gives us a representation of it, which bears a very accurate resemblance to that which I have mentioned to have seen in November 1790. No tumor or swelling is expressed in the figure; but the horn is coming directly out from the surface of the skin.

In the Natural History of Cheshire, a woman is mentioned to have lived in the year 1668, who had a tumor or wen upon her head for thirty-two years, which afterwards enlarged, and two horns grew out of it; she was then seventy-two years old.

There is a horny excrescence in the British Museum, which is eleven inches long, and two inches and a half in circumference at the base, or thickest part. The following account of this horn I have been favoured with by Dr. Gray, taken from the records of the Museum. A woman, named French, who lived near Tenterden, had a tumor or wen upon her head, which increased to the size of a walnut: and in the forty-eighth year of her age this horn began to grow, and in four years arrived at its present size.

There are many similar histories of these horny excrescences in the authors I have quoted, and in several others; but those mentioned above are the most accurate and particular with respect to their growth, and in all of them we find the origin was from a tumor, as in the two cases I have related; and although the nature of the tumor is not particularly mentioned, there can be no doubt of its being of the incisted kind, since in its progress it exactly resembled them, remaining stationary for a long time, and then coming forwards to the skin; and the horn being much smaller than the tumor previously to the formation of the horn, is a proof that the tumor must have burst, and discharged its contents.

From the foregoing account it must appear evident, that these horny excrescences are not to be ranked among the appearances called *lusus naturæ:* nor are they altogether the product of disease, although undoubtedly the consequence of a local disease having previously existed; they are, more properly speaking, the result of certain operations in the part for its own restoration; but the actions of the animal economy being unable to bring them back to their original state, this species of excrescence is formed as a substitute for the natural cuticular covering —*Philosophical Transactions, Vol.* 81.

Hoaxes and Impostures.
No. XI.
THE FORTUNATE YOUTH,
[Continued from p. 204.]

YOUNG CAUSTON now saw himself the object of general interest, not merely in a Newmarket circle, but amongst all ranks in every part of the kingdom, and he also found that even the most exaggerated absurdities fascinated more than probable narrative. Still he was not indifferent to the dumb shew of the drama. In all his views he seemed to be guided by the most disinterested and honourable feelings. His generosity was romantic, but still it was tempered with a delicate tact and refinement, with a knowledge of mankind, and a quick perception of character, surprising for his age, and rarely to be met with in the real transactions of life. With his intimate friends he avoided all conversation about his affairs; and before strangers he appeared to be retired in his habits, absorbed in thought, and overcome by intense application to business, and the anxieties attending the management of his important concerns at home and abroad. He generally read great part of the night, wrote and received many letters, pretended to despatch couriers to London and Liverpool, but without ostentation, and kept a German secretary (who once travelled with Lor-

Darlington) in constant employment. His expenses were not considerable, but still he was sometimes profuse, and his allowance of 200l. per annum to his groom appeared a culpable extravagance, until he justified it by stating that it was no more than a just compensation for the confidence he was obliged to repose in him, and the fatigue he encountered in carrying his most secret despatches to their various destinations. Sometimes a draft was accidentally suffered to fall out of his pocket-book, and he appeared eager to recover it, but not before the figures representing a considerable sum had been seen by some of the company.

Now and then he produced drafts signed by himself, but under assumed names, to verify some anecdote he might be relating to the mysterious transactions of the old man, and which obliged him to pursue the same alias system. Amongst those drafts was one on Hanbury and Lloyd, in favour of the Duke San Carlos, and in the name of Puerta, for 335,000l.; another on the same firm for 150,000l. after date, as he stated he had overdrawn the house 100,000l. for the moment, to make a Spanish loan. This draft not being on stamped paper, he said, was of no consequence, as the stamp might be affixed at any time, and then it would be rendered legally valid. Another in the name of Forrester, on the bank of Shrewsbury, for 37,000l.; and this draft he appeared to send instantly by the post, as he requested the bell might be rung for his servant to carry it there; and on his coming in gave him what was then presumed to be the letter he had shewn. Occasionally he embellished his tales with appropriate anecdotes, then expressing great apprehension that avarice would become his predominant passion, said that he felt it growing, and that the only antidote in his case was the acquisition of power.

He rejected all questions about the old man, but once he said that he had a sister living in Kent; that she was a lady of rank, but he could not mention her name, as it would endanger her happiness and interests; but that the estate she now enjoyed would devolve to him at her death. He also spoke of two noblemen, who had put themselves so completely in the power of the old man, that even their lives were compromised; that during the time he was on a visit to Sir J. H. near Edinburgh, the father of one of his schoolfellows, he had given up the fatal papers, which one nobleman had claimed, and who, in consequence, had placed at his disposition a living of 800l. a year; but he had refused 9,000l. for those which affected the other, and that he would never part with them, as he was resolved, in consequence of some pretended injury, on humbling him, and on making him an instrument of his will. Adverting to tenderer connections, he admitted an early attachment and indiscreet engagement to a lady at Shrewsbury; but as he had lent the family large sums of money, he had controlled their resentment at his subsequent defection from the lady's charms. He might have married a young lady of high rank in Scotland, connected with a person from whom he pretended to have received another incidental legacy of 3,000l.; and that General Bolivar, in gratitude for the services rendered by his benefactor, and continued by him, towards the South Americans, had recently offered him his daughter in marriage. Matrimony, however, was his professed object, and to ingratiate himself still more into the favour of a family who had countenanced him through life for his promising talents and unassuming manners, he insisted on being the adopted parent of a little boy, to whom he had once expected to be the tutor. Before the consent was actually given, he took the boy from his school, and removed him to the care of his own original instructor, the Rev. Mr. O. to whom he held out the assurance of a very large compensation for the attention he required of him, and which compensation would blend with a debt of gratitude which had been contracted on his own account.

Some time afterwards he solicited a union with the family, and with the consent of the respective parents he was allowed to express his admiration, "where for so many years he had confined his feelings to the language of acknowledgment for protection." The family being obliged to go to town, young C. affected a low nervous state, and earnestly requested permission to accompany his friends. In the first instance he occupied lodgings near Pall Mall, where he was attended by Mr. P. and Dr. H., to the latter of whom he almost immediately proposed the appointment of travelling physician during his journey to Spain (where he was obliged to go to take possession of his estates), with a salary of 10,000*l.* per annum as a compensation for the sacrifices of his professional business.

His nervous affection appearing to continue, his medical advisers recommended his removal to the more comfortable residence of his friend, who immediately wrote for his mother to come up to him, but received him in his house, on the 25th of November, until her arrival.

From his first coming to town he had entered freely into conversation with all classes of persons who approached him, and related particulars of his history, fortune, and prosperity, with many inconsistencies, as have since been discovered, but still he imposed on all hearers, and by exhibition of parchment documents (which there is a suspicion he engrossed himself, as blank parchment was seen in his possession) and of fictitious drafts of immense amount, he paralysed completely that good common sense which, if once exerted, must have discovered the imposition. As the first of January approached, his character seemed to change; instead of his usual gentleness, he displayed great violence of temper, and an irritation on the most trifling subjects, that greatly alarmed all about him for the state of his mind. At length his language was so extravagant that it was feared the acquisition of fortune had overpowered his faculties, and his physicians were consulted, but they contradicted the opinion, and vouched for his sanity of mind. It was nevertheless resolved, on the 30th of November, to remove him, and terminate an intercourse which could no longer exist with any prospect of happiness, whatever might be the wealth at his command, and Mr. W. the solicitor, was sent for, that a painful personal explanation with young C. might be avoided.

Before, however, this determination had been carried into execution, young C. had sent for the lawyer of the family, Mr. E. of Gray's Inn, and, after making him execute another will, gave him various instructions, amongst which was that of advertising for all claims on the estate of Gasper Quintella,* as the old man, his benefactor, had possessed an estate in that name, and from his books it appeared owed to some creditors about 6,000*l.* which he, young C. was anxious to pay immediately. This trait of honesty, and imagined proof of redundant money at command, added to the circumstance of the solicitor being sent for to the house of the family by whom he was regularly employed on their own important affairs, stifled every doubt of his mind, and he proceeded accordingly to execute the directions he had received.

To the family young C. had represented the employment of Mr. E. as the consequence of his connection with Mr. S. of Liverpool; but his anxiety to prevent any communication with Mr. E. until he had arranged, as he said, all his business, caused inquiries to be instituted by others, which convicted him of a fallacious representation of the affairs he was pretending to transact, for instead of a proposition to pay debts, he had stated he was selling to Mr. E. debts of the old man for ready money, as was his practice, to avoid the trouble of collection. Young C. foreseeing the hour of detection must arrive, had always insisted on the necessity of a journey to Spain, that he might enter into possession of his property in that country; and in his interview with Mr. E. had requested him to procure passports, not only for that country, but also for Germany, Switzerland, France, Italy, &c. which Mr. E. declined, as not being in his province, but he indicated the regular mode to obtain them.

A day or two afterwards the foreign secretary came to the family and announced his departure the same night on a mission to the Continent to collect 700,000*l.* which belonged to young C. from several bankers in Germany, and return with it so expeditiously that he should not be absent more than six weeks. The secretary accordingly took his leave, and remained in London, notwithstanding a person subsequently declared that he had gone to Dover to embark, but with an irregular passport, so that he was sent for to town again by the Alien Office; a declaration which, on inquiry at the Alien Office, proved not to be true. Such is the baneful influence of delusion, that few can resist the contagion of misrepresentation when veracity is to manifest their error.

At length, on the 3d of Dec. Mr. W. who had been too much occupied to attend the first summons, on the 30th of November arrived, and the letter was put into his hands which announced the necessity of his client's immediate removal. Some conversation ensued at the instigation of a person present, which on Mr. W.'s own denial of propositions attributed to him by young C. established still more clearly the fact of his being a lunatic or an impostor, and Mr. W. was expressly requested to make that statement to the father, with delicacy but candour, that he might take suitable measures to prevent further mischief being hazarded to the detriment of the young man, his family, and society. Mr. W., young C., and the father (who had come with Mr. W., but who had not been present at

---

* Don Pedro Joachim Quintella, the richest man in Portugal, had lately died, leaving two millions sterling.

the conference, as it was wished to spare him the pain of such an interview), withdrew from the house, and Mr. W. soon afterwards acquainted the family that young C. would not return, but would leave town that night, which he did in a postchaise and four (the chaise he took away without the consent of the owner) accompanied by the German secretary and groom.

So many circumstances had transpired which gave cause to suspect that the whole story of young C. was an invention, sustained by a tissue of falsehoods and disingenuous acts, that every person whom he had named in the course of his narration as a banker, agent, &c. was applied to for information, and all disowned knowledge of him, except from public report or schoolboy connection; every fact affirmed by him was examined, and not one was authenticated which related to money transactions. The whole was visionary, but still most artfully wrought, and so successful was his manner in making dupes, that to this hour there are many who confide in his reappearance with all the treasure to which he has pretended.

One very respectable person affirmed that he had seen a remittance to young C. from Spain amounting to 350,000*l.*, a draft of frightful amount from Liverpool, and that he knew that he possessed two millions in the funds; nay, that a banker, within a few doors of him, had but the day before said he would have paid his bill for 100,000*l.* if it had been presented, instead of the 300*l.* bill which was cashed. Other persons had heard a respectable solicitor declare he knew young C. had great estates in Scotland, from which 45,000*l.* had been received; that he had many diamonds at Rundle and Bridges's, and altogether 700,000*l.* per annum. Others, that he meant to buy an estate, and pay 500,000*l.* for it in gold; and some offered large bets he would be in possession of Houghton by the 1st of January: others cited noblemen and gentlemen of the greatest accuracy, who had known the old man at Shrewsbury, and who had heard it said at the time, "that he would cut up, when dead, for more money than any man in the empire:" others, that they had known those who had dealt in diamonds with him; and almost every one professed to have an authority which justified a general and still unshaken belief. Even those to whom property purchased by young C. but not paid for, had been returned, seemed to think an injury more than a service was likely to be done them by the restitution, and no statement of detected falsehood could counteract or weaken the infatuation.

In the course of a visit near Newmarket, young C. had announced the expected arrival of some Sicilian wines from his estates on Mount Etna : a hamper came, but he did not appear anxious to revert to the subject. When it was mentioned, he affected pleasure at being reminded of the circumstance, ordered the sample bottles to be brought in, descanted on the advantages he should derive by the improved cultivation of the Sicilian grape, and requested opinion as to the quality he should encourage. The Surchall, the Tinta, and the Crema di Vino, especially were approved. Young C. promised to allow his friends to partake of the quantity already imported by his agent, and to direct abundant stores to be supplied in future from his vineyard. One of the guests had at the time observed " Edwards, Crutched-friars," written on the cork of the bottles. To Edwards application was now made, and it resulted from that inquiry, that the son-in-law of Mr. Edwards was named Cawston, and had employed himself for some years in the Sicilian vintage ; " that, presuming on his namesake, he had written to recommend his father's Sicilian wines to young C. as doubtless he was about to stock the cellars of his various mansions." No proposition could ever come more happily, and an order was instantly given for samples to be sent; fourteen bottles, containing seven different sorts, were despatched accordingly, and the memorandum remains this day existing in Mr. Edwards's books. All these discoveries were communicated the ensuing day to Mr. W. who admitted that they authorized a bad opinion of the young man, but still he had faith in him, and as a proof, had paid that morning a bill of forty odd pounds, by verbal message, and without any other security; for he reported again, as he had done the preceding day, that he never had any reference given him, nor was any document ever shewn him to authenticate the boy's story, or prove his possession of one shilling. Never, indeed, was any confidence more sincere than Mr. W.'s, for he not only had been in treaty for Houghton with Lord C. and for other estates, but he had employed Mr. H. and Sir S. R. to make his client a ward in Chancery; and as some difficulty arose from the young man's property being personal, and conveyed by deed of gift, it was arranged that young C. should give his father 100,000*l.* ; and the father should make a settlement on him to this amount, which would enable the Chancellor to interfere

Mr. W. has himself mentioned, that he had moreover directed his banker, near Charing Cross, to open two accounts in his name, representing the account No. 2, as one that would be of a greater magnitude than any which was ever brought into the house. On the 10th of December, however, on reference being made to it, there appeared the solitary item of—No. 2, debtor to No. 1, forty-seven pounds seven shillings.

In consequence of what had transpired, it was thought a public duty to disconcert any further machinations which this young man might have in view, and therefore in the Morning Chronicle, on the 6th of December, a caution was inserted against the Fortunate Youth, who was designated an impostor, but the caution was worded with as much delicacy as possible for the feelings of his family and friends, by omission of his family name. This caution produced a letter from Mr. W. the solicitor and confidential friend of the Fortunate Youth; in which the youth's character was vindicated from the aspersion, and a threat of prosecution was hazarded against the libeller.

An answer was published in which the charge of imposition was mentioned, and the pledge made of proof being given to substantiate the charges before the menaced tribunal. Instead of returning to London to investigate the accusation, Mr. W. set off with the young man's father and brother to Houghton, and at the same time, in his own name, addressed a letter to the public, in which he stated, " he had no reason to disbelieve the story of the much abused youth; but if ever he did discover him to be an impostor he would give him no longer countenance." This letter was considered by many not merely a public defence against the charge, but an admission that Mr. W. had no proof to offer that he was not the dupe of his client. Still the journey to Houghton, the correspondence from thence with the conveyancer on the subject of the purchase; the declaration that the contract should be concluded, and that this act would be the best answer to the calumniators, and the high language held with regard to the prosecution of the newspaper editors, fortified many in their errors, and induced some of the most respectable persons, who had been made acquainted with every particular, to confess they were again wavering in their opinion—a confession which certainly does the highest honour to the character of Mr. W. Nevertheless, Mr. W.'s agents were not satisfied that his confidence was justified, and at length they persuaded him to return to town, when a letter which young C. had given to Mr. W. with orders that it should not be opened until the 1st of January, was under the urgent necessity of the case examined (the father thereto consenting,) and that letter being found to contain only false references, Mr. W. suffered the bandage to be drawn from his eyes, which a generous confidence had so perseveringly maintained. A letter from Messrs. S. and E. of Liverpool, removed the last lingering doubts, and Mr. W. immediately wrote and published the acknowledgment of his having been deceived by a lunatic or depraved impostor.

The charm being broken, a letter written by young C. and dated Paris, in which he anticipated the discovery of his false references, but yet affirmed the general truth of his story, although received the day preceding the publication of Mr. W.'s recantation, had no effect upon his decision, but it was so far satisfactory as to remove some of Mr. W.'s uneasiness as to the course taken by young C. after he reached Calais, since it is said he had letters of recommendation, which, if he had gone direct into Germany, he might have used to the great prejudice of Mr. W. who had rendered himself responsible, by his first published letter, for the money he might take up abroad, as well as the debts he had incurred in England.

Of the original 1,100*l.* advanced by the relative, young C. had drawn out all but 10*l.* by London and Newmarket checks; but he has left several hundred pounds to be paid by his family. There is indeed a report that the relative alluded to had previously advanced 800*l.* but this report wants confirmation. At all events, it is certain that this young man spent above sixteen hundred pounds in two months, without being at any expense for house, equipage, &c. But although this sum was large for one whose previous expenditure had been so very limited, still it is not of sufficient magnitude to justify the supposition that his objects were merely pecuniary.

Eccentric Biography.

MRS. MARY HONEYWOOD.

MRS. MARY HONEYWOOD was

daughter and one of the co-heiresses of Robert Waters, esq. of Lenham, in Kent. She was born in 1527; married in February 1543, at sixteen years of age, to her only husband, Robert Honeywood, of Charing in Kent, Esq. She died in the ninety-third year of her age, in May 1620. She had sixteen children, seven of whom were sons and nine daughters, of whom one had no issue, three died young, and the youngest was slain at Newport battle, June 20, 1600. Her grandchildren, in the second generation, were one hundred and fourteen; in the third, two hundred and twenty-eight; and in the fourth, nine. So that she could almost say the same as the distich doth, of one of the Dalburg family of Basil. "Rise up, daughter, and go to thy daughter; for her daughter's daughter hath a daughter."

Mrs. Honeywood was a very pious woman, but afflicted in her declining age with religious melancholy. Some divines once discoursing with her on the subject, she in a passion said, "*I shall be as certainly damned as this glass is broken*," (throwing a Venice glass against the ground, which she had then in her hand,) but the glass escaped breaking, "as credible witnesses," saith Derham, " have attested."

In Markshal church, in Essex, on Mrs. Honeywood's tomb, is the following inscription:

"Here lieth the body of Mary Waters, the daughter and coheir of Robert Waters, of Lenham, in Kent, Esquire, wife of Robert Honeywood of Charing in Kent, Esquire, her only husband, who had at her decease lawfully descended from her, 367 children. Sixteen of her own body, 114 grandchildren, 228 in the third generation, and nine in the fourth. She lived a most pious life, and in a christian manner died at Markshal, in the ninety-third year of her age, and in the forty-fourth of her widowhood."—May 11, 1620.

ROGER BRANAGH.

THERE is at present in Belfast, an ingenious young man named Roger Branagh, who was born without arms, and is of course devoid of hands, which may be justly classed among the most useful members of the human frame. His feet, however, serve him in their place, and enable him to perform various operations, for which, at first view, he would appear wholly incapacitated. He has been seen opening out, with his toes, a closed penknife, with which he trimmed a quill and made an excellent pen, in a very short space of time. He can write rapidly and distinctly, his small letters being well formed and his capitals formed with taste and ease. It is surprising with what expedition he can thread needles, and even tie a knot at the extremity of the thread with nearly as much facility as the most practised seamstress. He can darn his own stockings, and twist the thread or worsted line which he uses for that purpose to the proper degree of thickness. Branagh can row in a boat with singular energy, though it must be confessed his attitudes are more unique than graceful. On such occasions he leans his back against the stern and one foot on one of the seats, so as to keep the oar, which he propels with the other, in due position. With boys he can play at marbles, and clear the ring with remarkable skill;

his big toe bulking, as the phrase is, his taw to the mark with the precision of an air gun. He can convey his food to his mouth with his toes, and is by no means deficient as a carver. He is by no means a timid equestrian, but can even drive a cart or carriage. The reins, on such occasions, are placed round his body, and by moving to and fro, to the right or to the left, he so varies their position as to affect the horse's mouth and direct his motions.—Amongst his other accomplishments and acquirements, may be enumerated his powers of scourging tops with his left foot—his skill in sharpening knives—to say nothing of lighting fires, blowing bellows, picking up pins with his toes, cracking whips, and putting his hat on one extremity of his frame (the head) with the other (the foot.)—About fifty years ago there was in Ireland a man named Buckinshaw, who wrote elegantly with his toes. This extraordinary person was able to comprise the Lord's Prayer in the narrow bounds of a British sixpence. The letters were regular and distinct, the penmanship most exquisite.

Varieties.

A SAILOR'S WISH.

A few years since, in a public garden near Philadelphia, some of the company happened to express their wishes to possess this or that, when a sailor, who overheard the conversation, stepped up and said, "Gentlemen, permit me to tell you what I wish for." Being desired to proceed, he continued, " I wish that I had three ship-loads of needles—as much thread and cloth as the needles would make up into bags —and these bags full of gold."

Now, supposing that the ships might carry 1200 tons of needles, one hundred of which would weigh an ounce—that each needle, on an average, would make up 20 two-bushel bags, that the bushel contains 215,042 solid inches, and that a cubic inch of gold weighs 10 ounces, or 102 grains; the products, omitting fractions, would be 3,825,800,000 needles. 154,112,000,000 bushels of gold, or about 217,297,920,000,000 pounds, or 9,700,800,000 tons; enough to freight twenty-four millions, two hundred and fifty-two thousand ships, of 400 tons burden; and allowing these ships to range side by side, only thirty feet being admitted to each, they would reach about 70,429 miles, and form three complete bridges round the world.

WAR AND WEATHER.

A GERMAN author who conceives war to have considerable effect on the atmosphere, states, that in the seven years' war, clouds and vapours were dispersed by the explosions of the cannon; and he asserts that, during his travels through the Tyrol, he saw on several occasions, to use his own expression, the clouds " shot dead." He observed in the neighbourhood of Leignitz, while the regiment of Wartensleben were going through their exercise, that the clouds were broken by the explosions, and that the murmuring of the wind and the agitation of the leaves of the trees and small feathers suspended from any body, were sometimes stronger, sometimes weaker, according as the troops fired by battalions or companies. The barometer rose and fell at each explosion, and water in a vessel at the distance of five hundred paces was violently agitated. There have been instances of the noise of heavy cannonades being heard at the distance of more than forty miles. It is natural to suppose, too, that the thunder of cannon must penetrate even into the interior parts of the earth, and to the bottom of the sea; and the Dutch fishers have, accordingly, remarked, that every great naval engagement has the effect of frightening the fish far away from the scene of action, near which none are to be met with for some time after.

The author endeavours from these principles to account for certain singularities which prevailed in the weather in some parts of Germany, in the year 1797, and to shew that the quantity of gunpowder fired in time of war may have a sensible effect on the fertility of fields and gardens.

POWER OF IMAGINATION.

Dr. Darwin relates the following instance of the power of superstition on the mind, which, two centuries ago, would have been accounted witchery:—A young Warwickshire farmer, finding his hedge broken and robbed during a severe winter, determined to watch for the thief. He chose a moonlight night, and lay many hours beneath the shade and shelter of a haystack. He suffered much from cold, and at midnight was about to retire; but at that moment appeared a decrepid old woman, of appearance much corresponding with the popular notion of a witch: she hastily collected a bundle of sticks from the hedge, and was about to carry them off; the farmer sprang from his concealment, and seized the old woman, as the nightly thief of his property. After some struggling, the old woman, who displayed great personal strength and determination, suddenly knelt down upon her bundle of sticks, and, after silently raising her withered arms to the moon, then at the full, she thus addressed the already half-frozen farmer: "Heaven grant thou mayest never again enjoy the blessings of *warmth.*" The terrified farmer left her, and made his way home, under the full effect of the cold spell. He complained of extreme cold the following day; wore an extra upper coat—then another—and at length, in despair, took to his bed, which was continually heaped with blankets, which covered even his face—and in which he actually lay *until his death,* which did not happen until twenty years afterwards!

TRIFLING OCCUPATIONS.

Pliny represents to us a Greek philosopher, whose occupation, for several years together, was to measure the space skipped over by fleas. Without giving into such ridiculous researches, I can (says Borrichius in the "Acts of Copenhagen") relate an anecdote which chance discovered to me in regard to that insect. Being sent for to attend a foreign lady, who was greatly afflicted with pains of the gout, and having staid by desire to dine with her, she bade me take notice, after dinner, of a flea on her hand. Surprised at such discourse, I looked at the hand, and saw indeed a plump and pampered flea, sucking greedily, and kept fast by a little gold chain. The lady assured me, she had nursed and kept the little animal, at that time, full six years, with exceeding great care, having fed it twice every day with her blood; and, when it had satisfied its appetite, she put it up in a little box lined with silk. In a month's time, being recovered from her illness, she set out from Copenhagen with her flea; but, having returned in about a year after, I took an opportunity of waiting upon her, and, among other things, asked after her little insect. She answered me with great concern, that it died through the neglect of her waiting-woman. What I found remarkable in this story was, that the lady being attacked by chronical pains in the limbs, had recourse in France to a mercurial course of medicine, during six weeks; and all this time the flea had not ceased to feed upon her blood imbued with the vapours of mercury, and yet was not the worse for it. This shows, how much its constitution is different from that of the louse, to which mercury is a mortal poison.

The Scrap Book.

STRENGTH AND SAGACITY OF A FOX.

IN 1815, a fox was caught in a trap, at Bourne, Cambridgeshire, with which he made off. He was traced in the snow the following morning, by the Earl of De La Warr's gamekeeper, upwards of ten miles, and was taken out of the earth alive and strong. His pad was then in the trap, which, with three feet of chain at the end of it, is supposed to have weighed fourteen pounds. Another fox accompanied him the whole of the way, seldom being distant from him more than four or five yards.

A JOVIAL FUNERAL.

AT Egton near Whitby, in July 1768, died Mr. William Keld, Farmer and Grazier, who, from a very small fortune, acquired an estate worth near 30,000*l.* which he generously distributed amongst his poor relations and dependents. At his funeral were expended 110 dozen of penny loaves, eight large hams, eight legs of veal, twenty stone of beef, sixteen stone of mutton, fifteen stone of Cheshire cheese, and thirty ankers of ale, besides what was distributed among a thousand poor people, who had sixpence in money given them.

PHENOMENON IN LAKE ERIE.

A LETTER, dated Port Talbot, June 20, 1823, gives an account of a very singular phenomenon which lately occurred in the waters of Lake Erie. On the 30th of May, about sunset, the lake being calm and smooth, and the weather fair, the waters suddenly rose perpendicularly, rushed up the channel of Otter Creek, drove a schooner of thirty-five tons from her moorings, threw her on high ground, and rolled over the beach into the woods, completely inundating all the adjacent flats. This was followed by two others of equal height, which caused the creek to retrograde a mile and a half. The noise occasioned by its rushing was truly astonishing. The same phenomenon took place at Tittle Creek, twenty miles from the other.

Published by J. LIMBIRD, 355, *Strand*, *(East End of Exeter 'Change); and sold by all Newsmen and Booksellers. Printed by A. APPLEGATH, Stamford-street.*

THE CABINET OF CURIOSITIES,
OR
Wonders of the World Displayed

A world of wonders where creation seems
No more the works of Nature but her dreams.—MONTGOMERY.

No. XV.]   PRICE TWOPENCE.

WYBRAND LOLKES, THE DUTCH DWARF.

MYNHEER WYBRAND LOLKES was a native of Holland, and born at Jelst, in West Friezland, in the year 1730, of parents in but indifferent circumstances, his father being a fisherman, who, beside this most extraordinary little creature, had to support a family of seven other children, all of whom were of ordinary stature, as were both the father and mother. Wybrand Lolkes, at an early age, exhibited proofs of a taste for mechanism; and when sufficiently grown up, was by the interest of some friends placed with an eminent watch and clockmaker at Amsterdam, to learn that business: he continued to serve this master for four years after the expiration of his apprenticeship, and then removed to Rotterdam, where he carried on this trade on his own account, and where he first became acquainted with, and afterwards married, the person who accompanied him to England. His trade of a watchmaker however failing, he came to the resolution of exhibiting his person publicly as a show; and by attending the several Dutch fairs obtained a handsome competency. Impelled by curiosity and in hopes of gain, he came to England, and was visited at Harwich, (where he first landed) by crowds of people: encouraged by this early success, he proceeded to London, and on applying to the late Mr. Philip Astley, obtained an engagement at a weekly salary of five guineas. He first appeared at the Amphitheatre, Westminster Road, on Easter Monday, 1790, and continued to exhibit every evening during the whole season. He always was accompanied by his wife, who came on the stage with him hand in hand, but though he elevated his arm, she was compelled to stoop considerably to meet the proffered honour.

Mynheer Lolkes was a fond husband; he well knew the value of his partner, and repaid her care of him, with the most fervent affection; for he was not one of those men, who

——— are April when they woo,
December when they wed.

He had by this wife three children, one of which, a son, lived to the age of twenty-three, and was five feet seven inches in height.

This little man, notwithstanding his clumsy and awkward appearance, was remarkably agile, and possessed uncommon strength: he could with the greatest ease spring from the ground into a chair of ordinary height. He was rather of a morose temper and extremely vain of himself, and while discoursing in broken English was extremely (as he imagined) dignified. He continued in England but one season, and through the help of a good benefit, returned to his native country, with his pockets better furnished than when he left it.

SCYLLA AND CHARYBDIS.

" Here Scylla bellows from her dire
    abodes,
" Tremendous pest! abhorr'd by man
    and gods!
" Hideous her voice, and with less
    terrors roar
" The whelps of lions in the midnight
    hour!"   POPE.

SCYLLA and Charybdis, according to the fables of the poets, are two sea monsters, whose dreadful jaws are continually distended to swallow up unhappy mariners; the one situated on the right, and the other on the left extremity of the strait of Messina, where Sicily fronts Italy. Scylla is a lofty rock, twelve miles distant from Messina, which rises almost perpendicularly from the sea, on the shore of Calabria, and beyond which is the small city of the same name. Though there was scarcely any wind (says the Abbé Lazzaro Spallanzani, in his Travels, whence this account is taken,) I began to hear, two miles before I came to the rock, a murmur and noise, like a confused barking of dogs, and on a nearer approach readily discovered the cause. This rock in its lower part contains a number of caverns; one of the largest of which is called, by the people there, *Dragara*. The waves, when in the least agitated, rushing into these caverns, break, dash, throw up frothy bubbles, and thus occasion these various and multiplied sounds. I then perceived with how much truth and resemblance of nature Homer and Virgil, in their personifications of Scylla, had portrayed this scene, by describing the monster they drew as lurking in the darkness of a vast cavern, surrounded by ravenous, barking mastiffs, together with wolves to increase the horror.

The Greek poet, when he portrays the rock which is the habitation of Scylla, finishes the picture higher than the Latin, by representing it as so lofty that its summit is continually wrapped in the clouds; and so steep, smooth, and slippery, that no mortal could ascend it, though he had twenty hands and twenty feet.

Such, three thousand years ago, or nearly so, appeared the rock of Scylla, according to the observations of Homer; and such is nearly its appearance at this day.

The accuracy of this truly "first great painter of antiquity," (which has likewise been observed by scientific travellers) in other descriptions which he has given, shews that the level of the waters of the sea was at that time at nearly the same height as at present, since, had it sunk only a few fathoms, it must have left the foot of the rock, which according to my observations is not very deep, entirely dry. And this I consider as one among several strong arguments, that the most remarkable sinkings of the sea are anterior to the time of Homer.

Such is the situation and appearance of Scylla: let us now consider the danger it occasions to mariners.—Though the tide is almost imperceptible in the open parts of the Mediterranean, it is very strong in the strait of Messina, in consequence of the narrowness of the channel, and is regulated, as in other places, by the periodical elevations and depressions of the water. Where the flow or current is accompanied by a wind blowing the same way, vessels have nothing to fear, since they either do not enter the strait, both the wind and the stream opposing them, but cast anchor at the entrance; or, if both are favourable, enter on full sail, and pass through with such rapidity that they seem to fly over the water. But when the current runs from south to north, and the north wind blows hard at the same time, the ship, which expected easily to pass the strait with the wind in its stern, on its entering the channel is resisted by the opposite current, and, impelled by two forces in contrary directions, is at length dashed on the rock of Scylla, or driven on the neighbouring sands; unless the pilot shall apply for the succour necessary for his preservation. For to give assistance in case of such accidents, four and twenty of the strongest, boldest, and most experienced sailors, well acquainted with the place, are stationed night and day along the shore of Messina; who, at the report of guns fired as signals of distress from any vessel, hasten to its assistance, and tow it with one of their light boats. The current, where it is strongest, does not extend over the whole strait, but winds through it in intricate meanders, with the course of which these men are perfectly acquainted, and are thus able to guide the ship in such a manner as to avoid it. Should the pilot, however, confiding in his own skill, contemn or neglect this assistance, however great his ability or experience, he would run the most imminent risk of being shipwrecked. In this agitation and conflict of the waters, forced one way by the current, and driven in a contrary direction by the wind, it is useless to throw the line to discover the depth of the bottom; the violence of the current frequently carrying the lead almost on the surface of the water. The strongest cables, though some feet in circumference, break like small cords. Should two or three anchors be thrown out, the bottom is so rocky, that they either take no hold, or, if they should, are soon loosened by the violence of the waves. Every expedient afforded by the art of navigation, though it might succeed in saving a ship in other parts of the Mediterranean, or even the tremendous ocean, is useless here. The only means of avoiding being dashed against the rocks, or driven upon the sands, in the midst of this furious contest of the wind and waves, is to have recourse to the skill and courage of these Messinese seamen.

In proof of the truth of this assertion, I might adduce many instances related to me by persons deserving of credit. But I was myself an eye-witness to the situation of a trading vessel from Marseilles, which had one day entered the strait by the mouth on the north side, at the time that I was on a hill looking towards the sea. The current, and a north wind, which then blew strong, being both in its favour, the vessel proceeded under full sail into, and had passed one half of the strait, when, on a sudden, the sky became overcast with thick clouds, and violent gusts of wind arose, which in an instant changed the direction of the current, and turned up the sea from its bottom. The mariners had scarcely time to hand the sails, while the furious waves broke over the ship on every side. Whether they merely followed the practice usual with ships in distress, or whether they were acquainted with the laudable custom of the Messinese, I cannot say; but they fired two guns: immediately upon which one of the barks employed on this service hastened to the assistance of the distressed vessel, and, taking it in tow, began to make every exertion to carry it safely into the harbour.

If I had seen with fear and shuddering the danger of the sailors on board the vessel, which I expected every moment to be swallowed up in the waves; I beheld with wonder and pleasure the address and bravery of the Messinese mariners, who had undertaken to steer safely through so stormy a sea the ship intrusted to their care. They extricated it from the current which impelled it towards destruction; changed the helm to this side or to that; reefed or let out the sails, as the wind increased or abated; avoided the impetuous shocks of the waves by meeting them with the prow, or opposing to them the side, as either method appeared most proper to break their violence; and by these and other manœuvres which I am unable to describe, these brave mariners, amid this dreadful conflict of the sea and the winds, succeeded in their undertaking, and brought the vessel safe into the harbour.

But enough of Scylla:—we will now proceed to Charybdis. This is situated within the strait, in that part of the sea which lies between a projection of land named *Punta Secca,* and another projection, on which stands the tower called *Lanterna,* or the lighthouse, a light being placed at its top to guide vessels which may enter the harbour by night.

On consulting the authors who have written of Charybdis, we find that they all supposed it to be a whirlpool. The first who has asserted this is Homer, who has represented Charybdis as a monster which three times in a day drinks up the water, and three times vomits it forth.

The Count de Buffon adopts the idea of Homer in full confidence, and places Charybdis among the most celebrated whirlpools of the sea: " Charybdis, in the strait of Messina, absorbs and rejects the water three times in twenty-four hours." Strabo tells us, that the fragments of ships swallowed up in this whirlpool are carried by the current to the shore of Tauromenium (the present Taormina), thirty miles distant from Charybdis. In confirmation of this tradition, an amusing though tragical anecdote is related of one Colas, a Messincan diver, who, from being able to remain a long time under the water, had acquired the surname of *Pesce* (the fish.) It is reported that Frederic king of Sicily, coming to Messina purposely to see him, made trial of his abilities with a cruel kind of liberality, by throwing a golden cup into Charybdis, which, if he brought it up, was to be the reward of his resolution and dexterity. The hardy diver, after having twice astonished the spectators by remaining under water a prodigious length of time, when he plunged the third time appeared no more; but, some days after, his body was found on the coast near Taormina.

We will now inquire what foundation there is for the saying which became proverbial, that " he who endeavours to avoid Charybdis, dashes upon Scylla;" and which was applied by the ancients to those who, while they sought to shun one evil, fell into a worse.

On this subject I likewise made inquiries of the Messinese pilots above-mentioned, and to what better masters could I apply for the elucidation of such a proverb? They told me that this misfortune, though not always, yet frequently happens, unless proper measures are taken in time to prevent it. If a ship be extricated from the fury of Charybdis, and carried by a strong southerly wind along the strait, towards the northern entrance, it will pass out safely; but should it meet with a wind in a nearly opposite direction, it will become the sport of both these winds, and, unable to advance or recede, be driven in a middle course between their two directions, that is to say, full upon the rock of Scylla, if it be not immediately assisted by the pilots. They added, that in these hurricanes a land wind frequently rises, which descends from a narrow pass in Calabria, and increases the force with which the ship is impelled towards the rock.

Before I began to write on Scylla and Charybdis, I perused the greater part of the ancient authors who have written on the subject. I observe that they almost all represent these disastrous places in the most gloomy and terrifying colours, as continually the scene of tempests and shipwrecks. These terrors and this destruction, however, they are far from exhibiting in the present times; it rarely happening that any ships are lost in this channel, either because their pilots possess the knowledge requisite for their preservation, or because they apply for the necessary assistance. Whence then arises this great difference between ancient times and the present? Can we suppose that Scylla and Charybdis have changed their nature, and become less dangerous? With respect to the former, we have seen that this hypothesis is contradicted by fact; Scylla still remaining such as it was in the time of Homer; and with regard to the latter, from the strait of Messina becoming narrower, Charybdis must be at present more to be feared than formerly, as it is well known that an arm, channel, or strait of the sea, is the more dangerous in proportion as it is narrow. I am rather of opinion that this difference arises from the improvement of the art of navigation, which formerly, in its infancy, dared not launch into the open sea, but only creep along the shore, as if holding it with its hand—

" To shun the dangers of the ocean, sweep
" The sands with one oar, and with one the deep."

But time, study, and experience, have rendered her more mature, better informed, and more courageous; so that she can now pass the widest seas, brave the most violent tempests, and laugh at the fears of her childhood.

SALT MINES AND SALT SPRINGS OF CHESHIRE.

The Cheshire rock-salt, with very few exceptions, has hitherto been ascertained to exist only in the vallies bordering on the river Weaver, and its tributary streams in some places manifesting its presence by springs impregnated with salt, and in others being known by mines, actually carried down into the substance of the salt strata. Between the source of the Weaver and Nantwich, many brine springs make their appearance; and occur again at several places, in proceeding down the stream. At Moulton, a mine has been sunk into the body of rock-salt, and a similar mine is wrought near Middlewich. At Northwich, brine springs are very abundant; and there also many mines have been sunk for the purpose of working out the fossil salt. In that vicinity a body of rock-salt has been met with in searching for coal.

The brines in this district are formed by the penetration of spring or rain waters to the upper surface of the rock-salt, in passing over which they acquire such a degree of strength, that one hundred parts have yielded 27 of pure salt, thus nearly approaching to the perfect saturation of brine. Their strength is therefore much greater than that of the salt springs met with in Hungary, Germany, and France. The brine having been pumped out of the pits, is first conveyed into large reservoirs, and afterwards drawn off as it is needed, into pans made of wrought iron. Here heat is applied in a degree determined by the nature of the salt to be manufactured, and various additions are made to the brine, with a view either to assist the crystallization of the salt, or to promote the separation of the earthy particles, which exist in a very small proportion. The importance of the manufacture of Cheshire salt will be sufficiently obvious from the statement, that, besides the salt made for home consumption, the annual amount of which exceeds 16,000 tons, the average of the quantity sent yearly to Liverpool for exportation, has not been less than 140,000 tons.

The mine of rock-salt first worked was discovered by accident at Marbury, near Northwich, about a century and a half ago; and this bed had been wrought for more than a century, when, in the same neighbourhood, a second and inferior stratum was fallen in with, separated from the former by a bed of indurated clay. This lower stratum was ascertained to possess a very great degree of purity, and freedom from earthy mixture; on which account, and from the local advantages of Northwich for exportation, the fossil salt is worked in the vicinity of that place only. It occurs in two great strata or beds, lying nearly horizontally, and separated, the superincumbent from the subjacent stratum, by several layers of indurated clay, or argillaceous stone. These intervening beds possess, in conjunction, a very uniform thickness of from thirty to thirty-five feet, and are irregularly penetrated by veins of fossil salt. There is every reason to believe that the beds of rock-salt at Northwich, are perfectly distinct from any others in the salt district, and form what are termed, by mineralogists, *incumbent bodies* or *masses of mineral.*

These enormous masses stretch a mile and a half in a longitudinal direction from north-east to south-west; but their transverse extent, as measured by a line at right angles from the former, does not exceed 4,200 feet, somewhat more than three quarters of a mile. Without this area, the brine which is met with is of a very weak and inferior quality, and at a short distance disappears altogether. The thickness of the upper bed varies from sixty to ninety feet; and a general estimate made from its level, shows that its upper surface, which is ninety feet beneath that of the earth, is at least thirty-six feet beneath the low-water mark of the sea at Liverpool—a fact not unimportant in determining the nature of the formation of this mineral. The thickness of the lower bed has not hitherto been ascertained; but the workings are usually begun at the depth of from sixty to seventy-five feet, and are carried down for the space of fifteen or eighteen feet, through what forms the purest portion of the bed. In one of the mines a shaft has been sunk to a level of forty-two feet still lower, without passing through the body of rock-salt. There is thus an ascertained thickness of this bed of about a hundred and twenty feet, and without any direct evidence that it may not extend to a considerably greater depth.

Although two distinct beds only of fossil salt have been met with at Northwich, it has been ascertained that the same limitations do not exist throughout the whole of the salt district. At Lawton, near the source of the river Wheelock, three distinct beds have been found, separated by strata of indurated clay: one at the depth of 126 feet, four feet in thickness; a second, thirty feet lower, twelve feet in thickness; and a third, forty-five feet farther down, which was sunk into seventy-two feet, without passing through its substance. The intervening clay, the structure of which is very peculiar, is called the SHAGGY METAL, and the fresh water which passes through its pores has the expressive appellation of ROARING MEG. This epithet will not appear too strong, when it is mentioned that in a mine in which the section of strata was taken, and where the shaggy metal was found at the depth of about eighty feet, the quantity of water ascertained to issue from its pores in one minute, was not less than three hundred and sixty gallons; a circumstance greatly enhancing the difficulties of passing a shaft down to the body of rock-salt.

In many of these beds of argillaceous stone, a portion of salt, sufficiently strong to affect the taste, is found to exist; and this saltness increases, as might be expected, in proportion as the body of rock-salt is approached: in the strata or layers immediately above the rock, which in all the mines are perfectly uniform in their appearance and structure, it is particularly remarkable, notwithstanding there are not, in these strata, any veins of rock-salt connected with the great mass below. On the contrary, the line between the clay and rock-salt is drawn with great distinctness in every instance, without presenting any of those inequalities which would arise from a mutual penetration of the strata. Not any marine exuviæ, or organic remains, are found in the strata above the rock-salt; and the almost universal occurrence of gypsum, in connexion with beds of fossil salt, is a fact still more deserving of observation, because it appears, not only in these mines, but also in the salt mines of Hungary, Poland, and Transylvania, on which account Werner, in his geognostic system, assigns to the rock-salt and floetz gypsum a conjunct situation.

The fossil salt extracted from the Northwich mines is of different degrees of purity, and more or less blended with earthy and metallic substances. The purer portion of the lower bed yields a rock-salt, which, being principally exported to the Baltic, obtains the name of Prussian rock. The extent of the cavity formed by the workings varies in different mines, the average depth being about sixteen feet. In some of the pits, where pillars from eighteen to twenty-four feet square form the supports of the mine, the appearance of the cavity is singularly striking, and the brilliancy of the effect is greatly increased when the mine is illuminated by candles fixed to the side of the rock. The scene thus formed, almost appears to realize the magic palaces of the eastern poets. Some of the pits are worked in aisles or streets, but the choice here is wholly arbitrary. Among the methods employed in working out the rock-salt, the operation of blasting is applied to the separation of large masses from the body of the rock, and these are afterwards broken down by the mechanical implements in common use. The present number of mines is eleven or twelve, from which there are raised, on an annual average, fifty or sixty thousand tons of rock-salt. The greater part of this quantity is exported to Ireland and the Baltic, the remainder being employed in the Cheshire district, in the manufacture of white salt by solution and subsequent evaporation.

The general situation occupied by the rock-salt in Cheshire, is very similar to that of the Transylvanian and Polish mines, the beds of this mineral being disposed in small plains, bounded by hills of inconsiderable height, forming a kind of basin or hollow, from which there is usually only a narrow egress for the waters. The situation of the Austrian salt mines near Saltzburgh is, however, very different. The mineral there appears to be disposed in beds of great thickness, which occur near the summits of limestone hills, at a great elevation above the adjoining country. This is a singular fact; and if the hypothesis be allowed that rock-salt is formed from the waters of the sea, it is necessary to suppose the occurrence on this spot of the most vast and surprising changes!

THE DOG OF MONTARGIS.

THE fame of an English bull dog has been deservedly transmitted to posterity by a monument in basso-relievo, which still remains on the chimney-piece of the grand hall, at the castle of Montargis, in France. The sculpture, which represents a dog fighting with a champion, is explained by the following narrative.

Aubri de Mondidier, a gentleman of family and fortune, travelling alone through the forest of Bondi, was murdered, and buried under a tree. His dog, an English bull dog, would not quit his master's grave for several days; till at length, compelled by hunger, he proceeded to the house of an intimate friend of the unfortunate Aubri's, at Paris, and by his melancholy howling seemed desirous of expressing the loss they had both sustained. He repeated his cries, ran to the door, looked back to see if any one followed him, returned to his master's friend, pulled him by the sleeve, and with dumb eloquence entreated him to go with him.

The singularity of all these actions of the dog, added to the circumstance of his coming there without his master, whose faithful companion he had always been, prompted the company to follow the animal, who conducted them to a tree, where he renewed his howl, scratching the earth with his feet, significantly entreating them to search that particular spot. Accordingly, on digging, the body of the unhappy Aubri was found.

Some time after, the dog accidentally met the assassin; who is styled, by all the historians that relate this fact, the Chevalier Macaire; when, instantly seizing him by the throat, he was with great difficulty compelled to quit his prey.

In short, whenever the dog saw the chevalier, he continued to pursue and attack him with equal fury. Such obstinate virulence in the animal, confined only to Macaire, appeared very extraordinary, especially to those who at once recollected the dog's remarkable attachment to his master, and several instances in which Macaire's envy and hatred to Aubri de Mondidier had been conspicuous.

Additional circumstances increased suspicion; and at length the affair reached the royal ear. The king (Louis VIII.) accordingly sent for the dog, who appeared extremely gentle till he perceived Macaire in the midst of several noblemen; when he ran fiercely towards him, growling at and attacking him as usual.

In those rude times, when no positive proof of a crime appeared, an order was issued for a combat between the accuser and the accused. These were denominated the Judgments of God, from a persuasion that heaven would much sooner work a miracle than suffer innocence to perish with infamy.

The king, struck with such a

collection of circumstantial evidence against Macaire, determined to refer the decision to the chance of battle; in other words, he gave orders for a combat between the chevalier and the dog. The lists were appointed in the Isle of Nôtre Dame, then an uninclosed, uninhabited place; Macaire's weapon being a great cudgel.'

The dog had an empty cask allowed for his retreat, to enable him to recover breath. Every thing being prepared, the dog no sooner found himself at liberty, than he ran round his adversary, avoiding his blows, and menacing him on every side, till his strength was exhausted; then, springing forward, he griped him by the throat, threw him on the ground, and obliged him to confess his guilt in the presence of the king and the whole court. In consequence of which the chevalier, after a few days, was convicted upon his own acknowledgment, and beheaded on a scaffold in the Isle of Nôtre Dame.

The above curious recital is translated from the *Mémoires sur les Duels*, and is confirmed by many judicious critical writers; particularly Julius Scaliger and Montfaucon, neither of whom have ever been regarded as fabricators of idle stories. On this narrative the melodrame of the Forest of Bondi is founded.

Hoaxes and Impostures.
No. XII.
ROYAL IMPOSTORS.

FROM the earliest period to the present time impostors of every description have arisen. To trace them through the various scenes of life would be an endless task. Some have boldly aspired to thrones and dominions, and others have been contented with the humblest tricks of imposition or legerdemain. We might enumerate the regal impostors, the usurper, the courtier, the gambler, the quack, the swindler, &c.; and under each classification detail the various species of imposture practised on society; but we shall now simply confine ourselves to *Royal* impostors. For this purpose we need only advert to a few instances to prove the credulity of mankind, when impudence and hypocrisy have blinded the understanding.

From Smerdis the Magian to the present period many daring impositions have been practised on society. Some of them, either from the cunning and duplicity of the impostor, or the ignorance and credulity of men, have been peculiarly successful in transmitting the fruits of their fraud and imposture: such was the notorious Mahomet. Others, of subordinate importance, have emerged from obscurity; and, after disturbing the repose of society by a few plausible pretensions, like meteoric exhalations, have suddenly disappeared; or have otherwise been consigned to the ignominy they deserved. Of this latter class were, Demetrius of Russia, Pugatskef the Cossack, Symnel and Perkin Warbeck of England, the pretended Louis XVI. &c. &c.

We shall commence with Smerdis, as being the most daring impostor of early times. Cambyses, the King of Persia, murdered his brother Smerdis from jealousy and suspicion. At his departure from Susa on his Egyptian expedition, he left the administration of affairs, during his absence, in the hands of Patisithes, one of the chief of the

Magi. This man had a brother extremely like Smerdis the brother of Cambyses. As soon as Patisithes was assured of the death of that prince, which had been concealed from the public, he placed his own brother on the throne, declaring him to be the true Smerdis, the son of Cyrus. Cambyses immediately gave orders for his army to march from Egypt, and cut off the usurper; but receiving a wound in the thigh from his own sword, at Ecbatana, he died soon after. Before his death he represented the true state of the case to the assembled chiefs of the Persians, earnestly exhorting them not to submit to the impostor who had usurped the empire. The Persians, supposing he stated all this through hatred to his brother, disregarded his request, and quietly submitted to him whom they found on the throne, supposing him to be Smerdis the true son of Cyrus. He reigned for some months in undisputed sovereignty, until he was discovered to be Smerdis the Magian by the loss of his ears, of which he had been ignominiously deprived.

The success of that notorious impostor Mahomet is too manifest at this day to enter into the least detail. He has transmitted the fruits of his daring hypocrisy and fraud to posterity, and they are likely to remain as perpetual mementoes of the most impudent imposture that ever ruled the destinies of mortals.

In 1605 an impostor in Poland pretended that he was Demetrius, the son of John Basilowitz, Grand Duke of Muscovy. He was the cause of a sanguinary war betwixt Poland and Muscovy. He stated that he was to have been murdered by the order of Boris Gudenow, who hoped to obtain the succession to the empire after the death of Theodore the eldest son of the said John Basilowitz; but that another had been killed in his stead. This person having received great encouragement from George Mniszeck, the Vayvod of Sendomir, promised to marry his daughter. On this assurance, Vayvod, with the assistance of some other Polish lords, raised an army that marched with Demetrius into Muscovy. The Grand Duke Boris Gudenow dying soon after, Demetrius was warmly received by the Russians, and, having subdued those who opposed him, he was proclaimed Grand Duke of the city of Moscow. His conduct soon rendering him odious to the Russians, he was suspected to be an impostor, and they secretly raised an army of 20,000 men. At the celebration of his nuptials, they suddenly attacked the castle, and cut to pieces Demetrius, and a great number of Poles who had escorted the bride. After the death of Demetrius, Basilius Zuski was proclaimed Grand Duke in the public market, where he caused the usurper's body to be exposed to public view. Notwithstanding this (such is the credulity of mankind), a rumour prevailed that Demetrius had escaped the slaughter; and shortly after another individual appeared, who pretended to be the same. The Poles acknowledged him for Demetrius, and having formed a great army, marched against the Russians. They several times defeated Zuski, and set at liberty the captive bride of Demetrius, who acknowledged him for her husband. After much blood had been shed in various battles, this daring and successful impostor was slain by the Tartars who composed his guard.

During the reign of Catherine II. of Russia, Pugatskef, a Cossack, was induced, in consequence of his personal resemblance, to assume the name of Peter III. who had been privately murdered by his queen. He raised a revolt, which for some period threatened serious consequences, and even made Catherine herself to tremble. However, at the end of the year 1774 he was captured, and put to death.

Our own country has not been exempt from impostors of the same description, though of less consequence. In the reign of Henry VII. Lambert Symnel, son of a baker, assumed the name and person of Edward Earl of Warwick, and caused himself to be proclaimed King in Ireland. This imposture was first contrived by a priest, and encouraged by Margaret, the widow of Charles Duke of Burgundy, sister to Edward IV. Symnel transported an army out of Ireland into England. Being signally routed by Henry, he was taken prisoner, and made a turnspit in the king's kitchen.

In the year 1491, Margaret, duchess dowager of Burgundy, set up another impostor, whose name was Perkin Warbeck, who pretended to be Richard, a younger son of King Edward IV. He possessed talent much superior to his predecessor Symnel, and managed the business so well, that he caused a considerable sensation in England. However the Scotch, who supported him, having been defeated, Warbeck fled into Cornwall, and there caused himself to be proclaimed King; but receiving little support, he was compelled to surrender himself, when he was committed a prisoner to the Tower. Having twice made attempts to escape, he was at length hanged, according to his demerits.

After the fatal expedition of Sebastian, the youthful King of Portugal, to Morocco, in 1578, a bold adventurer aspired to the throne. He took the advantage of assuming Sebastian's name, in consequence of a similiarity of features. Like his deceased sovereign, he had but one eye. He gained numerous partisans, which enabled him, for some time, to carry on perpetual contests with Henry the uncle of Sebastian. At last he received the reward of his deserts.

In descending to our own times, we have a recent instance of ridiculous imposture, in the person of Mathurin Bruneau, the pretended Dauphin of France. His pretensions were prompted more by folly and puerile vanity, than cunning design, or studied hypocrisy. Although the strongest symptoms of insanity frequently betrayed his actions, he had the power of imposing on the credulity of numbers. Had he possessed intellect or energy, a serious commotion, excited by designing villains or credulous fools, might possibly have ensued. Fortunately his conduct in the court of justice evinced undoubted signs of idiotcy. On being sentenced to a fine and imprisonment, he impudently replied, "I am not less what I am." The process against this impostor induced a person named Sieur Dufresne to assume the title of Charles Navarre. He insisted on an audience with the King, and in this attempt was apprehended. He was discovered to be mad, and accordingly sent to Charenton, the Bedlam of Paris.

Anecdotes of Longevity.

JONATHAN HARTOP.

JONATHAN HARTOP, who died at Aldborough, near Boroughbridge in Yorkshire, in 1791, reached the astonishing age of 138 years, having been born in 1653. "His father and mother both died of the plague, at their house in the Minories, in 1666, and he perfectly remembers the great fire of London. He is short of stature, has been married five times, and has now alive seven children, twenty-six grandchildren, seventy-four great grandchildren, and a hundred and forty great great grandchildren. He can read without spectacles, and plays at cribbage with perfect recollection. Last Christmas day he walked nine miles to dine with one of his great grandchildren. He remembers Charles the Second perfectly well, and once travelled from London to York with the facetious Killigrew. He eats but little, and drinks nothing but milk; he enjoys also an uninterrupted flow of spirits. The third wife of this very extraordinary old man was an illegitimate daughter of Oliver Cromwell, who gave with her a portion amounting to about five hundred pounds. He has in his possession a fine portrait of the usurper by Cooper, for which the late Mr. Hollis offered him 300l. but was refused. Mr. Hartop lent the great Milton 50l. soon after the restoration, which the bard returned him with honour, though not without much difficulty, as his circumstances were very low. Mr. Hartop would have declined receiving it again, but the pride of the poet was equal to his genius, and he sent the money, with an angry letter, which is extant among the curious possessions of this venerable man."—*Universal Magazine*, 1790.

A NEGRESS.

DIED on the 14th of February 1813, at St. John's, Antigua, a black woman, named Statira, who, by information from herself, must have attained the advanced age of a hundred and thirty-two or a hundred and thirty-four. She was a slave, and was hired as a day labourer during the building of the gaol, and was present at the laying of the corner stone; which ceremony took place a hundred and sixteen years ago. She also stated she was a young woman grown when President Sharpe assumed the administration of the island, which was in 1706; so that, allowing her to be then only eighteen, it brings her age to that of 134.

SCOTTISH PENSIONER

THERE appeared in the Courtroom of Wester Portsburgh, John M'Donald, a pensioner, who resides in Cone's-close, Highstreet. It appears, from his instructions, that he was admitted an out-pensioner of Chelsea-hospital on the 16th day of February 1749, from the 15th regiment of foot, commanded by General Harrison. He was then about thirty-four years of age, and was afterwards called in 1807, and his instructions (issued anew to him on the 25th of June that year) shew that he was then ninety-two years of age, which now makes him a hundred and eight years old. The magistrate who signed his affidavit, accompanied by another gentleman, went to his residence, to make inquiry where he was born, &c.

He stated he was born in Glengarry's land, Inverness-shire, in 1715, enlisted as a soldier in early life;—recollects perfectly of seeing Prince Charles; but, as his memory is so much impaired, little more of his history could be obtained, except that he was wounded on the plains of Quebec, on the same day that General Wolfe fell. His wife is also an infirm old woman, and says she is about a hundred years old, but her faculties are apparently not so much impaired as those of the old man. They have lived nearly thirty years in the low hovel which they now occupy, in one of the most unhealthy closes in Edinburgh.—*Edinburgh Observer*, 1823.

Eccentric Biography.

MR. THOMAS GASCOIGNE.

Mr. Thomas Gascoigne, of East Retford, a well known penurious character, who died some months ago, was a native of Derby, and was born on the 24th of June, 1738, being the same month and year as that in which his late Majesty was born. At an early period of his life Mr. Gascoigne's parents removed from Derby to Ordsall, a village near Retford: when arrived at a proper age he was bound apprentice to a shoemaker, of Retford, who was a burgess of that place, and at the close of his apprenticeship Mr. G. was consequently entitled to the privilege of a freeman, and at his death he was the oldest burgess upon the list. Some time after the expiration of his apprenticeship, he obtained a situation in the Excise, and was appointed to fulfil the duties of his office at Derby, which he did to the satisfaction of his superior officers, as also those whom it was his duty to survey, till an accident obliged him to retire on a pension when about the age of forty. About this time an uncle of Mr. G.'s died, who left him the owner of several houses, situate in Derby, one of which is the Crown Inn; he now returned to Retford, and again followed his vocation as a shoemaker, which he continued to do till within the last ten years. During the whole of his long life he was never known to employ a doctor, and was generally his own tonsor, except upon particular occasions, such as the dinners of the freemen, which were about twice a year, and which he regularly attended, when he repaired to the hair-dresser's to be finished, having himself previously applied the scissors and razor, and taken off the greatest part, purposely with a view to save expense. He regularly went once a year to Derby to receive his rents, on which occasion he put on his best coat and boots, and cocked hat, each of which have now been in use more than forty years. It was his practice always to walk, carrying with him a pair of old saddle bags, hung over his shoulders, containing provisions necessary for his whole journey. On his way thither, as also on his return, he generally reposed during the night on Nottingham Forest, thinking himself and his property more safe there than sleeping in a public-house, and being too penurious to pay for a bed, or call at an inn for refreshment. His saddle bags, on these occasions, were not only used for the purpose of carrying the provisions necessary for his journey, but were also a subservient receptacle for potatoes, and every other eatable which might chance to fall in his way, and which he did not fail to carry home with him. During his absence on one of his tours to Derby, about five years since, his house was broke open and robbed of bills and cash to the amount of 500*l.* which was but a small sum compared with what was secreted in the house, and that escaped the scrutinizing search of the robbers. His punctuality as a paymaster for his rent, and that which necessity compelled him to purchase, was very strict, as was also his accuracy as a bookkeeper; for at the time of the robbery, he had carefully booked the number of every note, the name of the person who signed and entered them, and the date; he likewise kept an account of his expenditure, many weeks in which appeared to be only a penny and twopence, as he chiefly subsisted on what he picked up in the streets, particularly on market days, by which means he became well known to all who frequented the market, as he always wore a long coat, which, with his stockings, could not be said to contain a particle of the original, they being so patched and darned with worsted. A ton of coals would serve him seven years, in the use of which he was very sparing and economical; for in making his fire he first put a few sticks and coals, then a tier of stones, next a few more coals, and at top another tier of stones, which, in time, became red hot; but it was only to bake his bread that he made a fire, at which times he also roasted potatoes sufficient to serve him till he again baked. His house was indeed a miserable abode, and had more the appearance of a receptacle of filth, than the residence of a human being; it was indeed unfit for "mortal ken," the walls not having been whitewashed, nor the floor washed, for more than twenty years. In one corner lay a heap of stones for his fire, in another hundreds of pieces of leather, such as old soles, which he had gathered for the purpose of mending his own. Many other instances of his parsimonious disposition might be named, but they would occupy too much of our space. The principal part of his furniture consisted of an old clock, a table, bed, and several old chairs, all of which had been the property of his father; none of them appeared to have been cleaned for a number of years, or even removed from their situation, being covered and surrounded with dust to a great thickness. Mr. Gascoigne lived and died a bachelor; the full amount of his property is not known, but supposed to be some thousands, the whole of which will belong to his two nephews: Mr. G.'s patched coat, an ancient saddle which he used when in the Excise, and several other antiquities of the same description, it is said, would make a valuable addition to the curiosities in the British Museum. In an electioneering squib, printed in 1802, are the following lines, which shew the state of the coat at that time, and of a truth he continued to wear it ever after:—

"Had I been this fam'd poet, I'd have wrote
'Bout Gascoigne's bald old hat, or worsted coat:
No man dare undertake to count the stitches,
Or take the grease in nine days from his breeches."

MARCUS LEVI.

An eccentric individual died at Richmond, Virginia, in the United States, on the 2d of July 1823,

His name was Marcus Levi, and he was of the Hebrew congregation. He constantly wore his beard with great circumspection, and declared himself a prophet who had many peculiar favours from the Almighty.—Amongst which was one, that he should not die, but be removed as Enoch and Elijah were. Indeed his departure did not seem to partake of any of the pains of death. As he was returning from market near his own house, and in his usual health, he suddenly fell down—his tobacco pipe flew out of his mouth, and with the last puff of smoke, that then departed, his spirit fled, without one convulsive motion. Mr. Levi's appearance seemed to indicate penury, and sometimes great indigence—he lived quite solitary, having no wife, child, or other person in his house; yet, it is said, that there have been found in his house, since his departure, upwards of 60,000 dollars.—*American Paper.*

The Scrap Book.

BETTER LATE THAN NEVER.

THERE was married in September 1783, Mr. John Harrison, of Cowick, in Yorkshire, aged 101, to Mrs. Ann Heptonstall, aged ninety-eight. The bridemaid was seventy-four, and the bridegroom's man eighty-three. They were attended to and from church by a prodigious concourse of people. The lady to whom he is now married is the fourth within the space of two years and a few months; and, what is still more remarkable, the bridegroom expressed his hope, that he should be again called to that holy state, by the following address to the clergyman on this occasion:—

"Come, man; 'tis only 3s. 6d. I paid thee last, therefore don't advance upon us. I've been a good customer; and, if thou uses me well, I may be a customer to thee again in a little time."

HATCHING PARTRIDGES

IN the year 1819, as a cat belonging to Mr. W. Allwork of Goudhurst, was prowling through the meadows, it was observed to kill a partridge, and, on examining the spot, a nest was found, containing eighteen eggs, which were taken up and that evening deposited in an oven that had been recently used. On the following morning, when the oven was opened, the whole of the eggs were found hatched, and the young ones running about, but in catching them three were unfortunately killed; the remaining fifteen were put into the nest, and placed in the meadow where it was taken from on the preceding evening. In a short time the old cock partridge was attracted to the spot, and in a few minutes it departed with the whole brood, in the presence of several persons; since that time they have been frequently seen by the gamekeeper of T. Wallis, Esq.—*Edinburgh Paper.*

THE MULLET.

WHEN the mullet is dying it changes its colours in a very singular manner till it is entirely lifeless. This spectacle was so gratifying to the Romans, that they used to show the fish dying, in a glass vessel, to their guests before dinner.

Published by J. LIMBIRD, 355, Strand, (East End of Exeter 'Change); and sold by all Newsmen and Booksellers. Printed by A. APPLEGATH, Stamford-street.

THE CABINET OF CURIOSITIES,
OR
𝔚onders of the 𝔚orld Displayed.

A world of wonders where creation seems
No more the works of Nature but her dreams.—MONTGOMERY.

No. XVI.]   PRICE TWOPENCE.

PETER WILLIAMSON.

PETER WILLIAMSON, whose portrait forms our present engraving, is represented in the dress of a Delaware North American Indian, in which costume he exhibited himself in London, in the years 1760 and 1761. He was born within ten miles of Aberdeen, of parents who supported him in the best manner they were able, till he was sent to reside with an aunt at Aberdeen; where, playing on the quay, with others of his companions, he was taken notice of by two fellows belonging to a vessel in the harbour, employed by some of the *worthy* merchants of the town in the then prevalent villainous and execrable practice of kidnapping. Peter, then a child of only eight years old, was easily seduced on board the ship, which having shortly after got in the complement of unhappy youths for carrying on their inhuman commerce, set sail for America. On their arrival at Philadelphia, Peter was sold with his other companions, at about 16*l*. per head: what became of his fellows in misfortune, he never knew, but it was his chance to be sold for a term of seven years to a North Briton, who had, in his youth, undergone the same fate as Peter, having been kidnapped from St. John's Town in Scotland.

This new master, having no children of his own, and commiserating the condition of his fellow-countryman, took great care of him, till he was fit for business: with this master he continued till he was seventeen years old, when his master died, and as a reward for Peter's faithful services, left him about two hundred pounds currency, his best horse, saddle, and all his wearing apparel.

Being now his own master, and possessed of money as well as other necessaries, he employed himself in jobbing about the neighbouring plantations, for nearly seven years; when, considering himself sufficiently enriched to follow some better way of life, he carried into execution his resolution to settle, and married the daughter of a substantial planter. His father-in-law, in order to establish Peter and his wife, in an easy if not in an affluent manner, presented him with a tract of land on the borders of the forest of Delaware, of about two hundred acres. The situation pleased Peter so well, that he immediately settled on it; but his felicity was not of long duration; for in 1754, the Indians, in the French interest, who had for a long time before ravaged and destroyed other parts of America, began to be very troublesome to the Pensylvanians. On the second of October, 1754, his wife being then from home, Peter was sitting up later than usual, waiting her return, when about eleven o'clock at night, he heard the dismal war-whoop of the savages, and soon found that his house was attacked; he asked the Indians what they wanted, and they told him if he would come out and surrender they would not kill him. He accordingly went out with his gun in his hand; they immediately rushed on him, disarmed him, and bound him to a tree; they then went into the house, plundered and destroyed every thing that was in it, carrying off what moveables they could; they then set fire to the house and the barn, which with the cattle were all destroyed.

Having completed the object of their ravages, they untied him, and caused him to carry a great load, under which he travelled all night; at daybreak, he was ordered to lay down his load, and was again tied so close round a tree with a small cord, as to force the blood from his fingers' ends. They next kindled a fire, and for some time danced round him, whooping, hallooing and crying in a frightful tone: they then proceeded in a more tragical manner, taking the flaming sticks and brandishing them near his face, head, hands and feet, with seeming ferocious pleasure and satisfaction, at the same time threatening to burn him entirely, if he made the least noise, or cried out: thus tortured almost to distraction, he suffered their brutal pleasure without being allowed to express any anguish, otherwise than by shedding tears, which the savages observing, they again took flaming sticks, and placing them near his eyes, told him, his face was wet and they would dry it.; at length, they sat down, and roasted their meat, of which they had robbed Williamson's dwelling : having satisfied their hunger, they offered some to their unfortunate captive, which he pretended to eat. After having finished their repast, they proceeded onward to their winter habitations, and on their journey committed the most cruel outrages, till they reached Alamingo, where the severity of the cold increasing, they stripped him of his cloak for their own use, and gave him such as they usually wore themselves, being a piece of blanketing, and a pair of *mogganes*, or shoes, with a yard of coarse cloth to put round him instead of breeches. Thus, for nearly two months, naked as he nearly was, did he endure the inclemency of the weather, which rendered his limbs in a manner quite stiff, and unsusceptible of motion : he contrived however to erect a little *wigwam*, with the bark of the trees, covering the same with earth, which made it resemble a cave : and to prevent the ill effects of the cold which penetrated into it, he always kept a good fire near the entrance.

At length the time arrived, when the Indians were preparing for a new expedition, and the snow being quite gone, so that no traces of their footsteps could be perceived, they set forth on their journey towards the provinces of Pensylvania. One night, the Indians being much fatigued with their day's excursion, they fell so soundly asleep, that Williamson, trusting to Divine Providence for protection, effected his liberty; and after very narrow escapes of being retaken, he arrived, on the fifth day, at the house of John Bell, an old acquaintance, who kindly received him : here he remained some time; and on January 4, 1755, arrived at his father-in-law's house in Chester county, when scarcely one of the family would believe their eyes, thinking he had fallen a prey to the merciless cruelty of the Indians.

Shortly after his arrival at home, his wife having been dead two months before, he enlisted into Colonel Shirley's regiment, which was intended for the frontiers, to destroy the French ports : in this desultory kind of warfare, he continued till Oswego was captured by the French in August 1756, when the French, and the Indians in their interest, committed the most heart-rending barbarities and excesses.

Williamson was one of the persons taken prisoners at Oswego; and was, in November 1756, brought from America to Plymouth under a flag of truce; where, in about four months subsequent to his arrival, he was discharged as incapable of further service, occasioned by a wound in his left hand. He then published a narrative of his sufferings, in a tract, entitled "French and Indian Cruelty displayed in the Life and Adventures of Peter Williamson." Neither the strange vicissitudes of his own fortune, chequered with uncommon calamities, nor the good intention of his narrative, could protect him from the resentment of some merchants of Aberdeen, where he went in quest of his relations ; because, in the introduction to his narrative, he had noticed the manner in which he had been illegally kidnapped on board ship, and sold for a slave. For that publication he was imprisoned, and 350 copies of his book (the only means he had of obtaining his sustenance) were taken from him, and his enlargement only granted him on his signing a paper, disclaiming two or three pages of his book. However, as he soon after found a few of his relatives, he got the attestations of some, and the affidavits of others, proving he was the person taken away, as mentioned in the narrative.

THE MYSTICAL NUMBER SEVEN.

In No. XII. we gave an account of the mystical number *Three:* and we now insert a much greater number of coincidences relating to the still more mystical number *Seven.*

Seven is composed of the two first perfect numbers, equal and unequal—three and four; for the number two consisting of repeated unity, which is no number, is not perfect; it comprehends the primary numerical triangle, or trine, and is square or quartile; conjunctions considered by the favourers of planetary influence, as of the most benign aspect.

In six days creation was perfected, the 7th was consecrated to rest.—On the 7th of the 7th month, a holy observance was ordained to the children of Israel, who fasted 7 days, and remained 7 days in tents—the 7th year was directed to be a sabbath of rest for all things; and at the end of 7 times 7 years commenced the grand jubilee—every 7th year the land lay fallow: every 7th year there was a general release from all debts, and all bondsmen were set free. From this law may have originated the custom of our binding young men to 7 years' apprenticeship; and of punishing incorrigible offenders by transportation for 7, twice 7, or three times 7 years—every 7th year the law was directed to be read to the people—Jacob served 7 years for the possession of Rachel, and also another 7 years—Noah had 7 days warning of the flood, and was commanded to take the fowls of the air into the ark by sevens, and the clean beasts by sevens. The ark touched the ground on the 7th month; and in 7 days a dove was sent; and again in 7 days after. The 7 years of plenty and the 7 years of famine were foretold in Pharaoh's dream, by the 7 fat and the 7 lean beasts; and the 7 ears of full, and the 7 ears of blasted corn.—Nebuchadnezzar was 7 years a beast; and the fiery furnace was heated 7 times hotter to receive Shadrach, Meshech, and Abednego. The young of animals were to remain with the dam 7 days, and at the close of the 7th to be taken away. By the old law, man was commanded to forgive his offending brother 7 times; but the meekness of the last revealed religion extended his humility and forbearance to seventy times 7. " If Cain shall be revenged 7 fold, truly Lamech seventy times 7." In the destruction of Jericho 7 priests bare 7 trumpets 7 days.—On the 7th they surrounded the walls 7 times, and after the 7th time the walls fell.—Balaam prepared 7 bullocks and 7 rams for a sacrifice. Seven of Saul's sons were hanged to stay a famine—Laban pursued Jacob 7 days and 7 nights; 7 bullocks and 7 rams were offered as an atonement for wickedness —In the 7th year of his reign, King Ahasuerus feasted 7 days, and on the 7th directed his 7 chamberlains to find a queen, who was allowed 7 maidens to attend her—Miriam was cleansed of her leprosy by being shut up

7 days—Solomon was 7 years building the temple, at the dedication of which he feasted 7 days—In the Tabernacle were 7 lamps—7 days were appointed for an atonement upon the altar, and the priest's son was ordained to wear his father's garment 7 days—The children of Israel eat unleavened bread 7 days—Abraham gave 7 ewe lambs to Abimelech as a memorial for a well—Joseph mourned 7 days for Jacob—The Rabbins say that God employed the power of answering this number to perfect the greatness of Samuel, his name answering the value of the letters in the Hebrew word which signify 7; whence Hannah his mother in her thanks says, "that the barren had brought forth 7"—In Scripture are enumerated 7 resurrections — the widow's son by Elias, the Shunamite's son by Elisha, the soldier who touched the bones of the prophet, the daughter of the ruler of the synagogue — The widow's son of Nain—Lazarus, and our blessed Lord — The Apostles chose 7 deacons—Enoch, who was translated, was the 7th after Adam—and Jesus Christ the 77th in a direct line—Our Saviour spoke 7 times from the cross, on which he remained 7 hours; he appeared 7 times—after 7 times 7 days sent the Holy Ghost—In the Lord's Prayer are 7 petitions contained in 7 times 7 words, omitting those of mere grammatical connection—Within this number are connected all the mysteries of the Apocalypse, revealed to the 7 churches of Asia—There appeared 7 golden candlesticks, and 7 stars in the hand of him that was in the midst—7 lamps before the 7 spirits of God!—The book with 7 seals—The lamb with 7 horns and 7 eyes—7 angels with 7 seals—7 kings—7 thunders—7 thousand men slain—The dragon with 7 heads and 7 crowns—The beast with 7 heads — 7 angels bringing 7 plagues, and 7 phials of wrath—The vision of Daniel was 70 weeks—The Elders of Israel were 70—There are also numbered 7 heavens, 7 planets, 7 stars, 7 wise men, 7 champions of Christendom, 7 notes in music, 7 primary colours, 7 deadly sins, 7 sacraments in the Roman Catholic Church—The 7th son was considered as endowed with pre-eminent powers—The 7th son of a 7th son is still thought to possess the power of healing diseases spontaneously—Perfection is likened to gold 7 times purified in the fire; and we yet say, "you frighten me out of my seven senses." The opposite side of every face on the dice makes 7; whence players at hazard make 7 the main. Hippocrates says that the septenary number, by its occult virtues, tends to the accomplishment of all things, to be the dispenser of life and fountain of all its changes; and, like Shakspeare, he divides the life of man into 7 ages. In 7 months a child may be born and live, and not before; and anciently it was not named before 7 days, not being accounted fully to have life before that periodical day. The teeth spring out in the 7th month, and are shed and renewed in the 7th year, when infancy is changed into childhood. At twice 7 years puberty begins; at thrice 7 years the faculties are developed, manhood commences, and we become legally competent to all civil acts.—At four times 7 man is in full possession of his strength; at five times 7 he is fit for the business of the world; at six times 7 he becomes grave and wise, or never; at 7 times 7

he is in his apogee, and from that time decays; at eight times 7 he is in his first climacteric; at nine times 7, or 63, he is in his grand climacteric, or year of danger; and ten times 7, or three score years and ten, has by the Royal Prophet been pronounced the natural period of human life. The shield of Ajax consisted of 7 bulls' hides.—There were 7 chiefs before Thebes—The blood was to be sprinkled 7 times before the altar—Naaman was to be dipped 7 times in Jordan — Apuleius speaks of dipping the head 7 times in the sea for purification—In all solemn rites of purgation, dedication, and consecration, the oil or water was 7 times sprinkled.—The house of wisdom, in Proverbs, had 7 pillars.

REMARKABLE THUNDER-STORMS.

The effects of a thunder-storm on a house and its furniture the 8th of August 1707, at New Forge, Ireland, were very singular. It was observed that the day was throughout close, hot, and sultry, with scarcely any wind, until towards the evening, when a breeze came on with misling rain, which lasted about an hour. As the air darkened after sunset, several faint flashes of lightning were seen, and thunderclaps heard, as at a distance; but between ten and eleven o'clock they became, in their approach, very violent and terrible, progressively increasing in their intensity, and coming on with more frequency, until towards midnight. A flash of lightning, and clap of thunder, louder and more dreadful than all the rest, came simultaneously, and shook and inflamed the whole house. The mistress being sensible at that instant of a strong sulphureous smell in her chamber, and feeling a thick gross dust fall on her hands and face as she lay in bed, concluded that part of her house to have been thrown down by the thunder, or set on fire by the lightning. The family being called up, and candles lighted, both the bed-chamber and the kitchen beneath it were found to be filled with smoke and dust. A looking-glass in the chamber had been broken with such violence, that not a piece of it was to be found of the size of half a crown: several of the pieces were stuck in the chamber door, which was of oak, as well as on the other side of the room. The edges and corners of some of the pieces of broken glass were tinged of a light flame colour, as if they had been heated by the fire.

On the following morning it was found that the cornice of the chimney next the bed-chamber had been struck off, and a breach twenty inches in breadth, made in the wall. At this part there was seen on the wall a smutted scar or trace, as if left by the smoke of a candle, which pointed downward to another part of the wall, where a similar breach was made. Within the chamber, the boards on the back of a large hair trunk, filled with linen, were forced in: two thirds of the linen were pierced or cut through, the cut appearing of a quadrangular figure. Several pieces of muslin and wearing apparel, which lay on the trunk, were dispersed about the room, not in any way singed or scorched, notwithstanding the hair on the back of the trunk, where the breach was made, was singed. In the kitchen, a cat was found dead, with its legs extended as in a moving posture, without any other sign of being hurt, except that the fur was singed a little about the rump.

In the parish of Samford-Courtney, near Oakhampton, in Devon, on the 7th of October, 1811, about three in the afternoon, a sudden darkness came on. Several persons being in the church-porch, a great fire-ball fell among them, and threw them down in various directions, but without any one being hurt. The ringers in the belfry declared that they never knew the bells go so heavy, and were obliged to desist ringing. Looking down from the belfry into the church, they perceived four fire-balls, which suddenly burst, and the church was filled with fire and smoke. One of the congregation received a blow on the neck, which caused him to bleed both at the nose and mouth. He observed the fire and smoke to ascend to the tower, where a large beam, on which one of the bells was hung, was broken, and the gudgeon breaking, the bell fell to the floor. One of the pinnacles of the tower, next the town, was carried away, and several of the stones were found near a barn door, at a considerable distance from the church.

On the 15th of December, 1754, a vast body of lightning fell on the great hulk at Plymouth. It burst out a mile or two to the westward of the hulk, and rushed towards it with incredible velocity. A portion of the derrick (a part of the apparatus which serves to hoist in and fix the masts of the men of war) was cut out, of a diameter of at least eighteen inches, and about fifteen feet in length: this particular piece was in three or four places girt with iron hoops, about two inches broad, and half an inch thick, which were completely cut in two by the lightning, as if done by the nicest hand and instrument. The lightning was immediately succeeded by a dreadful peal of thunder, and that by a most violent shower of hail, the hailstones being as large as nutmegs, and for the greater part of the same size and shape.

Among the many fatal accidents by lightning which have befallen ships, the following is a remarkable instance. In the year 1746, a Dutch ship lay in the road of Batavia, and was preparing to depart for Bengal. The afternoon was calm, and towards evening the sails were loosed, to take advantage of the wind which then constantly blows from the land.

A black cloud gathered over the hills, and was brought by the wind towards the ship, which it had no sooner reached, than a clap of thunder burst from it, and the lightning set fire to the maintop-sail: this being very dry, burned with great fury; and thus the rigging and mast were set on fire. An attempt was immediately made to cut away the mast, but this was prevented by the falling of the burnt rigging from the head of the mast. By degrees the fire communicated to the other masts, and obliged the crew to desert the ship, the hull of which afterwards took fire, and, burning down to the powder magazine, the upper part was blown into the air, and the lower part sunk at the place where the ship was at anchor.

In crossing the Atlantic, in the month of November, 1749, the crew of an English ship observed a large ball of blue fire rolling on the water. It came down on them so fast, that before they could raise the main tack, they observed the ball to rise almost perpendicularly, and within a few yards of the main chains it went off with an explosion as if hundreds of cannon had been fired off simultaneously, and left behind it a great smell of brimstone. The maintop-mast was shattered into a thousand pieces, and spikes driven out of the mainmast which stuck in the maindeck. Five seamen were knocked down, and one of them greatly burnt, by the explosion. The fire-ball was of the apparent size of a large millstone, and came from the north-east.

The ingenious and indefatigable Professor Richman lost his life on the 6th of August, 1753, as he was observing, with M. Sokolow, engraver to the Royal Academy of St. Petersburgh, the effects of electricity on his gnomon, during a thunder-storm. It was ascertained that the lightning was more particularly directed into the Professor's apartment, by the means of his electrical apparatus, for M. Sokolow distinctly saw a globe of blue fire, as large as his clenched hand, jump from the rod of the right gnomon, towards the forehead of Professor Richman, who at that instant was about a foot distant from the rod, observing the electrical index. The globe of fire which struck the Professor, was attended with a report as loud as that of a pistol. The nearest metal wire was broken in pieces, and its fragments thrown on M. Sokolow's clothes, on which burnt marks of their dimensions were left. Half of the glass vessel was broken off, and the metallic filings it contained thrown about the room. Hence it is plain that the force of the lightning was collected on the right rod, which touched the filings of metal in the glass vessel.

On examining the effects of the lightning in the Professor's chamber, the doorcase was found split half through, and the door torn off, and thrown into the chamber. The lightning therefore seems to have continued its course along the chain conducted under the ceiling of the apartment.

In a Latin treatise, published by M. Lomonosow, member of the Royal Academy of Sciences of St. Petersburgh, several curious particulars are mentioned relative to this melancholy catastrophe. At the time of his death, Professor Richman had in his left coat-pocket seventy silver coins, called rubles, which were not in the least altered by the accident which befell him. His clock, which stood in the corner of the next room, between an open window and the door, was stopped; and the ashes from the hearth thrown about the apartment. Many persons without doors declared that they actually saw the lightning shoot from the cloud to the Professor's apparatus at the top of his house. The author, in speaking of the phenomena of electricity, observes that he once saw, during a storm of thunder and lightning, brushes of electrical fire, with a hissing noise, communicate between the iron rod of his apparatus at the side of his window, and that these were three feet in length, and a foot in breadth.

WHIMSICAL TRIAL IN FRANCE.

In January 1769, an important cause was brought forward in the highest court of judicature in Paris. This cause was of a most extraordinary nature, and the prevailing topic of conversation. It was bought with great avidity, and was at once to be found on the dusky desks of the lawyers, and the brilliant toilettes of the ladies. It was entitled, " For the coëffeurs de dames of Paris, against the corporation of master-barbers, hairdressers, and bagnio-keepers." It is proper to observe that the bagnio-keepers generally dressed the ladies' hair after bathing.

Those hairdressers, who presumed to dress both sexes, in this case, maintained that it was their exclusive privilege to dress the ladies; and indeed they had several of their adversaries imprisoned or fined, &c. These, in their turn defended themselves, and pretended that the exclusive privilege was in their favour; because, first, the art of dressing ladies' hair is a *liberal art*, and foreign to the profession of the *maîtres perruquiers*; secondly, that the statute of the *perruquiers* does not give them the pretended exclusive right; and, thirdly, that they have hitherto oppressed them, and are indebted to them in considerable damages and interests.

It is probable that some able pleader amused himself in drawing up this memoir. This frivolous case is conducted with art and elegance, and every where discovers the playful hand of a master, who perhaps thus unbended himself in the midst of more painful avocations. It will gratify the reader's curiosity to extract some of these brilliant passages.

In the first division the orator, who makes his clients speak in their own persons, maintains that the art of dressing the ladies' hair is a liberal art: and compares it to those of the poet, the painter, and the statuary. " By those talents," say they, " which are peculiar to ourselves, we give new graces to the beauty who is sung by the poet; it is when she comes from under our hands that the painter and the statuary represent her; and if the locks of Berenice have been placed among the stars, who will deny that to attain this superior glory she was first in want of our aid ?

" A forehead more or less open, a face more or less oval, require very different modes; every where we must embellish nature, or correct its deficiencies. It is also necessary to conciliate with the colour of the flesh, that of the dress which is to beautify it.

" This is the art of the painter; we must seize with taste the variegated shades; we must employ the *chiar' oscuro*, and the distribution of the shadows, to give more spirit to the complexion, and more expression to the graces. Sometimes the whiteness of the skin will be heightened by the auburn tint of the locks, and the too lively splendour of the fair will be softened by the greyish cast with which we tinge the tresses."

In another place, to prove that the art has claims to genius, the *coëffeurs de dames* add :—

" If the arrangement of the hair, and the various colours we give the locks, do not answer our intention, we have under our hands the brilliant treasures of Golconda. To us, belongs the happy disposition of the diamonds; the placing the pearl pins, and the suspending of the feathers. The general of an army knows what reliance he can make on a *half moon*, (a term of the then fashionable dress) placed in front; he has his engineers, who are distinguished by their titles; and we with a sparkling cross advantageously placed, know how difficult it is for an enemy not to yield. It is we, indeed, who strengthen and extend the empire of beauty."

Several legal discussions now follow, the aridity of which, do not permit our gay pleader to take his happy flights. But he appears with all his felicity of imagination in the peroration.

After having informed us that there exist above 1200 *coëffeurs de dames* at Paris, he thus closes his oration:

"Some rigid censurers will, perhaps, say that they could do very well without us, and that, if there were less art and ornaments at the toilettes of the ladies, things would be all for the better. It is not for us to judge, if the manners of Sparta were preferable to those of Athens; and if the shepherdess who gazes on herself in the glassy fountain, interweaves some flowers in her tresses, and adorns herself with natural graces, merits a greater homage than those brilliant citizens, who skilfully employ the refinements of a fashionable dress. We must take the age in the state we find it. We feel a congenial disposition to the living manners, to which we owe our existence, and while they subsist we must subsist with them."

Shortly afterwards, the case in favour of the *coëffeurs* was ordered to be suppressed, as unworthy of the majesty of the tribunal to which the suit was brought. The *coëffeurs*, however, gained their cause against the perruquiers, and the Graces triumphed over the Monster of Chicanery. The ladies had taken a warm interest in their favour, and formed for them most powerful solicitations. This important trial was crowded by a most brilliant assemblage, and when the grave decisions of the court were finally made, it was approved by a sudden clapping of hands from the anxious beauties of Paris, who considered the affair of their *coëffeurs*, as of the most national consequence.

The Book of Dwarfs.

We are men my liege.
Ay, in the catalogue ye go for men;
As hounds and greyhounds, mungrels, spaniels, curs,
Showghes, water-rugs, and demi-wolves are cleped,
All by the name of dogs.—SHAKSPEARE.

CHAPTER III.

THE following account of a dwarf is contained in a letter from John Browning, Esq. of Barton-hill, near Bristol, to Mr. Henry Baker, F.R.S. dated September 12, 1751. "I am just returned," says the writer, "from Bristol, where I have seen an extraordinary young man, whose case is very surprising: he is shown publicly for money, and therefore I send you the printed bill which is given about to bring company, and also a true copy of a certificate from the minister of the parish where he was baptized, together with the attestation of several of the neighbours of great credit and veracity, some of whom are personally known to me; to these I have likewise added my own observations, as necessary to clear up the case. The certificate is as follows:—

"This is to certify, that Lewis Hopkins, the bearer hereof, is a man of a very honest character, and has six children. His second son, Hopkins, whom you see now with him, is in the fifteenth year of his age, not exceeding two feet seven inches in height, and about twelve or thirteen pounds weight, wonderful to the sight of all beholders: the said little man was baptized the 29th of January, 1796, by me,

R. Harris,
Vicar of Lantrissent,
Glamorganshire.

The above is signed also by eight gentlemen of figure and fortune in the county of Glamorgan.

"I went myself," says Mr. Browning, "to view and examine this very extraordinary and surprising but melancholy subject; a lad entering the fifteenth year of his age, whose stature is no more than two feet seven inches, and weight thirteen pounds, labouring under all the miseries and calamities of old age, being weak and emaciated, his eyes dim, his hearing very bad, his countenance fallen, his voice very low and hollow; his head hanging down before, so that his chin touches his breast, consequently his shoulders are raised, and his back rounded not unlike a hump back; he is so weak that he cannot stand without support.

"His father and mother both told me, that he was naturally sprightly, though weakly, until he was seven years old, would attempt to sing and play about, and then weighed nineteen pounds, and was as tall, if not taller, than at present, naturally straight, well grown, and in due proportion; but from that period he had gradually declined and grew weaker, losing his teeth by degrees, and is now reduced to the unhappy state I have just been describing. The mother is a very jolly healthy woman, in the prime of life, the father enjoys the same blessing."

Another dwarf is thus described in the same work by William Arderon, F.R.S. "John Coan, a dwarf, was born at Twitshall in Norfolk, in 1728, and has been shown in this city for some weeks past, I weighed him myself, April 3, 1750, and his weight, with all his clothes, was no more than thirty-four pounds, I likewise carefully measured him, and found his height with his hat, shoes, and wig on, to be thirty-eight inches. His limbs are no bigger than a child of three or four years old, his body is perfectly straight, the lineaments of his face answerable to his age, and his brow has some wrinkles in it when he looks attentively at any thing. He has a good complexion, is of a sprightly temper, discourses readily and pertinently, considering his education, and reads and writes English well. His speech is a little hollow, though not disagreeable; he can sing tolerably, and amuses the company that come to see him with mimicking a cock's crowing, which he imitates very exactly. In 1744, he was thirty-six inches high, and weighed twenty-seven pounds and a half; his father says, when about a year old he was as large as children of that age usually are, but grew very little and slowly afterwards."

Hoaxes and Impostures.
No. XIII.
OYA POC! OR A CURE FOR THE TOOTHACHE.

In the year 1821, a man entered a coffee-house at Vienna, with his hand pressed close against his cheek, groaning, stamping and exhibiting every symptom of violent indisposition. He took a seat, called for some punch, and made useless efforts to swallow it. Several people collected round him, and inquired the cause of his illness; he replied, that he was tormented by a violent fit of toothache, which resisted every remedy. Various things were prescribed for him, but without effect. At length a man, who was playing at billiards in an adjoining room, stepped forward, and said, " Allow me to prescribe for the gentleman, I possess a remedy which I am certain will cure him in five minutes." He drew from his pocket a box, filled with small chips of a yellow kind of wood. " Here, sir," said he, " apply this to your tooth." The patient did as he was directed, and to the astonishment of every one present, he immediately experienced a diminution of pain; the remedy operated as if by enchantment, and in less than a quarter of an hour he was completely relieved, and drank his bowl of punch to the health of his deliverer. " Sir," said he," you have performed a most wonderful cure, and I shall be eternally grateful to you, if you will inform me where your valuable remedy can be purchased."—"No where," replied the billiard player : " I procured it during my last visit to South America, and brought it home with me for my own private use ; the Indians of *Oya Poc* never use any other remedy."—" Well, surely you will not refuse to let me have a few pieces of the wood."—" Impossible."—" I only ask for twenty pieces, and I will give you a ducat for each." " Well, I consent out of pure humanity ; but mind, you are the only person to whom I can grant such a favour." Every one present now wished to have some portion of the divine wood of *Oya Poc;* all were subject to the toothache ; all claimed the sacred rights of humanity, and the compassionate traveller was obliged to part with nearly all his chips of wood, and to fill his box with ducats. The master of the coffee-house himself, unwilling to suffer such an opportunity to escape him, had the good fortune to purchase ten pieces. When occasion came for putting the virtue of the wonderful wood to the test, it was found that it had none of those effects on the good people of Vienna, which it had on the savages of Oya Poc. Had it lost its virtues by carriage and keeping ?—So the happy few who had got bits of the rarity insisted; for, as usual, the greatly hoaxed were the last to acknowledge the ingenuity by which they had been fooled and cheated.

Eccentric Biography.

LUMLEY KETTLEWELL, ESQ.

LUMLEY KETTLEWELL, Esq., of Clementhorpe, near York, was a very eccentric character. He died at the age of seventy, of wretched, voluntary privation, poverty, cold, filth, and personal neglect, towards the close of the year 1819, in obscure lodgings in the street called the Pavement, whither he had removed from his own house a little while before. His fortune, manners, and education, had made him a gentleman ; but from some unaccountable bias in the middle of life, he renounced the world, its comforts, pleasures, and honours, for the life of a hermit. His person was delicate, rather below the middle size, and capable of great exertion and activity. His countenance, singularly acute and intelligent, reminded you of a French alchymist of the middle ages. His dress was mean, squalid, tattered, and composed of the most opposite and incongruous garments; sometimes a fur cap with a ball-room coat, bought at an old clothes shop, and hussar-boots; at another time a high-crowned London hat, with a coat or jacket of oil-skin, finished off with the torn remains of black silk stockings, and so forth. His manners were polished, soft and gentlemanly, like those of a courtier of the middle of the last century. Early in life he shone in the sports of the field; and he kept blood-horses and game dogs to the last; but the former he invariably starved to death, or put such rough, crude, and strange provender before them, that they gradually declined into so low a condition, that the ensuing winter never failed to terminate their career, and their places were as regularly supplied by a fresh stud. The dogs also were in such a plight that they were scarcely able to go about in search of food in the shambles or on the dunghills. A fox was usually one of his inmates, and he had Muscovy ducks, and a brown Maltese ass, of an uncommon size, which shared the fate of his horses, dying for want of proper food and warmth. All these animals inhabited the same house with himself, and they were his only companions there; for no human being was allowed to enter that mysterious mansion. The front door was strongly barricadoed within, and he always entered by the garden, which communicated with Clementhorpe Fields, and thence climbed up by a ladder into a small aperture that had once been a window. He did not sleep in a bed, but in a potter's crate filled with hay, into which he crept about three or four o'clock in the morning, and came out again about noon the following day. His money used to be laid about in his window seats, and on his tables, and, from the grease it had contracted by transient lodgment in his breeches pockets, the bank notes were once or twice devoured by rats. His own aliment was most strange and uninviting; vinegar and water his beverage; cocks' heads with their wattles and combs, baked on a pudding of bran and treacle, formed his most dainty dish, and occasionally he treated himself with rabbits' feet; he liked tea and coffee, but these were indulgences too great for every day. He read and wrote at all hours not occupied with the care of the aforesaid numerous domestic animals, and with what he called the sports of the field. His integrity was spotless; his word at all times being equal to other men's bonds. His religion was what is commonly understood by the "religion of nature;" he attended no place of worship; nor would he without great effort and much reluctance, vote at the city and county elections. But when he did, it was always in support of the candidate most favourable to the cause and rights of the people. "Never vote for the ministerial members," he used to say, "the king and the great men will always take care of themselves." He used to carry about with him a large sponge, and on long walks and rides he would now and then stop, dip the sponge in water, and soak the top of his head with it, saying it refreshed him far more than food or wine. He admitted no visitor whatever at his own house; but sometimes went himself to see any person of whose genius or eccentricity he had conceived an interesting opinion; and he liked on these visits to be treated with a cup of tea or coffee, books, and a pen and ink; he then sat down close to the fire, rested his elbow on one knee, and, almost in a double posture, would read till morning, or make extracts of passages peculiarly striking to him. His favourite subjects were the pedigree of blood-horses, the writings of freethinkers, chymistry, and natural history.

FRANK HALS, THE PAINTER

Among the many painters the city of Mechlin has produced, none excelled Mr. Frank Hals, who was born there, in 1584. He was a pupil of Charles Van Mander, and applied himself to the study of nature, as to find no competitor, except Vandyke, whom he equalled in every thing, but clearness and delicacy of colouring.

While Mr. Hals resided at Haerlem, Vandyke went purposely to visit him, and calling, as if by accident, to view his pictures, desired to sit for his portrait, which, as he had only two hours to stay, must be painted immediately.

Hals immediately began with his usual rapidity, and succeeded so well, that he desired Vandyke to view his progress; which he did, and observed to him that painting seemed so easy, that he thought he could paint a portrait himself; and desiring Hals to give him the pallet and pencils, begged him to sit, which he complied with, and in a quarter of an hour he produced a sketch, which threw the artist into such an extasy, that he rapturously exclaimed, it could only be Vandyke himself who had honoured him with a visit.

Mr. Frank Hals in his life and manners, was unfortunately (for himself) as dissipated as he was excellent in his profession; he was almost every night in a state of intoxication at some neighbouring tavern, whence it became regularly the business of his pupils to conduct him home to bed.

In this state of inebriety he would frequently fall to prayers, which were so loud as to be heard all over the house; his ejaculations often concluded with "Oh, Lord, take me quickly to thy highest heaven."

The pupils, among whom was that excellent artist Adrian Brouwer, having determined on a joke at the expense of their master, contrived so to fix some ropes under his bed, as in the midst of his prayer to draw him to the ceiling; which Hals perceiving, he roared out lustily, "Not quite so soon, Oh Lord! I shall be glad to stay here a little longer." He was afterwards heard to pray; but never expressed a wish to be taken hence so suddenly.

This celebrated painter was much entreated by Vandyke to visit England; but his unhappy turn for indolence, prevailed over his interest, and he died in indigence at the age of eighty, leaving a numerous family, all painters and musicians.

Varieties.

PROVIDENTIAL ESCAPE.

On a high steep promontory, called Ladder Hill, upon the island of St. Helena, the height of which cannot be much less than eight hundred feet, an extraordinary accident happened to a Dutch sailor, in 1759. This man coming out of the country after dark, and being in liquor, mistook the path then in use, and turned to the left, instead of the right; he continued his journey with great difficulty, till finding the descent no longer practicable, he took up his residence for the night in a chink of the rock, and fell asleep. Late in the morning he waked, and what was his horror and astonishment to find himself on the brink of a precipice one hundred fathoms deep! he attempted to return back, but found it impossible to climb the crags he had descended.

After having passed several hours in this dreadful situation, he discovered some boys on the beach at the foot of the precipice, bathing in the sea; hope of relief made him exert his voice to the utmost, but he had the mortification to find that the distance prevented his being heard.

He then threw one of his shoes towards them, but it unfortunately fell without being perceived. He threw the other and was more fortunate; for it fell at the feet of one of the boys who was just coming out of the water: the youth looked up, and with great surprise, saw the poor Dutchman waving his hat, and making other signs of distress.

They hastened to the town, and telling what they had seen, great numbers of people ran to the heights over head, from whence they could see the man, but were nevertheless at a loss how to save him. At last a coil of strong rope was procured, and one end being fastened above, the other was reeved down over the place where he stood. The sailor instantly laid hold of it, and with an agility peculiar to people of his profession, in a little time gained the summit.

As soon as he found himself safe, he produced an instance of provident carefulness, truly Dutch, by pulling out of his bosom a China punch bowl, which in all his distress he had taken care to preserve unbroken, though the latter must have alarmed the children at once by its noise, and the shoes must have left him to starve, if they had not fallen in sight.

EXTRAORDINARY INSTANCE OF THE EFFECTS OF SUPERSTITION.

The Northern Indians suppose that they originally sprang from a dog; and, about five years ago, a superstitious fanatic so strongly pressed upon their minds the impropriety of employing these animals, to which they were related, for purposes of labour, that they universally resolved against using them any more, and, strange as it may seem, destroyed them. They now have to drag every thing themselves on sledges. This laborious task falls most heavily on the women; nothing can more shock the feelings of a person, accustomed to civilized life, than to witness the state of their degradation. When a party is on a march the women have to drag the tent, the meat, and whatever the hunter possesses, whilst he only carries his gun and medicine case. In the evening they form the encampment, cut wood, fetch water, and prepare the supper: and then, perhaps, are not permitted to partake of the fare until the men have finished. A successful hunter sometimes has two or three wives; whoever happens to be the favourite, assumes authority over the others, and has the management of the tent. These men usually treat their wives unkindly, and even with harshness; except, indeed, at the time when they are about to increase the family, and then they show them much indulgence. With all this they have a strong affection for their children.—*Franklin's Journey to the Polar Sea.*

MOVING EARTH.

In July, 1823, at the Waen Wem lime rocks, near Llanymynech, the inhabitants of the neighbourhood were surprised to find that, during the preceding night, several thousand tons of limestone had parted *en masse* from the main rock, and moved four or five yards forward, pushing the earth before it with tremendous force, leaving a horrid chasm behind. This seems the more extraordinary, as there appears no adequate cause for such an effect. The rocks had not been worked for several years, and as the weather was perfectly dry at the time, it would seem that nothing but an earthquake could have produced the separation. In many similar situations near the spot in question, the cottagers have erected their dwellings, in the full confidence that they could not have a surer foundation; and nothing extraordinary had happened during the night in question to warrant the supposition that an earthquake was the cause. The matter must therefore remain at present a mystery, until some geologist shall be able to give a satisfactory reason for so unlooked for an event; which has not a little alarmed the cottagers in the neighbourhood, who flattered themselves on the security of the foundations of their humble dwellings.

The Scrap Book.

REPTILES.

The following may serve to elucidate the abode of some of the summer reptiles, during the cold season. Some men, who were employed by Mr. Skinner, of Rickmansworth, Herts, in removing a quantity of flints out of a large open chalk pit, for the repair of the roads, dug out twelve serpents or vipers, alive, but from the cold could scarcely move, and seemed to have lost the power of opening their mouth, though they patted the forked tongue freely. Six of the largest measured two feet, some twenty inches, and two, six inches in length; besides which was found one *slow* or blind worm in high vivid perfection, and a great number of the lizard kind, called the dry *eft*. They were found lying in the interstices of the flints; the flints had long lain there, it is supposed a century, as the root of a large beech tree was standing over them, which, from its size, could not be less than a hundred years of age, and the flints were covered with about three feet of chalk and mould, mixed, and open to a southern aspect.

CORNISH ARCHERS

The ancient Cornish men were most excellent archers; they would shoot an arrow 24 score; their arrow was a cloth yard long, wherewith they would pierce any ordinary armour. One Mr. Robert Arundel would shoot 12 score with his right hand, with his left hand, and behind his head; and one Robert Bone shot at a little bird upon a cow's back, and killed the bird without touching the cow.

Published by J. LIMBIRD, 355, Strand, (East End of Exeter 'Change): and sold by all Newsmen and Booksellers. Printed by A. APPLEGATH, Stamford-street.

THE CABINET OF CURIOSITIES,
OR
𝔚onders of the 𝔚orld 𝔇isplayed.

*A world of wonders where creation seems
No more the works of Nature but her dreams.*—MONTGOMERY.

No. XVII.] PRICE TWOPENCE.

ANNE MOORE OF TUTBURY.

THIS vile impostor, who pretended she could live without food, was born at Royston, near Ashborn, in the county of Derby, in the year 1761. Her parents were poor, and of the name of Peg. At the age of twenty-seven she married James Moore, a labourer, with whom she soon parted, after which she had two children by her master, a boy and a girl.— About the beginning of 1807, when residing at Tutbury, a village in Staffordshire, she first excited public attention, by declaring she could live without food. An assertion so repugnant to reason and nature was of course rejected. She therefore offered to prove the truth of her assertion by submitting to be watched for a considerable time.

In order to satisfy the public, she was removed from her home to the house of Mr. Jackson, grocer, of the same village, and all the inhabitants were invited to join in watching her. A Mr. Taylor, surgeon, superintended the watching, which continued sixteen days, during which time she was allowed a little water, on the three first days. When the watch had ended, she was removed to her own house; and Mr. Taylor published an account, declaring that she had lived for thirteen days, without taking any food, liquid or solid. This account, so attested, was believed by numbers, who flocked to see her, and few visited her without leaving some proof of their credulity or pity. By this means she collected about £250.

Though the declaration of the persons who formerly watched her, had obtained considerable credit, yet there were many who thought her an impostor, and demanded that she should be again watched. A committee was formed of the neighbouring clergymen and magistrates, who met on Tuesday, the 20th of April, 1813; and the time it was determined she should be watched was fixed at one month, to which she at last was obliged to assent.

Her bed was filled with chaff, and the clothes examined in the presence of the committee. The watch entered on their office at two o'clock on Wednesday. She received the watches with as much good manners as she was capable of, though she had been crying bitterly before they came. The first watch, which continued four hours, was begun by Sir Oswald Mosley and the Rev. Leigh Richmond, and followed by several other gentlemen. At the end of seven days the public was informed that she had during that time taken no food whatever. Great confidence was now expressed by her advocates that she would endure the ordeal with credit. But when the machine for weighing her was put under the bed, it was found that she lost weight rapidly. At last, on the ninth day, she insisted upon the watches quitting the room, declaring that she was very ill, and that her daughter must be sent for. She was now greatly reduced, and the watches who attended her were much alarmed, lest she should expire, and apprehensive of being implicated in the charge of murder, they quitted the room and admitted the daughter, who administered what she thought proper, when the mother began to recover.

One remarkable circumstance was, that on Friday, the 30th of April, after the watch broke up, she desired to take a solemn oath that she had not, during the time she was watched, taken any food whatever; which oath was administered unto her. This she did in hope, notwithstanding all, still to impose upon the public. But as her clothes gave evidence against her, to her utter confusion, she was brought at last to make the following confession:

"I, Anne Moore, of Tutbury, humbly asking pardon of all persons whom I have attempted to deceive and impose upon, and above all, with the most unfeigned sorrow and contrition, imploring the divine mercy and forgiveness of that God, whom I have greatly offended, do most solemnly declare, that I have occasionally taken sustenance for the last six years.

" Witness my hand, this fourth day of May, 1813.

"The mark ⋈ of ANNE MOORE."

The above declaration of Anne Moore, was made before me, one of his Majesty's Justices of the Peace for the county of Stafford.

THOMAS LISTER.

Witness of the above declaration and signature of my mother Ann Moore,

MARY MOORE.

This impostor was committed to prison, February 1816, for falsely collecting money under the pretence of charity.

DESCRIPTION OF MONT BLANC.

This mountain, so named on account of its white aspect, belongs to the great central chain of the Alps. It is truly gigantic, and is the most elevated mountain in Europe, rising no less than 15,872 feet, somewhat more than three miles, above the level of the sea, and 14,624 feet above the lake of Geneva, in its vicinity. It is encompassed by those wonderful collections of snow and ice, called "Glaciers," two of the principal of which are called Mont Dolent and Triolet. The highest part of Mont Blanc, named the Dromedary, is in the shape of a compressed hemisphere. From that point it sinks gradually, and presents a kind of concave surface of snow, in the midst of which is a small pyramid of ice. It then rises into a second hemisphere, which is named the Middle Dome; and thence descends into another concave surface, terminating in a point, which, among other names bestowed on it by the Savoyards, is styled "Dôme de Gouté," and may be regarded as the inferior dome.

The first successful attempt to reach the summit of Mont Blanc was made in August 1786, by Doctor Paccard, a physician of Chamouni. He was led to make the attempt by a guide, named Balma, who, in searching for crystals, had discovered the only practicable route by which so arduous an undertaking could be accomplished. The ascent occupied fifteen hours, and the descent five, under circumstances of the greatest difficulty, the sight of the doctor and that of his guide, Balma, being so affected by the snow and wind, as to render them almost blind, at the same time that the face of each was excoriated, and the lips exceedingly swelled.

On the first of August of the following year, 1787, the celebrated and indefatigable naturalist, M. de Saussure, set out on his successful expedition, accompanied by a servant and eighteen guides, who carried a tent and mattresses, together with the necessary accommodations and various instruments of experimental philosophy. The first night they passed under the tent, on the summit of the mountain of La Côte, 4986 feet above "the Priory," a large village in the vale of Chamouni, the journey thither being exempt from trouble or danger, as the ascent is always over turf, or on the solid rock; but above this place it is wholly over ice or snows.

Early next morning they traversed the glacier of La Côte, to gain the foot of a small chain of rocks, enclosed in the snows of Mont Blanc. The glacier is both difficult and dangerous, being intersected by wide, deep, irregular chasms, which frequently can be passed only by three bridges of snow, which are suspended over the abyss. After reaching the ridge of rocks, the tract winds along a hollow, or valley, filled with snow, which extends north and south to the foot of the highest summit, and is divided at intervals by enormous crevices. These shew the snow to be disposed in horizontal beds, each of which answers to a year, and, notwithstanding the width of the fissures, the depth can in no part be measured. At four in the afternoon, the party reached the second of the three great platforms of snow they had to traverse, and here they encamped at the height of 9312 feet above the Priory, or 12,768 feet, nearly two miles and a half, above the level of the sea.

From the centre of this platform, enclosed between the farthest summit of Mont Blanc on the south, its high steps, or terraces, on the east, and the Dôme de Gouté on the west, nothing but snow appears. It is quite pure, of a dazzling whiteness, and on the high summits presents a singular contrast with the sky, which, in these elevated regions, is almost black. Here no living being is to be seen; no appearance of vegetation; it is the abode of cold and silence. "When," observes M. de Saussure, "I represent to myself Dr. Paccard and James Balma first arriving, on the decline of day, in these deserts, without shelter, without assistance, and even without the certainty that men could live in the places which they proposed to reach, and still pursuing their career with unshaken intrepidity, it seems impossible to admire too much their strength of mind and their courage."

The company departed, at seven the next morning, to traverse the third and last platform, the slope of which is extremely steep, being in some places thirty-nine degrees. It terminates in precipices on all sides; and the surface of the snow was so hard, that those who went foremost were obliged to cut places for the feet with hatchets. The last slope of all presents no danger; but the air possesses so high a degree of rarity, that the strength is speedily exhausted, and on approaching the summit it was found necessary to stop at every fifteen or sixteen paces to take breath. At eleven they reached the top of the mountain, where they continued four hours and a half, during which time M. de Saussure enjoyed, with rapture and astonishment, a view the most extensive, as well as the most rugged and sublime in nature, and made those observations which have rendered this expedition important to philosophy.

A light vapour, suspended in the lower regions of the air concealed from the sight the lowest and most remote objects, such as the plains of France and Lombardy; but the whole surrounding assemblage of high summits appeared with the greatest distinctness.

M. de Saussure descended with his party, and the next morning reached Chamouni, without the smallest accident. As they had taken the precaution to wear veils of crape, their faces were not excoriated, nor their sight debilitated. The cold was not found to be so extremely piercing as it was described by Dr. Paccard. By experiments made with the hygrometer on the summit of the mountain, the air was found to contain a sixth portion only of the humidity of that of Geneva; and to this dryness of the air M. de Saussure imputes the burning thirst which he and his companions experienced. The balls of the electrometer diverged three lines only, and the electricity was positive. It required half an hour to make water boil, while at Geneva fifteen or sixteen minutes sufficed, and twelve or thirteen at the sea side. Not any of the party discovered the smallest difference in the taste or smell of bread, wine, meat, fruits, or liquors, as some travellers have pretended is the case at great heights; but sounds were of course much weakened, from the want of objects of reflection. Of all the organs, that of respiration was the most affected, the pulse of one of the guides beating ninety eight times in a minute, that of the servant one hundred and twelve, and that of M. de Saussure one hundred and one; while at Chamouni the pulsations respectively were forty-nine, sixty, and seventy-two. A few days afterwards, Mr. Beaufoy, an English gentleman, succeeded in a similar attempt, although it was attended with greater difficulty, arising from enlargements in the chasms in the ice.

SINGULAR TRIAL FOR MURDER, IN FRANCE.

The Assize Court of the department of the Landes, in the South of France, was occupied for some time in the month of July, 1822, with the trial of two men named *Begu* and *Lafforcade*, accused of the murder (in the year 1816) of a soldier, whose name is unknown. The trial lasted nine days, and a hundred and twelve witnesses were examined. Of course we can do no more than give the substance of their evidence, which disclosed a scene of shocking barbarity.

It appeared that the accused, and another man named Dugers, lived near the bridge of Oro, and there is every reason to believe that they were associated for the purposes of murder and robbery. When the French troops returned from Spain, some dragoons were billeted at Oro. One of them who lodged with Begu, who kept an inn, possessed a great number of quadruples, and upon one occasion he spread them out on a table. This dragoon being compelled to depart suddenly from Oro, buried his treasure in Begu's garden. In 1815, two individuals, who called themselves the brothers of the dragoon, came to Begu, and wished to dig in his garden, which Begu would not suffer. On the 7th of October, 1816, about six in the evening, a stranger alighted at Begu's house: the next morning a quantity of blood was discovered near the remains of a fire in a neighbouring wood; the blood was traced to the Luz, a deep river which bounds the forest. The river was dragged, and a naked body was found, which had been disfigured by fire, and to the neck and feet of which bags filled with stones were tied. The selection of the places where the body had been burned and drowned, and the arrangements which had been made, announced that the crime must have been committed by individuals who were acquainted with the locality of the neighbourhood. The bags which were tied to the body had been sewed by an experienced hand: Begu was a tailor. It appeared from an inspection of the footmarks in the forest, that the assassins were three in number; one wore shoes, another shoes and spatterdashes, and the third wooden shoes. It was proved that Lafforcade, Begu, and Dugers constantly wore shoes of this description. Begu admitted that a dragoon, possessing a quantity of gold, had lodged with him, and he also acknowledged that two persons had wished to dig in his garden; but he strongly denied that any stranger had come to his house on the 7th of October, 1816. To contradict this denial, three witnesses were called; the two first of whom merely proved that they saw a stranger in Begu's house on the 7th of October; the evidence of the third was more important. He deposed that he was a cowherd, and that he was in the habit of sleeping regularly at Begu's.

On the night of the 7th of October, 1816, he did not meet with so kind a reception as he was wont to experience from Begu. He was only allowed to sup and refresh his oxen, and could not even obtain permission to sleep in the stable. This witness also stated, that when he arrived at the inn, he found a supper preparing for several persons. He saw Lafforcade there, and a stranger, whose description he gave; when he left the house between ten and eleven o'clock, the stranger was still there. Some witnesses proved the complete identity of the dragoon who lived with Begu in 1813, the stranger who was seen at the inn on the night of the murder, and the corpse which was discovered in the river. The witnesses concurred in describing the dragoon and the stranger as being robust, and about five feet high, and as having very white hair, and finally, as wanting a front tooth. This description tallied exactly with that of the corpse. On the night of the murder, Dugers and Begu were seen conversing together, and the former said to one of the witnesses, "I have been assisting Begu to perform an operation; keep your counsel, or it is all over with you." Shortly after the commission of the crime, Begu wished to sell a waistcoat, which the person to whom it was offered refused to buy, because it was stained with large spots of blood, partly washed out. It appeared also, that from the period of the murder Begu had abandoned his business of tailor, and his circumstances had greatly improved. The prisoner Lafforcade stated that he did not see Begu on the night of the murder, and that he was in bed at nine o'clock. The former assertion had already been proved false, by the evidence of the cowherd, who saw Lafforcade at Begu's house on the night in question; and the latter statement was shown to be equally unworthy of credit by two witnesses, who deposed that Lafforcade had visitors in his house at a very late hour of the night. Another witness stated, that about midnight cries of suffering were heard to proceed from Lafforcade's house. Nothing of what passed in Lafforcade's house would have been known had not a little girl overheard a woman who lodged there, and who could not be found at the period of the trial, give the following details to one of her female acquaintances:— After supping at Begu's, the dragoon was brought to the house of Lafforcade, where Dugers was. The three wretches suddenly placed a noose round the neck of their victim, threw him on the ground, and strangled him. "You did not do it well," said Lafforcade: "And yet," replied Dugers, "I put the cord seven times round his neck." The assassins then, by favour of the night, carried the body into the forest, and there, like cannibals, delivered the yet quivering members to the flames, and afterwards threw it into the river. Divine retribution soon exercised itself on Dugers. He happened one day to say to an individual that he had assisted Lafforcade and Begu to commit a wicked act, that he had been badly paid for it, and that he intended to confess all he knew. Shortly after this, Dugers was found mortally wounded; he had only time to confess his participation in the murder of the soldier, and to tell that he had been himself killed by one of his associates in crime.

After the counsel for the accused had been heard, the jury immediately found the prisoners *guilty*. They heard the sentence of their death pronounced without exhibiting any emotion.

It was shown during the course of the trial, that two persons who had by some means obtained a knowledge of the prisoners' crime had died suddenly, under circumstances which left no room to doubt that their death was caused by poison. In the house of Lafforcade was found a rope with a slip knot, forming a noose, to which human hair of a different colour from that of the murdered soldier was found sticking.

HENRY MASERS DE LA TUDE

A Baron de Kolli, who was employed by the British government in 1809, to effect the liberation of Ferdinand VII. from Valençay, has published an account of his enterprise, which failed. The Baron was arrested and thrown into the castle of Vincennes, where he was confined four years, and attempted his escape; which he nearly effected. A more remarkable instance of escape from this prison occurs in the person of Henry Masers de la Tude, who suffered a confinement of thirty-five years in the state prisons of France.

This gentleman was born in Languedoc in the year 1725. He had scarcely attained his twenty-third year, when his father, who was a knight of the royal and military order of St. Louis, sent him to Paris, to improve a genius which he discovered early for the study of mathematics. At this time Madame de Pompadour was become the favourite of Louis XV.; and young Henry, learning that she was afraid of being poisoned, resolved to be of use to her, if possible; but the means which he used for this purpose were such as laid the foundation of his misery for the remainder of his life.

He went to Versailles to tell her that he had seen a box left at the post-office and addressed to her; and communicating his suspicions of the contents of this box, advised her to be upon her guard; assuring her at the same time that he was really alarmed for her welfare, after what he had heard, and that he thought himself very happy by having it in his power to give her such important information. She appeared sensible of his attention, and after having assured him of it, offered him her services.

The box arrived, for it was he that had left it at the post-office: it was filled with a powder, which had no pernicious qualities. But in reflecting on the information he had given, Madame de Pompadour ordered experiments to be made with the powder on animals, and finding that it had no bad effect, she soon discovered his stratagem. She made her complaint, and he was put into the Bastille, on the first of May, 1749.

In the month of September following, he was sent to the dungeon of Vincennes, where M. Berrier, lieutenant-general of the police, was very kind to him; giving him the best apartment in the dungeon, and permitting him to walk two hours a day in one of the gardens which are in the enclosure. The window of his chamber looked towards the governor's house, and that of the cabinet towards Paris. From this window he saw what passed in the other garden of the dungeon, which had been given to a clergyman who was a Jansenist. This clergyman enjoyed much liberty, and taught the son of the Marquis de Chatelet, and that of the turnkey to read and write. The elder of these was not sixteen. The appearance of ease and liberty in these young men excited the envy of Masers, and made him conceive the project of escaping. He profited by the permission which he had of walking two hours a day in the garden. There were two turnkeys, and at two o'clock precisely, the elder of the two went into the garden to wait for Masers, and the younger came to open the door of his chamber that he might go down. Having now conceived his project, he went down stairs quicker than the turnkey, and on his arrival in the garden, the latter found him by the side of his companion. Masers mended his pace every day in going down stairs, and after having accustomed the turnkey to this practice for a little time, on the 25th of June, 1750, he effected his escape in the following manner.

No sooner had the turnkey opened the chamber door than Masers flew down stairs, shut the door at the foot of the staircase, to gain a little time. He then knocked boldly at the outer door, on the other side of which was posted a sentinel, who immediately opened it. Without giving the sentinel time to speak to him, he cried out, "Zounds, the clergyman has been already waiting two hours for the Abbé de Saint Sauveur; have you seen this sorry fellow? Has he been long gone out? I am going to seek him, but he shall pay me for my trouble." In pronouncing these words, he still kept retiring from the door. When he had run a little way he met with another sentinel, and asked him the same question: he answered that he knew nothing of the matter, and let him pass by. He afterwards met a third sentinel, and asked him if he had not seen the Abbé Saint Sauveur go by? He answered no: Masers now began to skip like a schoolboy, and passed by the fourth sentinel, who did not so much as suspect him to be a prisoner.

Six days after his escape, conscious of having been guilty of imprudence only, he surrendered himself, by the mediation of the physician in ordinary to the king. He was however conducted to the Bastille. Madame de Pompadour, on being informed of this transaction, was piqued at his having had more confidence in the king's goodness than in hers, and notwithstanding the zeal and humanity of M. Berrier, the lieutenant-general of the police, who was interested in the fate of the prisoner, she caused him to be confined eighteen months in a cell, in company with another prisoner, named Delegré, detained likewise by the marchioness.

In this situation the two prisoners began to meditate whether it was not possible to make their escape. The high and thick walls of the Bastille, the iron-grates before the windows and in the chimney, the number of armed men who guard the prison, the depth of the ditches, in a word, every circumstance conspired to prove that the attempt was impracticable. But what may not be accomplished by ingenuity, impelled by an invincible thirst of freedom?

They had neither scissars, knives, nor any edged instrument; and for a hundred guineas, the turnkey would not supply them with an ounce of thread. Upon an exact calculation, they wanted fourteen hundred feet of cordage; they also stood in need of two ladders of wood, from twenty to twenty-five feet long, and another of a hundred and eighty feet long. It was necessary to pull several iron grates out of the chimney, and in one night to make a hole in a wall several feet thick, at the distance of only twelve or fifteen feet from a sentinel. They had to make and to do all these things to accomplish their design, and they had nothing but their hands to operate with. It was necessary to hide both the wooden ladder and that of cord, with two hundred and fifty rounds of a foot long and an inch diameter, as well as many other things prohibited in the apartment of a prisoner; and the officers accompanied by the turnkeys came to visit and search them several times a week.

[*To be concluded in our next.*]

FECUNDITY OF VEGETABLES.

The fecundity of various plants is very surprising. We have an account in the Philosophical Transactions, of a single plant of barley, that by steeping and watering with saltpetre dissolved in water, produced two hundred and forty-nine stalks, and eighteen thousand grains. In this case, indeed, art and force were made use of, but we have remarkable instances of this kind, effected by unassisted nature, particularly that of a pompion seed, attested by Mr. Edwards of Windsor. This seed, in the year 1699, was accidentally dropped in a small pasture, where cattle had been foddered for some time, and taking root of itself, without any manner of care, the vine ran along over several fences, and spread over a large piece of ground far and wide, continuing its progress till it was killed by the frost. The seed produced no more than one stalk, but it was a very large one, being eight inches round; and from this single vine they gathered two hundred and fifty pompions, one with another as big as a half peck measure, besides a considerable number of small ones, not ripe, which they left upon the vine. Add to this what M. Dodart observes, who has an express discourse on the fecundity of plants in the Memoirs of the Academy of Sciences, wherein he shows, that an elm, at a moderate computation, yields, one year with another, three hundred and twenty-nine thousand grains or seeds, each of which, if properly planted, would grow up to a tree. Now an elm ordinarily lives a hundred years, and consequently, in the course of its life, produces nearly thirty-three millions of grains, all coming originally from one single seed.

Mr. Luccock, of Birmingham, has published an account of the produce of twelve plants of rhubarb, as a proof of the astonishing fertility and value of that vegetable. He planted twelve roots of rhubarb in a plot of ground of eighteen square yards. In the third year, he had no less than five pounds at each gathering, repeated three times per week, for a period of five months, making a total weight of three hundred pounds. This amount divided by eighteen, the number of square yards, yields the extraordinary produce of sixteen pounds to the yard, or thirty-four tons and a half per acre. The rhubarb is sold in small bundles at threepence per pound, which is after the rate of four shillings per yard, or nearly £1000 per acre. This quantity refers to the stem or eatable part of the plant, leaving the fine luxuriant leaves, three feet in diameter, for other purposes. Pigs and cattle, it is said, will feast upon them. They weigh upon an average more than the stalks. Rhubarb for pies and puddings, can hardly be distinguished from gooseberries, and may, like them, be preserved through the winter. It may also be introduced, stewed in gravy, or fried in butter, as an excellent vegetable. There is also no doubt in Mr. Luccock's mind, but the root might be used as a substitute for the Turkish rhubarb, which our merchants sell us at half-a-crown per ounce. Of the three sorts, that with sharp pointed leaves and green stems is the most productive.

A single plant of Turkey corn (*Zea Mays*), bears 3000 seeds; the sun-flower (*Helianthus Animus*), 4000; the poppy (*Papaver Somniferum*), 32,000; and tobacco (*Nicotiana Tabacum,*) 40,320!

TRANS-ATLANTIC WONDERS!
From the United States Papers for August 1823.

How to catch an Owl.—When you discover one on a tree, and find that it is looking at you, all you have to do is to move quickly round the tree several times, when the owl, in the mean time, whose attention will be so firmly fixed, that forgetting the necessity of turning its body with its head, will follow your motion with its eyes, till it wrings its head off.

How to catch Rabbits.— Place apples in the parts where they frequent, after sprinkling them with snuff, and when they come to smell, the sudden effort to sneeze which they make never fails to break their necks, and even, in some cases, have been known to throw their heads a foot beyond their tails.

A paneful habit.—A lady of New York has contracted the habit of counting the panes of glass in a house the moment she casts her eyes upon the window. She has repeatedly assured her friends, it is impossible to cure herself of the habit, and that the sense of weariness and pain from associating the number of panes with the idea of a house or window is a hundred times worse than the labour of superintending the concerns of her family.

A whistler.—A boy in Vermont, accustomed to working alone, was so prone to whistling, that, as soon as he was by himself, he unconsciously commenced. When asleep, the muscles of the mouth, chest, and lungs, were so completely concatenated in the association, he whistled with astonishing shrillness. A pale countenance, loss of appetite, and almost total prostration of strength, convinced his mother it would end in death, if not speedily overcome; which was accomplished by placing him in the society of another boy, who had orders to give him a blow as soon as he began to whistle.

Animated Pedometer.—An attorney insensibly contracted a habit of numbering his steps when walking, and when in his office, of thinking how many paces distant were certain places in the neighbourhood. He found it nearly impossible to meditate on any other subject. He fancies a cure was effected by walking over the stream, on a pole, where he was in imminent danger of being drowned.

Trunk Maker and his Nails.— A trunk maker in the country

could never refrain from biting his nails at a moment of leisure. In 1816, every appearance of a nail on the left fingers and right thumb was obliterated.

Imitation.—A child in New Hampshire, who was usually seated in the meeting-house, on the Sabbath, opposite an old gentleman who laboured under *chorea sancti viti*, contracted the habit of imitating his distorted features to such a degree that its face was continually in a grimace. The child was cured by working at needlework before a mirror.

Ruling Employment.—A pious woman in the eastern section of New Hampshire, who drew large quantities of water from a deep well with a pole, was repeatedly observed at her evening devotions, before the Bible, unconsciously moving her arms all the while, as in drawing the bucket from the well.

Force of Habit.—Mr. C. who committed suicide two years since, was constantly pinching his left cheek, if his left hand was not otherwise employed. The consequence was, a hard callosity, of the size of a dollar, formed over the buccinator muscle, that materially injured his speech; he could not blow out a candle, nor bring his lips to the blowing the hole of a flute, on which he was formerly a good player.

Anecdotes of Longevity.

MRS. STARR BARRETT.

DIED at Charleston, on the 9th of January, 1820, Mrs. Starr Barrett, after fully completing one hundred and twenty years of an active and various life. This venerable lady was born in the year 1699 of the Christian æra, and 1078 (solar calculation) of the Hegira of the Mahomedans, about a year before the death of Charles II. King of Spain, to which country her family had emigrated at an early period of her life. She was born in one of the Barbary States, which is not ascertained, but it is supposed under the empire of Morocco. Peter I. was then Czar of Muscovy, a title now enlarged to that of Emperor of all the Russias; Frederick Augustus was King of Poland; Charles XII. was King of Sweden; Frederick IV. (son to Christian V.) was King of Denmark; William III. King of England; Peter IV. King of Portugal; and Louis XV. King of France.. Mrs. Barrett possessed a constitution truly Arabian; she was seldom or never sick, and rather withered away like some majestic tree, which gradually loses its moisture, but which the tempest has always spared. A variety of circumstances formed her a great traveller, and she had visited, with no unobservant eye, the four quarters of the globe. She spoke English, Spanish, Italian, and French, with great fluency; was perfectly acquainted with the Morisco or Frank, as it is spoken by the traders along the southern shores of the Mediterranean; was mistress of the Hebrew, and wrote, spoke, and translated the pure Arabic with ease and elegance. Her memory was very tenacious of impressions made in early youth, but for the last half century she was apt to forget occurrences from one day to another. She recollected the public joy in Spain, upon the important discovery of the Philippine Islands, by the Spanish navigators, as well as the battle of Almanza, which was fought on the frontiers of the kingdom of Valencia, when the army of Philip V. King of Spain, obtained a complete victory over the Imperialists under the Archduke Charles. Both these events occurred in 1707, when the subject of this notice was only eight years of age. She was near the scene of action when Gibraltar was besieged by the Spaniards, in 1727. Mrs. Barrett was of an easy and cheerful disposition, even after her blindness, which continued during the last thirty years of her life. Latterly, extreme debility had reduced her to second infancy. She ate every thing within the pale of the Hebrew rule, (being a Jewess, and strict in her religious duties) drank and slept well, and was remarkably cleanly and particular about her person. After dwelling thirty or forty years in London she went to America, in 1780, being then in the eightieth year of her age, and lived in Charleston ever since. Her mortal sickness did not last a fortnight, when, having completed a truly patriarchal age, she was gathered to her fathers, leaving behind her half a dozen generations, to the fifth and sixth removal. She died esteemed by all who knew her, and greatly beloved by her family for her amiable qualities and fervent piety. They were accustomed to look upon her with a feeling approaching to religious veneration; nor could the reflecting mind regard her person or face for a moment, without a sentiment that would thrill the heart and make the countenance turn pale. Her great age had caused her to behold the sons and daughters of men fall before her like the leaves in autumn; and yet that life, extended as it was to the utmost span, must have appeared to its possessor but as a troubled dream, from which she was at length awakened by the hand of death. The soul has burst its mortal prison-bonds:

" Svegliata fra gli spiri etetti,
 Ove nel suo Fattor l'Alma s'interna!"

Eccentric Biography

MR. A. PENTHENEY.

A YOUNG Irishman of the county of Meath, named Peter Gaynor, resolved to go to the West Indies, to make, as the saying is, his fortune. On the day he set out on his travels, he had on a pair of shoes of such enormous size, that his friends and acquaintance, who had assembled in great numbers to wish him long life and good luck, unanimously dubbed him with the name of Peter Big Brogues. Peter, with a great deal of eccentricity, was shrewd, industrious, persevering, and obliging; in the course of years he acquired a large fortune, and lived to see his only child married to Sir George Colebrook, chairman to the East India Company, and a banker in London, to whom Big Brogues gave with his daughter two hundred thousand pounds.

Big Brogues had a nephew of the name of Augustine Pentheney, who was very early in life encouraged to make a voyage to the West Indies, to follow his trade of a cooper, under the patronage of his uncle, and acquired, like him, an immense fortune. He became, indeed, the richer, though not the better, man of the two; he accumulated at least £300,000, but used it in a way that was a disgrace to him and nature. He was a miser of the most perfect drawing, perhaps, that nature has given to the world.

Mr. A. Pentheney saw mankind only through one medium; his vital powers were so diverted from generous or social subjects, by his prevailing passion for gold, that he could discover no trait in any character, however venerable or respectable, that was not seconded by riches; in fact, any one that was not rich, he considered only as an inferior animal, neither worthy of notice, nor safe to be admitted into society. This extraordinary feeling he extended to female society, and, if possible, with a greater degree of disgust. A woman he considered only as an incumbrance on a man of property, and therefore he never could be prevailed upon to admit one into his confidence. As to wedlock, he utterly and uniformly rejected the idea of it. His wife was the public funds, and his children, guineas; and no parent or husband paid more deference or care to the comforts of his family. He was never known to separate his immense hoard, by rewarding a generous action, or alleviating an accidental misfortune, by the application of one shilling to such purposes. It could scarcely be expected, indeed, that a man who was so niggardly of comforts to himself, would bestow a gift, or extend charity, to others. The evening before he died, some busy friend sent a respectable physician to him; the old miser did not show any apparent dislike to the visit, until he recollected the doctor might expect a fee; this alarmed him, and immediately raising himself in the bed, he addressed the Irish Esculapius in the following words: "Doctor, I am a strong man, and know my disorder, and could cure myself; but as Mr. Nangle has sent you to my assistance, I shall not exchange you for any other person, if we can come to an understanding: in fact, I wish to know what you will charge for your attendance till I am recovered." The doctor answered, eight guineas. "Ah sir," said the old man, "if you knew my disorder, you would not be exorbitant: but to put an end to this discussion, I will give you six guineas and a half." The doctor assented, and the patient held out his arm with the fee, and to have his pulse considered, and laid himself down again. His relations were numerous, but not being, in his opinion, qualified, for want of experience, in the management of money, to nurse his wealth, he bequeathed the whole of it to a rich family in the West Indies, with the *generous* sum of £4 annually to a faithful servant, who had lived with him twenty-four years. In the will, he expresses great kindness for poor John, and says he bequeathed the £4 for his kind services, that his latter days may be spent in comfortable independence. Like Thelluson, he would not allow his fortune to pass to his heirs immediately, as he directed the whole should be funded for fourteen years, and then, in its improved state, be at the disposal of the heirs he had chosen. For the regulation of his last will and testament, he appointed Walter Nangle, Esq. and Major O'Farrell, of the Austrian army, his executors; and the Right Hon. David La Touche and Lord Fingal trustees.

Varieties.

THE SUPERSTITION OF DRYDEN.

The poet Dryden was particularly fond of judicial astrology, and always used to calculate the nativity of his children.

When his lady was in labour with his son Charles, he being told that it was decent to withdraw, he laid his watch on the table, begging one of the ladies, then present, in a very grave manner, to take notice of the exact minute of the child's birth, which she observed, and acquainted him therewith.

About a week after, when his lady was pretty well recovered, Mr. Dryden took occasion to tell her, that he had been calculating the child's nativity; and observed with grief, that he was born in an evil hour; for Jupiter, Venus, and the Sun were all under the Earth, and the lord of his ascendant afflicted with a hateful square of Mars and Saturn. If he lives to the eighth year (continued he) he will go near to die a violent death on his very birth day; but if he should then escape, of which I see but little hopes, he will in his twenty-third year be under the same evil direction; and if he should then also escape, the thirty-third or thirty-fourth is, I fear——Here he was interrupted by the immoderate grief of his lady, who could no longer hear so much calamity prophesied to befall her son.

The time at last came, and August was the inauspicious month in which young Dryden was to enter into the eighth year of his age.

Mr. Dryden being then at leisure to leave town, he was invited to the country seat of the Earl of Berkshire, his brother-in-law, to spend the long vacation with him at Charlton, in Wilts; his lady going at the same time on a visit to pass the remaining part of the summer at her uncle Mordaunt's. When they came to divide their children, his lady would have had him take his son John, and let her have Charles; but Mr. Dryden was too absolute, and they parted in anger, he took Charles with him, and she was obliged to be content with John.

When the fatal day arrived, the anxiety of the lady's spirits caused such an effervescence of blood, as threw her into so violent a fever, that her life was despaired of, till a letter came from Mr. Dryden, reproving her for womanish credulity, and assuring her that her child was well, which revived her spirits, and in six weeks after she received an eclaircissement of the whole affair.

Mr. Dryden, either through fear of being reckoned superstitious, or thinking it a science beneath his study, was extremely cautious of letting any one know that he was a dealer in astrology; therefore could not excuse his absence on his son's birth day, from an hunting match, which Lord Berkshire had made, to which all the neighbouring gentlemen were invited. When he went out, he took care to set his son a double exercise in the Latin tongue, which he taught his children himself, with a strict charge not to stir out of the room till his return, well knowing that the task which he had set him, would take him up longer time than he could be absent from him.

Charles was performing his exercise, in obedience to his father's command, when, as ill-fate would have it, the stag made towards the house, and the noise alarming the servants, they hasted out to see the sport; one of them taking young Dryden by the hand, led him out along with him, when just as they came to the gate, the stag being at bay with the dogs, made a bold push and leaped over the court wall, which being low, and very old, the dogs followed, threw down a part thereof, and poor Charles was buried in the ruins. He was presently got out, but much bruised, so that he languished for six weeks in a very dangerous way, which accomplished the former part of his father's prophecy.

In his twenty-third year, being at Rome, he fell from the top of an old tower belonging to the Vatican, occasioned by a swimming in his head, with which he was seized by the heat of the weather. He recovered this also; but ever after remained in a languishing sickly state, till the thirty-third year of his age, when being returned to England, he was drowned at Windsor, being taken with the cramp as he was bathing in the Thames with another gentleman, to whom he called for assistance, but too late. Thus his father's prophetical calculation proved but too true.

RUTLAND CAVERN.

RUTLAND CAVERN, within the mountains of Abraham's Heights, Matlock Bath, is the largest in these kingdoms. The discovery and opening of this tremendous cemetry of nature, has given to this country a rich treasure of the most brilliant gems, rare fossils, and numerous minerals, forming the most splendid natural grotto in the world. Philosophers, mineralogists, and the public, may now avail themselves of a visit to this treasure—this grand lesson and lecture on science; capacious as a city, and extending many miles, with pillars, arches, and bridges of every denomination and order—nature the great architect. The lakes, fish ponds, fountains, and rivulets of the most delicate rock water. The labyrinths, arcades, walls, roofs, and floors, embellished with the most glittering crystals, and the ores of silver, lead, copper, and zinc in every combination:—

Here, ranging through her vaulted ways,
On nature's alchymy you gaze:
See how she forms the gem, the ore,
And all her magazines explore.

The Rutland Cavern, as an object of general curiosity, and the terrific grandeur of the immense natural cavities, far exceeds the wildest pictures of romance, or the fearful scenes of enchantment, and gives a most interesting and perfectly new subject for the mind. From the finest terrace, commanding all the beauties of Matlock, you enter the rock by a dry, roomy, and even mountainous archway, perfectly safe and pleasant for the most timid female. The external surface of the Heights of Abraham abounds in rare botanical plants, and from the Serpentine and Moon Battery Walks, shaded by fine and lofty cedars, the most sublime scenery is taken, rich and romantic as the imagination can conceive. The pure air of this delightful region, and the extraordinary instances and facts of the lengthened periods of existence of its inhabitants, proclaim this to be really the seat of health and beauty.

The principal objects of general observation within the Cavern, are the rocky mountain archway, imbedding marine shells; the druses, or grottos; fish ponds; Ossian's hall; an arcade to the Hall of Enchantment, in the Castle of Otranto, of indescribable grandeur; the den of lions; a grand cave, with the extraordinary distant glimmering of daylight; a fine arcade to Jacob's well and fountain; the waters of life; the ascent by one hundred steps to the ancient mine, worked by the Romans; other fish ponds, with fish living in perpetual darkness; the dark and gloomy cave of black stone; the enemy of miners; the den of wolves and bears; a romantic bridge; a fine rocky scene. These recesses lead to the most fantastic, grotesque, and whimsical distribution of rocks, imbedding the most rare and delicate fossils, grottos, and druses, that defy all attempts at description or relation.

The Scrap Book.

QUADRUPED TURNED BIPED.

WHAT would *Lord Monboddo* have given for such a fact as the following, recorded in the *American Farmer* of 20th June last? 'Extracts from a letter to the editor, dated Allentown, N. J. June 10, 1823: "A few days ago, in passing a flock of sheep, at some distance from me, I observed something of uncommon appearance moving about amongst them: it was owing, I found upon approaching nearer, to a lamb following its dam, *walking* upon its *fore-feet*, with its *body* erect. Its hind feet, I was told upon inquiry, and legs as far as the gambrels, were frozen off, the night it was lambed, and very soon afterwards it acquired this extraordinary kind of motion. It is three months old, quite fat, and of ordinary size for its age. It grazes and sucks, resting wholly upon its fore-feet, with its body in the position just mentioned; and will walk, if not urged too fast, a quarter of a mile at once, without inconvenience.

LOSS OF HAIR.

A VERY remarkable case has occurred with a man in the Schoolwynd of Paisley. The hair of his head, and likewise his beard, has entirely come away from his skin, without any apparent cause for so striking a change. He is perfectly well in health, and can assign no reason for the loss of his hair. He had formerly a good head of hair, and an ordinary strong or rough beard, and in the short space of six weeks he has been marvellously deprived of both. He was nearly eleven years in a militia regiment, during which period, in order to attend parade in a decent and cleanly manner, he was necessitated to shave his beard generally once a day; and now, to the astonishment of all his friends, he has not to perform any labour of the kind.—*Glasgow Chronicle.* We know a Captain in the Navy who has been both bald-headed and beardless for several years. He wears a wig, but needs no razor. He is unable to account for the loss of his beard.—*Edinburgh Star.*

WILD CAT.

A FEW days ago, at Tan y lan, near Llanrwst, a wild cat was caught in a trap, measuring three feet seven inches in length, and fourteen inches high.

Published by *J. LIMBIRD,* 355, Strand, (East End of Exeter 'Change); and sold by all Newsmen and Booksellers. Printed by *A. APPLEGATH, Stamford-street.*

THE CABINET OF CURIOSITIES,
OR
Wonders of the World Displayed.

A world of wonders where creation seems
No more the works of Nature but her dreams.—MONTGOMERY.

No. XVIII.]　　　PRICE TWOPENCE.

OLD BOOTS.

NEVER certainly were the nose and chin of any human being on more friendly terms than those of Old Boots, of whom, at the request of a Correspondent, we present a portrait. In No. XII. of THE CABINET, we gave a brief notice of this singular individual, who lived at an Inn at Rippon in Yorkshire, in the humble but useful capacity of Boots; and though his singular appearance subjected him to a thousand jokes, yet poor Boots good naturedly bore them all; particularly (which was frequently the case) when they were paid for by a present of money. Many a thrifty traveller was led to crack a joke on Boots' nose, and then present him with sixpence or a shilling to place between it and his chin, and thus go whistling out of the room. Eating would almost

T

seem to have given Boots some difficulty; but on such occasions, the two prominent features of his face were very accommodating, and by distending his mouth pretty wide, he could contrive at any meal to introduce in a short time a pound of bacon with a due proportion of bread, beer, and vegetables. He was, however, an inoffensive creature, kind to his equals, and humble to his superiors, which made poor Boots a great favourite with all the visitors at the inn, where he long lived, and died.

SYMPATHIES AND ANTIPATHIES.

The seeds of our aversion and antipathy to particular things are often lodged so deep, that in vain we demand a reason of ourselves for what we do or do not love.

Cardinal Don Henrique de Cardona would fall into a swoon upon the smell of a rose, saith Ingrassia. And Laurentius, Bishop of Uratislavia, is said to have been killed by the smell of roses.

Cardinal Oliverius Caraffa, during the season of roses, used to enclose himself in a chamber, not permitting any to enter his palace, or to come near him, that had a rose about him.

The smell of a rose, or sight of it at a distance, would cause a noble Venetian of the family of the Barbaragi to swoon: he was therefore advised by the physicians to keep at home, and not to hazard his life by going abroad while roses continued.

I knew a stout soldier, says Donatus, who was never able to bear the smell or sight of the herb rue, but would ever betake himself to flight at his first notice of its presence.

Johannes e Querceto, a Parisian, and Secretary to Francis the First, King of France, was forced to stop his nostrils with bread, when there were any apples at table; and so offensive was the smell of them to him, that if an apple had been held near his nose, it would fall a bleeding. Such a peculiar and innate hatred to apples had the noble family of Fystates in Aquitain.

I have seen, saith Brassavolus, the younger daughter of Frederick, king of Naples, that could not eat any kind of flesh, nor so much as taste of it; and as often as she put any bit of it into her mouth, she was seized with vehement fits, and falling to the earth, and rolling herself thereupon, would lamentably shriek out; this she would continue to do for the space of half an hour, after which time she would return to herself.

Antonius Postellus, a French boy, would eat nothing that was roasted, boiled, or fried, contenting himself with bread, fruits and milk; nor could he eat the finer sort of bread, but such only as had coarse bran in it. In the winter time he ate dried apples, pears, cherries, nuts, &c.; his milk also must be cold, for he could eat nothing hot or warm.

I saw a noble Countess, saith Horstius, who (at the table of a Count) tasting of an udder of beef, had her lips suddenly swelled thereby: observing that I took notice of it, she told me that she had no dislike to that kind of dish, but as often as she did eat of it, she was troubled in this manner.

A learned person told me, saith the same author, that he knew one at Antwerp, that would immediately swoon, as oft as a pig was set before him, upon any table where he was present.

There lives a person amongst us, saith Henricus of Heersberg, of prime quality, who at the sight of an eel is presently cast into a swoon, even though it be brought to the table enclosed in paste; he falls down as one that is dead, nor doth he return to himself till the eel is taken off from the table.

A noble count of Arustadht had such an antipathy to olive oil, that all kind of sauces that were prepared with it, and set in the room where he was, must suddenly be taken thence, or else he would immediately fall into deadly faintings.

Rondeletius saith, he knew a Bishop of France, who, when he was by no means able to take any physic, as often as he had need, used to have it prepared for him in a great quantity; that done, he caused it to be poured hot into a clean basin, where he used to stir it to and fro with a small stick, and to hold his mouth and nostrils over the steam of it, by which he was purged as plentifully as if he had taken any convenient medicine for that purpose.

When I was at Pisa, saith Fallopius, and was physician to the nuns of St. Paul's in the East, I often prescribed pills to the Abbess of that place, who never swallowed them, but crushed them flat with her fingers, forming them as it were into little cakes, then she moistened them on the one side with her spittle, and so applied them outwardly to the region of the ventricle, binding them on with a swathing band; and in the space of four or five hours, she would be as well purged as if she had swallowed down the pills themselves. This I observed in her for two years together, and it seemed wonderful to me.

That is wonderful, saith Donatus, which was observed in a boy, the son of a count; that if at any time he ate of an egg, his lips would swell, in his face would rise purple and black spots, and he would froth at the mouth, after the same manner as if he had swallowed poison.

I knew, saith Bruyerinus, a maid born at Chauniacum in Flanders, who being sixteen years of age or more, had been brought up only with milk, without any other kind of food; for she was not able to endure so much as the smell of bread, and if the smallest particle of it was put into her milk, even at a distance, she would discover it by the smell.

Germanicus could not endure the sight or voice of a cock; and the Persian Magi were possessed with an extreme hatred to mice.

There was (saith Weinrichus) a person of a noble family, who was not able to bear that an old woman should look upon him: and being once drawn out by force from his supper to look upon one such, that which was only intended for merriment, as to him, ended in death, for he fell down and died upon it.

There was in Hafnia a man, in other respects strong, healthful, and of a good courage, who yet as often as he saw a dog (though it be ever so small a one) was not only affrighted, but also seized with convulsions in his left hand.

I know, says Henricus, a nun in the monastery of St. Clare, yet living, who at the sight of that insect we call a beetle is strangely affected. It fell out that some young girls, knowing this disposition of hers, cast a beetle into her bosom, betwixt her breasts; which when she perceived, she presently fell into a swoon to the earth, deprived of all sense, and remained four hours in cold sweats; when she came to herself, and recovered her spirits by degrees; yet she could not obtain her former strength in many days after, but continued trembling and pale.

Marcellus Donatus speaks of a nobleman of Mantua, that could not endure the sight of a hedgehog without falling into fits and cold sweats immediately upon it.

Mathiolus tells us of a German, who coming in winter-time into an inn to sup with him and some other of his friends, the woman of the house, being acquainted with his temper, had beforehand hid a young cat in a chest, in the same room where they sat at supper. But though he had neither seen nor heard it, yet after some time that he had sucked in the air, infected by the cat's breath, that quality of his temperament that had antipathy to that creature being provoked, he sweated, and a sudden paleness came over his face; and to the wonder of all that were present, he cried out, that in some corner or other of the room there was a cat that lay hid.

Mrs. Raymond, of Stowmarket, says Dr. Fairfax, whenever she hears thunder, even afar off, begins to have a bodily distemper seize on her: she grows faint, sick in her stomach, and ready to vomit.

Mrs. Mary Brook, of Yoxford, says the same author, has such an aversion to wasps, that whilst their season of swarming about in houses lasteth, she is forced to confine herself to a little close chamber, and dares not then appear at table, lest their coming there should put her into such distempers as cheese doth those who have an antipathy to it.

HENRY MASERS DE LA TUDE.

[Concluded from p. 265.]

The mind of Masers was constantly occupied with his project of escape from the Bastille. He had several times mentioned it to his companion, who was a very sensible man, but his answer constantly was, that the thing was impossible. But his reasons, instead of discouraging, fortified the resolution of Masers.

Being satisfied, from some observations, that the cieling of the apartment was double, some hope was formed of the practicability of opening a passage in that direction. After holding a conference on this subject the whole day, the two prisoners, immediately after they had supped, wrenched an iron hinge from their table, with which they took out a pane of the wainscot, and began to take away the mortar. In six hours they had penetrated the first cieling, and to their great satisfaction, they found there was another at three feet distance. From this moment they looked upon their escape as certain; they replaced the pane in the wainscot, so as not to appear to have been taken out. The next day Masers broke their steel, and converted it into a little pin or common knife, with which instrument they made handles to the two hinges of the table. They gave each of them an edge. Afterwards they unthreaded two of their shirts; that is, after having ripped and unhemmed them, they drew out one thread after another; they tied these threads together, and made of them several balls, each containing an equal and determinate quantity: all these being finished, they divided them into two, and they became two great cushions. There were about fifty threads to each, of sixty feet long; they then plaited them, and made of them a cord of about fifty-five feet long; with which, and the wood which was brought them for their fire, they made a ladder of twenty feet long.

They next attempted the most difficult part of the enterprise; which was to take the iron bars out of the chimney. For this purpose they fastened their rope ladder with a weight to one end of the bars; it easily twisted about them, and by means of the wooden steps they supported themselves in the air whilst they were at work. In six months they had taken out all the bars, and restored each of them to its place, in such a manner as to be able to take it instantly away when an opportunity offered. This work is said to have been very painful: they never came out of the chimney without their hands covered with blood; and their bodies were in such a position when at work, as to make it impossible for them to continue for more than an hour at a time.

This done, they wanted a wooden ladder of twenty feet long, to ascend from the fosse to the parapet, where the guards were posted, and afterwards to get into the garden of the government house. Several pieces of wood were every day given them to make their fire; they were from eighteen to twenty inches long. They now wanted pulleys and several other things. Their hinges were unfit for this work, and still more so for sawing of wood. In less than six hours, Masers made with an iron candlestick, and the other half of the steel, an excellent saw, with which he could, in less than a quarter of an hour, have cut in two a log of wood as thick as his thigh. With the knife, the hinge and the saw, they chipped and smoothed the logs, and made at the ends mortises and tenons that they might be inserted one within the other; as soon as they had finished a part of their ladder, they hid it between the two cielings.

As in the daytime the officers and turnkeys frequently entered their chamber, when they least expected them, it was necessary to hide, not only their utensils, but the least chip or shaving which they made, as the least of them would have betrayed them.

All round the Bastille there is an entablature, which has a projection of three or four feet. They doubted not, but at each step which they descended, the ladder would wave from one side to another, and in these moments the best organized head may become giddy. To prevent either of them from being beaten to pieces if they should fall, they made a second rope, in the same way as the former, of three hundred and sixty feet long, or twice the height of the towers. This rope was to be passed through a kind of pulley, which they had made without a wheel, that the rope might not slip between it and the cheeks; and in this manner one of them might, either from above or below, support his companion, and prevent him descending quicker than he would wish in case his head was affected. They likewise made other shorter ropes, to tie their ladder to a piece of cannon, and for other unforeseen necessities. They worked almost eighteen months day and night in putting together these materials.

The moment of attempting their dangerous enterprise now arrived. As soon as their supper was served, Masers, notwithstanding a rheumatism which he had in his left arm, climbed the chimney, and it was with the greatest difficulty he got to the top. He was near being stifled with soot; for he was not aware of the precaution used by chimney sweepers of covering their elbows, girding their loins, and putting something over their heads, to save them from the dust of chimneys. Therefore all the skin of his elbows and knees was rubbed off. At length he arrived at the chimney top, where setting himself astride, he let down a ball of packthread which he had in his pocket, at the end of which it was agreed that his companion should tie the strongest cord, which was fastened to Maser's portmanteau: by this means he drew it up to him, and let it down upon the platform. He let down the cord again to his companion, who tied it to the wooden ladder. He afterwards drew up in the same manner the two iron bars, and all the other things of which they were in need. After this he let down his cord again, to get up the rope ladder; leaving his companion enough of it to get up the chimney more commodiously than he himself had done. Being both now on the top, they drew up the rest of the ladder; and they descended at once upon the platform, serving as a counterpoise to each other.

Two horses would not have been able to carry all their apparatus. They began to roll up their rope ladder, which made a volume of five feet high, and of a foot thick: they rolled it upon the tower of the treasury which they judged most favourable to their descent. They fixed their ladder to a piece of cannon, and afterwards let it gently down into the fosse. They fixed their pulley also, and passed through it their rope of three hundred and sixty feet long. After having brought all their packages to this side, Masers tied himself fast by the thigh to the end of the pulley cord: he got upon the ladder; and as he descended, his companion let go the rope. At length he arrived safe in the fosse. His companion immediately let down his portmanteau, the iron bars, the wooden ladder, and all their equipage. This being done Dalegré next descended; and during all the time, the sentinel was not more than ten fathoms length from them, walking upon the corridor. This would have prevented them from getting up to it to go into the garden, as they had at first intended; they therefore were under the necessity of making use of their iron bars. Masers took one upon his shoulder with the wimble, and his companion took the other. Masers did not forget to put a bottle of usquebaugh into his pocket, and they went straight to the wall which separates the fosse of the Bastille from that of the gate Saint Antoine, between the garden and the governor's house. In this place there had formerly been a little fosse, a fathom wide, and one or two feet deep. There the water was up to their armpits.

The moment Masers began with the wimble to make a hole between two stones, to introduce their levers, the round-major passed by with his great lantern, at the distance of ten or twelve feet over their heads. To prevent their being discovered, they sunk up to their chins in the water. As soon as the major had passed, Masers made two or three little holes with his wimble, and they took out the great stone they had begun with. From this moment he assured Dalegré of their success: he drank some usquebaugh, and made his companion do the same. They attacked a second stone, and afterwards a third. A second round came by, and they again sunk until the water was up to their chins. They were obliged to repeat this ceremony every half hour when the round came by, which greatly distressed them.

Before midnight, they pulled out upwards of ten cart loads of stone, and in less than six hours, had entirely pierced the wall, which is more than four feet and a half thick. They drew the portmanteau out of the hole, abandoning every thing else without regret. They descended into the deep fosse of the gate Saint Antoine, where, after a narrow escape from perishing, they got upon dry ground, and took refuge at the abbey of Saint Germain des Prez.

Such is the narrative of an escape perhaps the most extraordinary of any that ever was effected by the ingenuity and resolution of man. La Tude was afterwards taken and reconducted to the Bastille, where he continued till 1784, when he was liberated, after passing a period of thirty-four years in person.

BONAPARTE AND HIS FAMILIAR.

The following singular story was circulated almost immediately after the fall of Napoleon, and with the credulous obtained ready belief:—

Ever since the retreat of Napoleon across the Rhine, and his return to his capital, a visible change had been observed in his habits and his conduct. Instead of wearing the livery of woe for the discomfiture of his plans of ambition, he had dismissed his usual thoughtfulness; smiles played on his lips, and cheerfulness sat on his brow. His manners had become light and easy, and his conversation lively. Business seemed to have lost its charms for him, he sought for amusement and pleasure, and, like another hero of an inferior rank, whenever his spirits sunk, he had recourse to the sparkling cup, to " raise them high with wine." Balls and entertainments succeeded each other, and the Parisians began to fancy either Napoleon was certain of making an advantageous peace with the Allies whenever he thought proper, or were convinced that his downfal was at hand, and therefore he wished to spend the last weeks of his imperial dignity in enjoyment and ease. A new conscription had been ordered, and the legislative body had been dismissed; but these were signs of his existence, not of his activity. Indolent, at least in appearance, he remained buried in pleasure, whilst the invaders crossed the Rhine, and, rapidly approaching Paris, threatened 'to destroy at once his throne and the metropolis. On a sudden his conduct experienced a second change— his face assumed his deep and habitually thoughtful gloom—his attention was once more entirely engrossed by the cares due to his armies—and every day witnessed new reviews of regiments in the Place du Carrousel. Sleep could no longer seal his wakeful eyes, and his wonted activity, in which perhaps no other mortal ever equalled him, was displayed with more energy than ever. All the time he could spare from his armies and cabinet, he bestowed on the State Council. So striking an opposition between his present and past conduct, could not fail to excite a powerful agitation in the minds of the Parisians, and to make them strive to trace a change so abrupt in the manners of the Emperor, to its true cause; but to the still greater astonishment of the whole city, the report of an interview of Napoleon with his genius, under the shape of a mysterious red man, transpired. The gentleman from whom this curious communication was received, heard it related, with the following particulars, on the 1st of January, at Paris, where he spent the whole of the winter:—The 1st of January, 1814, early in the morning, Napoleon shut himself up in his cabinet, bidding Count Mole, then Counsellor of State, and since made Grand Judge of the Empire, remain in the next room, and to hinder any person whatever from troubling him, while he was occupied in his cabinet. He looked more thoughtful than usual. He had not long retired to his study, when a tall man, dressed all in red, applied to Mole, pretending that he wanted to speak to the Emperor. He was answered, that it was not possible. "I must speak to him; go and tell him that it is the red man that wants him, and he will admit me." Awed by the imperious and commanding tone of that strange personage, Mole obeyed reluctantly, and trembling, executed his dangerous errand. "Let him in," said Bonaparte sternly. Prompted by curiosity, Mole listened at the door, and overheard the following curious conversation :—The red man said, "This is the third time of my apparition before you; the first time we met was in Egypt, at the battle of the Pyramids. The second, after the battle of Wagram. I then granted you four years more, to terminate the conquest of Europe, or to make a general peace; threatening, that if you did not perform one of these two things, I would withdraw my protection from you. Now I am come, for the third and last time, to warn you, that you have but three months to complete the execution of your designs, or to comply with the proposals of peace which are offered you by the Allies; if you do not achieve the one, or accede to the other, all will be over with you—so remember it well."—Napoleon then expostulated with him to obtain more time, on the plea that it was impossible, in so short a space, to reconquer what he had lost, or to make peace on honourable terms. "Do as you please, but my resolution is not to be shaken by entreaties, nor otherwise, and I go." He opened the door, the Emperor followed, entreating him, but to no purpose; the red man would not stop any longer. He went away, casting on his Imperial Majesty a contemptuous look, and repeating, in a stern voice "three months —no longer." Napoleon made no reply; but his fiery eyes darted fury, and he returned sullenly into his cabinet, which he did not leave the whole day. Such were the reports that were spread in Paris, three months before the fall of Napoleon Bonaparte, where they caused an unusual sensation, and created a superstitious belief among the people, that he had dealings with infernal spirits, and was bound to fulfil their will, or perish. What is more remarkable, in three months the wonderful events justified the red man's words completely; more unfortunate than Cæsar, or Henry IV. of France, these presages did but foretell his ruin, and not his death. Who the man really was who visited Napoleon, in a red dress, has never been known; but that such a person obtained an interview with him, seems to be placed beyond a doubt. Even the French papers, when Bonaparte was deposed, recurred to the fact, and remarked, that his mysterious visitant's prophetic threat had been accomplished.

Hoaxes and Impostures.
No. XIV.
THE DEMETRIUSES.

IN our account of Royal Impostors in No. XVI. of THE CABINET, we alluded to the Pretenders to the throne of Russia, but a more detailed account may be deemed interesting:—

History hardly furnishes a more extraordinary event, than that of the pretender Demetrius, who raised such disturbances in Russia, after the death of John Basilides. In 1584, this czar left two sons; one named Fedor, or Theodore, the other Demetri, or Demetrius. Fedor succeeded his father; and Demetrius was confined to a village called Uglis, with the czarina his mother. As yet the rude manners of that court had not, like the Turkish sultans and the ancient Greek emperors, adopted the policy of sacrificing the princes of the blood to the security of the throne. A prime minister, named Boris Gudenou, whose sister had been married to the czar Fedor, persuaded his master, that he would never reign quietly unless he imitated the Turks, and assassinated his brother. An officer was therefore sent to the village, where young Demetrius was brought up, with orders to kill him. The officer, at his return, said he had executed his commission, and demanded the reward that had been promised him. All the reward Boris gave the murderer was to kill him also, in order to suppress every proof of the guilt. It is said that Boris poisoned the czar Fedor some time after; and though he was suspected of the crime, yet this did not prevent his ascending his throne.

There appeared at that time, 1597, in Lithuania a young man who pretended to be prince Demetrius, that had escaped out of the hands of the assassin. Several, who had seen him at his mother's, knew him again by particular marks. He bore a perfect resemblance to the prince; he shewed the golden cross, enriched with precious stones, that had been tied about Demetrius's neck. The palatine of Sandomir immediately acknowledged him for the son of John Basilides, and for the lawful czar. The diet of Poland made a solemn inquiry into the proofs of his royal extraction, and, finding them past all doubt, he lent him an army to drive out the usurper Boris, and to recover the throne of his ancestors.

In the mean while Demetrius was treated in Russia as an impostor, and even as a magician. The Russians could not believe that a Demetrius, who was supported by the Poles, a Catholic nation, and who had two Jesuits for his council, could be their real king. So little did the boyars question his being an impostor, that, upon the decease of the czar Boris, they made no difficulty to place his son, then only fifteen years of age, on the throne.

During these transactions in 1605, Demetrius was upon his march into Russia with a Polish army. They who were dissatisfied with the Muscovite government, declared in his favour. A general of that nation, advancing within sight of Demetrius's army, cried out, "He is the only lawful heir of the empire;" and immediately went over to him with the troops under his command. The revolution was sudden and complete, and Demetrius ceased to be a magician. The inhabitants of Moscow ran to the palace, and dragged the young Boris and his mother to prison. Demetrius was proclaimed czar without opposition. It was given out that young Boris and his mother had killed themselves in prison; but it is more likely that Demetrins put them to death.

The widow of John Basilides, mother of the real or pretended Demetrius, had been banished long since to the north of Russia; the new czar sent a kind of coach, as magnificent as any that could be had at that time, to bring her to Moscow. He went himself part of the way to meet her; they embraced each other with transport and tears of joy in the presence of a prodigious multitude, so that nobody doubted but Demetrius was the lawful emperor. He married the daughter of the palatine of Sandomir, his first protector, and this was what ruined him. The people were shocked to see a Catholic empress, a court composed of foreigners, and, above all, a church built for the Jesuits; so that Demetrius was no longer looked upon as a Russian.

In the midst of the entertainments at the marriage of the czar, a boyar, whose name was Zuski, put himself at the head of a number of conspirators, who, entering the palace, with the sword in one hand, and a cross in the other, cut the Polish guard in pieces. Demetrius was loaded with chains. The conspirators confronted him with the czarina, widow of John Basilides, who had so solemnly acknowledged him for her son. The clergy obliged her to declare upon oath the real truth in regard to Demetrius. Whether it was that the apprehension of death forced this princess to take a false oath, and to get the better of nature, or whether she did it out of regard to the real truth, she confessed, with tears in her eyes, that the czar was not her son, that the real Demetrius had been murdered in his infancy, that she had only followed the example of the whole nation in acknowledging the new czar, and to be revenged for the blood of her son upon a family of assassins. Demetrius was now said to be a low fellow, named Grisba Utropoya, who had been for some time a monk in a Russian convent. Before, they used to reproach him with not following the Greek religion, and with differing entirely from the customs and manners of Russia; but now, they called him a Russian peasant, and a Greek monk. Let him be what he would, Zuski, the chief of the conspirators, killed him with his own hand, and succeeded to the empire in 1606.

This new czar, having suddenly mounted the throne, sent back the few Poles that had escaped the massacre, to their own country. As he had no other right to the crown, than that of having assassinated Demetrius, the rest of the boyars, dissatisfied with being subject to a person so lately their equal, soon pretended that the deceased czar was not an impostor, but the real Demetrius; and that the murderer was unworthy of the throne. The name of Demetrius became dear to the Russians. The chancellor of the late czar declared, that he was not dead, but would quickly recover of his wounds, and appear again at the head of his loyal subjects.

This chancellor made a progress through Muscovy, with a young man in a litter, whom he called Demetrius, and treated as his sovereign. At the very sound of Demetrius's name the people rose up; they fought some battles in behalf of his cause, without so much as seeing him; but the chancellor's party having been defeated, this second Demetrius soon disappeared. However, the people were so mad after the name, that a third Demetrius presented himself in Poland. This man was more fortunate than the rest; being supported by Sigismond, king of Poland, he laid siege to Moscow, where Zuski resided. The tyrant was shut up in this capital; but he had still in his power the widow of the first Demetrius, and the palatine of Sandomir, that widow's father. The third Demetrius demanded the princess as his wife. Zuski delivered up both the father and the daughter, hoping perhaps to soften the king of Poland, or flattering himself that the palatine's daughter would not acknowledge the impostor. But this impostor was victorious; the widow of the first declared this third Demetrius to be her real husband; so as the first of that name found out his mother, the third as easily found out his wife. The palatine swore that this was his son-in-law; and the people made no longer any doubt of it. The boyars, divided betwixt the usurper Zuski and the impostor, would acknowledge neither. They deposed Zuski, and shut him up in a convent. This was still a superstition of the Russians, as it had been of the ancient Greek church, that a prince who had been once a monk, was incapable of ever reigning again: and this same opinion had been insensibly introduced into the Latin church. Zuski appeared no more; and Demetrius was assassinated at a public entertainment by a party of Tartars.

The boyars then offered their crown to prince Ladislaus, son of Sigismond, king of Poland. Ladislaus was preparing to take possession, when behold a fourth Demetrius started up, and entered the lists with him. This man gave out, that God had constantly preserved him, though he had been in all appearance assassinated at Uglis by the tyrant Boris; at Moscow, by the usurper Zuski; and afterwards by the Tartars. He found partisans that believed in these three miracles. The town of Pleskou acknowledged him as czar. Here he fixed his residence a few years; during which time the Russians, repenting, they had called in the Poles, drove them back again; and Sigismond renounced all hopes of seeing his son Ladislaus seated on the throne of Russia. In the midst of these disturbances, the son of the patriarch Fedor Romanow was made czar. This patriarch was related by the females to the czar John

Basilides. His son, Michael Federowitz, that is, son of Fedor, was chosen to this dignity at the age of seventeen, by his father's influence. All Russia acknowledged this Federowitz, and the city of Pleskou delivered up the fourth Demetrius, who was hanged.

There remained still a fifth, a son of the first, who had been really czar, and married the daughter of the palatine of Sandomir. His mother removed him from Moscow, when she went to meet the third Demetrius, and pretended to acknowledge him for her real husband. She retired afterwards (1613) among the Cossacks along with this child, who was looked upon, and might be really the grandson of John Basilides; but as soon as Michael Federowitz was seated on the throne, he obliged the Cossacks to deliver up the mother and the child, who were both drowned.

One would not have expected a sixth Demetrius. Yet, during the reign of Michael Federowitz in Russia, and of Ladislaus in Poland, another pretender of this name appeared in the czar's dominions. As some young people were bathing one day with a Cossack of their own age, they took notice of Russian characters on his back, which were pricked with a needle; and they found them to be, "Demetrius, son of the czar Demetrius." He was supposed to be the same son of the first Demetrius, by the palatine of Sandomir's daughter, whom the czar Federowitz had ordered to be drowned. God had operated a miracle to save him; he was treated as the czar's son at the court of Ladislaus; and they intended to make use of him in order to excite fresh disturbances in Russia. The death of his protector Ladislaus blasted all his hopes. He retired first to Sweden, and from thence to Holstein; but, unfortunately for this adventurer, the duke of Holstein having sent an embassy into Russia, in order to open a communication for a silk trade with Persia, and the ambassador having had no other success but to contract debts at Moscow, the duke of Holstein discharged the debts by delivering up this last Demetrius, who was quartered alive.

Anecdotes of Longevity.

The following instances of longevity have been selected.

Year.		Age.
1759	Don Cameron	130
1766	Jno. Delasomer	130
——	George King..	130
1767	John Taylor..	130
1774	William Beattie	130
1778	John Watson	130
1780	Robert M‘Bride	130
——	William Ellis	130
1764	Eliza Taylor	131
1775	Peter Garden	131
1761	Eliza Merchant	133
1772	Mrs. Keith	133
1767	Francis Ange.	134
1777	John Brookey	134
1714	Jane Harrison	135
1759	James Sheille	136
1768	Catherine Noon	136
1771	Margaret Foster	136
1776	John Mariat	136
1772	J. Richardson	137
1793	— Robertson	137
1757	William Sharpley	138
1768	J. M‘Donough	138
1770	— Fairbrother	138
1772	Mrs. Clum	138
1766	Thomas Dobson	139
1765	Mary Cameron	139
1732	William Leyland	140
——	Countess of Desmond	140
1770	James Jands	140
1778	Swarling (a monk)	142

Year.		Age.
1773	Charles M'Finlay	143
1757	John Effingham	144
1782	Evan Williams	145
1766	Thomas Winsloe	146
1772	J. C. Dradkenberg	146
1652	William Mead	148
1768	Francis Confi	150
1542	Thomas Newman	152
1656	James Bowels	152
——	Henry West	152
1648	Thomas Damme	149
1635	Thomas Parr	152
1762	A Polish Peasant	157
1797	Joseph Surrington	160
1668	William Edwards	168
1670	Henry Jenkins	169
1780	Louisa Truxo	175

The following aged persons have died of late years:—

1821	Cato Overing, a black	110
1823	Ellen Tate	110
——	Mrs. Ormesby	110
——	Mr. J. Larling*	110
1808	Col. J. Stewart	111
1820	Bridget Byrne	111
1822	Joseph Mills	111
1823	J. Mackenzie	111
1821	Ann M'Rae	112
1822	Sam. Welch, an American †	112
1818	Thomas Botwell	113
——	William Napier	113
1823	A Woman in Finland	115
1818	Ann Smallwood	116
——	Alexander Campbell	117
1822	A Female Slave, Jamaica	120
——	T. Gilbert	120
——	J. Woods	122
1818	David Ferguson	124
1822	Thadey Doorley ‡	
1821	Marg. Darby, a black	130

* He left 130 children and grandchildren.
† His father was near 90, his mother 100, a sister 100, and a brother upwards of 90.
‡ This person was married when 107 years of age, to a woman aged 31.

Year.		Age.
1822	Lucretia Stewart	130
1819	Roger Hope Elliston, a Negro	140
1820	Solomon Nibet	143

The following aged persons were living in the several years set against their respective names:—

1821	A widow, named Millar, at Lynn	107
1823	John Macdonald	108
1818	John Dorman, Strabane, Ireland	109
1820	At Adria, in Lombardy, a Catholic Priest	110
1823	Peter Grant, a Highlander	110
1821	At Ballyragget, Michael Brennan *	112
1822	Felix Buckley, Esq.	113
1818	At Charleston, a Negro	118
1823	A female at Calabria	125
1819	Henry Francisco, an American	130
1819	At Lake Champlain, a German	135
1821	At Freesneen, Wœvre Verdem, a female	155

Eccentric Biography.

MR. LANGLEY.

Mr. JOHN LANGLEY, an Englishman, who settled in Ireland, where he died, left the following extraordinary will:—

"I, John Langley, born at Wincaunton in Somersetshire, and settled in Ireland in the year 1651, now in my right mind and wits, do

* His father was 117 years of age, his mother 109, and his wife 105.—He was the father of fifteen children.
† He had had several wives, and his youngest child was twenty-eight years old at his death, making him 107 when she was born.

make my will in my own handwriting. I do leave all my house, goods, and farm of Black Kettle, of two hundred and fifty-three acres, to my son, commonly called Stubborn Jack, to him and his heirs for ever, provided he marries a protestant woman, but not Alice Kendrick, who called me Oliver's whelp. My new buckskin breeches, and my silver tobacco stopper, with J. L. on the top, I give to Richard Richards, my comrade, who helped me off at the storming of Clonmel, when I was shot through the leg. My said son John shall keep my body above ground six days and six nights after I am dead; and Grace Kendrick shall lay me out, who shall have for so doing five shillings. My body shall be put upon the oak table, in the brown room, and fifty Irishmen shall be invited to my wake, and every one shall have two quarts of the best *aqua vitæ*, and each one a skein, dish, and knife, laid before him; and when the liquor is out, nail up my coffin, and commit me to the earth, whence I came. This is my will. Witness my hand, this third of March, 1674.

"John Langley."

Some of Mr. Langley's friends asked him why he would be at such expense in treating the Irishmen he so much hated? He replied, that if they got drunk at his wake they would probably get to fighting and kill one another, which would do something toward lessening the breed.

Varieties.

VIOLENT STORM.

On August 26, 1823, at three o'clock in the afternoon, the sudden heat of the atmosphere announced an approaching storm, which shewed itself coming from the S. E. over the village of Boncourt (Canton of Anet,) and not far from there a remarkably large waterspout made its appearance. Its base touched the earth, and its summit was lost in the clouds. It was formed of a dense dark vapour, and flames frequently darted through its centre. In its course onwards, it tore up or broke the trees for a space of a league, destroying between seven and eight hundred trees, and at length burst with vast impetuosity on the village of Marchefroy, destroying in one instant the half of the houses. The walls were shook to their foundations, and crumbled down in every direction; they were torn off and split, and the pieces carried half a league away by the force of the wind. Some of the inhabitants who remained in the village were knocked down and wounded; those who were at work in the field, fortunately the greater number, were also thrown down by the violence of the storm, which destroyed the harvest and wounded or killed the beasts. Hailstones, as big almost as a man's fist, stones and other bodies, showered down by this impetuous wind, wounded several individuals very severely. Waggons heavily laden were broken in pieces, and their burdens dispersed. Axle-trees capable of supporting the weight of eight or ten tons were broken, and large wheels were carried two or three hundred paces from where the storm found them. One of these waggons, almost entire, was even carried over a brick-kiln, some portions of which were carried to a considerable distance. A steeple, several hamlets, and isolated houses, and new walls were blown down, and other villages were considerably damaged. The spout occupied about a hundred toises at its base, if we may judge from the durable and disastrous marks it made in its progress.—*French Paper.*

CURIOUS CALCULATIONS.

The immensity of the National Debt will appear by the following calculation. On the 5th of January, 1811, the debt funded and unfunded was £811,898,811, which is equal to 773,236,267 guineas, which, at five dwts. eight grains each guinea, weigh 6312 tons, 11 cwts. three quarters, five pounds, one ounce, six drachms nearly, avoirdupois. Now, supposing a waggon and five horses to extend in length twenty yards, and to carry two and a half tons of the said guineas, the number of teams necessary to carry the whole would extend in length twenty-eight miles and twenty-three yards. To count the debt in shillings, at the rate of thirty shillings in a minute, for ten hours a day, and six days a week, would take 2469 years, 306 days, seventeen hours, and thirty minutes nearly. Its height in guineas, supposing twenty to be an inch, would be 610 miles, 339 yards, and nine inches; and supposing each guinea an inch in diameter, they would extend in a right line 12,203 miles, 150 yards, and seven inches; moreover, the said guineas would cover in space 348 acres, two roods, and 202 yards nearly; and lastly, in shillings, each an inch in diameter, would cover 7319 acres, one rood, and thirty-four yards.

The last wars have, it is said, cost Great Britain not less than £2,040,000,000 of our money. To aid our conceptions of the vastness of this sum, suppose this money were in gold, and valued at 5*l.* per ounce, it would weigh about 14,400 tons, which would load, at three tons each, 4,800 waggons; and if in silver, at 5*s.* per ounce, about 76,000 waggons; and, allowing twenty yards to a waggon, would reach, in a direct line, about 864 miles. If an ounce of gold can be drawn into a wire of 1,000 feet long, the above sum would be sufficient to make a girdle for the whole globe!

LIZARDS FOUND IN A CHALK ROCK.

A pit having been opened, in the summer of 1814, at Eden, Suffolk, for the purpose of raising chalk, (says a Clergyman in a paper read before the Bath Philosophical Society) I had the good fortune to be present at the discovery of two lizards imbedded in the solid chalk, fifty feet below the surface. So completely devoid of life did the lizards appear on their first exposure to the air, that I actually considered them in a fossil state; judge then of my surprise when, on my attempting to take them up, I perceived them move! I immediately placed them in the sun, the heat of which soon restored them to animation. In this state I carried them home, and immersed one in water, keeping the other in a dry place. The mouths of the lizards were closed up with a glutinous substance. This obstruction seemed to cause them great inconvenience, which was evident from the agitation perceptible in their throats, and from the frequent distentions of the jaws, or around the jaws and the head; indeed, they seemed in a state little short of suffocation. The next which had been immersed in the water, after violent struggles, was at length enabled to open his mouth: this afforded it instant relief, and it evidently derived much satisfaction and comfort from its new element. The other lizard, notwithstanding its repeated endeavours, was unable to open its mouth. It died in the course of the night, probably from being debarred the use of its proper element. The remaining lizard continued alive in the water for several weeks, during which it appeared to increase in size. It disliked confinement; and after many attempts, at length to my great mortification, effected its escape, nor could I ever after find it.

The Scrap Book.

PIGEON FLYING.

SEVERAL persons residing at Liege have lately been engaged in the establishment of pigeon stations. A few days since twenty-two pigeons returned from Paris to Liege, having travelled seventy-five leagues, (as the bird flies, in four hours, which gives eighteen leagues an hour.) Another experiment has been made between Frankfort and Liege. A third was made at Coblentz. The object was to send off for Liege a great number of pigeons. Two among them arrived at Liege in two hours and a half. The distance is only thirty leagues, about twelve leagues an hour. Making observations upon the different results, and following the roads upon the map, we are led to conclude, that the winding of rivers is an assistance to pigeons finding their way back, while woods and heights impede their flight, or, at least, occasion uncertainty in the direction they must take. It ought to be known that the famous pigeons which travel between Aleppo and Alexandria are of a particular class—the *columba tabellaria*.—*Paris Paper, August,* 1823.

AN INVETERATE PIKE.

As two gentlemen were fly-fishing at South Newton, near Salisbury, in July, 1823, one of them hooked a grayling, or umber, on the opposite side of the river. In playing it, a pike seized it. In order to land the fish, it was found necessary to draw it over a large spot of weeds in the middle of the river; the pike still kept his hold, and although on the weeds, and indeed out of water, shook his prey as a dog would a rat, and continued so to do for several minutes. At length both were drawn to the bank, and taken out together in a landing net, the pike never quitting his prey until enclosed in the net. The grayling weighed twelve ounces, and the pike two pounds only.

SINGULAR DEATH.

ON the 8th of August, 1823, a young man, named Thomas Clements, lost his life in a manner as dreadful as it was extraordinary. He was fishing with a draw net, near Elizabeth Castle, Jersey, and taking a little sole out of the net, he put it between his teeth to kill it, when the fish, with a sudden spring, forced itself into his throat, and choked him. The unfortunate man had just time to call for assistance, but it came too late; he expired soon after in dreadful agony.

Published by J. LIMBIRD, 355, Strand, (East End of Exeter 'Change): and sold by all Newsmen and Booksellers. Printed by A. APPLEGATH, Stamford-street.

THE CABINET OF CURIOSITIES,
OR
Wonders of the World Displayed.

*A world of wonders where creation seems
No more the works of Nature but her dreams.*—MONTGOMERY.

No. XIX.]   PRICE TWOPENCE.

THE PYRAMIDS OF EGYPT.

The pyramids of Egypt rank among the seven wonders of the ancient world; and even in the present day, when manual labour has received so many aids from science, their construction is viewed with astonishment.

The origin and object of the construction of the pyramids has been the theme of continued discussion among antiquaries, some of whom think they were erected as sepulchres; while the more probable conjecture is, that they were edifices built for the celebration of cavern mysteries, like the caves of Delphi, Trophonius and Mithra.

The largest of these stupendous monuments, equally famous for the enormity of their size and their remote antiquity, are those of Djiza, so called from a village of that name on the bank of the Nile, distant from them about eleven miles. The three which most attract the attention of travellers stand near one another on the west side of the river, almost opposite to Grand Cairo, and not far from the site of the ancient Memphis. When viewed from a distance, peering above the horizon, they display the fine transparent hue they derive from the rarefied air by which they are surrounded. M. Savary having approached to within three leagues of them, in the night time, while the full moon shone bright upon them, describes them as appearing to him, under this par-

U

ticular aspect, like two points of rock crowned by the clouds. On a nearer approach, their sloping and angular forms disguise their real height, and lessen it to the eye; independently of which, as whatever is regular is great or small by comparison, and as these masses of stone eclipse in magnitude every surrounding object, at the same time that they are inferior to a mountain, to which alone the imagination can successfully compare them, a degree of surprise is excited on finding the first impression produced by a distant view so much diminished in drawing near to them. On attempting, however, to measure any one of these gigantic works of art by some known and determinate scale, it resumes its immensity to the mind; since, on drawing near to the opening, the persons who stand beneath it appear so small that they can scarcely be taken for men.

The base of the great pyramid of Cheops, or Cheospes, so named after a king of Egypt, is estimated by Denon at seven hundred and twenty feet, and its height at four hundred and forty-eight feet, calculating the base by the mean proportion of the length of the stones, and the height by the sum of that of each of the steps or stages. Its construction required so many years, and employed such a multitude of labourers, that the expenditure for garlic and onions alone, for their consumption, is said to have amounted to one thousand and sixty talents, upwards of one fourth of a million sterling. Its interior is thus accurately described by the above traveller.

"The entrance of the first gallery is concealed by the general outer covering which invests the whole of the pyramid. It is, however, probable, that the attention of the earlier searchers was by some particular appearance directed to this spot. This gallery goes towards the centre of the edifice, in a direction sloping downward to the base: it is sixty paces in length; and at the further end are two large blocks of granite, an obstacle which caused some uncertainty in the digging. A horizontal passage has been made for some distance into the mass of stone; but this undertaking was afterwards abandoned.

"Returning to the extremity of the first gallery, and working upward by the side of the two granite blocks, you come to the beginning of the first sloping staircase, which proceeds in an oblique direction upward for a hundred and twenty feet. You mount the steep and narrow gallery, helping your steps by notches cut in the ground, and by resting your hands against the sides. At the top of this gallery, which is formed of a calcareous stone cemented with mortar, you find a landing place about fifteen feet square, within which, to the right of the entrance, is a perpendicular opening called the well. This appears, from its irregularity, to have been the result of a fruitless attempt at a search, and has a diameter of about two feet by eighteen inches. There were no means of descending it; but by throwing down a stone, it was ascertained that its perpendicular direction could not be very considerable. On a level with the landing is a horizontal gallery, a hundred and seventy feet in length, running directly towards the centre of the pyramid; and at the extremity of this gallery is a small room, called the Queen's chamber. This is an oblong square of eighteen feet two inches, by fifteen feet eight inches; but the height is uncertain, the floor having been turned up by the avidity of the searchers. One of the side walls has also been worked into, and the rubbish left on the spot. The roof, which is formed of a fine calcareous stone, very neatly brought together, has the form of an angle nearly equilateral; but contains neither ornament, hieroglyphic, nor the smallest trace of a sarcophagus. Whether it was intended to contain a body, is uncertain; but, in this case, the pyramid must have been built with a view of containing two bodies, and would not therefore have been closed at once. If the second tomb was really that of the queen, the two blocks of granite, at the end of the first gallery, must have been finally reserved to close all the interior chambers of the pyramid.

"Returning again from the queen's chamber to the landing place, you ascend a few feet, and immediately find yourself at the bottom of a large and magnificent staircase, or rather inclined plane, one hundred and eighty feet in length, taking a direction upward, and still bearing towards the centre of the edifice. It is six feet six inches in breadth, in which are to be included two parapets, each nineteen inches in diameter, and pierced, every three feet six inches, by oblong holes twenty-two inches by three. The sarcophagus must have ascended this passage, and the series of holes must have been intended to receive a machine of some description, to assist in raising so heavy a mass as the sarcophagus up so steep an ascent.

"The side walls of this ascending gallery rise perpendicularly for twelve feet, and then form a sloping roof of an excessively high pitch, not by a regular angle, but by eight successive projections, each of them six feet in height, rising above the other, and approaching nearer to the corresponding projection on the opposite side, till the roof is entirely shut in. The height of this singularly-contrived vault may be estimated at sixty feet from the part of the floor immediately beneath. The ascent of the staircase is facilitated by pretty regular but modern footings cut in the floor; and at the top is a small platform, in which is a thick block of granite, resembling an immense chest, imbedded in the solid building, and hollowed out so as to leave alternate projections and retirings, into which are let blocks of the same material, with corresponding grooves and projections intended for ever to conceal and protect the entrance to the principal chamber which is behind them. It must have required immense labour to construct this part of the edifice, and not less to have broken an opening through; so that the zeal of superstition has here been opposed to the eagerness of avarice, and the latter has prevailed. After mining through thirteen feet of solid granite, a door, three feet three inches square, has been discovered, which is the entrance to the principal chamber. This is a long square, sixteen feet by thirty-two, and eighteen in height. The door is in the angle facing the gallery, corresponding to the door of the queen's chamber below. When it is said that the tomb is a single piece of granite, half polished, and without cement, all that is remarkable in this strange monument, which exhibits such rigid simplicity in the midst of the utmost magnificence of human power, will have been described. The only broken part is an attempt at a search at one of the angles, and two small holes nearly round and breast high. Such is the interior of this immense edifice, in which the work of the hand of man appears to rival the gigantic forms of nature."

To the above account by the accurate Denon, we subjoin the following pleasing one by the celebrated Doctor Clarke. The impression made by these monuments, when viewed at a distance, can never, he observes, be obliterated from his mind.

"By reflecting the sun's rays, they appeared as white as snow, and of such surprising magnitude, that nothing we had previously conceived in our imagination had prepared us for the spectacle we beheld. The sight instantly convinced us that no power of description, no delineation, can convey ideas adequate to the effect produced in viewing these stupendous monuments. The formality of their structure is lost in their prodigious magnitude: the mind, elevated by wonder, feels at once the force of an axiom, which, however disputed, experience confirms, — that in vastness, whatsoever be its nature, there dwells sublimity !

"Having arrived at the bottom of a sandy slope, leading up to the principal pyramid, a band of Bedouin Arabs, who had assembled to receive us upon our landing, were much amused by the eagerness excited in our whole party, to prove who should first set his foot upon the summit of this artificial mountain. As we drew near its base, the effect of its prodigious magnitude, and the amazement caused in viewing the enormous masses used in its construction, affected every one of us; but it was an impression of awe and fear, rather than of pleasure. In the observations of travellers who had recently preceded us, we had heard the pyramids described as huge objects which gave no satisfaction to the spectator, on account of their barbarous shape and formal appearance: yet to us it appeared hardly possible, that persons susceptible of any feeling of sublimity could behold them unmoved. With what amazement did we survey the vast surface that was presented to us, when we arrived at this stupendous monument, which seemed to reach the clouds! Here and there appeared some Arab guides upon the immense masses above us, like so many pigmies, waiting to shew the way up to the summit. Now and then we thought we heard voices, and listened; but it was the wind, in powerful gusts, sweeping the immense ranges of stone. Already some of our party had begun the ascent, and were pausing at the tremendous depth which they saw below. One of our military companions, after having surmounted the most difficult part of the undertaking, became giddy in consequence of looking down from the elevation he had attained; and being compelled to abandon the project, he hired an Arab to assist him in effecting his descent. The rest of us, more accustomed to the business of climbing heights, with many a halt for respiration, and many an exclamation of wonder, pursued our way towards the summit. The mode of ascent has been frequently described; and yet, from the questions which are often proposed to travellers, it does not appear to be generally understood. The reader may imagine himself to be upon a staircase, every step of which, to a man of middle stature, is nearly breast high, and the breadth of each step is equal to its height, consequently, the footing is secure; and although a retrospect, in going up, be sometimes fearful to persons unaccustomed to look down from any considerable elevation, yet there is little danger of falling. In some places, indeed, where the stones are decayed, caution may be required; and an Arab guide is always necessary, to avoid a total interruption; but, upon the whole, the means of ascent are such that almost every one may accomplish it. Our progress was impeded by other causes. We carried with us a few instruments; such as our boat-compass, a thermometer, a telescope, &c.; these could not be trusted in the hands of Arabs, and they were liable to be broken every instant. At length we reached the topmost tier, to the great delight and satisfaction of all the party. Here we found a platform, thirty-two feet square; consisting of nine large stones, each of which might weigh about a ton; although they are much inferior in size to some of the stones used in the construction of this pyramid.

"The view from the summit of the pyramid amply fulfilled our expectations; nor do the accounts which have been given of it, as it appears at this season of the year (in the month of August), exaggerate the novelty and grandeur of the sight. All the region towards Cairo and the Delta resembled a sea, covered with innumerable islands. Forests of palm-trees were seen standing in the water; the inundation spreading over the land where they stood, so as to give them an appearance of growing in the flood. To the north, as far as the eye could reach, nothing could be discerned, but a watery surface thus diversified by plantations and by villages. To the south we saw the pyramids of Saccara; and, upon the east of these, smaller monuments of the same kind, nearer to the Nile. An appearance of ruins might indeed be traced the whole way from the pyramids of Djiza to those of Saccara; as if they had been once connected, so as to constitute one vast cemetery. Beyond the pyramids of Saccara we could perceive the distant mountains of the Said; and upon an eminence near the Libyan side of the Nile appeared a monastery of considerable size. Towards the west and south-west, the eye ranged over the great Libyan Desert, extending to the utmost verge of the horizon, without a single object to interrupt the dreary horror of the landscape, except dark floating spots, caused by the shadows of passing clouds upon the sand.

"The stones of the platform upon the top, as well as most of the others used in constructing the decreasing ranges, from the base upwards, are of soft limestone. Those employed in the construction of the pyramids, are of the same nature as the calcareous rock on which they stand, and which was apparently cut away to form them, Herodotus says, however, that they were brought from the Arabian side of the Nile.

(*To be continued.*)

LA CHEVALIERE D'EON.

IN the Sixth Number of THE CABINET, we gave a memoir of

the eccentric Chevalier D'Eon, whose doubtful sex so long exercised the curiosity of Europe. In a Magazine of the year 1792, we find the following singular correspondence between the Chevalier and the celebrated Anacharsis Cloots, "the Orator of the Human Race," as he was then called, which forms an appropriate appendage to our memoir.

Anacharsis Cloots to Genevieve D'Eon, greeting.

Paris, May 12, 4th Year of Liberty.

The portrait of the Gaulish Minerva was conveyed to me by the hand of the Graces. Instead of expressions of thanks, I shall submit to the heroine of our age, that now is the time to put the seal to her glory, by arming herself cap-a-pee, like another Thalestris, or Joan of Arc, to aid us in delivering the world from the infernal race of tyrants. The episode of La Chevaliere D'Eon is yet wanting to complete our epic poem. You sleep, D'Eon, you sleep, while despots are awake; you prefer the ornaments of a toilet to the victorious arms of Achilles. March, for shame! your country calls you. An Amazonian phalanx will swiftly follow you against the oppressors of the human race. Come, and the victory is ours.

ANACHARSIS CLOOTS.

La Chevaliere D'Eon's Answer to the Orator of the Human Race.

Just as I am despatching my nephew for Paris, I am favoured with your charming billet of invitation to resume the arms of Mars, or, as you will have it, of Achilles. When I receive a friendly summons to the field of battle, I am not the woman to hang back. Paint to those generous founders of French liberty my situation, and my desire of being released from it to fight for Liberty, the Nation, the Law, and the King. If I do not succeed, the fault shall not be mine —it shall be wholly yours. In the mean time, despatch my nephew, either for the army of Rochambeau, of Luckner, La Fayette, or Biron. He has a letter from M. Chauvelin, our minister at London, and another from me, to M. Biron, and also letters for the other commanders in chief. On your part, do for him and recommend him the best you can. He is young, brave, robust, fit to kill or be killed, to learn to live or die for the safety of his country. The study of the Rights of Man made him quit the English service: three of his brothers are already combating for a cause so noble.

Madam * * * will deliver you a packet containing twenty-four medals of the Little Minerva, who, *invita magna Minerva Græca*, admires, esteems, and loves you with all her heart. Judge what will be her gratitude, if you remount her on horseback to conquer or die gloriously.

I by no means employ myself, illustrious Anacharsis, as you seem to think, in the frivolous decorations of the toilet. All who know me here, know that I pay much more attention to my books than to my robes. I detest the female garb as much as those who have compelled me to wear it. Dressed always in a plain black gown, I wear perpetual mourning as the widow *du secrète de* Louis XV.

Since 1777, when I left London to repair to Versailles, and since 1785, when I returned to London with the King's permission, I have always worn the dress of my sex, to prove to his Majesty my submission to his orders, as well in a foreign country as in France. But now, when I see the Nation, the Law, and the King in great danger, I feel my love for the King and my country revive, and my warlike spirit revolts against my cap and my petticoats. My heart fiercely demands my casque, my sabre, and my horse, and, above all, my rank in the army, to go and fight against the enemies of my King and my country. This rank is justly due to me by the date of my former commissions, by my services, and my wounds.

Join me, therefore, in supplicating the president and all the honourable members of the National Assembly, the representatives of the majesty of the French nation, and of the first people in the world, when they shall have finished the grand work of a wise Constitution, to request for me the King's permission to lay aside the dress of a woman, and to go and fight against his enemies and the enemies of France.

I want his consent, being unwilling that he should suspect me of disobedience and ingratitude, after all that his great grandfather and he have been pleased to do for me. In his present situation and my own, it is my duty to obey him so much the more willingly as his powers are less; this is a delicacy of sentiment which I ought to cherish, and at sixty-five years of age not run after vain-glory like a giddy girl, at the expense of my feelings. The wife of Cæsar ought not to be suspected of infidelity and ingratitude. *I render to God the things that are God's, and to Cæsar the things that are Cæsar's.*"

(Signed)   LA CHEV. D'EON.

In the French National Assembly, in the session of the 11th of June, an extract of a petition from Madame D'Eon was read, setting forth, that although she had worn the dress of a woman for fifteen years, she had never forgotten that she was formerly a soldier; that since the Revolution she feels her military ardour revive, and demands, instead of her cap and petticoats, her helmet, her sabre, her horse, and the rank in the army to which her seniority, her services, and her wounds entitle her; and that she now requests permission to raise a legion of volunteers for the service of her country. Unconnected with any party, she has no desire of brandishing her sword in processions in the streets of Paris, and wishes for nothing but actual service; war nobly made, and courageously supported.—" In my eager impatience," adds she, " I have sold everything but my uniform and the sword I wore in the last war, which I wish again to wear in the present. Of my library nothing remains but the shelves and the manuscripts of Marshal Vauban, which I have preserved as an offering to the National Assembly, for the glory of my country, and the instruction of the brave generals employed in her defence. I have been the sport of nature, of fortune, of war and peace, of men and women, of the malice and intrigue of courts. I have passed successively from the state of a girl to that of a boy; from the state of a man to that of a woman; I have experienced all the odd vicissitudes of human life. Soon I hope, with my arms in my hands, I shall fly on the wings of liberty and victory to fight and die for the Nation, the Law, and

HOBBIES.—HERMITS.

We all have our hobbies. Some, however, very much encumbered by wealth and *virtu*, collect shells, teapots, military saddles, wigs, turnpike tickets, shop bills, stained glass, stuffed birds, cameos, bronzes, prints, halters, (if duly authenticated by Jack Ketch,) watchmen's rattles, staves, lanterns, and knockers, armour, and other nick-nackery. But who would have thought that there should have existed a mania for *live* hermits? A stuffed one, in a grotto, we have seen, and considered as not unappropriate; but, to get a live one, is an experimental species of penance, that none but the yellow-faced Dives would ever think of inflicting. M. Hamilton, however, once the proprietor of Payne's Hill, near Cobham, Surrey, advertised for a person, who was willing to become a hermit in that beautiful retreat of his. The conditions were, that he was to continue in the hermitage seven years, where he should be provided with a Bible, optical glasses, a mat for his bed, a hassock for his pillow, an hour glass for his timepiece, water for his beverage, food from the house, but never to exchange a syllable with the servant. He was to wear a camlet robe, never to cut his beard or nails, nor ever to stray beyond the limits of the grounds. If he lived there, under all these restrictions, till the end of the term, he was to receive seven hundred guineas. But on breach of any of them, or if he quitted the place any time previous to that term, the whole was to be forfeited. One person attempted it, but a three weeks' trial cured him.

Mr. Powyss, of Marcham, near Preston, Lancashire, was more successful in this singularity: he advertised a reward of £50 a year for life, to any man who would undertake to live seven years under ground, without seeing any thing human; and to let his toe and finger nails grow, with his hair and beard, during the whole time. Apartments were prepared under ground, very commodious, with a cold bath, a chamber organ, as many books as the occupier pleased, and provisions served from his own table. Whenever the recluse wanted any convenience, he was to ring a bell, and it was provided for him. Singular as this residence may appear, an occupier offered himself, and actually staid in it, observing the required conditions for four years!

RATTLE AND OTHER AMERICAN SNAKES; THEIR POWER TO CHARM, &c.

Extracts from Mr. Heckewelder's Letters.

In the summer of 1770, says Mr. H., while I was fishing under the bank of the Lehigh, I heard, for the space of near an hour, the sound of a ground squirrel, seemingly in distress, on the top of the bank. At length I went up to see what was the matter with the squirrel, when, to my utter astonishment, I discovered the animal about half way up a bush, but running sometimes higher up, sometimes lower down, and a very large rattlesnake at the root of the bush on which the squirrel was. Here I was immediately struck with the idea that the snake was in the act of enchanting, and I hoped now to be fully convinced that the rattle snake obtained its prey altogether in this manner, as I have often heard reported. I therefore sat down quietly upon a log about six yards distant, where I had a full view of both the snake and squirrel. Sometimes I thought I saw the squirrel going down for the last time, and to enter the jaws of the snake; but it would again return up the bush with the same liveliness it had run down. Finding, finally, no alteration in the squirrel or its motions, and my patience being exhausted, I determined on killing the snake, and examining into the case of the squirrel, viz. what strength, &c. it yet retained after being charmed for so long a time; for by this time the supposed charm had lasted near three hours. I struck at the snake with a long pole, but missed it; upon which it ran down the bank where I had been fishing. Remaining on the bank by the bush on which the squirrel was, I hailed a man on the opposite side of the river, desiring him to cross in a canoe and kill the snake under the bank, with which he immediately complied; but likewise missing his stroke on account of the bushes, the snake took up the bank again, where I killed it. We now both joined to shake the squirrel down, but it had both strength and sense enough to climb to the very top, I suppose nearly twenty feet high. However, we brought it down to the ground, and though it had fallen about two yards from the bush, it well knew its hole in which it dwelt, and this was at the root of the bush, and exactly at the spot where the snake had lain. Here the mystery was cleared up to us at once. We conjectured that the snake was either watching the squirrel to come down to enter its hole, or for its companion or young, which were probably in the hole, to come out, all which were sufficient to cause anxiety to the squirrel on the bush. The dexterity, however, of the squirrel in making its way into the hole, and the very place where we stood, showed plainly that it retained its full strength and sagacity, and had by no means suffered from the charm of the snake."—Dated at Bethlehem, August 5, 1796.

"Having questioned Indians a number of times with respect to snakes having the power of charming, and always being answered in the negative, I was at length desired," says Mr. Heckewelder, "to give the reason the white people had for believing such a thing; which not being satisfactory, Pemaholend (an aged and much-respected Delaware Indian) declared the rattlesnake obtained its food merely from sliness and persevering patience. It knows as well where to watch for its prey as a cat does, and succeeds as well. It has and retains its hunting ground. In spring, when the warm weather sets in and the woods seem alive with smaller animals, it leaves its den. It will cross a river and go a mile and further from its den, to the place it intends to spend the summer, and in fall, when all the young animals bred this season are become strong and active, so that they are no more so easily overtaken or caught, it directs its course back again to its den, the same as a hunter does to his camp.

"The white people continued Pemaholend, probably have taken the idea of this snake having the power of charming, from a tradition of ours (the Indians) which our forefathers have handed down to us from many hundred years back, and long before ever the white people came into this country. Then (they tell us) there was such a snake, and a rattlesnake too, but there was only *this one* snake that had this power, and it was afterwards destroyed; it hath never been said that any other of the kind had ever made its appearance."

Hoaxes and Impostures.

No. XV.

SIR JOHN FIELDING.

Sir John Fielding, the brother of the celebrated novelist, appears to have inherited no small portion of the family humour, although he has left no record in a lettered form of his comic propensity. On one occasion, after paying a visit to a country gentleman of eminent hospitality, Sir John mounted his horse, in company with several brother convivialists. The knight, though "a thick drop serene" had quenched the lustre of his orbs, was a fearless horseman. In fact, his steed was trained to obedience, and was familiar with the rider's haunts. Sir John rode forwards; but when he arrived at Hartley Row, under the impulse of the gay purpose of the hour, he checked his horse, and the animal entered the paved yard of an inn. Our traveller was in the habit of wearing a shade over his sightless eyes, which the apprehensiveness and surprise of the innkeeper and his wife converted into a mask. It was during the time of a general panic throughout the country, in consequence of a threatened invasion from France. Sir John found, by the tremulous accents of the people at the inn, that his appearance had produced a striking effect on their imagination, and he accordingly humoured their apprehensions. He with many significant shrugs, and divers protestations of extreme haste, informed his auditors that the French had landed in great numbers, and were far advanced on their march to the metropolis; that he himself had been captured by the foe, and only released on condition of wearing a mask, or bandage, till six hours were expired. After communicating this intelligence, he quitted the inn.

It happened that the innkeeper's wife was one of the most credulous among the weak. Terrified beyond measure, she hastened and buried all the money she could collect, and threw the household plate into the well for safety. The whole house was in commotion, from the stableyard to the topmost garret. The joke was, of course, soon detected, and the identity of the knight shortly ascertained. So high was the indignation of the silly host, when he discovered the extent of his duplicity, that he commenced an action against the waggish alarmist. The cause was tried at Winchester, when the plaintiff was nonsuited.

BOBART THE NATURALIST.

Dr. Grey, in one of his notes to Hudibras, tells the following story of this eminent naturalist, who was keeper of the physic garden at Oxford, in the reign of Charles II.:—" He made a dead rat resemble the common picture of dragons, by altering its head and tail, and thrusting in taper sharp sticks, which distended the skin on both sides till it resembled wings. He let it dry as hard as possible.—The learned immediately pronounced it a dragon; and one of them sent an accurate description of it to Dr. Magliabechi, Librarian to the Grand Duke of Tuscany. Several fine copies of verses were wrote on so rare a subject; but at last Mr. Bobart owned the cheat: however, it was looked upon as a masterpiece of art, and as such deposited in the Museum."

BATTLE BETWEEN TWO SNAKES.
(By an American Farmer.)

As I was one day sitting solitary and pensive in my arbour, my attention was engaged by a strange sort of rustling noise at some paces distant. I looked all around, without distinguishing any thing, until I climbed one of my great hemp stalks; when, to my astonishment, I beheld two snakes of considerable length, the one pursuing the other with great celerity through a hemp stubble-field. The aggressor was of the black kind, six feet long; the fugitive was a water-snake, nearly of equal dimensions. They soon met, and in the fury of their first encounter, they appeared in an instant firmly twisted together; and whilst their united tails beat the ground, they tried with open jaws to lacerate each other. What a fell aspect did they present! Their heads were compressed to a very small size; their eyes flashed fire; and after this conflict had lasted about five minutes, the second found means to disengage itself from the first, and hurried toward the ditch. Its antagonist instantly assumed a new posture, and half creeping and half erect, with a majestic mien, overtook and attacked the other again, which placed itself in the same attitude, and prepared to resist. The scene was uncommon and beautiful; for, thus opposed, they fought with their jaws, biting each other with the utmost rage; but notwithstanding this appearance of mutual courage and fury, the water-snake still seemed desirous of retreating toward the ditch, its natural element. This was no sooner perceived by the keen eyed black one, than twisting its tail twice round a stalk of hemp, and seizing its adversary by the throat, not by means of its jaws, but by twisting its own neck twice round that of the water-snake, it pulled the latter back from the ditch. To prevent a defeat, the water-snake took hold likewise of a stalk on the bank, and by the acquisition of that point of resistance became a match for its fierce antagonist. Strange was this to behold; two great snakes, strongly adhering to the ground, fastened together, by means of the writhings which lashed them to each other, and stretched at their full length, they pulled, but pulled in vain; and in the moments of greatest exertions, that part of their bodies which was entwined seemed extremely small, while the rest appeared inflated, and now and then convulsed with strong undulations, rapidly following each other. Their eyes seemed on fire, and ready to start out of their heads: at one time the conflict seemed decided; the water-snake bent itself into two great folds, and by that operation rendered the other more than commonly outstretched; the next minute the new struggles of the black one gained an unexpected superiority;

it acquired two great folds likewise, which necessarily extended the body of its adversary in proportion as it had contracted its own. These efforts were alternate; victory seemed doubtful, inclining sometimes to the one side, and sometimes to the other: until at last the stalk, to which the black snake was fastened, suddenly gave way, and in consequence of this accident they both plunged into the ditch. The water did not extinguish their vindictive rage; for by their agitations I could trace, though not distinguish, their mutual attacks. They soon reappeared on the surface, twisted together, as in their first onset; but the black snake seemed to retain its wonted superiority, for its head was exactly fixed above that of the other, which he incessantly pressed down under the water, until it was stifled, and sunk. The victor no sooner perceived its enemy incapable of farther resistance, than abandoning it to the current, it returned on shore, and disappeared.

Eccentric Biography.

BUCKHORSE.

BUCKHORSE, one of nature's vagaries, whose real name is said to have been John Smith, first saw the light in the house of a *sinner*, in that part of London known by the name of Lewkener's Lane,—a place notorious in the extreme, for the eccentricity of characters it contained: *here* the disciples of Bamfylde Moore Carew were to be found in crowds, and here *beggars* of all descriptions resorted to regale themselves upon the *good things of this life*, laughing at the credulity of the public in being so easily duped by their impositions; groups of the frail sisterhood also adorned its purlieus. The juvenile *thief* was soon taught to become an adept in the profession, by taking out a handkerchief or a snuff-box from the pocket of a coat *covered with bells*, without ringing any of them; and the finished thief *roosted* here from the prying eye of society, and laid plans for his future depredations: those timber-merchants who reduce their logs of wood to *matches*, to light the public, might be observed issuing out in numbers from this receptacle of *brimstones!* Costermongers, in droves, were seen mounting their *neddies*, decorated with hampers, *scorning* the refined use of saddles and bridles; and *Lewkener's Lane* was not only celebrated amongst all its other attractions, in being the residence of a finisher of the law, (Tom Dennis) *slangly* denominated Jack Ketch, but acquired considerable notoriety by giving birth to the ugliness of a Buckhorse.

It appears then, that few places could boast of more originality of character than *that* from which Buckhorse sprang; and from the variety of talent here displayed, there is little doubt he did not remain long a *novice*. As we have never been troubled with any account, to what *good-natured* personage he owed his origin, we cannot determine; but suffice it to observe, that *little* Buckhorse and his mother were turned out upon the wide world long before he knew its slippery qualities, by the cruel publican, their landlord; which inhuman circumstance took place about the year 1736.

This *freak* of Nature, it should seem, was indebted to his mother for what little instruction he received, the principal of which was an extraordinary volubility of speech; and from his early acquaintance with streets, he picked up the rest of his qualifications.

Buckhorse's composition, however rude and unsightly, was not without *harmony;* and although his fist might not appear *musical* to his antagonist by its potent *touch,* yet when applied to his own chin, was capable of producing a variety of popular tunes, to the astonishment of all those who heard and saw him, by which peculiar trait he mostly subsisted. It was a common custom with him to allow any person to beat a tune on his chin for a penny; and which was a source of much profit: and added to that of selling switches for a halfpenny a piece, were his only means of subsistence for many years. His *cry* of "Here is pretty switches to beat your wives" was so singular, that Shuter, the celebrated comedian, among his other imitations, was more than successful in his attempts of Buckhorse, and which was repeatedly called for a second time.

As a pugilist, Buckhorse ranked high for courage and strength among the boxers of his day, and displayed great muscular powers in the battles he had contested. He is represented as a most impetuous character, and his principal qualifications were—Love and Boxing.

Buckhorse was the person whom the late Duke of Queensbury selected to ride for him, when he won his celebrated wager against time.

Varieties.

THE CRYSTALLIZED CAVERN.

THE Crystallized Cavern, the new wonder of the Derbyshire Peak, has been recently discovered in the vicinity of the village of Bradwell. We extract the following particulars of this singular and beautiful natural excavation from Hutchinson's late Tour in the High Peak.

The entrance is rather terrific than grand; and the descent for about thirty paces very abrupt. The visitor has then to pass along an inclined way for nearly a quarter of a mile, the opening being so low that it is impossible to proceed, in particular parts, in an erect posture. The different crystallizations which now attract his attention on every side, soon make him forget the irksomeness of the road, and banish every idea of fatigue. New objects of curiosity crowd one on the other: in a place called the *Music Chamber,* the petrifactions take the semblance of the pipes of an organ; while in other parts, these stalactites are formed into elegant small colonnades, with as exact a symmetry as if they had been chiseled by the most skilful artist. Candles, judiciously disposed within them, give an idea of the imaginary palaces of fairies, or of sylphs and genii, who have chosen this for their magnificent abode.

Still he has seen nothing comparable to what he is now to expect; for, at the distance of about a hundred paces further, by a rugged descent, he enters what is called the *Grotto of Paradise.* This heavenly spot, for it cannot be compared to any thing terrestrial, is, of itself, a beautiful crystallized cavern, about twelve feet high, and in length twenty feet, pointed at the top, similar to a gothic arch, with a countless number of large stalactites hanging from the roof.

Candles placed among them give some idea of its being lighted up with elegant glass chandeliers; while the sides are entirely incrusted, and brilliant in the extreme. The floor is chequered with black and white spar. It has altogether, Mr. Hutchinson observes, the most novel and elegant appearance of any cavern he ever beheld. This glittering apartment would be left by the visitor with a certain degree of regret, did he not expect to see it again on his return.

Still continuing a route similar to the one he has passed, in the course of which his attention is occasionally arrested by the curiosities of the place, and by the gentle droppings of the water, which scarcely break the solemn silence of the scene, he at length reaches the *Grotto of Calypso*, and the extremity of the cavern, upwards of 2000 feet from the entrance. To see this grotto to advantage, he has to ascend about six feet, into a recess. There, the beautiful appearances of the different crystallizations, some of them of an azure cast, and the echoes reverberating from side to side, make him fancy that he has reached the secluded retreat of some mythological deity.

Returning by the same path for a considerable distance, another cavern, which branches in a south-western direction from the one already explored, presents itself. The roads here are still more difficult of access, but the stalactites are certainly most beautiful. Many of them, more than a yard in length, are pendent from the roof, and the greater part do not exceed the dimension of the smallest reed. The top and sides of this cavern are remarkably smooth, particularly at the part called the *Amphitheatre*. In general, the stone is of a very dark colour, to which the transparent appearances before mentioned, with each a drop of water hanging at its extremity, form a fine contrast.

EXTRAORDINARY IMBECILITY.

Jane Molisson, of the town of Richlieu, was, on the 6th of September 1743, struck into a state of insanity, and refused to see either husband, relations, or friends; nor would she walk, but was carried to bed, hiding her face with her hands, that she might neither see nor speak to any body, though she was sensible of her condition, as she has since declared.

She kept her bed, would not eat before any body, but often complained of pains all over her body; she was obliged to be taken out of bed, like a child, when it was thought necessary to make it, and replaced in the same manner, not suffering any body to look at her, and still hiding her face with her hands.

About the year 1758 her husband died: this gave her no uneasiness; her effects were carried off, and she was taken to her husband's brother without uttering a single word: the priests attending her often, without being able to get any thing out of her but continued sighs: her brother died about six years after; but she still remained insensible: in short, a thousand surprising circumstances attend this little affair.

On the 6th of September 1760, just seventeen years on that day since this unaccountable malady seized her, she came down from her chamber, embraced her sister-in-law and her nephews, as if she had been ill but one night, and recollected all that had passed during the seventeen years: she went to mass, and at her return fell to her usual occupation. She perfectly remembered every thing that she had learnt, even her prayers, which she had not once said during her illness; the sudden air had no effect upon her, though she had been so long confined: she says she never slept one hour together during the whole time, and never was in any other attitude than sitting, with her head leaning upon her breast. Now she eats, drinks, and works, and is as well as ever she was; she appears to be about fifty-five. — This extraordinary case, says the letter-writer, I had ocular proof of; and it can be attested by almost every inhabitant of this place.—*Magazine of* 1768.

WHITE NEGRESS.

SOME years ago a white negro woman, who was born at Kingston, in Jamaica, was sent to this country, where she married an Englishman of the name of Newsham, by whom she had six children. She was the daughter of black parents, and though perfectly white herself, all her children were mulattoes. Previous to her marriage she was exhibited for some time in London and in the country, where she used to address her visitors in the following lines:

In me you see the Almighty's wondrous power,
Who works new wonders each succeeding hour;
Who calms the seas and bids the tempest roar;
Darts down his fiery flashes from on high;
Who rolls loud peals of thunder from the sky.
His potent arm can all things overthrow,
And crush the world to nothing at one blow;
Make nature change her course whene'er he list—
Or from black parents how could I exist?
My nose, my lips, my features all explore,
The just resemblance of a blackamoor;
And on my head the silver-coloured wool,
Gives further demonstration clear and full.
This curious age may with amazement view,
What after ages won't believe is true!

ON POPULATION.

SUPPOSING the earth to be peopled with one thousand millions of inhabitants, and allowing thirty-three years for a generation, the deaths of each age amount to 30,000,000—of each day, to 82,000—and of each hour, to 3446. But as the number of deaths to the number of births is as ten to twelve, there are born yearly 36,000,000—daily, 98,630—and hourly, 4109. Reckoning only the generations to a century, and supposing the world has existed 5700 years, there have been only 172 generations from the Creation, 125 since the Deluge, and fifty-five since the Christian Æra.

Out of every thousand there die annually thirty; and the number of inhabitants of every city and country is renewed every thirty years. Of 200 children, one dies in the birth; but more than one-third of the births die within two years of age.

The births are more numerous than the deaths, in any given place; and the proportion of the births of male and female are not in a wide proportion, not an uncertain accidental number, but nearly equal. Major Graunt's tables, formed about 150 years ago, stated, for the bills of mortality, fifteen males to thirteen females; whence he justly inferred, that the Christian religion, prohibiting polygamy, is more agreeable to the law of nature than Mohammedanism, and all other persuasions that allow it. The majority of males is a wise dispensation to provide for their dangers and losses by wars, sea voyages, excess of labour, &c.

Every marriage, upon a general view, produces four births—allowing for those which produce none, and those which produce an extraordinary number of children.

This curious proportion is every where preserved, and is a manifestation of the order of Divine Providence, by which the world has never been overstocked with population, notwithstanding the great increase and doublings of each species of animals since the repeopling of it by the sons of Noah and their widely spread descendants.

The Scrap Book.

ACCOUNT OF THE PSYLLI AT TRIPOLY.

These extraordinary people, of whom mention is frequently made by ancient writers, have, as it is said, the qualification of curing the bites of serpents. Previous to their going abroad they prepare themselves by a particular regimen, which produces a species of frenzy, and then they imagine themselves to be inspired. The rabble regard them as saints, and when the Psylli desire to astonish them, they sally forth, half naked, foaming at the mouth, and exhibiting every sign of madness, except that of biting the Moors. If they meet a Christian, they make many attempts to seize him alive: they are actually known to devour live cats, dogs, and fowls. They are taken to visit sick persons, it being supposed they are endowed with the power of curing all diseases. Their madness subsides in a few days, and they are not then heard of for several months.

FASCINATION.

A very singular fact occurred in Manchester, in the United States, in the summer of 1823. As Mr Samuel Cheever was at work in the field, his attention was arrested at the sight of a number of fowls, with heads erect and wings extended, standing in a circular manner. On going near to ascertain the cause, he saw a large black snake, of five feet in length, within the circle, and his squamous head elevated eight or nine inches above the surface of the earth, while his posterior parts remained in a spiral form. And so complete was the fascination, that Mr. Cheever was under the necessity of getting a pole to disperse the fowls, in order to kill the snake, in which he happily succeeded. The serpent, which had power over our mother Eve, hath power also over the beasts of the field and the fowls of the air.

MAMMOTH SUNFLOWER.

We have been presented by Mrs. Vedder, of Guilderland, with a prodigious large sunflower, which grew in her garden, in that town; and which, although contracted by the frost, is yet fourteen inches in diameter. It is of that kind which produces white seeds, and is by far the largest plant of the species we have ever seen.—*American Paper.*

Published by J. LIMBIRD, 355, Strand, (East End of Exeter 'Change); and sold by all Newsmen and Booksellers. Printed by A. APPLEGATH, Stamford-street.

THE CABINET OF CURIOSITIES,
OR
𝕴𝖆𝖔𝖓𝖉𝖊𝖗𝖘 𝖔𝖋 𝖙𝖍𝖊 𝖂𝖔𝖗𝖑𝖉 𝕯𝖎𝖘𝖕𝖑𝖆𝖞𝖊𝖉.

A world of wonders where creation seems
No more the works of Nature but her dreams.—MONTGOMERY.

No. XX.] PRICE TWOPENCE.

THE INCARNATION OF VISHNU.

THE whole system of Hindoo theology is founded upon the doctrine that the Divine Spirit, as the soul of the universe, becomes, in all animate beings, united to matter; that spirit is insulated or individuated by particular portions of matter, which it is continually quitting, and joining itself to new portions of matter; that the human soul is, in other words, God himself. The complete deliverance from the degrading and polluting influence of material objects, the Hindoos teach, may be obtained in the present state by separation from human intercourse, the practice of bodily austerities, and entire abstraction of mind; and that if not obtained in one birth, it is to be sought through every future transmigration till obtained.

The Hindoo mythology, in its

present mixed state, has gods of every possible shape and for every possible purpose; but most of them appear to refer to the doctrine of the periodical creation and destruction of the world—the appearance of nature—the heavenly bodies—the history of deified heroes—the poetical wars of the giants with the gods—or to the real or imaginary wants of mankind. The Hindoos profess to have 330,000,000 of gods, not that they have the names of such a number, but they say that God performs all his works by the instrumentality of the gods; and that all human actions, as well as all the elements, have their tutelar deities.

Many of the Hindoo idols are monstrous personifications of vice; and there is scarcely a single virtuous idea communicated by any one of them. One of these idols represents a female, with inflamed eyes, standing on the body of her husband, bespattering her bosom with the blood of her enemies, and wearing a necklace of skulls. Another, the image of Doorgon, is that of a female warrior so athirst for blood, that she is represented as cutting off her own head; and the severed head, with the mouth distended, is seen devouring the blood streaming from the trunk. The effect of this idolatry is not only the grossest moral darkness, but also an universal corruption of manners; nor is this to be wondered at when their religious rites are indecent and disgusting. Mr. Ward says:—

"It is a fact too, that the festivals in honour of the gods have the most pernicious effects on the minds of the people. During the ceremonies of worship before the image, the spectators are very few, and these feel no interest whatever in the mummery going forward; and were it not for those who come to pay a visit of ceremony to the image, and to bring their offerings, the temple would be as little crowded on festival, as on common days: but as soon as the well-known sound of the drum is heard, calling the people to the midnight orgies, the dance and the song, whole multitudes assemble, and almost tread one upon another; and their joy keeps pace with the number of loose women present, and the broad obscenity of the songs. Gopalu Turkkalunkaru, a pundit employed in the Serampore printing-office, and a very respectable man among the Hindoos, avowed to a friend of mine, that the only attractives on these occasions were the women of ill-fame, and the filthy songs and dances; that these songs were so abominable, that a man of character, even amongst them, was ashamed of being present; that if ever he (Gopalu) remained, he concealed himself in a corner of the temple. He added, that a song was scarcely tolerated which did not contain the most marked allusions to unchastity; while those which were so abominable that no person could repeat them out of the temple, received the loudest plaudits. All this is done in the very face of the idol; nor does the thought, 'Thou, God, seest me,' ever produce the slightest pause in these midnight revels. What must be the state of morals in a country, when its religious institutions and public shows, at which the whole population is present, thus sanctify vice, and carry the multitude into the very gulf of depravity and ruin!

"There is another feature in this system of idolatry, which

increases its pernicious effects on the public manners. The history of these gods is a highly coloured representation of their wars, quarrels, and licentious intrigues; which are held up in the images, recitations, songs, and dances, at the public festivals. At the separate recitations, which are accompanied with something of our pantomime, these incredible and most indecent fables are made still more familiar to the people: so familiar indeed, that allusions to them are to be perceived in the most common forms of speech. Many works of a pernicious tendency in the European languages are not very hurtful, because they are too scarce and expensive to be read by the poor; but the authors of the Hindoo mythology have taken care, that the quarrels and revels of the gods and goddesses shall be held up to the imitation of the whole community."

Although the deities in the Hindoo Pantheon amount to three hundred and thirty millions, yet all these gods and goddesses may be resolved into the three principal ones, Vishnu, Shivu, and Brumha; the elements; and the three females, Doorga, Lukshmee, and Suruswutee. Each of these are worshipped, in a variety of forms, as distinct or subordinate gods. To attempt even an outline of the varied forms which the superstitions of the Hindoos assume, would far exceed our limits: we must therefore content ourselves with noticing some of the most remarkable. Among the forms in which the goddess Doorga is worshipped, one is denominated Kalee, which Sir W. Jones considered as the Proserpine of the Greeks.

In the images commonly worshipped, Kalee is represented as a very black female, with four arms; having in one hand a scimitar, and in another the head of a giant, which she holds by the hair; another hand is spread open bestowing a blessing; and with the other she is forbidding fear. She wears two dead bodies for ear-rings, and a necklace of skulls; and her tongue hangs down to her chin. The hands of several giants are hung as a girdle round her loins, and her tresses fall down to her heels. Having drank the blood of the giants she has slain in combat, her eyebrows are bloody, and the blood is falling, in a stream, down her breast; her eyes are red like those of a drunkard. She stands with one leg on the breast of her husband Shivu, and rests the other on his thigh.

This deity is equal in ferocity to any of the preceding forms of Doorga. In the Kalika pooranu, men are pointed out, amongst other animals, as proper for sacrifice. It is here said that the blood of a tiger pleases the goddess for one hundred years, and the blood of a lion, a rein-deer, or a man, a thousand. But by the sacrifice of three men, she is pleased 100,000 years! We insert two or three extracts from the sanguinary chapter of the Kalika pooranu:—" Let a human victim be sacrificed at the place of holy worship, or at a cemetery where dead bodies are buried. Let the oblation be performed in the part of the cemetery called héruku, or at a temple of Kamakshya, or on a mountain. Now attend to the mode: the human victim is to be immolated in the east division, which is sacred to Bhoiruvu; the head is to be presented in the south division, which is looked upon as the place of skulls sacred to Bhoiruvu: and the blood is to be presented in the west division, which is denominated héruku. Having immolated a human victim, with all the requisite ceremonies, at a cemetery or holy place, let the sacrificer be cautious not to cast his eyes upon it. The victim must be a person of good appearance, and be prepared by ablutions and requisite ceremonies, (such as eating consecrated food the day before, and by abstinence from flesh and venery,) and must be adorned with chaplets of flowers, and besmeared with sandal wood. Then causing the victim to face the north, let the sacrificer worship the several deities presiding over the different parts of the victim's body: let the worship be then paid to the victim himself by his name."

A part of the mythology of India seems to be blended with the history of that country: it relates to the different *awatars* or incarnations of Vishnu, who, with Brama and Sheeva, form the Indian trinity, or the Supreme Being himself, under the triple character of Creator, preserver, and destroyer.

The first of these awatars has a reference to that general deluge of which all nations have preserved some tradition. Vishnu, we are told, metamorphosed himself into a fish to save king Sattiavriden and his wife during the deluge, and which had been sent as a punishment for the crimes and wickedness of mankind. In this form he acted as a rudder to the vessel which this king had constructed, and watched incessantly over his safety.

The second incarnation is that of Kourma, or the tortoise. The gods and the giants wishing to obtain immortality by eating *amourdon*, delicious butter formed in one of the seven seas of the universe, which the Indians call the sea of milk, transported, by Vishnu's advice, the mountain of Mandreguivi into that sea; they twisted round it the serpent Adissechen, and alternately pulling, some by his hundred heads, others by his tail, they made the mountain turn round in such a manner as to agitate the sea and to convert it into butter; but they pulled with such rapidity that Adissechen, overcome with weakness, could no longer endure it. His body shuddered; his hundred trembling mouths made the universe resound with hisses; a torrent of flames burst from his eyes; his hundred black pendent tongues palpitated and vomited forth a deadly poison, which immediately spread all around. The gods and giants betook themselves to flight. Vishnu, bolder than the rest, took the poison and with it rubbed his body, which became quite blue.

The gods and the giants, encouraged by Vishnu's example, fell to work again. After they had laboured a thousand years, the mountain was on the point of sinking in the sea, when Vishnu, in the form of a tortoise, quickly placed himself beneath, and supported it. A number of gods and goddesses arose from the sea of milk, seized a full vessel of *amourdon*, which they devoured; and the giants, disappointed in their expectations, dispersed over the earth, prevented mankind from paying worship to the gods, and strove to attain adoration for themselves. Their insolence occasioned the subsequent incarnation of Vishnu, who endeavoured to destroy this race, so inimical to the gods.

The third incarnation of Vishnu,

of which we this week give a figurative engraving has the name of *Varaguen*. A giant called Paladas, having rolled up the earth like a sheet of paper, carried it on his shoulders to the bottom of the sea. Vishnu, in the form of a man with a boar's head, attacked the giant, and ripped open his belly; he then plunged into the sea to bring up the earth, which he seized with his tusks and placed on the surface of the water, as it was before, putting several mountains on it to keep it in equilibrium.

There are several other incarnations of Vishnu; but the three we have enumerated are the most remarkable.

PYRAMIDS OF EGYPT.

[Concluded from p. 293.]

The French (says Dr. Clarke) attempted to open the smallest of the three principal pyramids; and having effected a very considerable chasm in one of its sides, have left this mark behind them, as an everlasting testimony of their curiosity and zeal. The landing of our army in Egypt put a stop to their labour. Had it not been for this circumstance, the interior of that mysterious monument would probably be now submitted to the inquiry which has long been an object among literary men.

" Having collected our party upon a sort of platform before the entrance of the passage leading to the interior, and lighted a number of tapers, we all descended into the dark mouth of the larger pyramid. The impression made upon every one of us, in viewing the entrance, was this: that no set of men whatever could thus have opened a passage, by uncovering precisely the part of the pyramid where the entrance was concealed, unless they had been previously acquainted with its situation; and for these reasons: First, because its position is almost in the centre of one of its planes, instead of being at the base. Secondly, that not a trace appears of those dilapidations which must have been the result of any search for a passage to the interior; such as now distinguish the labours of the French upon the smaller pyramid, which they attempted to open. The persons who undertook the work, actually opened the pyramid in the only point, over all its vast surface, where, from the appearance of the stones inclined to each other above the mouth of the passage, any admission to the interior seems to have been originally intended. So marvellously concealed as this was, are we to credit the legendary story of an Arabian writer, who, discoursing of the wonders of Egypt, attributed the opening of this pyramid to *Almamon*, a Caliph of Babylon, about nine hundred and fifty years since?

" Proceeding down this passage, which may be compared to a chimney about a yard wide, we presently arrived at a very large mass of granite: this seems to have been placed on purpose to choke up the passage; but a way has been made round it, by which we were enabled to ascend into a second channel, sloping, in a contrary direction, towards the mouth of the first. Having ascended along this channel, to the distance of one hundred and ten feet, we came to a horizontal passage, leading to a chamber with an angular roof, in the interior of the pyramid. In this passage we found, upon our right hand, the mysterious well, which has been so often mentioned. Pliny makes the depth of it equal to one hundred and twenty-nine feet; but Greaves, in sounding it with a line, found the plummet rest at the depth of twenty feet.

"We threw down some stones, and observed that they rested at about the depth which Greaves has mentioned; but being at length provided with a stone nearly as large as the mouth of the well, and about fifty pounds' in weight, we let this fall, listening attentively to the result from the spot where the other stones rested. We were agreeably surprised by hearing, after a length of time which must have equalled some seconds, a loud and distinct report, seeming to come from a spacious subterraneous apartment, accompanied by a splashing noise, as if the stone had been broken into pieces, and had fallen into a reservoir of water at an amazing depth. Thus does experience always tend to confirm the accounts left us by the ancients; for this exactly answers to the description given by Pliny of this well.

"After once more regaining the passage whence these ducts diverge, we examined the chamber at the end of it, mentioned by all who have described the interior of this building. Its roof is angular; that is to say, it is formed by the inclination of large masses of stone leaning towards each other, like the appearance presented by those masses which are above the entrance to the pyramid. Then quitting the passage altogether, we climbed the slippery and difficult ascent which leads to what is called the principal chamber. The workmanship, from its perfection, and its immense proportions, is truly astonishing. All about the spectator, as he proceeds, is full of majesty, and mystery, and wonder. Presently we entered that 'glorious roome,' as it is justly called by Greaves, where, ' as within some consecrated oratory, art may seem to have contended with nature.' It stands 'in the very heart and centre of the pyramid, equidistant from all its sides, and almost in the midst between the basis and the top. The floor, the sides, the roof of it, are all made of vast and exquisite tables of Thebaick marble.' So nicely are these masses fitted to each other upon the sides of the chamber, that, having no cement between them, it is really impossible to force the blade of a knife within the joints. This has been often related before; but we actually tried the experiment, and found it to be true. There are only six ranges of stone from the floor to the roof, which is twenty feet high; and the length of the chamber is about twelve yards. It is also about six yards wide. The roof or ceiling consists only of nine pieces, of stupendous size and length, traversing the room from side to side, and lying, like enormous beams, across the top."

Mr. Salt, the traveller, having paid a recent visit to the principal pyramid, in company with a British officer, it has been ascertained that the short descending passage at its entrance, which afterwards ascends to the two chambers, is continued in a straight line through the base of the pyramid into the rock on which it stands. This new passage, after joining what was formerly called the well, is continued forward in a horizontal line, and terminates in a well, ten feet in depth, exactly beneath the apex of the pyramid, and at the depth of a hundred feet beneath its base. Mr. Salt's companion has likewise discovered an apartment immediately above the king's chamber, exactly the same size, and of the same fine workmanship, but only four feet in height.

The base of the pyramid of Cephrenes, the next in magnitude, of the pyramids of Djiza, to that of Cheops, is estimated at six hundred and fifty-five feet, and its height at three hundred and ninety-eight feet. The pyramid of Miserinus has a base of two hundred and eighty feet, and an elevation of a hundred and sixty-two feet.

The pyramids of Saccara, which are numerous, are interesting on account of the peculiarities of their structure. The largest of them is of an irregular form, the line of the terminating angle being sloped like a buttress reversed. Another, of a middling size, is composed of stages rising one above the other. The smaller ones are greatly decayed; but the whole occupy an extent of two leagues. This multitude of pyramids scattered over the district of Saccara, Denon observes, prove that this territory was the *Necropolis* (city of the dead) to the south of Memphis, and that the village opposite to this, in which the pyramids of Djiza are situated, was another Necropolis, which forms the northern extremity of Memphis. The extent of that ancient city may thus be measured.

At an inconsiderable distance from the great Egyptian pyramids, and by an almost imperceptible descent, the traveller arrives at the Sphynx, the enormous bulk of which instantly attracts his attention. It is cut out of the solid rock, and is said to have been the sepulchre of Amasis. The height of this figure is twenty-seven feet; and the beginning of the breast thirty-three feet in width. The nose has been shamefully mutilated. " Although," Denon remarks, " the proportions are colossal, the outline is pure and graceful; the expression is mild, gracious, and tranquil; the character is African; but the mouth, the lips of which are thick, has a softness and delicacy of execution truly admirable; it seems real life and flesh. Art must have been at a high pitch when this monument was executed; for, if the head is deficient in what is called *style*, that is, the straight and bold lines which give expression to the figures under which the Greeks have designed their deities, yet sufficient justice has been rendered to the fine simplicity and character of nature displayed in this figure."

LARGE FOSSIL ANIMAL OF MAESTRICHT.

THE large animal, whose fossil remains are found in the quarries of Maestricht, has been deservedly a frequent object of admiration; and the beautiful appearance which its remains possess, in consequence of their excellent state of preservation, in a matrix which admits of their fair display, has occasioned every specimen of this fossil to be highly valued. The lower jaw of this animal, with some other specimens, which were presented by Dr. Peter Camper to the Royal Society, and which are now in the British Museum, are among the most splendid and interesting fossils in existence.

In 1770, the workmen having discovered part of an enormous

head of an animal imbedded in the solid stone, in one of the subterraneous passages of the mountain, gave information to M. Hoffman, who, with the most zealous assiduity, laboured until he had disengaged this astonishing fossil from its matrix. But when this was done, the fruits of his labours were wrested from him by an ecclesiastic, who claimed it as being proprietor of the land over the spot on which it was found. Hoffman defended his right in a court of justice; but the influence of the chapter was employed against him, and he was doomed not only to the loss of this inestimable fossil, but to the payment of heavy law expenses. But in time, justice, M. Faujas, says, though tardy, at last arrived—the troops of the French Republic secured this treasure, which was conveyed to the National Museum.

The length of the cervical, dorsal, and lumbar vertebræ appears to have been about nine feet five inches, and that of the vertebræ of the tail about ten feet; adding to which the length of the head, which may be reckoned, considering the loss of the intermaxillary bones, at least at four feet, we may safely conclude the whole length of the skeleton of the animal to have approached very nearly to twenty-four feet.

The head is a sixth of the whole length of the animal; a proportion approaching very nearly to that of the crocodile, but differing much from that of the monitor, the head of which animal forms hardly a twelfth part of the whole length.

The tail must have been very strong, and its width, at its extremity, must have rendered it a most powerful oar, and have enabled the animal to have opposed the most agitated waters, as has been well remarked by M. Adrian Camper. From this circumstance, and from the other remains which accompany those of this animal, there can be no doubt of its having been an inhabitant of the ocean.

Taking all these circumstances into consideration, M. Cuvier concludes, and certainly on fair, if not indisputable, grounds, that this animal must have formed an intermediate genus between those animals of the lizard tribe, which having an extensive and forked tongue, include the monitors and the common lizards, and those have a short tongue, and the palate armed with teeth, which comprise the iguanas, marbrés, and anolis. This genus, he thinks, could only have been allied to the crocodile by the general characters of the lizards.

FOSSIL STAGS' HORNS.

Among the fossils of the British empire, none are more calculated to excite astonishment than the enormous stags' horns which have been dug up in different parts of Ireland. Their dimensions, Dr. Molyneux informs us, were as follows :—

	Feet.	In.
From the extreme tip of each horn	10	10
From the tip of the right horn to its root	5	2
From the tip of one of the inner branches to the tip of the opposite branch	3	7½
The length of one of the palms, within the branches	2	6
The breadth of the same palm, within the branches	1	10½
The length of the right brow antler	1	2

Hoaxes and Impostures.

No. XVI.

FRIAR JETZER.

At a time when the pretended miracles of Prince Hohenlohe are occupying so much of the public attention, it may not be uninteresting to point out some of the artifices formerly resorted to by the Roman Catholics, to impress the vulgar with a belief in the superhuman power of their priests. A remarkable instance of this occurs in the history of Friar Jetzer, of Berne, in Switzerland.

About the beginning of the sixteenth century, a Franciscan happened to preach in Frankfort, and one Wigand, a Dominican, coming into the church, the Cordelier seeing him, broke out into exclamations, praising God that he was not of an order that profaned the virgin, or that poisoned princes at the sacrament (for a Dominican had poisoned the emperor Henry VII. with the sacrament.) Wigand, being extremely provoked with this severe reproach, gave him the lie; upon this a dispute arose, which ended in a tumult that had almost cost the Dominican his life; yet he got away.

The whole order resolved to take their revenge; and in a chapter held at Vimpsen, in the year 1504, they contrived a method for supporting the credit of their order, which was much sunk in the opinion of the people, and for bearing down the reputation of the Franciscans. Four of the friars undertook to manage the design: for they said, that since the people were so much disposed to believe dreams and fables, they must dream on their side, and endeavour to cheat the people as well as the others had done. They resolved to make Berne the scene in which the projcet should be put in execution: for they found the people of Berne at that time apt to swallow any thing, and not disposed to make severe inquiries into extraordinary matters. When they had formed their design, a fit tool presented itself; for one Jetzer came to take the habit as a lay-brother, who had all the dispositions that were necessary for the execution of the project; for he was extremely simple, and much inclined to austerities. Having observed Jetzer's temper well, they began to execute their projcet the very night after he took the habit, which was on Ladyday, 1507, when one of the friars secretly conveyed himself into his cell, and appeared to him, as if he had been in purgatory, in a strange figure; and he had a box near his mouth, which as he blew, fire seemed to come out of his mouth. He had also some dogs about him, that appeared as his tormentors.

In this posture he came near to Jetzer, while he was in bed, and took up a celebrated story, which they used to tell to all the friars, to beget in them a great dread of laying aside their habit: which was, that one of their order, who was superior of their house at Soloturn, had gone to Paris, but laying aside his habit, was killed in a lay habit. He told him further, that he was that person, and was condemned to purgatory for that crime; but that he might be rescued out of it by his means; and he seconded this with most horrible cries, expressing the miseries which he suffered. The poor friar Jetzer was excessively frightened; but the other advanced, and required a promise of him to do that which he should desire, in order to the delivering him out of his torments. The frightened friar promised whatever he should ask. Then said the other, " I know thou art a great saint, and thy prayers and mortifications will prevail; but they must be very extraordinary. The whole monastery must for a week together discipline themselves with a whip, and thou must lie prostrate in the form of a cross, in one of the chapels, while mass is saying, in the sight of all that shall come together to it. If thou doest thus, thou shalt find the good effects thereof in the love that the blessed virgin doth bear thee: but I will appear again unto thee, accompanied with two other spirits; and I assure thee that all that thou shalt suffer for my deliverance shall be most gloriously rewarded.

Morning was no sooner come, than the friar gave an account of this apparition to the rest of the convent, who all seemed extremely surprised at it, and pressed him to undergo the discipline that was enjoined him, and every one undertook to bear his share: so the deluded friar performed it all exactly in one of the chapels of their church. This drew a vast number of spectators together, who all considered the poor friar as a saint; and in the mean time the four friars that carried on the imposture magnified in their sermons the miracle of the apparition. Friar Jetzer's confessor was in the secret, and by this means they knew all the little passages in the poor friar's life, even to his thoughts, which was no small help to them in this affair. The confessor gave him a host with a piece of wood, which was, as he pretended, a true piece of the cross, and by these he was to fortify himself, if any more apparitions should come to disturb him, since evil spirits would certainly be chained up by them.

The next night the former apparition was renewed, and with him two other friars, whom poor Jetzer thought were devils indeed. According to his confessor's directions, he immediately presented the host to them, which gave them such a check; that he was fully satisfied of the virtue of the preservative; and the friar, who pretended he was suffering in purgatory, said so many things relating to the secrets of Jetzer's life and thoughts, that the poor man had now no reason to doubt of the reality of the apparition.

In two of these visions, that were managed both in the same manner, the friar in the mask talked much of the Dominican order, which he said was excessively dear to the Blessed Virgin, who knew herself to be *conceived in original sin*; and that the doctors, who taught the contrary, were in purgatory. That the story of St. Bernard's appearing with a spot on him, for having opposed the feast of the conception, was a forgery; but that it was true that some hideous flies had appeared on St. Bonaventure's tomb, who taught the contrary: that the Blessed Virgin abhorred the Cordeliers for making her equal to her son; that Scotus was damned, whose canonization the Cordeliers were then soliciting hard at Rome, and that the town of Berne would be destroyed for harbouring such plagues within their walls.

When the enjoined discipline was fully performed, the spirit appeared again; and said he was now relieved out of purgatory;

but before he could be received into heaven, he must receive the sacrament, having died without it; and that he would say mass for those, who had by their great charities rescued him out of his pains. Jetzer fancied the voice resembled the prior's; but he was then so far from suspecting any deceit, that he gave no great heed to this suspicion. Some days after, the same friar appeared as a nun, all in glory, and told the poor friar that she was St. Barbara, for whom he had a particular devotion; and added, that the Blessed Virgin Mary was so pleased with his charity, that she intended to come and visit him. He immediately called the convent together, and gave his brethren an account of this apparition, which was entertained by them all with great joy, and the friar languished with desire for the accomplishment of the promise that St. Barbara had made him.

After some days the longed for delusion appeared to him, clothed as the virgin used to be on the great festivals, and indeed in the same habit. There were some angels hovering about her, which he afterwards found were the little statues of angels, which they set upon their altars on the great holydays; and by a pulley and cord were made to rise up and fly about the virgin, which increased the delusion. The virgin, after some endearments to him, extolling the merit of his charity and discipline, told him, that she was conceived in original sin, and that Pope Julius II. who then sat in the chair, was to put an end to the dispute, and was to abolish the feast of the conception, which Sixtus IV. had instituted; and the friar was to be the instrument of persuading the pope of the truth of this matter. She then gave him three drops of her son's blood, which were three tears of blood that he had shed over Jerusalem; and signified that she was three hours in original sin, after which she was by his mercy delivered out of that state. She also gave him five drops of blood in the form of a cross, which were tears of blood that she had shed when her son was on the cross: and to convince him more fully, she presented him with a host that appeared as an ordinary host, but suddenly changed its colour into deep red. These visits were often repeated to the abused friar. At last the virgin told him, that she was to give him such marks of her son's love to him, that the matter should be past all doubt. She said, that the five wounds of St. Lucia and St. Catharine were real wounds, and she would also imprint them on him. So she bid him reach out his hand. He had no great mind to receive a favour in which he was to suffer so much; but she forced his hand, and struck a nail through it. This threw him out of a supposed transport into a real agony! but she seemed to touch his hand, and he thought he smelt an ointment with which she anointed him, though his confessor persuaded him that was only his imagination, for that was healed by miracle without ointment.

The next night the virgin returned again, and brought him some linen cloths, which had the virtue to allay his torments, and the virgin said they were some of the linen in which her son was wrapped. She then gave him a soporiferous draught; and while he was asleep the other four wounds were imprinted on his body in such a manner, that he felt no pain.

When he awoke he felt this wonderful impression on his body, and was transported beyond measure, and fancied himself to be acting all the pains of our Saviour's passion. He was exposed to the people on the great altar, to the great amazement of the whole town, and to the no small mortification of the Franciscans. The Dominicans gave him some other draughts, which threw him into convulsions; and when he came out of these, a voice was heard proceeding from the image of the virgin with a little Jesus in her arms, and the virgin seemed to shed tears; which a painter had drawn upon her face so lively, that all the people were deceived by it. The voice came through a hole, which yet remains, and runs from one of the cells along great part of the wall of the church: a friar spoke through a pipe, and at the end of the hole was the image of the virgin. The little Jesus asked his mother why she wept? She answered, because his honour was given unto her, since it was said, that she was born without sin. In conclusion, the friars so overacted this matter, that at last even the poor deluded *friar* himself came to discover it, and resolved to quit the order.

It was in vain to delude him with more apparitions, for he almost killed a friar that came to him, personating the virgin in another shape with a crown on her head. He also overheard the friars once talking amongst themselves of the contrivance and success of the imposture so plainly, that he discovered the whole affair; upon which, as may easily be imagined, he was filled with all the horror with which such a discovery could inspire him.

The friars fearing that an imposture carried on hitherto with so much success should be quite spoiled and turned against them, thought the surest way was to own the whole matter to him; and to engage him to carry on the cheat, they told him in what esteem he would be, if he continued to support the reputation he had acquired, and would become the chief person of the order: they therefore persuaded him to go on with the imposture. But afterwards, fearing least he should discover all, they resolved to poison him: of which he was so apprehensive, that once a loaf being brought to him, prepared with some spices, he kept it some time, and then it growing green, he threw it to some wolves' whelps that were in the monastery, who died immediately. His constitution was so vigorous, that though they gave him poison five several times, he was but little hurt by it. At last they forced him to take a poisoned host, which he vomited up soon after he had swallowed it. Then they whipped him with an iron chain, and girded him about so tight with it, that to avoid further torments, he swore, in the most imprecating terms, that he would never discover the secret, but would still carry it on. Thus he deluded them till he found an opportunity of getting out of the convent, and throwing himself into the hands of the magistrates, to whom he discovered all.

The four friars were seized and put into prison, and an account of the whole affair was sent first to the bishop of Lausanne, and then to Rome; and it may easily be supposed that the Franciscans took all possible care to have it fully examined into. The bishops of Lausanne and Zyon, with the provincial of the Dominicans, were appointed to form the process. The four friars first excepted to Jetzer's credit; but that not availing them, they confessed the imposture. About a year after a Spanish bishop came, authorized with full powers from Rome; and the whole cheat being particularly examined into, and fully proved, the four friars were solemnly degraded from their priesthood, and, on the last day of May 1509, were burnt in a meadow on the other side of the river, over-against the great church.

The place of their execution was shewn me (says bishop Burnet) as well as the hole in the wall through which the voice was conveyed to the image. It was certainly one of the blackest, and yet the best carried on cheats that has ever been known. And no doubt had the poor friar died before the discovery, it had passed down to posterity as one of the greatest of miracles; and it gives a shrewd suspicion, that many of the other miracles of that church were of the same nature, but more successfully finished.

Eccentric Biography.

MRS. SARAH DAWBER.

LATELY died at East Retford, Mrs. Sarah Dawber. Her peculiarity of manners and singularity of disposition rendered her very conspicuous, and obtained for her in Retford, the well-known appellation of " Old Granny Dawber." She was born in the same year as his late Majesty, consequently was in the 86th year of her age; and though having past the number of years which by the royal prophet has. been stated as the common period of human life, still nature seemed to revive again, until Monday the 2d ult., when, having incautiously placed a lighted candle too near her, her clothes took fire, in consequence of which she was much scorched, and her right ear nearly burnt off, so that she lingered in great misery until Monday last, when death, who is the soother of all sorrows, put a period to her afflictions. For several years, of late, her mind was impressed with the idea that every person who seemed to look at her wanted to rob her; and in order to frustrate their designs, she kept constantly well armed, having a small room nearly full of missiles, brickbats, stones, &c., and at times, when irritated, did not fail to send a plentiful shower of the same from out of her chamber windows. Her lower room front windows were constantly shut up, and for several years had not seen the vivifying rays of the sun, until the last enemy ' shot his dart at her vitals,' and we hope removed her to that place where ' thieves break not through nor steal.' — *Stamford News*, Sept. 1823.

MR. JAMES HURST.

THE Doncaster races of 1823 were attended by the " Old Miser," as he is termed, Mr. James Hurst, of Roliffe, near Wakefield. This eccentric old man, who appears to be about 77 years of age, has not missed the race for the cup for several years. His carriage he made himself, which is composed of rude pieces of stick tied together, and without springs. It stands very high, and is covered with a piece of patchwork quilt. Mr. Hurst being determined not to pay duty for any thing about his person, he keeps an otter instead of a dog about his house, and generally rides out upon a bull instead of a horse. He had on a dingy, felt, coarse, white hat, and his trowsers were made of a piece of a woman's gown. He had a sack full of apples, and to those persons he recognised as his acquaintances he presented one. Mr. Hurst and his vehicle excited a great deal of curiosity; and, upon the whole, it is one of the most eccentric performances that can be imagined.

Varieties.

CUCKOO-SPITTLE.

EVERY person must have observed what the naturalist calls froth-spittle, or cuckoo-spittle, a sort of white froth or spume very common in the spring and the first months of summer, on the leaves of certain plants, particularly on those of the common white field lychnis, or catch-fly, thence called by some spattling-poppy. All writers on vegetables have taken notice of this froth, though few have understood the cause or origin of it, till of late. Many imagined it an exhalation of the earth; some have esteemed it, as its name expresses, the saliva of the cuckoo; others the extravasated juices of the plant; and some a hardened dew. But all these are erroneous opinions, and the true account of it is, that it owes its origin to a small insect.

There are very frequently to be seen in the summer months a sort of small leaping animal, called by some the flea grasshopper, because they are very small, and leap like a flea: these little creatures have each a pointed proboscis, by means of which they suck the juice of the plants they are found upon. These animals lay their eggs in autumn, from which in the spring following the young ones are hatched; and these are at first tenderly sheltered from injuries by a delicate and thin membrane, which makes a sort of nymph, having the lineaments of all the parts of the animal which is to issue from it. When it is at first hatched from the egg, it is a small white point on the leaf, not larger than the point of a needle; a few days after, it is greenish, its colour changing with the juices of the plant on which it feeds: in this state it not unaptly resembles that small species of frog, called the tree-frog, which is common on the branches of trees in many places: it moves about very swiftly in this state, though still covered with its membrane; but, till it gets rid of that, it can neither leap nor fly.

The manner in which the little creature forms this froth upon the plant, is this: it applies itself close to the leaf, and discharges upon it a small drop of white viscous fluid, which, containing some air in it, is soon elevated into a small bubble; before this is well formed, it deposits such another drop, and so on, till it is every way overwhelmed with a quantity of these bubbles, which form the white froth which we see. It adds to this upon occasion, but never moves from under it, till it has got rid of its enveloping membrane, or has arrived from the nymph state to that of the perfect animal. It throws out these globules of viscous humour, by a sort of dilatation and contraction of its belly; and, as they succeed one another, it disposes them every way round it with its feet. A proof that, while these animals are in this imperfect state, and covered with froth, they yet feed on the juices of the plant, is, that, if one of them be placed on a leaf of mint, or any other such plant, the leaf on which they live will never grow beyond the size it was of, when the animal was placed upon it, while the opposite leaf will acquire its full dimensions. When the animal has quitted its nymph state, it makes no more froth, but leaves that under which it had lived, and takes its course freely about the plant.

This is the true nature of the froth so often observed on plants; and may serve, as one instance, how careful nature is in preserving every species in the creation, by methods best adapted to that purpose.

SWEDISH METHOD OF BREEDING TURKEYS.

MANY of our housewives, says an ingenious author, have long despaired of success in rearing turkeys, and complained, that the profit rarely indemnifies them for their trouble and loss of time: whereas, continues he, little more is to be done, than to plunge the chick into a vessel of cold water, the very hour if possible, but at least the very day it is hatched, forcing it to swallow one whole peppercorn; after which let it be returned to its mother. From that time it will become hardy, and fear the cold no more than a hen's chick. But it must be remembered, that this useful species of fowls are also subject to one particular disorder while they are young, which often carries them off in a few days. When they begin to droop, examine carefully the feathers on their rump, and you will find two or three whose quill part is filled with blood. Upon drawing these the chick recovers, and after that requires no more care than what is commonly bestowed on poultry that range the court-yard.

The truth of these assertions is too well known to be denied; and as a convincing proof of the success, it will be sufficient to mention, that three parishes in Sweden have, for many years, used this method, and gained several hundred pounds by rearing and selling turkeys.

NATURAL WONDERS IN AMERICA.

IT is very surprising, that two of the greatest natural curiosities in the world are within the United States, and yet scarcely known to the best informed of our geographers and naturalists.

The one, a beautiful fall in Franklin (Habersham) county, Georgia, the other a stupendous precipice in Pendleton district, South Carolina: they are both faintly mentioned in the late edition of Morse's Geography, but not as they merit. The Tuccoa fall is much higher than the Falls of Niagara. The column of water is propelled beautifully over a perpendicular rock, and when the stream is full, it passes down without being broken. All the prismatic effect seen at Niagara illustrates the spray of Tuccoa. The Table mountain, in Pendleton district, South Carolina, is an awful precipice of 900 feet. Many persons reside within five, seven, or ten miles of this grand spectacle, who have never had curiosity or taste enough to visit it. It is now, however, occasionally visited by curious travellers, and sometimes by men of science.

Very few persons who have

once cast a glimpse into the almost boundless abyss, can again exercise sufficient fortitude to approach the margin of the chasm. Almost every one, in looking over, involuntarily falls to the ground senseless, nerveless, and helpless, and would inevitably be precipitated and dashed to atoms, were it not for measures of caution and security that have always been deemed indispensable to a safe indulgence of the curiosity of the visitor or spectator. Every one, on proceeding to the spot whence it is usual to gaze over the wonderful deep, has, in his imagination, a limitation, graduated by a reference to distances with which his eye has been familiar. But, in a moment, eternity, as it were, is represented to his astonished senses, and he is instantly overwhelmed. His system is no longer subject to his volition or reason, and he falls like a mass of mere matter. He then revives, and in a wild delirium surveys a scene, which, for a while, he is unable to define by description or imitation.

The Scrap Book.

CURE OF A PALSY BY A STROKE OF LIGHTNING.

Mr. SAMUEL LEFFERS, of the county of Carteret, in North Carolina, had been attacked with a palsy in the face, and particularly in the eyes. While he was walking in his chamber, a thunderstroke threw him down senseless. At the end of twenty minutes he came to himself; but he did not recover the entire use of his limbs till the evening. Next day he found himself perfectly recovered; and he could now write without the use of spectacles. The palsy did not return.

THE HIPPOPOTAMUS.

"You are aware," says the writer of a letter from St. Mary's, Madagascar, dated December 29, 1822, "that that huge beast the Hippopotamus abounds in the rivers of southern and eastern Africa. One of them came in contact with the Leven's cutter, called the Cockburn, and bit out six planks at one bite; the boat immediately filled, but being close to the bank of the river soon reached the shore. On another occasion, one of them sprang from the bank of the river, open mouthed, at one of the boats, but without doing any injury to either the boat or crew. They were so surprised and terrified by this huge animal, that it was under water before a shot could be fired at it."

TAME PHEASANT.

A SPOTTED cock pheasant, of beautiful plumage and large size, has, during the last and present season, forsaken his own species in the woods, and attached himself to the domestic poultry of the Rev. George Bowness, at the rectory, Rokeby. It is seldom absent till the evening, when he generally walks off to roost in his native haunts, but returns with the dawn, to give the maids the benefit of his "clarion" in the morning. He is so tame as nearly to feed from the hand, and has occasionally ventured to enter the dwelling. During the heavy snow in the spring he was invisible, but reappeared with the thaw, in full feather and beauty.

Published by J. LIMBIRD, 355, Strand, (East End of Exeter 'Change): and sold by all Newsmen and Booksellers Printed by A. APPLEGATH, Stamford-street.

THE CABINET OF CURIOSITIES,
OR
Wonders of the World Displayed.

*A world of wonders where creation seems
No more the works of Nature but her dreams.*—MONTGOMERY.

No. XXI]   PRICE TWOPENCE.

JEFFERY HUDSON IN THE PIE.

JEFFERY HUDSON, the famous English dwarf, who contributed to the amusements of the court of Charles II., was born at Oakham, in Rutlandshire, in the year 1619. When about the age of seven or eight, being then but eighteen inches high, he was retained in the service of the Duke of Buckingham, who resided at Burleigh on the Hill. Soon after the marriage of Charles I, the king and queen being entertained at Burleigh, little Jeffery was served up to table in a cold pie, and presented by the duchess to the queen, who kept him as her dwarf. Of this scene, which must have been eminently ludicrous, we this week give an original engraving. From seven years of age till thirty he never grew taller; but after thirty he shot up to three feet nine inches, and there fixed. Jeffery took a considerable part in the entertainments of the court. Sir William Davenant wrote a poem, called "Jeffreidos," on a battle between him and a turkey-cock; and in 1638 was published a very small book, called "The New Year's Gift," presented at court from the Lady Perceval to the Lord Minimus (commonly called little Jeffery,) her majesty's servant, &c. written by Microphilus; with a little print of Jeffery pre-

Y

fixed. Before this period Jeffery was employed on a negotiation of great importance: he was sent to France to fetch a midwife for the queen; and on his return with this gentlewoman and her majesty's dancing-master, and many rich presents to the queen, from her mother, Mary de Medicis, he was taken by the Dunkirkers. Jeffery, thus made of consequence, grew to think himself really so. He had borne with little temper the teazing of the courtiers and domestics, and had many squabbles with the king's gigantic porter. At last, being provoked by Mr. Crofts, a young gentleman of family, a challenge ensued; and Mr. Crofts coming to the rendezvous armed only with a squirt, the little creature was so enraged, that a real duel ensued, and the appointment being on a level, Jeffery with the first fire shot his antagonist dead. This happened in France, whither he had attended his mistress in the troubles. He was again taken prisoner by a Turkish rover, and sold into Barbary. He probably did not remain long in slavery; for at the beginning of the civil war he was made a captain in the royal army, and in 1644 attended the queen to France, where he remained till the restoration. At last, upon suspicion of his being privy to the popish plot, he was taken up in 1682, and confined in the Gate-house, Westminster, where he ended his life, in the sixty-third year of his age.

SYMPATHIES AND ANTIPATHIES.
No. II.

"That a human body," says Mr. Boyle, "is so framed as to suffer great changes from seemingly gentle impressions of external objects, appears from many instances already mentioned. Thus, likewise, to go suddenly into the sunshine will sometimes instantly occasion that violent motion we call sneezing. To look from a precipice will make the head giddy; the sight of a whirlpool has caused men to fall into it; and to fix the eyes upon the water beneath a ship under sail will prove emetic; as I, for my health's sake, have sometimes experienced. If a person be ticklish, stroke the sole of his foot with a feather, and it shall, against his will, affect the remote muscles of his face and provoke him to laughter. As the tickling of a straw in the nostrils excites sneezing, many kinds of grating noise will set the teeth on edge; and a servant of mine complained that the whetting of a knife would make his gums bleed. Henricus ab Heer mentions a lady who would faint at the sound of a bell, or any loud noise, even that of ringing, and lie as if she were dead; but as she was thoroughly cured by a course of physic, it appears that this disposition proceeded from some particular texture in her body. With regard to sounds, one hysterical woman in fits shall even communicate them to another by aspect; and to show that distempered bodies may receive alterations, while sound ones remain the same, we need only consider that the subtile effluvia which float in the air before any change of weather, are felt by those valetudinarians who have formerly received bruises, wounds, or other injuries, and that too only in the very parts where they happened. Others we daily see, who are disordered by riding backwards in a coach; and the scent of musk or ambergris, though grateful to others, will throw hysterical women into strange convulsions. Zacutus Lusitanus tells us of a fisherman, who, having spent his life at sea, and coming accidentally to the reception of the king of Portugal, in a maritime town where perfumes were burnt, he was thereby thrown into a fit, judged apoplectic by two physicians, who treated him accordingly; till three days after, the king's physician guessing the cause, ordered him to be removed to the sea-side, and there to be covered with sea-weed, which soon recovered him.

"But there are many strange peculiarities," says the same author, "in some persons both in sickness and health. These differences, indeed, between healthy men may not be greater than those observable in the same person when in a sound or distempered state; yet we frequently see that some bodies are so framed as to be strangely disordered by such things as either not at all, or else differently affect those of others. Thus it is common for men to express great uneasiness, and fall into fits of trembling, at the sight of a cat. This was the case of the late gallant and noble Earl of Barrymore, who had the like aversion to tansy; and I, myself, cannot behold a spider near me without a great commotion in my blood, though I never received any hurt from that creature, and have no abhorrence of toads, vipers, or other venomous animals. I also know an excellent lady who is remarkable for a strange antipathy to honey. Her physician supposing this in some measure imaginary, mixed a little honey in a remedy he applied to a very slight scratch she happened to receive in her foot; but he soon repented of his curiosity; for it caused a strange and unexpected disorder, which ceased upon the removal of that medicine and the application of others. The same excellent person complained to me, that the vulgar pectoral remedies did her no service in coughs wherewith she was troubled, and which nothing relieved but either the fumes of amber received by a pipe with that of proper herbs, or the balsam of sulphur. I know an ingenious gentlewoman on whom cinnamon, which generally is considerably astringent and stomachic, has a quite contrary effect, and this in a strange degree; so that, having found by two or three accidental trials that a very little cinnamon seemed to disorder her stomach and prove laxative, she once resolved to satisfy herself whether these discomposures came by chance or no; and having strewed some powdered cinnamon on a toast, she ate it, and was thereby purged for two days together with such violence that it caused convulsions and a spasmus, which she continues to be troubled with from time to time, though it is three years since she made the experiment, as was averred to me by her husband, a physician.* A person of quality lately asked me, whether he should continue the use of coffee as an emetic, because he had found it operate very violently with him. Inquiring particularly into this odd effect, I found that an ordinary wine glass full of the common liquid coffee, would in two hours'

* On the other hand, M. Lemery tells us that he knew a chymist who could eat *mercurius dulcis* as if it were bread; and that he has seen him chew and swallow down four ounces at once, without any sensible effect. Hist. de l'Académ. An. 1699, p. 69.

make him vomit more severely than the infusion of *crocus metallorum*, or other usual emetics. That this had been for several years his constant vomit; that scarcely any one was more irksome than this of late grew to take, so that the scent of a coffee-house would make him sick; and lastly, that he himself had formerly used it long together for the fumes which offended his head, without observing any emetic quality therein."

M. Zimmerman relates the following instance of antipathy to spiders: "Being one day in an English company," says he, "consisting of persons of distinction, the conversation happened to fall on antipathies. The greater part of the company denied the reality of them, and treated them as old women's tales; but I told them that antipathy was a real disease. Mr. William Matthew, son of the governor of Barbadoes, was of my opinion, and as he added that he himself had an extreme antipathy to spiders, he was laughed at by the whole company. I showed them, however, that this was a real impression of his mind, resulting from a mechanical effect. Mr. John Murray, afterward Duke of Athol, took it into his head to make, in Mr. Matthew's presence, a spider of black wax, to try whether this antipathy would appear merely on a sight of the insect. He went out of the room, therefore, and returned with a bit of black wax in his hand, which he kept shut. Mr. Matthew, who in other respects was a sedate and amiable man, imagining that his friend really held a spider, immediately drew his sword in a great fury, retired with precipitation to the wall, leaned against it, as if to run him through, and sent forth horrible cries. All the muscles of his face were swelled, his eyeballs rolled in their sockets, and his whole body was as stiff as a post. We immediately ran to him in great alarm, and took his sword from him, assuring him at the same time that Mr. Murray had nothing in his hand but a bit of wax, and that he might himself see it on the table where it was placed. He remained some time in this spasmodic state, and I was really afraid of the consequences. He, however, gradually recovered, and deplored the dreadful passion into which he had been thrown, and from which he still suffered. His pulse was exceedingly quick and full, and his whole body was covered with a cold sweat. After taking a sedative, he was restored to his former tranquillity, and his agitation was attended with no other bad consequences." We must not be surprised at this antipathy: the largest and most hideous spiders are found in Barbadoes, and Mr. Matthew was born in that island. Some one of the company having formed of the same wax, in his presence, a small spider, he looked at it, while making, with the utmost tranquillity, but it would have been impossible to induce him to touch it. He was not, however, of a timid disposition.

SUBTERRANEOUS FORESTS.

In the year 1708, a breach made by the Thames, at an extraordinary high tide, inundated the marshes of Dagenham and Havering, in Essex. Such was the impetuous rush of the water, that a large passage or channel was torn up, three hundred feet in width, and in some parts twenty feet in depth. In this way, a great number of trees, which had been buried there many ages before, were exposed to view. With one exception, that of a large oak, having the greatest part of its bark and some of its heads and roots in a perfect state, these trees bore a greater resemblance to alder than to any other description of wood. They were black and hard, and their fibres extremely tough. Not any doubt was entertained of their having grown on the spot where they then lay; and they were so numerous, that in many places they afforded steps to the passengers. They were imbedded in a black oozy soil, on the surface of which they lay prostrate, with a covering of grey mould.

In passing along the channel torn up by the water, vast numbers of the stumps of these subterraneous trees, remaining in the posture in which they grew, were to be seen, some with their roots running down, and others branching and spreading about in the earth, as is observed in growing trees. That they were the ruins, not of the deluge, but of a later age, has been inferred from the existence of a bed of shells, which lies across the highway, on the descent near Stifford bridge, leading to South Okendon. At a perpendicular depth of twenty feet beneath this bed of shells, and at the distance of nearly two hundred feet, in the bottom of a valley, runs a brook which empties itself into the Thames at Purfleet. This brook is known to ebb and flow with the Thames; and, consequently, if the bed of shells, as has been conjectured, was deposited in that place by an inundation of the Thames, it must have been such as to have drowned a vast proportion of the surrounding country, and have overtopped the trees near the river, in West Horrock, Dagenham, and the other marshes, overturning them in its progress. In support of this hypothesis, it should be remarked, that the bed of earth in which the trees grew, was entire and undisturbed, and consisted of a spongy, light, oozy soil, filled with the roots of reeds, of a specific gravity much less than that of the stratum above it.

The levels of Hatfield Chase were, in the reign of Charles I., the largest chase of red deer in England. They contained about one hundred and eighty thousand acres of land, about one half of which was yearly inundated; but being sold to one Vermuiden, a Dutchman, he contrived, at great labour and expense, to dischase, drain, and reduce these lands to arable and pasture grounds, not subject to be overflowed. In every part of the soil, in the bottom of the river Ouse even, and in that of the adventitious soil of all marsh land, together with the skirts of the Lincolnshire Wold, vast multitudes of the roots and trunks of trees of different sizes are found. The roots are fixed in the soil, in their natural position, as thick as they could have grown; and near to them lie the trunks. Many of these trees appear to have been burned, and others to have been chopped and squared; and this in such places, and at such depths, as could never have been opened, since the destruction of the forest, until the time of the drainage. That this was the work of the Romans, who were the destroyers of all the woods and forests which are now found underground in the bottoms of moors and bogs, is evidenced by the coins and utensils, belonging to that nation, which have been collected, as well in these levels, as in other parts of Great Britain where these subterraneous forests have been discovered.

THE APPARITION OF SOUTER FELL.

SOUTER FELL is a mountain about half a mile in height, enclosed on the north and west sides by precipitous rocks, but somewhat more open on the east, and easier of access. At Wilton Hall, within half a mile of this mountain, on a summer's evening, in the year 1743, a farmer and his servant, sitting at the door, saw the figure of a man with a dog, pursuing some horses along Souter Fell side, a place so steep that a horse could scarcely travel on it. They appeared to run at an amazing pace, till they got out of sight at the lower end of the fell. On the following morning the farmer and his servant ascended the steep side of the mountain, in full expectation that they should find the man lying dead, being persuaded that the swiftness with which he ran must have killed him; and imagining also that they should pick up some of the shoes which they thought the horses must have lost, in galloping at so furious a rate. They were, however, disappointed, as not the least vestige' of either man or horses appeared, nor so much as the mark of a horse's hoof on the turf.

On the 23d of June of the following year, 1744, about half past seven in the evening, the same servant, then residing in Blakehills, at an equal distance from the mountain, being in a field in front of the farm house, saw a troop of horsemen riding on Souter Fell side, in pretty close ranks, and at a brisk pace. Having observed them for some time, he called out his young master, who, before the spot was pointed out to him, discovered the aerial troopers; and this phenomenon was shortly after witnessed by the whole of the family. The visionary horsemen appeared to come from the lowest part of Souter Fell, and were visible at a place called Knott: they then moved in regular troops along the side of the Fell, till they came opposite to Blakehills, when they went over the mountain. They thus described a curvilinear path, and their first, as well as their last appearance, was bounded by the foot of the mountain. Their pace was that of a regular swift walk; and they were seen for upwards of two hours, when darkness intervened. Several troops were seen in succession, and frequently the last, or last but one in the troop, would quit his position, gallop to the front, and then observe the same pace with the others. The same change was visible to all the spectators, and the sight of the phenomenon was not confined to Blakehills, but was witnessed by the inhabitants of the cottages within a mile; it was attested before a magistrate by the two above-cited individuals in the month of July, 1785. Twenty-six persons are said in the attestation to have witnessed the march of these aerial travellers.

It should be remarked that these appearances were observed on the eve of the rebellion, when troops of horsemen might be privately exercising; and as the imitative powers of the Spectre of the Broken Mountain demonstrate that the actions of human beings are sometimes pictured in the clouds, it seems highly probable, on a consideration of all the circumstances of this latter phenomenon on Souter Fell, that certain thin vapours must have hovered round the summit of the mountain when the appearances were observed. It is also probable that these vapours may have been impressed with the shadowy forms which seemed to "imitate humanity," by a particular operation of the sun's rays united with some singular but unknown refractive combinations then taking place in the atmosphere.

THE CORNISH MURDER

Lillo, the author of the tragedy of George Barnwell, wrote another tragedy called the "Fatal Curiosity," which was founded on the following dreadful murder.

"In September, Anno Christi 1618, there lived a man at Perin in Cornwall, who had been blessed with an ample possession and fruitful issue; unhappy only in a younger son, who, taking liberty from his father's bounty, joined with a crew like himself, who, weary of the land, went roving to sea, and, in a small vessel, southward made prize of all whom they could master; and so increased in wealth, number, and strength, that in the Straits they adventured upon a Turkish man of war, where they got great booty: but their powder by mischance taking fire, our gallant, trusting to his skilful swimming, got to shore upon the Isle of Rhodes, with the best of his jewels about him; where, after a while, offering some of them for sale to a Jew, he knew them to be the governor's of Algiers, whereupon he was apprehended, and for a pirate condemned to the gallies, among other Christians, whose miserable slavery made them use their wits to recover their former liberty; and accordingly watching the opportunity, they slew some of their officers, and valiantly released themselves. After which, this young man got on board an English ship, and came safe to London, where the experience he had acquired in surgery preferred him to be servant to a surgeon, who, after a while, sent him to the East Indies: there, by his diligence and industry he got money, with which he returned home: and longing to see his native country, Cornwall, in a small ship from London, he sailed westward; but ere he attained his port, he was cast away upon that coast: where, once more, his excellent skill in swimming brought him safe to shore. But then, having been fifteen years absent, he understood that his father was much decayed in his estate, and had retired himself to live privately in a place not far off, being indeed in debt and danger.

"His sister he finds married to a mercer, a meaner match than her birth promised. To her he first appears as a poor stranger, but after a while privately reveals himself to her, shewing her what jewels and gold he had concealed in a bow-ease about him; and concluded that the next day he intended to appear to his parents, yet to keep his disguise, till she and her husband should come thither, to make their common joy complete.

"Being come to his parents, his humble behaviour, suitable to his poor suit of clothes, melted the old couple into so much compassion, as to give him shelter from the cold season, under their outward roof; and by degrees, his stories of his travels and sufferings, told with much passion to the aged people, made him their guest so long by the kitchen fire, that the husband bade them good night, and went to bed. Soon after, his true stories working compassion in the weaker vessel she wept, and so did he; but withal, he, taking pity on her tears, comforted her with a piece of gold, which gave her assurance that he deserved a lodging, which she afforded him, and to which she brought him: and being in bed he shewed her his wealth, which was girded about him, which he told her was sufficient to relieve her husband's wants, and to spare for himself: and so being weary, he fell asleep.

"The old woman being tempted with the golden bait that she had received, and greedily thirsting after the enjoyment of the rest, she went to her husband, and awaking him, presented him with this news, and her contrivance what further to do; and though with horrid apprehensions he oft refused, yet her pewling eloquence (Eve's enchantment) moved him at last to consent, and to rise to be master of all that wealth, by murdering the owner thereof: which accordingly they did, and withal, covered the corpse with clothes, till opportunity served for their carrying of it away.

"The early morning hastens the sister to her father's house, where with signs of great joy, she inquires for a sailor that should lodge there the last night. The old folks at first denied that they had seen any such, till she told them that he was her brother, and lost brother, which she knew assuredly, by a scar upon his arm, cut with a sword in his youth, and they were resolved to meet there the next morning and be merry.

"The father hearing this hastily runs up into the room, and finding the mark, as his daughter had told him, with horrid regret for this monstrous murder of his own son, with the same knife wherewith he killed him, he cut his own throat. The mother, soon after, going up to consult with her husband what to do, in a strange manner beholding them both weltering in blood, wild and aghast, finding the instrument at hand, readily rips up her own belly.

"The daughter, wondering at their delay in returning, seeks about for them, whom she found out too soon, and with the sad sight of this bloody scene, being overcome with sudden horror and amazement for this deluge of destruction, she sank down and died, the fatal end of that family. The truth of these things was soon made known, and quickly flew to King James's court, clad with these circumstances: but the imprinted relation conceals their names, in favour of some neighbour of repute and kin to the family."—*Sanderson's History of King James.*

Eccentric Biography.

SIMEON STYLITES.

This remarkable man, who is honoured with a niche in the Roman Catholic calendar, was the son of a poor shepherd of Cilicia, on the borders of Syria, and entered on his eccentric career towards the close of the fourth century. Simeon was brought up to keep his father's sheep, but, at a very early age, the imagination of the poor boy was excited, or, more rationally speaking, disordered, into an extravagant admiration of the glory at that time to be acquired by bodily mortification and self-denial. To a wise and benevolent deity, the misery endured for his sake was thought to be peculiarly acceptable; and the voluntary rejection of his best gifts entitled the wretched devotee not only to the applause of heaven, but to a reverence of his fellow-creatures approaching to adoration. The mind of Simeon, thus prematurely stimulated, was so struck, in his thirteenth year, with the tenour of the text, "Blessed are they that mourn," that he instantly resolved to forsake all earthly employment, and to dedicate his future life to sorrow and suffering for the faith in Christ. In conformity to this holy resolution, the unfortunate youth first applied at the gates of a neighbouring monastery, requesting to be received within its walls, and to be employed in the vilest drudgery for the service of the brotherhood. His offer was accepted; but it seems that the order was not sufficiently strict for the devout ambition of Simeon, who at the end of two years removed to the monastery of Heliodorus, a person, says Theodoret, in the way of praise, who had spent sixty-two years so abstracted from the world, that he was ignorant of the most obvious things in it. Under the auspices of this judicious personage, the aspiring penitent first began to display that loftiness of spiritual conception, by which he was subsequently so eminently distinguished. The brothers of the community being restricted to one meal a day, which they took towards evening, Simeon improved the regulation in his own case to a single repast a week, but was obliged to moderate his rigour at the desire of the superior. This unpleasant restriction led him to adopt greater privacy in his subsequent mortifications; thus, esteeming the wearing of haircloth and other known body-tormenting apparatus as too lenient, he secretly appropriated the rough well-rope of the monastery to his own especial use. This ingenious substitute, which was formed of twisted palm-tree leaves, the saint tied so tightly round his naked body, that it ate into his flesh, and the fact was discovered by the noisomeness of the ulcer which it created. So severely was his body lacerated, it was three days before the rope could be disengaged from the wound, and it was at last separated by the knife of the surgeon, at the immediate hazard of the holy man's life. However indicative of zeal and piety, these extraordinary penances were found exceedingly troublesome to the less gifted brethren; and a ray of good sense breaking in upon the Abbot, he dismissed Simeon, as either above or below monastic discipline.

Upon this event, the ungovernable saint repaired to an hermitage at the foot of Mount Thelanissa, where, in imitation of the Saviour, he endeavoured to pass the forty days of Lent without food. This wonderful undertaking he is asserted not only to have accomplished at that particular time; but the learned Theodoret, a contemporary, vouches, upon his own knowledge, for the same abstinence during twenty-six Lents of his subsequent life. His manner of passing the forty days is thus detailed by the above writer:—" The first part of his Lent he spent in praising God *standing*; growing weaker, he continued his prayer *sitting*; and towards the end, being exhausted, he *lay* upon the ground." In all these situations he was continually seen by thousands of devotees, who crowded to witness so edifying a spectacle.

After spending three years in this hermitage, Simeon removed to the top of the mountain on which it was situated, when, throwing together some loose stones in the form of a wall, he made for himself an enclosure, but without roof or shelter, and to confirm his resolution of passing his holy life in it, had his right leg fastened to a rock, with a great iron chain. The interference of the dignified clergy of his vicinity was never required to increase the vivacity of Simeon, but sometimes humanely stepped in to moderate it. In the present instance, Meletius, Vicar to the Patriarch of Antioch, considering the chain as rather out of saintly costume, told him that a firm will, supported by God's grace, was sufficient to make him abide in his solitary enclosure, without having recourse to bodily restraint. "Whereupon," says a modern clerical narrator, "the obedient *servant of God* sent for a smith, and had his chain knocked off."

In whatever form it exhibits itself, the love of fame is a very restless propensity; it rendered the life of Simeon a continual progression in his own line of sanctity. The multitudes of people who flocked to receive his benediction, most of whom were desirous of touching so holy a personage, became at length a great annoyance; and to remove so obvious a cause of distraction without offence, he projected for himself a manner of life, altogether new and unprecedented. The result of this bright thought was, the erection of a pillar within his enclosure six cubits high, in the summit of which he resided *four* years; on a second, twelve cubits high, he perched himself for *three* years; on a third, twenty-two cubits high, for *ten* years; and finally, on a fourth, forty cubits high, built for him by the people, he abode *twenty* years. Thus, in the whole, he lived *thirty-seven* years on *pillars*, receiving the name of Stylites, from the Greek word Stylos, which signifies pillar, and hence his usual appellation of Simeon Stylites.

The various pillars of this poor lunatic, did not exceed a few feet in diameter at the top, which was enclosed round with rails; on which, and on his staff, the wretched man reclined when he slept. The space being so small, it was impossible for him to lie down, and a seat he wholly declined. His usual food was vegetables and water, with which he was supplied as he required them, by admirers and disciples. His garments were formed of the skins of wild beasts, an iron collar adorned his neck, and such was his ungallant tenacity, with respect to women, he would never suffer one to come within the enclosure which surrounded his pedestal. From his elevated rostrum, this ghastly and frightful spectre regularly harangued the admiring multitude twice a day; when not addressing them, they were equally edified by his significant acts of adoration and reverence. Gibbon quotes the still-existing account of a curious *spectator*, who counted twelve hundred and forty-four genuflections or bows, of the indefatigable Simeon on his pillar, during the time that he looked on. He sometimes prayed in an erect posture, with his outstretched arms in the figure of a cross; but his most usual practice was that of bending his meagre skeleton from the forehead to the feet. The Eucharist was frequently conveyed to him by a *Saint* Domus; and during Lent, he often fasted on his pillar, as rigidly as he had done on *terra firma*. During a few of the first and last years, indeed, he was obliged to attach himself to a pole, to support him under his abstinence; but in the zenith of his career he was frequently enabled to fast the whole time without requiring aid of any kind, so strong was his constitution, and so gradually had he habituated himself to a long endurance of inanition.

It is curious to observe the watchful tenacity of the hierarchy of that period, even with respect to the extravagances which it countenanced. 'Madness and folly were only roads to heaven, as coupled with obedience.' When Simeon first took to his pillar, the singularity of his choice was universally condemned as vanity or extravagance; and to make trial of his obedience an order was sent to him, in the name of the neighbouring bishops and abbots, to quit his new manner of life. The saint instantly prepared to comply, which when the messenger perceived, agreeably to his instructions, he informed him, that as he had shown so willing an obedience, he was at liberty to follow his vocation in God. The result has been narrated. Simeon spent thirty-seven years in the air—a monument of human folly and degradation, disgraceful to the Christian name. He died at last of a mortification produced by an ulcer in his foot, which brought him to his end on the 2d of September, A. D. 459, when the poor man bowing on his pillar, as if intent on prayer, silently expired, in the sixty-ninth year of his age.

Were the above particulars verified only by the Catholic legends, or even by writers like Theodoret, Cosmo, and Simeon's own disciple, Anthony, who wrote his life, they would be undeserving of credit; but this poor maniac's extraordinary manner of living has been attested by witnesses of all kinds, in consequence of the impression made by it on the whole Christian world of his day. Pilgrims of all ranks visited Syria to obtain his prayers; the emperors Theodosius and Leo sought his inspired advice in religious difficulties; and another emperor, Marcian, even went to behold him in disguise. These are facts; the legends, of course, go much farther: according to them, miracles of all kinds attended his prayers and benedictions; and even surrounding nations of barbarians sought the benefit of his intercession. When dead, he was carried to Antioch in solemn procession, attended by all the prelates of the neighbouring country; and even to this day, many Catholic writers refer to him, as a glorious confessor of the cause of Christ.

But it is pleasant to see that the folly of such sanctity was not altogether invisible to some acute observers, even in the saint's own time: Gibbon relates a jocose piece of scandal propagated at his expense, which proves that the latent cause of so much absurdity was not mistaken by *all* the world. The squib alluded to, took its rise from the ulcer in his foot that caused his death, which was thus accounted for:—The ever-watchful Satan, it seems, discovered no small portion of spiritual vanity lurking in the heart of Simeon, which he was permitted to correct by assuming the form of the prophet Elijah. In this holy character the father of lies waited upon the saint, in a chariot of fire, and informed him that his merits were so regarded on high, that the penance of death would be spared him, and he had only to seat himself to be borne directly to heaven. The vanity of Simeon (continued these satirists) leading him to give implicit credit to the plausible tale, he instantly put his foot into the chariot, and not only got laughed at for his credulity, but so burnt in the too ready limb, that an ulcer ensued, which brought him to his end—a fiction so far pleasant, as it proves the existence of a little humour and common sense in an age of superstition and extravagance.

So different, however, was the general impression in those dark and declining days, that the example of Simeon produced many imitators all over eastern Christendom, where alone the mildness of the climate would admit of so insane a devotion. Magelli, a domestic prelate to Pope Benedict XIV. wrote a grave dissertation on these fanatics, and gave a plate in the work, representing the Pillar of Simeon, whose image on his column, carved in silver, or in ivory, was at one time very common among devotees. According to this author, the Stylites prevailed in the east until the conquest of the Saracens put an end to the degrading absurdity. The climate of the west rendered similar infatuation impracticable to any great degree. However, Gregory of Tours relates that one Vulfilaic, a Lombard, placed himself on a pillar in the neighbourhood of Triers, but after a short abode thereon, was ordered by his bishop to quit a life not endurable in that country. He is the only recorded Stylite of the west.

The 5th of January is the day appropriated to Simeon Stylites in the Roman Catholic calendar, and it is still observed.

Varieties.

A SHORT MODE OF BRINGING A GHOST TO LIGHT.

Mrs. Water, a widow lady, who, with her family, occupied a cottage at Hampstead, during the autumn of 1817 was much alarmed by unusual noises in various parts of her premises at the dead hour of the night. At first she was induced to believe these sounds proceeded from thieves, but having missed nothing to confirm her suspicions, this idea was abandoned, and one of a more solemn description found place in her breast; namely, that the disturbance arose from some supernatural agency; a belief which was confirmed by both her servant maids, who affirmed most positively that they had seen things which had the appearance of a human figure clothed in white, flitting through the garden after nightfall. The terror arising from the continuance of these supposed visitations from the other world, which were kept a secret from the neighbourhood, at length induced Mrs. Water to apply to her nephew, who at once suspected the cause, and by agreement was secretly admitted on the premises, in company with a friend, without the knowledge of the servants, on the night fixed upon; when taking their station behind some trees in the shrubbery, they patiently waited the midnight hour, being provided with a dark lantern, in the event of artificial light being necessary to unravel the mystery. Soon after one, a figure enveloped in white entered the garden from a door leading into an adjoining field, and approaching directly to the house, rattled several of the shutters and doors. This turned out to be the signal of his arrival, and in a few seconds a female came from the house and joined the aerial visitant, which, without much ceremony, encircled her not in his shadowy, but sinewy arms. While in this state of bliss the friends approached with as much silence as possible, but not with sufficient precaution, to prevent alarm, and before they could secure the spirit he vanished, not into the air, but into an adjoining pig-sty, which happened to be untenanted, and was filled with dry straw. The female vanished with as much celerity into the house, and shut the door, waiting in a state more easily conceived than imagined the issue of their untoward interruption to her joys. The friends having approached the pig-sty, exhorted the evil spirit to come forth, with every argument of which they were masters, but all in vain, till at length one of them very deliberately set fire to the straw, the light and smoke of which produced the desired effect, and to their infinite surprise and amusement out crept a young gentleman, whose parents resided in the vicinage, and who had adopted this mode of carrying on an intrigue with the housemaid. It is needless to say that the shame of his exposure, as well as the danger which he had incurred, operated as a sufficient caution to prevent the repetition of similar idle and mischievous expedients, by which on more occasions than one the lives of our fellow-creatures have been sacrificed.

CURIOUS DISCOVERY OF MURDER.

THE men who lately committed a murder in the county of Clare, upon a person named Ryan, have been, through the activity of the police, apprehended, in the following curious manner:—A party of the police, commanded by Sergeant Jameson, reached the spot within about an hour after the perpetrating of the horrid deed, and followed the foot-prints of the murderers with the most persevering assiduity. The men remarked from the impression upon the ground, that one of them wore new brogues, or strong shoes, the soles of which were thickly set with nails; and so vigilant were they, that they observed the vacancy left by the head of a nail being wanting in one of them. This track they pursued to the ruffian's house, where they took him into custody, with the identical shoes yet wet upon his feet! They immediately measured the shoe with the impression upon the fatal spot, and found it to answer in every respect, even to the absent nail. The other man, they observed, had on but one shoe. This track they also followed, and actually took him into custody in his own house, having on a wet and a dry shoe! This circumstantial evidence, we are glad to say, has been strengthened by the identification of both the prisoners, by the family of the unfortunate victim. We cannot but recognise a remarkable Providence in the apprehension of these men, and we wish it may impress upon the minds of the evil-disposed the awful warning, that the murderer will not, even upon earth, be suffered to escape the vengeance due to his crime. Both the above men have been committed to gaol, and the family of Ryan has been brought into town for safety.—*Waterford paper, Sept.* 1823.

FECUNDITY OF FISH.

The prolific powers of fishes are scarcely credible. Immense tracts of the ocean are so thickly and deeply covered with their spawn, that, as the waves break, and ships dash through them, the phosphoric light, emitted from the substance which surrounds the animalculæ, gives the waters, during a dark night, the appearance of flames of fire, terrific, but harmless. Liewenhoek calculated that a cod fish, of ordinary size, contained more young than there are inhabitants upon the face of our globe.— The writer had once the curiosity to count the young in a herring seven inches in length, and found 40,000! But these things sink into insignificance before the following, taken from *Scoresby's Account of East Greenland*, lately published. Perceiving the waters of the sea, to a wide extent and a great depth, to be of a beautiful but deep yellow colour, he had some of the water taken up. Applying a microscope of moderate powers to the same, he found that the colour of the water proceeded from the number of animalculæ in it, each so inconceivably small, that a single drop contained 26,000! An ordinary sized glass tumbler contained 150 millions of these creatures, which lived, and moved, and sported about, each in his place, without disturbing or pressing upon its neighbour.

THE INFANT LAMBERT.

A REMARKABLE fat child, says the *Journal de l'Empire* of 1813, has been for some time exhibited at Paris. If we may believe his parents he is not more than five years and nine months old; but an examination of his teeth proves him to be eight years old: be that as it may, he exhibits a combination of very singular *phenomena*. He is three feet four inches in height. He weighs fifty pounds. He has the thighs, arms, and body of an adult in size, though not in development of bone and muscle. His hands and feet are not in proportion with his other limbs, they do not exceed in size those of a child from eight to ten years of age. His head is large, his hair woolly, and his eyebrows thick. His face is very fat and high coloured, and his neck short. He has fine black eyes. His figure is not disgusting, it bears some resemblance to that of a very fat woman of thirty. His smile has much in it of archness and infantine grace. The breasts of the child are as large as those of a very large woman, but they have neither nipples nor glands. They are extremely soft, and are, as it were, curved from the armpits towards the sternum, so that the two ends meet, notwithstanding which curvation, they resemble the breasts of a woman. The muscles of this enormous child are a soft, light fat, which feels like hogs' lard, and covers the fleshy parts. It would appear as if all the vital powers were directed to the developement of fat, at the expense of the muscles and bones. The back is covered with a mass of soft fat, which floats as it were beneath the skin. It is easily taken up by the hand in distinct masses. This fat increases in such a degree beneath the armpits, that the child cannot but with difficulty raise his hand to his mouth. His respiration is laborious, and he cannot without much difficulty rise from his chair. When he is up, it is easy to perceive that the weight of his fat is very distressing to him. There is every reason to suppose that an apoplexy will put an end shortly to his existence. His manners are childish, nor is his understanding above that of ordinary children. His voice is not strong. He articulates badly when answering the questions put to him, but when he gets into a passion, which is not unfrequently the case, his voice becomes loud and vehement, and something like that of irritable market women. Buried in his fat he speaks only in monosyllables, when he is not enraged. Whenever he is contradicted, he upbraids his adversary in very gross terms, which appear to have been taught him with a view to the amusement of those who visit him. The avarice of the person who exhibits the child induces him to envelope his moral existence with ridiculous mystery; in consequence of which it is impossible to obtain any information with respect to it, such as would be useful to the naturalist. His answers to the simplest questions consist of stupid and irrelevant arguments.

WATERSPOUT.

On Saturday the 23d August, the town and neighbourhood of Pediham were thrown into consternation by the appearance of a very large waterspout. When first seen, it seemed to have risen from clouds which were gathering thick round Hamilton: soon after it assumed a more terrific appearance, and veered to the north-west. In this quarter it displayed every symptom of immediate explosion, but suddenly made a rapid circuit to the west. In its passage, the noise which it created represented the distant roar of the sea on a rocky shore; but as it continued to ascend, the tone was altered, and resembled more the compressed discharge of steam from a boiler. The revolutions which it made in its transit were awfully grand; and its attractive faculties of re-uniting the volumes of mist which issued from its side were beyond description beautiful. After repeated ascents and descents, it varied its form with astonishing rapidity: at one period its longitudinal extent must have been very considerable, and in the next moment, the point, which left no more than eighty yards from itself to the earth, was embosomed in the mass. It continued these transmutations for an hour, and then was buried in the clouds. Immediately on its disappearance, the atmosphere became densely dark, and the most vivid lightning and tremendous thunder that has been heard in the neighbourhood for many years ensued.—*Blackburn Mail.*

FATAL EFFECTS OF FEAR.

A man of colour, of middle age, rather above the common stature, robust, and apparently in good health, was received into the London Hospital, labouring under a moderate sized aneurism of the femoral artery. An operation was proposed to him, to which he readily assented: on entering the theatre, however, he fainted; some wine and water was given to him, which he distinctly swallowed, and the operation was proceeded in, the artery exposed, and the ligature applied, but not tightened. During the operation, it was observed that no pulsation could be felt in the tumour, but this was accounted for by the fainting; before tightening the ligature, it was suggested by the operator to wait until the pulsation was reestablished; some increased attention was then paid to arouse the dormant energies of the patient, and it was remarked that the syncope had continued an unusual time; after the attempts had been some time persevered in, a more attentive observation proved that he was quite dead. All the usual resuscitative means were tried, but without effect. On dissection, both sides of the heart were found empty, and the lungs turgid with blood: no other particular appearance was observable.

The Scrap Book.

NUMBER OF THE KNOWN SPECIES OF ORGANIZED BEINGS.

From the collections in the Paris Museums, M. Humboldt estimates (Ann. de Chimie, xvi.) the known species of plants at 56,000 and those of animals at 51,000; among which, 44,000 insects, 4,000 birds, 700 reptiles, and 500 mammalia. In Europe live about 400 species of birds, eighty mammalia, and thirty reptiles; and on the opposite southern zone on the Cape, we find likewise almost five times more birds than mammalia. Towards the equator the proportion of birds, and particularly of reptiles, increases considerably. However, according to Cuvier's enumeration of fossil animals, it appears that in ancient periods the globe was inhabited much more by mammalia than birds.

RATS AND FLORENCE OIL.

A gentleman receiving a present of some Florence oil, the flasks were set in his cellar, at the bottom of a shallow box; the oil not being wanted for use, they remained there some time; when the owner, going one day by chance into the cellar, was surprised to find the wicker-work, by which the flasks were stopped, gnawed from the greater part of them, and upon examination the oil sunk about two inches or two and a half from the neck of each flask. It soon occurred to him, that it must be the work of some kind of vermin; and being a man of a speculative turn, he resolved to satisfy the curiosity raised in his mind; he accordingly found means to watch, and actually detected three rats in the very fact. The neck of the flasks was long and narrow, it required therefore some contrivance: one of these stood upon the edge of the box, while another, mounting his back, dipped his tail into the neck of the flask, and presented it to a third to lick; they then changed places; the rat which stood uppermost descended, and was accommodated in the same manner with the tail of his companion, till it was his turn to act the porter, and he took his station at the bottom. In this manner the three rats alternately relieved each other, and banqueted upon the oil till they had sunk it beyond the length of their tails.

Published by J. LIMBIRD, 355, Strand, (East End of Exeter 'Change); and sold by all Newsmen and Booksellers. Printed by A. APPLEGATH, Stamford-street.

THE CABINET OF CURIOSITIES,
OR
𝔚onders of the 𝔚orld Displayed.

A world of wonders where creation seems
No more the works of Nature but her dreams.—MONTGOMERY.

No. XXII.] PRICE TWOPENCE.

HINDOO AND MUSSULMAN DEVOTEES.

In India there are numerous penitents of different sects called Fakeers, Yogees, Tadins, Pandaroons, &c. who make a vow to live at the expense of the public and travel about begging. The Yogees and Fakeers, who are often mistaken the one for the other, are both penitents and mendicants, but the former are Hindoos, and the latter Mussulmans; in other respects they resemble one another in cunning, hypocrisy, and impudence. They are often to be seen in the bazars in the markets, and in all other public places. Let our readers figure to themselves a fanatic stark naked, with the exception of a small piece of stuff which is fastened round his middle, bedaubed all over with a whitish powder, his hair so twisted that it might be taken for Medusa's serpents, setting up from time to time the strangest howls, running like a madman, with a face proof against shame, red and wild looking eyes, and they will have some idea of a Fakeer. The wretches strive to surpass one another in extravagance, and try by all possible means to attract the notice of the multitude, some wounding themselves on the forehead, arms, or thighs, to excite the compassion of the charitable and obtain alms from them. Others will lie on their backs motionless in the streets, and there exposed on the scorching sand to the intense heat of the sun, sing hymns and affect to be totally indifferent to all that is passing about them, as if they were absorbed in profound meditation, but at the same time leering to observe if any thing is thrown to them.

These Fakeers sometimes assemble in troops of eight or ten thousand, levying contributions wherever they go. The total number of the Fakeers is estimated at 800,000. They class themselves in particular orders.

The *Dundee* is so called from *dundu*, a staff, or pole, which he carries in one hand : in the other he bas an alms-dish. He does not beg his food, nor cook with his own hands; but is a guest at the houses of Brahmins, who will prostrate themselves before these men : the Dundee pretends to bless persons who thus fall down before him. His chief business is—to repeat the name of his god; to meditate on him, with closed eyes, by the side of the Ganges; and to bathe therein once a day, having first besmeared himself all over with the mud of the river. He shaves his head and beard every four months; wears a narrow cloth round his loins, and a loose red cloth over his body; and abstains from fish, flesh, oil, common salt, and rice which has been wetted in cleansing. The Hindoos believe, that as soon as their souls leave their bodies, they go into other bodies : this they call transmigration : but Dundees are said, after death, to be united to their god; so that some Brahmins, when death approaches, enter into this order, that they may obtain that fancied happiness, and not pass into other bodies.

The *Brumhucharee* subsists by begging, resides at temples, or holy places, wears red clothes, and binds round his arms and neck, and suspends from his ears, strings made of the seeds of grapes. He shaves his head, but sometimes wears a beard. He differs in appearance from the Dundee, chiefly in having no staff in his hand. His time is principally taken up in repeating the name of his god, and counting the number of times on his bead-roll. All these men drink spirits, smoke, eat intoxicating drugs, and reject no kind of food. People of the Sudra Caste may not enter into this order : those of the other three may.

The *Ramatu* worships a god called Ramu. They rub their bodies with the ashes of cowdung, and wander to holy places, many of them armed with spears or swords. They do not beg one by one, but quarter themselves, in a body, on rich men. They make fires in the night, and sleep near them, in the open air. They smoke intoxicating herbs to great excess.

The *Voishnuvu* goes about singing the praises of his gods, before the doors of persons where he begs; sometimes adding a musical instrument. They generally remain in towns, and mix with the inhabitants; being much more social in their manners than any other tribe of Hindoo beggars.

The *Mussulman Fakeer* is not a Hindoo, but a follower of the false prophet Mahomed; but these men are, in many things, like the Hindoos : they crowd to idolatrous shows, and sing and dance before the idols. In a great forest, called the Sunderbunds, which abounds in wild beasts, several of these men live in huts, pretending to be in possession of charms to keep the wild beasts from hurting them. The natives, who go to cut firewood, make offerings to these saints, that they may be protected in their work; and the assurances of these Fakeers arm them with new courage. If one of the woodcutters perishes, the faith of the rest is not shaken; though, for the time, they tremble. So long as the tigers spare the Fakeers, these deceivers are greatly venerated by the superstitious natives : the longer any one escapes, the greater saint he is esteemed; and, at last, if he should be snatched away, they say his time was come. This trade of deceiving is a tolerable livelihood to the few men who are hardy enough to follow it.

The missionary, Mr. Ward, from whose " Account of the Hindoos" we have extracted the above description of the beggars in the east, makes some remarks on them, which will serve to throw some light on the deplorable condition of millions of British subjects.

" These persons renounce the world because it has frowned upon them; or because the state of a religious beggar in a warm climate is preferred by an idle people to that of the lowest order of day-labourers. When I asked a learned Brahmin, whether there were not some instances of persons, from religious motives, renouncing the world and becoming mendicants, he said, there might be, but he did not know of a single instance.

" These mendicants, so far from having subdued their passions, frequently curse those who refuse to give them food. Many are common thieves : almost all live in an unchaste state : and others are almost continually drunk by smoking intoxicating drugs. They are total strangers to real purity of heart and righteousness of life. They dread to kill an insect, to reproach a Brahmin, or to neglect a ceremony; but their impure thoughts or unjust actions never disturb their peace.

" I have endeavoured to ascertain the probable number of Hindoos who embrace a life of mendicity; and am informed that scarely less than an eighth part of the whole population abandon their proper employments, and live as religious mendicants by begging. Supposing that there are 16,000,000 of Hindoos in Bengal and Bahar, and that each mendicant requires only one rupee monthly for his support, it will appear, that not less than 2,000,000 rupees, or 250,000 pounds sterling, are thus devoured annually by persons, the great majority of whom are well able to support themselves by manual labour. What a heavy tax this must be on the industrious, the great body of whom among the Hindoos are comparatively poor!

" When we add to this, the baneful effects of this system on the morals of the mendicants themselves as well as on the public manners, every benevolent mind must exceedingly deplore such a state of things. These beggars are not frowned upon like those who have nothing but their misery to plead for them; but are privileged and insolent harpies, boldly demanding the contributions of the abject and superstitious Hindoos. Their indolent habits too, and the filthy songs which they sing, lead to every species of impurity and to perpetual acts of private plunder.

" Many of the more enlightened Hindoos, especially the Brahmins, hold these mendicants in the utmost contempt; and would consider their being compelled to work as a great blessing conferred upon the country. On the other hand, some persons of property treat them with the greatest reverence; and sometimes invite a number of them to their houses, drink the water with which they have washed their feet, and, at the end of the entertainment, eat of the refuse from the plate of each!"

Various are the modes of self-torment adopted by these Fakeers. One man will travel through the country with one of his legs tied up, another will stand in the midst of fires kindled round him, to show that he is got above all feeling: a third acquires the art of making his feet and hands exchange their natural places; and another will suspend himself by his legs from a tree, and there continue for some time. Of the two latter Fakeers we have given an engraving.

Some years ago there was a singular Fakeer who laid on a bed of spikes, and took the name of Purrum Soatuntre, which means, in their language, "self-possession" or "independence;" because he thought himself a wonderful man, and able to endure any thing that he pleased. Mr. Duncan, an English gentleman, saw this man at Benares, a very large city in India, and gives the following account of him, which he got from his own mouth.

When only ten years of age, this man began a life of self-mortification, and used to lie on thorns and pebbles. He went on thus for ten years, and then began to wander about as a Fakeer, going from one of their pretended holy places to another.

At one place, he shut himself up in a cell, where he vowed to do penance for twelve years. There he stayed till vermin gnawed his flesh, and left marks which remained when Mr. Duncan saw him. At the end of a year, the rajah, or chief of that country, taking pity on him, opened the door of his cell, hoping to persuade him to leave off tormenting himself: but the poor wretch was full of fury to be thus interrupted; and told the rajah that he should have his curse on his head (and all the Hindoos dread the curses of these men) for breaking in upon him. What! did he think that he was not above such sufferings as these! They were nothing to him! Let the rajah get him a bed of spikes, that he might lie on it night and day, and shew him what he was able to do, and then perhaps he might forgive him!

The rajah, frightened at the thought of the curse of this ferocious man lighting on him, got him a bed of spikes; and this bed of spikes became a sort of triumphal car for the wretched man. He set out immediately to take very long journeys; and was drawn on this horrid bed all round the country for thousands of miles, the poor people every where worshipping him as a sort of god. He travelled about in this manner for thirty-five years. Having no longer, as he said, any inclination to roam, he wished to spend the rest of his days in Benares.

But this poor man was not contented with the supposed merit of his self-torture on the bed of spikes, but he tried to put himself to greater pain. He boasted to Mr. Duncan, that he had caused water to fall on his head, night and day, in the cold season, from a pot with holes in it, placed over him, drop by drop so that he might be constantly uneasy: and, when the hot weather came, he mortified himself in an opposite manner, by causing logs of wood to be kept burning round him, to make his sufferings from the heat greater!

But a more remarkable Fakeer than any of these, was Praoun Poury, who was living at Benares in 1792. This man held his arms over his head till the circulation of the blood stopped, his nails grew to be talons, and his arms withered and became stiff, so that he could not take them down again; and he sat with his legs tucked up under him, till they became almost useless. Every day he was brought out and placed on the seat raised upon a leopard's skin, and leaning against a cushion; and there the people came and supplied him with the most delicate food.

SINGULAR VORTEX.

In the month of March 1792 the ground in a meadow, part of the estate of Stanley, the property of the earl of Lonsdale, in Cumberland, suddenly sunk to the depth of some feet, making a circular break on the surface. Immediately after, a torrent of water was heard, which appeared to rush out from various parts of the broken soil; and falling, as it was conjectured, into a receptacle which could not at that time be perceived, occasioned a tremendous noise, while the shrinking was evidently increasing upon the surface.

In the morning, the aperture exhibited the appearance of an immense funnel: it was yet enlarging, consequently no admeasurement could be made: but the computation generally agreed to, was from sixty to seventy yards in diameter, and thirty yards in depth to the vortex, the diameter of which appeared to be six or seven yards.

During this time, large heaps of earth was falling from the sides, and water gushing out in an amazing abundance; the water also was sometimes forced up a considerable height above the vortex, as if from a *jet d'eau*; the whole presenting to the eye a scene of the most awful grandeur, while the ear was filled with the most terrifying sounds; often resembling distant thunder, as the deluge poured into the subterraneous workings of Scalegill colliery. The people employed in this colliery had quitted their work a short time before the sinking happened.

The aperture kept increasing for several hours, still preserving its circular form, till a shoot of earth from one part of its margin altered the figure in a small degree. It remained without any perceptible change for three days, when a rivulet, which runs at a small distance, was let into it by a trench, with a view to prevent any further shrinking of the surrounding earth.

The ground, thus almost instantaneously lost, is one acre, one rood, and twenty-four perches.

THE ASSASSIN OF COLOGNE.

An individual accused of many murders has been arrested at Beul, a village on the right bank of the Rhine, opposite to Bonn. He has already confessed three murders, the recital of which is enough to make the mind shudder. The following is an account of the means by which these atrocious crimes were discovered. An inhabitant of Beul, named Moll, a shoemaker, and Henry

Ochs, of Cologne, a tailor, had served together in the same company of the 28th regiment, and were united in the closest bonds of friendship: they returned to their houses after some years' service, and resumed their former occupations. Moll came frequently to visit his friend Ochs, who was married at Cologne. The young married folk always received and treated him with much affection. The judicial authority took cognizance last year of the double disappearance of Moll's step-mother, 28 years old, and of his own young brother: search was made after their persons but in vain. Moll, having given rise to some suspicions, was arrested; but for want of sufficient proof was discharged from arrest after a detention of some months, and resumed his connection with Ochs as before. The latter wishing to make purchases at the fair of Putzyen, not far from Beul, held on the 8th of September, set out on the 7th, having procured sixty Prussian crowns, informing his wife that he would take lodgings at the house of his friend Moll. After she had waited the return of her husband for eight days, she began to feel considerable anxiety, and sent a confidential person to make inquiries for him. This messenger arrived at Beul on the 18th, and saw Moll wearing the clothes and using the pipe of his friend Ochs: struck with these signs he returned to Bonn, and communicated them to the officers of justice. The judge instructor instantly despatched the civil power; who, having surrounded Moll's residence, proceeded to make a domiciliary visit. They presently discovered some loose planks on the floor of the work-house; on raising which, they perceived the extremities of mutilated bones sticking out from a hole filled with earth, like those in which peasants usually preserve their potatoes. They dug out three bodies in succession: the first of which was recognised as that of the unfortunate Ochs. While the officers were busied in the work of exhumation, Moll escaped through a window, and baffled the vigilance of the police with such caution, that they were not able to retake him until about nine o'clock at night, when he was discovered in the middle of a field, in which he had laid down through excessive fatigue. He was brought back to the judge's office, where he found before him the three bodies exposed to view: at first he wished to deny every thing, but the impressive and ingenious interrogations of the judge pressed him so closely, that he became confused and inconsistent in his answers, and in the end, the voice of conscience succeeded in wringing from him the horrible confession of his crimes. He then confessed, with a flood of tears, that fifteen months ago he assassinated his step-mother. He afterwards avowed that he assassinated his own brother, because he possessed the power of revealing the former deeds; he moreover confessed the murder of his friend Ochs, which he committed on the night of the 7th of Sept. 1823. An inquiry into many other murders is on foot, which also are attributed to this monster, and on which he still continues to undergo examinations. M. Schiller, son to the celebrated poet, is employed in conducting the investigation of this affair.

We understand that the inhabitants of Beul, fired with detestation of the murderer Moll, assembled last Saturday, and destroyed his house, which was situated in an isolated spot at the extremity of the village. After they had demolished it from roof to foundation, they collected the combustible materials, set them on fire, and scattered the ashes to the winds. This act of simultaneous indignation was performed in a moment, and (we are happy to learn) was followed by no other excess.

DAVIS THE SOMNAMBULIST.

A REMARKABLE instance of this affection of the nerves occurred on Sunday evening last, October 5, to a lad named George Davis, sixteen and a half years of age, in the service of Mr. Hewson, butcher, of Bridge-road Lambeth. At about twenty minutes after nine o'clock, the lad bent forward in his chair, and rested his forehead on his hands; and in ten minutes started up, went for his whip, put on his one spur, and went thence to the stable; not finding his own saddle in the proper place, he returned to the house and asked for it. Being asked what he wanted with it, he replied to go his rounds. He returned to the stable, got on the horse without the saddle, and was proceeding to leave the stable: it was with much difficulty and force that Mr. Hewson, junior, assisted by the other lad, could remove him from the horse; his strength was great, and it was with difficulty he was brought in doors. Mr. Hewson, sen. coming home at this time, sent for Mr. Benjamin Ridge, an eminent practitioner, in Bridge-road, who stood by him for a quarter of an hour, during which time the lad considered himself stopped at the turnpike gate, and took 6d. out of his pocket to be changed; and holding out his hand for the change, the sixpence was returned to him. He immediately observed, " None of your nonsense—that is the sixpence again, give me my change." When threepence half-penny was given to him, he counted it over, and said, " None of your gammon; that is not right. I want a penny more;" making the fourpence half-penny, which was his proper change. He then said " Give me my castor" (meaning his hat), which slang term he had been in the habit of using, and then began to whip and spur to get his horse on: his pulse at this time was 136, full and hard; no change of countenance could be observed, nor any spasmodic affection of the muscles, the eyes remaining closed the whole of the time. When stripped, he asked for his jacket; his coat was given to him; he said, " This is not my jacket, it is my best coat; but never mind, I am behind my time." When he had put it on, he began the motion of whipping and spurring; he was held in the chair by force, and his observations were, to " get out of his way, and let go his horse.—Ah, damn you, won't you, I will soon make you let him go: go along Jack." He then whipped and spurred in motion to make his horse kick, in order to get away, saying, " Let go my horse's tail, or I will soon make you." He was then brought out of the parlour into the front shop, and was asked what orders he had? He there went through the regular list of all the customers living at Brixton, &c. which he had been in the habit of calling on, and named the kind and exact quantity of meat to be supplied to each, as regularly as if he had been sent out in a morning. He was then told to clean the shop;

he stripped off his coat, and turned up his sleeves to begin washing the benches, and was obliged to be held to prevent his doing it. After two or three minutes he observed, "There is no pigs' victuals mixed up, let me go; when master comes home he will be angry at that." A gentleman present then told Mr. Hewson, that if he had the boy on board ship he would tie him up and ropesend him. It was agreed that the experiment should be tried: he was held by the arms in front, and Mr. Hewson, jun. a stout young man, took a hand whip, which he applied with all his force across the shoulders, but which did not appear to make any impression, although a dozen lashes were applied. Immediately after this the operation of bleeding was had recourse to. His coat was taken off his arm, shirt sleeve stripped up, and Mr. Ridge bled him to thirty-two ounces; no alteration had taken place in him during the first part of the time the blood was flowing; at about twenty-four ounces, the pulse began to decrease; and when the full quantity named above had been taken, it was at eighty—a slight perspiration on the forehead. During the time of bleeding, Mr. Hewson related the circumstance of a Mr. Harris, optician in Holborn, whose son some years since walked out on the parapet of the house in his sleep. The boy joined the conversation, and observed he lived at the corner of Brownlow-street. After the arm was tied up, Mr. Hewson, jun. told him to take some lights to a customer; he answered that he had taken them in the morning. He was then told by Mr. Hewson, sen. to take some more. "That is of no use," answered he, "I shall have to bring them back again." In three or four minutes from this he awoke, unlaced one boot and said he would go to bed: in three minutes from this time he got up, and asked what was the matter (having then been one hour in the trance), not having the slightest recollection of any thing that had passed; except having fetched in water, and of having moved from one chair to the other in the kitchen, being the last two acts previous to sinking into the trance, and wondering at his arm being tied up, and at the blood, &c. A strong aperient medicine was then administered, he went to bed, slept well, and the next day appeared perfectly well, excepting debility from the bleeding and operation of the medicine, and has no recollection whatever of what had taken place. Neither his family nor himself were ever affected in this way before. His eyes were several times opened by force, and the pupils regularly contracted and dilated, but he was not sensible to vision. It was ascertained from his mother on the Tuesday following, that twelve months previously he had been attacked with fever, which affected his brain, and for which he was sent to the Fever House at Battlebridge, where his head was shaved and blistered. Could this latter circumstance have in any way affected the particular nerves oppressed in this trance?

The Book of Dwarfs.

We are men my liege.
Ay, in the catalogue ye go for men;
As hounds and greyhounds, mungrels, spaniels, curs,
Showghes, water-rugs, and demi-wolves are cleped,
All by the name of dogs.—SHAKSPEARE.

CHAPTER IV.

IN the year 1746, the Academy of

Sciences gave an account of the strange history of a young child called Nicholas Feny, who when born was not quite nine inches long, and weighed but twelve ounces, and at the age of five was absolutely formed without having attained to a greater height than twenty-two inches; this singularity proved the child's happiness, the King of Poland, Duke of Lorraine, saw and honoured him with his beneficence. From that moment Bebe, which was the name he gave him, never quitted his august benefactor, and he died in his palace. The Count de Tressan, who had been attached to the fortunes of that monarch, sent the history of this singular being to the academy, and it was this history which induced M. Merand, to make researches on the subject, which were read in a public meeting on the 14th of November, 1746, and accompanied by the statue of Bebe in wax, modelled from his own person, with a wig of his own hair, and dressed in his own clothes. The following is an abstract of Count de Tressan's relation, and M. Merand's reflections.

Nicholas Feny was born at Plaisnes, a principality of Salins, in Vosges. His father and mother were of hale constitutions, and of good stature: we have mentioned how little he was at his birth, but did not add how puny he was. He was carried to church on a plate overspread with the tow of flax, and a wooden shoe served him for a cradle: he never could suck his mother; his mouth was too small to take hold of the nipple, so that a goat was pitched upon to suckle him, and he had no other nurse than that animal, which on her part seemed to be very fond of him.

He had the smallpox at six months' old, and the goat's milk was at the same time his only nourishment and his only remedy. At the age of eighteen months he began to speak; at two years he walked almost without help, and it was then that his first shoes, which were eighteen lines long, were made.

The coarse food of the villagers of Vosges, such as pulse, bacon, and potatoes, was that of his infancy, till the age of six years, and during that time he had some very bad fits of sickness, from which he fortunately recovered.

King Stanislaus, the Titus of the age, having heard of this extraordinary child, desired to see him; he was therefore brought to Luneville, and soon after had no other abode than the palace of that beneficent prince, to whom on his part he was singularly attached, though he commonly showed very little sensibility, and it was then he took the name of Bebe, which was given him by that prince. With all the care that was taken of Bebe's education, it was impossible to bring him to any exertions of judgment or reason, the very small measure of knowledge he had been able to acquire having never been susceptible of any notion of religion, nor capable of reasoning on any subject, so that his mental faculties never rose much above those of a well-trained dog. He seemed to love music, and sometimes beat time with some justness; he likewise danced pretty well, but it was only by looking attentively at his master, to direct all his steps and motions according to the signs he received from him. Once in the fields he entered a meadow, where the grass was higher than himself; he thought himself lost in a copse, and cried out for help. He was susceptible of passions, such as desire, anger, and jealousy, and his discourse was without connection, and his ideas confined. In short, he showed that kind of sentiment which arises from circumstances, from objects as they present themselves, and from momentary impressions made on the senses, and the little reason he showed did not seem to rise much above the instinct of some animals.

The Princess of Talmond endeavoured to give him instructions, but notwithstanding all her wit, she could not light up a spark of it in Bebe. The only natural consequence from her familiarity was his being greatly attached to her, and even so jealous, that once seeing the lady fondle a little dog before him, he forced him out of her hands in a violent passion, and threw him out of the window, saying "Why do you love him more than me?"

Till the age of fifteen Bebe had his organs free, and his whole diminutive figure very exactly and agreeably proportioned: he was then twenty-nine inches high. His weak and frail body, however, soon became enervated, and his strength exhausted; on which his backbone was incurvated, his head sunk forward, his legs were enfeebled, one shoulderblade was dislocated, his nose grew large, and losing his cheerfulness, he became valetudinary; but in the four following years he grew four inches taller.

The Count de Tressan, who had attentively noted the progression of nature in Bebe, foresaw that he would die of old age before he was thirty years of age; and in fact he fell after twenty-two into a sort of caducity, and those who took care of him, observed in him a childhood which did not resemble that of his first years, but rather seemed created by decrepitude. The last year of his life he seemed quite spent: he had a difficulty in walking; the external air, unless very hot, incommoded him; he was made to bask in the sun, which seemed to refresh him, but he could scarcely walk a hundred paces without resting. In the month of May, 1764, he had a slight indisposition, succeeded by a cold, accompanied with a fever, which threw him into a kind of lethargy; he however got the better of it at intervals, but without being able to speak. During the last four days of his life, his knowledge was much more perfect, and clearer and better connected ideas than he had during his greatest vigour astonished all those that were about him: his sufferings were long, and he died on the 9th of June 1764, aged nearly twenty-three, at which time he was thirty-three inches in height. The skeleton that was kept of him presents a remarkable singularity; at first sight it appears to be that of a child of four years; but when examined on the whole, and according to proportions, one is astonished to find in it the skeleton of an adult.

Anecdotes of Longevity.

M. NEUMARK, of Ratisbon, has just published a curious treatise on the means of attaining to an advanced age. The examples which he has quoted of persons who have lived to between ninety and a hundred years of age, are from twelve to twenty of every year in that interval. Those of centenaries, and up to a hundred and fifteen years, are more numerous; but the number diminishes of those who have attained the age of from a hundred and sixteen to a hundred and twenty-three years, being not more than from four to nine.—The examples of persons of a greater age than a hundred and twenty-three years, are naturally more rare.—M. Neumark has quoted only one of two hundred, two of two hundred and ninety-seven, and one of three hundred and sixty. The individual who reached the last-mentioned age was called Jean de Temporibus; he was equerry to Charlemagne, and died in Germany in 1128. It is remarkable that there are few people of rank, and few physicians, among the centenaries. Hippocrates and Dufournel (the latter of whom died at Paris, in 1805, aged a hundred and fifteen years) are almost the only ones. Among monarchs, except Frederic the Second, who lived to the age of seventy-six years, few have passed seventy. Among three hundred popes, only seven have reached the age of eighty years. Among philosophers who have became old, may be reckoned Kepler, Bacon, Newton, Euler, Kant, Fontenelle, &c. Among poets, Sophocles, Pindar, Young, Haller, Voltaire, Bodmer, Goethe, &c. The most numerous examples of longevity have been furnished by Russia, Sweden, Norway, Denmark, Hungary, and Great Britain.

DENIS COOROBEE.

Mr. Denis Coorobee died at Gloves, near Athenry, Ireland, in December 1804, aged 117. He retained his faculties to the last; and until two days previous to his death he never remembered to have had any complaint or sickness whatever, toothache only excepted. Three weeks before his death he walked from his house to Galway, and back the same day, which is twenty-six miles. He could, to the last, read the smallest print without the assistance of glasses, which he never accustomed himself to, with as much ease as a boy of sixteen. It has been acknowledged by the most intelligent men of this kingdom, that, for the present age, he was the most experienced farmer, and the brighest genius for the improvement of agriculture; it is upwards of seventy year since he propagated that most useful article to the human species, called the Black Potato. He was married seven times, and when married to the last he was ninety-three years old; by them all he had 48 children, 236 grandchildren, 944 great grandchildren, and 25 great great grandchildren, the oldest of whom is four years old; and his own youngest son, by the last wife, is about eighteen years old.

RUTH WOOD.

Died in 1804, at Philadelphia, at the house of Samuel Wheeler, Esq. in the 100th year of her age, Ruth Wood, a native of that place. She remembered the city when the high forest trees stood in Walnut-street from Fourth-street to the river.

Eccentric Biography.

SAMUEL STRETCH THE MISER.

In November, 1804, there died at Madeley, in Staffordshire, Mr. Samuel Stretch, aged 72, who may with justice be ranked in the catalogue of eccentric misers. He was a native of Market Drayton, in that county, and the early part of his life was spent as a private in the army, in which capacity he experienced some service, in fighting the battles of his country. For a length of time he resided in an obscure dwelling at Madeley, into which, he did not for many years admit either male or female; it was indeed a dwelling of complete wretchedness. It was about fifteen years before that he purchased a load of coals, a part of which were left at the time of his death. His chief employ was to go about to the adjacent towns, carrying letters and small parcels, and doing errands for his neighbours. His person bespoke the most abject penury; he usually appeared in an old slouched hat and tattered garments, scarcely sufficient to cover his nakedness, with a ragged bag hung over his shoulder, in which he mostly carried a little parsley, or some other kind of herb, the produce of his garden: these he generally offered as a present at the different places where he had to do business; and when accepted, he took care to deal them out with a very sparing hand. This show of generosity, together with his eccentric dress and conversation, usually produced him a tenfold return. On searching his tattered satchel after his death, it was found to contain old bones and shoe soles, pieces of paper, &c. which articles he usually collected in his peregrinations. His stock of linen consisted of two old shirts and a pair of sheets; in his hat were found several articles of silver plate, &c. His death was occasioned by a violent cold, brought on by his falling into a ditch in a state of intoxication on his return from Newcastle the Saturday preceding. By his penurious disposition he had amassed a considerable sum of money, (exclusive of a loss of 500l. which he experienced a few years before) a part of which he left to purchase an additional bell for the church at Madeley, and an annual salary for it to be rung every night at nine o'clock during the summer months, and at eight during the winter; a chandelier for the church; a bell for the use of the free school; 5. per annum towards the organist's salary for that place, and a like annual amount for the Drayton organist; a further sum to be applied to the enlarging and repairing the Madeley almshouses, and clothing and educating two poor children, until of a proper age to be put apprentice; and to his relations, TWO SHILLINGS AND SIXPENCE EACH.

THE MUSICAL SHRIMP MAN.

A SHORT time ago Old Jack Norris died suddenly and an inquest was held on the body, before Mr. Stirling, Coroner, at the Black Horse, George-street, St. Giles's. It was reported the deceased was starved to death. The evidence proved, that latterly the deceased, who was nearly seventy years of age, was unable to pursue his occupation of a dealer in shrimps, which, from his peculiar cry, gained him the appellation of the "Musical Shrimp Man;" he shortly since applied for parochial relief, and received a trifling sum from the overseers of St. Giles's, and a pass to his own parish, St. Margaret's, Westminster; but of this he did not avail himself, as he retired to his lodgings in

George-street, where he was found in a few days, dead. Norris was considered the father or veteran chief of the votaries of "low life" in St. Giles's; he was, it is said, down to every thing, and his advice on the subject of "cadging" (begging) was considered of the first order: no man could in finer style than he evade the clauses of the Vagrant Act, and none in his day, when he could work, could make a more profitable harvest of a cadging ramble, in his profession of shrimp-dealer. He had by fighting, and mere dint of beating, driven out of a certain walk all the dealers in that way, and monopolized to himself the business. In this monopoly he always could command a party to defend him and substantiate his pretensions: he was known for the last fifty years at the markets; in fact, the whole of his life was a busy round of cecentric trickery and begging. The Black Horse is the house where Holloway and Haggerty, the murderers of Mr. Steele on Hounslow-heath, were secured. "Old Jack Norris" was present, and was instrumental in the capture of the murderers. The Jury found a verdict of—"*Died by the Visitation of God.*"

Varieties.

IDENTITY EXTRAORDINARY.

THE editor of that cock and bull journal, the *Dumfries Courier*, who outstrips Munchausen in marvels, lately gave the following extraordinary narrative:—

"Of late we have heard rumours of a most extraordinary child which is living at Newton Stewart; rumours so incredible, that we neither ask nor expect our readers to believe them. Nevertheless, the truth of the story was so strongly asserted, and that by different individuals, that we were induced to solicit information on the subject; and the following is the substance of a letter which we received last night from a most respectable quarter:—
'You may safely insert a paragraph regarding the child you write about. The story is simply this: in the year 1817, a woman in the parish of —— became pregnant, and some time before her infant was born, gave as the father a married man of the name of John Wood. The man strongly protested his innocence, and repeatedly said that he would not confess until his name was stamped on its forehead. In a short time the woman was delivered of a boy, and in about ten days thereafter, the letters 'John Wood,' on the right, and 'born 1817,' on the left eye, became plain and legible. These words and figures are on the part of the eye which surrounds the pupil, betwixt the ball and the white of the eye, so that they cannot for a moment be supposed to have been traced by any human hand. The form of the letters is truly beautiful. The mother afterwards married an Irishman, who, with his stepson, has been living in Newton Stewart for sometime past. Most of the gentlemen in the town and neighbourhood have inspected the boy's eyes, who all seem to think there is no imposition in the matter. The child is afflicted with water in the head, and although between five and six years old, it can neither stand nor walk. This is a most singular circumstance, so much so that it is hardly credible. Nevertheless you may rest assured of the ac-

curacy of my information. Dr. Smith examined it yesterday, and I have myself repeatedly seen it, and examined its father.' (At the end of the letter is a drawing of the eyes.)—Here then is a marvellous story with a vengeance; and whether the disease with which the child is afflicted may have biassed the imaginations of its visitors in the same way as we sometimes see castles in the air, we leave others to determine. Just as we had received the above letter, a Mr. Glover, from Newton Stewart, called on us, who, after repeating the same story, said, if we had any doubt of the statement, we might put his name to it."—*Dumfries Courier.*

EXTRAORDINARY RESEMBLANCES.

There are now living and well, in Oldham-road, Manchester, twin brothers, about six years old, whose resemblance to each other in growth, make, feature, voice, and complexion has been so exact, that it was found difficult for any one, the parents excepted, to distinguish one from the other. Their names are Joseph and James ———. Some time since, as James was viewing himself in a glass, he started back as if unconscious of the resemblance, and exclaimed, in a tone of surprise, "See, mammy, there is Joseph's face in the glass looking at me!" It was with difficulty he could be persuaded of his error, or that it was his own features, and not those of his brother Joseph, he had been contemplating. At the present time, one of these twins is in a very slight degree lustier than the other, but the resemblance is such as to excite admiration, and is heightened by both being dressed alike.—*Bolton Express.*

WILD ELEPHANT.

Bombay, July 3, 1822.—Khasgur, a town in the province of Agra, sixty-four miles N. W. from Furruckabad, has for some time been ravaged by a wild elephant with only one tusk, who had taken up his abode in a wet dike near the town, from which he issued whenever he happened to be so disposed, and without fear or mercy devoured men and beasts, villagers and travellers, as they came in his way. The Sahibina Alashan having been moved to compassion by the lamentations of the inhabitants, undertook the deliverance of the town, and resolutely bound up their *kurimi himet* to destroy him. They accordingly provided themselves with twelve good elephants, and under the supposition that the wild elephant would show symptoms of mildness at the sight of a female, they determined to take a female elephant in their train—placing her, however, in front, with an advanced guard under seven bold Burkardaz, well mounted on seven elephants, with a great concourse of people. The Sahabina Alashan then took post in the rear, and gave the word to advance. On arriving at the ditch the wild elephant was discovered, and a shot was immediately fired at him. This did not in the least alarm him; on the contrary it excited his utmost choler, and he turned his face towards the Sahabina Alashan, and began to shake both his ears at them in a manner at once wild and terrific. Upon this the armed Burkardaz on the elephants advanced within 160 yards of the spot in a most courageous style supported by the Sahabina Alashan in the rear. The elephant, wild as he was, very judiciously took alarm at this formidable advance, and endeavoured to retreat. The hunters upon this opened a heavy fire, which drove the animal out of the ditch. The whole body then pursued and crossed the dike, and after a severe contest this formidable animal was slain by a ball entering his left eye. On opening him no less than eighty balls were found in his head. He measured nine and a half cubits high, twelve feet in length, and seven and a half round the neck. He had been a resident of the ditch Khasgur for upwards of four years, and had killed during the time about fifty of the inhabitants.

BIRDS' NESTS.

HAD Providence left the feathered tribe unendued with any particular instinct, the birds of the *torrid zone* would have built their nests in the same unguarded manner as those of Europe ; but in India the lesser species, having a certain prescience of the dangers that surround them, and of their own weakness, suspend their nests at the extreme branches of the trees ; conscious of inhabiting a clime replete with enemies to them and their young ;— snakes that twine up the bodies of the trees, and apes that are perpetually in search of prey ; but, heaven-instructed, they elude the gliding of the one and the activity of the other.—Some form their pensile nest in the shape of a purse, deep and open at top, others with a hole in the side, and others still more cautious, with an entrance at the very bottom, forming their lodge near the summit.

But the Tailor-Bird seems to have greater diffidence than any of the others ; it will not trust its nest even to the extremity of a slender twig, but makes one more advance to safety, by fixing it to the leaf itself. It picks up a *dead* leaf, and, surprising to relate, *sews* it to the side of a living one, its slender bill being its needle, and its thread some fine fibres,—the lining, feathers, gossamer, and down.

The colour of these ingenious flying tailors is a light yellow, its eggs are white, its length is three inches, its weight only three-sixteenths of an ounce ; so that, the materials of the nest, and its own size, are not likely to draw down an habitation that depends on so slight a tenure.

A FEAST.

GEORGE NEVIL, brother to the great Earl of Warwick, at his instalment into his archbishopric of York, in the year 1470, made a feast for the nobility, gentry, and clergy, wherein he spent— 300 quarters of wheat, 300 tuns of ale, 104 tuns of wine, one pipe of spiced wine, eighty fat oxen, six wild bulls, 300 pigs, 10,004 wedders, 300 hogs, 300 calves, 3000 geese, 3000 capons, 100 peacocks, 200 cranes, 200 kids, 2000 chickens, 4000 pigeons, 4000 rabbits, 204 bitterns, 4000 ducks, 400 hernsies, 200 pheasants, 500 partridges, 4000 woodcocks, 400 plovers, 100 curlews, 100 quails, 1000 eggets, 200 roes, 4000 bucks, and does and roe-bucks, 155 hot venison pasties, 1000 dishes of jellies, 4000 cold venison pasties, 2000 hot custards, 4000 ditto cold, 400 tarts,

300 pikes, 300 breams, eight seals, four porpoises.—At this feast the Earl of Warwick was steward, the Earl of Bedford treasurer, the Lord Hastings comptroller; with many noble officers servitors.—1000 cooks, 62 kitcheners, 515 scullions.

The Scrap Book.

CURIOUS WAGER.

In August, 1823, a man undertook to carry thirteen sieve-baskets, piled one upon another on his head, from Dean-street, Westminster, to Perry's potato-warehouse in Covent Garden. The wager was for a sovereign; and the conditions were, that he was to walk through the public streets, and to arrive at the place named with eleven on his head, without resting. He walked with great caution, sometimes in the carriage road, and sometimes on the pavement, followed by numbers of people, who, however, at once encircled and cleared the way for him. His greatest difficulty seemed to be to avoid the lamp irons when upon the pavement, as the upper sieve, which poised the whole, had a continual inclination to the right side. He succeeded in gaining the middle of Southampton-street without losing one sieve, having passed coaches and carts of all descriptions; when here, the upper sieve fell to the ground. He halted for a moment, and poised the remaining sieves, with which he proceeded full into the market, where he cast the whole down, amid the cheers of the populace. Though the weight must have been considerable, the poising the sieves was the greatest difficulty he had to encounter, as they reached the second floor windows. He won his wager; and many gentlemen, who were highly delighted with the novelty of the scene, subscribed to reward his ingenuity and perseverance.

INTERMARRIAGE.

Mr. Hardwood had two daughters by his first wife, the eldest of whom was married to John Coshick: this Coshick had a daughter by his first wife whom old Hardwood married, and by her had a son; therefore John Coshick's second wife could say:

My father is my son, and I'm my mother's mother;
My sister is my daughter, and I'm grandmother to my brother.

A curious circumstance occurred at West Farleigh, Kent, lately. A man who is *deaf* and *dumb* went into a house occupied by two men, named Larkin and Savage, who are both totally *blind*, and stole a loaf of bread. The wife of Savage soon discovered the robbery, and went in pursuit of the thief, accompanied by her husband and his blind companion. They ran a considerable distance, led on by the wife, and at length overtook the robber, with whom they had a desperate scuffle; the blind men were, however, victorious, and succeeded in capturing their antagonist, although the latter, from his strength and eyesight, had decidedly the advantage over his afflicted brethren.

Published by J. LIMBIRD, 355, Strand, (East End of Exeter 'Change); and sold by all Newsmen and Booksellers Printed by A. APPLEGATH, Stamford-street.

THE CABINET OF CURIOSITIES,
OR
Wonders of the World Displayed.

A world of wonders where creation seems
No more the works of Nature but her dreams.—MONTGOMERY.

No. XXIII.]   PRICE TWOPENCE.

FIGHT BETWEEN A TIGER AND A CROCODILE.

FREQUENT rencontres take place between the tiger and the crocodile, in which case both frequently perish. When the tiger deecnds to the river to allay his thirst, the crocodile raises its head above the surface in order to seize him as it does animals on whom it preys. When this happens the tiger instantly strikes his claws into the eyes of his antagonist, the only vulnerable part within reach; the latter, immediately plunging into its element, drags in the tiger likewise, by which means both perish. A singular adventure of this sort was observed by the crew of a Dutch East India ship, who certified the truth of it before the Judges of the Admiralty at Amsterdam. This ship having cast anchor in the river Ganges, sent out a boat with eight mariners to catch fish: as they were casting their nets one of the men got out of the boat and climbed up the bank, either led by a desire to view the country, or some other design, but he had not proceeded above twenty paces when he perceived a crocodile very near him. Surprised and terrified at this bitter enemy of the human race, which he saw getting up the bank towards him, he was about to retreat, but at that very instant, he beheld a tremendous tiger rush out of an adjacent forest, running with the utmost speed towards him. Either actuated by fear, or led by prudence, he threw himself aside, and the tiger having taken his leap with too precipitate a force flew directly over him, and fell into the river, where the crocodile seized on his new adversary, and with impetuosity drew him to the middle of the stream, where they killed each other. Of this terrific scene our engraving presents a good view.

SNIPE.

The following is a description of a very beautiful snipe, shot Dec. 13, 1791, near Dereham, Norfolk, by Mr. Collison, of that town:—"This bird is unique in the peculiar elegance of its plumage, which appears to a common observer orange and white. It corresponds in its principal particulars with the common snipe of Pennant, the *scolopose gallenago* of Linnæus, its weight being nearly four ounces, the length to the end of the tail twelve inches; its bill is three inches long, of a dusky colour at the base, and of a dark cinereous green at the end; the head is a dull white, and divided lengthwise, with three light coloured orange lines, one passing over the middle of the head, and one over each eye; the chin is cream-coloured; the neck and breast cream-coloured and yellow, or rather varied with light orange and white undulated. The scapulars are beautifully striped lengthwise with light orange spots; the quill feathers white; the back an intermixture of deep orange and white, with a few feathers spotted with brown; the belly white; coverts of the tail orange and white; near its bottom a broad bar of orange, like the common snipe, but not quite so deep, and ends in a light orange and white; the legs like the common snipe."

A GIFTED FAMILY.

There at present resides near Versailles, a retired subaltern officer, who accompanied Napoleon in most of his wars, who is the father of nine children, and whose nine children, born in nine different countries, speak nearly as many different languages or idioms. His wife was an Italian, whom he married in Italy on the first invasion of that country by the French. His first child (Marie) was born at Milan, and speaks Italian, the language of her mother. His second (Guillaume) saw the light in Switzerland. His third, called Ali, came into the world in Egypt, and speaks on occasion a kind of Coptic. His fourth child was born at Boulogne-sur-Mer, when Bonaparte threatened a descent on England from that port. His fifth child was born in Germany, and speaks German. His sixth is a Neapolitan, and consequently is called Genaro (or Januarius.) His seventh is a little Spaniard, called Diego, who has not forgotten the language of his infancy. His eighth is a little Prussian, of the name of Frederick; and his ninth, Mademoiselle Nicholina, saw the light in Elba. The eldest of these children is said to be twenty-eight, the youngest eight. The mother is dead. These nine children still reside under the paternal roof, and render the house something like the tower of Babel.

ON VAMPIRES AND VAMPIRISM.

VOLTAIRE was astonished that, in the eighteenth century, people should believe in vampires; and that the doctors of the Sorbonne should give their *imprimatur* to a dissertation on these unpleasant personages. The philosopher of Ferney would scarcely have experienced less surprise had he lived to see them introduced into popular novels, represented as figuring at the drawing-rooms, shining in fashionable assemblies, favourites with the ladies, and this not alone in barbarous London, but forming the delight and admiration of elegant audiences in the superlatively polished capital of his own country. Indeed, their success among our refined and delicately-nerved neighbours has infinitely surpassed what they have met with among ourselves. We are not aware that many of our dramatists have hitherto attempted to draw tears from the pathetic amours of these interesting bloodsuckers — that " source of sympathetic tears has been only sparingly unlocked"— and except the strange history of the " leaden-eyed" vampire Lord Ruthven, which the circumstances attending its composition principally contributed to force into the hands of all the lovers of the marvellous, we are not aware that the " Broucolaca" has hitherto become a favourite in the English closet. But at Paris he has been received with rapturous applause at almost all the spectacles, from the Odeon to the Porte St. Martin; all the presses of the Palais Royal have for the last few years been employed in celebrating, and describing, and speculating on him and his adventures, and in putting forth perpetual *nouveautés* on all the cognate topics—" Infernal Dictionaries" — " Demoniana" — " Ombres Sanglantes"—" Diable peint par lui-même," &c. &c. Where are the descendants of the Encyclopedists and the worshippers of the goddess Reason, when Parisian readers and audiences are running mad after " *loups-garoux*" and " *apparitions nocturnes,*" " *cadavres mobiles,*" &c., all " *puisées dans les sources réeles.*" Thirty years ago, what bookseller in the Palais Royal would have risked the conflagration of his whole stock by exposing for sale any of these superstitious treasures drawn from sacred legends and monkish impositions? The revulsion has indeed been somewhat sudden, and does not tend to remove prevalent impressions on the instability of Parisian sentiments and opinions. From believing in the eternal sleep of death, and persecuting every one who hinted a suspicion unfavourable to the absolute supremacy of matter, it is rather a rapid bound to the study of demonolatry, and a lively interest in apparitions and spectres of all sorts.

If *we* are disposed to partake any interest in these subjects, it may, perhaps, be forgiven to *us* who have never professed ourselves votaries of Diderot and Bayle. We call our readers to witness, we have never said a syllable derogatory to the ghost of Mrs. Veal, or General Clavering, or any other respectable individual of spiritual memory. We have, therefore, a fair right, without inconsistency of fickleness, to say a few words on the subject of that most appalling of the whole *corps démoniaque*, the Vampire. The belief in the existence of vampires is one of the most extraordinary and most revolting superstitions which ever disturbed the brains of any semi-barbarous people. It is the most frightful embodying of the principle of evil, the most terrific incarnation of the bad demon, which ignorance and fanaticism ever suggested to the weak and the deluded. It displays superstition in its grossest and most unrelieved horrors. Other creatures of fanatical creation have a mixture of good and bad in their composition — their mischief is sometimes distinguished by sportiveness and mingled with good humour — they are malicious, but not malignant — and the lightness and triviality of their spite against human nature is often united with an airiness of movement and a spirituality of character which render them amusing, and often highly poetical.— Puck, Will-with-the-wisp, the Bogles, the Ogres, the Nixies, and *id genus omne*, if they are to be considered as emanations of the Evil principle, are at least inspired with much of his drollery, and only a small portion of his gall and malignity;—the Gnomes are sulky and splenetic persons, but there is a certain impotence about them which prevents their becoming very terrific;—the Lamiæ and the Larvæ of the ancients were, indeed, horrid creations—but the latter were mere shadows, which takes off much of their monstrosity:—but the Vampire is a corporeal creature of blood and unquenchable blood-thirst—a ravenous corpse, who rises in body and soul from his grave for the sole purpose of glutting his sanguinary appetite with the life-blood of those whose blood stagnates in his own veins. He is endowed with an incorruptible frame, to prey on the lives of his kindred and his friends—he reappears among them from the world of the tomb, not to tell its secrets of joy or of woe, not to invite or to warn by the testimony of his experience, but to appal and assassinate those who were dearest to him on earth — and this, not for the gratification of revenge or any *human* feeling, which, however depraved, might find something common with it in human nature, but to banquet a monstrous thirst acquired in the tomb, and which, though he walks in human form and human lineaments, has swallowed up every human motive in its brutal ferocity. The corporeal grossness, the substantiality " palpable to feelings as to sight," of this monster of superstition, renders it singularly terrific, and lays hold on the mind with a sense of shuddering and sanguinary horror which belongs to few of the aërial demons of imagination, however ghastly or malignant. Fancy, (for such tricks will flit across the fancy of the least superstitious)—fancy your friend with whom you are walking arm-in-arm, or your mistress on whose bosom your head reposes, a spirit—a Gnome or an Undine —or any mere spirit—the idea is startling; if pursued it may lead an active imagination, to a disagreeable sense of the possibility of happiness being an imposition, and pleasure " an unreal mockery,"—but it is not overpoweringly painful;—but let the idea of your companion or your mistress being a Vampire, cross the brain—the blood would run chill, and every sense be oppressed by the bare supposition, childish and absurd as it would be felt to be—

——" 'twould shake the disposition
With thoughts beyond the reaches of our
  souls."

We remember once spending two days at Brighton at the same hotel with a renowned old money-lender. The man was lean and stooping,—dressed in rusty black —with grey hairs that inspired no respect—a dull large grey eye "without *speculation*," (unless, perhaps, at the look of a post-obit)—hollow cheeks, a vulture nose, and a blotchy truculent sort of complexion, which, with long clawy hands, made up a character of most uninviting appearance. He was quite alone— prowled about a great deal with a quiet creeping step—spoke little—read the papers—and never took above two meals in a day, which, indeed, he seemed to order more for form than any thing else, as his daily consumption certainly could not extend to two ounces. There was altogether something repulsive to sympathy about this old Shylock; and whether or not from any involuntary associations connected with his known profession (which certainly of itself might entitle him to succeed to the distinction of the monks, whom Voltaire called the modern vampires), or more, as we believe, from his *red hollow* cheeks, *adunque* nose, and small appetite for *butchers' meat*, we wrote this man down in our imagination a Vampire. We involuntarily avoided meeting him, and felt much disposed to think that his nightly abode was in the burying-ground of St. James's, or St. Martin's, and that he was only at Brighton on a foraging excursion; not in quest of title-deeds and annuity-bonds, but of the richer dainties which the assemblage of youth of both sexes might afford to a being of his presumed propensities. Our acquaintance with Vampires at that period was but slight—had we then known all we have since learnt of them, we should infallibly have given information at the Pavilion of the suspicious *vampyrio-fœnerator*, and have taken a place in the Dart with all possible speed. Not long after this circumstance, we (yes *we*, the magnificent *we*) were at a ball in London, and, with a modest resignation of our collective dignity, were forming not a whole quadrille, but, *one* in a quadrille together with a young lady of a mind and person both exquisitely poetical. She complained of being fatigued, saying, as she sat down on a sofa, "I was up half last night."—" Were you dancing?" was the reply. "No! I was reading Calmet on Vampires with my brother!!"—Calmet on Vampires, in such a scene of brilliancy, and beauty, and innocent and splendid enjoyment! Calmet on Vampires perused by the midnight lamp by those pure and lovely eyes of the blue of sixteen summers! What a contrast of images!—The book was bought and read.

(*To be continued.*)

SUBTERRANEOUS VAULTS AT MAESTRICHT.

By Colonel Bory de Saint-Vincent.

PETERSBURG, or the Hill of St. Peter, is situated between the Jaar and the Meuse, and extends along the distance of nearly a league. The earth which is contained in the cavities in the interior of the hill, furnishes materials for building; but principally for manure, and for this double purpose it has been excavated from the most remote ages of antiquity. In the symmetrical galleries of Petersburg the Roman pickaxe has imprinted a kind of monumental character, and the feudal spade has left its gothic traces. Workmen have, from time immemorial, been employed in extracting the bowels of the earth to fertilize its surface. For ages the pickaxe and wheelbarrow have worked passages in every direction, and the traveller in this subterraneous labyrinth is happy, if with the aid of his torches, he can return the way he entered. Streets, squares, and cross-roads appear on every side; in short, the vaults of Petersburg present the appearance of a town, in which there are only wanting houses, inhabitants, theatres, carriages, and gas lamps. Mr. Bory de Saint-Vincent draws the following picture of this gloomy region:—" If any thing," he says, " can add to the horror of the perfect darkness, it is the total silence which reigns in these dismal vaults. The voice of man is scarcely sufficient to disturb it; sound is, as it were, deadened by the thickness of the gloom. Echo itself, which the bewildered traveller may interrogate in the desert, dwells not in these silent cavities."

It may naturally be conjectured, that superstition has peopled these subterraneous vaults with demons and hobgoblins. Tradition has even allotted a hell and a paradise to the cavities of Petersburg. The huge pieces of coal, which an equal temperature has protected from the ravages of time, imagination has converted into monsters with claws, long tails, and horns. In various places, names, inscriptions, and remote dates record the history of the origin of the excavations, and relate numerous adventures and unfortunate deaths, of which Petersburg has been the theatre. In one part of the vaults a workman, whose torch became extinguished, perished amidst the pangs of hunger and the horrors of darkness; his hat and some fragments of his clothes still remain, to attest his melancholy fate. In another part the walls present the history of four friars, who purposed to erect a chapel at the remotest point of these cavities. The thread by which they were to trace back their way to the opening of the vaults, broke, the unfortunate men perished, and their bodies were subsequently found at the distance of a few paces from each other. However, catastrophes of this terrible kind presented fewer horrors to the conscripts of the Lower Meuse than the pursuits of the gendarmerie, and, according to the testimony of the author, many preferred these dismal retreats to the laurels of Wagram and Jena.

The interior of the Hill of St. Peter, has given rise to anecdotes worth collecting: the Austrians, having possession of the Fort of Petersburg, discovered a secret communication with the vaults of the hill, of which the French troops guarded some of the entries. With torch in hand and fixed bayonets, the Austrians attempted to surprise the French, but the latter, warned by the subterraneous lights, rushed upon the enemy, who were dazzled by their own torches, and a conflict ensued, which resembled a combat of the infernal deities.

The following story is of a less serious nature. Maestricht had fallen into the power of the French, and long continued a most formidable garrison. A portion of the Austrian population fled to the vaults beneath the Hill of St. Peter. They took their cattle with them, and in the subterraneous cavities they hastily constructed rooms and stables. The French were unable to account for the miraculous disappearance of a portion of the conquered inhabitants, when a pig, which had escaped from its sty, rushed along the subterraneous galleries, squeaking tremendously. It was heard by the French sentinels, and this circumstance led them to suspect the retreat of the Austrians. They adopted means to make the pig squeak still louder, in the hope of attracting the fugitives, when to the great surprise of the French soldiers, several pigs rushed out to answer the summons of the imprudent deserter. In ancient times the Roman capitol was saved by geese, and on this occasion a pig caused the destruction of the little republic of Petersburg. The Austrians were routed from their retreat, and their cattle and pigs, as may well be supposed, were speedily roasted and devoured.

SIMULATED DEATH.

A VERY extraordinary case of this nature occurred a few weeks ago, at Hammersmith, in the person of Harriet Smith, a young woman of interesting appearance, who served as housemaid in the family of Robert Emmerson, Esq., of Oxford-street. This girl, it seems, had, about three years ago, been thrown from the top of a stage-coach, and received many severe contusions both internal and external, which seriously affected her strength, and brought on a gradual decay of nature. Being incapable of performing her customary business, she relinquished her situation, and obtained an asylum beneath the roof of a female relative at Hammersmith. Here, notwithstanding her total cessation from all corporeal labour, her complaint still advanced; she every day grew weaker and was frequently subject to long faintings. Through the kind attention of some ladies with whom she had formerly lived, every aid that eminent professional advice could afford was rendered to her, with a constant supply of such necessaries and comforts as her helpless situation demanded. On Thursday week she had been taken out for an airing, and returned home with renewed strength, and in rather better spirits than usual. After taking some refreshments, she complained of excessive inclination to sleep, and was therefore placed in bed, betwixt the hours of six and seven in the afternoon. In apparent enjoyment of profound repose, she remained until a very far advanced hour the following day, when, on attempting to arouse her, she was found to be quite cold; her lips were colourless, and her eyes glazed; all pulsation had ceased; every thing bore testimony to the power of the fell destroyer death. The last offices to her remains, which are directed by decency, were then performed; the corpse was attired in the usual grave-clothes, and laid on a bed, where it remained from Friday noon until Sunday morning, the afternoon of which day was fixed for the interment. Happily, however, the horrible event was frustrated. On the removal of the body from the bed to the coffin, one of the persons engaged, inadvertently, placed her hands on the bosom, and fancying its touch imparted a sensation far more warm than the damp and clayey feel of a corpse she naturally expressed her opinion to those who were assisting in the melancholy office; a closer examination convinced them that they were about to commit to the cold grave a living subject. The cheeks and the lips were still livid and colourless; the eye exhibited no sensation of vision, but the vital principle reigned about the region of the heart, and on the application of a glass breathing was once more perceptible. The physician who had attended during her illness was instantly sent for; on his arrival, signs of returning animation were so manifest, that he concluded bleeding and the application of warm bricks would be productive of immediate restoration. He therefore opened a vein, first in one arm, and then the other, but without effect; every other effort proved equally unavailing, until about five o'clock in the evening, when a rapid change took place; the throbbing of the heart and the pulse became audible, the cheeks and lips partially regained their crimson, respiration returned with ease and vigour, and in a few moments all the animal powers assumed their functions. During the interesting interval, the various insignia of death were removed, in order that she should not be terrified by their appearance when perception returned, but being questioned as to her health in the customary manner, she manifested no knowledge of what her situation had been, merely saying, that she felt cold and weak, with an extraordinary oppression and a sensation of fear, not unlike that which is experienced in dreams when afflicted with the complaint commonly called nightmare. She has since improved not only in health but in spirits.

EFFECTS OF LIGHTNING ON THREE SHIPS IN THE EAST INDIES.

"On August 1, 1750, in 1° 56' north latitude, at two and a half A. M. a violent clap of thunder burst, as was judged by the report, about midway between the head of the mast and the body of the ship, or it might be higher, and in descending might cause that appearance, and just over it. This made the ship tremble and shake as if she was going to burst into pieces, and great pieces and splinters of the mast had fallen upon different places of the ship; but it was so very dark we could not see from which of the masts they were forced. This was followed by a second clap, much more terrifying than the former.

"At daylight we found that the fore-mast and mizzen-mast had escaped, and the main-mast had suffered as follows: all the maintop-gallant-mast (which is the uppermost piece of the mast) from the rigging at the top of it, to the cap at the head of the maintop-mast, was entirely carried away; part falling overboard, and part into the ship in different places. The maintop-mast had great pieces carried from it, from the hunes down to the cap at the head of the main-mast, so that it could but just stand, being hardly strong enough to bear its own weight and that of its rigging. The main-mast being composed of three pieces towards the top of it; those of the sides being of oak (called the cheeks) were not hurt! but the middlemost part, being of fir, was shivered in several places,' and pieces were carried out of it six or seven inches in diameter, and from ten to twelve feet long, and this in a circular descending manner from the parrel of the main-yard down to the upper-deck of the ship; the pieces being taken out crooked, or circular, or straight, according as the grain of the wood ran. It must be remarked, that these claps were not one single explosion, but successive explosions, about the dimensions, as near as we could guess, of small shells, and continued some time cracking after each other; and as the lightning is observed to run not in a straight line, but zig-zag, so these different explosions might be differently placed in the air; that when they came to take fire and burst, they might take the pieces out of the different sides of the mast, as above related.

INUNDATION IN WORCESTERSHIRE.

In April 1792, the inhabitants of Bromsgrove, in Worcestershire, were one day alarmed by one of the most sudden and violent inundations ever known. Between three and four o'clock, during a storm accompanied with loud and continued claps of thunder, and the most vivid lightning, a waterspout fell upon that part of the Lickey which is nearest the town. The pouring down of the cataract was heard to a great distance, and the body of water, taking a direction towards Bromsgrove, soon swept every thing before it, laid down the hedges, washed quantities of grain from barns and malt-houses, destroyed tan-yards, and so strong was the current, that it floated through the town a waggon loaded with skins. The inhabitants of the place had no time to take the necessary precautions; almost in an instant the cellars and under kitchens were filled to the top, and every thing in them overturned. In a few minutes the water entered at the parlour windows, covered the counters of shops, and in the principal street it rose and continued upwards of five feet perpendicular from the pavement. The horses in some of the inn stables stood up to their tails in water. Pigs, washed from their stys, were swimming through the passages of the houses situated between the brook and the principal street; down which quantities of furniture, brewing utensils, and clothing, shop articles, grain, garden-pales, gates, wheelbarrows, pigs, dogs, timber, &c. were carried in one mass by the impetuous torrent. Many of the inhabitants, who happened to be at their neighbours, could not that evening return home. A house on the borders of the Lickey was thrown down by the force of the water; but the damage sustained by shopkeepers (and particularly the hucksters) was very great. The hedges and other fences to fields and gardens on this side of the town, were entirely demolished; a horse and a number of sheep and pigs were drowned, and are sorry to say, that some young children were also missing.

This tremendous fall of water happened near the eleven milestone, on the edge of the Lickey: it has beat the ground there (which is chiefly gravel) into small pits. At Bromsgrove, and the upper part of the Lickey, nothing more than a common fall of rain was experienced.

HUMAN VICTIMS.

The tribe of Brahmins, called Caradec, formerly had a horrid custom of yearly sacrificing a young Brahmin of a different sect to their household god, Sukhtee, who delights in human blood, and is represented with three fiery eyes covered with red flowers, in one hand holding a sword, and in the other a bottle. The prayers of his votaries are directed to him only during the first nine days of the Dusserah feast; and on the evening of the tenth day a feast is prepared, to which the whole family are invited, and an intoxicating drug is continued to be mixed with the victuals of the unsuspecting stranger, whom the master of the house has for several months, or perhaps years, treated with the greatest attention and kindness, and even, to lull him into a fatal security, given him his daughter in marriage. As soon as the effects of the poisonous and intoxicating drug appear, the master of the house, unattended, takes the death-devoted victim into the temple, leads him three times round the idol, and when he prostrates himself, takes the opportunity of cutting his throat, and with the greatest care collects the flowing blood into a small bowl, which he first applies to the lips of his ferocious god, and then sprinkles it over the dead body, which is put into a hole dug for its reception, at the foot of the idol.

After the perpetration of this cruel action, the innocent Brahmin returns to his family, and spends the night in mirth and revelry; his mind perfectly satisfied, that for the praiseworthy action, the favour of his blood-delighting deity will remain upon him for the space of twelve years. On the morning of the following day the corpse is taken from the hole into which it had been thrown, and then the idol is deposited until next Dusserah, and until the sacrifice of another victim.

This horrible custom, however, has been greatly discontinued of late years, from the following circumstance, which happened at Poonah during the time of the Paishwah Ballagee Bagee Row.

A young and handsome Carnatick Brahmin, fatigued with travel, and oppressed with the scorching heat of the sun, sat himself down in the veranda of a rich Brahmin (of the Caradee sect), who, in a short time passing that way, and perceiving that the young man was a stranger, kindly invited him into his house, to remain until he perfectly recovered from the fatigues of his journey. The young and unsuspecting Brahmin readily accepted the kind invitation, and was for several days treated with so much attention and kindness, that he showed no inclination to depart, especially since he had seen the Brahmin's beautiful daughter, for whom he conceived a most violent attachment, and before a month elapsed he asked and obtained her in marriage. They lived hapily together until the time of the Dusserah, when the deceitful old Brahmin, as he had all along intended, determined to sacrifice his son-in-law to the household god of his caste; accordingly, on the tenth day of the feast, he succeeded in mixing a poisonous and intoxicating drug in his victuals, not however without being perceived by his daughter, who was passionately fond of her husband. She contrived, without being observed, to exchange his dish with that of her brother, who, in a short time, became intoxicated and senseless. The unhappy father seeing the helpless state of his son, and despairing of his recovery, carried him to the temple, put him to death with his own hands, and made an offering of his blood to the idol Sukhtee. This being perceived by the young Brahmin, he asked his wife the reason of an action so shocking and so unnatural, and was informed by her of the particulars of the whole affair, and of his recent danger. He, alarmed for his own safety, and desirous that justice should be inflicted on the cruel Brahmin, contrived to make his escape, and immediately repairing to the Paishwah, fell at his feet and related the whole affair.

Orders were instantly given to seize every Caradee Brahmin in the city of Poonah, and particularly the infamous perpetrator of the horrid deed, who was immediately put to death, together with several hundred Brahmins, who were convicted of similiar practices. All of the same sect were expelled the city, and strict injunctions laid upon the inhabitants to have with them as little connection as possible for the future.

By this well-timed severity, the Paishwah effectually prevented the repetition of similar crimes; and the Caradee Brahmins are now contented with sacrificing a buffalo or a sheep, instead of a human victim.—*Asiatic Journal.*

THE VAMPIRE OF THE OCEAN.

The following copy of a letter, from the president of the New York Lyceum of Natural History to the members, dated New York, September 11, 1823, gives an account of a singular sea animal.

"On the 9th day of September, 1823, returned from a cruise off Delaware Bay, the fishing smack *Una.* She had sailed about three weeks before from New York, for the express purpose of catching an enormous fish, which had been reported to frequent the ocean, a few leagues beyond Cape Henlopen. The adventurers in this bold enterprise have been successful. They have brought, for the enlargement of science and the gratification of curiosity, an uncommon inhabitant of the deep, which has never been seen on the land before.

"The creature is one of the huge individuals of the family of Raja; or perhaps may be erected, from his novelty and peculiarity, into a new genus, between that, the Squalas, and the Acipenser. Its strength was such, that after the body had been penetrated by two strong and well formed gigs of the best tempered iron, the shank of one of them was broken off, and the other singularly bent. The boat containing the three intrepid men, John Patchen, Theophilus Beebe, and William Porter, was connected, after the deadly instrument had taken hold, with the wounded inhabitant of the deep by a strong warp or line. The celerity with which the fish swam could only be compared to that of the harpooned whale, dragging the boat after it with such speed, as to cause a wave to rise on each side of the furrow in which he moved several feet higher than the boat itself.

"The weight of the fish after death was such, that three pair of oxen, one horse, and twenty-two men, all pulling together, with the surge of the Atlantic wave to help, could not convey it far to the dry beach. It was estimated from this, and probable estimate, to equal four tons and a half, or perhaps five tons.

"The size was enormous; for the distance from the extremity of one wing or pectoral fin to the other, expanded like the wing of an eagle, measures eighteen feet;

over the extremity of the back, and on the right line of the belly, sixteen feet; the distance from the snout to the end of the tail, fourteen feet; length of the tail, four feet; width of the mouth, two feet nine inches.

"The operation of combat and killing lasted nine hours. It was an heroic achievement, and was witnessed by crowds of citizens, on the shores of New Jersey and Delaware, and by the persons on board the flotilla of vessels in the bay and offing.

"During the scuffle, the wings, side flaps, or vast alated fins of the monster, lashed the sea with such vehemence, that the spray rose to the height of thirty feet, and rained round to the distance of fifty feet. It was a tremendous encounter. On shore, all was awe and expectation.

"Mr. Patchen, whose taste and zeal in zoology are well known, has attended very much to the manners of *the Vampire* of the ocean; to the preservation of the skin and external parts; to the osseology and skeleton, the internal organizations; and, in short, to every circumstance that was practicable during such a hazardous business, and the tempestuous weather which distressed them almost from the beginning to the end of their voyage.

"I merely mention, before I lay down my pen, that this animal is viviparous, and of course connects fishes with mammiferous animals; and that the respiratory motion, generative and sensitive organs, present an extraordinary amount of rare and interesting particulars. Incomprehensible as well as wonderful are thy works, O Creator! in consummate sagacity thou hast executed them all!

"This is but an outline: I intend to finish this sketch; and prepare it as well as I can for the Society's formal notice.

"While I express full approbation of our friends, whom neither difficulty nor danger could discourage, I utter a further sentiment, that they may be well paid by their intended exhibition.
"SAMUEL L. MITCHILL."

Hoaxes and Impostures.
No. XVII.
AQUATIC HOAX.

In December 1783, when the air-balloons were the object of public attention, there appeared in the *Journal de Paris*, a letter from a watchmaker, who, without subscribing his name, offered to traverse the river Seine, between the Pont Neuf and the Pont Royal so quickly, that a fast trotting horse, which was to set off at the same time, should not reach the opposite extremity before him. To make this experiment, he asked for his reward, two hundred louis, when he reached the appointed spot; and which were merely to pay his travelling expenses to, and lost time at Paris. He appointed the first of January, if the river were not frozen, for the experiment. The town was immediately agitated; subscriptions filled rapidly, and at the court and in the city the only subject of conversation was the watchmaker who was able to walk on the water faster than a horse could trot. As some, however, appeared to doubt its practicability, he satisfied the inquirers by describing his apparatus. This consisted of a pair of elastic wooden shoes, joined by a thick bar. Each *sabot*, or shoe, was to be one foot long and seven inches high, on an equal breadth; and if necessary, he was to hold in each hand a bladder fully blown. He assured the public he could repeat the miracle fifty times in an hour. The city of Paris began to erect scaffolds for the convenience of the subscribers; but before the appointed time the hoaxer, M. Combles, confessed that he had done this only to try the credulity of the Parisians; but the humorist had nearly endangered his liberty by the joke; for he had not only imposed on several distinguished persons, but a society at Versailles had subscribed a thousand livres, and which society was formed by Monsieur (Louis XVIII.) who was too grave a prince to suffer with impunity any personal ridicule. M. Combles applied to the lieutenant of the police, who solicited his majesty's pardon. The king laughed, and amused himself at the expense of Monsieur and the count; and it was thought best to conclude this affair by informing the public, that the watchmaker was insane, and that he was neither desirous nor capable of performing his engagement.

Eccentric Biography.

THE HERMITESS OF SALEM.

The following account of a singular character, residing in the neighbourhood of Salem, in Duchess County, in the State of New York, in 1804, is from the *Political Barometer,* printed at Poughkeepsie:

Sarah Bishop (for this was the name of this hermitess) is a person of about fifty years of age. About thirty years ago, she was a lady of considerable beauty, with a competent share of mental endowments, and education; she was possessed of a handsome fortune, but she was of a tender and delicate constitution, and enjoyed but a low degree of health, and could be hardly comfortable without constant recourse to medicine and careful attendance; and was often heard to say, that she had no dread of any animal on earth but man. Disgusted with them, and consequently with the world, about twenty-three years ago she withdrew herself from all human society, and in the bloom of life resorted to the mountains, which divide Salem from North Salem: where she has spent her days to the present time, in a cave, or rather cleft of the rock, withdrawn from the society of every living creature. Yesterday, in company with the two Capt. Smiths of this town, I went into the mountains to visit this surprising hermitage; a just portrait of which is contained in the following lines:—

" As you pass the southern and most elevated ridge of the mountain, and begin to descend the southern steep, you meet with a perpendicular descent of a rock of about ten feet, in the front of which is this cave. At the foot of this rock is a gentle descent of rich and fertile ground, extending about ten rods, when it instantly forms a frightful precipice, descending about half a mile to the pond, known by the name of Long Pond.

" On the right and left of this fertile ground, the mountain rises in cliffs, and almost encloses it, being a square of about one half acre. In the front of the rock on the north, where the cave is, and level with the ground, there appears to be a large frustrum of the rock, of a double fathom size, thrown out of the rock by some unknown convulsion of nature, and lies in front of the cavity from whence it was rent, partly enclosing the mouth, and forming a room of the same dimensions with the frustrum itself; the rock is left entire above, and forms the roof of this humble mansion.

"This cavity is the habitation of this hermitess, in which she has spent twenty-three of her best years, self-excluded from all human society. She keeps no domesticated animal, not even a fowl, a cat, or a dog. Her little plantation consisting of one half acre, is cleared of its wood, and reduced to grass; but she makes little use of it, excepting that she has raised a few peach trees on it, and she plants yearly a few hills of beans, cucumbers, and potatoes. The whole plat is surrounded with a luxuriant growth of grape vines, which overspread all the surrounding wood, and produce grapes in the greatest abundance. On the opposite side of this little tenement, or cave, is a fine fountain of excellent water, which issues from the side of the mountain, and loses itself in this little place.

"At this fountain we found the wonderful woman, whose appearance it is a little difficult to describe; indeed, like nature in its first state, she was without form; that is, she appeared in no form or position I had ever seen before; her dress appeared little else but one confused and shapeless mass of rags, patched together without any order, which obscured any human shape, excepting her head, which was clothed with a luxuriancy of lank grey hair, depending on every side, just as nature and time had formed it, wholly devoid of any artificial covering or ornament.

"When she had discovered our approach, she exhibited the appearance of any other wild and timid animal. She started, looked wild, hastened with the utmost precipitation to her cave, which she entered, and barricadoed the entrance with old shells which she pulled from the decayed trees. To this humble mansion we approached, and after some conversation with her, we obtained liberty to remove the pallisadoes, and look in; for we were not able to enter, the room being only sufficient to accommodate a single person. We conversed with her for some considerable time, found her to be of a sound mind, a religious turn of thought, and to be entirely happy and contented with her situation: of this she has given to others repeated demonstration, who have in vain solicited her to quit this dreary abode. We saw no utensil, either for labour or cookery, excepting an old pewter basin, and a gourd-shell; no bed but the solid rock, unless it were a few old rags, scattered here and there upon it; no bedclothes of any kind; nor the least appearance of any sort of food, and no fire.

"She had, indeed, a place in one corner of her cell, where she kindles a fire at times; but it does not appear that any fire has been kindled there this spring. To confirm this opinion, a gentleman says that he passed her cell five or six days after the great fall of snow in the beginning of March last, that she had no fire then, and had not been out of her cave since the snow had fallen. How she subsists during the severe seasons is yet a mystery. She says she eats but little flesh of any kind; and it is difficult to imagine how she is supported through the winter season. In the summer she subsists on the berries, nuts, and roots, which the mountains afford. It may be, that she secrets her winter store in some other fissure in the rock, more convenient for that purpose than the cell she inhabits.

"She keeps a Bible with her, and says she takes much satisfaction, and spends much time in reading in it, and meditating therein."

Varieties.

AN INDIAN FOREST.

"An Indian Forest," says Mr. Forbes "is a scene the most picturesque that can be imagined; the trees seem perfectly animated; the fantastic monkies give life to the stronger branches; and the weaker sprays wave over your head, charged with vocal and various plumed inhabitants. It is an error to say, that nature hath denied melody to the birds of hot climates, and formed them only to please the eye with their gaudy plumage. Ceylon abounds with birds equal in song to those of Europe, which warble among the leaves of trees, grotesque in their appearance, and often loaded with the most delicious and salubrious fruit. Birds of the richest colours cross the glades, and troops of peacocks complete the charms of the scene, spreading their plumes to a sun that has ample power to do them justice. The landscape in many parts of India corresponds with the beauties of the animate creation. The mountains are lofty, steep, and broken; but clothed with forests, enlivened with cataracts, of a grandeur and figure unknown to this part of the globe."

MINUTE WONDERS OF NATURE.

Human hair varies in thickness, from the 250th to the 600th part of an inch. The fibre of the coarsest wool is about the 500th part of an inch in diameter, and that of the finest only the 1,500th part. The silk line, as spun by the worm, is about the 5,300th part of an inch thick; but a spider's line is perhaps six times finer, or only the 30,000th part of an inch in diameter, insomuch, that a single pound of this attenuated, yet perfect substance, would be sufficient to encompass our globe.

A single grain of musk has been known to perfume a room for the space of twenty years. At the lowest computation, the musk had been subdivided into 320 quadrillions of particles, each of them capable of affecting the olfactory organs. The diffusion of odorous effluvia may also be conceived from the fact, that a lump of *assafœtida*, exposed to the open air, lost only a grain in seven weeks. Again, since dogs hunt by the scent alone, the effluvia emitted from the several species of animals, and from different individuals of the same race, must be essentially distinct, and being discerned over large spaces, must be subdivided beyond our conception or powers of numbers.

The human skin is perforated by a thousand holes in the space of a square inch. If, therefore, we estimate the surface of the body of a middle-sized man to be sixteen square feet, it must contain not fewer than 2,304,000 pores. These pores are the mouths of so many excretory vessels, which perform the important function in the animal economy of *insensible perspiration*.

If a candle be lighted, it will then be visible above two miles round; and consequently were it placed two miles above the surface of the earth, it would fill with luminous particles a sphere whose diameter is four miles, and before it had lost any sensible part of its weight.*

A quantity of vitriol, being dissolved and mixed with 9,000 times as much water, will tinge the whole; consequently it will be divided into as many parts as there are visible portions of matter in that water.

The Scrap Book.

PIG EXTRAORDINARY.

Dr. Hickman, of Ludlow, Shropshire, has in his museum a pig, the anatomical structure of which is as extraordinary as it is unaccountable. The minute anatomy is not given; but the external appearances are—one head, two eyes, four ears, eight legs, two tails. The internal structure—one tongue, one windpipe, one œsophagus and stomach, one heart, having four circulations (viz.) two aortæ to supply the body, and two vessels to supply the lungs, two livers, four kidneys, two bladders, two spleens, and two sets of intestines. The body forms a division at right angles from the navel downwards. Dr. H. in a paper on the Monstrosity of the Fœtus, concludes by saying: " Philosophers and anatomists have, in general, attempted to account for the unnatural formation of the fœtus (as produced by different animals) on principles relative to the anatomical structure in the generative parts of the female, but such principles tend to mislead others, and urge them on to wild and extravagant theories. That such monsters are formed we all know; but how they acquire an unnatural shape and superabundance of structure, we are at present totally ignorant."

SPARROWS.

It is proved that a pair of sparrows, during the time they have their young to feed, destroy on an average, every week, 3,360 caterpillars. This calculation is founded upon actual observation. Two parents have been known to carry to the nest forty caterpillars in an hour; and supposing the sparrows to enter the nest only twelve times during each day, which would cause a consumption of 480 caterpillars, this sum gives 3,360 caterpillars extirpated weekly from a garden. But the utility of these birds is not limited to this circumstance alone, for they likewise feed their young with butterflies and other winged insects, each of which, if not destroyed in this manner, would become the parent of hundreds of caterpillars.

It is not, however, to be hence presumed that the space is filled with luminous rays, for rays of light travel 200,000 miles in a second, and 20 per second produce continuous vision. Hence if we divide the circumference, 12 miles, or 7,200,000 tenths of an inch, there will at one time be but 1,440 rays emanating from the candle, so as to produce distinct vision two miles distant in every tenth of an inch.

Published by J. LIMBIRD, 355, Strand, (East End of Exeter 'Change); and sold by all Newsmen and Booksellers. Printed by A. APPLEGATH, Stamford-street.

THE CABINET OF CURIOSITIES,
OR
𝔚onders of the 𝔚orld Displayed.

*A world of wonders where creation seems
No more the works of Nature but her dreams.*—MONTGOMERY.

No. XXIV.]   PRICE TWOPENCE.

THE HINDOO GOD SIVA.

In No. XX. of "THE CABINET," we gave an engraving and description of the Hindoo God Vishnu, and we now present another of their principal deities, Siva and his wife Parvati. Our engraving is copied from an image cast in brass made in India, and presented to the London Missionary Society. Images of this kind are kept in the houses of the natives who worship the deity, whom they suppose to reside in the image.

In this engraving, Siva has his wife, named Parvati, on his knee. Both are highly ornamented, and so is the animal whereon they ride, which is meant to represent a white bull. As Siva is considered to be the God of Justice, he is seated on this animal, which the Hindoos look on as a symbol of divine justice, the colour pro-

2 B

bably denoting the purity of that justice.

Among the three chief gods of India, Siva is considered as the destroyer, or changer of things; for the Hindoos suppose, that, at the end of certain very long periods of time, he puts an end to all things as they then are, and changes or reproduces them. His images are accompanied by emblems, denoting the destruction and change connected with the revolutions of time. Some of these are seen in this engraving. The third eye—which is usually given to Siva, as denoting his knowledge of the past, the present, and the future—is seen in his forehead: Parvati has the same; and this third eye seems peculiar to him and his supposed family. A crescent on his head intimates the measuring of time, by the changing phases of the moon.

Siva is sometimes seen with two hands; at others, with four, eight or ten: in the engraving he has four. In the upper right hand is seen his trident; in the lower, what is supposed to be meant for an hour-glass. In his upper left hand is an antelope, joined behind him to the trident; in the lower left hand, is a lotos flower.

A multitude of tales are told of Siva and Parvati; and a vast number of names are given to them, all which are supposed to have some hidden meaning. The Brahmins profess to explain all these things, and all the emblems and ornaments about their idols.

Both indecent and cruel rites are practised in the idolatrous worship of these supposed deities. Well might St. Peter brand the worship of the heathen as " abominable idolatries !"

At an annual festival in honour of this god, many Hindoo devotees inflict on themselves the greatest cruelties.

THE SAVAGE GIRL OF CHAMPAGNE.

The following account of a savage girl, caught wild in the woods of Champagne, extracted from a curious pamphlet published about the year 1771, is a translation from the French, to which the translator prefixed a preface, containing a variety of particulars, not in the original, which he had an opportunity of learning from the girl herself, when in France in the year 1765. He gives the following account of the authenticity of this publication.

This narrative was drawn up under the immediate inspection of M. de la Condamine, whose curiosity and accuracy in matters of this sort, is universally known. It not only bears the plainest marks of truth and authenticity, but, if any doubt on this head remained, the facts it relates could be still attested by many living witnesses. The woman herself is yet alive, at least she was so in the year 1765, when the translator had an opportunity of seeing her, in several different conversations that she had with a Scots gentleman of distinction, then at Paris, who was introduced to her by M. de la Condamine, and who again mentioned her to most of the British persons of distinction then at Paris, to some of whom he likewise introduced her. To that gentleman Le Blanc confirmed with her own mouth, in the hearing of the translator, every circumstance in this relation; mentioning at the same time several particulars not here taken notice of. The translator likewise attended the same gentleman in a journey which he made, merely with a view of searching to the bottom every circumstance of this curious history, all the way from Rheims to Chalons, in a convent of which town Le Blanc was placed very soon after being taken; and from thence to Songi, the place of her capture. In that journey he had occasion to hear all these particulars amply confirmed, both by the abbess of the convent in which she had resided at Chalons, as well as by several other persons of that place, and likewise by several of the inhabitants of the village of Songi, who had been witnesses to her capture, and to the facts which immediately followed. These persons, too, particularly the abbess, mentioned several anecdotes of Le Blanc omitted in this narrative; such as some instances of her surprising agility in climbing walls, and running on the tops of houses, and of her imitating the notes of singing birds, such as the nightingale, and that so naturally, as often to deceive the people of the convent. One of the chief objects of this gentleman's journey to Songi, was to view the bludgeon used by Le Blanc as her principal weapon, in her wild state, which she said was in the possession of the Viscount d'Epinoy, the proprietor of Songi. From some characters which Le Blanc informed him were engraved on this bludgeon, this gentleman hoped to have been able to form more certain conjectures about her native country, and the more early part of her history and adventures.

The history proceeds as follows: "One evening, in the month of September 1731, a girl, nine or ten years old, pressed, as it would seem, by thirst, entered about the twilight into Songi, a village four or five leagues south of Chalons in Champagne. She had nothing on her feet; her body was covered with rags and skins, her hair with a gourd leaf, and her face and hands were black as a negro's. She was armed with a short baton, thicker at one end than the other, like a club. Those who first observed her, took to their heels, crying out " There is the devil." And, indeed, her dress and colour might well suggest this idea to the country people. Happy were they who could soonest secure their doors and windows; but one of them, thinking, perhaps, that the devil was afraid of dogs, set loose upon her a bull-dog with an iron collar. The little savage seeing him advance in a fury, kept her ground without flinching, grasping her little club with both hands, and stretching herself to one side, in order to give greater scope to her blow. Perceiving the dog within her reach, she discharged such a terrible blow on his head as laid him dead at her feet. Elated with her victory, she jumped several times over the dead carcass of the dog. Then she tried to open a door, which not being able to effect, she ran back to the country towards the river, and, mounting a tree, fell quietly asleep.

The late Viscount d'Epinoy happened to be then at his country seat of Songi; where, having heard the various accounts of the little savage that had appeared on his grounds, he gave orders to catch her, and particularly to the shepherd who had first discovered her.

One of the country people, by a very simple thought, but which was attributed to his great knowledge of the manners and customs of savages, conjectured that she was thirsty, and advised to place a pitcher full of water at the foot of the tree in which she was sitting, to tempt her to come down. They followed his advice; and, after placing the pitcher, retired from the tree, but still kept privately a close watch on her. Upon which the little savage, after having first looked sharply around, to see whether any body observed her, came down the tree, and went to drink at the pitcher, plunging her chin into the water; but something having startled her, she regained the top of the tree before they had time to apprehend her.

This first stratagem having failed, the same person by whom it had been suggested, again advised to place a woman and some children near the tree, because savages commonly are not so shy of them as men; and he bade them above all show her a friendly air, and a smiling countenance. His directions were complied with. A woman with a child in her arms walking near the tree, carried different sorts of roots, and two fishes in her hands, which she held out to the savage, who, desirous to have them, descended a branch or two, but went back again. The woman, still continuing her invitation with an affable pleasant countenance, accompanied with all possible signs of friendship, such as laying her hand upon her breast, as if to assure her that she loved her, and would do her no harm; the savage was at last emboldened to come down the tree to receive the roots and fishes that were offered her in so kindly a manner: but the woman enticing her from the tree, by retiring insensibly, gave time to the men, who were lying in wait for her, to advance and seize her.

The shepherd and the rest, who had caught and brought her to the castle, carried her first into the kitchen, till M. d'Epinoy should be informed of her arrival. The first thing there that appeared to draw her attention, was some fowls which the cook was dressing; at these she flew so greedily, and with such amazing agility, that the astonished cook beheld one of them between her teeth before he imagined she had reached it. M. d'Epinoy arriving in the mean time, and seeing what she was eating, caused them to give her an unskinned rabbit, which she instantly stripped of the skin and devoured.

Those who considered her then, were of opinion that she was about nine years of age. She supposes she was a child only about seven or eight years of age, when she was carried away from her own country; yet, by that time, she had learnt to swim, to fish, to shoot with the bow and arrow, to climb, and to leap from one tree to another like a squirrel. She was taken up at sea, where she was, with other children, set in a little round canoe, which was covered with a skin that drew about her middle like a purse, and prevented the water from getting in; for, she says, it is the manner in her country, to put the children early to sea in such canoes, in order to accustom them to bear the sea, which breaks over them; and though it may overturn the canoe, does not sink it. When she was taken up, she was put aboard a great ship, and was carried to a warm country, where she was sold for a slave; the person who sold her having first painted her all over black, with a view, no doubt, to make her pass for a negress.

She says further of the country from which she was thus carried away, that the people there had no clothing but skins, and had no use of fire at all; so that when she came to France, she could not bear the fire, and hardly even the close air of a room, or the breath of persons who were near her. There were, she says, another sort of men in this country, who were bigger and stronger than her people, and all covered with hair; and those people were at war with her people, and used to eat them when they could catch them.

In the hot country to which she was first carried, she says she was reembarked, and performed a very long voyage, during which the master, to whom she had been sold, wanted to make her work, particularly, at a sort of needlework, which obliged her to crouch and then look up; and when she would not work he beat her; but her mistress, who, she thinks, spoke French, was very kind to her, and would hide her when her master was seeking her to make her work. The ship having been wrecked, the crew took to the boat; but she, and a negro girl that was on board, were left to shift for themselves. The negro girl, she says, could not swim so well as she, and therefore she was obliged to assist her, and she kept herself above water, by taking hold of Le Blanc's foot; and, in this way, they both got on shore. They then traversed a great tract of country, commonly travelling all night, and sleeping in the daytime on the tops of trees; and they subsisted upon roots which she dug out of the ground with her fingers, and particularly with her thumb, which by that, and by the use she made of it in climbing and leaping from tree to tree, was much broader, and every way larger than the thumbs of other people. They also catched as much game as they could, which they eat raw with the hot blood in it, in the manner as a hawk or wild beast does; and she remembers particularly, that they killed a fox, of which they only sucked the blood, finding the flesh very disagreeable. She remembers also that they catched a hind. She says farther, that besides the being able to subsist herself in the manner above-mentioned, she had learned the use of several roots and herbs, which were good for the stomach and head, and could cure wounds. She seemed black, as I have already said; but it soon appeared, after washing her several times, that she was naturally white, as she still continues. They observed likewise, that her fingers, and particularly her thumbs, were extraordinarily large, in proportion to the rest of her hand, which was otherwise neat enough; and to this day her thumbs retain somewhat of that largeness. By her account, these large strong thumbs were very useful to her during her wild life in the woods; for when she had a mind to pass from one tree to another, without being at the trouble of descending and remounting, if the branches of the two trees were but at a small distance from each other, and though of no greater thickness than her finger, would place her thumbs on a branch of the tree in which she happened to be, and by their means spring to the other just like a squirrel.

(To be continued)

THE VINE-FRETTER.

You have frequently (says M. Bonnet in his "Contemplation of

Nature") seen little flies fastened in great numbers to the upper extremities and leaves of plants, and twist them round in various forms: these are vine-fretters, whose species are almost as numerous as those of vegetables, and whose remarkable properties are multiplied in proportion to the attention we pay them. They bring forth living young ones. Their births are easy to trace, there needs only good eyes and a little patience. Take up a little one as soon at it is produced; enclose it immediately in the most perfect solitude, and in order to be the better assured of its virginity, carry your precautions to a degree of scrupulousness; be with respect to it a more vigilant Argus than the fabulous one. When the little recluse has acquired a certain growth, it will begin to have young, and after some days, you will find it amidst a numerous family. Make the same experiment on one of the individuals that you have tried on its chief: the new hermit will multiply like its *father*, and this second generation brought up in solitude, will not prove less fruitful than the first. Repeat the experiment from one generation to another; abate nothing of your cares, your precautions, your suspicions; proceed, if your patience will permit you, to the ninth generation, and they will all present you with fecund virgins. After these experiments so decisive and reiterated, you are easily persuaded that there is no distinction of sex in vine-fretters. What indeed would be the use of such a difference among a people, where all the individuals are constantly sufficient for themselves? Natural history is the best logic, because it best teaches us to suspend our judgment. Vine-fretters are really distinguished by sexes, and their amours are the least equivocal of any in the world. I do not know whether there are in nature any males more amorous than they. What then is the use of coupling between insects that multiply without its assistance? Of what service can an actual distinction of sex be to real androgynes. The clearing up of this point depends on another singularity afforded us by these little animals. During the summer season they are viviparous; they all bring forth living young. Towards the middle of autumn they become oviparous; they all then lay real eggs, which are hatched at the return of spring. The males begin to appear exactly at the time the females begin to lay. There are always found in the bodies of the females, eggs and young ready to be produced. The young then were originally enclosed in eggs. During the fine season they are hatched in the belly of the mother, and are brought into the world alive. Plants at that time furnish them with proper nourishment. The developement depends ultimately on nutrition: vine-fretters that are produced alive, are more unfolded in the matrix than those which are brought forth enclosed in eggs. The former then have received a nourishment in the matrix. Had not coupling, then, for its primary end, the supplying the defect of this nourishment in such germs as were not to be hatched till after they had issued from the belly of the mother?'

How astonishing must the activity of these laborious insects be, by which they are enabled to collect the materials necessary for the construction of their nest! Behold their sagacity in uniting together, and assisting each other in scooping out the earth, in order to transport to their habitation bits of herb, straw, scraps of wood, and other bodies of the like kind, which they employ in their work. They seem only to pile it up in heaps at random; but under this apparent confusion is couched art and design, which is perceived upon a strict examination. Under this little heap, of which their lodging consists, and whose form facilitates the passage of the water, are discovered galleries, which communicate with each other, resembling the streets of a little city. We are particularly struck with the solicitude of ants for their nurslings, with the care they take to convey them, in proper time, from one place to another, their nourishing them, and causing them to shun every thing that may prove hurtful to them. One cannot but admire the readiness with which they withdraw from danger, and the courage they shew in defending them. An ant has been seen, after being cut asunder in the middle, to transport eight or ten of its nurslings, one after another. They seek their provisions at a great distance from their abode. Various paths, which are often very winding and intricate, terminate at their nest. The ants pass over them in rows, without ever missing their way, any more than the republican caterpillars. Like the latter they leave tracks wherever they pass. These are not discernible to the eye; they are much more sensible to the smell; and it is well known that ants have a very penetrating one. However, if we draw a finger several times backward and forward along the wall, by which the ants pass and repass up and down in rows, they will be stopped on a sudden in their march, and it will afford some amusement to observe the perplexity they are in.

The foresight of ants has been greatly celebrated. Near three thousand years ago it was remarked, that they amassed provisions for the winter; and were skilful in building magazines for containing the grain they had collected during the fine season. It would seem that these magazines must be altogether useless to them, insomuch that they sleep during the whole winter, like dormice and many other animals. A small degree of cold would be sufficient to benumb them. We may conclude thence that they have no use for these pretended magazines; and consequently do not build them. The corn they convey with so much activity to their dwelling, is by no means intended by them for food; but consists only in simple materials, which contribute to the construction of their edifice, in the same manner as little bits of wood, straw, &c.

THE HIMALAYA MOUNTAINS IN THE EAST INDIES.

In the twelfth volume of the Transactions of the Asiatic Society, recently published, an account is given of the height of the stupendous mountains of Himàlaya in the East Indies, till lately inaccessible to Europeans. They have been long believed, in India, to surpass in height all other mountains on the earth. The Himálaya chain is visible from Patna, on the southern banks of the Ganges, as a continued well-defined line of white cliffs, extending through more than two points of the compass, at a distance of about sixty leagues; while at an equal distance, Chimborazo, the highest of the Andes, is seen as a single point, the rest of the Cordillera being invisible. It appears from Captain Turner's account, that the Peak of Chamalasi, near which he passed, after crossing the frontier of Thibet, is the same mountain which is seen from various stations in Bengal, the most remote of which is not less than 238 English miles distant. This, in the mean state of the atmosphere, requires an elevation of 28,000 feet. The President himself observed the usual altitude of a peak of the Himálaya to be 1° 1', as viewed from a station in Bengal, distant not less than 150 English miles, which, after a due allowance for terrestrial refraction, would give a height of not less than 26,000 feet. According to the mean of several observations of a peak, taken by lieutenant-colonel Colebrook, its height above the level of the plains of Róhilkhand, is 22,291 feet, or about 22,800 feet above the level of the sea. According to the observations communicated to the President, Mount Dhaibún, is 20,140 above Cat'hmándu, which is itself more than 4500 above the level of the sea; and another exceeds the elevation of the same station, by 17,819 feet—another by 20,025 —another by 18,662 feet. All these are visible from Patna, the nearest being nearly 170 English miles distant, and the farthest about 226 miles. The Dhawalagiri, or white mountain, supposed to be situated near the source of the Glandac River, was found, by observations of bearings, taken by Mr. Webb, from four points, and of altitudes from three, to be (allowing one-eighth for refraction) 26,784 feet; and, allowing one-eleventh, 27,551. Supposing the errors arising from refraction, and those from observation, to be the highest possible, and both in excess, the President calculates that its height, above the plains of Gorakhpur, cannot fall short of 26,462 feet, or 26,863 above the level of the sea. Since the publication of the above volume of the Transactions of the Asiatic Society, Lieutenant Webb, of the Bengal establishment, has transmitted to Europe the result of his observations for ascertaining the heights of some of the principal mountains belonging to the Himálaya or Himāyā-chain, in the Nepaul territory. He has ascertained that several of these mountains exceed in height any known before. Of twenty-seven peaks, nineteen are higher than Chimborazo. This mountain of South America, according to Reddel's chart, is 20,900 feet above the level of the sea; but the highest of the Asiatic peaks has an elevation of not less than 25,669 feet, exceeding it by 4,769 feet, considerably more than three-fourths of a mile, or nearly one-fourth of its own height. Several others of these Asiatic peaks have an altitude of more than four miles.

GHOST STORY.

In the year 1704, a gentleman, to all appearance of large fortune, took furnished lodgings in a house in Soho-square. After he had resided there some weeks with his establishment, he lost his brother, who had lived at Hampstead, and who on his death-bed particularly desired to be interred in the family vault in Westminster Abbey. The gentleman requested his landlord to permit him to bring the corpse of his brother to his lodgings, and to make arrangements there for the funeral. The landlord, without hesitation, signified his compliance.

The body, dressed in a white shroud, was accordingly brought in a very handsome coffin, and placed in the great dining-room. The funeral was to take place the next day, and the lodger and his servants went out to make the necessary preparations for the solemnity. He staid out late, but this was no uncommon thing. The landlord and his family, conceiving that they had no occasion to wait for him, retired to bed as usual, about twelve o'clock. One maid-servant was left up to let him in, and to boil some water, which he had desired might be ready for making tea on his return. The girl was accordingly sitting alone in the kitchen, when a tall, spectre-looking figure entered, and clapped itself down in a chair opposite to her.

The maid was by no means one of the most timid of her sex; but she was terrified beyond expression, lonely as she was, at this unexpected apparition. Uttering a loud scream, she flew out like an arrow, at a side-door, and hurried to the chamber of her master and mistress. Scarcely had she awakened them, and communicated to the whole family some portion of the fright with which she was herself overwhelmed, when the spectre, enveloped in a shroud, and with a deathlike paleness, made its appearance, and sat down in a chair in the bed-room, without their having observed how it entered. The worst of all was, that this chair stood by the door of the bed-chamber, so that not a creature could get away without passing close to the apparition, which rolled its glaring eyes so frightfully, and so hideously distorted its features, that they could not bear to look at it. The master and mistress crept under the bed-clothes, covered with profuse perspiration, while the maid-servant sunk nearly insensible by the side of the bed.

At the same time the whole house seemed to be in an uproar; for, though they had covered themselves over head and ears, they could still hear an incessant noise and clatter, which served to increase their terror.

At length all became perfectly still in the house. The landlord ventured to raise his head, and to steal a glance at the chair by the door; but, behold, the ghost was gone! Sober reason began to resume its power. The poor girl was brought to herself after a good deal of shaking. In a short time, they plucked up sufficient courage to quit the bed-room, and to commence an examination of the house, which they expected to find in great disorder. Nor were their anticipations unfounded. The whole house had been stripped by artful thieves, and the gentleman had decamped without paying for his lodging. It turned out that he was no other than an accomplice of the notorious Arthur Chambers, who was executed at Tyburn in 1706, and that the supposed corpse was this arch rogue himself, who had whitened his hands and face with chalk, and merely counterfeited death. About midnight he quitted the coffin and appeared to the maid in the kitchen. When she flew up stairs, he softly followed her, and seated at the door of the chamber, he acted as a sentinel, so that his industrious accomplices were enabled to plunder the house without the least molestation.

Eccentric Biography.

MR. DANIEL LAMBERT.

Mr. Daniel Lambert was born at Leicester, in the year 1769: during the younger period of his life, no particular circumstances worthy of record occurred. He was apprenticed to an engraver, and until he arrived at the age of nineteen, he was not of more than ordinary bulk,—neither were his parents, nor any of his family above the common stature.—The rapidly increasing size of Mr. Lambert, after this period, cannot be attributed to want of exercise, for he was, on the contrary, remarkably active, and took great pleasure in field sports, and particularly delighted in shooting.— To the breed of dogs, Mr. Lambert paid the most marked attention; and the delight he received from that celebrated Leicestershire Nimrod, (Mr. Meynell) first impressed his mind with the love of that faithful and sagacious animal.

Mr. Lambert perceived that there was no hound in Mr. Meynell's pack, whose *tongue* his master did not instantly recognise, nor any one which did not obey his master's voice.—Until Mr. L. became too corpulent for riding on horseback, he partook of the pleasures of the chase, with inexpressible delight; and even after that event, frequently accompanied the hounds to *cover,* receiving high gratification from a *view halloo!* The improvement of the breed of spaniels and setters was the peculiar object of Mr. Lambert; and to such a degree of celebrity had his name attained in consequence of his exertions, that a brace of puppies was sold at Tattersall's for seventy guineas; and for a small white terrier bitch, which he had at the time of his death, and which was supposed one of the most beautiful in the kingdom, he had refused the astonishing sum of nearly one hundred guineas. Mr. Lambert had also been much attached to coursing, and he was equally celebrated for possessing some excellent greyhounds, which were patterns of symmetry and high breeding · in the most distinguished parts of the country through which he passed, his dogs were constantly running with those in the neighbourhood where he was staying, and they were justly allowed to have been of tried bottom. Mr. Lambert himself occasionally went in his carriage to see the matches.— Before he left Leicester he was the keeper of the gaol, as his father previously had been; and frequently, when sitting at the door smoking his pipe, many a stranger, attracted by his extraordinary size, would enter into conversation with him. Indeed, in his own neighbourhood he was greatly respected, and more especially amongst the sporting part of it. This circumstance, added to the knowledge he had acquired by reading and otherwise cultivating his mind, rendered Mr. Lambert a remarkably pleasant companion, and few men were better calculated to add to the pleasures of the festive board. His person was tall and his countenance manly. His disposition and general suavity of manners very prepossessing, and he sang with much taste. He was also a good judge of painting, and more particularly of the portraits of animals, from the great attention he had paid to the breed of dogs, and the observations he had been accustomed to make on that nobler animal the horse in the first field of sportsmen in the united kingdom. He well knew the different proportions of symmetry, and whether or not the painter had depicted nature in her truest colours, and if he had caught her in her happiest moods. Replete with anecdote and of a lively turn of mind, possessing a genius naturally mechanical, and with a choice selection of words, and a variety of subjects, to which his active thoughts were ever inclined, it is not to be wondered that Mr. Lambert was respected by those who were in a higher rank of life, and beloved by those who were his most intimate acquaintances.—There is one circumstance in support of this assertion, which we particularly wish not to pass unnoticed, as it also shews that he entertained that high sense of honour which will ever command respect from *all* ranks. Mr. Lambert, at an early period of his life, was riding to view some coursing matches, and just before he arrived at the appointed spot, he met a brace of greyhounds coursing a hare, which they killed very near him; not far behind and much ahead of the rest of the company, was a person of considerable property, who was much interested in the match, and who declared his own dog had won the race. Mr. Lambert immediately contradicted him, observing that he was surprised he should make that declaration, when there was any one present, who must have known that such was not the case. Mr. Lambert was answered in so rude a manner as to call forth from him some menacing words, and he appealed, to his sporting friends present, to say if they ever had any reason to doubt his word, adding that he neither knew the dogs which had been running nor the person to whom they belonged. Their reply was "Mr. Lambert, we are perfectly satisfied that you never will tell an untruth, and we shall abide by *your* decision." Mr. Lambert left the town of Leicester to the great regret of many intimate friends, on April 4, 1806, in a very handsome carriage; the dimensions of which were accommodated to his convenience and comfort, and wherever he went, he was received with the greatest civilities, and had every attention shewn him from all ranks, so highly was he respected. One nobleman, Lord S., during Mr. Lambert's stay in his neighbourhood, every day sent his keepers to know what game he would like, either at his own table, or to send to his distant friends. Numerous are the occasions which could be related of similar attentions which were shewn him, and never was a frown seen on Mr. Lambert's countenance, except it was justly raised by the impertinent remarks and rude observations of those whose situation in life should have taught them a better behaviour. Amongst this number, Mr. Lambert often mentioned, that when a *distinguished* nobleman paid him a visit, he asked him such unmanly and such disgusting questions, that he looked at his *distinguished* visitor with ineffable contempt, and would not condescend to answer him. Mr. Lambert was enabled not only to discern a wellbred man, but also by his own deportment and polite acquiescence in the wishes of others, to shew that he himself, was well acquainted with both men and manners. With all that corpulency which at an early period deprived Mr.

Lambert of his life, yet he did not give way to sloth. Though latterly he could not walk, and evidently was a burden to himself, suffering much pain in his legs, yet he was cheerful in the extreme. He rose early in the morning, and appeared at breakfast refreshed by his sleep, and either read or sang. In the forenoon, when free from visitors, he read the news of the day, or some recent publication, from which he could obtain information. At dinner, he was particularly abstemious, but his friends partook the cheerful glass with him, and the evening was often devoted, not only to the enjoyment of society from the ability of others, but also by his own exertions, to add by his vocal and mental powers to the pleasures of those around. In his political sentiments, Mr. Lambert appeared, like a true Englishman, to have no other view than that of applauding or condemning measures, and not men, being satisfied with whatever he believed was for the welfare of his native land, and regretting those public transactions which he conceived brought either disgrace or misfortune upon his country. Mr. Lambert certainly was well aware, that every hour " his mortal coif was likely to be shuffled off," and the thought of another and a better world, frequently occupied his mind. He was well aware, that in all probability his death would be sudden, and that his life would be short. Yet the cheerfulness which ever accompanied him, and his general character, leave no room to doubt but that he was *prepared* for this awful event, although he had no immediate previous warning of its approach. When indeed his astonishing weight is recollected, and it is known that his bones were not larger, nor his frame higher or more gigantic, than that of much smaller men, when it is recollected that he was incapable of that activity and of partaking of those pleasures which he had engaged in the earlier periods of his life, it may by his friends be considered a happy release for him from a world of trouble and fatigue; yet his relatives must ever regret that Providence did not a short time longer spare his life, to enable him to reach that home he was anxious again to visit, and which he very soon expected to behold, after an absence of more than three years. He would there have been welcomed with all the ardour of sincere affection, and with the heartfelt salutations of his numerous friends.

Mr. Lambert had determined that Stamford should be the last town in which he would publicly receive company, and he went there on Tuesday the 27th of June, the races commencing at that period. Mr. Lambert came from Huntingdon to Stamford, and in the evening sent for the printer, that he might have handbills published immediately, announcing his arrival. His orders were given with his usual cheerfulness, and he retired to rest fatigued with his journey, but apparently unusually anxious to have his bills printed, that he might admit his visitors by nine o'clock on the following morning. Till within a few minutes of the expiration of that very hour, he had no reason to suppose that it was to be the last of his life, that he was not to survive its duration. At about half past eight o'clock, nature worn out with a trespass she could no longer endure, sunk beneath the pressure of such unusual corpulency, and after a faint struggle yielded to that power which no mortal can resist. Mr. Lambert was in his fortieth year, and his weight a few days previous, at Ipswich, was found to be fifty-two stone eleven pounds, (fourteen pounds to the stone,) which is ten stone eleven pounds more than the great Mr. Bright, of Essex, ever weighed. As might naturally be supposed, within a few hours after Mr. Lambert's decease, all identity of features were lost, and in forty-eight hours it was become necessary to remove him to his mother earth. His coffin was six feet four inches long, four feet four inches wide, and two feet four inches deep, the immense size of his legs making it almost a square case, which was built around him upon two axletrees and four clog-wheels. The window and wall of the room in which he lay were obliged to be removed to allow of his exit, and having thus been extricated, his remains were drawn by eight men with ropes to the burial ground, for into the church it was not possible to take him. A regular descent to the grave was made, by cutting away the earth slopingly for some distance, and thus were his remains rolled into it, amidst an immense concourse of people, besides whom, during the day, hundreds attended to visit the place of his interment.—The circumference of the body of this astonishing man, was three yards four inches, and that of his leg, one yard one inch; and his height five feet eleven inches. Indeed, we may with great propriety exclaim of Mr. Lambert, as did the royal Dane of his mysterious father, that—

"Take him for all in all,
We shall not look upon his like again."

THE REV. EMANUEL GLEBE.

THE following is an anecdote of an eccentric, though worthy and excellent divine, (the Reverend Emanuel Glebe,) and may afford some amusement to the lovers of eccentricity. Having, a few summers ago, determined to make a tour, he took leave of his flock, over whose souls his care was extended, with more than ordinary feelings of good-will; but, as he was what the world calls "a good liver," he extended his care likewise over that generous and inspiring beverage which promotes "the feast of reason and the flow of soul;" in short, he possessed a cellar well stored with the true Falernian. This store must be allowed to have naturally demanded his attention before he left home, and its security in his absence was what every man of common care would have endeavoured to promote as far as possible. With this intention, therefore, the Doctor rang his bell, and his faithful servant John immediately stood before him: then, taking out of his purse a half-crown, he said, "Here John, take this: go to the blacksmith's in the village, and buy with it three tenpenny nails immediately." John, delighted with his errand, immediately repairs to the habitation of this disciple of Vulcan, and, paying him for the three nails, quietly profits by his master's ideas of the number of tenpenny nails to be had for two shillings and sixpence, by pocketing the difference, and then, crowding all sail, appears again in his master's presence. "Very well, John," says the Doctor, "now bring me a candle and a hammer, and go with me into the wine-cellar, to nail up the door." Picture to yourself now the worthy Doctor and John, in the subterraneous vaults, consulting the safety of the choice spirits there immured. "Give me the candle, John, shut the door, and drive a nail in here at the top." John hammered. "Hit it hard, John, drive it up to the head." "I have, Sir." "Now drive another in here above the lock, John." "Yes, Sir." "Up to the head, John." "I will, Sir." "Now the third here, a little way from the bottom, John." "Yes, Sir." This being accomplished, both paused to view the work, when the Doctor exclaimed, with exultation. "Now, John, I think we have done the business cleverly; you don't think any body can manage to get in now John, do you?" John, however, it seems, during the pause at the conclusion of driving the nails, had reflected that he was on the wrong side of the door to run away, and had nailed himself and his master up in the cellar, along with the wine, in their anxiety to prevent others from getting in: he, therefore, very laconically observed, in answer to this question, "No, Sir: I am afraid nobody can get in: but how are we to get out?" Conviction then first flashed upon the Doctor's mind, and being considerably annoyed at his situation, he replied with warmth, "You stupid fellow, John, why, why, why, did you not tell me at first, John; you great fool, John: shout, John. Oh dear, we are fast! shout and raise the house, John; the servants must get assistance and break the door down." How the worthy Doctor and John were liberated from the cellar, we have never heard.—*American Paper.*

Varieties.

GAME OF TURKS AND CHRISTIANS.

The story of the fifteen Turks and fifteen Christians which has given rise to the amusing trick practised with cards, or by the aid of the men of the backgammon table, is probably known to many of our readers; but as a new method of killing the Turks has been lately proposed by a writer in a contemporary journal, we shall repeat the little tale as it is related in "Hutton's edition of Montucla's and Ozanam's Recreations," and then give the *variations* to this amusing winter evening's pastime.

Fifteen Turks and fifteen Christians being at sea in the same vessel, a dreadful storm came on, which obliged them to throw all their merchandise overboard; this, however, not being sufficient to lighten the ship, the Captain informed them there was no possibility of its being saved, unless half the passengers were thrown overboard also. Having, therefore, caused them all to arrange themselves in a row, by counting from nine to nine, and throwing every ninth person into the sea, beginning again at the first of the row; when it had been counted to the end, it was found that after fifteen persons had been thrown overboard, the fifteen Christians remained. How did the Captain arrange these thirty persons so as to save the Christians?

The method of arranging the thirty persons may be deduced from these French verses:

Mort, tu ne falliras pas
En me livrant le trepas.

Or from the following Latin one, which is not so bad of its kind:

Populeam virgam mater regina ferebat.

Attention must be paid to the vowels, *a, e, i, o, u,* contained in the syllables of these verses; observing that *a* is equal to one, *e* to two, *i* to three, *o* to four, and *u* to five.

You must begin them by arranging four Christians together, because the vowel in the first syllable is *o;* then five Turks, because the vowel in the second syllable is *u;* and so on to the end. By proceeding circularly in this manner, it will be found, taking every ninth person circularly, that is to say, beginning at the first of the row, after it is ended, that the lot will fall entirely on the Turks.

THE MERMAID.

Mr. Lawrence Edmonston, a surgeon of Zetland, in a letter recently published, says, that an animal answering to the following description, so far as the account of six fishermen, who captured it, can be depended on, was actually in their possession for three hours, but unluckily, from some superstitious dread of injuring it, they returned it to its native element, and thus prevented the scientific identification of an animal, which appears to have very nearly resembled what has been generally regarded as a merely fabulous creation. Length of the animal, three feet; body without scales or hair; silver gray above, whitish below, like the human skin; no gills were observed; no fins on the back or belly; tail like that of a dogfish; body very thick over the breast; by the eye the girth might be between two and three feet; the neck short, very distinct from the head and shoulders; the body rather depressed; the anterior extremities very like the human hand, about the length of a seal's paw, webbed to about an inch of the ends of the fingers; mammæ as large as those of a woman; mouth and lips very distinct, and resembling the human.

THE GOSSAMER SPIDER.

The manner by which spiders form those long filmy lines that are frequently met with at this season of the year, crossing our path betwixt hedge-rows, and sometimes stretching across streams of considerable width, I had often puzzled myself to account for, till I chanced to make the following observation: —Amusing myself in a garden some years ago, I happened to find a spider of the above description, of an unusually large size, which I secured upon a twig, and stationed myself on the top of the wall, with a view to observe by what method the insect should endeavour to extricate itself. The spider, after having travelled backwards and forwards upon the twig, and finding no means of escape from his novel situation, suddenly dropped by its thread; and, at short intervals of rest and apparent consideration, gradually lowered itself to about twelve feet. Unable to reach our planet with this length of line, he ascended back to the twig I held in my hand, and remained motionless. I shortly observed, glancing in the sunbeams, another line, which was gradually drawn out by the wind from the abdomen of the spider in a horizontal direction, to about three yards distance, where, coming in contact with a tree, it was fastened, thus forming one of those lines alluded to, and by which it would appear they transport themselves from one object to another.

Dr. Paley, in his work on *Natural Theology*, under the article "Compensation," seems to suppose that those spiders are wafted through the air on this substance, which from its specific lightness he has compared to a balloon. The above experiment shows that the spider does not venture upon it till it has been carried by the wind to some remote object, serving them rather as a bridge than a balloon, and trusting more to the strength than to the buoyancy of their aerial pathway.

The Scrap Book.

OAK TREES.

Some oak trees were, in 1817, discovered in deepening the channel of the Caledonian Canal through Loch Dochfour; they were in seven feet water, and buried under a depth of ten feet of gravel. After injuring the dredging machine, with a power of thirty tons, another of fifty was applied, which succeeded in dragging to the surface three trees of a very large size; one of them was of a magnitude altogether beyond the ordinary growth of this country, in the present day; it was in circumference twenty and a half feet at the insertion of the limbs, three in number; and fourteen feet two inches at the root end; one of the limbs was eight feet eleven inches in circumference, and the three trees measured one hundred and ninety-eight solid feet; the wood appeared to be perfectly fresh and sound.

NUMEROUS PROGENY.

It is sometimes mentioned as extraordinary, that an individual should be surrounded by descendants (children, grandchildren, and great grandchildren,) to the number of a hundred and fifty. Our sister kingdom can at this time boast of something much more wonderful, something never before heard of, we believe, on this side of Turkey. A nobleman of that kingdom has, we understand, the distinguished honour of being the father of a hundred and seventy children. The late Mr. Lovel Edgeworth, another Irishman, was, perhaps, with respect to legitimate children, at the head of the fathers of this part of Europe. This rivalry of the east would almost seem to be confined to the extreme west. Extremes sometimes meet. The Laird of Mænal, of whom there was a fine picture, by Raeburn, in the exhibition a year or two ago, was nothing to our Irish hero, though the Scots talk of his seventy children as a wonder.

COURSING EXTRAORDINARY.

While a gentleman of Kirkaldy was lately enjoying the amusement of coursing, along with some friends, a favourite dog sprung after a hare. In the course of the chase a rabbit came in his way, which he picked up and carried along with him, continning the original pursuit till within reach of his prey, when he dropped the rabbit and seized the hare. Both animals were killed.

Published by J. LIMBIRD, 355, Strand, (East End of Exeter 'Change); and sold by all Newsmen and Booksellers. Printed by A. APPLEGATH, Stamford-street.

THE CABINET OF CURIOSITIES,
OR
𝔚onders of the 𝔚orld Displayed.

A world of wonders where creation seems
No more the works of Nature but her dreams.—MONTGOMERY.

No. XXV.]   PRICE TWOPENCE.

THE HINDOO DEITY, GANESA.

GANESA is, like Vishnu and Siva, one of the principal deities of the Hindoos. His name Ganesa signifies a Governor or Leader of Gods; and when the Hindoos offer sacrifices, or enter on any other religious ceremonies, they begin by praying to Ganesa.

When they mean to address **any** of their greater gods, for they have *gods many and lords many,* they beg Ganesa to help them. When they sit down to write, even a letter, they write an invocation to Ganesa at the top. Few books are begun without the words, " Salutation to Ganesa." All worldly affairs of any moment are begun in the same way. In some parts of India, in particular, the natives would not, on any account, build a house, without having first placed on the ground an image of this deity, which they sprinkle with oil, and adorn every day with flowers: and, in those parts, they set up his figure in all their temples, in the streets, on the high roads, and in open plains at the foot of some tree.

The figure of the Idol in our Engraving has the head of an elephant, and has four arms and hands. In his hands he holds different things, which are probably meant to represent what may be expected from him by his worshippers. The animal on which he rides is intended for the figure of a huge rat. Over his head are some sacred letters, enclosed in the figure of a serpent.

When the Hindoos worship this Idol, they cross their arms, close their fists, and in this manner strike themselves on their temples: then, still with their arms crossed, they take hold of their ears, and bow their bodies and bend their knees three times; after which, with the hands joined, they address to him their prayers, striking on their foreheads. Many persons keep in their houses a small metal image of this god, and worship it daily.

Idle tales are common among the people, by which they pretend to account for several things about this Idol.

One fable tells us how he came to have an elephant's head. It is this:—

Ganesa and another of their pretended gods were one day fighting together; when, as the story goes, Ganesa would have conquered, but a third god came in and cut of Ganesa's head. His mother was greatly displeased and distressed at this; and, in revenge, began to make great confusion, as she was a pretended goddess. Nothing could quiet her but the restoration of her son. His head could not, however, be found: it was determined, therefore, to fix on his trunk the head of the first animal that should be found, which happened to be an elephant.

Another fable pretends to shew why Ganesa rides on a rat. It is this:—

His rat, it is said, was a giant, of great power; but he abused his power, and inflicted much evil on mankind. Ganesa attacked him, and threw him down. Instantly the giant turned himself into a rat as large as a mountain; and was just going to attack Ganesa, when Ganesa leaped on his back, crying out, "From henceforth thou shalt be my beast of burthen!"

VOLCANIC MOUNTAIN OF ALBAY.

The following details of the dreadful eruption of the volcano of Albay, in the island of Luconia, one of the Philippines, on the 1st of February, 1814, are from an eyewitness of the dreadful scenes it presented.

"During thirteen years the volcano of Albay had preserved a profound silence. It was no longer viewed with that distrust and horror with which volcanoes usually inspire those who inhabit the vicinity. Its extensive spacious brow had been converted into highly-cultivated and beautiful gardens. On the first day of January 1814, no person reflected, in the slightest degree, upon the damages and losses which so bad a neighbour had once occasioned. Previously to the former eruptions there had been heard certain subterraneous sounds, which were presages of them. But upon the present occasion we remarked nothing, except that on the last day of January we perceived some slight shocks. In the night the shocks increased. At two in the morning one was felt more violent than those hitherto experienced. It was repeated at four, and from that time they were almost continual until the eruption commenced.

"The day broke, and I scarcely ever remarked in Camarines a more serene and pleasant morning. I observed, however, that the ridge nearest to the volcano were covered with mist, which I supposed to be the smoke of some house that might have been on fire in the night. But at eight o'clock the volcano began suddenly to emit a thick column of stones, sand, and ashes, which, with the greatest velocity, was elevated into the highest regions of the atmosphere. At this sight we were filled with the utmost dread, especially when we observed that in an instant the brow of the volcano was quite covered. We had never seen a similar eruption, but were convinced that a river of fire was flowing towards us, and was about to consume us. The first thing which was done in my village was to secure *the holy sacrament from profanation!* we then betook ourselves to flight. The swiftness with which the dreadful tide rolled towards us, did not give us time either for reflection or consultation. The frightful noise of the volcano caused great terror even in the stoutest hearts. We all ran, filled with dismay and consternation, endeavouring to reach the highest and most distant places to preserve ourselves from so imminent a danger. The horizon began to darken, and our anxieties redoubled. The noise of the volcano continually increased, the darkness augmented, and we continued our flight. But, notwithstanding our swiftness, we were overtaken by a heavy shower of huge stones, by the violence of which many unfortunate persons were in a moment killed. This cruel circumstance obliged us to make a pause in our career, and to shelter ourselves under the houses; but the flames and burnt stones which fell from the above, in a short time reduced them to ashes.

"The sky was now completely overcast, and we remained enveloped and immersed in a thick and palpable darkness. From that moment reflection was at an end. The mother abandoned her children, the husband his wife, and the children forgot their parents.

"In the houses we had no longer any shelter. It was necessary to abandon, or perish with them; yet, to go out uncovered, was to expose one's self to a danger not less imminent, because many of the stones were of an enormous size, and they fell as thick as drops of rain. It was necessary to defend ourselves as well as we could. Some covered themselves with hides, others with tables and chairs, and others with boards and tea-trays. Many took refuge in the trunks of trees, others among the canes and hedges, and some hid themselves in a cave, where the brow of the mountain protected them.

"About ten o'clock the heavy stones ceased to fall, and a rain of thick sand succeeded. At half past one the noise of the volcano began to diminish, and the horizon to clear a little; and at two it became quite tranquil; and we now began to perceive the dreadful ravages which the darkness had hitherto concealed from us. The ground was covered with dead bodies, part of whom had been killed by the stones, and the others consumed by the fire. Two hundred perished in the church of Budiao, and thirty-five in a single house in that village. The joy the living felt at having preserved themselves, was in many converted into the extremity of sorrow at finding themselves deprived of their relations and friends. Fathers found their children dead, husbands their wives, and wives their husbands, in the village of Budiao, where there were very few who had not lost some of their nearest connections. In other places we found many persons extended upon the ground, wounded or bruised in a thousand ways. Some with their legs broken, some without arms, some with their sculls fractured, and others covered with wounds. Many died immediately, others on the following days, and the rest were abandoned to the most melancholy fate, without physicians, without medicines, and in want even of necessary food.

"Five populous towns were entirely destroyed by the eruption; more than twelve hundred of the inhabitants perished amidst the ruins; and the twenty thousand who survived the awful catastrophe, were stripped of their possessions and reduced to beggary.

"The subsequent appearance of the volcanic mountain was most melancholy and terrific. Its side, formerly so well cultivated, and which afforded a prospect the most picturesque, is become a barren sand. The stones, sand, and ashes, which cover it, in some places exceed the depth of ten and twelve yards; and on the ground where lately stood the village of Budiao, there are spots, in which the cocoa-trees are almost covered. In the ruined villages, and through the whole extent of the eruption, the ground remains buried in the sand to the depth of half a yard, and scarcely a single tree is left alive. The crater of the volcano has lowered more than one hundred and twenty feet; and the south side discovers a spacious and horrid mouth, which is frightful to the view. Three new ones have opened at a considerable distance from the principal crater, through which also smoke and ashes are incessantly emitted.' In short, the most beautiful villages of Camarines, and the principal part of that fine province, are deeply covered with barren sand."

THE SAVAGE GIRL OF CHAMPAGNE.
(Continued from p. 373.)

M. D'EPINOY committed the Savage girl of Champagne to the care of the shepherd, who dwelt near the castle, recommending her to him, and promising to reward him handsomely for his pains. The man accordingly took her to his house, in order to begin to tame her; and on this account they called her, in the neighbourhood, *The shepherd's beast*. We may well conceive, that it would require a considerable space of time, and some harsh usage, to wean her from her former habits, and to temper her fierce and savage disposition; and I have good reason to believe, that she was very closely confined in this house; for she informed me herself, that she found means to make holes in the walls, and in the tiles of the roof, upon which she would run with as much unconcern as on the ground, never suffering herself to be retaken without a great deal of trouble, and passing so artfully (as they afterwards told her) through small holes, that they could scarcely believe their eyes, after they had seen her do it. It was thus that she escaped once, among several other times, out of his house, in a most severe storm of frost and snow; on which occasion, after making good her escape, she betook herself for shelter to a tree. The dread of the resentment of M. d'Epinoy threw the whole family that night into a hurry and confusion; who never imagining that, in so excessive a frost, she would have ventured into the country, rummaged every corner of the house; but finding all their researches in vain, they at last resolved, that they might leave no means untried, to look for her out of the house likewise; when, behold, they find Miss perched, as I have just said, on the top of a tree; from whence, however, they were lucky enough to prevail on her to descend.

I myself have been an eye-witness of some instances of the ease and swiftness with which she ran, than which nothing could be more surprising; and yet what I saw was but the remains of her former agility, which long sickness, and the want of practice for many years, have greatly impaired. Without having seen it, it is hardly possible to imagine her singular and agile manner of running. It was not at all by setting one foot before the other alternately, as we do; it was a sort of flying gallop, almost too quick for the eye. It was rather jumping than running, one foot being kept constantly behind the other. One could scarcely observe the motion either of her body or feet; and to run along with her was impossible. The small example I was shown, which was but a trifle, having been performed only in a hall of no great length, convinced me, nevertheless, of the truth of what she had told me before, that even for several years after she was caught, she could overtake the game in the chase. Of this she gave proof in presence of the queen of Poland, mother to the queen of France, about the year 1737, as she was going to take possession of the duchy of Lorraine. That princess, in passing by Chalons, having heard of the young savage, who was at that time in the convent *des Regentes*, had her brought before her. Though she had been then several years tamed, yet her disposition, her behaviour, even her voice and speech, were, as she affirms herself, but like those of a child four or five years old. The sound of her voice, though weak, was sharp, shrill, and piercing; and her words were short and confused, like those of a child, at a loss for terms to express its meaning. In a word, her childish and familiar gestures and behaviour shewed plainly, that as yet she only took notice of the persons who caressed her the most; which the queen of Poland did extremely. On being informed of the swiftness of her running, the queen desired that she might accompany her to the chase. There finding herself at liberty, and giving full scope to her natural inclination, the young savage pursued the hares and rabbits that were started, took them, and returning at the same pace, delivered them to the queen.

Mademoiselle le Blanc, the name by which she is now called, remembers perfectly well her having passed a river two or three days before she was taken; and we shall see by and by, that this is one of the most certain facts of her history. She was then accompanied by another girl, a little older than herself, and a black likewise; but whether that was her natural colour, or whether she was only painted like Le Blanc, is uncertain. They were swimming across a river, and diving to catch some fish, when they were observed by one M. de St. Martin, a gentleman of that neighbourhood, as Mademoiselle le Blanc was afterwards told, who, seeing nothing but the two black heads of the children now and then appearing above the water, mistook them, as he says himself, for two water-cocks, and fired at them from a good distance. Luckily, however, he missed them; but the report made them dive, and retire farther off.

The little Le Blanc, on her part, had a fis in each hand, and an eel in her teeth. After having gutted and washed their fish, she and her companion eat, or rather devoured it; for, by her account, they did not chew their meat; but holding it in their hands, tore it with their fore teeth into small pieces, which they swallowed without chewing. After finishing their repast, they directed their course into the country, leaving the river at their back. Soon after, she who is now become Mademoiselle le Blanc, perceived the first, a chaplet on the ground, which, no doubt, had been dropt by some passenger. Whether the novelty of the object delighted her, or whether it brought to her remembrance something of the same kind that she had seen before, is not known; but she immediately fell a dancing and shouting for joy. Being apprehensive lest her companion should deprive her of her little treasure, she stretched out her hand to take it up; upon which the other, with her baton struck her so severe a stroke on the hand, that she lost the use of it for some moments. She had, however, strength enough left, as with the weapon in her other hand, to return the blow on the forehead of her antagonist, with such a force as to knock her to the ground, screaming frightfully. The chaplet was the reward of her victory, of which she made herself a bracelet. Touched in the mean time, as it would seem, with compassion for her companion, whose wound bled very much, she ran in search of some frogs, and finding one, she stripped off its skin, which she spread on her forehead, to stop the blood, binding up the wound with a thread of the bark of a tree, which she peeled off with her nails. After this they separated; she that was wounded taking the road towards the river, and the victorious Le Blanc that towards Songi.

There is much greater uncertainty still as to what happened to these two children, previous to their arriving in Champagne; Le Blanc's memory on that head being very indistinct and confused.

The squeaking cries she uttered through her throat, by way of language, were, I believe, not the least occasion of the harsh treatment she sometimes underwent: she has lost almost entirely the language of her country, remembering only the tone of it, and manner of speaking, and some wild cries, with which she used to frighten the French people after she was first caught; and it was by these cries, and by signs, that she conversed with her companion, the negro girl, who did not speak nor understand her language, but had a language of her own, of which Le Blanc only remembered one word, viz. "Broutut," signifying any thing that was eatable. As to her own language, she says it was all spoken from the throat, with very little use of the tongue, and none at all of the lips; and this she represented in a very lively manner, so as to convince every body who heard her, that her language was no more than a collection of guttural sounds, with very little articulation. Her mouth she says, when she was caught, was much less than it is now, and almost round; and when she laughed, she did not open her mouth as we do, but made a little motion with her upper lip, and a noise in her throat, by drawing her breath inwards. She remembers some of the idioms of her language; such as, for wounding a man, "to make him red;" and instead of killing, she used the phrase, "to make him sleep long;" and that the common salutation in her country, is, "I see you." She remembered also a good deal of the funeral ceremonies used in her country; and, particularly, that the dead man was set up in a kind of case, something like an arm-chair, and was addressed by his nearest relation, in a speech, of which she gave the substance in French, importing, that he had eyes, yet could not see; ears, yet could not hear; legs, yet could not walk; a mouth, yet could not eat; what then was become of him? and whither was he gone? And the ceremony was concluded with what she called "*un cri de tristesse*," which was a horrid shriek that she used first when she was caught, upon every occasion of surprise or distress, to the terror and astonishment of every body that heard her.

Her screams were indeed frightful, those of anger or fear especially, which I could easily conceive from a specimen exhibited by her in my presence, of one of the most moderate, expressive of her joy or friendship; and at which, had I not been put on my guard beforehand, I should have been heartily frightened. The most terrible of all were uttered by her on the approach of any unknown person, with an intention to take hold of her, at which she discovered a horror that appeared altogether extraordinary. Of this she once gave a strong instance in the house of M. de Beaupre, at present a counsellor of state, but at that time intendant of the province of Champagne, to whom she had been brought soon after being placed in the hospital-general of St. Maur at Chalons; which, by the certificate of her baptism, is fixed to the thirtieth of October, 1731. A man, who had heard of her abhorrence of being touched, resolved nevertheless to embrace her, in spite of the danger that he was told, as an unknown person, he ran in going too near her. She had in her hand at the time a piece of raw beef, which she was devouring with great satisfaction: and, by way of precaution, he kept fast hold of her clothes. The instant she saw the man near her, in the attitude of taking hold of her arm, she gave him such a violent stroke on the face, both with her hand and the piece of flesh she held in it, that he was so stunned and blinded as to be scarcely able to keep his feet. The savage, at the same time, believing the strangers around her to be so many enemies, who intended to murder her, or dreading, perhaps, punishment for what she had done, sprang out of their hands towards a window, through which she had a view of trees and a river, intending to jump into it, and so make her escape; which she would certainly have done, if they had not again caught hold of her.

The weaning her from feeding on raw flesh, and the leaves, branches, and roots of trees, was the most difficult and dangerous part of her reformation. Her stomach and constitution having been constantly accustomed to raw food, full of its natural juice, could by no means endure our artificial kinds of food, rendered by cookery, according to the opinion of several physicians, much more difficult of digestion. While she continued at the castle of Songi, and for the two first years that she staid in the hospital of St. Maur at Chalons, M. d'Epinoy, who took care of her, gave orders to carry her, from time to time, the raw fruits and roots of which she was fondest; but in the hospital she was entirely deprived of raw flesh, and raw fish, which she had found in great plenty about the castle of Songi. She appeared particularly fond of fish, either from her natural taste, or from her having acquired, by constant custom from her childhood, the faculty of catching them in the water with more ease than she could the wild game by speed of foot. M. de L—— remembers that she retained this inclination for catching fish in the water, two years after her capture: and the same gentleman informed me, that the little savage having been one day brought, by order of the Viscount d'Epinoy, to the castle of Songi, where M. de L—— then happened to be, no sooner perceived a door open which led to a large pond, than she immediately ran and threw herself into it, dressed as she was, swam round all the sides of it, and landing on a small island, went in search of frogs, which she eat at her leisure. This circumstance puts me in mind of a comical adventure which she told me herself.

(*To be continued.*)

ANECDOTES OF EXTRAORDINARY STRENGTH.

MANY years since there was well known throughout all Italy, a famous dancer upon the rope, a Venetian by birth, and called Venetianello, because of the lowness of his stature: yet was he of that strength and firmness that he broke the thickest shank bones of oxen upon his knee: three rods of iron as thick as a man's finger, wrapping them about with a napkin, he would twist and writhe as if they were softened by fire. A beam of twenty feet long, or more, and a foot thick laid upon his shoulders, sometimes set on end there, he would carry without the use of his hands, and shift from one shoulder to another. My son Theodorus (says Wierus) was an eyewitness of all this, and related it to me.

George le Feur, a learned German, writes, that in his time, in the year 1529, there lived at Misnia in Thuring, one called Nicholas Klunher, provost of the great church, who was so strong, that without rope or pulley, or any other help, he brought up out of a cellar a pipe of wine, carried it out of doors, and laid it upon a cart.

I have seen a man, saith Mayolus, an Italian bishop, in the town of Aste, who, in the presence of the Marquis of Pescara, handed a pillar of marble three feet long, and one foot in diameter, which he cast high in the air, then received it again in his arms, then threw it up again, sometimes after one fashion, sometimes after another, as easily as if he had been playing with a ball.

There was, saith the same author, at Mantua, a man called Rodomas, of little stature, but so strong, that he broke a cable as thick as a man's arm, as easily as if it had been a small twine-thread.

Froisard, (a man much esteemed for the truth and fidelity of his history) reports, that about two hundred years since, lived one Ornando Burg, a Spaniard, who was companion to the Earl of Foix: one time attending the earl, he accompanied him into a higher room, to which they ascended by twenty-four steps; the weather was cold, and the fire not answerable. But seeing some asses laden with wood in the lower court, he goes down thither, lifts up the greatest of them, with his burthen, upon his shoulder, and carrying it to the room from whence he came, laid them both on the fire together.

Lebelski, a Polander, in his description of the things done at Constantinople in the year 1581, at the circumcision of Mahomet the son of Amurath, emperor of the Turks, writes, that amongst many active men who there showed their strength, one was very memorable, who, for proof thereof, lifted up a piece of wood which twelve men had much ado to raise from the earth; and afterwards, lying down flat upon his back, he bore upon his breast a weighty stone, which ten men had with much ado rolled thither: and this he made but a jest of.

Many, says Jovius, know how strong and mighty George Froasberg, baron of Mindleheim, was; he was able, with the middle finger of his right hand, to remove a very strong man out of his place, though he sat ever so firm. He stopped a horse suddenly that ran in full career, by only touching the bridle: and with his shoulder would easily shove a cannon whither he pleased. His joints seemed to be made of horn: and he wrested twisted ropes and horse-shoes asunder with his hands.

Cardan writes, that himself saw a man dancing with two men in his arms, two upon his shoulders, and one hanging about his neck.

Of later days and here at home, Mr. Carew, a worthy gentleman, in his Survey of Cornwall, assures us that one John Bray, well known to himself, as being his tenant, carried upon his back at one time, for the space of near a bow-shot, six bushels of wheaten meal, reckoning fifteen gallons to the bushel, together with the miller, a stout fellow of twenty-four years of age: whereunto he addeth, that John Roman, of the same shire, a short clownish fellow, would carry the whole carcass of an ox.

Julius Capitolinus, and others, report of the tyrant Maximinus (who murdered the good emperor Alexander Severus) that he was so strong, that with his hands he drew carts and waggons full laden. With a blow of his fist he struck out a horse's tooth, and with a kick broke his thighs. He crumbled stones betwixt his fingers: he cleft young trees with his hands; so that he was surnamed Hercules, Antæus, and Milo.

Trebellius Pollio writes of Caius Marius, a cutler by his first occupation (and who in the time of Galienus was chosen emperor by the soldiers,) that there was not any man who had stronger hands to strike and thrust than he; the veins of his hands seemed as if they had been sinews: with his fourth finger he stayed a cart drawn with horses, and drew it backward. If he gave but a fillip to the strongest man that then was he would feel it as if he had received a blow on his forehead with a hammer: with two fingers he would wrest and break many strong cords twisted together.

Tritanus, a Samnite fencer, was of such a make, that not only his breast, but his hands and arms were furnished with sinews both longwise and across: so that without any pain, and with the least blow, he overthrew all that encountered him. The son of this fencer, of the same name and make, a soldier in Pompey's army, when he was challenged by an enemy, set so light by him that he overcame him by the blows of his bare hand; and with one finger took him up and carried him to Pompey's camp.

Flavius Vopiscus writes, that the emperor Aurelian was of a very high stature, and marvellous strength: that, in the war against the Sarmatians, he slew in one day, with his own hands, eight-and-forty of his enemies; and in divers days together he overthrew nine hundred and fifty. When he was colonel of the sixth legion, called Gallica, at Mentz, he made strange havoc of the Franci, who overran all the country of Gaul: for he slew with his own hands seven hundred of them, and sold three hundred at Portsale, whom he himself had taken prisoners: so that his soldiers made a military song in praise of him.—*Wanley's Wonders.*

EXTRAORDINARY DELUSION.
From Madame du Noyer's Letters.

The following story will appear to you incredible and fabulous, and perhaps I need not assure you that I had great difficulty in believing it; but as I had it from the lips of the individual who forms the subject of it, and as he was a visionary, I attributed it to the effects of a disturbed imagination. The event (at least as far as this person's mind was concerned) occurred in our day, and is attested by many in the city of Nismes. The tale is thus told: Mr. Graverol was alone in his study one day, about two o'clock in the afternoon, when a stranger was ushered in. As soon as he was seated, a conversation started up between the two. The stranger addressed Mr. G. in elegant Latin, saying, that he had heard his learning spoken highly of, and he had come from a distant country to converse with him on things which had embarrassed the ancient philosophers. After Mr. G. had replied suitably to the compliment offered to his talents, some very abstruse subject was introduced, and handled in a scientific manner. The stranger did not confine himself to the Latin language, but he spoke Greek and some Eastern tongues, which Mr. G. also understood perfectly. The latter was astonished and delighted with his guest's profound information; and from fear some person should call on him and interrupt it, he proposed a walk, which was readily acceded to by the stranger. The day was delightful, and you know there are some beautiful walks in the neighbourhood of Nismes. They left the house with the design of going through the gate called the Crown-gate, which leads to some gardens and a very fine avenue of noble trees; but as Mr. Graverol's house was a considerable distance from the place above-mentioned, they were obliged to cross several streets before they reached it. During the walk, Mr. G. was observed by many of his acquaintances, he being well known in the city, to use much gesture, and he was also noticed to be speaking at intervals: what added to the surprise was, that no person was seen accompanying him. Some of his friends sent to his wife, expressing their fear that he was deranged, describing the manner in which he was noticed to pass through the streets. She, being greatly alarmed at intelligence so extraordinary, despatched several persons in search of him; but they could not find him, as he had gained the shady walks outside the city with his new acquaintance. After expatiating on the subjects of ancient and modern philosophy, and reasoning on the secrets of nature, they entered on the wide fields of magic and enchantment. The stranger argued with great ingenuity and power, but he exceeded the bounds of probability; and Mr. G. cried out "Stop, stop! Christianity forbids us proceeding to such lengths—we should not pass the prescribed boundaries." He had no sooner said this (at least according to the narration spread abroad) than the stranger vanished. Mr. Graverol being at that moment at the extreme end of one of the avenues, which was terminated by some palisades, was compelled to return the same way he went. On turning round, and not perceiving his companion, he became greatly alarmed, and uttered a dreadful shriek, which brought some men, who were employed in pruning the trees, to him. When these people perceived how pale and frightened he was, they gave him some wine which they had in a flagon, and used all the means they could devise to restore him to himself. As soon as he recovered his recollection, he inquired if they had noticed where the gentleman had gone with whom he had been walking. He was very much agitated when these good people informed him that no one was with him when he passed under the trees where they were at work; neither had a single individual been in his company since he came in their sight, and they had observed him some distance before he reached them. They added, moreover, that when he passed, it struck them as being somewhat singular that he should be so deeply engaged in apparent conversation, although he was alone. Mr. G. on learning this, went immediately home, where he found his house in disorder and alarm concerning the reports which had reached his wife. He then related his adventure. When the story was noised abroad, it was publicly asserted all over the city that the devil had visited Mr. Graverol. He was a very gentlemanlike man and an advocate, and related the circumstances to me as I have detailed them. When he concluded, he said "This is accurately what happened: you now are acquainted with the facts as well as myself, and you may exercise your judgment respecting them as shall best seem fit. And all that I can add is, the stranger was a very learned and eloquent man, and reasoned like a philosopher."

Eccentric Biography.

MAURICE QUILL.

Died on Friday morning, the 15th of August, 1823, at his quarters in the New Barrack, Cork, Maurice Quill, Esq., Surgeon of the 1st Veteran Garrison Battalion.

Mr. Quill was a native of Tralee, the capital of " the kingdom of Kerry," as it is called in Ireland. He was appointed Assistant-Surgeon of the 31st Regiment of Foot, about the year 1809, and followed that regiment to the Peninsula. Subsequent to his landing, he contrived to remain for many months at Baylen in Portugal; but, after much manœuvring to avoid "joining" at head-quarters, Maurice was " ordered up" peremptorily by the Duke of Wellington. His reputation for wit, originality, and consequently for " idling," all who came within the sphere of his influence knew was such, that the morning after he had " joined," his Colonel (the gallant Duckworth) waited upon Lord Hill (of whose division of the army the 31st formed a part), and with unaffected regret and gravity reported the arrival of Maurice, and the consequent termination of discipline in the regiment. The General uttered the most dreadful denunciations against " Mr. Maurice," as he called him, should the fears of the Colonel be realized—but he became ultimately extremely partial to the droll, eccentric Maurice.

Quill was one of the finest specimens of Irish character that has appeared in our day. He possessed in an extraordinary degree all the wit, humour, and love of *badinage* that distinguish his countrymen. To the originality of his conceptions, the oddness of his remarks, and the strangeness of his phraseology, the richness of his brogue gave peculiar poignancy. He loved ease, good living, and society; of the latter he was always certain, if, indeed, he happened not to be in a desert; for so attractive was he, that his quarters were the rendezvous of all the officers who could, by possibility, repair to them to " beguile the tedium of the winter's night;" unless such as were, unfortunately, from their rank, denied that pleasure in observance of military etiquette. The rushlight in his tent or lodging was a beacon to the exhausted and dispirited soldier. I have said that he loved *badinage*, and was witty; but his wit was never barbed by the slightest touch of ill-nature or offensive personality. He was brave, but affected cowardice; and gave such whimsical expression of his assumed fears, as provoked laughter in the hottest engagement. Of this his conduct at the dreadful and bloody battle of Albuera will be a sufficient example.

Quill had unnecessarily followed the regiment " into fire," as it is termed; creeping on his hands and knees, with boyish tricks, he traversed the rear of the line, pulling the officers by their coats, and tendering his brandy bottle, saying, " Here, take a *slug*[*] before you get a *bullet.* Have a *deoch an dhurras* (a drink at the door) *before you depart.*" A mass of the enemy's cavalry, including a regiment of Polish Lancers, prepared to charge the 31st. Colonel Duckworth ordered the regiment to form in square, in the

[*] Slug—*Anglice* a dram.

centre of which he discovered Maurice, shaking from head to foot with well-dissembled terror. " This is no place for you, Mr. Maurice," said the lamented Duckworth, a few moments before his fall.—" By J——, I was just thinking so, Colonel," replied the *droll;* " I wish to the Holy Father that the greatest rascal in Ireland was kicking me this moment up Dame-street, and that even though every friend I have in the world was looking at him!" Finding it impossible to break the square, the enemy's cavalry retired with great loss, when ordering the regiment to deploy, " Fall *in*," said the Colonel; " Fall *out*," said Maurice, and scampered off; but hearing that a captain of the regiment was severely wounded, he returned into fire, and dressed him. He had just finished this operation, when a twelve-pound shot struck the ground near Maurice and his patient, and covered them with earth. " By J——, there is more where that came from," said Quill, and again took to his heels.

Of the nature of his replies to the many questions with which he was assailed by his Colonel, who was induced to ask them by the suggestions of those better acquainted with his manner—and to give a striking specimen of Quill's character, I shall add one more instance :—" I am desirous to know, Mr. Maurice," said the Colonel, " to what good fortune we can ascribe your appointment to the thirty-first?" —" Why, Colonel," (with affected embarrassment,) " I left the —— because some of the spoons belonging to the mess were found in my kit, and you know that would not do in one of the crack regiments, Colonel. I joined the *thirty-first* because I had a brother in the *thirty-second*, and I wanted to be *near* him."

Of his professional abilities I know nothing: that they were not held in high estimation would appear from the fact of his not having been promoted during the Peninsular war. That he despaired of advancement after the war had terminated, was obvious, from his reply to a friend who asked him what rank he held— " Why, I have been thirteen years an Assistant-Surgeon, and, with the blessing of GOD—that is, if I live and *behave* myself, I shall be so for thirteen years more." I am pleased to observe, that this prophecy was not verified, and that he had been promoted to the rank of full Surgeon before his death. Mr. Quill died young— he must have been under forty years of age. Of poor Maurice it might be truly said, that he possessed

Spirits o'erflowing — wit that did ne'er offend—
He gained no enemy, and he lost no friend.

The tear of many a veteran will fall when he shall learn that Maurice Quill is no more.

MR. CHRISTOPHER BARTHOLOMEW.

MR. CHRISTOPHER BARTHOLOMEW, who was proprietor of White Conduit House Tea Gardens, and the Angel Inn at the top of the City Road, exhibited a singular instance of attachment to speculating in the lottery, amidst all the fluctuations of fortune. He rented land to the amount of two hundred pounds a year in the neighbourhood of Islington and Holloway; and was remarkable for having the greatest quantity of hay-stacks of any grower in the neighbourhood of London. At that time, he is believed to have been worth £50,000, kept his carriage and servants in livery; and upon one occasion, having been unusually successful at insuring in the lottery, gave a public breakfast at his tea-gardens, "*to commemorate the smiles of fortune,*" as it was expressed upon the tickets of admission to this fête champêtre. He at times had some very fortunate hits in the lottery, and which, perhaps, tended to increase the mania which hurried him to his ruin. He has been known to spend upwards of 2000 guineas in a day for insurance; to raise which, stack after stack of his immense crops of hay have been cut down and hurried to market, as the readiest way to obtain the supplies necessary for these extraordinary out-goings. Having at last been obliged to part with his house from accumulated difficulties and embarrassments, he passed the last thirteen years of his life in great poverty, subsisting by the charity of those who knew his better days, and the emolument he received as a juryman of the Sheriffs' Court for the County. Still his propensity to be engaged in this ruinous pursuit, never forsook him: and meeting one day, in the year 1807, with an old acquaintance, he related to him a strong presentiment he entertained, that if he could purchase a particular number in the ensuing lottery (which he was not then in a situation to accomplish), it would prove successful. His friend, after remonstrating with him on the impropriety of persevering in a practice that had been already attended with such evil consequences, was at last persuaded to go halves with him in a sixteenth part of the favourite number; which, being procured, was most fortunately drawn a prize of £20,000. With the money arising from this extraordinary turn of fortune, he was prevailed upon by his friends to purchase an annuity of sixty pounds *per annum*; yet, fatally addicted to the pernicious habit of insurance, he disposed of it, and lost it all. He has been known frequently to apply to those persons who had been served by him in his prosperity, for an old coat, or some other article of cast-off apparel; and not many days before he died, he solicited a few shillings to buy him necessaries.

Varieties.

MIDNIGHT TERRORS.

A PERSON in 1813, carrying from the east coast of Fife a hundred rabbits, to occupy a warren in the western islands, hired a room for them for the night at an inn, at Cupar, and putting them into it, and giving them greens and food, he shut the door; and having refreshed himself, went to bed. A gentleman arrived just afterwards, who had supper, and went to bed, which happened to be in the room contiguous to the rabbits, but he knew nothing of their being there. About the middle of the night, and in the midst of his sleep, the door between his room and the rabbits not being locked, a gale of wind arising, the door suddenly opened, and the whole of the rabbits rushing from their own room, ran into the gentleman's, some running over his face, hands, and other parts of the body, both above and below the bed, and many of them seeking for shelter under the blankets. The gentleman, awaking suddenly, was much alarmed, and roared out for help, but none appeared. Their keeper was asleep, as well as every one else in the house. Thinking himself surrounded by a thousand evil spirits, which he found before, behind, and round him, he at length found the door, and ran down stairs naked, in the dark. The rabbits, as much afraid as the gentleman, following him, were down stairs before him; and it was not many minutes before the whole house was in an uproar. When the candle was lighted nothing appeared. The rabbits had dispersed, and hid themselves in different parts of the house. Hungary waters, spirits, &c. were brought to recover the gentleman; and it was not till the rabbit man appeared, and found his rabbits gone, that he could comprehend what had happened.

SUPERSTITION THE BEST DOCTOR.

The eldest daughter of a French lady residing in Bouverie-street, has been afflicted with a most severe and excruciating nervous complaint for the period of eighteen months. When she attempted to leave her bed, the depending posture of the legs produced the greatest agony in the stomach and bowels; and after the attempt, she would lie for several hours suffering under acute hysterical flatulence, distension, and violent head-ache. In short, her agony was extreme, and she became completely bed-ridden. She was constantly bedewed with clammy perspirations, her face was exanguine, her body emaciated. The most eminent physician in this city attended this young lady; by expostulations and entreaties he endeavoured to rouse her to exertion— by medicines and diet to correct the deranged state of the human system; but to no purpose. Six days after his last visit he received a long letter from this young lady, stating herself to be perfectly recovered. She had written to Prince Hohenlohe. He ordered her to say mass thrice, and pray for him; at the same time he would pray for her, and after the third mass she would be restored to perfect health. The attempts to kneel down at the two first masses were prevented by the tortures usually experienced upon trying to quit her bed. Dread and apprehension lest she should lose the chance of recovery, enabled her to perform genuflexion at the third mass, though her attempts to quit her bed were equally excruciating. She rose quite well from her last devotions. [The *Times* contains the above, and adds, "In conformity with the wish of the writer, we withhold his name: he is, however, an eminent physician, and he has given, as vouchers of his statement, the names of two other physicians of the very first rank."]

A WHISTLING SWAN.

In January, 1822, a sportsman of Reading, Berks, shot on the Thames, a whistling swan, of which the following account was published at the time.—It is much smaller than the tame species, the bill is three inches long, yellow to the middle, but black at the end; the whole plumage is white, and the legs are black. This species is an inhabitant of the northern regions, never appearing in England but in hard winters, when flocks of five or six are now and then seen. In Iceland these birds are objects of chase. In the month of August they lose their feathers to such a degree, as not to be able to fly. The natives at that season resort in great numbers to the places where they most abound, and are accompanied with dogs and active strong horses, trained to the sport, and capable of passing nimbly over the boggy soil and marshes. The swan will run as fast as a tolerably fleet horse. The greater number are caught by dogs, which are taught to seize them by the neck—a mode of attack which causes them to lose their balance, and become an easy prey. The bird is now in the possession of Mr. Holgate, gunmaker, of Reading, where it may be seen by the curious

The Scrap Book.

LONDON AND SHEFFIELD CUTLERS.

When Sheffield first became famous for its cutlery, a very curious knife, calculated for a variety of uses, was executed with great care, and sent to the Cutler's Company in London. On one of the blades was engraved the following challenge :

"Sheffield made both haft and blade; London for thy life shew me such another knife."

The London cutlers, to show that they were not inferior to their more northern brethren, finished, and sent down to Sheffield, a penknife, containing only one well-tempered blade, in which was a cavity, and in the cavity a piece of straw, fresh and unsinged. Some lines on the blade mentioning this fact, induced the Sheffield cutlers to break it, when they found a straw, and unable to account for the manner in which it was done, or to imitate it, they confessed themselves surpassed in ingenuity.

AN EXTRAORDINARY CAT !

In 1821, a shoemaker in the south side of Edinburgh, while engaged in cleaning a cage in which he kept a lark, left the door of the cage open, of which the bird took advantage, and flew away by a window at which its owner was then standing. The lark being a favourite, its loss was much lamented. But it may be imagined what was the surprise of the house, when about an hour after, a cat, belonging to the same person, made its appearance with the lark in its mouth, which it held by the wings over the back, in such a manner that the bird had not received the least injury. The cat, after dropping it on the floor, looked up to those who were observing her, and mewed, as if to attract attention to the capture. The lark now occupies its wiry prison, with the same noisy cheerfulness as before its singular adventure.

SINGULAR ACCIDENT.

On the 25th of February 1823, a span of horses with a sleigh and lumber box, broke away from the five mile house on the old Schenectady road, and were not heard of until the 17th of March inst. when they were found in a swamp, about a mile and a half from the four mile house. One of the horses, having been thrown down, had, in this situation, eat off half the neck yoke, and the end of the tongue of the sleigh. He was found dead. The other was alive, having remained twenty days, during the most inclement part of the season, without food or water, except what he obtained from browsing in the short space of a hundred feet. Both horses were still in the harness when found, and the articles in the sleigh were found as they had been left.—*American paper.*

Published by J. LIMBIRD, *355, Strand, (East End of Exeter 'Change); and sold by all Newsmen and Booksellers. Printed by A.* APPLEGATH, *Stamford-street.*

THE CABINET OF CURIOSITIES,
OR
Wonders of the World Displayed.

A world of wonders where creation seems
No more the works of Nature but her dreams.—MONTGOMERY.

No. XXVI.]   PRICE TWOPENCE.

AUTO-DA-FE IN SPAIN.

The restoration of absolute power in Spain, and the clamours of the priesthood for the restoration of the Inquisition, naturally excite an alarm that the cruelties for which the church of Rome has been too much distinguished, in Spain, may be revived. We need not ransack the dungeons of the Inquisition to learn that thousands have fallen victims to persecution in that country, for independent of those who perished within its walls there have been frequent immolations in public; and sanguinary murder, by every species of cruelty that ingenuity could invent, was called an *Auto-da-Fé*, or Act of Faith. What an insult to the Deity, who is merciful and forgiving! One of these murders took place in

1680, in order to celebrate the marriage of Charles II. of Spain, with a princess of the Bourbons, and in the presence of the royal family. Our engraving will convey some idea of the horrid ceremony, but the following narrative is necessary to exhibit its atrocity. The Auto-da-Fé took place at the capital.

The ministers of religion, monks, and their attendants, within many leagues of Madrid, being summoned, a solemn procession took place on the 30th of May, for the purpose of proclaiming the approaching ceremony, calling on the faithful to attend, and promising those indulgences which the sovereign pontiffs had ordained in their various decrees. The following is a literal translation of the proclamation, which was repeated eight times, in different parts of the city, and before the royal family, who were seated in a balcony of the alcazar, or palace, as the procession passed :— " Be it known to all the inhabitants of Madrid, and those of the neighbouring districts, that the holy office of the kingdom of Toledo, will celebrate a public Auto-da-Fé in the Great Square of this city, on the 30th June, when all the graces and indulgences granted by the sovereign pontiffs, will be conceded to those who accompany and assist at the said Auto; which is thus proclaimed, that it may come to the knowledge of all the faithful."

While several thousand workmen were employed under the direction of an architect especially appointed to prepare the amphitheatre, a company of soldiers of the faith were organized, and nearly all the grandees solicited permission to act as *familiars*,—a privilege allowed only to the purest blood in Spain. " Many of the highest nobility," says our author, " immortalized their names by this memorable act of piety; and, in order that future generations may enjoy the consolation of seeing our age ennobled, that the present may admire what those who come after will, without doubt, imitate ; as also that the ministers of the holy tribunal may enjoy the pleasure of witnessing the estimation in which its rank and dignity are held by the most illustrious names in the universe, the names of those who asked the favour of being allowed to act as familiars, and assumed the habit of the Holy Inquisition, on this occasion, are inserted." Of the eighty-five names which follow, a fourth were grandees of the first class, forty counts and marquesses, and the remainder either their immediate heirs or relatives.

The procession of the green and white crosses took place on the 29th of June, when all those destined to take an active part in the ceremony of the following day attended; and, amongst others, the Duke of Medinaceli, bearing the standard of Faith.

Passing before the palace, to the sound of instruments, and chaunting the Miserere, the procession moved on to the Brasero, or place of execution, where one of the symbols of Christianity was planted and consecrated on a pedestal prepared for its reception. As to the standard and green cross, they were destined to ornament the arena of the amphitheatre, to which the procession went, after quitting the Brasero.

The procession of the criminals followed that of the crosses and standard : they were conducted to the amphitheatre, to have their respective sentences read; this part of the rehearsal, for so it may be called, is compared by the author to that which will be seen in the "tremendous day of the universal judgment; because, if the ignominy of the guilty creates horror there, the glory of the just and sovereign majesty of Christ and his Apostles, who, following the standard and cross, assisted by choirs of angels, will bend their way to the Valley of Jehosaphat, where the Supreme Judge will occupy his throne," &c.

Although the preparations commenced as early as three in the morning of the 30th, the victims, living and dead, were not led forth before seven o'clock; at which hour the procession commenced. Of the number who graced this horrible triumph, twenty-one were condemned to the flames, and thirty-four to be burnt in effigy.— There were eleven penitents who had abjured the Jewish faith, and fifty-four reconciled Israelites, wearing sanbenitors and carrying wax tapers. Judging from the author's description, the procession must have been at once one of the most magnificent and terrific ever witnessed in Spain. Though attended by upwards of two hundred thousand spectators, not a sound was heard to break the awful silence, as it passed along; nothing could exceed the order and regularity preserved throughout: these are subjects of panegyric with the author, but his chief admiration is reserved for the Inquisitor-General, Don Diego Sarmiento de Talladares. "There was much to admire," says Don Jose, "in each individual of this marvellous assemblage; but the majesty with which the Inquisitor-General upheld the dignity of his office, was so transcendent, that he appeared to have exceeded himself! As the cause was so much of God, it pleased him to grant greater light to his minister; because, when he predestines men for high employment, he prepares them with the knowledge necessary for their intended occupations."

That part of the amphitheatre appropriated to the royal family and the court, was resplendent with gold and silver ornaments, displayed on damask, silk, and velvet draperies of all hues. After having exhausted his power of description, in detailing the other portions of the edifice, Don Jose del Olmo concludes by observing, that it might justly be regarded as one of the wonders of the world.

Those parts of the theatre thrown open for the public, were crowded to excess, and the King, attended by the whole of his family and court, had taken their seats some time before the procession had arrived. When high mass was over, the Inquisitor-General proceeded to the royal balcony, and administered the usual oath; after which it was taken by the municipality.

A sermon was then preached by the king's chaplain, which being ended—

A secretary began to read the sentences of those condemned to the flames: this ceremony occupied the attention of the auditory till four o'clock, when the victims were conducted to the Brasero, under an escort, and accompanied by the Corregidor and Alcaldes, appointed to see the sentences put into execution. Don Fernandez Alvarez Valdes, an officer high in the sacred tribunal, followed, to bear testimony to the event. When those victims, who are described in another account as pale, languid, and woebegone, the very emblems of despair, had been led off, the secretaries proceeded with the trials and sentences of those convicted of superstition, sorcery, bigamy, and as impostors and hypocrites. It was nine o'clock before the prisoners were assembled round the Grand Inquisitor, to go through the different forms of abjuration. The Articles of Faith were then put to each penitent, who was required to give his answer in an audible voice.

Giving absolution, saying mass, and chaunting *Te Deum*, took up another hour; after which, the royal family withdrew, and thus ended the ceremony of the 30th of June, 1680.

The process of strangling and burning continued all night: as to those who were condemned to be flogged and publicly degraded, their punishment was reserved for the following day. Nearly a third of the whole number, whether destined to be burned, flogged, or degraded, were women. When the executions had terminated, another grand procession was performed, for the purpose of restoring the crosses and standard to the cathedral.

The persecuting spirit of the 'holy office,' as the most diabolical tribunal that demon or man ever invented was called, was not confined to native Spaniards, but more than one Englishman has suffered by its Autos-da-fé and tortures. What those tortures were, we will not stop to inquire; it is sufficient to say, that the ingenuity of the priesthood was continually exercised in order to devise new means of augmenting human sufferings.

FECUNDITY OF FLIES.

A FLY lays four times during the summer, each time eighty eggs, which makes	320
Half of these are supposed to be females, so that each of the four broods produces forty.	
1. First eighth, or the forty females of the first brood, also lay four times in the course of the summer, which makes	12,800
The first eighth of these, or 1600 females, three times	384,000
The second eighth, twice	256,000
The third and fourth eighth, at least one each	256,000
2. The second eighth, or the forty females of the second brood, lay three times, the produce of which is.	9,600
One sixth of these, or 1600 females, three times	384,000
The second sixth, twice	256,000
The third sixth, once..	128,000
2. The third eighth, or the forty females of the third brood, lay twice, and produce	6,400
One fourth of these, or 1600 females lay twice more	256,000
4. The fourth eighth, or forty females of the fourth brood, once..	3,200
Half of these, or 1600 females, at least once.	128,000
Total produce of a single fly, in one summer	2,080,320

ICE ISLANDS.

The interest which the return of Captain Parry has given to subjects connected with the Polar sea, induces us to give an account of Ice Islands. This name is bestowed by seamen on the huge solid masses of ice which float on the seas near or within the Polar circles. Many of these fluctuating islands are met with on the coasts of Spitzbergen, to the great danger of the vessels employed in the Greenland fishery. In the midst of these tremendous masses, navigators have been arrested and frozen to death. In this manner the brave Sir Hugh Willoughby perished, with all his crew, in 1553; and in the year 1773, Lord Mulgrave, after every effort which the most accomplished seaman could make to reach the termination of his voyage, was caught in the ice, and nearly experienced the same unhappy fate. The scene he describes, divested of the horrors attendant on the eventful expectation of change, was most beautiful and picturesque. Two large ships becalmed in a vast basin, surrounded on all sides by ice islands of various forms; the weather clear; the sun gilding the circumambient ice, which was low, smooth, and even covered with snow, except where pools of water, on a portion of the surface, shot forth new icy crystals, and the smooth surface of the comparatively small space of sea in which they were hemmed. Such is the picture drawn by our navigator, amid the perils by which he was surrounded.

After fruitless attempts to force their way through the fields of ice, the limits of these became at length so contracted, that the ships were immoveably fixed. The smooth extent of surface was soon lost: the pressure of the pieces of ice, by the violence of the swell, caused them to pack; and fragment rose upon fragment, until they were in many places higher than the main-yard. The movements of the ships were tremendous and involuntary, in conjunction with the surrounding ice, actuated by the currents. The water having shoaled to fourteen fathoms, great apprehensions were entertained, as the grounding of the ice, or of the ships, would have been equally fatal: the force of the ice might have crushed them to atoms, or have lifted them out of the water, and have overset them; or, again, have left them suspended on the summits of the pieces of ice at a tremendous height, exposed to the fury of the winds, or to the risk of being dashed to pieces by the failure of their frozen dock. An attempt was made to cut a passage through the ice; but after a perseverance truly worthy of Britons, it proved ineffectual. The commander, who was at all times master of himself, directed the boats to be made ready to be hauled over the ice, till they should reach navigable water, proposing in them to make the voyage to England; but after they had thus been drawn over the ice for three progressive days, a wind having sprung up, the ice separated sufficiently to yield to the pressure of the ships in full sail. After having laboured against the resisting fields of ice, they at length reach the harbour of Smeeringberg, at the west end of Spitzbergen.

The vast islands of floating ice which abound in the high southern latitudes, are a proof that they are visited by a much severer degree of cold than equal latitudes towards the north pole.

Captain Cook, in his second voyage, fell in with one of these islands in latitude 50° 40′ south. It was about fifty feet high, and half a mile in circuit, being flat on the top, while its sides, against which the sea broke exceedingly high, rose in a perpendicular direction. In the afternoon of the same day, the 10th of December, 1773, he fell in with another large cubical mass of ice, about two thousand feet in length, four hundred feet in breadth, and in height two hundred feet. Mr. Foster, the naturalist of the voyage, remarks that, according to the experiments of Boyle and Marian, the volume of ice is to that of sea water nearly as 10 to 9: consequently by the known rules of hydrostatics, the volume of ice which rises above the surface of the water, is to that which sinks below it as 1 to 9. Supposing, therefore, this mass of ice to have been of a regular figure, its depth under water must have been 1800 feet, and its whole height 2000 feet: estimating its length, as above, at 2000 feet, and its breadth at 400 feet, the entire mass must have contained 1600 millions of cubic feet of ice.

Two days after, several other ice islands were seen, some of them nearly two miles in circuit, and 600 feet high; and yet such was the force of the waves, that the sea broke quite over them. They exhibited for a few moments a view very pleasing to the eye; but a sense of danger soon filled the mind with horror: for had the ship struck against the weather side of one of these islands, when the sea ran high, she must in an instant have been dashed to pieces. The route to the southward was afterwards impeded by an immense field of low ice, the termination of which could not be seen, either to the east, west, or south. In different parts of this field were islands, or hills of ice, like those which had before been found floating in the sea.

At length these ice islands became as familiar to those on board as the clouds and the sea. Whenever a strong reflection of white was seen on the skirts of the sky, near the horizon, then ice was sure to be encountered; notwithstanding which, that substance itself was not entirely white, but often tinged, especially near the surface of the sea, with a most beautiful sapphirine, or rather a berrylline blue, evidently reflected from the water. This blue colour sometimes appeared twenty or thirty feet above the surface, and was probably produced by particles of sea water which had been dashed against the mass in tempestuous weather, and had penetrated into its interstices. In the evening, the sun setting just behind one of these masses, tinged its edges with gold, and reflected on the entire mass a beautiful suffusion of purple. In the larger masses were frequently observed shades or casts of white, lying above each other in strata, sometimes of six inches, and at other times of a foot in height. This appearance seemed to confirm the opinion entertained relative to the increase and accumulation of such huge masses of ice, by heavy falls of snow at different intervals: for snow being of various kinds, small-grained, large-grained, in light feathery locks, &c., the various degrees of its compactness may account for the different colours of the strata.

In his third attempt to proceed southward, in January, 1774, Captain Cook was led, by the mildest sunshine which was, perhaps, ever experienced in the frigid zone, to entertain hopes of penetrating as far toward the south pole as other navigators had done toward the north pole; but on the 26th of that month, at four in the morning, his officers discovered a solid ice-field of immense extent before them, bearing from east to west. A bed of fragments floated around this field, which was raised several feet above the surface of the water. While in this situation, the southern part of the horizon was illuminated by the rays of light reflected from the ice, to a considerable height. Ninety-seven ice-lands were distinctly seen within the field, beside those on the outside; many of them very large, and looking like a ridge of mountains, rising one above the other until they were lost in the clouds. The most elevated and most rugged of these ice-islands were surmounted by peaks, and were from two to three hundred feet in height, with perpendicular cliffs or sides astonishing to behold. The largest of them terminated in a peak not unlike the cupola of St. Paul's.

The outer, or northern edge, of this immense field of ice, was composed of loose or broken ice closely packed together, so that it was not possible to find any entrance. Such mountains of ice, Captain Cook was persuaded, were never seen in the Greenland seas, so that not any comparison could be drawn; and it was the opinion of most of the persons on board, that this ice extended quite to the pole, to which they were then within less than nineteen degrees; or, perhaps, joined to some land to which it had been fixed from the earliest time.

Our navigator was of opinion that it is to the south of this parallel that all the ice is formed, which is found scattered up and down to the northward, and afterward broken off by gales of wind, or other causes, and brought forward by the currents which are always found to set in that direction in high latitudes. "Should there," he observes, "be land to the south behind this ice, it can afford no better retreat for birds, or any other animals, than the ice itself, with which it must be wholly covered. I, who was ambitious, not only to go farther than any one had been before, but as far as it was possible for man to go, was not sorry at meeting with this interruption; as it in some measure relieved us, or at least shortened the dangers and hardships inseparable from the navigation of the southern polar regions."

The approximation of several fields of ice of different magnitudes produces a very singular phenomenon. The smaller of these masses are forced out of the water, and thrown on the larger ones, until at length an aggregate is formed of a tremendous height. These accumulated bodies of ice float in the sea like so many rugged mountains, and are continually increased in height by the freezing of the spray of the sea, and the melting of the snow which falls on them. While their growth is thus augmented, the smaller fields, of a less elevation, are the meadows of the seals, on which these animals at times frolic by hundreds.

The collision of great fields of ice, in high latitudes, is often attended by a noise, which, for a time, takes away the sense of hearing any thing beside; and that of the smaller fields with a grinding of unspeakable horror. The water which dashes against the mountainous ice, freezes into an infinite variety of forms, and presents to the admiring view of the voyager ideal towns, streets, churches, steeples, and almost every form which imagination can picture to itself.

ICEBERGS.

ANALOGOUS to the ice-fields described above, are those large bodies of ice, named ICEBERGS, which fill the vallies between the high mountains in northern latitudes. Among the most remarkable are those of the east coast of Spitzbergen. They are seven in number, and lie at considerable distances from each other, extending through tracts unknown, in a region totally inaccessible in the internal parts. The most distant of them exhibits over the sea a front three hundred feet in height, emulating the colour of the emerald: cataracts of melted snow fall down in various parts; and black spiral mountains, streaked with white, bound the sides, rising crag above crag, as far as the eye can reach, in the back-ground. At times immense fragments break off, and precipitate themselves into the water with a most alarming dashing. A portion of this vivid green substance was seen by Lord Mulgrave, in the voyage above referred to, to fall into the sea; and, notwithstanding it grounded in twenty-four fathoms water, it spired above the surface fifty feet. Similar icebergs are frequent in all the arctic regions; and to their lapse is owing the solid mountainous ice which infests those seas.

The frost sports wonderfully with these icebergs, and gives them majestic, as well as other most singular forms. Masses have been seen to assume the shape of a gothic church, with arched windows and doors, and all the rich drapery of that style of architecture, composed of what the writer of an Arabian tale would scarcely have ventured to introduce among the marvellous suggestions of his fancy—*crystals of the richest sapphirine blue.* Tables with one or more feet; and often immense flat-roofed temples, like those of Luxor on the bank of the Nile, supported by round transparent columns of cerulean hue, float by the astonished spectator. These icebergs are the creation of ages, and acquire annually additional height by falls of snow and rain, which latter often freezes instantly, and more than repairs the loss occasioned by the influence of the sun's heat.

THE ANACONDA.

THE following extract from M'Leod's voyage of the British ship Alceste, furnishes decisive evidence that the accounts of the celebrated snake, called the Anaconda, are not altogether fabulous:

"After the Alceste was wrecked, and the people taken off, the ship Cæsar, Taylor, was engaged to carry Lord Amherst and his suite, and the officers and crew of the Alceste, to England. She sailed from Batavia on the 12th of April, 1816.

"Notwithstanding the crowded state of the Cæsar, two passengers, of rather a singular nature, were put on board at Batavia, for a passage for England: the one a snake of that species called the Boa Constrictor; the other, an Ourang Outang. The former was somewhat small of his kind, being only about sixteen feet long, and of about thirteen inches in circumference; but his stomach was rather disproportionate to his size, as will presently appear. He was a native of Borneo, and was the property of a gentleman (now in England) who had two of the same sort; but, in their passage up to Batavia, one of them broke loose from his confinement, and very soon cleared the decks, as every body very civilly made way for him. Not being used to a ship, however, or taking, perhaps, the sea for a green field, he sprawled overboard and was drowned. He is said not to have sunk immediately, but to have reared his head several times, with a considerable portion of his body out of the sea. His companion, lately our shipmate, was brought safely on shore, and lodged in the court-yard of Mr. Davidson's house, at Ryswick, where he remained for some months, waiting for an opportunity of being conveyed hence in some commodious ship sailing directly to England, and where he was likely to be carefully attended. This opportunity offered in the Cæsar, and he was accordingly embarked on board of that ship with the rest of her numerous passengers.

"During his stay at Ryswick, he is said to have been usually entertained with a goat for dinner, once in every three or four weeks, with occasionally a duck or a fowl, by way of a dessert. He was brought on board, shut up in a wooden crib or cage, the bars of which were sufficiently close to prevent his escape; and it had a sliding door, for the purpose of admitting the articles on which he was to subsist. The dimensions of the crib were about four feet high, and about five feet square; a space sufficiently large to allow him to coil himself round with ease. The live stock for his use during the passage, consisting of six goats of the ordinary size, put with him on board, five being considered as a fair allowance for as many months. At an early period of the voyage, we had an exhibition of his talent in the way of eating, which was publicly performed on the quarter deck, upon which he was brought. The sliding door being opened, one of the goats was thrust in, and the door of the cage shut. The poor goat, as if instantly aware of all the horrors of its perilous situation, immediately began to utter piercing and distressing cries; butting instinctively at the same time, with its head towards the serpent, in self-defence.

"The snake, which first appeared scarcely to notice the poor animal, soon began to stir a little, and turning his head in the direction of the goat, it at length fixed a deadly and malignant eye on the trembling victim, whose agony and terror seemed to increase; for, previous to the snake seizing its prey, it shook in every limb, but still continuing its unavailing show of attack, by butting at the serpent, who now became sufficiently animated to prepare for the banquet. The first operation was that of darting out his forked tongue, and at the same time rearing a little his head; then suddenly seizing the goat by the fore leg with his mouth, and throwing him down, he was encircled in an instant in his horrid folds. So quick, indeed, and so instantaneous was the act, that it was impossible for the eye to follow the rapid convolution of his elongated body. It was not a regular screw-like turn that was formed, but resembling rather a knot, one part of the body overlaying the other, as if to add weight to the muscular pressure, the more effectually to crush his object. During this time he continued to grasp with his mouth, though it appeared an unnecessary precaution, that part of the animal which he had first seized. The poor goat, in the mean time, continued its feeble and half-stifled cries for some minutes, but they soon became more and more faint, and at last expired. The snake however retained it for a considerable time in its grasp, after it was apparently motionless. He then began slowly and cautiously to unfold himself, till the goat fell dead from his monstrous embrace, when he began to prepare himself for his feast. Placing his mouth in front of the head of the dead animal, he commenced by lubricating with his saliva that part of the goat; and then taking its muzzle into his mouth, which had, and indeed always has, the appearance of a raw lacerated wound, he sucked it in as far as the horns would allow.

"These protuberances opposed some little difficulty, not so much from their extent as from their points; however, they also, in a short time, disappeared; that is to say, externally—but their progress was still to be traced very distinctly on the outside, threatening every moment to protrude through the skin. The victim had now descended as far as the shoulders; and it was an astonishing sight to observe the extraordinary action of the snake's muscles when stretched to such an unnatural extent—an extent which must have utterly destroyed all muscular power in any animal that was not, like itself, endowed with any peculiar faculties of expansion and action at the same time. When his head and neck had no other appearance than that of a serpent's skin stuffed almost to bursting, still the workings of the muscles were evident; and his power of suction, as it is erroneously called, unabated; it was, in fact, the effect of a contractile muscular power, assisted by two rows of strong hooked teeth. With all this he must be so formed as to be able to suspend, for a time, his respiration, for it is impossible to conceive that the process of breathing could be carried on while the mouth and throat were so completely stuffed and expanded by the body of the goat, and the lungs themselves (admitting the trachea to be ever so hard) compressed, as they must have been, by its passage downwards.

"The whole operation of completely gorging the goat occupied about two hours and twenty minutes—at the end of which time, the tumefaction was confined to the middle part of the body, or stomach, the superior parts, which had been so much distended, having resumed their natural dimensions. He now coiled himself up again, and laid quietly in his usual torpid state for about three weeks or a month, when his last meal appearing to be completely digested and dissolved, he was presented with another goat, which he devoured with equal facility. It would appear that almost all he swallows is converted into nutrition. He had more difficulty in killing a fowl than a larger animal, the former being too small for his grasp.

"As we approached the Cape of Good Hope this animal began to droop, as was then supposed, from the increasing coldness of the weather, (which may probably have had its influence,) and he refused to kill some fowls which were offered to him. Between the Cape and St. Helena he was found dead in the cage.

"It may here be mentioned that during a captivity of some months at Whidah, in the kingdom of Dahomey, on the coast of Africa, the author of this narrative had opportunities of observing snakes more than double the size of the one just described; but he cannot venture to say whether or not they were of the same species, though he has no doubt of their being of the genus of Boa. They killed their prey, however, precisely in a similar manner; and from their superior bulk, were capable of swallowing animals much larger than goats or sheep. Governor Abson, who had for thirty-seven years resided at Fort William, described some desperate struggles which he had either seen, or came to his knowledge, between the snakes and wild beasts, as well as the smaller cattle, in which the former were always victorious. A negro herdsman, belonging to Mr. Abson, had been seized by one of these monsters by the thigh; but from his situation in a wood, the serpent in attempting to throw itself around him, got entangled with a tree; and the man being thus preserved from a state of compression, which would have instantly rendered him quite powerless, had presence of mind enough to cut, with a large knife which he carried about with him, deep gashes in the neck and throat of his antagonist, thereby killing it, and disengaging himself from his alarming situation. He never afterwards, however, recovered the use of that limb, which had sustained a considerable injury from his fangs, and the mere force of his jaws."

THE SAVAGE GIRL OF CHAMPAGNE.

(Concluded from p. 392.)

WHEN any company visited M. d'Epinoy at Songi, he used to send for the girl, who soon became more tame, and began to discover much good humour, and a softness and humanity of disposition, which the savage life she had been obliged to follow for self-preservation, had not been able altogether to efface; for when she did not appear apprehensive of any harm, she was very tractable and good humoured. One day when she was present at a great entertainment in the castle, observing none of the delicacies she esteemed, every thing being cooked, she ran out like lightning, and traversing all the ditches and ponds, returned with her apron full of living frogs, which she spread very liberally on the plates of all the guests; and, quite overjoyed at having found such good cheer, cried out, *tien man, man, donc tien,* (hold man, man, hold then) almost the only syllables she could then articulate. We may easily figure to ourselves the confusion and bustle this occasioned among the guests, every one endeavouring to avoid or throw away the frogs that were hopping all about. The little savage, quite surprised at the small value they seemed to set on her delicate fare, carefully gathered up the scattered frogs, and threw them back again on the plates and table. The same thing has happened several times in different companies.

It was with the utmost difficulty that they prevented her

from eating raw flesh, and, by slow degrees, reconciled her to our cooked victuals. The first trials she made to accustom herself to victuals dressed with salt, and to drink wine, cost her her teeth, which, together with her nails, were preserved as a curiosity. She recovered, indeed, a set of new teeth just like ours, but she irrecoverably hurt her health, which continues to be extremely delicate. From one dangerous disorder she immediately fell into another, all occasioned by intolerable pains in her stomach and bowels, but especially in her throat, which became parched and inflamed, owing, as the physicians asserted, to the little exercise and nourishment derived to these parts from her new regimen, in comparison of what they had received from the raw victuals she formerly fed upon. These pains frequently produced an universal spasm over the whole body, and weaknesses irreparable by all the arts of cookery.

I was informed by M. L——, that M. d'Epinoy, who was solicitous to save her at any expense, sent a physician to see her, who being at a loss what to prescribe, hinted, that it was necessary to indulge her now and then with a bit of raw flesh. Accordingly, she says, they gave her some, but she could, by that time, only chew it and suck out the juice: not being able to swallow the flesh. Sometimes too, a lady of the house, who had a great affection for her, would bring her a chicken or pigeon alive, of which she immediately sucked the blood warm, which she found to be a kind of balsam that penetrated every part of her body, softened the acrimony of her parched throat, and brought back her strength. It was with all this trouble, and these narrow escapes, that Mademoiselle le Blanc, by slow degrees, gave over her raw diet, and accustomed herself to the cooked victuals we eat; and that so entirely, that at present she has a disgust at raw flesh.

As to her two embarkations, of which she has preserved a pretty distinct idea, and about which she has never varied; the truth of them, as well as her having remained some time in a hot country, such as our West India islands, seems to be in some measure confirmed by this, that sugar-canes, cassave or manioc, the known productions of the hottest climates, were by no means new or unknown objects to her, for she remembers to have eat of them; and the first time they were shewn her in France, she seized them very greedily. I take notice of these circumstances, because they tend to form a connection between the several parts of the adventures that may have conducted Mademoiselle le Blanc from the northern regions, of which she appears to be a native, first into the West Indies, and from thence into Europe, somewhere near to the frontiers of France.

She and her companion caught the fish with their hands, either in the sea, in lakes, or in rivers; for Mademoiselle le Blanc could not explain to me which; nor could she give me any other description of their manner of fishing, except, that when they saw in the water, where their sight was extremely acute, any fish, they instantly pursued and caught them, then returned to the surface of the water to gut and wash them, immediately afterwards eat them, and then went in quest of more. It must therefore have been either in some river, or if in the sea, it could only be when the ship was at anchor in some port or road, that they fished in this manner. Of this I was persuaded by one of her adventures; for she told me, that having one day thrown herself into the water, not to fish, as it would seem, because she did not choose to return again, but to make her escape, on account of some harsh usage, and having swam about a considerable time, she betook herself at last to a steep rock, on which she scrambled, as she says, like a cat; and having been pursued thither by a boat or canoe, she was retaken with much difficulty, being found concealed among some bushes. All this shews, that the ship was not far from land; though it is not unlikely that this escape may be the same with that mentioned above, of which M. de L—— was an eyewitness at Songi.

On account of this flight, perhaps, or some other attempts of the same kind, the two little savages were confined to the hold of the ship; but this precaution had like to have proved fatal both to them and to the rest of the crew likewise. Perceiving themselves near the water, their favourite element, they formed a scheme of scratching a hole in the ship by which they might make their escape into the water: the crew, however, luckily discovered their operations time enough to prevent the effect of them, and thereby escaped an unavoidable shipwreck. This attempt made them chain the two little savages in such a way as to put it out of their power to resume their work.

It appears, that after the escape of these two children, from whatever place it was, being then incapable of any other views or intentions than those of liberty and self-preservation, they pursued no other route than chance or necessity presented. At night, when, according to Le Blanc, they saw more distinctly than in the day, (which, however, must not be understood literally, though her eyes do still retain somewhat of that faculty) they travelled about in search of food and drink. The small game which they caught sitting, and the roots of trees, were their provisions; their arms and nails supplying the place of caterer and cook. They passed the day either in holes, in bushes, or upon trees, as the nature of the place permitted. The trees were their refuge against the wild beasts which they discovered; they served them likewise as their watch-towers, from whence they could observe at a distance whether any of their enemies were near, when they wanted to come down; and it was here they waited, as it were in ambush for the passing of any game, upon which they either leaped all of a sudden, or went in pursuit of them. Providence, which bestows on every creature the instincts and faculties necessary for the preservation of its kind, had endued those with a power of motion in the eyes quite inconceivable; their movement was so extremely quick, and their sight so sharp, that they might be said to see in the same instant on every side of them without hardly moving their heads. The little of this faculty that Le Blanc still retains, is astonishing, when she chooses to show it; for at other times her eyes are like ours; which she reckons a lucky circumstance, it having cost a great deal of pains to deprive them of their quick motion, and in which she had almost despaired of succeeding.

The trees were likewise their beds, or rather their cradles; for, according to her description, they slept soundly in them, either sitting, or probably riding on some branch, suffering themselves to be rocked by the winds, and exposed to every inclemency of the weather, without any other precaution than the securing themselves with one hand, and using the other by way of pillow.

The largest rivers did not at all stop their journey either by day or night; for they always crossed them without any dread: sometimes they entered merely for the sake of drinking, which they performed by dipping in their chins up to the mouth, and sucking the water like horses. But they most frequently entered the rivers to catch the fish they perceived at the bottom, which they brought ashore in their hands and mouths, there to open, skin, and eat them.

The French author imagines this savage girl to have been of the Esquimaux nation of Indians; the translator, however, thinks there is much greater probability of her being of the Huron race, and advances many ingenious arguments in support of his opinion.

Eccentric Biography.

MR. JOSEPH CAPPER.

Mr. Joseph Capper, who died in August 1804, was, perhaps, the most eccentric character living since the celebrated miser Elwes. He was born in Cheshire, of humble parents: his family being numerous, he came to London at an early age (as he used to say) to shift for himself, and was bound apprentice to a grocer: Mr. Capper soon manifested great quickness and industry, and proved a most valuable servant to his master It was one of the chief boasts of his life, that he had gained the confidence of his employer, and never betrayed it. Being of an enterprising spirit, Mr. Capper commenced business as soon as he was out of his apprenticeship, in the neighbourhood of Rosemary-lane. His old master was his only friend, and recommended him so strongly to the dealers in his line, that credit to a very large amount was given to him. In proportion as he became successful, he embarked in various speculations, but in none was so fortunate as in the funds. He at length amassed a sum sufficient to enable him to decline all business. Mr. Capper, having now lost his old master, was resolved to lead a sedentary life. This best suited his disposition; for, although he possessed many amiable qualities, yet he was the most tyrannical and overbearing man living, and never seemed so happy as when placed by the side of a churlish companion. For several days he walked about the vicinity of London, searching for lodgings, without being able to please himself. Being one day much fatigued, he called at the Horns at Kennington, took a chop, and spent the day, and asked for a bed in his usual blunt manner; when he was answered in the same churlish style by the landlord, that he could not have one. Mr. Capper was resolved to stop, if he could, all his life, to plague the growling fellow, and refused to retire. After some altercation, however, he was accommodated with a bed, and never slept out of it for twenty-five years. During that time he made no agreement for lodging or eating, but wished to be considered as a customer only for the day. For many years he talked about quitting this residence the next day. His manner of living was so methodical, that he would not drink his tea out of any other than a favourite cup. He was equally particular with respect to his knives and forks, plates, &c. In winter and summer he rose at the same hour, and when the mornings were dark, he was so accustomed to the house, that he walked about the apartments without the assistance of any light. At breakfast he arranged, in a peculiar way, the paraphernalia of the tea-table, but first of all he would read the newspapers. At dinner he also observed a general rule, and invariably drank his pint of wine. His supper was uniformly a gill of rum, with sugar, lemon-peel, and porter, mixed together; the latter he saved from the pint he had at dinner. From this economical plan he never deviated. His bill for a fortnight amounted regularly to 4*l.* 18*s.* He called himself the Champion of Government, and his greatest glory was certainly his country and king. He joined in all subscriptions which tended to the aid of government. He was exceedingly choleric, and nothing raised his anger so soon as declaiming against the British constitution. In the parlour, he kept his favourite chair, and there he would often amuse himself with satirizing the customers, or the landlord, if he could make his jokes tell better. It was his maxim, never to join in general conversation, but to interrupt it, whenever he could say any thing ill-natured. Mr. Capper's conduct to his relations was exceedingly capricious; he never would see any of them. As they were chiefly in indigent circumstances, he had frequent applications from them to borrow money. "Are they industrious?" he would inquire; when being answered in the affirmative, he would add, "Tell them I have been deceived already, and never will advance a sixpence by way of loan, but I will give them the sum they want; and if ever I hear they make known the circumstance, I will cut them off with a shilling." Soon after Mr. Townsend became landlord of the Horns, he had an opportunity of making a few good ready-money purchases, and applied to the old man for a temporary loan:—" I wish (said he) to serve you, Townsend; you seem an industrious fellow; but how is it to be done, Mr. Townsend? I have sworn never to lend, I must therefore give it thee;" which he accordingly did the following day. Mr. Townsend proved grateful for this mark of liberality, and never ceased to administer to him every mark of comfort the house would afford; and what was, perhaps, more gratifying to the old man, he indulged him in his eccentricities. Mr. Capper was elected a steward of the parlour fire; and if any persons were daring enough to put a poker in it without his permission, they stood a fair chance of feeling the weight of his cane. In summer time, a favourite diversion of his was killing flies in the parlour with his cane; but, as he was sensible of the ill opinion this would produce among the bystanders, he would with great ingenuity introduce a story about the rascality of all Frenchmen, " whom," says he, " I hate and detest, and would knock down just the same as these flies."

This was the signal for attack, and presently the killed and wounded were scattered about in all quarters of the room. This truly eccentric character lived to the age of seventy-seven, in excellent health; and then died suddenly. In his boxes were found 100*l.* in bank notes, a few guineas, a great many government securities, and a will, which the parties present proceeded to read. It was curiously worded and made on the back of a sheet of banker's checks. It was dated five years back, and the bulk of his property, which was then upwards of 30,000*l.*, he left equally amongst his poor relations. The two nephews were nominated executors, and were bequeathed between them 8000*l.* in the three per cents. What has become of all the property which has been accumulating since the will was made, does not appear. From Mr. Capper's declarations in his lifetime, there was reason to suppose he had made another will, as the one found did not appear to be witnessed.

The Scrap Book.

CONGLOMERATED HAIL.

PERHAPS we shall be thought desirous of taxing the credulity of our readers, by publishing the following dimensions of a mass of ice, said to have fallen in the presence of several respectable persons, during a hail storm, in July 1823, in Munson (Mass.) The appearance is said to have been that of a compact body of hail stones, as firmly united as ice usually is:—Extremes, four feet long, three ditto wide, two ditto thick. After removing the rough parts of the body, there remained a solid block of two feet three inches long, one foot six inches wide, and one foot three inches thick.—*American Paper.*

SEA SERPENT.

WE are informed that the Sea Serpent was seen off Squam Bar on Wednesday last, and again on Thursday, in Sandy Bay harbour. At the latter place, he was visible for some time, within fifty yards of the shore, and was fired at a number of times with muskets; two balls were seen to strike him and rebound. He was distinctly seen by as many as fifty people; and is described as appearing perfectly calm, with his head about two feet out of water, and his body visible only in parts or humps, as he has been before described, with a space of about two feet between each. He was judged to be at least seventy or eighty feet long.—*Salem Gazette.*

A PELICAN was lately wounded and taken in the Alleghany river. This immense bird measures, from the tip of the bill to the end of the tail, five feet one inch and a half; from tip to tip of the wings eight feet, in height of body one foot seven inches, neck one foot six inches long, head and bill one foot eight inches and a half; mouth one foot six inches; round the body three feet. The pouch, under its mandible, would contain three quarts. The bird was very poor, and not supposed to weigh sixteen pounds.—*Philadelphia Gazette.*

Published by J. LIMBIRD, 355, Strand, (East End of Exeter 'Change); and sold by all Newsmen and Booksellers. Printed by A. APPLEGATH, Stamford-street.

THE CABINET OF CURIOSITIES,

OR

Wonders of the World Displayed.

A world of wonders where creation seems
No more the works of Nature but her dreams.—MONTGOMERY.

No. XXVII.] PRICE TWOPENCE.

ASSASSINATION OF DORISLAUS.

WHEN Oliver Cromwell wished to form an alliance between the Commonwealth of England and the Republic of Holland, he sent over an envoy of the name of Dorislaus, a doctor in civil law, who was born at Delft, and educated at Leyden, but had lived long in London. Dr. Dorislaus was one of the Professors of Gresham College, and had from the commencement of the civil war exercised the office of judge advocate in the Earl of Essex's army.

When Dr. Dorislaus arrived at the Hague, he took a temporary lodging until better accommodation could be provided for him. While he was at supper on the evening on which he arrived at the Hague, in company with many others, who lodged at the same house or hotel, six gentlemen entered the room with their swords drawn, and requested all those who were at table not to stir, for that "there was no harm intended to any one but the agent who came from the rebels in England, who had newly murdered their king." One of the assassins, who knew Dorislaus, pulled him from the table, and killed him at his feet; upon which they all put up their swords and walked leisurely out of the house, no attempt being made to arrest any of them. Clarendon says, the assassins were Scotchmen, and most of them servants or dependents on the Marquis of Montrose.

THE ABBE OF CALVADOS.

IN a village of Calvados, in the month of October, 1820, was buried an old man, who had retired from business, and owned some national property. Before his death, he was desirous of receiving the sacrament, and the priest gave him absolution, on condition that he would restore some acres to the church, which he promised to do; but death came before the notary. — His property, therefore wholly descended to his son, a simple youth. On the night after his father's funeral, the young man was awakened by a violent noise, accompanied with a vivid light; which in a moment disappeared. Being no stranger to fear, he shook as he lay in his bed, and tried to call out for help; but a cold and moist hand closed his lips, and completed his amazement. He fancied that he beheld a spectre, covered with a long white mantle, pass before him, and a sepulchral voice uttered these words: " *Badly obtained— The soul of P— must go into torments, if his son makes not restitution.*" Another voice, weak and failing, continued, " *My son, restore the ill-gotten property, or else*" —the sepulchral voice added— " *I shall come night after night to drag you by your feet.*" These words were followed by total silence; the youth slept no more; and the next morning he went to relate to the priest and his family the vision of the night. The priest and some of the neighbours advised him to give up his property; but a young kinsman, just come from school, maintained that the dead do not come back again, and that the possessors of national property are no more likely to have their feet dragged by ghosts than their neighbours. Then taking the young heir aside, he offered to lie in the bed in his place, if he would keep it a secret, and would promise to wait one day more before he gave up the property. This proposal was accepted, and the young kinsman took possession of the other youth's bed for that night. Between twelve and one o'clock, he heard some person gently open the window, and at the same time he beheld a phantom enter, who came up as if to speak to him with a threatening gesture. "So far so good;" said he mentally, " as he mistakes me for another person, spirits are not omniscient." He then slipped out of bed as quietly as he could, seized the phantom with both his hands, and threw him in a moment into a little dark closet, which he shut and locked very carefully. The spectre finding himself a prisoner, began to cry out for mercy; but the youth went to call in his neighbours, who soon recognised, in the semblance of a ghost, a young abbé, who although as yet only in deacon's orders, had been desirous to give a proof of his zeal for the church of Rome.

THE FLYING DUTCHMAN.

A LARGE luminous body, of a circular form, called the Flying Dutchman, gliding along the surface of the sea, in lat. $36\frac{1}{2}$, lon. 75, at seven o'clock P. M., drew the attention and curiosity of the passengers on board the schooner Angenora, on her passage from Charleston. The seamen state that it appears seldom, but is the certain indication of a storm (as was afterwards proved, being followed by one on the 4th inst.) It is supposed to be a species between the Starfish and Sea Nettle.

CHILTON THE SOMNAMBULIST.

The following singular account of a most remarkable somnambulist, is copied from a scarce tract by Dr. William Oliver, Fellow of the Royal Society and of the College of Physicians, published in 1707, and entitled " A Relation of a very extraordinary Sleeper, at Tinsbury, near Bath." We give the narrative in the author's own words.—Edit.

" May the 13th, 1694, one Samuel Chilton, of Tinsbury, near Bath, a labourer, about twenty-five years of age, of a robust habit of body, not fat, but fleshy, and dark brown hair, happened, without any visible cause, or evident sign, to fall into a very profound sleep, out of which no art used by those that were near him, could rouse him, till after a month's time; then rose of himself, put on his clothes, and went about his business of husbandry as usual; slept, could eat and drink as before, but spake not one word till about a month after. All the time he slept victuals stood by him; his mother fearing he would be starved, in that sullen humour, as she thought it, put bread and cheese, and small beer before him, which was spent every day, and it is supposed by him, though no one ever saw him eat or drink all that time.

" From this time he remained free of any drowsiness or sleepiness till about the 9th of April, 1696, and then fell into a sleeping fit just as he did before. After some days they were prevailed upon to try what effect medicines might have on him, and accordingly one Mr. Gibs, a very able apothecary of Bath, went to him, bled, blistered, cupped and scarified him, and used all the external irritating medicines he could think of, but all to no purpose, nothing of all these making any manner of impression on him; and after the first fortnight he was never observed to open his eyes. Victuals stood by him as before, which he eat of now and then, and sometimes they have found him fast asleep with his mouth full of meat. In this manner he lay for about ten weeks, and then could eat nothing at all, for his jaws seemed to be set, and his teeth clenched so close, that with all the art they had with their instruments they could not open his mouth, to put any thing into it to support him. At last, observing a hole made in his teeth, by holding his pipe in his mouth, as most great smokers usually have, they, through a quill, poured some tent into his throat now and then; and this was all he took for six weeks and four days, and of that not above three pints or two quarts, some of which was spilt too.

" August the 7th, which was seventeen weeks from the 9th of April, (when he began to sleep) he awoke, put on his clothes, and walked about the room, not knowing he had slept above a night, nor could he be persuaded he had lain so long, till going out into the fields he found every body busy in getting in their harvest, and he remembered very well when he fell asleep they were sowing of barley and oats, which he then saw ripe and fit to be cut down.

" There was one thing observable, that though his flesh was somewhat wasted with so long lying in bed, and fasting for above six weeks, yet a worthy gentleman, his neighbour, assured him, when he saw him, which was the first day of his coming abroad, he looked brisker than ever he saw him in his life before; and asking him whether the bed had not made him sore, he assured him and every body, that he neither found that, nor any other inconveniency at all; and that he had not the least remembrance of any thing that past or was done to him all that while. So he fell again to his husbandry as he used to do, and remained well from that time till August the 17th, 1697, when in the morning he complained of a shivering and coldness in his back, vomited once or twice, and that same day fell into his sleeping fit again.

"Being then at Bath, and hearing of it, I took horse on the 23d, to inform myself of a matter of fact I thought so strange. When I came to the house, I was by the neighbours (for there was no body at home at that time besides this man) brought to his bedside, where I found him asleep, as I had been told before, with a cup of beer, and a piece of bread and cheese, upon a stool by his bed, within his reach: I took him by the hand, felt his pulse, which was at that time very regular; I put my hand on his breast, and found his heart beat very regular too, and his breathing was easy and free; and all the fault I found was, that I thought his pulse beat a little too strong: he was in a breathing sweat, and had an agreeable warmth all over his body. I then put my mouth to his ear, and, as loud as I could, called him by his name several times, pulled him by the shoulders, pinched his nose, stopt his mouth and nose together, as long as I durst, for fear of choking him, but all to no purpose, for in all this time he gave me not the least signal of his being sensible. I lifted up his eyelids, and found his eyeballs drawn up under his eyebrows, and fixed without any motion at all. Being baffled with all these trials, I was resolved to see what effects *spirit* of *sal ammoniac* would have, which I had brought with me, to discover the cheat, if it had been one; so I held my vial under one nostril a considerable time, which being drawn from quicklime, was a very piercing spirit, and so strong I could not bear it under my own nose a moment without making my eyes water; but he felt it not at all. Then I threw it several times up the same nostril, it made his nose run and gleet, and his eye-lids shiver and tremble a very little, and this was all the effect I found, though I poured up into one nostril about a half ounce bottle of this fiery spirit, which was as strong almost as fire itself. Finding no success with this neither, I crammed that nostril with powder of *white hellebore*, which I had by me, in order to make my farther trials, and I can hardly think any impostor could ever be insensible of what I did. I tarried some time afterwards in the room, to see what their effects altogether might be upon him; but he never gave any token that he felt what I had done, nor discovered any manner of uneasiness, by moving or stirring any one part of his body, that I could observe. Having made these my experiments I left him, being pretty well satisfied he was really asleep, and no sullen counterfeit, as some people thought him.

"Upon my return to Bath, and relating what I had observed, and what proofs this fellow had given me of his sleeping, a great many gentlemen went to see him, as I had done, to satify their curiosity in a rarity of that nature, who found him in the same condition I had left him in the day before; only his nose was inflamed and swelled very much, and his lips and the inside of his right nostril blistered and scabby with my *spirit* and *hellebore,* which I had plentifully dosed him with the day before. His mother upon this for some time after would suffer nobody to come near him, for fear of more experiments upon her son. About ten days after I had been with him, Mr. Woolmer, an experienced apothecary at Bath, called at the house, being near Tinsbury, went up into the room, finding his pulse pretty high, as I had done, takes out his lancet, lets him blood about fourteen ounces in the arm, ties his arm up again, nobody being in the house, and leaves him as he found him; and he assured me he never made the least motion in the world when he pricked him, nor all the while his arm was bleeding.

"Several other experiments were made by those that went to see him every day from Bath, but all to no purpose, as they told me on their return: I saw him myself again the latter end of September, and found him just in the same posture, lying in his bed, but removed from the house where he was before about a furlong or more; and they told me, when they removed him, by accident, carrying him down stairs, which were somewhat narrow, they struck his head against a stone, and gave him a severe knock, which broke his head, but he never moved any more at it than a dead man would. I found now his pulse was not quite so strong, nor had he any sweats, as when I saw him before. I tried him again the second time, by stopping his nose and mouth, but to no purpose; and a gentleman then with me ran a large pin into his arm to the very bone, unknown to me, but he gave us no manner of token of his being sensible of any thing we did to him. In all this time they assured me nobody had seen him either eat or drink, though they endeavoured it all they could, but it always stood by him, and they observed sometimes once a day, sometimes once in two days, all was gone. It is farther observable, he never fouled his bed, but did his necessary occasions always in the pot.

"In this manner he lay till the 19th of November, when his mother hearing him make a noise, ran immediately up to him and found him eating; she asked him how he did? He said, very well, thank God. She asked him again, which he liked best, bread and butter, or bread and cheese? He answered, bread and cheese; Upon this, the poor woman overjoyed, left him to acquaint his brother with it, and they came straight up into the chamber to discourse with him, but found him as fast asleep again as ever, and all the art they had could not awake him. From this time to the end of January, or the beginning of February, (for I could not learn from any body the very day) he slept not so profoundly as before, for when they called him by his name he seemed to hear them, and be somewhat sensible, though he could not make them any answer. His eyes were not now shut so close, and he had frequently great tremblings of his eyelids, upon which they expected every day he would awake, which happened not till about the time just now mentioned, and then he awoke perfectly well, not remembering any thing that happened all this while.

It was observed he was very little altered in his flesh, only complained the cold pinched him more than usually, and so presently fell to husbandry, as at other times."

GROTTOES AND CAVERNS.

There are few countries which have not to boast of a variety of natural excavations; and these have, from their extent, structure, and the curious phenomena they exhibit, in the formation of petrifactions, &c. been at all times objects of popular attention. Among those particularly deserving of notice are the following:

The volcanic country bordering on Rome is peculiarly diversified by natural cavities of great extent and coolness, on which last account it is related by Seneca, that the Romans were accustomed to erect seats in their vicinity, to enjoy their refreshing chilness in the summer season. He gives a particular account of two such grottoes belonging to the villa of Vatia; and it was in a place of this kind that Tiberius was nearly destroyed while at supper. Its roof suddenly gave way, and buried several of his attendants in its ruins; which so alarmed the others that they fled and abandoned the emperor, with the exception of Sejanus, who, stooping on his hands and knees, and covering the body of Tiberius with his own, received all the stones which fell at that part from the roof, insomuch that, although he himself sustained considerable injury, the emperor escaped unhurt.

The grottoes of the Cevennes mountains, in Lower Languedoc, are both numerous and extensive. The principal one is not to be explored without much precaution, and without a safe guide.

The entrance, which is low and narrow, leads to a spacious amphitheatre, the petrifactions hanging from the roof of which have a most splendid effect by the light of torches. Hence the visitor has to descend to several chambers, one of which is named the Chamber of the Winds; another, of Echo; another, of the Cascade; another again, of the Statue, &c.; on account of their exhibiting these different phenomena. In the grotto of Valori, at a small distance, the different natural curiosities which are to be found at every step, may be viewed at leisure, and without apprehension, as the visitor never loses sight of the light at the entrance, and is, therefore, not under any dread of returning in safety. Here he is gratified by a view of the most singular petrifactions, representing flowers, fruits, beehives, and, in short, a variety of objects, in many of which the resemblance is nearly as accurate as if they had been sculptured.

In a wood, about five leagues from Besançon, in the province of France, called Franche Comté, an opening, formed by two masses of rock, leads to a cavern more than nine hundred feet beneath the level of the country. It is in width sixty feet, and eighty feet high, at the entrance, and exhibits within side an oval cavity of one hundred and thirty-five feet in breadth, and one hundred and sixty-eight in length. To the right of the entrance is a deep and narrow opening, bordered with festoons of ice, which distilling in successive drops on the bottom of the cavern, form a mass of about thirty feet in diameter. A similar one, but somewhat smaller, produced by the water which drips in less abundance from these imperceptible fissures in the roof, is seen on the left. The ground of the cavern is perfectly smooth, and covered with ice eighteen inches thick; but the top, on the outside, is a dry and stony soil, covered with trees, and on a level with the rest of the wood. The cold within this cavern is so great, that however warm the external atmosphere may be at the time it is visited, it is impossible to remain in it for any continuance.

These natural ice-houses are not unfrequent in France and Italy, and supply this agreeable luxury at a very cheap rate. Thus, in the same province, in the vicinity of Vesoul, is a cavern which, in the hot season, when it is eagerly sought, produces more ice in one day than can be carried away in eight. It measures thirty-five feet in length, and in width sixty. The large masses of ice which hang pendant from the roof, have a very pleasing effect. When mists are observed in this cavern, they are regarded by the neighbouring peasantry as infallible prognostics of rain; and it is worthy of observation, that although the water in the interior is always frozen in the summer, it becomes liquid in the winter season.

A grotto near Douse, also in Franche Comté, forms a similar ice-house, and is remarkable on account of the various forms of its congelations, which represent a series of columns, sustaining a curious vault, which appears to be carved with figures of men, animals, trees, &c.

The caverns of Gibraltar are numerous, and several of them of a great extent. The one more particularly deserving attention is called St. Michael's Cave, situated on the southern part of the mountain. Its entrance is one thousand feet above the level of the sea, and is formed by a rapid slope of earth, which has fallen in at various periods, and which leads to a spacious hall, incrusted with spar, and apparently supported in the centre by a large stalactical pillar. To this succeeds a long series of caves, of difficult access. The passages leading from the one to the other are over precipices which cannot be passed without the aid of ropes and scaling ladders. Several of these caves are three hundred feet beneath the upper one; but at this depth the smoke of the torches, carried by the guides, becomes so disagreeable, that the visitor is obliged reluctantly to give up the pursuit and leave other caves unexplored. In these cavernous recesses, the process and formation of the stalactites is to be traced, from the flimsy quilt-like cone suspended from the roof, to the robust trunk of a pillar, three feet in diameter, which rises from the floor, and seems intended by nature to support the roof from which it originated.

The variety of forms which this matter takes in its different situations and directions, renders this subterraneous scenery strikingly grotesque, and in some places beautifully picturesque. The stalactites of these caves, when near the surface of the mountain, are of a brownish yellow colour; but, in descending towards the lower caves, they lose the darkness of their colour, which is by degrees shaded off to a pale yellow. Fragments are broken off, and, when wrought into different forms, and polished, are beautifully streaked and marbled.

About seven English miles from Adlersberg, in Carniola, is a remarkable cavern, named St. Magdalen's Cave, The road being covered with stones and bushes, is very painful; but the great fatigue it occasions is overbalanced by the satisfaction of seeing so extraordinary a cavern. The visitor first descends into a hole, where the earth appears to have fallen in for ten paces, when he reaches the entrance, which resembles a fissure, caused by an earthquake, in a huge rock. The torches are here lighted, the cave being extremely dark. This wonderful natural excavation is divided into several large halls, and other apartments. The vast number of pillars by which it is ornamented give it a superb appearance, and are extremely beautiful: they are as white as snow, and have a semi-transparent lustre. The bottom is of the same materials; insomuch that the visitor may fancy he is walking beneath the ruins of some stately palace, amid noble pillars and columns, partly mutilated, and partly entire. Sparry icicles are every where seen suspended from the roof, in some places resembling wax tapers, which, from their radiant whiteness, appear extremely beautiful. All the inconvenience here arises from the inequality of the surface, which may make the spectator stumble while he is contemplating the beauties above and around him.

In the neighbourhood of the village of Szelitze, in Upper Hungary, there is a very singular excavation. The adjacent country is hilly, and abounds with woods, the air being cold and penetrating. The entrance into this cavern, fronting the south, is upwards of one hundred feet in height, and forty-eight in breadth, consequently sufficiently wide to receive the south wind, which here generally blows with great violence; but the subterraneous passages, which consist entirely of solid rock, winding round, stretch still farther to the south. As far as they have been explored, their height has been found to be three hundred feet, and their breadth about one hundred and fifty. The most inexplicable singularity, however, is, that in the midst of winter the air in this cavern is warm; and when the heat of the sun without is scarcely supportable, the cold within is not only very piercing, but so intense that the roof is covered with icicles of the size of a large cask, which, spreading into ramifications form very grotesque figures. When the snow melts in spring, the inside of the cave, where its surface is exposed to the south sun, emits a pellucid water, which congeals instantly as it drops, and thus forms the above icicles: even the water which falls from them on the sandy ground freezes in an instant. It is observed, that the greater the heat is without, the more intense is the cold within; so that, in the dog-days every part of this cavern is covered with ice. In autumn, when the nights become cold, the ice begins to dissolve, insomuch that when the winter sets in, it is no longer to be seen; the cavern then is perfectly dry, and has a mild warmth.

TURPIN THE HIGHWAYMAN.

DICK TURPIN was one of the most desperate and cruel highwaymen that ever took to the road. He was notorious in the shires of York and Lincoln: and after innumerable minor offences, was tried for horse-stealing, and he immediately wrote to his father for a character, as though it could be sent by post. He behaved in York Castle with great impudence.

His villainies were heavy and manifold. His behaviour at the place of execution (for he suffered for horse-stealing) was curious. The morning before his execution, he gave three pounds ten shillings amongst five men, who were to follow the cart as mourners, with hatbands and gloves to several persons more. He also left a gold ring, and two pair of shoes and clogs to a married woman at Brough, that he was acquainted with; though he at the same time acknowledged he had a wife and child of his own.

He was carried in a cart to the place of execution, on Saturday, April 7, 1739, with John Stead, condemned also for horse-stealing; he behaved himself with amazing assurance, and bowed to the spectators as he passed. It was remarkable, that as he mounted the ladder, his right leg trembled, on which he stamped it down with an air, and with undaunted courage, looking round about him; and after speaking near half an hour to the topsman, threw himself off the ladder, and expired directly.

His corpse was brought back from the gallows about three in the afternoon, and lodged at the Blue Boar, at Castle-gate, till ten the next morning, when it was buried in a neat coffin in St. George's church-yard, within Fishergate Postern, with this inscription: L R. 1739, R. T. aged 28. He confessed to the hangman that he was thirty-three years of age. The grave was dug very deep, and the persons whom he appointed his mourners, as above-mentioned, took all possible care to secure the body; notwithstanding which, on Tuesday morning, about three o'clock, some persons were discovered to be moving of the body, which they had taken up, and the mob having got scent where it was carried to, and suspecting it was to be anatomized, went to a garden in which it was deposited, and brought away the body through the streets of the city, in a sort of triumph, almost naked, being only laid on a board covered with some straw, and carried on four men's shoulders, and buried it in the same grave, having first filled the coffin with slacked lime.

Turpin was, perhaps, as desperate a ruffian as ever pulled trigger in the face of a traveller. He shot people like partridges! Many wild and improbable stories are related of him; such as his rapid ride to York, his horse chewing a beef-steak all the way; but setting these aside, he was a desperate and extraordinary villain.

Hoaxes and Impostures.
No. XVIII.
A WATER QUACK.

In the year 1728, one Villars told his friends, in confidence, that his uncle, who had lived almost a hundred years, and who died only by accident, had left him a certain preparation, which had the virtue to prolong a man's life to a hundred and fifty years; if he lived with sobriety. When he happened to observe the procession of a funeral, he shrugged up his shoulders in pity. "If the deceased," said he, "had taken my medicine, he would not be where he is." His friends, among whom he distributed it generously, observing the condition required, found its utility, and extolled it. He was thence encouraged to sell it at a crown the bottle; and the sale was prodigious. It was no more than the water of the Seine, mixed with a little nitre. Those who made use of it, and were attentive at the same time to the regimen, or who were happy in good constitutions, soon recovered their usual health. To others he observed: "It is your own fault if you be not perfectly cured; you have been intemperate and incontinent, renounce these vices, and believe me, you will live at least a hundred and fifty years." Some of them took his advice, and his wealth grew with his reputation. The Abbé Pones extolled this quack, and gave him the preference to the Marischal de Villars; the latter, says he, kills men, the former prolongs their existence. At length it was discovered, that Villars's medicine was composed chiefly of river water; his practice was now at an end, men had recourse to other quacks.

Villars was certainly of no disservice to his patients, and can only be reproached with selling the water of the Seine at too high a price.

THE MOUNTAIN DOCTOR.

A wealthy farmer, much affected with hypochondria, came to Langenau, to consult Michael Scuppach, better known by the appellation of the *mountain doctor*. "I have seven devils in my belly," said he, "no fewer than seven." "There are more than seven," replied the doctor, with the utmost gravity; "if you count them right you will find eight." After questioning the patient concerning his case, he promised to cure him in eight days, during which time, he would every morning rid him of one of his troublesome inmates, at the rate of one louis d'or each. "But," added he, "as the last will be more obstinate and difficult to expel than the others, I shall expect two louis d'ors for him. The farmer agreed to these terms: the bargain was struck, and the doctor, impressing upon all present the necessity of secrecy, promised to give the nine louis d'ors to the poor of the parish. Next morning the imaginary demoniac was brought to him, and placed near a kind of machine which he had never seen before, by which means he received an electric shock. The farmer roared out lustily. "There goes one!" said the doctor, with the utmost gravity. Next day the same operation was repeated: the farmer bellowed as before, and the doctor coolly remarked, "Another is off!" In this manner he proceeded to the seventh. When he was preparing to attack the last, Scuppach reminded his patient that he now had need of all his courage, for this was the captain of the gang, who would make a more obstinate resistance than any of the others. The shock was at this time so strong, as to extend the demoniac on the floor. "Now they are all gone!" said the doctor, and ordered the farmer to be put to bed. On recovering himself the latter declared he was completely cured; he paid the nine louis d'ors with abundance of thanks, and returned in the best spirits to the village. Creditable witnesses attest this extraordinary cure, which proves the acuteness of the doctor, as well as the truth of Solomon's proverb, that with the fool we must sometimes talk like a fool.

Anecdotes of Longevity.

THE following is a remarkable instance of the longevity of a family, a majority of which are now living.

The father died about twenty years ago, in the 93d year of his age............ 93
The mother died about eighteen years ago, in the 95th year of her age...... 95
They lived together in a married state upwards of seventy years, and had nine children.
The eldest son is a healthy and intelligent old gentleman, in his 92d year...... 92
The eldest daughter died in her 88th year.......... 88
The second son died in his 87th year.............. 87
The third son died in his 75th year, of the fifteenth attack of pneumonia.. 75
The fourth son is living in the 82d year of his age.... 82
The fifth son is in his 80th year................ 80
The second daughter is in her 78th year........... 78
The sixth son is in his 76th year.................... 76
The seventh son, a respectable physician, (one of course) is in his 73d year.. 73
—
919
—

The above facts can be substantiated by three physicians living in as many towns in the State, on the banks of Connecticut River, who are the sons of the seventh son and physician.
Amount of their ages...,919
Average age............83½
United States' Paper.

Eccentric Biography.

SIR GEORGE HASTINGS.

At Winborne, St. Giles, is a whole length portrait of Sir George Hastings, formerly Lord of the Manor of Woodland, Dorset. Under the picture is the following account of him, drawn by Shaftesbury, the noble author of the Characteristics.

"He was peradventure, an original in our age, or rather the copy of our ancient nobility in hunting, not in warlike times. He was low, very strong, and very active; of reddish flaxen hair; his clothes always green cloth, and never worth, when new, five pounds. His house was perfectly of the old fashion, in the midst of a large park, well stocked with deer; and near the house, rabbits for his kitchen; many fishponds, great store of wood and timber, a bowling green in it, long, but narrow, full of high hedges, it being never levelled since it was ploughed; they used round sand bowls; and it had a large banqueting-house, like a stand, built in a tree. He kept all manner of sport hounds, that ran buck, fox, hare, otter, and badger; and hawks, long and short winged. He had a walk in the forest and the manor of Christ church; this last supplied him with red deer; sea and river fish; and indeed all his neighbours' grounds, and royalties, were free to him, who bestowed all his time on these sports, but what he borrowed to caress his wives and daughters, there being not a woman in all his walks, of the degree of a yeoman's wife, or under, and under the age of forty, but it was her own fault if he was not intimately acquainted with her. This made him very popular, always speaking kindly to the husband, brother or father, who was to boot very welcome in his house. Whenever he came there, he found beef, pudding, and small beer, in great plenty, the house not so neatly kept as to shame him, or dirty his shoes, the great hall strewed with marrow bones, full of hawks, paches, hounds, spaniels, and terriers; the upper side of the hall hung with fox skins of this and the last year's killing; here and there a polecat, intermixed with game keepers' and hunters' poles in great abundance. The parlour was a large room as properly furnished. On a great hearth, paved with brick, lay some terriers, and the choicest hounds and spaniels. Seldom but two of the great chairs had litters of cats in them, which were not to be disturbed, he always having three or four attending him at dinner, and a little white stick of fourteen inches long, lying by his trencher, that he might defend such meat as he had no mind to part with to them. The windows, which were very large, served for places to lay his arrows, cross bows, and stone bows, and such like accoutrements; the corners of the rooms full of the best chosen hunting poles; his oyster table, at the lower end, which was in constant use twice a day all the year round, for he never failed to eat oysters both dinner and supper at all seasons; the neighbouring town of Poole supplied him with them. The upper part of the room had two small tables and a desk, on one side of which there was a church bible, and on the other side the Book of Martyrs; on the tables were hawks' hoods, bells, and such like; two or three old green hats with the crown thrust in, so as to hold ten or a dozen eggs, which were of the pheasant kind of poultry; these he took much care of, and fed himself. Tables, dice, cards, and books, were not wanting. In the hole of the desk were a store of tobacco-pipes that had been used. On one side of this end of the room, was the door of the closet, wherein stood the strong beer, and the wine, which never came from thence but in single glasses, that being the rule of the house exactly observed, for he never exceeded in drink, or permitted it. On the other side was the door of an old chapel, not used for devotion; the pulpit, as the safest place, was never wanting of a cold chine of beef, venison pasty, gammon of bacon, or a great apple pie, with thick crust extremely baked. His table cost him not much, though it was good to eat at. His sports supplied all but beef or mutton, except on Fridays, when he had the best of salt fish, as well as any other fish he could get: and this was the day his neighbours of best quality visited him. He never wanted a London pudding, and always sang it in ' With my part lyes therein a'.' He drank a glass or two of wine at meals, very often put syrup of gilly-flowers in his sack, and had always a tun glass without feet, standing before him, holding a pint of small beer, which he often stirred with rosemary. He was well natured but soon angry.

"He lived to be a hundred, and never lost his eye-sight, but always wrote and read without spectacles, and got on horseback without help. Until past fourscore, he rode to the death of a stag as well as any."—*Percy Anecdotes.*

Varieties.

EXECUTION OF AN INNOCENT MAN.
(From an American Paper.)

It was stated some months since that John C. Hamilton was executed at Kentucky in 1817, for the murder of Dr. Sanderson, of Natchez, Mississippi, and that a man had been executed in Mobile, who confessed himself the murderer of Sanderson, and declared that Hamilton was innocent. The following are the particulars of this melancholy affair, the perusal of which is sufficient to wring tears of anguish from the heart of apathy itself:—

"The annals of judicial proceedings rarely afford a report of a trial and execution of a more extraordinary and distressing character than this, and it should be universally circulated, that judges and jurors may be guarded against condemning supposed culprits on circumstantial evidence. Young Hamilton, through life, supported an unblemished character, and obtained the love, esteem, and admiration of all who had the pleasure of his acquaintance. As is common with the young gentlemen of Kentucky, he was in the practice of spending the winter season in the more genial climate of the Mississippi. On his return from a winter residence in that quarter, he accidentally fell in company with Dr. Sanderson, who being in ill health, was journeying to the celebrated watering-place at Harrodsburg Spa, with hopes of recovering his lost health; as he was anxious to make something out of his pilgrimage, he took with him a large sum of money, with which he contemplated purchasing negroes on speculation. On his way up the country, his infirmities increased, and as he was apprehensive he might expire on the road, he committed to the charge of Hamilton his treasure, having in his short acquaintance discovered that he was worthy of unlimited confidence. In a few days, however, his indisposition abated, when he pursued his journey and finally arrived in safety at the residence of Hamilton, in Barren County, Kentucky, where he remained during the summer, and received from his young friend every mark of courtesy, attention, and hospitality. In the month of October, Dr. Sanderson made arrangements to depart, and on taking leave of his hospitable host, young Hamilton accompanied him several miles on the road, and then took an affectionate farewell. Ten or twelve days after, as some hunters were rambling through the forest, they discovered the body of Dr. Sanderson in a state of corruption, shot in several places, and mangled in the most shocking manner. As Hamilton was last seen with him, and as it was known that he had, from time to time, made use of sums of money originally the property of Sanderson, suspicion fell on his head, and he was arrested, tried, and executed.

"Previous to his arrest, he was advised to leave the country, to avoid danger; but as he was conscious of his innocence, he disdained to take a step which would cast a cloud of obloquy and disgrace upon his character, and resolutely remained at home. As the inhabitants of the county were divided in their opinions as to his guilt, the affair gradually died away; but Hamilton, being anxious that a trial should take place, firmly believing that in such an event his reputation would remain unspotted, he solicited at the hands of justice a trial, which, to his astonishment and sorrow, closed with his condemnation. The only evidence against him was circumstantial, viz. that near the body of Sanderson were found a bloody pair of pantaloons and a pistol, both bearing the name of Hamilton. Through the whole of the trial he manifested that fortitude and determined coolness characteristic of innocence, and expired with a full conviction that the real murderer would ultimately be discovered. When on the scaffold, he took a manly leave of the world, expressed not the least regret for his fate, but lamented that his misfortunes would cloud the prospects of his family, and shed an indelible disgrace on his memory. Thus through the weakness of the law, was an interesting young man and a worthy citizen hurried from the world, and doomed to expiate on the gallows that crime committed by the hands of a villain and assassin."

RECENT MARTYRDOM.

The following event, occurred at Smyrna, April, 1819.

Athanasius, a Greek Christian, twenty-four years of age, was the son of a boatman, who carried on a small trade in the Archipelago. —The gains of the father being unable to support the son, and the business not sufficiently great to require his assistance, he was obliged to look out for employment in some other way. He engaged in the service of a Turk, who, being pleased with his conduct, considered him as a proper object for exercising his influence in converting him to the Mahometan faith. After holding out great offers, he ultimately prevailed on him to renounce Christianity, in presence of the Meccamay, who is the Turkish Judge and Bishop. He continued in the service for about a year after, when he quitted it, and having experienced severe reproofs of conscience for his apostasy, he made a pilgrimage to Mount Achas, where there are many convents, from which he returned some months after.

On his arrival at Smyrna, in the costume of a Greek monk, he proceeded instantly to the Meccamay, expressed his repentance at renouncing the Christian faith, and his resolution to abjure the tenets of the Mahometan. On this he was confined in a dungeon, and endured the torture with the greatest fortitude, persisting in his resolution to die a Christian. A day was then appointed for his execution in the most public part of Smyrna, and opposite one of the principal mosques; and he was led to the scaffold bound, attended by the Turkish guards. Here he was offered his life, nay, houses, money, in short riches, if he would still continue in the Mahometan creed; but no temptation could induce Athanasius again to apostatize.

On this occasion a Turkish blacksmith was employed to decapitate him. As a last attempt, however, to effect, if practicable, a change of opinion, the executioner was directed to cut part of the skin of his neck, that he might feel the edge of the sword. Even this, however, failed of success. He was then ordered to kneel on the ground, when he declared, with a calm and resigned countenance, that "he was *born* with Jesus, and would *die* with Jesus!" at one blow the head was struck off. The guards then instantly threw buckets of water on the neck and head of the corpse, to prevent the multitude of surrounding Greek spectators from dipping their hankerchiefs in his blood, to keep as a memorial of an event so remarkable. The body was publicly exposed for three days, the head placed between the legs, on the anus, and afterwards given up to the Greeks, by whom it was decently interred, in the principal church-yard of Smyrna. This is the third instance of the kind which has occurred at Smyrna during the last twenty years.

BARON TRENCK BEATEN.

In January 1823, Howard Trask, a prisoner in the county gaol in Boston, United States, made his escape. He was tried, says an American Paper, in the Supreme Court for murder committed in the state prison, and acquitted on the plea of insanity, and who, being committed for safe keeping to the gaol in this town, in September 1822, killed two of his fellow-prisoners, who had been permitted to accompany him in his room, to assist him in reading the bible. Since the commission of this last act, he has been kept in irons. A short time since, he entirely stripped himself of his irons, and they were replaced by a new set much stronger. There were shackles upon his legs, by which he was chained to the floor, a double pair of handcuffs, and an iron collar with a chain passing from it to the irons between his hands. These irons had been strictly examined on the Monday, and were entirely sound, and they were apparently so on Tuesday. He, however, succeeded on Tuesday night in breaking both pair of handcuffs, the chain of his collar and the chain by which he was fastened to the floor. He then removed two or three thick oak planks which formed a part of the ceiling, and were fastened by several bolts, broke two large bars of iron, removed a number of small stones in the wall, and forced out a large stone forming a part of the outer face of the wall, which fell upon the platform, and left an opening large enough for him easily to escape. By the assistance of a plank from his room, he made his way to the top of a shed, from which he escaped into the street, carrying with him probably his collar and handcuffs. Soon after the shifting of the gaol watch, at one o'clock, the stone was discovered upon the platform, and the room was found deserted. From a noise that was heard it is supposed that the escape was effected a little before twelve o'clock. A person, supposed to be him, was soon afterwards seen by the watchmen near the market, and challenged by them, but he gave such an account of himself that they suffered him to pass on. It does not appear that he had any instrument to assist in relieving himself from his irons, or in removing the wall.

AN AMERICAN MONSTER.

The Lexington, (Kentucky) Gazette contains the following account of a strange animal which has been recently seen:—

" We learn from Russellville that a gentleman discovered an animal of alarming appearance, a few miles from town, and hastened to the nearest house, where he was joined by three men, two of whom were armed with guns, and attended by a dog. The strange monster was again discovered, and while bayed by the dog, the two guns continued to fire on him at the distance of about fifty yards, without forcing him to move from his stand; a furious look, and appalling brow frightened the two men without guns, who fled to town. Experienced marksmen continued to fire, and on the twelfth shot the beast put off at full speed, marking his way by blood flowing from many wounds that it must have received. The dog was too much frightened to continue his pursuit, and the huntsmen dare not venture, although one of them was as fearless as Boone himself, and accustomed to the chase from early life.

"When the news reached Russellville, about forty gentlemen repaired to the spot, and had a full view of the ground. The print which the paws of this animal made in the earth, corresponds with the account given of his great bulk by those who had an opportunity of viewing him at a short distance for several minutes: he was of a brindle colour with a most terrific front—his eyes are described as the largest ever seen in any animal. We are well acquainted with the party engaged in the attack, and give the fullest credit to the account we have received.

"The conclusion drawn is, that the animal in question was a tiger, of the largest order, from Mexico, and that it has, like the monsters of the deep, thought proper to wander into distant regions. There is nothing remarkable in his passing such a distance unobserved. Wolves have been seen of late years low down in the northern necks of Virginia, a distance of nearly two hundred miles from the Blue Ridge, the supposed residence of those animals; they had to pass through a country of the thickest population, unprotected by large forests, until they arrived on the Potomac river, where cedar and pine thickets shelter them from all future danger.

"The above tiger was seen a few days after braving a dozen shots, making its way into the state of Tennessee, and there is still a prospect of its being taken, and the public gratified with a more correct description."

The Scrap Book.

SEA SERPENT.

A GENTLEMAN of the strictest probity and honour declares to us, he was on board a small boat, and had, for the space of half an hour, a leisurely survey of this monster. He was lying at his ease, and appeared no way disposed to do injury. The gentleman describes his appearance and his length much in the same way as they both have been described already. The monster approached the boat in a direct line, and fears were entertained by the passengers for their personal safety. On his coming alongside, however, like a quiet citizen of the deep, he gently sunk under the water, and rose on the other side, litle dreaming of the dismay and consternation that he had excited above.—*Baltimore Paper.*

THREE LEGGED RABBITS.

WE have this week, through favour of Mrs. Ridler, of the Lower George Inn, in this city, visited a litter of rabbits, of most extraordinary deformity; consisting of *ten* in number, two only of which are perfect; two have no ears, two but one ear each, two have only three legs each, and two others are blind. They are all living.—*Gloucester Herald.*

Published by J. LIMBIRD, 355, Strand, (East End of Exeter 'Change); and sold by all Newsmen and Booksellers. Printed by A. APPLEGATH, Stamford-street.

Printed in Poland
by Amazon Fulfillment
Poland Sp. z o.o., Wrocław